THE WHISKY DISTILLERIES OF THE UNITED KINGDOM

THE CENTENARY EDITION

ALFRED BARNARD

FOREWORD BY DAVID DAICHES

INTRODUCTION BY MICHAEL MOSS

MAINSTREAM PUBLISHING

in conjunction with

LOCHAR PUBLISHING

EDINBURGH

1987

First published in 1887 by *Harper's Weekly Gazette*.
Reprinted in 1969 by David & Charles Ltd with an introduction by Dr I. A. Glen.
This centenary edition published in 1987 by
MAINSTREAM PUBLISHING COMPANY (EDINBURGH) LTD.
7 Albany Street
Edinburgh EH1 3UG
and
LOCHAR PUBLISHING
Bankhead, Annan Water
Moffat DG10 9LS

British Library Cataloguing in Publication Data

Barnard, Alfred
The whisky distilleries of the United Kingdom
1. Distilling industries——Great Britain
——History——19th century 2. Whiskey——
Great Britain——History——19th century
I. Title
338.4'766352'0941 HD9395.G72

ISBN 1-85158-087-5

Printed by Butler & Tanner, Frome, Somerset.

ACKNOWLEDGEMENTS

The co-publishers gratefully acknowledge the assistance of the staff of the Rare Books & Manuscripts Department, Mitchell Library, Glasgow in the production of this edition.

PICTURE CREDIT

Front cover, black and white portrait: Royal Commission on the Ancient Monuments, Scotland.
Front cover, colour photographs: Steve Johnston.
Rear cover, photograph courtesy of John Ryan, Irish Distillers Ltd.
Dust-jacket (inside rear, portrait of D. Daiches): Courtesy of the *Glasgow Herald*.

Acknowledgement

IN 1886, the writer Alfred Barnard made one of the most remarkable pilgrimages of the Victorian era. Over a period of months he journeyed by rail, horse, carriage and boat around every distillery in England, Scotland and Ireland creating one of the most important records the industry has ever known. In particular, his Hebridean travelogue has been compared to the earlier works of Martin Martin, Thomas Pennant and Sam Johnson, in whose footsteps he followed. Cataloguing every conceivable detail of distillery location, operation, manning and output, he became acquainted with some of the most famous (and infamous) distillers of his time.

One year later, *Harper's Weekly Gazette* published his findings in what is now one of the rarest volumes of its type. As a tribute to Alfred Barnard's pioneering spirit, and to make his remarkable work more accessible, Lochar and Mainstream Publishing are delighted to present this Centenary Edition.

EDINBURGH

1987

FOREWORD

THIS book was first published in 1887 by *Harper's Weekly Gazette* (later *Harper's Wine and Spirit Gazette*) with which Alfred Barnard and his family were involved although he himself was not a distiller and had no connection with the whisky trade. It was a work prompted by curiosity about the processes involved in the production of whisky and enthusiasm for Scotland's landscape. The result is not only an engaging Victorian travelogue of Scotland but also a detailed analysis of every distillery in the United Kingdom, for in 1886 there were also 28 in Ireland and four in England.

It is Barnard's curiosity and enthusiasm that carry the book along in what can only be called an affectionate personal account of his travels and modes of transport, the landscapes through which he passed, the people he met and the hostelries he frequented, as well as the lay-out, equipment and plant of every distillery he visited. The liveliness of this account, the obvious enjoyment of his experiences, and openness with which he encountered people and places, give the book a flavour that cannot possibly be anticipated by anyone merely judging the title.

In 1886 Barnard recorded that there were 129 distilleries in Scotland, of which 120 produced pot-still malt whisky and nine produced large quantities of grain spirit with three of the latter producing both malt and grain whisky and one producing "grain with an admixture of malt". Pot-still whisky was the original Highland Malt Whisky, made solely from malted barley but grain whisky was made in large industrial Coffey stills named after the Irishman Aeneas Coffey who invented the process in 1830. And whereas pot-still malt whisky was the product of at least two distillations, the Coffey still used a variety of cereals to produce greater quantities of spirit (albeit of no great flavour or quality) more quickly and cheaply, doing so in one continuous process. It was the blending of the Coffey still product with a selection of different pot-still malt whiskies which produced the great whisky boom of the late 19th Century and made Scotch a household name the world over.

By 1896, the number of distilleries in Scotland had risen by 32 to 161 and it looked as though the Scotch whisky boom would continue indefinitely. But unrestrained production brought the failure of Pattisons of Leith in 1898 and created mayhem amongst producers, many of whom went to the wall. A period of limitation and amalgamation followed in an effort to avoid the circumstances which had so very nearly destroyed the prosperity of the entire industry. Barnard had written during the heyday of the expansion of the Scotch whisky industry when it had completed the transition from a farmyard activity to a great national commercial asset. It still had its roots with family firms interested in the quality and style of their product unwilling to lose control of generations of craftsmanship.

Barnard thus captured a highpoint in the history of Scotch whisky, and his account of the distilleries reflects the confidence and goodwill prevalent throughout the industry at that time. The splendid illustrations betray Barnard's interest in the surrounding landscape and local characteristics, while his tone of happy reminiscence beautifully conveys the mood in which his tour of investigation was made.

> As we drove along home, the last lingering rays of the setting sun were falling on the russet coverings of the trees, and the hills, which now began to darken the horizon, were flushed by the sunset, and before we reached home the sea, which now almost appeared at our feet, was enveloped in mist.
>
> We rattled along in high spirits, enjoying the drive, and regretting that we should not have the same pleasure for many a long day.

That is a characteristic conclusion — here is a characteristic opening.

> We left Elgin by the night train for Keith, where we found excellent quarters at the Gordon Arms, one of those rare old-fashioned hostelries, which are fast passing away. Mr. Barclay, the jolly landlord, received us on our arrival and made us exceedingly comfortable, during our fortnight's sojourn at his house. The next morning we again entered the train, this time bound for beautiful Craigellachie.

(Try getting a train from Elgin to Craigellachie today and you will see how superior the Victorian railway system was compared to the present network.)

One of my favourite remarks by Barnard comes at the end of the short account of his visit to the now defunct Auchnagie Distillery at Ballinluig.

> One exciseman is employed at the Distillery, who informed us that he leads quite a pastoral life here, and spends his summer days in his garden and little farm-yard.

In its comprehensive and detailed authority Barnard's book stands alone as the great reference book on the distilling of whisky in Scotland. It is an outstanding contribution to social as well as industrial and economic history. It also possesses — quite uniquely for a work of this nature — a freshness, a personal charm and an ability to communicate the author's enjoyment in all the aspects of travel, inspection, conversation, encounter and reportage that make it such a pleasure to read.

EDINBURGH
JULY 1987.

DAVID DAICHES

INTRODUCTION

Then hey for the barley corn
The bonny barley corn;
No grain or flower
Has half the power
Of the bearded barley corn

WHEN Alfred Barnard set out in the mid-1880s to visit all the distilleries in the United Kingdom and compile this fascinating volume, he was paying tribute to the growing popularity of Scotch whisky. This change in taste had come about more through good luck than good judgement.

During the 1870s, wine and spirit merchants throughout the United Kingdom had begun mixing grain whiskies and 'self' whiskies, as they were termed, to produce blends on a large scale while some malt distillers had developed a market for their well-matured 'self' whiskies. However, brandy remained the spirit that the majority of drinkers preferred. In the late 1870s disaster struck the French brandy growers in Charante when the phylloxera aphid imported from America laid waste their vineyards. Over the next decade more than two-thirds of the vineyards were destroyed and much of the brandy that was distilled was unwholesome. Bereft of brandy and many other wines the trade turned to whisky. Sales grew rapidly and nearly every grocery shop in Britain had its own blend, normally made up by a wine and spirit merchant, not necessarily in Scotland. Although the Scotch malt whiskies gave each blend its distinctive flavour, they often contained other whiskies, particularly Irish Whiskey — a pot-still grain whiskey, which confusingly was produced not only in Ireland but also in England and Scotland. The sudden growth in demand for whisky to replace brandy was a reflection of the increased wealth of Britain in the late 19th Century.

Since the 1860s drinking of wines and spirits had climbed steadily and drinkers had become much more discerning in their tastes. Wine and spirit merchants proliferated throughout the British Isles and their suppliers, who were usually agents for continental producers, domestic distillers and brewers, found it difficult to keep track of the reliability and financial probity of the myriad of small businesses. This problem was brought sharply into focus by the very serious depression in the British economy which began in 1877 and lasted for almost eight years. A great number of concerns collapsed, particularly those trading in the luxuries of life like wines and spirits. As in many other trades, there was a pressing need for an organisation to publish and distribute, regularly and rapidly, information relating to firms in difficulty or suspected of trading fraudulently. In some industries this requirement was answered by representative companies combining to form an association. However, in the case of the wine and spirit trade, it was left to one man, E. Norton Harper, to establish, at the height of the crisis, The London Provincial Agency for Protecting the Interests of the Wine Trade. From the outset, it was his intention to produce a regular periodical containing 'private and confidential' information for members who were to pay an initial subscription of two guineas, rising to three guineas in 1879.

Edward Norton Harper came from a family long-connected with the trade. His family firm of wine shippers had been founded in the late 18th Century by his great-uncle and had secured the monopoly to ship all the wines and spirits to the East India Company. In managing the business, Norton Harper's greatest claim to fame was that he was the first to introduce into India, the ales of Michael Bass, the Burton-on-Trent brewer. When their popularity amongst the British residents was assured, Michael Bass named this beer 'East India Ale' in recognition of Norton

Harper's achievement. As well as being a skilled connoisseur of wines, beers and spirits, Norton Harper was also an accountant. He retired from the family business in 1869 to help his sons, Alfred C. Harper, Herbert E. Harper and F. Bernard Harper, to set up an accountancy practice in the heart of London's wineland to cater for the needs of the trade. He was a founding member of the Society of Accountants in England and served as its president in 1880-81. On assuming this office, he gave up his involvement in the London & Provincial Agency for Protecting the Interests of the Wine Trade, leaving its future direction to his second son, Herbert. Immediately Herbert Harper changed the name to the Wine Trade Creditors Association and started publishing a weekly magazine. Five years later, in 1885, this periodical became *Harper's Weekly Gazette*, devoted to the interests of the wine, spirit and brewing trade. This alteration in title reflected a widening of the coverage to include more general articles on the trade and its personalities.

There is no record of when Alfred Barnard first became associated with *Harper's Weekly Gazette*. He was born in 1837, possibly of Jewish parents and by the time he was 30 he was married to Fanny Ruffle and living at 1 Princes Street, Marleybone, London. Although this house was divided up into flats occupied by tradesmen, domestic servants and cleaning ladies, he described himself rather grandly as a 'gentleman'. His first son, Harold Alfred, was born in Princes Street on 10 March 1869. He moved before the census of population was taken in 1871 and consequently it is impossible to discover where he was born and other children he may have had. It seems almost certain that by then he had opened an advertising agency at No. 49 Fleet Street, moving later in the decade to No. 40. His choice of career was linked to the explosion in the number of periodicals like *Harper's Weekly Gazette* which depended in large measure on advertisements for their circulation. There is no trace of the names of his clients but there is enough to suggest that he had strong connections with the London wine and spirit trade. He was commissioned by *Harper's Weekly Gazette* to undertake his tour of the *Whisky Distilleries of the United Kingdom* in the spring of 1885. This was evidently a full-time job as he gave up his advertising agency and for the rest of his life described himself as either a journalist or an author.

He unashamedly delighted in this adventure — 'It is well known that most of the Scotch and Irish Distilleries, in addition to the interest they awaken as important sources of commercial interest, are invested with no ordinary attractions, by their picturesque surroundings, and the magnificent country in which they are placed.' Such enthusiasm for the Scottish countryside was by no means universal at the time. Writing just four years earlier in his *Thorough Guide Series — The Highlands of Scotland*, MJB Baddeley was harsh in his criticism.

> As to Scotch mountains themselves there are far too many of them. Their multiplicity is wearisome . . . Healthy appreciation of a beautiful scene can hardly be enhanced by the knowledge that some desperate deed of rapine or revenge has been perpetuated in it; and sooth to say, such deeds, best fitted for record in the pages of a "penny dreadful" form the staple commodity of Highland tradition.

These attitudes which permeate this guide did not affect Alfred Barnard. Everywhere he went he found much to marvel at, accepting local tradition and legend for what they were. He even enjoyed a rough crossing of the Pentland Firth on his way to Orkney after a day and a half's journey from London. Wherever possible he had prepared the ground for his visit well in advance of his arrival, usually through correspondence with the proprietors. Nearly always he was accompanied by a local photographer to take the pictures from which Walker and Boutall subsequently made the etchings for the book. By the end of 1886 he had visited and recorded 129 distilleries in Scotland, 28 in Ireland, and four in England. The manuscript was ready for publication in January 1887. The printers were Sir Joseph Causton & Sons of Eastcheap, London, who specialized in printing various types of record books that the Customs and Excise required distillers, brewers and bonded warehouse keepers to maintain. *The Whisky Distilleries of the United Kingdom* was well received, finding a ready market amongst the readers of *Harper's Weekly Gazette*, many of whom were English wine and spirit merchants, carrying some 'self' whiskies on their list.

After publication, Alfred Barnard seems to have worked full-time for Harpers in their office at No. 39 Crutched Friars in the heart of London's wineland. Sharing this Queen Anne house with the *Gazette* were Kennedy Reuss & Co, sole agents for Pol Roger & Co's champagne, and H Walbaum & Tosetti, a well-known firm of continental forwarding and shipping agents. A central feature of the editorial office was a large hexagonal oak table made from the sounding board of the old 'three-decker' pulpit which was removed from St Olav's church in Hart Street in 1853.

Since none of the articles in the *Gazette* are attributed to individual journalists, it is impossible to discover what Alfred Barnard contributed. However, he was soon busy with another monumental task. Encouraged by the reception of his whisky book and fascinated by the processes he had seen on his tours, he embarked on a similar survey of the United Kingdom brewing industry. With over 15,000 companies and individuals licensed to brew beer, Alfred Barnard appreciated that he could not possibly carry out the same comprehensive review as he had for the whisky industry. Accordingly, as he explained, he limited himself to the largest brewers, like Allsopps, Bass and Worthington:

> My pilgrimage was undertaken firstly with a view to acquaint my reader with a knowledge of the colossal trade and manufacture of beer, and the vast resources of the great breweries, and secondly to make known the history and antecedents of some of the eminent breweries.

To qualify for inclusion the breweries had not just to be large, but the proprietors had to pay an entry fee to Alfred Barnard of 25 guineas. Much to the annoyance of some brewery companies, he insisted that failure to contribute would lead to exclusion. The subscriptions were used to underwrite the printing of four volumes of the survey of the industry between 1889 and 1891. Unlike the whisky book, these volumes were not published by *Harper's Weekly Gazette* but by Sir Joseph Causton & Sons directly. Just as with the whisky book, the reception was enthusiastic with excellent reviews in the trade press. The review in the *Brewers' Guardian* of 5 August 1890 was typical — 'This is the third volume of this very interesting work and the manner in which it has been written reflects the highest praise on the author, whose entertaining style has never flagged in any of the volumes.'

Four years after the appearance of the last instalment of his brewery study in August 1891, Alfred Barnard received an invitation to write a book from William Whiteley, the department store owner. Alfred Barnard was a surprising choice since William Whiteley had built up his business over the previous 40 years by denying himself all the luxuries of life, including drinking and smoking, and had invested every penny he could. By the mid 1890s, apart from his original store in Westbourne Grove, Bromsgrove, he had several other shops, an estate agency, and a model fruit farm. Adopting the title the 'Universal Provider', he claimed, with some justification that he could provide everything from a pin to an elephant. Using the same technique as in his previous books, Alfred Barnard lavishly described in great detail William Whiteley's huge enterprise, illustrating the text with photographs and line drawings. Published by Sir Joseph Causton & Sons under the title *Orchards and Gardens*, William Whiteley anticipated 'enormous sales through his shops. He took 50,000 copies and stocked his windows and counters with piles of them, offered at five shillings apiece. But his expectations were sadly disappointed. Few copies were bought and the work proved a dead loss to him.' No doubt Alfred Barnard received a handsome fee for his troubles.

There is no trace of any further publications by Alfred Barnard until 1898 when he was commissioned by Highland Distilleries Company Limited of Glasgow to write a book about their four distilleries. Coincidentally this company had been established in the same year that the *Whisky Distilleries of the United Kingdom* was published through the amalgamation of the Islay Distillery Co, owners of the Bunnahabhain Distillery by Port Askaig and William Grant & Co, owners of Glen Rothes distillery at Rothes on Speyside. Since then the company had gone on to

acquire two further distilleries, Glenglassaugh at Portsoy in Banffshire (founded in 1875) and Tamdhu-Glenlivet distillery (founded in 1896) not far from Craigellachie on the Spey. In undertaking this project Alfred Barnard could not hide his happiness that whisky had become by far and away the most popular drink since he first wrote about the industry.

> During the past ten years the manufacture of whisky has increased by leaps and bounds until it has become a gigantic industry. Scotch whisky is daily penetrating regions hitherto unknown to commerce. This statement is borne out of the fact that wherever on the face of the globe Britons do congregate Scotch whisky is found to be the leading beverage and source of profit to the enterprising merchant who dispenses it.

> A fig for Horace and his juice,
> Falernian and Massic;
> Far better drink can we produce,
> Though is not quite so classic.

He was ecstatic at the opportunity to revisit some of the most remote parts of Scotland and even more lavish in his praise of the countryside. The account of Bunnahabhain distillery opens with a word of warning for the ordinary tourist.

> The untoward fate which condemns some of the most beautiful flowers and plants to spread their breath and beauty in the darkly haunts of the forest, seems also to take a perverse pleasure in keeping some of the most admirable scenes of which our islands can boast shut away from the steps of the tourists, who, following one another in the beaten track marked out by guide books, little dream how much beauty and grandeur they are leaving behind them on

either hand as they are dragged onward in the wake of the excursionist.

He was unequivocal in his praise of the Spey — 'A more beautiful country is not to be found anywhere, possessing as it does grouping mountains with deep cloughs and valleys intersecting them, picturesque torrents streaming down their sides, woods that climb the hills, and swift-flowing rivers.' Designed and printed again by Sir Joseph Causton & Sons Ltd, the book was illustrated with photographs of all their distilleries and the Glasgow head office of the company. Although by the time it was ready for the press, there were clear indications that the whisky trade was seriously overstocked, Alfred Barnard gave no hint of any trouble ahead, except possibly in his valedictory verse on leaving Glenglassaugh:

> But I must bid these pleasing scenes adieu;
> Farewell ye grazing herds and warbling birds.
> I go to seek the savage haunts of men.

The book appeared under the whimsical title *'Willie Brewd a Peck o' Maut' — A Run through some famous Scotch Distilleries.*

Back in the savage haunts of men in London, Alfred Barnard, now in his early sixties, continued to contribute articles to *Harper's Weekly Gazette.* He was now comfortably off, living in a villa in South Norwood with the appropriately Scottish name of 'Glenalmond'. His son Herbert Alfred had also joined him at the office in Crutched Friars assisting with the administration of the enterprise. In 1902 the Harper family decided to widen the ownership of the *Gazette* by forming a limited liability company and selling shares to their employees and other interested individuals. Registered under the title Wine and Spirit Gazette (Harper's Weekly) Ltd, the new company had a capital of some £19,000. Alfred Barnard was appointed a director along with HE Harper and John N. Bishop and Herbert Barnard became company secretary.

The opening years of the 20th Century were difficult times for the wine and spirit trade due partly to a serious recession in the economy and, perhaps more importantly, to a swelling tide of anti-drink opinion. These problems reached a climax in 1909 with massive increases in duty imposed by the Liberal Chancellor of the Exchequer, Lloyd

George, a confirmed teetotaller. At the same time, Herbert Barnard died unexpectedly of pneumonia at the early age of 41. His father took over his responsibilities as secretary in addition to his duties as a director. He was immediately faced with a serious crisis in the company's affairs. The circulation of the *Gazette* had been falling for some years and the company had been losing money. The sharp increase in duty had knocked the stuffing out of the trade and in the prevailing mood of little confidence in the future, their was nothing to be done to save the company. Early in 1910 Wine and Spirit Gazette (Harper's Weekly) Ltd went into liquidation and the shareholders, including Alfred Barnard lost all their investment. *The Gazette* was sold by the receiver and manager F. Bernard Harper to the Straker family for the value of the office fittings and there was little interruption in publication.

Alfred Barnard, now in his early seventies, ceased to have any connection with the periodical. The loss of both his son and his investment was a heavy blow and he was forced to remove from his villa to a flat over a row of shops in Royal Mansions, Croydon. He had, however, managed to recoup some of his finances by the following year and acquired a house at 6 Cheltenham Villas in Croydon. Within a year he had moved once more to 11 Grenaby Road, also in Croydon and it was here that he died in the spring of 1918 at the age of 81. His death went unnoticed by either the distillers or brewery press. There was no obituary in *Harper's Weekly Gazette.* It was to be another 50 years before a surge in popularity for whisky and beer was to lead to the re-discovery of his two fascinating books. He would probably like best to be remembered by the two lines in praise of the common ingredient in whisky and beer with which he ended the introduction to his book for Highland Distilleries.

For men of sense must own it is better,
To live on malt than to starve on water.

UNIVERSITY OF GLASGOW
JULY 1987

MICHAEL S. MOSS

THE

Whisky Distilleries

— OF —

The United Kingdom.

JAMES POWER ESQ, FOUNDER OF THE FIRM OF SIR JOHN POWER & SONS, DUBLIN
FROM A CONTEMPORARY PICTURE IN IVORY AND NEEDLEWORK.

THE

Whisky Distilleries

— OF —

The United Kingdom

BY

ALFRED BARNARD.

WITH ILLUSTRATIONS AND MAPS.

EDITED AND PUBLISHED BY THE

PROPRIETORS OF "HARPER'S WEEKLY GAZETTE,"

39 CRUTCHED FRIARS, LONDON, E.C.

1887.

London:

Printed by SIR JOSEPH CAUSTON AND SONS,

9, Eastcheap, E.C.

PREFACE.

THE object of this Work is to give a familiar description and history of all the Whisky Distilleries of Great Britain, the product of which brings the largest revenue to the Imperial Exchequer of any industry in the Kingdom. Also to draw attention to the rapid increase of the Whisky Trade, and the vast field of Distillery enterprise now existing in this country; the annual output of Scotland alone being for the year 1885-6 17,982,338 gallons, whilst that of Ireland was 10,620,584 gallons. In these pages I have made no pretensions to observations, scientific or otherwise, on the art of distilling malt and grain spirit, but have simply given a description of the Distilleries and what I have seen therein. That I am not a practical distiller or connected with the trade is not an assumption of merit, as will probably be proved by the censure which, from some quarters, the book may receive; therefore, I earnestly bespeak the leniency of the Distillers, who will doubtless see faults and technical errors in my description of the various methods, now in use for making malt and grain whisky at the different establishments herein described. The book makes no pretension to literary merit of any sort, and should not be judged by any such standard. It is simply the product of a run through the Distilleries, with an endeavour to give descriptive sketches upon each in more or less detail. So far as is known to the author, there has never been a work of the kind published before, and as many blenders and whisky merchants have very little knowledge of the "inner workings" of a Distillery, it may, I trust, prove in some measure interesting, if not useful, to them. Again, I wish to stimulate an interest in the art of distilling among those who trade in whisky, and to aid in demonstrating, what I am convinced is correct, that good whisky, as a beverage, is the most wholesome spirit in the world. Should I succeed in doing this, and my book proves of interest to my readers, I shall be gratified, and the publication of this volume will afford me pleasure to the end of my days. I may state that at first I found my descriptive task beset with difficulties far exceeding what I had contemplated; but, after a few weeks' experience, I got acquainted with the nature of the business, the names of the vessels, and the process of mashing and distilling, when my interest grew with the work, making it easier for me; until, after a time, I acquired quite a zest for these distillery studies.

It is well known that most of the Scotch and Irish Distilleries, in addition to the interest they awaken as important sources of commercial interest, are invested with no ordinary attractions, by their picturesque surroundings and the magnificent country in which they are planted. In these pages I have endeavoured to give permanence to impressions made on my mind by the beautiful scenery it was my good fortune to behold in the most favourable weather during a two years' tour. If my readers think that I have gone rather too freely into the history and description of the lovely places visited, I trust that I shall be pardoned, and some allowance made for the exuberance of one in "city pent" who has been released to enjoy the pure air of heaven among the mountains, lakes, and valleys of Scotland and Ireland. I have endeavoured to confine myself exclusively to observations on the most striking objects that presented themselves to my view in passing through the Distilleries, even at the risk of repetition, and although many chapters may appear alike, in reality there is a difference in detail of each one of them. In several "out of the way" places I was detained a day or two waiting for a steamer or other conveyance, which gave me the opportunity of exploring the locality, hence some of the sketches are much longer than others.

I cannot refrain from expressing the delight with which I look back upon my visits and associations with the Distillers themselves, as apart from my extremely pleasurable intercourse with them, without their assistance this book could not have been written, and from stating that a more agreeable and hospitable class does not exist. Everywhere I was received courteously, and in many places with kindly hospitality,

> "When death's dark stream I ferry o'er,
> A time that surely shall come,
> In heaven itself I'll ask no more
> Than just a Highland welcome!"
>
> BURNS.

In alluding to those persons who have rendered me assistance, I must not omit to mention a dear friend, who will not let me "prent him," for his able article on "Distillation," whose talent has left nothing for me to say on the subject, and to whom I feel deeply indebted. Also to Messrs. A. & C. DAWSON for the admirable reproduction of an old family relic, which appears as the frontispiece to the work, and which has been photo-engraved on copper direct from the object; also for the maps. To Messrs. WALKER & BOUTALL for many of the etchings which have done much to embellish and increase the value of the work.

LONDON,
JANUARY 1887.

ALFRED BARNARD.

CONTENTS.

SCOTLAND.

SCOTLAND.

IRELAND.

ENGLAND.

A The Still
B The Worm tub
C The Pump
D Water tub
E A Press
FFF Tubs to hold the goods
GGGG Canns of different size
H A Wood Funnel with a iron nosel
I A large Vessel to put the Fains or after runnings
K Tin pump
L A Pewter Crane
M A Pewter Valencia
N Hippocrates bag or Flannel Sleeve
O Poker Fire-shovel Cole rake
P A Box of Bungs
Q The Worm within the Worm tub mark'd with prick'd lines
R A Piece of Wood to keep down the Head of the Still to prevent flying of

P. Fourdrinier Delin et Sculp

A DISTILLERY IN THE YEAR 1729,

From an old work on the subject.

DISTILLATION.

TO compile a history of the art of Distillation is beyond the province of the present work, but a few remarks upon the subject will not be out of place before commencing the more important task before us, of a description of the various Distilleries in the United Kingdom.

At the outset it may be stated that any inquirer seeking to find the origin and discovery of the art of Distillation, is doomed to disappointment. Many reliable authorities have carefully studied the subject, and many interesting works have been devoted to its consideration, but none have been able to get beyond the range of assumption; of conjecture drawn from the writings and history of past ages. It is curious to note how each writer who takes the subject in hand resorts largely to those who have written before him, and few fresh facts are brought to bear upon the origin of this most important industry. We do not presume to deviate from this rule ourselves, but to follow the authorities who have written on distillation and its history. Of the many to select from, Morewood, an officer of excise, in his exhaustive treatise on "Inebriating Liquors," published at Dublin in 1838, is by far the most interesting and complete, and all writers on the subject since that date rely largely upon him for their facts and data; and taking him as our authority for much that is written in the following pages, we propose to briefly review the history of the art from the earliest ages to the present time.

It may fairly be assumed that the art was unknown to either the Greeks or Romans, for nowhere in their poems, plays or writings which have been handed down to us, is any reference made to alcohol or any distilled spirit. Xenophon, it is true, in his history of the retreat of the ten thousand after the battle of Cunaxa, makes some vague reference to the inhabitants of Armenia "filling their vessels with barley and water;" the liquor is described as very strong if not mixed with water, but from the fact that he makes no reference to fermentation, or to the method of making the liquid, it may be inferred that the drink he describes was no product of the still. Hippocrates, the most famous among Greek physicians, and author of the first attempt at the scientific treatment of medicine, who lived, according to the generally received account, about 400 years before Christ, in none of his works makes the slightest reference to any alembic or retort being used by him. Pliny again, who lived in the first century of the Christian era, wrote an excellent treatise on vines and wine, but makes no mention of its spirit, which he surely would have done had he been possessed of so valuable a secret. In addition to the works of early writers, we have the discoveries during the last hundred years of ancient cities and monuments, and nothing has revealed the slightest clue to the existence of alcohol in early ages. Herculaneum and Pompeii, said to have first been occupied by the Oscans, subsequently by Tyrrhenians and Pelasgians, and afterwards by the Samnites, have been excavated after a burial of some eighteen hundred years, and nothing in the ruins suggests in any way that spirit, in any form, was known among the inhabitants of these ancient cities.

Hitherto reference has only been made to the Greeks and Romans, but from what is known of the Egyptian, the Arabian, and even the Chinese races, it is probable that the secret of the power of the alembic was known to them in ages, the records of which have been lost in the long course of events. Smith writing in 1729, attributes the invention of the art of distillation, by general consent of all learned men, to the Arabian physicians. M. le Normand, a great authority, in his work entitled "L'art du Distillateur des eaux-de-vie et des esprits," published in Paris in 1817, takes the same view. Speaking on the subject he says:—"Les Arabes s'occupèrent, de temps immémorial, à extraire, par la distillation, les parties aromatiques des fleurs et des plantes, dont leurs princes faissaient un très-grand usage. L'on croit que ce sont eau qui, les premiers, ont soumis le vin à la distillation, et qu'ils en ont extrait la liqueur qu'ils appeletent *aqua vitæ*, et que nous avons nommée *eau-de-vie.* Les Arabes, dans les incursions qu'ils firent en Europe, portèrent successivement leurs procédés en Italie, en Espagne et en France." (page 29). Morewood, however, is of a different opinion. He gives credit to the Arabians as the "improvers" of the art, but looks to other nations for its origin; he is rather of opinion that the art was long known in the east, by the Egyptians, the inhabitants of India, and the Chinese.

Leaving the discovery of the art shrouded in the mystery of bygone ages, we pass to that period when learned writers began to give it prominence in their works. Rhazes, Albucassis and Avicenna, three celebrated Arabian physicians and philosophers, who lived about the tenth and eleventh centuries, mention the distillation of Roses, a process in their country much in esteem as affording a perfume greatly valued by their kings and nobles; but they do not allude to the distillation of wine. Geber, commonly called the Arab, who lived according to generally accepted account in the seventh century, in his celebrated work on chemistry, gives an elaborate account of distillation, but only refers to it as a means of extracting the aroma of plants and flowers; he also makes no reference to the distillation of wine. Passing, however, to the thirteenth century, we find several celebrated writers alluding to the product of the still. Arnold de Villa Nova, a physician who lived during that century, writing on the subject, declares that the ancients knew nothing of spirit of wine. He informs us that this extraordinary liquor had been then lately discovered; and that it was believed to be the universal panacea which had been so long sought after. This would appear to be the first authentic reference to the distillation of wine. Raymund Lully, who was born in 1236, and died in 1315, and was the contemporary and pupil of Arnold, affirms that this admirable product from wine, which one can consider, says he, in no other way than as an emanation of the divinity, was concealed from the ancients, because the human race was too young; so precious a discovery, he adds, was reserved for the renovation of its decrepit old age. To Lully the credit is given for giving the name of *alcohol* to the strongest spirit. Friar Bacon, who also lived about this time, did much to develope the early and practical knowledge of the chemical labours of the Arabians, and his *elixir vitæ* must have been the result of experiments in distillation.

France was for a series of years the seat of the great Distilling interest in Europe, as her wines afforded a constant supply for the distillation of Brandy, but as the knowledge of agriculture advanced, and grain became plentiful, a new industry was opened up, especially in our own northern latitudes, where the grape has to give place to the more hardy products of the soil. Dim as are the records of the introduction of the art of distillation into Europe, almost more obscure are those of its introduction into what is now known as the British Isles. That the art was known at an age prior to any authentic record may fairly be assumed, and to the sister isle must be awarded the palm, as the pioneer of the industry. The history of Ireland is so romantic that the records of bygone ages read almost like fiction; as a nation we may be proud of our antiquity, but all parts of England, Scotland, and Wales must give way to the Emerald Isle in historic fame. As regards England the introduction of distillation is generally attributed to the time of Henry II, a date which will fairly coincide with the introduction of the art into Europe generally, as contained in the writings of the authorities already referred to. History tells us that *aqua vitæ* was first known in Europe about this time; but it is more than probable that it was known in Ireland before the English were acquainted with it. Morewood is strong on this point and says, that the strong affinity between the Irish language and the primitive languages of Asia, as stated by Vallancey and other etymologists, and the intercourse the Irish had with that quarter of the world, lead to the supposition that the art of distillation was introduced indirectly from India; but it is more likely that it was received from Spain or Italy, where it was earlier known under the epithet of *acqua vitæ* or *aqua de vite* (water of the vine), the grape being the material from which a spirit was originally extracted in these countries. The monasteries being the repositories of science and the original dispensaries of medicine, it is a natural surmise that the term *acqua vite*, was there corrupted into the Latin and universal appellation *aqua vitæ* (water of life), from its salutary and beneficial effects as a medicine; and from the Latin tongue being the general conveyancer of scientific discovery, as well as of familiar correspondence, the term *aqua vitæ* may have crept into use to signify an indefinite distilled spirit, in contradistinction to *acqua vite*, the mere extract of the grape.

We learn from Ware and Ledwich that the *aqua vitæ* or *usquebaugh* of the Irish, was of a less inflammatory nature than that made in England, because the latter is supposed to be of more recent invention. We find the virtues of usquebaugh and a receipt for making it in the red book of Ossory. The Irish distilled spirits from malt in 1590, and imitated foreign liqueurs in adding aromatic seeds and spices. This manufacture of *usquebaugh* leads us to an opportunity of making a few remarks upon the derivation of the word Whisky, by which we know the modern products of the Irish and Scotch Distilleries. Johnson, in the early edition of his famous dictionary, does not quote the word under the letter W, but under usquebaugh he explains that "it is an Irish and Erse word, which signifies the water of life. It is a compounded distilled spirit, being drawn on aromaticks: and the Irish sort is particularly distinguished for its pleasant and mild flavour. The Highland sort is somewhat hotter, and by corruption in Scotch they call it *Whisky*."

Webster spells the word "Whisky," giving the derivation "from the Irish *uisge*, water, whence usquebaugh; Welch, wysg, a stream." His definition says "a spirit distilled from grain. In the north of England, the name is given to the spirit drawn from barley. In the United States, whisky is generally distilled from wheat, rye, or maize." Morewood adopts the "e," and speaking of the derivation of the word says, "The Latin epithet, *aqua vitæ*, the Irish term usquebaugh, and the modern word, Whisky, are, in point of fact, synonymous. *Aqua vitæ*, signifying the *water of life*, and *usquebaugh*, which should be written *Iskebaghah* or *Isque beoh*, the former implying *water of life*, and the latter, living water. As *Isque,* or *iske* means water, it must appear evident that the word Whisky is only a slight alteration in the pronunciation of the Irish term. Both O'Brien and Vallencey admit that *ai, ay,* or *ey,* are old terms for water, and *Isque,* or *Iske* implying water, the compound word, literally means *water of waters.* Mr. Tovey in his work on British and Foreign Spirits published in 1864, objects to the method of spelling the word as adopted by Morewood, but beyond stating "that it will be clear to our readers that he is not eminently successful as an Etymologist," he has nothing to say upon the subject, nor does he give any reason for his adoption of the now more generally used spelling of the word.

Thus it will be seen that, like the discovery of the art of distillation, the derivation of the word "Whisky" is very obscure. It may, however, be fairly assumed that it is a corruption of the Gaelic word *uisge,* and upon this point most authorities agree. With regard to the spelling of the word, it would seem to have, in former times, been spelled with the "e," and is by many at the present day. In the present work the more generally accepted spelling of the word has been adopted; it after all being a matter of fancy or fashion rather than of etymology. It is certain that the word has been coined within the past hundred years, for in none of the older works on distillation is it to be found. In fact, in Ireland and Scotland plain whisky, such as we have it at the present day, was no doubt only known among a few consumers, who chiefly derived their supplies from the produce of illicit distillation. What may be termed plain Whisky was not the common beverage, a fact that is borne out by all who have written upon the subject. Many persons believe Whisky to be synonymous with the *usquebaugh* of the Irish; but beyond the presumed derivation of the word "Whisky" it has nothing in common. Usquebaugh seems to have been a general name for all compound spirits, and in no work can it be found referred to except as such. Smith, in his work entitled "The Compleat Body of Distilling," published in 1729, refers to Usquebaugh, and gives various receipts for its composition; but he, in common with others too numerous to mention, always refers to it as a compound by rectification of proof spirits. Here is one receipt he gives:—

Fine Usquebaugh.

	l.	*s.*	*d.*
5 gallons of proof Molossus spirits at 2*s.* 7*d.*½	00	13	01½
6 gallons of proof rectify'd Malt spirits at 20*d.*	00	10	00
Mace and Cloves each one ounce and a half	00	03	09
Nutts 4 ounces and a half: Cinnamon 3 ounces	00	05	01½
Coriander-seed, Ginger, each 3 ounces	00	00	03
Cubebs 1 ounce and half	00	00	04½
Raisins 4 pound½	00	01	06
Dates 3 pound	00	04	00
Liquorise 2 pounds ¼	00	01	06
Best English Saffron 4 ounces and a half	00	11	03
10 pound Lisbon Sugar at 7*d.*½	00	06	03
	02	17	01½

For sale.

	l.	*s.*	*d.*
10 gallons of fine Usquebaugh at 20*s.* *per* gallon	10	00	00

Directions in making fine Usquebaugh.

Charge your Still with the Brandy, Mace, Cloves, Nutts, Cinnamon, Coriander-seeds, Ginger and Cubebs adding 5 or 6 gallons of liquor, and draw off your goods very gently, and no longer than proof; and against your Still comes to work prepare ready the English Saffron, well dissevered and put into a linen cloth, and hung at the worm's end; whereby all the goods running through the Saffron (which must be oftentimes turn'd over and over) all the tincture will be extracted, and run amongst the distill'd Goods.

In the interim take the Raisins and Dates and stone them, and scrape the Liquorise, and slice them all very thin, and put'em into an earthen pot, with three gallons of liquor, and covered with thick cap paper, and set to stand in a moderate oven 5 or 6 hours; then let it stand 'till it be fully cold, and strain it into the goods drawn from the Still, and with liquor make up the ten gallons wanting from the Still, dissolving your Sugar therein, and add it to your goods, which when well mix'd together must stand 8 or 10 days in a cask with a cock in it, to become clear, and then put into your cask for sale.

From this it would appear that given the demand a very fair profit might have been made out of the compound. We give a fac-simile of this interesting recipe as a curiosity of past ages. Following the directions for making this usquebaugh, Smith writes at length upon its beneficial qualities, from which it would appear to be a perfect panacea for all human ills.

But returning to the main subject of our remarks, and leaving the art of distillation, its introduction into Europe and into the British Isles, and the derivation of the word Whisky, all buried in the dim obscurity of early and unrecorded ages, let us pass into matters of fact connected with the vast home industry of the manufacture of British Spirits. In England, for a long period, the use of the alembic was confined to the manufacture of medicinal compounds by apothecaries. The introduction of distillation from grain, as we have shown, is not authentically recorded, but from the fact that in the reign of Charles the Second it had assumed proportions to make it an article productive of revenue, we may from that time, a little over two hundred years ago, mark the first epoch in the industry. On the 25th December, 1661, a duty of fourpence was imposed on every gallon of *aqua vitæ* distilled in the kingdom; at this date, of course, it only applied to England and Wales. As showing the gradual development of trade in spirits it may be interesting to note that in 1694 the produce of all stills in England amounted to 1,885,752 gallons of *low wines*, or 754,300 gallons of spirits, and in 1743 it had increased to 12,498,800 gallons of *low wines* or 4,999,520 gallons of spirits. As regards Scotland the earliest record of the quantity of spirits made is in the year after the Union, 1708, when the quantity made was 50,844 gallons; in 1756 we find the quantity increased to 433,811 gallons. About 1776 the export to England commenced which further increased the manufacture. As showing the vast trade in the manufacture of spirits in Ireland, the following is of interest; in 1720 the number of gallons distilled was 136,675; fifty years later, in 1770, it was 801,174 gallons; in 1820 it was 4,636,192. From the earliest duty of twopence per gallon on spirits distilled in England, various additions and alterations have been made; at one time on proof gallons, at another on the capacity of the stills; but it is not our present intention to follow the history of the past too closely.

Leaving the earlier ages of the art of distillation buried in much obscurity, we come to what, without hesitation, is the most important epoch of the Whisky Industries of the United Kingdom. Prior to the year 1825 distillation was in the hands of a few capitalists, and English spirits, although made from the finest materials, could not, from the grossness and richness of the wash, be rendered palatable or saleable without undergoing rectification to remove their coarseness and harshness. Accordingly, says Morewood, a number of traders, denominated rectifiers, were called into action between the distillers and consumers. These rectifiers re-distilled the spirits with the addition of certain drugs and flavouring materials, such as juniper berries, spirits of turpentine, &c., by which they made a sort of compound called British Gin; or else with spirits of nitre, prunes, &c., manufactured an imitation of Brandy and Foreign Liqueurs.

This period may be said to be the infancy of the Whisky Industries, for it is within the last sixty years only that this enormous home industry has existed as such. Prior to 1825, as we have said, plain Whisky was not a common beverage, and all spirits, whether manufactured in England, Scotland, or Ireland, were obliged to pass through the medium of the rectifiers, who held the position of arbiters of public taste. To the liberal views of the Earl of Ripon, the then Chancellor of the Exchequer, must be attributed the correction of this abuse and the destruction of this monoply. "He saw that were the distillers enabled to make a good pure spirit, not only would there be a direct supply to the consumer, but the liquor would be unquestionably more palatable and wholesome in the natural state, than when compounded and impregnated with such materials as have been described. From this the most beneficial effects would ensue, the trade would become prosperous, and an augmented consumption increase the revenue; Geneva and Brandy would decrease in proportion—smuggling be checked—foreigners no longer enrich themselves at our expense—and an impetus be given to our agriculture." We quote the foregoing from a writer of that day; how far the views of the then Chancellor of the Exchequer have been fulfilled, one has only to turn to the present annual Revenue returns for a complete fulfilment of his anticipations.

Taking this period as the actual foundation of the Whiskey industries, we may pass rapidly on, during which times various alterations were made in the duties in England, Scotland and Ireland, till we arrive at the year 1858, when Mr. Disraeli by adding a further 1s. 10d. to the duty on Irish Spirit, brought the spirit duties throughout the United Kingdom to one uniform rate of 8s. per gallon. In 1860, the duty was raised by Mr. Gladstone to 10s. per gallon, the rate at which it now stands.

So vast has this industry grown, that for the financial year 1884-5, the duty on British Spirits realised no less than £13,987,422, being a sum nearly one-sixth of the entire Revenue of the Nation, and being more than sufficient to entirely provide for the expenses of the Navy; and its importance can only be fully realised by a careful consideration of these vast figures of revenue.

Our few remarks upon Whisky in general would be incomplete without some reference to the smugglers of old, to whom we owe much for the spirit which we now value so highly. Both in Scotland and Ireland the smugglers may be looked upon as the pioneers of the Whisky trade. To them is largely due the superior quality of the Fine Old Malt Whisky that is made in these days, and the "Sma' Stills," and the "Illicit Potheen" may be said to be the foundations upon which the vast Whisky Distilling interests were founded. It is difficult in these days, when cases of illicit distillation are few and far between, and then of small importance, to realise the extent to which this traffic grew in the early days of the present century. The produce of the smugglers' stills being from malt without adulteration, found great favour among the inhabitants of Scotland and Ireland, its distinct flavour making it most agreeable to those who had acquired the habit of drinking it. Added to this, the high rates of duties, and the want of a ready market for the disposal of grain grown in many remote districts, induced many to embark in this illicit traffic to an extent, which was not only injurious to the agriculture and revenue of the country, but to the morals and peaceful habits of the community. To such an extent was it carried in Ireland, that in 1806, out of 11,400,030 gallons (the consumption of spirits in Ireland in that year), 3,800,000 gallons were allowed to be the produce of illicit manufacturers; and in 1811, 1812 and 1813 there were no less than 19,067 illicit distilleries destroyed by the revenue and military.

To put down this illicit trade, various enactments were framed by the Legislature, among which that of fining the townlands on which any portion of a still, wash, low wines, or other materials for distillation were found, was not the least oppressive. The annual average of fines levied for seven years under the act for the suppression of this evil, amounted to £50,989 for all Ireland, while in one county alone the sum laid for 1806, was £2,620; in 1807, £2,750; and in 1814, £18,125. How could it be expected to be otherwise, when it was proved before the Parliamentary Commissioners, that many men were found to declare that they had never done a day's work in their lives but at illicit distillation, and that they knew nothing else by which they could gain subsistence?

Many interesting and curious facts might be related of the extraordinary contrivances of the people to evade the law and prevent detection, such as the artful construction of distilleries on the boundaries of townlands, in the caverns of mountains, on islands in lakes, on boats in rivers; of carrying away and secreting revenue officers for weeks together to prevent their giving testimony, the romantic manner of their treatment while in confinement, and the various other schemes and devices to defeat the intentions of the Government.

Among these, Morewood mentions the instance of a person who had constructed a distillery so artfully, that it eluded the vigilance of the most expert officers of excise, though known to have long existed in the neighbourhood. A determined gentlemen of this department resolved to find it out at all hazards, and, on one moonlight night, unaccompanied by any person, he followed a horse led by a peasant, having a sack across the back of the animal, which, he suspected contained materials for this mysterious manufactory. When the horse had arrived at a certain place, the sack was removed from his back, and suddenly disappeared. The officer made his observations, returned to his residence, and having procured military assistance, repaired to the place where the horse had been unloaded, all was silent, the moon shone bright, the ground was unmarked by any peculiar appearance, and he was almost inclined (as well as those who accompanied him) to think that he laboured under a delusion. Perceiving, however, some brambles loosely scattered about the place, he proceeded to examine more minutely, and on their removal, discovered some loose sods, under which was found a trap door leading to a small cavern, at the bottom of which was a complete distillery at full work, supplied by a subterraneous stream, and the smoke conveyed from it through the windings of a tube that was made to communicate with the funnel of the chimney of the distillers' dwelling-house, situated at a considerable distance.

Another distillery has been known to be worked on the site, and in conjunction with a limekiln, which, from the kiln being continually in operation, kept the other for years without detection. So cunningly were some of those still-houses situated, and so artfully constructed, that the smoke proceeding from them was made to issue as if from burning heath, or sods of peat, ignited for manure. Their position was, for the most part, either on a commanding eminence, in the centre of a bog, or in a well-secured fastness; but always calculated to prevent the identity of townland or proprietorship, while the portability and easy removal of the apparatus rendered the discovery and seizure of their stills difficult and hazardous. On the approach of a stranger, an alarm was given either by deputing a messenger of sounding a horn, while the machinery was removed, and the potale always destroyed or conveyed into receptacles under ground prepared for such exigencies. Thus the still-hunter was often disappointed of his expected prize, the poor distiller put to the loss of many a brewing, and the excise officer rendered the object of the hatred and vindictive feeling of the unreflecting peasantry.

The subjoined curious engraving from an old plate represents a distillery of this description at full work, with a party of police approaching to seize it, while two peasants may be seen on the rocks, sounding their horns to alarm the smugglers.

Another account is given by Morewood, of an attempt to obstruct a revenue officer in the discharge of his duty. On the approach of the assizes in 1803, when many were about to be prosecuted for illicitly distilling, an officer, stationed at Dunfanaghy, in the county of Donegal, who was to support the informations, was suddenly seized, blindfolded, and carried away by a body of men in disguise, and brought to the island of Aran on the western coast. From thence he was conveyed to the islands of Goal, Inishmaan, &c., where he was closely confined, often threatened with the loss of life, and was even obliged by way of humiliation for his active services, to assist in the working of an illicit still; while, like another Tantalus, the cup of pleasure was held to his parched lips, without the liberty of gratifying his thirsty desires. At the end of thirteen days, when the necessity for his confinement had ceased, he was again blindfolded, taken from the island, and sent a considerable distance into the interior of the country, when the mask was removed from his face, and he was allowed in the solitude of the night, to make his way to his disconsolate family, who, all the time had looked upon his restoration as hopeless. Another officer, on a similar occasion, was hurried from his bed, without any covering except his shirt and trousers, put into a sack, thrown across the back of a horse, and, in this manner, was conducted to the margin of a lake, when, in his own hearing, a consultation was held whether he should be drowned by tieing a stone to the sack and committing it to the deep, or that he should be put to a more lingering and torturing death. In this awful state of suspense he was removed to a mountainous part of the country, where he was subjected to every kind of insult and privation, continually menaced with death in every shape of barbarity, led out at night as if about to be executed, and again conducted to his solitary habitation, anticipating a renewal of further cruelties. In this state he was retained for a considerable time, till the judge, who presided at the assizes during the trial of some persons for illicit distilling, suspecting the parties as being accessory to this outrage, told them, that if the officer who had been taken away, were not immediately liberated, he would pass such a sentence on them as would for ever put it out of their power to commit such another offence, and gave them but twenty-four hours for his restoration. This had the desired effect; the unfortunate man was again put into a sack and restored to his family in the same manner as that in which he had been carried away.

An adventure of a singular nature is said to have befallen a gentleman who was paying a visit to the Hebrides. While making some geological researches, he was induced to descend a precipice to examine the nature of the strata of a rock, and entering a cave that attracted his attention, he was astonished to hear the noise of persons, as if revelling at a banquet. Being fearful of danger he was about to retire, when he was accosted by a person inside and requested to advance. Considering compliance the best policy, and his curiosity being a good deal excited, he followed the individual into the cavern, and was no little astonished to find himself introduced to a number of persons seated on benches round a table, regaling themselves with as much apparent satisfaction as if in a palace. On looking round, he perceived a number of casks of spirits ranged as if in a cellar, with old swords and other weapons of defence, plainly indicating that he had fallen in with a party of smugglers. Apprehensive that he was an officer of the revenue, he was eyed with great distrust, and questioned most particularly as to his pursuits; but finding that his profession was of a different nature, they told him candidly what they were, treated him with much kindness, and, after enjoining secrecy, suffered him to depart, but not without partaking of a hearty glass, and a share of all the luxuries of their solitary grotto.

Many other authentic stories could be told of the old smuggling days, but we have not space to follow them here. But before leaving the subject of illicit distillation, it may be interesting to give an account of a visit to one of these pioneer establishments. In the following pages will be found descriptions of the various licensed Distilleries of the present day, and as it were to complete our wanderings in the lands of Spirits, we give the following account of a visit to an illicit potheen distillery, as described by Donovan in 1830. He says:— Some time since, being on a journey amongst the mountains in the most northern parts of Ireland, I learned that there was a potheen distillery at work; and having despatched an emissary well known to the distiller to procure me admission, I was permitted to inspect the process. This place was famous for producing good spirit.

The distillery was a very small thatched cabin, at one end of which was a large turf fire kindled on the ground, and confined by a semicircle of large stones. Resting on these stones, and over the fire, was a forty-gallon tin vessel, which answered both for heating the water and as the body of the still. Over the fire was an opening in the thatch, with a very low chimney; and through this was conveyed away the smoke, after traversing the whole of the apartment. The fumes of the burning turf were so acrimonious that my eyes were exceedingly smarted; on perceiving which, the distiller desired me to sit down as a certain remedy. I did so, and immediately the pain ceased; the fumes occupied the upper statum only of the air, they consisting chiefly of pyroligneous acid in vapour.

The mash-tun was a cask hooped with wood, at the bottom of which, next the chimb, was a hole plugged with tow. This vessel had no false bottom; in place of it, the bottom was strewed with young heath; and over this, a stratum of oat-husks. Here the mash of hot water and ground malt was occasionally mixed up for two hours; after which time the vent at bottom was opened, and the worts were allowed to filter through the stratum of oat-husks and heath. The mashing with hot water on the same grains was then repeated, and the worts were again withdrawn. The two worts being mixed in another cask, some yeast was added, and the fermentation allowed to proceed until it fell spontaneously, which happened in about three days. It was now ready for distillation, and was transferred into the tin body, which was capable of distilling a charge of forty gallons. A piece of soap, weighing about two ounces, was then thrown in to prevent its running foul; and the head, apparently a large tin pot with a tube in its side, was inverted into the rim of the body, and luted with a paste made of oatmeal and water. The lateral tube was then luted into the worm, which was a copper tube of an inch and half bore, coiled in a barrel for a flake-stand. The tail of the worm where it emerged from the barrel was calked with tow. The wash speedily came to a boil, and then water was thrown on the fire; for at this period is the chief danger of boiling over. The spirit almost immediately came over: it was perfectly clear; and by its bead, this first running was inferred to be *proof*. Its flavour was really excellent; and it might well have passed for a spirit of three months old. As soon as the upper statum of water in the flake-stand became warm, a large pailful of cold water from an adjoining stream was dashed in with sufficient force, as he said, to make the hot water run over, it being lighter; and this cooling process was continually applied to. In this way the singlings were drawn off in about two hours; and the singlings of four distillations made one charge of the still to produce the potheen.

The malt was prepared by enclosing the barley in a sack, and soaking the sack and its contents for some time in bog water, which is deemed the best; then withdrawing and draining it. The malt was then made to germinate in the usual manner. When it had grown sufficiently, it was conveyed in a sack to the kiln, along with some sacks of raw corn, for the purpose of concealment. The raw corn was spread out on the kiln; but during the night when the kiln owner had retired to rest, the raw corn was removed, the malt spread on, dried, and replaced by the raw grain before day. The owner of corn drying on a kiln sits up all night to watch it. In this way discovery was eluded, and the malting completed.

The body of this still cost one pound; its head about four shillings; the worm cost twenty-five shillings; the mash-turn and flakestand might both be worth twelve shillings. The whole Distillery was, therefore, worth about three pounds; and it is purposely constructed on this cheap plan, as it holds out no inducement to informers or excisemen. Sometimes they have been on an extensive scale.

But all is now changed; the working of our Distilleries has grown into a legalized and vast revenue-producing industry, and illicit distillation has been almost stamped out. Under an able staff of revenue officers the evil has been almost entirely overcome, as the following decennial statement, which shows the number of detections made during the past fifty years, will show:—

	England.	Scotland.	Ireland.	Total.
1834	314·	692·	8,192·	9,198·
1844	213·	177·	2,574·	2,964·
1854	301·	73·	1,853·	2,227·
1864	84·	19·	2,757·	2,860·
1874	12·	6·	796·	814·
1884	5·	22·	829·	856·

Illicit distillation may now be said to exist only among a few isolated evaders of the law; but they are unable to continue their operations for any length of time, and soon get discovered by the revenue authorities. The true smuggler of old exists no longer; he belongs to a bygone age, when what is now considered to be a crime was looked upon as justifiable evasion of undue laws. With all their faults one can but admire the smugglers of old, who had in their veins much of the pluck and daring that has been, and still is, the backbone of the British race. As we have said, they may be looked upon as the pioneers of the Whisky Trade; no men understood better the localities where they could turn out good spirit, and this fact may be seen to this day, when we find many of the oldest distilleries existing upon sites which have been well-known to have been chosen by smugglers of old as places where the purest mountain streams, flowing over moss and peats, could be used to distil and produce spirits of the finest descriptions.

Having thus far cast our glances back into the past of the Whisky Trade, and having in the body of our work its present extent and circumstances practically set forth, there remains for us only the somewhat risky, yet not unnecessary, duty of attempting to forecast the future of this extensive branch of our native industries. Prophecy is proverbially a thankless task, and it has been our experience that it is in their own domain especially prophets have no honour. Yet, as dealing with commercial men, we are entitled to lay before our readers the legitimate deductions from the facts and circumstances which are within our knowledge. At the present moment the Whisky Trade stands in possession, broadly speaking, of the key of the situation. French Brandy is, as an article of general consumption, hopelessly discredited, the *phylloxera* and other diseases of the vine have destroyed the material for the production of a spirit which will suit the ordinary purse. Rum, for some occult reason, nobody that is anybody drinks, except for the medicinal treatment of a cold. Gin, with all its many merits, fails to gain new drinkers, while the old consumers seem to be dying out. The opportunity of Whisky is, therefore, overwhelming. What will it do with it? England is the market in which both Irish and Scotch

Distillers are contending for the pre-eminence; while Caledonia drinks her own Whisky, Hibernia prefers *her* own make, so that the Saxon taste is the pivot upon which, in these days, hangs the prosperity of the Distilling Trade of either nation. To this we have to add the by no means unimportant weight of our Colonial taste, and the fact that wherever on the face of the civilised world Englishmen do congregate, a "good tap" of Whisky is found to be irresistible to the British, and a source of profit to "mine host" who has had the luck to secure for his customers something worth their drinking. Thus it may be said that even in its greatest markets, at home or abroad, Whisky is still in its youth, while in certain still scarcely-penetrated regions it is yet in its infancy.

We shall be treading on delicate grounds when we refer to the fact that there are those who hold that the future of the Whisky trade lies with Malt Whisky. Certainly "the present" is not entirely in the hands of that product. Blenders without number can be found who will strenuously affirm that to give the public a moderate priced article with sufficient age, there is no way but to use good old Patent Still Grain Spirit as a basis. Certainly, most palatable Whiskies are now being consumed by the public which, the blenders say, could not be sold at the money, were it not for the cheapening, and—they add—the improving qualities of old Grain Spirit. Into the controversy between Malt and Grain we do not care to enter at greater length; still, all who have a knowledge of the various makes of Whiskies will bear us out in affirming that in many cases they are unsuitable for sale unblended. What is the best qualifier of their potent flavour and body we must leave to those who have to please the public to determine. Our province is merely to lay before our readers the facts of the business as they are, and not as conflicting "judges" may say they ought to be.

"Four be the elements:
Here we assemble 'em
Each of man's world
Or existence an emblem.

"Press from the lemon
The slow flowing juices—
Bitter is Life
In its lessons and uses!

"Bruise the fair sugar lumps—
Nature intended
Her sweet and severe
To be everywhere blended.

"Pour the still water—
Unwarning by sound,
Eternity's ocean
Is dark'ning around!

"Mingle the Spirit
The life of the bowl—
Man is cold mortar
Unwarmed by a soul.

"Drink of the stream
Ere its potency goes—
No bath is refreshing
Except while it glows."

INDEX TO DISTILLERIES ON MAP OF SCOTLAND.

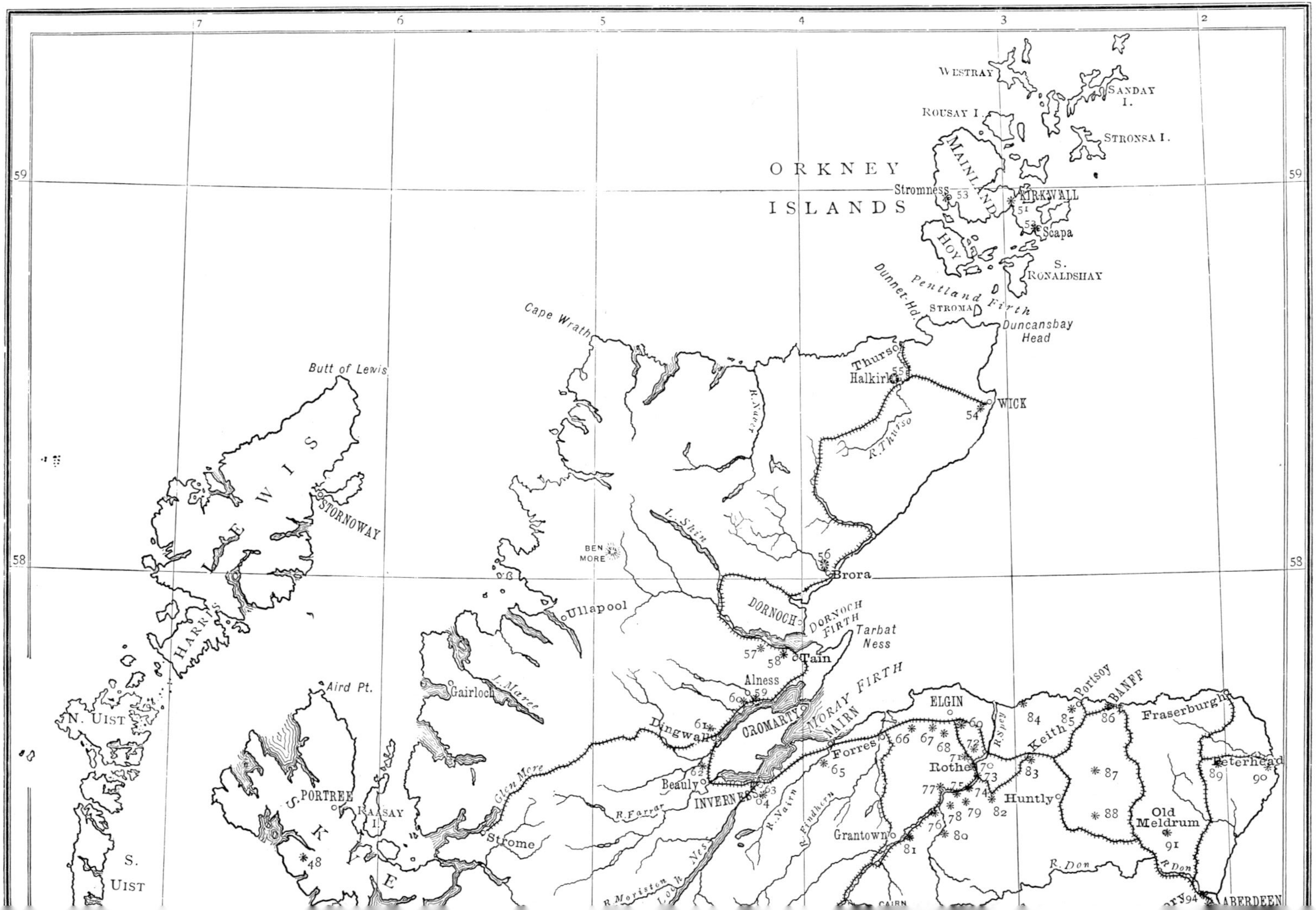
ORKNEY ISLANDS
WESTRAY
ROUSAY I.
SANDAY I.
STRONSA I.
MAINLAND
Stromness
KIRKWALL
Scapa
HOY
S. RONALDSHAY
Pentland Firth
STROMA
Dunnet-Hd.
Duncansbay Head
Cape Wrath
Thurso
Halkirk
WICK
R. Naver
R. Thurso
L. Shin
BEN MORE
Brora
DORNOCH
DORNOCH FIRTH
Tarbat Ness
Tain
Ullapool
Alness
CROMARTY
MORAY FIRTH
NAIRN
Dingwall
Beauly
INVERNESS
R. Farrar
R. Nairn
R. Findhorn
Gairloch
L. Maree
Glen More
Strome
R. Moriston
Loch Ness
Butt of Lewis
LEWIS
STORNOWAY
HARRIS
N. UIST
S. UIST
Aird Pt.
PORTREE
RAASAY I.
SKYE
ELGIN
Forres
Rothes
R. Spey
Keith
Portsoy
BANFF
Fraserburgh
Peterhead
Huntly
Grantown
Old Meldrum
R. Don
ABERDEEN
CAIRN

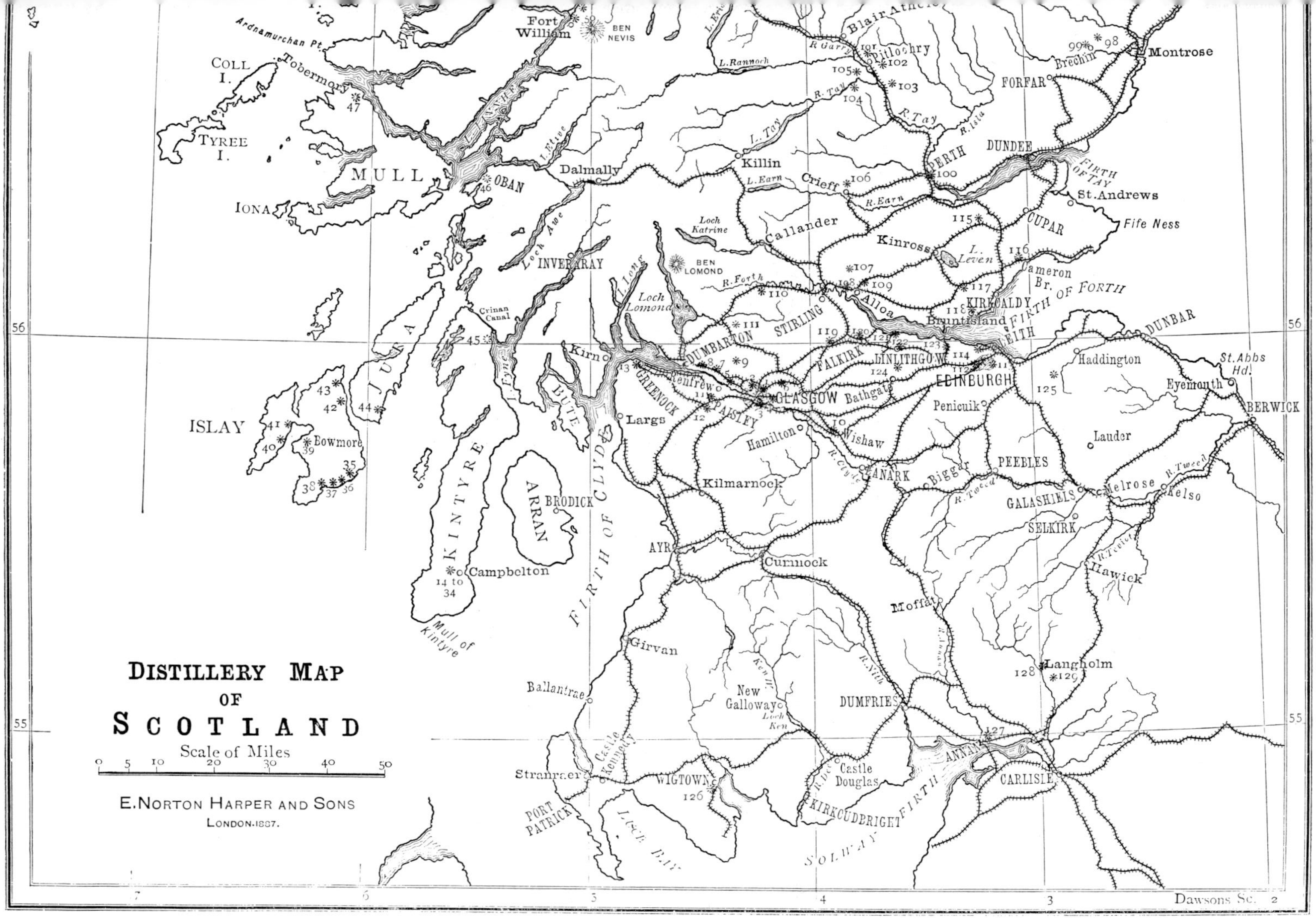
DISTILLERY MAP
OF
SCOTLAND
Scale of Miles
0 5 10 20 30 40 50
E.NORTON HARPER AND SONS
LONDON.1887.
Dawsons Sc.
Montrose
Brechin
FORFAR
DUNDEE
PERTH
FIRTH OF TAY
St.Andrews
Fife Ness
CUPAR
Kinross
L. Leven
Cameron Br.
KIRKCALDY
Burntisland
FIRTH OF FORTH
LEITH
DUNBAR
St.Abbs Hd.
Eyemouth
BERWICK
Haddington
EDINBURGH
Penicuik
Lauder
PEEBLES
GALASHIELS
Melrose
Kelso
R. Tweed
SELKIRK
Hawick
R. Teviot
Langholm
CARLISLE
ANNAN
Moffat
DUMFRIES
R. Nith
Castle Douglas
KIRKCUDBRIGHT
SOLWAY FIRTH
New Galloway
Loch Ken
WIGTOWN
LUCE BAY
Stranraer
PORT PATRICK
Castle Kennedy
Ballantrae
Girvan
Cumnock
AYR
Kilmarnock
Hamilton
Wishaw
LANARK
Biggar
R. Clyde
GLASGOW
Bathgate
PAISLEY
Renfrew
GREENOCK
Largs
DUMBARTON
FALKIRK
LINLITHGOW
STIRLING
Alloa
Callander
Crieff
L. Earn
R. Earn
Killin
L. Tay
R. Tay
Pitlochry
Blair Athole
R. Garry
L. Rannoch
R. Isla
Loch Katrine
BEN LOMOND
Loch Lomond
L. Long
R. Forth
Kirn
BUTE
ARRAN
BRODICK
FIRTH OF CLYDE
KINTYRE
Campbelton
Mull of Kintyre
Crinan Canal
L. Fyne
INVERARAY
Loch Awe
Dalmally
L. Etive
OBAN
Fort William
BEN NEVIS
MULL
IONA
Tobermory
Ardnamurchan Pt.
COLL I.
TYREE I.
JURA
ISLAY
Bowmore
14 to 34
56
55
7
6
5
4
3
2

INDEX—*continued.*

INDEX—*continued.*

INDEX—*continued.*

INDEX—*continued.*

CANAL WHARF, PORT DUNDAS DISTILLERY.

No. 1.

Port Dundas Distillery, Glasgow.

PROPRIETORS, THE DISTILLERS' COMPANY, LIMITED.

Registered Office: 12, TORPHICHEN STREET, EDINBURGH.

E. F. DUDGEON, *Secretary.*

Managing Director of the Distillery: RICHARD MACFARLANE.

HAVING long been possessed with an ardent desire to see the Distilleries of Scotland and Ireland, I took the first opportunity that presented itself, and, knowing the task set before me would occupy at least two years, made arrangements to transfer my duties to others. It was at first thought desirable that my tour should commence at the Orkneys; but, the weather proving unfavourable, my plan of entering the land of Whisky by the sea was abandoned in favour of the iron road to Glasgow. We—for I was not doomed to travel alone—started from Euston by the night mail, having previously invested in a copy of "Morewood" and one or two other books on Distillation to study on our journey. Nothing of note occurred on the journey, except that we got a little amusement out of our fellow travellers—one of them a gentleman in clerical attire, catching some fragments of our conversation on spirits, evidently mistook us for important officers in the Salvation Army. Seeing this we puzzled him, and in answer to his enquiries, informed him that we had just started on a long and tedious pilgrimage to the spirit land, and that ours was a mission of investigation into the creation, development and perfection of crude spirits into "spirits made perfect." One of our party here produced his flask and explained to our reverend friend what kind of missionaries we were, when, to our surprise, after taking a "wee drappie," and like Oliver Twist, asking for more, the pious-looking brother offered to join us in our excursions, that he might do the tasting, and we the writing. This generous offer we declined.

Arriving at Glasgow we drove to the Victoria Hotel, where the cheery landlord, Angus Mackay, a stalwart young "Hielander," gave us a hearty welcome. After a substantial breakfast we engaged a good horse and trap, and soon found ourselves trotting along Buchanan Street, up several steep hills, until we finally arrived at our destination. Port Dundas, from whence the Distillery takes its name, was so called in honour of Thomas, Lord Dundas. It is the basin of the celebrated Forth and Clyde Canal, and is situated, strange to say, at the top of a hill over-looking the city. The appearance of ships' masts in such a position, over-topping the houses, presented to us a peculiar surprise. The canal, which is a direct water-way from the Clyde to the Forth, a distance of some thirty-seven miles, over the whole of its progress through bustling towns and quiet villages, commands fine views of the country, pretty water scenes, and the magnificent background of the Forth. Port Dundas itself, however, is the scene of great commercial activity, and the prominent feature of the locality is the Distillery. Established more than a century ago, Port Dundas has, by the energy and enterprise displayed by its founder, Robert Macfarlane, and latterly by his son Daniel, been so developed that it has become one of the largest Distilleries in the world; and although amalgamated with the Distillers' Company, Limited, Richard Macfarlane, son of the Daniel before mentioned, is now Managing Director for the Company at this Distillery. The works, covering nine acres of ground, are situated on a steep hill near to and overlooking the city of Glasgow and surrounding districts, and are close to the railway and canal. Having previously communicated by telephone with Mr. W. Bruce, the operative manager, we found that gentleman waiting to receive us. Under his guidance we commenced our inspection at the Barns or Granaries, situated at the north end of the Distillery on the higher slopes of the hill. They consist of buildings, four stories high, and some idea of their magnitude may be formed by the following facts. Number One at the time of our visit contained 10,000 quarters of American corn, and Number Two, 14,000 quarters of barley and rye, and then they were not even full; at times they have stored as many as 45,000 quarters. The grain is imported by rail, canal, and carts, direct into the works, where it is emptied into hoppers, and taken by elevators and screws to any part of the buildings at will. We next entered the two malting floors, which are situated at the west end of the Granaries, and were amazed at their dimensions; they are quite the size of feeding parks, and a volunteer regiment could drill in them with ease. The cisterns connected with these buildings each wet 2,400 bushels at one time. South of the Granaries, standing all in a line, are the seven Kilns, which are of great dimensions, one of them drying 2,000 quarters of grain at a time. Five of them are used for grain, the other two for malt, and all are heated by hot air. The dried malt and grain is then passed through screws to the malt and grain Store-rooms, five in number, each capable of holding 14,000 bushels of malt, and used alternately. The grain and malt passes from these rooms into the Mill, which building has the appearance of having been hewn out of a rock, nothing being seen but solid masonry and iron girders, while it is covered by a large water tank communicating with all parts of the works where fire might originate, and capable of flooding the whole place in a few minutes. In the Mill there are eight pairs of large mill-stones, working night and day, driven by a powerful engine, upwards of 150 horse power. Emerging from the clouds of dust we found ourselves in the court-yard, where the scene was indeed striking. The engine department was before us, which is quite an important division in this mammoth establishment, as besides the ponderous engine which drives the Mill there are sixteen others ranging from 1 to 160 horse power, or a total of about 300 indicated horse power. In the Boiler-house there are ten of Galloway's Patent Steel Boilers, 30 feet long by 8 feet in diameter, worked at 60 lbs. pressure; eight of them are placed in a row, as seen in the illustration, and two near the Warehouses. These patent boilers are capable of evaporating 7,900 lbs. of water per hour, with average coal and draught which will drive 395 indicated horse with an engine consuming 20 lbs. of water per horse power per hour. The shell plates of these boilers are $\frac{7}{16}$ of an inch thick and other parts in proportion, and are composed of steel plates capable of withstanding a tensile strain of 26 to 30 tons per square inch with not less than 20 per cent. elongation in 10 inches. The grist, or ground grain, is conveyed from the Mill to the large grist-pits by screws, and thence not (as is usual in smaller distilleries) in bags or barrows, but in cart loads of from 26 to 30 cwts. The house in which the four pulping tuns are placed is on

THE BOILERS, PORT DUNDAS DISTILLERY.

the west side of the grist pits, near the Mash-tun, and is three stories high. The tuns are all wooden vessels, closely hooped and covered in. Having passed over weighing machines, the grist reaches the elevators, which raise it into patent Mashing Machines, through which it passes into four Pulping Tuns, and thence into two Mash Tuns of enormous size, measuring 30 feet in diameter and 9 feet 6 inches in depth. After the fine worts are drained off, the grains are pumped into a large Draff Tun, and when properly exhausted the draff is dropped through into carts, which come from various parts of the neighbourhood. For feeding cattle, and more especially dairy cows, the draff from this wort is unsurpassed.

The fine worts drained from the mash are collected in two large Underbacks, placed at the foot of the Mash-tuns, and holding about 14,000 gallons. From thence they are pumped into the Wort Receivers. In the adjoining house there are seven of Miller & Co.'s Patent Refrigerators, over which the wash flows into the Fermenting Backs. At the north end of the Mash House is the Tun Room, an extensive, lofty, and spacious apartment, which runs along and forms a greater part of Vulcan Street. It contains thirty-five Washbacks, some of them holding as much as 53,000 gallons apiece, from which the fermented liquor runs into the Wash and Intermediate Chargers, which together hold 270,000 gallons, and are situated in the vicinity of the Still Houses. The wash is afterwards pumped to the Stills by pumps of great size and power, driven by steam.

At this period of our inspection we paused for a short rest and slight refreshment; and resuming our tour at the Still House, a lofty structure forming the main body of the building, we were shown the three Coffey's Patent Stills. These handsome town-like vessels are 70 feet high; and after a full inspection, we passed on to No. 2 Still House, where are five Pot Stills, one of them having a capacity of 24,000 gallons, and said to be the largest in the kingdom. Here also are the pumps for water, wash, hot-feints and wash-heater pumps, some of them are three-throw, others centrifugal, some of these latter are huge machines of immense power and capable of throwing from 400 to 600 gallons per minute to a height of 40 feet. From the Still Houses we passed into the Receiver Room, which also contains the Safes and Sampling Safes. In front of the Patent Still House there is a Worm Tub, 30 feet long, 10 feet wide, and 6 feet deep, also for the Pot Stills as many as four Worm Tubs, each 40 feet long, 10 feet wide, and 6 feet deep, all constructed with metal, and filled with huge copper coils and pipes.

There are nine large Low-wines and Feints Receivers, and three Spirit Receivers, all great size, the latter being connected with the Spirit Store, to which the spirits run by gravitation, and are received into the Vats and casked in the usual way. During our progress through the Distillery we were delighted with the order, everywhere remarkable. All the work is accomplished with almost military precision, and the workmen attend to their duties in a quiet, methodical manner. The Still Houses and Receiver Rooms are models of brightness, the pipes and vessels being painted blue, red, white, or black, according to their contents; by those who are acquainted with the operations and process of distilling grain Whisky, this department is much admired.

The next object which attracted our attention was the Spirit Store, a large building conveniently situated for Stills, Receiver House, and Warehouses, containing three Vats of great capacity, holding respectively 7,387, 6,859, and 5,550 gallons. About fifty feet distant is the fine range of Warehouses, facing the canal.

They are immense buildings of from four to six stories high, forming part of the boundary of the works, and having 50,000 square yards of floorage. Here were stored over 16,660 casks of Whisky of various sizes and ages, containing 1,504,000 gallons of spirits. We next proceeded to the Cooperage, situated higher up the hill, which is quite a work in itself. The casks are stored here in thousands, and put in order before being conveyed to the Spirit Store. To the north of this we stepped into an open space of ground in which is a piggery accommodating over four hundred pigs fed on the distillery refuse. Some of them are highly bred animals of great size, and on entering one of the breeding sheds the visitor is surprised to see the wall literally covered with prize-cards. Employed upon the premises are 250 men, and the collection of the Inland Revenue necessitates a staff of 21 officers, including two supervisors. On the left hand side of the main entrance are the handsome and extensive offices for the Directors, Managers, and clerks. The operative Manager's office is in the centre of the works, with sampling rooms, &c., and is in telephonic communication with the offices and principal departments all over the Distillery. We may mention that this Distillery pays in duties annually about £430,000.

KILNS AND WAREHOUSES, PORT DUNDAS DISTILLERY.

The arrangements for extinguishing fire are on a very extensive scale in this Distillery, and consist of fire-plugs and hose distributed all over the premises.

The water used is taken from Loch Katrine and the Canal, each being made subservient to its special work in driving and distilling.

The annual output of this Distillery is no less than 2,562,000 gallons.

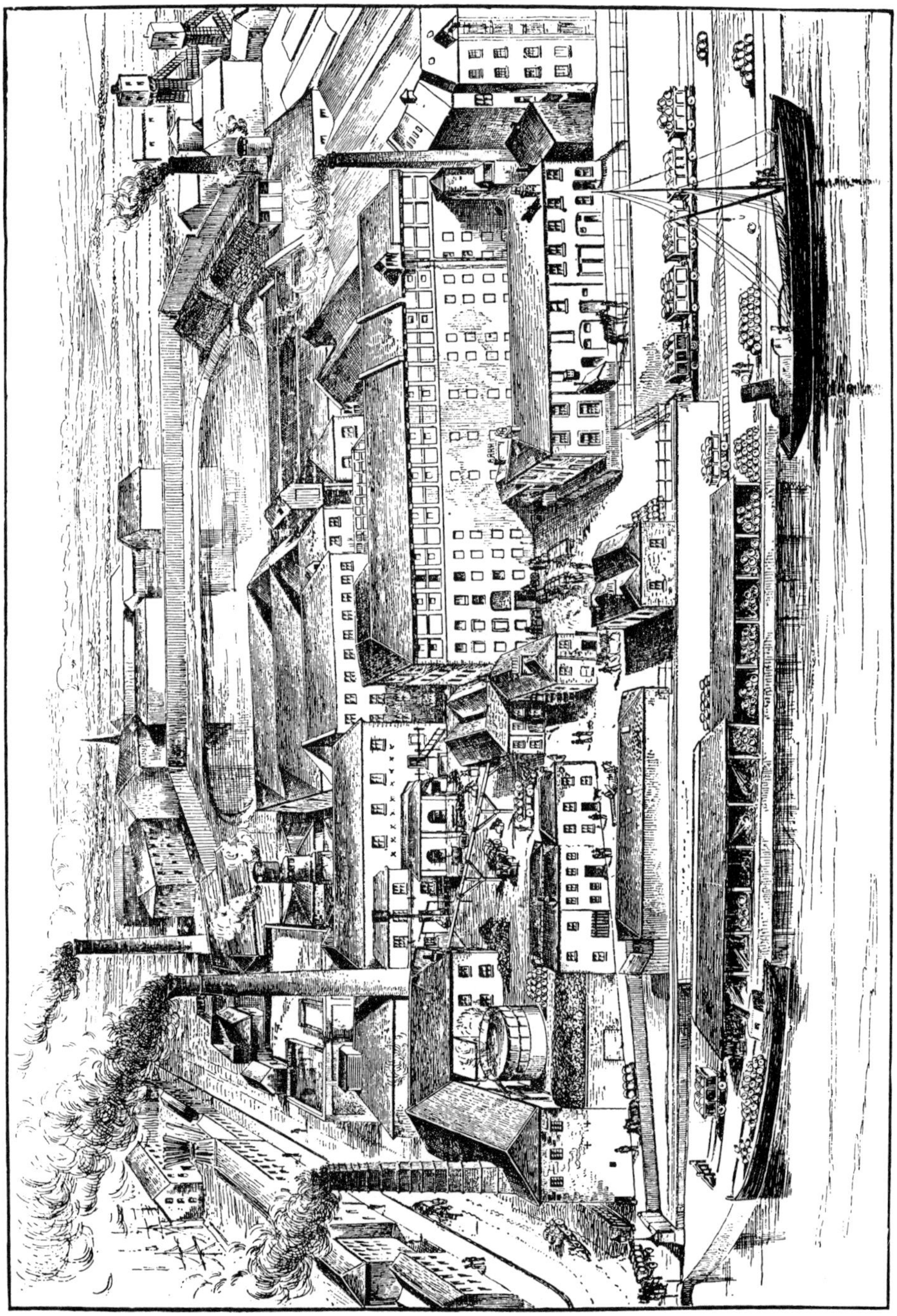

DUNDASHILL DISTILLERY, GLASGOW.

No. 2.

Dundashill Distillery, Glasgow.

PROPRIETORS, JOHN AND ROBERT HARVEY & Co.

THE next morning we drove to Dundashill Distillery, situated about a quarter of a mile from the work described in the previous chapter. It is built on the side of a steep hill, the extensive buildings and premises covering five acres of ground. Some of the buildings in connection with the Distillery are of a great height, the top of one of them forming the highest point in Glasgow, and from which a splendid view can be obtained. Immediately below lies spread out the City of Glasgow, giving one a good idea of the magnitude of the commercial Metropolis of Scotland, and claimed to be the second City of the Empire; a city which, unlike many others, has a history to boast of, dating from the remotest times, when elsewhere trade was unknown.

We were informed that on a clear day a magnificent panorama of hills can be seen to the west and north, including Goatfell in Arran, Ben Lomond, Ben Ledi, and Ben Lawers. Ben An and Ben Venue are also visible, whose base rises from Loch Katrine, the lake from which is obtained the splendid supply of water for Glasgow; also the beautiful wooded valley bounded by the Kilpatrick and Campsie Hills, by which route, as described by Sir Walter Scott in "Rob Roy," Baillie Nicol Jarvie and his companion passed through on their way from Glasgow to the Clachan of Aberfoyle, in order to keep their appointment with the famous outlaw chief. But to return to the Distillery, the subject of our sketch. The business was founded in the year 1770 by John Harvey (grandfather of the present proprietors), who was one of the first three licensed Distillers in Scotland, and we think we are safe in saying that Dundashill may claim to be one of the very first distilleries established in Glasgow.

We commenced our tour of inspection at the Granaries, of which there are several, and at the time of our visit they were all filled to overflowing, containing upwards of 20,000 quarters of fine barley. The barley is elevated from the level of the wharves and railway sidings in front of the Distillery, a height of about sixty feet, and from there distributed to the various Granaries, which are all arranged in the most convenient manner. The Steeps, which are four in number, are situated immediately below the Granaries, and are each capable of wetting 1,600 bushels of barley per week. The barley is run into them from the Granaries by

COURT-YARD OF DUNDASHILL DISTILLERY, GLASGOW.

means of iron shoots, and the Malt-barns being constructed on lower levels than the Steeps, the entire malting process is conducted by gravitation, thus saving an immense amount of labour.

These Barns are four in number, varying in extent from 1,200 to 1,600 square yards, and some idea of their enormous size may be estimated when we mention that they cover a total area of close on 6,000 square yards, and give ample floor room for the 6,400 bushels of barley malted weekly. Attached to the Barns are four Kilns, covering over 900 square yards ; one of them is a plate floored Kiln, and the other three wire cloth. The malt is dried with peat or coke according to the flavour required. Immediately adjoining the Kilns are sheds capable of stowing 1,000 tons of peat, and as the season previous to our visit was specially favorable for the cutting and securing of peats, not only were the sheds filled quite full, but we noticed several large stacks in addition, erected throughout the yard, containing, we should think, half as much again. The peats used are all of the best quality that can be procured, and come from various parts of the Highlands.

The Malt-deposits immediately adjoin the Kilns, and command the Mill-hopper, which is situated above a very powerful set of rollers, from which the crushed malt is conveyed by an elevator to the grist loft situated in the Mash House. This was the first building we entered more particularly connected with the manufacture of the Whisky, and at first sight the multiplicity of pipes, pumps, brewing tanks, mash tuns and refrigerators are somewhat confusing, but on further inspection we found that they are admirably arranged for the purposes for which they are intended. The Mash Tuns are two in number, one being 23 feet in diameter, the other 20 feet, their total capacity being 30,000 gallons, and are fitted with the usual revolving stirring machine, only in this case by a clever arrangement the driving power comes from below, which gives the whole apparatus a light and neat appearance, thus doing away with cumbrous beams and shafting, so prominent where the power is got from above.

The grist and the hot water used for mashing meet in the mashing machines, and run in a stream into the Mash Tuns. This not only avoids loss, but prevents the spread of the dust all over the Mash House, a source of discomfort, as well as risk of danger from fire. After more hot liquor has been added, and the whole has been mashed or mixed up by the revolving stirring machine before mentioned, it is allowed to settle for some time, so that the saccharine may be thoroughly extracted from the malt, the liquor (technically termed wort) is then drained off through the strainers, or false bottoms in the Mash Tuns, into the Worts Receiver, and the grain thus left behind is called "draff" in Scotland, but known in England as grains. The system of gravitation so largely adopted in this Distillery, and which is greatly facilitated by its situation on the side of a hill, is most advantageously utilised in the removal of the draff, or grains, from the Mash Tuns, which vessels are supported on massive stone arches forming the roof of a spacious Draff house, which, being directly underneath, allows the draff to be quickly and expeditiously removed through the openings in the bottom of the Mash Tuns. The draff is sold to farmers and cowfeeders in the neighbourhood of Glasgow.

From the Worts Receiver the liquor immediately passes through two Morton's Refrigerators, and without loss of time is pumped into the Wash-backs in the Tun room which adjoins the Mash-house ; these vessels are nine in number, and vary in capacity from 16,000 to 24,000 gallons. A certain quantity of yeast having been added, the process of fermentation commences, which occupies about two days, converting the saccharine matter in the worts, into alcohol. Notwithstanding the ample capacity of the tuns, or backs, the fermentation from the pure malt is so brisk that what are called switchers, are required to prevent loss by the overflow; these switchers are driven by an engine situated in the Tun-room. Overhead are still in existence the old air coolers used before the introduction of the Morton's Refrigerators, and it is from this point that the magnificent view before referred to, can be obtained. In the Tun-room what is called the brewing process terminates, and immediately thereafter, the distilling part of the manufacture begins. On the fermentation being completed the fermented liquor, now termed "wash" is run down from the tuns or wash backs to the wash chargers in the Still houses, which are situated on a lower level than the Tun-room.

WASH & LOW WINES STILLS, DUNDASHILL DISTILLERY.

We were next conducted to the Still houses, two in number, the first house containing two very large Wash-stills, with a capacity of 6,500 gallons each, and the other, ten smaller Stills, their sizes averaging from 600 to 1200 gallons each. In both houses all the Stills are of the old Pot Still pattern, same as those in use at the Highland Distilleries, but so arranged that Whisky is produced, either on the two or three distillation principle. The first process gives a spirit, with greater flavor and body; the latter a more highly rectified and silent spirit. The ancient process of heating the stills by fire is used in this Distillery, and the vapour as it rises from the stills, is entirely condensed in the old fashioned copper worms, one being attached to each still. Though this may not appear the most scientific mode either of boiling or condensing the spirit, the all but unanimous opinion among Scotch malt distillers seems still to be in favour of this old process.

The condensed spirit is run from the twelve worms into what are termed safes, being copper boxes with plate glass lids, secured with the Inland Revenue locks. Immediately adjoining are most elaborate-looking sampling boxes, for the testing of the strength and quality of the spirit produced, and the men in

SPIRIT STILLS, DUNDASHILL DISTILLERY.

charge, called ballmen, by a neat arrangement in the safes, can run the liquid, either into the Spirit-receiver as finished Whisky, or into the other Receivers of which there are several, to be subjected to a further distillation. When from three to five thousand gallons has been collected in the Receiver it is removed to large vats in the Spirit-store, the next building visited. The vats have ample capacity for reducing five thousand gallons at a time, and from them, the Whisky is filled off into puncheons, hogsheads or quarter-casks as may be required. The contents of the casks are ascertained by weight and by means of the indication or specific gravity of the spirit, which is taken by the Inland Revenue Officers and checked by one of Messrs. Harvey's clerks. After being filled off the Whisky is generally allowed to remain in the Spirit-store for forty-eight hours ; the strength is then carefully tested by the excise officers, checked again by the clerk, and thereafter the casks are filled full to the bung, and removed to the bonded Warehouses. These Warehouses are seven in number and very extensive We first visited the No. 2 bond, a fine vaulted building immediately below the No. 5, which latter is a very large warehouse comprising five flats, the others are all on the ground floor. These Bonds vary in size from 138 feet in length by 51 feet in width to 216 feet by 76 feet, and some conception of their enormous storing capacity may be formed, when we mention that in all they cover an area of 72,000 square feet, or 8,000 square yards, and at the time of our visit there were stored over 7,000 casks of all sizes containing upwards of 600,000 gallons, and there was room for at least another thousand casks. We were informed that almost all the Whisky in these warehouses is sold and lies to the order of customers, and the whole of it was of course manufactured at Dundas Hill, as by the Excise Regulations no other spirit can be introduced.

The Warehouses are mostly stone buildings with slated roofs, every bond being separated from each other by means of fire proof walls, which run up through the roofs, and all are detached from the manufacturing parts of the premises as a safeguard against fire. We may here mention that the means of extinguishing fire are very complete throughout the Distillery. The Loch Katrine water is led through all the premises, and there is a plentiful supply of fire *extincteurs* as well as other appliances kept at convenient places. Further, the Distillery is in telephonic communication with the Glasgow fire brigade one of the finest in the kingdom, and in the event of fire, the engines can be in the work within a few minutes after the alarm is given.

Regarding the water used in this Distillery, after the introduction of Loch Katrine water into the city of Glasgow, more than thirty years ago, it was exclusively used in the manufacture of Whisky at Dundashill, but the proprietors are now convinced that after an exhaustive trial, a superior quality of Whisky can be produced from the canal water immediately adjoining the Distillery. It is rather a remarkable fact that almost all the famous and successful distilleries in the Lowlands of Scotland are situated on the canal system. and use this water in their manufacture. The Loch Katrine water is of course used for reducing the Whisky. There is a fifty horse power engine, besides several smaller ones, for driving the machinery, in connection with the Distillery, and for the purpose of pumping the water to a large reservoir (270 feet in length by 65 feet in width and 15 feet in depth,) situated at the back of the work so as to command the various barley steeps and brewing tanks. Besides the usual industries, such as engineers, joiners and masons' shops, etc., there is a large cooperage, with all the usual facilities for steaming and seasoning new casks, and where the immense stock of casks, over 12,000, are overhauled and repaired as they are returned.

Regarding the means of transit, as already indicated, the Forth and Clyde Canal is situated close to the Distillery, and there is a railway siding into the works from the Caledonian Railway. The Distillery is also situated within a short distance of all the great railway systems, and the Broomielaw on the river Clyde, the one connecting with all parts of England, and the other with the shipping, trading to all parts of the world : so that both for the receiving of barley and coals, as well as for forwarding the Whisky, it has exceptionally favorable facilities of transit by rail, canal, and sea. In addition to the large and spacious distillery offices, there is a Manager's office, in which is fitted up a neat little model still, with connections for experimental purposes. The Excise department have also a comfortable and commodious office in which are six Inland Revenue Officers. Seventy-five persons are employed in this Distillery when at full work. The Brewer and Manager of the Distillery department comes from the Speyside where he had charge of one of the famous Glenlivet Distilleries for some years. The Manager in charge of the maltings is also a Highland man and previous to coming to this Distillery, he had charge of one of the Distilleries in Islay.

As will be seen from the foregoing, this is a very extensive work, and considered to be the largest Pure Malt Distillery in Scotland, and being the first of its kind we had visited, we have entered somewhat fully into details. The Whisky produced from the Malt dried with peat is known as "Highland Malt," and that from the Malt dried without peat as "Old Still Malt." These Whiskies are largely sold for blending purposes, as well as for single Whiskies, the principal market being in England; they are also largely consumed in Scotland, Ireland, and the Colonies.

The output from November to May will average about 10,000 gallons per week, thereafter a slight reduction is made, the annual quantity manufactured from 320,000 to 360,000 gallons.

In connection with the Distillery the firm have several large Dairy farms, in which are kept over four hundred milch cows. In this way a very large quantity of the draff, *i.e.*, grains, is consumed. The late Mr. Robert Harvey, uncle of the present proprietor, had at one time as many as a thousand cows in milk, but since his death the stock has been reduced to its present dimensions.

No. 3.

Adelphi Distillery, Glasgow.

(CHARLES AND DAVID GRAY.)

PROPRIETORS, A. WALKER & CO.

A TEN minutes' walk from our hotel, along Buchanan Street, the finest thoroughfare in Glasgow, and through busy Argyle Street, across the beautiful bridge which spans the Clyde, and we find ourselves at the Adelphi Distillery. Sixty-five years ago the site upon which it stands was a fine orchard, but in 1826 the trees were cut down to make room for the Distillery. The works cover upwards of two acres of ground, and are situated close to the banks of the Clyde. The course of this noble river, through the heart of the city, forms one of the most striking panoramas of its kind in the United Kingdom. From the centre of Jamaica Bridge, the scene presented to the eye is one never to be forgotten; a forest of masts extending as far as the eye can reach; the open centre of the silver stream; the wharves piled with wares from every nation, and alive with men from all parts of the world; the continuous flow of passengers passing to and from the various steamers; and the endless variety of sounds and sights complete a picture unequalled in any other city in the world. The bustle and activity of modern days is here seen to its fullest advantage.

The Distillery Buildings occupy nearly a whole street on both sides of the way, and, as we approached, presented an appearance of great activity. We entered through a Gothic archway, across a courtyard, to the principal office, where we secured a guide, and set forth upon our tour of inspection. We first proceeded to the Grain Lofts or Warehouses, buildings of lofty elevation, one of them 112 feet long by 100 feet broad, and another 96 feet long and 20 feet broad, which, with the warehouses at Port Dundas, are capable of storing 15,000 quarters of grain; the delivery of the grain to the various warehouses is accomplished by the aid of steam and hydraulic machinery. Adjoining the warehouses is the Malting Loft, a building 86 feet by 21 feet. The Steeps here are arranged in German fashion on an upper floor, beneath which the barley is malted in trays, of which there are some thousands, each sliding from out an upright frame fixed to the ceiling, in order that the operator may watch the progress of the acrospire; from this chamber the malt is elevated to the Kiln, which is floored with wire-cloth and heated by hot air. We next passed to the Malt Deposit, a spacious floor used for this purpose, measuring 50 feet by 22, and placed in close proximity to the Mill. We should here observe that the principal Maltings are at Port Dundas, consisting of three blocks of buildings four stories high, built on the banks of the canal, containing three barley floors with steeps, a malting floor and two kilns, the latter approached by a gangway from the lofts. They are handsome apartments, open roofed, about 60 feet square and floored with iron plates. These kilns are fired with peat in open furnaces.

We next entered the Mill Building which adjoins the engine house. The whole grain is conveyed to the mill by screws, and the grist carried by machinery to the grist lofts and hoppers, which command the Mash Tuns. The mill contains 3 pairs of stones and a set of rollers. From this building we proceeded to the Grist Loft which adjoins the Malting House, and from thence descended to the Mash House, which contains three large heating coppers for hot water, and two circular mash tuns; a large underback is situated below the three boilers. Ascending a steep stair we next visited the Back House, in which are ten wash-backs, containing on an average 16,000 gallons each; there are two more in course of construction in a building immediately adjoining. In addition there are three wash chargers, holding in all 45,000 gallons, which in turn command the stills. On a floor above this department the coolers and refrigerating apparatus are placed. Following the wash, as the liquor is now called, we next proceeded to the Distillery proper, where the important change in its nature takes place. There are two Still Houses, one of which contains a Coffey's Patent Still for the production of Grain Whisky, the other for Malt. The latter is a fine lofty and well-lighted building, some 60 feet high and 35 feet square, and contains four handsome Pot Stills, two with a capacity of 6,067 gallons, and the other 4,314 and 4,500 gallons respectively; here are also the usual safe and receivers. The power of the Stills has hitherto been much in excess of the brewing power of the works; but the two huge backs in course of construction will increase their capacity.

Our guide next conducted us, first, to the Spirit Store, where the spirit is received from the Stills, hence to the two large Bonded Warehouses, four stories high, and crowded with casks of Whisky of various ages, and afterwards to the engine house which adjoins the pump room. The engine house contains one beam engine of 80 horse-power, a horizontal engine of 10 horse-power, a table engine of 20 horse-power, two donkey engines for the boilers, and a blast engine. There are six boilers, two of them 23 by 9 feet, two of Galloway's 1875 patent, 28 feet by 7 feet 6 inches, one multitubular, and a smaller one. In the pump room are three different and handsome sets of three-throw pumps, capable of pumping 50,000 gallons of liquor per hour. The water used is entirely Loch Katrine, the proprietors being of opinion that it contains all the properties necessary for the making of good Whisky. Connected with the Distillery is a large cooperage, cask yard, stables and cart sheds; also a joiner's shop and other industries. The railway runs at the back of the buildings, and the wharf is within two hundred yards of the works.

In addition to this establishment Messrs. A. Walker & Co. are owners of a fine Distillery in Limerick, Ireland, and another in Liverpool, particulars of which will be found in another portion of this work.

The Whisky made is both Malt and Grain, and the output, taken upon the return for the season 1884-5, is 516,053 gallons.

No. 4.

Loch Katrine Distillery, Camlachie, Glasgow.

PROPRIETORS, BULLOCH, LADE, & CO.

THE morning we had fixed for our visit to this Distillery broke most miserably, and the rain poured down in torrents. We did not, however, start until eleven o'clock, and by that time the sun had begun to struggle through the clouds. When we arrived at the gates of the Distillery the sky had cleared, and the damp roofs of the buildings glittered in the sunshine. It requires a great stretch of imagination to believe that this was once the pleasantest suburb of Glasgow—the resort of well-to-do citizens, and that Camlachie was, in remote days, a pretty village, and its then sylvan stream much frequented by anglers. What a change! The village is now absorbed into the great city, and the little old-fashioned Distillery on the banks of the stream has disappeared, giving place to a handsome pile of buildings, and claimed to be one of the largest Malt Distilleries in Scotland.

The Loch Katrine Distillery was re-built in the year 1849, and the buildings alone cover an area of nearly six acres. They are arranged in two divisions with a spacious roadway down the centre, and some idea of their magnitude may be gathered from the following. The five Barley Lofts alone cover an area of over 5,000 square yards, and there are besides two germinating floors, one of which is 180 feet long by 90 feet wide, and the other 170 by 70 feet, and all the rest of the buildings are in similar proportions. In passing we examined the immense stock of barley on hand, and found the various kinds to be of the finest description and quality, an important factor, no doubt, in the desired results. A powerful steam engine is here placed for hoisting barley to the several flats of the buildings. The Steeps are two large cast-iron receptacles of over 3,000 bushels capacity, and here the first process in the manufacture of pure malt Whisky begins. In these vessels the grain is allowed to remain under water for a time, after which the water is drained off, and the now "steeped" barley drops through valves in the bottom of the vessels to the germinating floors below. Malting now begins, and occupies a more or less time according to the kind of barley and mode of working. When matured the malt is kiln-dried in two Kilns worked on a new scientific principle. The drying process is effected by pure air heated by steam in two copper machines of tubular construction, and the firm considers that it has the advantage of purity and economy, the malt possessing none of the deterrent effects which frequently follow the usual method of drying by fire alone. When the malt has remained long enough under the action of heated air and peat, and is perfectly dry, it is removed to a spacious store-house called the Malt Deposit. On our entrance here, a sweet agreeable odour pervaded the place, and between ten and twenty thousand bushels of matured malt lay before us. The next process is the "grinding," and we were taken to the adjoining Mill Room, where the malt is crushed between two cylindrical rollers on the ground floor, and conveyed by elevators to the floor above, where the grist is put into sacks preparatory to the next process of "mashing." The first room is capable of holding 5,000 bushels.

We next proceeded to the Mash House, containing a large mash tun capable of mashing 1,500 bushels at one time ; it is fitted with a double set of patent rakes of the most approved kind which do their work admirably. This part of the operations is called the "infusion," the grist being collected in a hopper above, at the end of which is attached a patent mashing machine in which the hot water and malt amalgamate and descend to the Mash Tun below, to be operated upon by the revolving rakes; the water for mashing purposes is heated by steam in three large coppers. After the "infusion" the worts are drained off to a Wort Receiver situated below the mash tun and of almost equal capacity. Two large patent pumps throw the vast volume of worts to another Wort Receiver situate in another part of the buildings commanding the Tun Room, which we shall notice later on. One of these pumps is composed principally of brass, and is capable of throwing 10,000 gallons per hour, while the other is a direct acting steam-pump of equal power, the two being able to be worked separately or together as required. The action of the steam-pump may be described as a combination of eccentric and hydraulic compensation principle in governing the slide valve. The whole of the machinery in this department is driven by a horizontal steam engine of 40 horse power.

Still following the process we next found ourselves in the Refrigerating House, where the worts are cooled down to the required degree of temperature. This house contains the large Wort Reservoir, before referred to, which supplies a constant flow of worts to three large patent refrigerators. The Refrigerating House is situate at the top of the premises adjoining the Tun Room, where the worts are conveyed in copper pipes to the Tuns or Washbacks. The Tun Room, which is of great length and width, contains eleven Washbacks, the largest of which has a content of 18,000 gallons. A modern style of "switching" is adopted, the "switchers" receiving their power from two main parallel shafts running the whole length of the buildings, and driven by a 20 horse power vertical engine.

Attenuation ended, the "wash," as it is now called, is pumped by a patent "centrifugal" to the Wash Charger. The Still House has a most attractive and handsome appearance, not to be excelled, we think, in Scotland. It contains four brightly polished Stills, one Spirit Receiver, three Low-wines and Feints Receivers, Wash Charger, Spirit Safes, and Refrigerator. The utensils are beautifully painted and kept scrupulously clean. The mirror-like Spirit Safes are of modern construction, and perfect examples of skilled workmanship. The Safe proper is a very large one, and the Sampling Safe a perfect work of art. Two of the Stills are used for distillation of wash, and two for low-wines and feints. The Spirits, Low-wines, and Feints Receivers have a content of nearly 4,000 gallons each respectively. A Prince of Wales' feather water gauge keeps playing like a little fountain near the Safes, and has an imposing and artistic effect as it glistens in the sunlight. This gauge shows whether or not the pumps that supply water for condensation are working. The Worm Tub is a huge utensil, containing an immense length of copper worms, over which a deluge of cold pure sparkling water is constantly flowing supplied by two pumps situated on the ground floor of the Still House. These pumps differ entirely in principle from the others we have referred to, each being a steam engine in itself, and may be described as of positive and direct action, with fly wheel.

The Draff House is situated at the extreme end of the yard, and is easy of access for horses and carts. It is a capacious apartment of great height and breadth, and is supplied with draff by a set of monster elevators; the draff commands a ready sale. Adjoining this house we were introduced to the Desiccated Grain Factory, a separate building and complete institution in itself, and a notable feature at this Distillery. It contains six patent revolving desiccating machines wherein the draff is dried and converted into a useful meal for cattle. There is a great demand for draff in this form, as it has the advantage of keeping any length of time without in the least impairing its quality. It is put up in bags for the market and sold at about £5 : 10 : 0 per ton. Opposite the Warehouses, and adjoining the Still House, stands the Spirit Store containing three Spirit Vats of a capacity of 4,100 gallons each, into which the Whisky flows by gravitation. Here it is filled into casks and, after remaining a day or so, it is transferred to the Duty Free Warehouses. These Warehouses are four in number and contain upwards of 4,000 casks.

We next directed our steps to the steam boiler department, situated on the opposite side of the yard to the Malt-houses, and adjoining the Still House. Here are three boilers for generating steam, each 27 feet long by 7 feet in diameter, with two furnaces to each boiler. The boilers are fed by injectors, a direct acting steam pump, and the engine pumps. The water used in this Distillery comes from Loch Katrine, and the Whisky produced is "Pure Malt," and is sold at home and abroad.

The annual output is 300,000 gallons.

A block of Counting Houses adjoins the Spirit Store with the Inland Revenue Department above, but the principal Glasgow Offices are at 4, Bothwell Street, where all business is transacted in connection with this, and also the Benmore Distillery, Campbeltown, and the Caol Ila Distillery, Islay, which belong to the same firm.

The Cooperage is at the top of the yard, and forms in this Distillery quite an industry in itself, many men being employed in keeping their department abreast of the rest. In front of the Cooperage is piled a perfect pyramid of empty casks, mostly belonging to customers, and there waiting their turn to be filled. The Engineer's Workshop, an iron erection near the Mash House, is replete with forge, heavy screw cutting lathe and fitter's bench, and a complete set of tools for repairing machinery.

The firm have their own Fire Brigade on the premises, a well drilled body of men who know how to act in case of emergency, and as this is not the least important department in all Distilleries, and more especially in this one, we detail the various safeguards and precautions taken against fire and explosions. Hydrants or fire plugs, reels and hose, extincteurs, water force pumps and hand grenades abound all over the buildings at the most commanding points. In addition to these, special precautions are taken against accidents in the Mill and Grist Room ; hydrants are placed at available points both outside and inside, and there is a large perforated steam pipe in connection with the boilers, whereby, in case of fire breaking out the building can be instantly filled with steam. A precaution against explosions is worthy of note ; these dust explosions do occasionally occur in grain or flour mills, and are sometimes attended with serious consequences, and even with fatal results. Here the safeguard consists by simply connecting a large metal pipe from the interior of the top of the grist elevators to the exterior of the roof, the outside of the pipe being fitted with a safety valve so that in case of an explosion the valve flies open, and the force harmlessly expands itself in the open air.

We returned to our hotel by way of Glasgow Green, a public park, covering upwards of 104 acres, with a ride or carriage drive around it of 2½ miles in length. The Green was at one time the fashionable promenade of the inhabitants, and was the scene of all the grand military exercises in the stirring times when "George the Third was King." Here, too, all the washing, drying, and bleaching operations of the whole city were performed, as, in those days, the ground abounded in springs and marshy rivulets, "lasses lilting o'er the pail" might be seen or heard by the hundred. Wilson, in his poem of "The Clyde," says:

> "Here barefoot beauties lightly trip along ;
> Their snowy labours all the verdure throng :
> The linen some with rosy fingers rub,
> And white the foam o'erflows the smoking tub."

The aristocracy of Glasgow no longer frequent the park, having migrated westward, but the militia and volunteers make it their rendezvous and parade ground. After his unfortunate expedition into England and his disastrous retreat from Derby, the Chevalier Charles Edward came to Glasgow, and made the citizens clothe his naked host and maintain his army for ten days, during which time he treated the inhabitants to a grand review on The Green, which they did not appreciate or countenance.

During the Radical ferment of 1819-20, The Green was a popular resort of the insurrectionists, who kept the citizens of Glasgow in a painful state of suspense. Those who escaped the lash of the law fled to America, but one James Wilson was hanged and beheaded for his share in the riots. This is said to be the last occasion on which the axe and block were used in Great Britain.

No. 5.

Yoker Distillery, near Glasgow.

PROPRIETORS, JNO. & WM. HARVEY & CO.

THE easiest and best way to reach Yoker is to go by the North British Railway; you book at the Queen Street Station, which is a short distance from the Victoria hotel, and in twenty-five minutes you find yourself in the Distillery. We started by an early train, so as to have a long day for our inspection of this old work. The route lies through the prettiest suburb of Glasgow, and our journey was a pleasant one. Just before we reached our destination we noticed an all pervading odour of Whisky in the air, and were not surprised shortly afterwards to see the buildings of the Distillery rearing their heads above the houses, and thick volumes of smoke belching forth from the chimney stacks.

YOKER DISTILLERY.

Yoker Distillery has been in the hands of the Harvey family since the year 1770, and was in existence previous to that remote date. It covers five acres of ground, and there is a dairy farm of a hundred acres connected with it, farmed by Messrs. Harvey. The buildings are of an ancient style, and some of the vessels of an antique pattern. We were shown the "Ballman's chair" in the Still-house; it is of oak in the Queen Anne style, and of great age.

There is an abundant supply of water connected with the Distillery. The Yoker Burn, which rises in the Kilpatrick Hills, flows through the premises into the Clyde; it is the boundary between Renfrew and Dumbarton shires. Across the paddock, about 200 yards distant, flows the Clyde, and it is a grand sight to stand on the wharf, and watch the steamers and ships passing to and fro. The wharf is a private landing place for the use of Messrs. Harvey & Co. only, and they have enjoyed this right from time immemorial; they can land barley and maize by lighters direct from the ships at Glasgow free of all dues and charges. They have also the right to draw water from the Clyde, and there is a circular reservoir for filtering purposes 90 feet in diameter and 8 feet deep in the grounds opposite the Distillery. On the property are also several wells of spring water; but for distilling purposes Loch Katrine water is used. On the opposite side of the river Clyde are the beautiful grounds of the Blytheswood Estates, and a quarter of a mile higher up, the Elderslie policies.

After visiting the offices and hunting up some of the old documents and deeds connected with the works, we commenced our tour of inspection, under the guidance of Mr. Glen, the manager, who first took us to the No. 1 Barley Loft, which is a spacious floor, being 62 feet long and 36 wide. Underneath is a Grain Warehouse of same dimensions, holding 140 tons of grain. These floors form part of a stone building which faces the main road, the whole covering a frontage of 200 feet. On the same level as the Grain Loft there is a yeast receptacle and Worts Receiver, and on an elevated platform are two of Morton's Refrigerators, and the entire roof of this building is devoted to the old-fashioned Coolers which were previously in use. We now ascend a staircase to the other Grain Loft, which is under the same roof, and measures 100 feet long and 30 feet broad. The slanting roof of this floor is boarded in and used for storage purposes.

We next retraced our steps, and came to a handsome red brick tower, 60 feet high and nearly 30 feet square, called the Malt Mill, the roof of which is entirely covered by a water tank. It is divided into several floors, the first being the Grist Floor commanding the Mash Tuns; the malt rollers are also here, the rest of the building being used as malt stores. It may here be mentioned that all the malt used in this establishment is brought from their Malt Distillery (Messrs. Jno. & Robt. Harvey & Co.) at Dundas Hill, Glasgow. Close to the Malt Mill is the Grain Mill containing three pairs of millstones; it is three storeys in height, the upper storeys being used as Granaries. Once again we entered the main building, and climbed a ladder to a gangway, crossing which amid a labyrinth of pipes and machinery we came to a huge brick recess, wherein are placed three heating coppers of enormous size and picturesque shape. Two of these vessels are made of copper and the other of metal.

We then descended by a stone staircase into the Mash-house, a large and separate building with windows looking out on green fields, beyond which is to be seen a forest of masts on the river Clyde. Depending from the roof is a Steel's patent mashing machine, which mixes the grist with the hot water before it descends to the Mash House, whilst underneath, resting on the floor, is a handsome new circular Mash Tun 23 feet in diameter and 6 feet deep, with the double action revolving stirring gear, also an Underback below the surface of the floor of large capacity ; whilst elevated on iron columns overhead in the next building is the large square iron return-worts Receiver, holding 6,000 gallons. It is designated the "Black Prince" seeing that it was erected and put up in its place on the same day as the "Black Prince" was launched on the Clyde. At the top of a ricketty staircase, in close proximity to this vessel, and projecting from the wall, there is an ancient apartment that brought our memories back to the houses of the last century. It is low pitched and lighted with three small dormer windows, and is in the oldest part of the Distillery buildings. It contains a desk and an eight-day clock of the last century style. Here Mr. Glen has a small laboratory for experiments, and a library of scientific books. We experimented on one or two varieties of Whisky and thus fortified retraced our steps through the brewing department and up a stair into the Back house, which is a peculiarly shaped brick building in the form of the letter L, 209 feet long by 30 feet wide. This old fashioned place has been mended and patched up very many times during the last century ; the beams of the ceiling are as thick as a man's body and so protrude from the low pitched roof that we had to doff our hats several times to avoid a collision. There are sixteen Wash-backs, three of which hold 25,000 gallons, one 17,000, and twelve 10,000 gallons each. In the same apartment are placed the Wash charger, an iron vessel holding 30,000 gallons, two Feints Receivers, holding about 8,000 gallons each, and an oil Separator, connected with the Patent Stills. On returning to the yard we mounted an outside staircase, crossing a platform between boilers and machinery and passing a water heater, by Miller, of Glasgow, which is elevated on stone piers, and heated by the spent wash, we duly arrived at the first floor of the Still house, a lofty building 70 feet high, of several floors, through which run the two Coffey's Patent Stills. These lofty erections built on the ground, run through four floors so that each section is come-at-able by the still men. On one of the lower floors we noticed one of Stein's Patent Stills for the manufacture of malt whisky, the same as that described hereafter at Cameron Bridge Distillery. The analyzer of the No. 2 Coffey's Patent Still is made of copper, and not of wood as is generally the case. The intermediate Wash charger, which holds 10,000 gallons, is placed on a gallery above the analyzer.

We then made our exit through a doorway, and found ourselves on an outside platform, where there is fixed a Morton's Refrigerator for cooling the spirit direct from No. 2 Coffey's Still, also a large Worm-tub, communicating with the No. 1 Coffey's Still, for the same purpose. At the suggestion of Mr. Glen we climbed by a ladder into the roof of the Still-house, where, from the windows, we obtained a splendid view of the Valley of the Clyde, bounded by the Campsie Hills to the north, the Kilpatrick Hills on the left, and the Gleniffer Braes opposite.

One of the lower floors of the Still-house is used for the Ballman's platform, and contains the safe and sampling apparatus, two Spirit Receivers, and a Feints Receiver, all these vessels are called "dishes" in this establishment, as they were a century ago. We then crossed to the Spirit Store, a large brick building with asphalted floor, which contains two spirit vats, each with a capacity of 1,500 and 1,600 gallons respectively, and from thence to the Racking Store, which is under the same roof, and only used for local trade. The Bonded Warehouses are very extensive, and eight in number. They are built of brick with slated roofs, and are well ventilated; the Whiskies therein date from 1873. The No. 7 Warehouse is not devoted to storage purposes, although it is equally under the surveillance of the Excise. It is a smaller building than the others, and contains a Patent "Ageing Apparatus," where new Whisky is subjected to an immense pressure of heat. This process is said to have the power of destroying the aldehyde or fieriness of new Whisky and converting it into a mature spirit of three to five years old. This patent is at present in its infancy, but arrangements are being made to work it in this Distillery on a larger scale.

On returning to the yard we pass a large Draff-house, and two huge spent Wash Tanks. The draff is largely used in the dairy farm attached to the Distillery. The cooperage and store houses, etc., are in close proximity to the engine department, which is on a large scale. As we entered the chief engine room we were struck with the order and brightness displayed; it is a square building and contains a compound horizontal sixty-horse power engine, seventeen years old, which works as well now as when new; also a horizontal pumping engine of ten-horse power for the Stills, and a three-horse power champion pump by Clarkson, of Glasgow, for feeding the boilers. Distributed elsewhere there are a Gwynn's centrifugal engine for pumping wash, three double-action pumps for worts and wash, and another centrifugal for same purpose, also a force pump for hot feints, three water pumps, and an old-fashioned single bucket pump for water. There are altogether four steam boilers, one 25 feet long and 7½ in diameter, one 26 feet long by 8 in diameter, one 23 feet long by 8 diameter, and one 28 feet long by 8 diameter; we noticed also two sight feed lubricators, for lubricating the cylinders of engines. There is a railway siding from the North British Railway direct through the works, and the Distillery is in telephonic communication with the office at 48, St. Enoch Square, Glasgow.

The Whisky is Grain with an admixture of Malt, and no acids have ever been used in the Distillery. At present the annual output is 600,000 gallons.

Fifty to sixty persons are employed in the establishment and six Excise officers, the supervisor being Mr. Macfarlane. We visited the farmsteading to see the cattle; it consists of two sets of byres, both neatly arranged buildings, well drained and easily kept clean, where are one hundred and twenty head of cattle, fed on the Draff of the Distillery. Across the roadway is the Dairy where the churns are all driven by steam power, and the butter made on the most approved principle. Glasgow is only six miles off, and the butter is sent there daily, and fetches the highest price in the market.

Mr. Barnett Harvey resides on the property; his house is quaint and picturesque, with an old-fashioned garden in front, whilst on one side there is a large bowling green, kept up by Mr. Harvey for the use of the men in the Distillery and the village.

The whistle of the train in the distance reminded us that we must be off, and, as it takes five minutes to reach the station, we shook hands with our guide and brought our interesting day's work to a close.

No. 6.

Provanmill Distillery, Millerston, Glasgow.

PROPRIETORS, MOSES RISK & SONS.

THIS Distillery is situated a few miles north-east of the City of Glasgow, in the vicinity of what in the old coaching days was the high road between that city and Stirling. The district is not without its historical associations; Robroystone, the place where tradition says that Sir William Wallace was captured, being within a mile of the Distillery; the village of Millerston, the postal town of the district, is within a short distance of the works.

The Distillery which lies in a hollow some few hundred yards from the high road, was built about the year 1815, and although small portions of the original buildings still remain, we fancy that the architect and builder, could they come to life again, would have some difficulty in recognising any of the original plans in the greatly altered and extended work which would meet their view. The Maltings, Mashing and Distillery Buildings, may be said to form three sides of a square, and are so arranged that the barley being put into the Steeps at one end, keeps continually moving forward through its various processes, until it emerges as Whisky at an almost corresponding point on the opposite side of the square. The work possesses all the most recent appliances and improvements for the production of pure malt Whisky, and has an abundant supply of water from three different sources, Hogganfield Loch, Loch Katrine, and from a copious spring upon the property. The arrangements are such that, on the same set of pipes may be turned any one of the three waters which all rise by gravitation to the highest part of the works. The Distillers, however, prefer the Hogganfield water for mashing, as from it they consider the best Whisky can be made; it is also a considerable auxiliary to the steam power in driving the machinery.

With regard to the buildings we may say that there is a large well ventilated Granary, connected with the Steeps by a gangway or bridge, so that they can be filled with ease and rapidity. The two Malt Houses or Barns are spacious and well suited to their purpose, being laid with a special composition, which has been found to be most satisfactory in producing first-rate malt; the Kiln, which is of recent construction, measures forty feet square. The floor of the Kiln is of wire cloth, and peat, which is brought from a long distance from a famed moss rented by the proprietors, and burned in a *chaffeur*, is the only fuel used for drying purposes. The Malt Store and Mill Room are large and complete, being fitted with elevators and all the latest appliances. The Mash Tun, a cast iron vessel of 26 feet diameter and 7 feet 6 inches deep, is fitted with a patent Mashing Machine, and stirring gear of modern improvements. The underback, also of cast iron, has a capacity of some 3,000 gallons, and there are two coppers of a capacity of 12,000 gallons each. In addition to the coolers there are two large refrigerators, one by Morton and the other by Miller and Co. The wash-backs, eight in number, vary from a capacity of 3,000 to 12,000 gallons; the Wash charger having a capacity of 12,000 gallons. There are three pot Stills, two heated by fire and the other by steam, with chargers, receivers, worm tubs. The Spirit Store, in which is a commodious Spirit Vat, completes this portion of the works. There are eight Warehouses, capable of containing some 2,000 casks. The Distillery and Excise Offices are well fitted and of recent construction. The Excise Officers are Messrs. Jas. Bridgman and Danl. J. Hickey; there are in all, including clerks, about twenty hands.

The Caledonian Railway passes close by the works and is most convenient for the carrying of grain, fuel, &c., and the dispatch of the Whisky.

The annual output is about 130,000 gallons, and nothing but pure malt is used in the manufacture of the Whisky.

No. 7.

Auchintoshan Distillery, Old Kilpatrick, Dumbartonshire.

PROPRIETORS, C. H. CURTIS & CO., GREENOCK.

ON our way to Bowling we stopped at Old Kilpatrick, and paid a hasty visit to the little Distillery which heads this chapter. It is situated in a romantic glen with a stream of water running past it, and is about one mile from the Station. At the time of our visit the haymakers were busy in the fields connected with the Distillery, and consequently the Works were almost abandoned. We were informed that the Distillery was founded in the year 1825. The Barley Barn and Malting are in an oblong building connected by a gangway with the Malt Kiln. The Tun Room contains four washbacks, and there is a good sized Mash Tun. The two Stills are "Old Pot Stills," and the Whisky is principally sold in the Home Trade. Nine persons are employed, and the annual output is 50,000 gallons. The water used comes from the Cochna Loch, on the Kilpatrick Hills, and is said to be of fine quality.

No. 8.

Littlemill Distillery, by Bowling, Dumbartonshire.

PROPRIETORS, WM. HAY FAIRMAN & CO.

THIS Distillery is planted at the base of the Kilpatrick Hills, on the banks of the Clyde, and is close by Bowling Railway Station. It is twelve miles from Glasgow, on the North British Railway, and a quarter of a mile from the Forth and Clyde Canal. The locality abounds in charming landscapes not unlike Richmond on the River Thames. The quiet beauty of the hill slopes and wooded plantations, the hedges covered with summer roses, and the numerous mountain rills, has made this place the favourite resort of artists, whilst at the front flows the great river, with its nautical stir, and the Bowling Bay, with its wharves and shipping, giving life to the scene.

The Distillery is a very old work, having been built about the year 1800, but considerably improved and enlarged by the late Mr. Hay in 1875 to meet the increased demand for his product. The Whisky is Malt only, and the peat used in drying is brought from Stornaway and Perthshire; the water comes from a shady glen away up in the Kilpatrick Hills, and is brought down to a reservoir close by.

There are four Malt Barns, one of them being 131 feet long and 21 feet wide, with Steeps of a proportionate size. The Granaries are on the upper floors of the Malt Barns; in the latter they make upwards of 3,000 bushels of Malt weekly, and there is a Kiln at each end of the buildings, with wire flooring capable of drying the same quantity. The Mash Tun mashes 350 bushels at one time; there are eight washbacks, holding over 5,000 gallons each. Three Pot Stills are in use, the largest containing 4,000 gallons. Two of them are Low Wines Stills, one containing 1,500 gallons and the other of smaller capacity. The two Brewing Vats will each hold 2,000 gallons. The machinery in the Distillery is worked by a twenty horse power steam engine, and additional power is obtained by a water wheel, which is so arranged that they can work together, or separately; the steam boiler is 30 feet long and 8 feet in diameter. The Vat in which the products of the Stills are collected is capable of holding 3,500 gallons.

There are four Duty free Warehouses holding 6,500 casks and there is a compact little cooperage employing two men all the year round.

The Whisky is sent to England, Ireland, India and the Colonies. The Firm has a Warehouse at 36, Douglas Street, Glasgow, where they blend, rack, and bottle for home use and exportation.

The annual output is 150,000 gallons.

No. 9.

Tambowie Distillery, by Milngavie, Dumbartonshire.

PROPRIETOR, DAVID CHRYSTAL.

OUR next journey was to Milngavie, a village eight miles from Glasgow on the North British Railway, from which we had to drive two miles to Tambowie Distillery. It is planted in the midst of undulating scenery of wood and park, and stands at the foot of one of the Tambowie Hills, from whence it derives its name. Opposite the works and across the valley the Strathblane Hills are visible, with the picturesque hill of Dungour in the background. The view embraces glimpses of sylvan scenery stretching over a distance of thirty miles, including the stately policies and picturesque grounds of Caigend and Mudock Castles, Edinbarnet, Mains, Carbeth Guthrie, and also the great reservoir of Loch Katrine water which supplies the city of Glasgow.

This old-fashioned Distillery, situated as it is in the country of Rob Roy, brings us back to the old smugglers' days, for this place was actually the scene of their illicit exploits, and the cave cut out of the solid rock, wherein they carried on their nefarious practices, is converted into and now used as Stores. The old work has under the present proprietor, been greatly enlarged and modernized to suit the requirements of an increasing business, nevertheless it still retains its old character. The water is brought direct from the Tambowie Hills into the works, and the stream provides an ample and unfailing supply both for driving power and distilling.

To preserve the original design and appearance of the Distillery, the alterations referred to have as far possible been adapted, and consequently the buildings have a smaller bulk than the output would lead one to expect. The machinery and utensils are all of the most approved description, and a notable feature connected with the cooling department is the employment of the perpendicular refrigerators made by Wilson, of Stockton-on-Tees. After inspecting the new offices, Mr. Watt, the manager, proffered his services as guide, and took us first of all to the Barley Barns; these quaint buildings placed above the Distillery on a terrace of the hill, are capable of storing 500 quarters of barley; underneath, at the end, there is an iron Steep. The manager informed us that Morayshire barley alone is used, and great attention is paid to its quality and weight; he further informed us that Mr. Chrystal gained his experience and learned his business, first at the Camlachie and afterwards at the

Benmore Distilleries. The Maltings, which are partly underneath the Barley Loft, are concreted; when the barley is sufficiently vegetated it is lifted by a hoist to the Kiln, a stone building 23 feet long and 24 feet broad, situated at the end of the Barns. The furnaces are fired entirely with peats brought from Tambowie moss. Leaving the Kiln we directed our steps to the Malt Deposit, a chamber over part of the Malt House, and from thence to the Mill. This little building is placed contiguous to the Mash House, and to reach it we descended a long flight of steps on a level with the Maltings; it contains a pair of metal malt cylinders and the usual machinery driven by water or steam. The bruised malt is taken from the Mill Room to the Grist Loft situated over the Mash Tun, wherein there is a hopper which feeds a Steel's mashing machine. Descending from this apartment we again found ourselves in the courtyard, and ascending a few steps arrived at the Mash House, a neat and well lighted building, containing a circular metal Mash Tun 12 feet in diameter and 6 feet deep, with the usual stirring gear, which is driven either by steam or water power. Beneath this is the Underback, a square vessel holding 1,000 gallons, and above is a Wort Receiver. Following our guide we next came to the fermenting department; in this hall are ranged four Wash-backs, each holding 4,200 gallons, switched by steam. The coolers are above, and the Wash Charger, which holds 4,500 gallons, is placed on beams in the Still House. The worts by the process of fermentation have now been changed into wash, and following the process we were next conducted to the Still House, the most antique of all the buildings, projecting from the Maltings, and measuring 200 feet long by 40 feet wide built of ordinary stone and brick. It contains two Pot Stills, a Wash and Spirit, the former holding 1,730 gallons, and the latter 1,230 gallons, both heated by furnaces. On a gallery elevation outside is a wooden Worm Tub, containing two copper worms, over which there is an abundant supply of water, the overflow from which is used for driving a small wheel attached to gearing for stirring the contents of the Wash Still. Part of the Still House is set apart as a Receiver room and contains one Low wines and a Feints Receiver and Charger holding 2,100 gallons and one Spirit Receiver holding 1,491 gallons, and a brass Safe.

We next retraced our steps and came to the Spirit Store which contains a Vat holding 1,900 gallons; Cooperage, and a Racking Store. From thence we proceeded to inspect the two Warehouses, one of them being the smugglers cave already referred to, and to reach which we had to descend some broken steps when we found ourselves in a low arched gallery of some considerable extent, where the casks of Whisky are ranged along the sides and down the middle. It is a curious old vault and well adapted for a hiding place and subterranean distilling. After tasting a "wee drappie" we returned to the surface, and paid a visit to the small farmyard, stables and cart sheds.

The Whisky is pure Malt, and the output in the year 1885 was 48,000 gallons.

No. 10.

Clydesdale Distillery, Wishaw, Lanarkshire.

PROPRIETORS, J. M. MACKENZIE & Co.

THIS Distillery is situated in the valley of the Clyde, six miles from the celebrated falls, in the neighbourhood of beautiful scenery; it faces the Wishaw House policies, which come up almost to the very gateway. The banks of the Clyde are very charming, whilst the woods, orchards and fruit gardens combine to give this district the well-known designation of the "Garden of Scotland." The water used in this Distillery comes from the Cambusnethan peat-moss, a natural burn in the hills, where wild flowers and heather grow in rich profusion. This burn has been diverted from its course and is brought by a stone conduit through the grounds of Coltness (the property of James Houldsworth, Esq.) direct into the works. Peat of excellent quality is dug from the Greenhead moss in the neighbourhood, so that the firm do not need to import any.

The Distillery is solidly built in the form of a square, and was founded in the year 1825; it covers five acres of ground, is about fourteen miles from Glasgow, on the Caledonian Railway, and a quarter of a mile from the Railway Station. The works, which cost Lord Belhaven nearly ninety thousand pounds, were leased to Patrick Chalmers (brother to the celebrated Dr. Chalmers) who was the originator of the "Cask Brand P. Chalmers." The establishment was afterwards purchased by the senior partner of the present firm, and as the business increased additions and improvements have continually been made.

The following are a few particulars of the establishment. There are four large Granaries at the top of the building and eight malting floors, four of the latter are 125 by 44 feet, and the other four 85 by 30 feet with Steeps of a proportionate size. The malt is hoisted by machinery to the large Kilns where it is dried by Peat; two of these Kilns are 44 feet square, the other 35 feet square, floored with perforated iron plates, and with the new improved sheet iron furnaces which cause a saving of fuel and give a greater amount of heat. The Malt Stores and Mill Rooms are in close proximity, and the malt after being bruised by steel rollers is sent up by Elevators into the Mash Tun—a vessel 24 feet in diameter and 6 feet deep holding 15,271 gallons, with the usual stirring gear. The Under-back holds 5,676 gallons and from here the wort goes through the coolers and two of Morton's Refrigerators into the four Wash-backs each containing 18,000 gallons. Thence after being fermented it is pumped to the Wash Charger, which holds 18,000 gallons, afterwards through the four Stills which are of the plain Pot kind with a capacity of 5,500, 3,500 2,650 and 1,000 gallons respectively. The worm tubs are in the open air, and it may here be mentioned that the Whisky in this establishment undergoes three distillations. There is of course the usual safe; also sampling safe and a Receiver, the latter a large wooden vessel holding 3,000 gallons, from this the spirit flows into the vat (holding 5,000 gallons) placed in the spirit store where it is casked, weighed, and branded in the usual way, and sent to the Warehouses of which there are ten, solid stone buildings with slated roofs, some of these 156 feet long by 96 feet wide. These Warehouses at the time of our visit contained 3,500 casks of Whisky of various ages. There is an extensive apparatus on the premises for distilling water for reducing purposes, also a powerful steam engine with two boilers 30 feet long by 7 feet diameter, and steam injectors with fire hose attached. The Coppers for heating water are pure copper vessels of large capacity each of them capable of filling the Mash Tun. There is a capital Cooperage for repairs and storage—we also noticed upwards of 100 Sherry Butts just imported from Spain.

Forty persons are employed in the works, and the Manager, Brewer, and other employés have dwellings within the enclosure. There are capital Offices for the Partners, Clerks, and Excise gentlemen. There is a railway siding direct into the works, so that barley can be brought to the very doors of the Granaries.

The Whiskey is pure Malt, and the Registered Trade Mark is "Clydesdale."

The name of the chief excise officer is Mr. Wm. Wight, with two divisional officers and two assistants.

The annual output is 170,000 gallons.

No. 11.

Saucel Distillery, Paisley.

PROPRIETORS, JAMES STEWART & CO.

THIS Distillery is situated in the suburbs of the town of Paisley, and in the parish of Saucel, close by the river Cart, and near to the celebrated abbey, which was founded in the year 1163, by "Walter the Good," the then High Steward of Scotland, who built it for the Benedictines of Wenlock Priory in Shropshire. He richly endowed it, and eventually it became one of the most opulent in Scotland. This fine old abbey is rich in history; the Stewarts made it their burial ground; Robert II, his two wives, Robert III, and other princes were here interred. In the seventeenth century the Abbey was rebuilt, and although the transept and a great part of it is now in ruins, the nave is still used as the parish church, and is said to be the most magnificent place of worship in Scotland. A hundred years ago this beautiful Abbey with its orchards, gardens, and deer park, was surrounded by a magnificent stone wall, upwards of a mile in circumference, and adorned with fine statues; but in 1781 the Earl of Abercorn sold the stones to build the new town of Paisley, which absorbed the beautiful grounds of the Abbey.

The Saucel Distillery is a large work and occupies nearly both sides of King Street, Saucel, covering in all eight acres of ground. It was built early in the century, and from time to time important additions have been made to the works, and tablets bearing date of the same are affixed to the various buildings; the first is dated 1832, the next 1853, and the third 1857, thus showing in a marked way the progress of the business. At the time of its establishment the Distillery was fortunate in having such a river as the Cart splashing by its walls, and the Espedair Burn running through the works. An old writer describes it as a beautiful impetuous stream flowing direct from the Stanley Braes, through fine scenery, falling into the river Cart, near the Abbey and Distillery. Owing to the close proximity of the dye works, &c., neither of these streams is now used, and Messrs. Stewart & Co., have made a large reservoir high up in the Hawkhead Hills. The water is collected therein from the Oldbar Burn, and conveyed two miles direct into the Distillery. They also have another valuable water supply from an Artesian Well upon the premises, 400 feet deep, which yields water of a good quality for distilling and mashing purposes.

There are six large Granaries nearly 300 feet long and 56 feet wide, holding in all eight thousand quarters of grain, and eight well ventilated Malt Barns of an average of 150 feet long by 50 feet broad. The six Kilns are of an average each of 40 feet square, and all of them are fitted with the good old fashioned furnaces, where nothing but peat is used. Some of the peats are brought from the Gleniffer Hills in the district, but a large quantity is shipped from Ireland

and the Hebrides. All the Kilns are floored with the patent wire cloth flooring The four Malt Stores, which are nearly 200 feet long by 50 feet broad, adjoin the Kilns, and the Malt is conveyed by Hoppers, of which there are two sets, and three pairs of Mill Stones. From this department it is dropped by sluices into the Tun Room which is 60 feet long, which contains three large Mash Tuns, two of which measure 24 feet in diameter and 6 feet in depth, and the other about half that size; the two former having a capacity of 16,000 gallons, and each fitted with the usual stirring gear. Here also are three heaters and three tanks heated by steam. From the Mash Tuns the worts run into one of the two Underbacks beneath, which are capable of holding 12,000 and 5,000 gallons respectively. It may here be mentioned that the Draff is conveyed by a screw and elevator to the Draff House adjoining the Mash House, and carts can be drawn in and remove the same without any trouble. From the Underbacks the worts are pumped into Coolers away up in the roof of the buildings, and to the three large Miller's patent Refrigerators. From these it descends to the Washbacks, of which there are twenty, holding from 12,000 to 45,000 gallons respectively. It is then pumped by Centrifugal Pumps into the large Wash Chargers, holding 14,000 and 28,000 gallons respectively. From thence it passes to the intermediate Wash Chargers, one holding 14,000 and the other 45,000 gallons. From these it is pumped into the Stills, of which there are eighteen. The two Still Houses are lofty buildings each 100 feet long, and the Stills which are capable of holding in all 45,000 gallons, are mostly of the old Pot kind, and there is besides a Coffey's Patent Still.

The Spirit from the Stills passes to the Worm Tubs, and thence through a vast safe and sampling safe to the Low Wines and Feints Receivers, large wooden vessels holding 3,000 and 5,000 gallons respectively. From these it passes to the four Spirit Vats, capable of holding 20,000 gallons, which are situated in the Spirit Store, a large and lofty building measuring 70 feet by 40 feet. Here it is casked, weighed and branded, and taken to the Warehouses, which are eight in number, and containing several thousands of casks. They are mostly 140 feet long by 30 feet broad, and contain Whiskies of various ages. The four principal ones, together with the Excise Offices, are enclosed in a walled-in yard on the opposite side of the Still House. Within this enclosure is also an export bottling and case department, a two decker building 50 feet by 60 feet, wherein the Whisky—for export only—is labelled under the Trade Marks of the "Lion & Crown" James Stewart & Co. and cased. These Warehouses contain many cases sealed and bearing the Excise Stamp, waiting for shipment.

In the Engine House there are two forty horse power engines, and eight Boilers, 23 feet long by 8 feet in diameter. Within the works there is an extensive Cooperage for the repair and storage of casks; also a Joiner's and Engineer's Shop, Smithy, and Stabling for six horses.

The precautions against fire are very complete, every floor having a plentiful supply of water laid on with the necessary hose attached. About one hundred persons are employed in the works.

The Whisky made is pure Malt and Grain, and is chiefly sold in Scotland, England, Ireland and the Colonies. The annual output of this Distillery is about One Million gallons.

The Chief Excise Officer is Mr. Mathison, and there are fourteen others besides engaged on the premises.

No. 12.

Gleniffer Distillery, near Paisley, Renfrewshire.

PROPRIETOR, JAMES JOHNSTON.

CONTINUING our pilgrimage, we again took train at Paisley, and after a run of about twenty minutes found ourselves at the town of Johnstone, where we were supplied with a dog-cart and a fast stepper. The drive of some two or three miles on a bright summer day, with a perfume of hawthorn scenting the air, smiling hedgerows, and rich plantations thick with foliage, was far too short, and lingers on our memory still.

Gleniffer Distillery is situated on the slopes of the Gleniffer Braes, a beautifully wooded range of hills. These braes are sacred to the memory of the poet Tannahill, and they inspired him to write—

Keen blaws the wind o'er the braes o' Gleniffer,
The auld castle turrets are cover'd wi' snaw;
How chang'd frae the time when I met wi' my lover,
Among the broom bushes by Stanley green shaw.
The wild flowr's o' summer were spread a' sae bonnie,
The mavis sang sweet frae the green birken tree;
But far to the Camp they hae march'd my dear Johnnie,
An' now it is winter wi' nature an' me.

These braes were his Sunday and week day haunts, and a great many of his poems were composed and written there. From their heights can be seen the river Clyde, the Grampians, and a boundless expanse of plain and valley. The Distillery is ten miles from Glasgow, and was built in the year 1834. It is embowered and almost hidden among trees, which in summer are covered with the most luxuriant foliage, and sloping flower gardens, which extend almost to the very doors of the Granaries. There is a bright sparkling burn flowing swiftly over miniature waterfalls, which, running through the Distillery grounds, drives the Mill Wheel. The works are old fashioned and quaintly built, and consist of two large Barley Barns, Malting Houses, a Mill Building, with two pairs of stones, a Mash House, Tun Room, and Still House, in the latter of which are two old Pot Stills. There are three Warehouses, containing a quantity of Whisky in bond, one of them a new building; capital stabling, cart sheds, and other outhouses. The water used for distilling purposes comes from the Glen Burn, which rises at the top of the Gleniffer Braes. Peat only is used in drying.

The Whisky is pure Malt, and the annual output is 70,000 gallons.

No. 13.

Greenock Distillery, Greenock, Renfrewshire.

PROPRIETORS, JOHN RENNIE AND JOHN H. BALLANTINE.

A SHORT railway journey brought us to Greenock, which is twenty-two miles from Glasgow on the South Western Railway. Early in the seventeenth century it was a small fishing village of some twenty cottages; now it is the sixth largest town in Scotland in point of population, and does an immense shipping trade with North and South America, the East and West Indies, and many other parts of the globe. It is a busy manufacturing town, with closely packed streets and some fine buildings. The hills at the back of the town rise to the height of 800 feet, and command the finest views of mountain, loch and river in Scotland. If Greenock had been built in terraces on the slopes of the hills instead of on the shore, it would, from its position on the Clyde, have been the most beautiful seaport in the world, and even now it is unrivalled in the United Kingdom.

The Greenock Distillery, an old-fashioned structure in Tobago Street, is not without its history. Early in the century it was an ancient brewery celebrated for its ale, and the fine quality of its brew has been chanted in many a song. The town has always been celebrated for its malt, and the first pier, or harbour, ever erected there, was built out of the proceeds of a malt-tax of one shilling and fourpence on every sack of malt brewed within the boundary of the town.

Let other poets raise a fracas
'Bout vines, and wines, and drunken Bacchus,
And crabbit names and stories wrack us,
And grate our lug.
I sing the juice Scotch bear can mak' us
In glass or jug.

BURNS.

In the year 1824 this fine old brewery was turned into a Distillery, and ever since that date it has been in the same proprietorship. The whole establishment covers three acres of ground; the water used for distilling is brought from Lochgryfe. Only the best Scotch barley is used by the proprietors, which is carted from the railway, distant about half a mile, direct into the Granaries, of which there are three; one of them being 128 feet long and 122 feet wide; the other two are not quite so large. From the Granary Floors the barley is dropped through traps into the Steeps beneath. There are three Malting Floors, each 130 feet long by 124 feet, two of them contiguous to the Kilns, the other across the yard connected by a bridge or gangway. The Kilns are covered with the wire flooring, and peat only, which is dug from the hills at the back of the work, is used in drying. The malt, after removal from the Kilns to the Mill Stores, is dropped by a hopper into the Mill rollers below, and thence conveyed through the Mashing Machine into the Mash Tun, a solid iron vessel, 17 feet in diameter and 5 feet deep, holding 573 bushels and containing the usual stirring gear.

The Underback is sunk into the ground under the Mash Tun, and holds 3,933 gallons. The Worts are pumped up to the coolers, and a Morton's Refrigerator above; thence into the eight iron Wash-backs—the only ones of that kind we have seen in Scotland—faced with timber and lined with felt covering, an excellent contrivance to retain the heat. These Wash-backs have each a capacity of 5,500 gallons. From there, by gravitation, the liquid flows into the Wash Charger, another iron vessel containing 5,122 gallons, and from thence to the Wash Stills holding 4,931 gallons. From there it is sent on to the Worm Tubs or Condensers out in the open air, and through the Safe into the Low Wines Receiver, holding 1,842 gallons. From here the Spirit is pumped into the Low Wines and Feints Charger, an iron vessel holding 1,980 gallons, and thence into the Low Wines Still containing 1,007 gallons. Passing again through the Worms it flows into the No. 1 Feints Receiver, containing 930 gallons. Thence it passes on to the Low Wines Charger again, and on to No. 1 and 2 Stills, containing 879 and 776 gallons respectively. Once more passing through the Worm into No. 2 Feints Receiver, containing 925 gallons, it flows on again to the Feints Chargers to Nos. 1 and 2 Stills and Safe, direct into the Spirit Receiver, which holds 820 gallons, and has a patent index thereon which shows at a glance the position of the stop-cock.

From the foregoing explanation it will be seen that the product is really distilled three times, and the consequent result is a pure Spirit. The Whisky is afterwards pumped from the Receiver into the Vat in the Spirit Stores, a vessel containing 1,451 gallons. These Spirit Stores which are underground, are very antiquated and have the appearance of having been formerly a smuggler's cave. They are reached by stone steps at the end of the yard; here the pure Spirit is casked, weighed and branded, and then removed to one of the six Warehouses, the whole of which are capable of holding 4,000 casks.

The Stills are of the old-fashioned "Pot Still" pattern, and although very aged they are exceptionally good vessels, and the proprietors would not change them for any price. The Wash Still contains in its interior the ancient chain arrangement for agitating the liquid. There is a good Racking Store conveniently arranged, and a 12 h.p. engine. There are two steam boilers, an extra one for heating water for mashing, one 18 feet by 8 feet, and the other 14 feet by 7 feet. On one side of the gateway there is a good Cooperage, on the other Clerks' Offices. Twenty-four persons are employed and most of the work is performed by manual labour.

The Whisky, which is pure Malt, is sold principally in Glasgow, London, Liverpool and Manchester. The annual output is 130,000 gallons.

The Chief Excise Officer is Mr. Moon, Supervisor.

HAZELBURN DISTILLERY.

No. 14.

Hazelburn Distillery, Campbeltown.

PROPRIETORS, GREENLEES & COLVILL, LIMITED.

WE had decided on going to Campbeltown by the steamer "Davaar," but hearing that it would be crowded with Glasgow Fair holiday people, together with the prospect of a number of women and children tumbling about in all directions in the event of the voyage proving unfavourable, we thought it better to abandon our original intention of entering the land of Whisky by way of the sea, and finally decided to go by the Tarbert Route. We joined the "Columba" at Princes Pier, Greenock, and soon found ourselves fairly under weigh and moving rapidly down the river. After so much railway travelling we found this mode of locomotion a very agreeable change. The perpetual bustle on board, the freedom of movement and the interchange of communication with so many fellow passengers was quite a relief to us. Passing Gourock, with its little bay crowded with yachts, and Dunoon, whose beach was thronged with summer visitors, we soon began to approach the grander scenery of the lochs and mountains. As we steamed along, rock and wood appeared to view, blended together in exquisite harmony, whilst over and above all, ridges on ridges of mountain stretched far away to the horizon. When we reached Rothesay the rain came down in torrents, and did not cease until we left the Kyles of Bute.

Rounding the point into Loch Fyne, the island of Arran came into full view, and we could plainly discern its highest mountain, "Goatfell," which rises three thousand feet above sea level; also Skipness Point, which marks the entrance to the Loch, and upon which the fine old ruin of the castle is placed. It is in a good state of preservation; its two quadrangular towers, which rise from opposite corners of the ruins, being prominent objects from the sea. Skipness Bay is a safe retreat for the herring fleet in stormy weather. Loch Fyne stretches from Kilbranan to Inverary, a distance of thirty-two miles, and its breadth varies from twelve to three miles; half way up is Loch Gilp, whence is cut the Crinan Canal to the Sound of Jura. This broad inlet of the sea is from sixty to seventy fathoms deep, and has from time immemorial been noted for its herrings, which are of a superior quality to any found in the western seas. Crossing the Loch we soon reached our destination.

On leaving the boat at East Loch, Tarbert, we hastened to the coach and secured the box seat, much to the chagrin of two of our fellow travellers who were not quite so quick in their movements. It is forty miles to Campbeltown from East

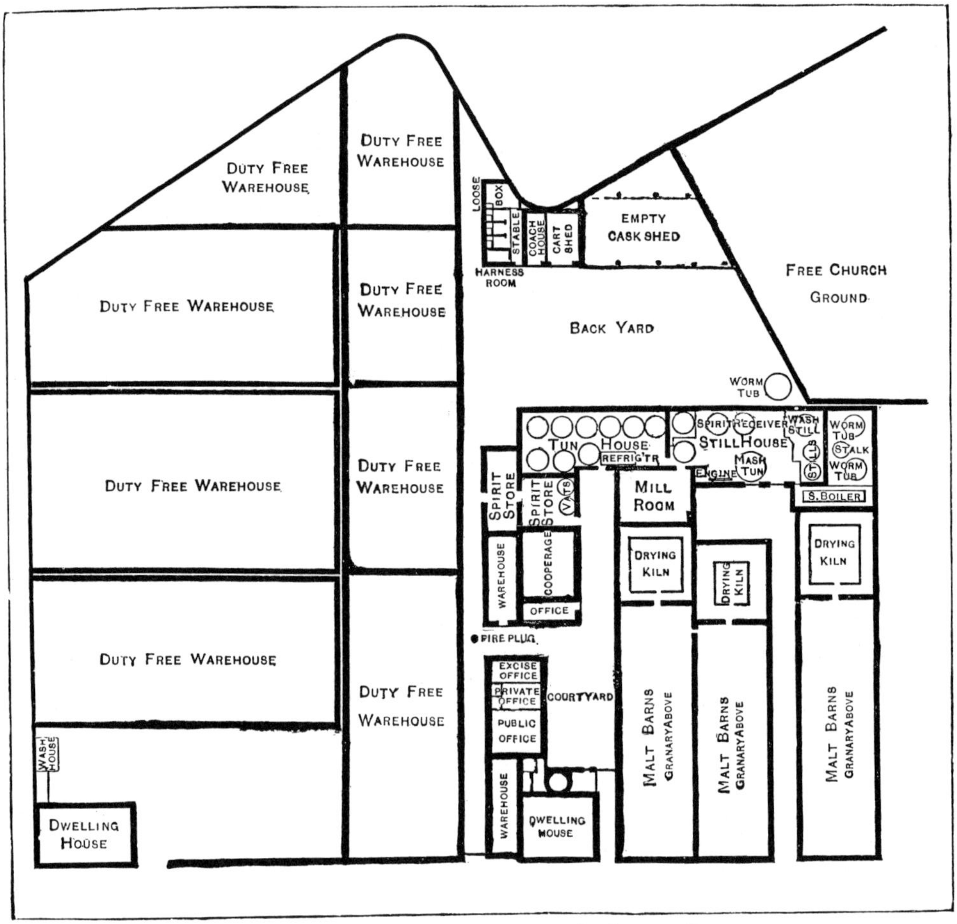

GROUND PLAN OF HAZELBURN DISTILLERY.

Tarbert Pier, and the journey by coach usually occupies six hours. We had a splendid day for our journey, and the road lay through some of the most delightful and romantic scenery in the county. After passing through the village of Tarbert, crossing the peninsula to the West Loch Tarbert Pier, from whence the Islay boats depart, we came in sight of the sea which we had in view for the rest of our journey. In this part of Kintyre most of the charms of nature are united. First we passed country lanes overshadowed with trees and farm houses mostly of a superior kind, whose smiling cornfields testify that cultivation is carried on to the highest perfection, then villages, so called, which scarcely reach the size of hamlets, and wide natural meadows on which herds of cattle were grazing. Coaching merrily along we were soon sunk into the recesses of a small valley, shut in by woods and overlooked by romantic elevations, and then in a few moments we were out of this seemingly remote concealment, looking down upon the broad waters of the loch, and across an expanse of luxuriant country terminating in a rocky shore and the wide ocean. Slight showers fell at intervals during our journey, which conduced to our comfort in one way by effectually laying the dust. After we had passed Tayinloan the road became more winding, and although we had left the foliage behind us the route was as interesting as ever. At every fresh step we discovered new features of beauty, new hills disclosed themselves and new rocks started up, whilst on our right there was always the beautiful sea. We reached Campbeltown soon after six and were deposited at the door of the "White Hart" Hotel, where, after some difficulty, the town being full of visitors, we were able to secure quarters. After satisfying the cravings of an eager appetite we strolled forth to take stock of the town which was to be our place of residence for the next fortnight.

Campbeltown is certainly a most attractive place and we were charmed with its appearance. It is situated at the head of a beautiful bay, which is almost land locked and engirt by heath covered hills. The foremost of these is Bengullion—Hill of the Wind—1,124 feet high, which is on the southern shore, and Knock Scalbert of nearly the same altitude on the northern shore. At the entrance to the bay like a sentinel stands the bold and rocky island of Davaar on which there is a Beacon Tower. The harbour, which is two miles long and one broad, is admitted to be the best roadstead in Scotland; at the time of our visit its waters were teeming with life and hundreds of sail were riding safely at anchor on its ample bosom. Campbeltown is a royal burgh and one of the most interesting towns of Scotland. It was the original seat of the Scottish monarchy which was founded there by King Fergus I. Anciently called Dalruadhain its name was changed into Claunloch, until finally it was called Campbeltown, in compliment to the Duke of Argyll. In former times the only trade of the place was herring fishing, net making and smuggling.

During the last century and up to seventy years ago the unlawful occupation of distilling Whisky was carried on to the greatest extent, the landed proprietors rather encouraging the practice. Those found smuggling by the Excise Officers were brought before the Court of Justice and fined; but usually the judge was one of the landed proprietors, so the fines were small and many got off free. When legal distilling was first introduced the Distillers met with a good deal of opposition and resentment from the smugglers, but they managed to live it down, and owing to the quality of the product, the trade developed so rapidly that it has now become the staple article of commerce, and there are no less than twenty-one Distilleries in Campbeltown.

A capital story is told of an aged woman who resided near Hazelburn. She was of a rather doubtful character and was charged before the Sheriff with smuggling. The charge being held proven, it fell to his lordship to pronounce sentence. When about to do so he thus addressed the culprit, "I daresay my poor woman it is not often you have been guilty of this fault," "deed no Sheriff" she readily replied "I haena made a drap since youn wee keg I sent to yersel."

The Hazelburn Distillery was founded in the last century, and rebuilt in the year 1836. It is said to be planted on the site of the Parliament House, where James IV. held a parliament when he emancipated the vassals of the McDonalds. The works cover three acres of ground and have a commanding appearance from Longrow. They are built chiefly with stone and have a frontage to the road of 372 feet, with a depth therefrom of 247 feet. Most of the Distilleries in Campbeltown are built on the same plan and surround a courtyard, but in the case of Hazelburn two courts are embraced in one distillery, besides which, it is intersected by three roadways. From the front there is a pleasant look out on

HAZELBURN DISTILLERY, STILL HOUSE

green hills and pastures. During our visit the haymakers were very busy in the fields opposite, carrying the hay, and the atmosphere was filled with its fragrance. The water used in Hazelburn comes from various sources, that for mashing is brought from the Crosshill Loch, for other purposes there are two excellent wells on the premises forty feet deep, containing spring water of the finest quality. The Barley used comes principally from Moray and Perthshire, and is brought by steamer to the quay, distant half a mile, and carted therefrom direct to the Granary doors. We entered the establishment through a covered archway and soon made ourselves known to Mr. Greenlees, who gave us every information and provided us with a guide. We commenced our circuit of the buildings at the Maltings, which, in this Distillery are on a large scale, and some idea of their magnitude may be gathered from the following particulars :—They consist of three Granary floors averaging 110 feet long and 31 feet wide, capable of storing ten thousand quarters of barley ; and five Malt barns with tiled or concrete floors of the same dimensions as the Granaries, each possessing a stone Steep capable of wetting 175 quarters at one time. These spacious floors are commanded by three Kilns each of which is 36 feet square ; all of them are floored with Hermano's patent wire cloth and fired with peat. The Malt is conveyed from the Malting floors to these Kilns by elevators. Communicating with each of the three Kilns and forming a central chamber is the Malt Deposit, underneath which is the Mill Room containing a large pair of metal rollers for crushing the malt. The machinery is driven by steam and grinds 2,500 bushels every ten hours. In close proximity to the Mill is the Grist-Loft, which contains a Hopper in connection with a Steel's Patent Mashing Machine over the Mash-tun.

We were next taken to a building which, besides other vessels hereafter to be described, contained two heating tanks, each holding 2,500 gallons for the supply of hot water to the Mash Tun, afterwards to the Mash and Still House combined, a neat building 64 feet long, 32 feet broad, and 42 feet high. At the east end there is placed a Circular Mash Tun, 14 feet in diameter and 6 feet deep, which is fed by the mashing machine and contains the usual stirring rakes driven by steam. In the same building, but at a lower level, is the Underback from which the worts are pumped up to a Worts Receiver placed at a high elevation. From this receptacle the Worts run through a large Morton's Refrigerator to the Fermenting Tuns.

Passing through another doorway we now come to the Tun Room, a spacious Hall, wherein are placed against the wall nine Washbacks, each holding 6,000 gallons, all of which are switched by machinery. We then ascended a staircase and found ourselves on a gallery in the Still House on which is placed the Wash-charger, a fine timber vessel holding 5,000 gallons, and a Low-wines and Feints Charger, a similar dish holding 2,800 gallons. Descending, we found ourselves on the ground floor of the House. It contains three Stills, one of them the Wash Still holding 7,000 gallons is the largest in Campbeltown, the other two are Low-wines and Feints Stills, each of a capacity of 1,800 gallons. The bodies of these two Stills are of the ordinary Pot Still pattern made entirely of copper, but built to certain exact proportions. They are surrounded by brick work ; underneath is a furnace so arranged that the flues carry the heat all round, and there is no heating by steam to these Stills. There is, however, a peculiarity in the form of the heads which we have not seen at any other Distillery. The tops instead of being of the ordinary pear-shaped heads are composed of 32 chambers or tubes in each Still, terminating in a dome just before passing into the worm.

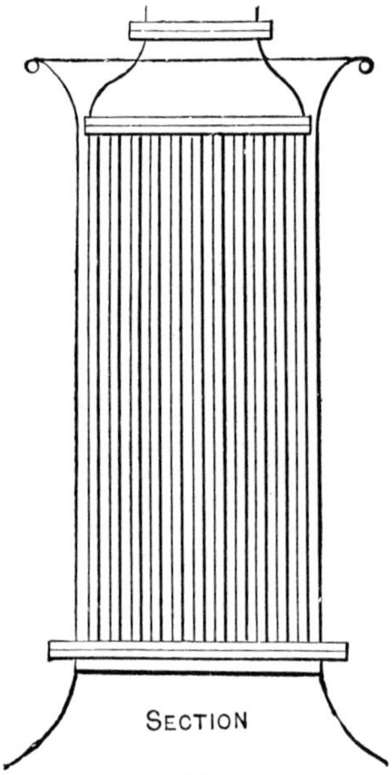

SECTION

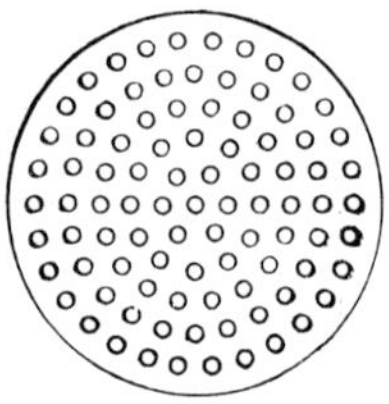

PLAN

These tubes are enclosed in a copper case which serves as a condenser, a stream of cold water being kept flowing around the pipes whilst the Stills are "at work." By this means a large proportion of the fusel oil which otherwise would pass off in the form of vapour along with the spirit is thrown back into the Still, and the pure spirit is allowed to pass through the columns into the worm free from impurity. The heated water is run off by an overflow pipe from the top of the case. The accompanying sections of these Still Heads will explain the system.

We next passed out into the Court to inspect the three Worm Tubs connected with the Stills. They are all constructed with timber and hold 10,000, 8,000 and 6,000 gallons respectively, and afterwards to the Ball Room, where we were shown the safe through which the spirit passes on its way from the Worm to the Spirit Receiver, a vessel holding 1,700 gallons, and partly sunk into the floor; also a Low Wines and Feints Receiver holding 2,000 gallons, from which the spirit is pumped up to the Low Wines and Feints Charger before referred to, which vessel commands the Stills. Retracing our steps to the outer courtyard we reached the Spirit Store, which contains three large Spirit Vats and the usual casking and weighing apparatus. Adjoining is a Racking Store, and the Engine Department is on the other side; this latter consists of a capital fourteen horse-power engine and a steam boiler 23 feet long by 9 in diameter. We then inspected the Bonded Warehouses, which are so spacious that they occupy a third section of the works. They are nine in number and cover 70,700 square feet, and the whole contained at the time of our visit 302,000 gallons of Whisky. The Manager informed us that when full they will hold half a million gallons. The principal Warehouses of the firm are, however, in Glasgow, which on our return to that city we visited. They are situated in Osborne Street, and have a superficial area of 39,357 square feet with a frontage of 254 feet, and contained 15,000 casks of Whisky distributed over seven large stores. The casks are placed on timber gauntrees, puncheons nearest the ground, hogsheads in the centre, and quarter casks on the top. Each cask is locked in position by a system of wedge-like blocks, and with comparatively little trouble every cask can be removed. But to return to Hazelburn. Adjoining the Racking Store, there is a cask shed and cooperage, also a carpenter's shop, and at the principal entrance gates are the clerks and manager's offices, where there are also sampling rooms and the Excise Offices. Twenty-two persons are employed in the Distillery, and there are three Inland Revenue Officers. The make is called Campbeltown Malt and the output for 1885 was 192,000 gallons. The works are however capable of turning out 250,000 gallons.

No. 15.

Springbank Distillery, Campbeltown.

PROPRIETORS, J. & A. MITCHELL & CO.

AFTER leaving Hazelburn we accepted the offer of a drive, from one of the Distillers who coached us along the sea coast, that we might inhale the bracing sea air and shake off the fatigue of a long day. The next morning we commenced our visitations at Springbank, which Distillery is situated in the heart of the Whisky City, and stands in its own grounds of upwards of ten acres. The buildings, which cover three acres, have a frontage to the street of 600 feet, and at the back there is a small grass park. The Distillery was built in the year 1828, by the father-in-law of one of the present proprietors, and is more conveniently arranged than some of the old works. The establishment is built in the form of a quadrangle, and there is only one gateway. On entering the enclosure the Brewer took us in hand, and we first visited the two Granaries, each 100 feet long and 44 feet wide; and then the four Malt Floors, which are of the same dimensions. Three of these floors each contain a Steep capable of wetting 80 quarters at one time. The malt when properly germinated is raised to the kiln floors by means of a steam lift and hand elevators. The two Kilns are contiguous to the Maltings; they are large and lofty, and floored with English perforated tiles. Peat is principally used in drying the malt, and the furnaces are both enclosed. We next passed on to the Malt Deposit, and from thence to the Mill, which contains the usual malt rollers and machinery driven by steam. The ground malt is raised to the Grist-loft by elevators, and when required is shot into hoppers over the mash-tun. Following our guide we reached the Mash-house, a lofty building as clean as white-wash and paint could make it, containing a metal Mash-tun, 14 feet in diameter by 5 feet deep, an Underback, a huge Heating Tank for hot water, and a Morton's Refrigerator. Passing through this apartment we came to the Tun-room, wherein are to be seen seven Washbacks, each holding 6,000 gallons, and a Wash-charger of 7,000 gallons capacity. Descending a few steps we retraced our way to the Still-house, where we were shown three Pot Stills, holding 3,000, 1,700, and 1,500 gallons respectively, whilst on an elevation were placed the Chargers and Receivers, and at the back the Worm-tub. In close proximity to the Mash-house there is a capital 16 horse-power Steam Engine, and a Boiler 21 feet long by 6½ feet in diameter; also a small Cooperage and Cask-shed, and good Offices for the Distillers and Excise Clerks.

The Distillery is about half a mile from the pier, and the water used in the works for all purposes comes from the Crosshill Loch. Fifteen persons are employed on the premises, and three excise officers, the chief being Mr. A. M. O'Brien.

The make is Campbeltown Malt, and the annual output is 145,000 gallons, which is principally sold in London and Glasgow.

DALINTOBER DISTILLERY.

No. 16.

Dalintober Distillery, Campbeltown.

PROPRIETORS, REID & COLVILLES.

AFTER living in Campbeltown a few days we began to feel quite at home in the town, and were on familiar terms with most of the Distillers and a good many of the inhabitants. Before starting on our usual pilgrimage we accepted the invitation of Mr. MacCallam to join him in a sail. It was just the morning for a cruise; a brisk breeze was blowing off the land, and the white crests of the billows were gleaming and dancing in the sunbeams. Off we started, and were soon scudding through the water at a great rate, the white wings of the yacht skimming the rippling waves, and all of us enjoying the delightful sensation of rapid movement through the air without the slightest bodily exertion. We made almost straight for the bluff Isle of Devaar, and the view of Campbeltown we got from that point was very beautiful. Our friend landed us close to the Distillery, whither we proceeded. Dalintober signifies the valley of wells, of which there are upwards of a score in the district. The Distillery buildings cover nearly two acres of ground, and have a frontage to Kinloch Park of five hundred feet, hence they command the finest view of any of the Distilleries, which includes the town, mountains and bay. The works were erected in the year 1832, and are within a quarter of a mile of the Steam Boat Pier and Harbour. The establishment consists of a double range of stone building enclosed at each end, built with stone, of neat elevation and conveniently arranged for the various processes of Malting and Distilling. We entered beneath a stone archway and found ourselves in an oblong court, with the various buildings disposed all round. On the right hand are the offices, stores and warehouses, on the left the Maltings and Grain Loft, and also the Distilling and Brewing Houses. The Manager, Mr. Archibald Pursell, a well-known Distiller, not only directed us through the establishment, but spent several hours with us, in explaining the whole process of the manufacture of Campbeltown Whisky, which we here detail for the benefit of our readers. The Barley is carted direct from the Wharf in the Distillers' own carts, and hoisted at once to the three Granary floors, which hold together 3,500 quarters of grain. When required the Barley is dropped through a sluice into the Steeps below, which are partly filled with water, where it soaks 48 to 50 hours, after which the water is drained off by means of false bottoms. The moistened Barley is next laid out by manual labour, on to the Malt floors, four in number, which are all concreted, capable of working 2,400 bushels per week. It is then spread out over the floors, and turned at frequent intervals according to the state of the atmosphere, until it is properly germinated, that is, until the "acrospire" is about two-thirds through the grain. It is now called Malt and is next removed to the drying kilns, where it is spread out on the floor some fifteen feet above the peat fires, to be thoroughly dried, after which the Malt is removed to the Stores which adjoin the Kiln, from whence when required it is dropped through a hopper into the Mill below. From the Mill-floor the crushed Malt is raised by elevators to the Grist-loft, which is situated over the Mash-house, and from whence it falls through a sluice direct into the Mash-Tun. This vessel is fourteen feet in diameter and five feet deep, inside it possesses double action revolving stirring gear driven by steam. As the crushed Malt falls into this vessel, water of a sufficiently high temperature is added, followed by two similar processes at increasing temperature. After this, the liquor, which is now called worts, is drained off from the Tun, into a dish called the Underback, nine feet in diameter and five deep, placed on the floor. From this receptacle the worts are pumped to the coolers above, where they are naturally cooled, until they become of a suitable temperature, and afterwards run by gravitation direct into the Wash-backs or Fermenting Tuns. There are six of these large vessels, each of which holds nearly 8,000 gallons, placed against the walls of a lofty and well-lighted Hall. As soon as the liquor has run from the coolers into these six Tuns, yeast is added and fermentation commences immediately, and continues for about 36 hours more or less After this process the liquor is called Wash, and is pumped into the Wash Charger, a large timber vessel placed on a gallery in the Still House, which building we next entered. It is a spacious apartment and contains three Pot Stills heated by furnaces. The Wash runs by gravitation into the Wash Still, a copper vessel holding 3,293 gallons. From this Still the product goes into the worm or condenser; there are two sets of worms, each placed in a large timber tank placed at a lofty elevation in the open, continuously renewed with cold water. These worms are circular tubes of about eleven inches in diameter, decreasing to five inches at the end. From the worm, the spirit passes through a safe, an instrument for testing, into the Low Wines Receiver, a timber vessel 10¼ feet in diameter and 3½ feet deep, from which receptacle it is pumped up to the Low Wines and Feints Charger, a vessel placed at an elevation and which holds 2,462 gallons. This Charger is so placed that it commands the other two Stills, to which the impure spirit next runs to undergo redistillation. They are called Low Wines and Feints Stills and hold 1,073 and 1,066 gallons respectively. From these Stills the product again goes through condensing worms, emerging therefrom as a pure spirit and running direct into the Spirit Receiver, from whence it is afterwards pumped into a vat which holds 2,426 gallons placed in the Spirit Store. The spirit is next filled into casks, weighed and marked by the Excise Officers, and placed either in the bonded warehouses at the Distillery, or sent direct to the orders of customers. There are five Warehouses at Dalintober, which contained sixteen hundred casks. At the time of our visit an addition was being made to the No. 4 Warehouse, and we were informed that when completed it will be one of the largest in Campbeltown. Following our guide we next visited the Engine Department, which contains an excellent eighteen-horse power engine and a steam boiler, twenty feet long by six in diameter. Adjoining there is a capital cooperage and cask sheds, also clerks' and Excise offices. The water used in the Distillery comes from the hills in front, and a deep well on the premises; the latter is of fine quality and highly suitable for mashing purposes.

The Whisky is Campbeltown Malts, and the annual output in 1884-5 was 120,000 gallons.

No. 17.

Benmore Distillery, Campbeltown.

PROPRIETORS, BULLOCH, LADE & CO.

A WALK of a quarter of an hour, past the quay and across the Kinloch Park, brought us to Benmore Distillery. We could never quite understand why this piece of land reclaimed from the sea, and without a shrub or flower thereon should be called a Park; at present it is a nursery ground for children, and sacred to the repairs of fishing nets and domestic washing. What might have been made a smiling paradise of flowers and greenery down to the very borders of the sea, is left a wilderness by a parsimonious local board. It may be that the Campbeltown magnates are satisfied with making fine Whisky, and let things remain as they are rather than as they might be. A thousand times during our stay in the Whisky Metropolis did we wish for the shade of trees, or some quiet sheltered seat whereon to rest and gaze at the beautiful sea, and distant hills which guard the entrance to the bay, and are the redeeming features of the scene. We grew quite fond of these hills; it may be because there was so little else to admire. We saw them from various points of view, from land and sea, under different influences of cloud and sunshine, and to us they often had very striking charms. Westward from Benmore Distillery stood Dalruadhain, the ancient capital of Scotland, where kings and nobles were wont to assemble, and whose streets and courtyards were thronged with gallant courtiers and armed hosts. What a change! In the place of strongholds and castles, huge Distilleries have sprung into existence, and in the place of tumult and warlike gatherings we find a peaceful industry and a contented people.

The Benmore establishment is situated in Saddell Street, about a quarter of a mile from the quay, and municipal buildings, and facing the Loch and Kinloch Park. It was the first of the three new Distilleries in Campbeltown, and its outside appearance resembles a public building rather than a manufactory of "Barley Bree." The edifice, which includes a Manager's house on the right hand side of the gateway, consists of one square block of buildings erected round a handsome paved court-yard; the whole covering upward of two acres of ground, entirely enclosed. As we pass through the entrance gates a handsome chimney stack comes into view, recently built to replace one blown down some time since in a gale of wind; it is a fine chimney, quite an ornament to the place, and rears its head far above its fellows.

The Manager, Mr. Ferguson, first conducted us to the three large Granaries, which at the time contained upward of 4,000 quarters of barley. From thence we descended to the Malt Barn, said to be the largest in Campbeltown, measuring 156 feet long by 48 feet broad, having a concrete floor and being well lighted. The Steep is made of cast-iron, and when sufficiently soaked with water, the barley is dropped through valves in the bottom, to the withering floor below. From here we passed on to the Kiln, a lofty building 48 feet square, and floored with wirecloth. We noticed a new furnace arrangement connected with this Kiln recently constructed, in which brick had been substituted for sheet iron, which not only saves fuel but creates a greater draught. The Malt Store is 42 feet by 30 feet, and adjoins the Kiln. From here the dried malt is sent through hoppers and elevators to the Mill where it is passed through a fine pair of steel rollers driven by steam. The grist falls into a hopper, from whence it is conveyed by elevators to the grist-loft over the Mash Tun.

We next followed our guide across a short passage and found ourselves in the Mash House, an oblong building wherein is a circular Mash Tun, capable of mashing 400 bushels at each mash, and fitted up with the usual revolving gear, which is driven by steam. Above this vessel we were shown one of Steel's Mashing Machines, through which the grist is passed, together with scalding water, before it reaches the Mash Tun. Leaving the Tun, the worts descend into the Underback, a vessel made of cast-iron and holding 1,600 gallons. From thence they are pumped into the Coolers, and through a large patent Refrigerator into the Wash Backs. Our guide next conducted us to the Tun Room, a cheerful and beautifully clean apartment, wherein are placed six Wash Backs, each holding 5,400 gallons. The liquor—now called wash—runs from the Backs by gravitation to the Wash Charger, which vessel commands the Stills. By a short cut across a platform we descended a step-ladder, and followed our guide to the Still House, said to be quite a model of its kind, both as regards the arrangement of the vessels and the construction of the building. It contains two Pot Stills beautifully polished, each possessing a patent air valve, and heated by furnaces. They are of the following capacities, 1,200 and 2,500 gallons respectively. From the Stills the vapour passes through the worm-tub a large wooden vessel which stands in the open, and is continually renewed with cold water. The Spirit then passes through the Safe which is placed in the Running-Room, to which place we next directed our steps. It contains one Spirit Receiver, two Lowwines and Feints Receivers and Chargers, and Sample Safe. The spirit flows from the Spirit Receiver through a copper pipe into the Vat, which holds about 2,000 gallons, in the Spirit Store, where it is casked, weighed, and branded, and sent across the yard to the duty-free Warehouses, of which there are four, substantially built of stone and brick, and which contained at the time about 3,000 casks. All the work in this Distillery is on the principle of gravitation, and there is only one pump upon the premises. There is a capital Cooperage, Cart-sheds, and Out-buildings.

To guard against fire, every floor is provided with extincteurs and hand grenades, besides a complete arrangement of fire-plugs and sets of hose and reels. The draff is pumped up into a drainer, and by a very simple contrivance is afterwards tumbled into the farmers' carts below.

The water used in the distilling process is from springs inside the work, and the proprietors consider it superior to the loch water ; anyway the sample we saw was clear, bright, and sparkling.

The Whisky produced is pure Malt, and the annual out-put is 125,000 gallons.

No. 18.

Ardlussa Distillery, Campbeltown.

PROPRIETORS, THE ARDLUSSA DISTILLERY COMPANY.

THE morning of our visit to Ardlussa broke ominously, and the rain poured down in torrents. Fortunately, the establishment is only ten minutes from the Hotel; so we donned our waterproofs and umbrellas, and thus equipped, marched forth defying the elements. We were much impressed with Ardlussa; it is one of the newest works in the town, and was built in 1879.

We first inspected the Maltings, which consist of a spacious building 180 feet long by 48 feet wide and nearly 40 feet high, divided into three flats; the top is the granary floor, and contains in its centre two Steeps, from which, by means of valves, the wetted barley can be dropped on to the floor below. Underneath are two Malt-barns with concreted floors, from which the malt, when properly grown, is raised by elevators to the Kiln, which is floored with perforated tiles. The Malt-deposit adjoins the Kiln, and underneath is the Mill, containing a pair of malt crushers and the usual machinery. We next followed our guide into the adjoining building, which is the Mash House. It is a lofty and light apartment, kept beautifully clean, and contains a metal Mash-tun, 15 feet in diameter and 6 feet deep, possessing the usual stirring rakes. The ground malt falls from a hopper above in the Grist-loft, from thence direct through a Mashing Machine into the Tun, so that no sacks are required. Most of the work in the Distillery is accomplished by gravitation, thus saving manual labour. The worts are pumped from the Tun to a number two Mash-tun in the roof, which vessel discharges the draff by gravitation. Our guide next drew attention to a Morton's Refrigerator and a set of Coolers placed in the open, which latter cool 3,000 gallons in half an hour. In close proximity to the Brewing House there is a large Hall with open roof, and well lighted, called the Tun Room, where are placed six Wash-backs, each holding 8,200 gallons, and a Wash Charger of similar capacity. We then crossed over to the Still House, another fine building, which contains a Wash Still holding 18,000 gallons and a Spirit Still 3,560, one heated by steam, the other by fire. On a gallery are placed the usual Chargers, Receivers, and Safe, and in close proximity is a large Worm Tub. Retracing our steps, we reached the Spirit Store, 42 feet by 27, containing a Vat which holds 2,776 gallons, and afterwards visited the two large Bonded Warehouses. One of them is 195 feet long and 63 wide, the other 160 feet long and 48 wide; both possess handsome arched roofs, requiring neither pillars nor central supports, and at the time of our visit held 18,000 casks.

On the premises there is a small Cooperage, peat sheds, stables, and clerks' offices. The Engine House contains a 15-horse power engine and a steam boiler 22 feet long by $7\frac{1}{2}$ feet in diameter.

The make is called Campbeltown Malt, and the output for 1885 was 118,000 gallons. Mr. Hilly is the chief Excise Officer. The Public Offices of the Company are in Glasgow.

No. 19.

Dalaruan Distillery, Campbeltown.

PROPRIETORS, DAVID COLVILL & CO.

MANAGING PARTNER, CHARLES COLVILL GREENLEES.

CONTINUING our Distillery visitations we wended our way to Lochend, the classic part of the town, where is situated the Dalaruan Distillery, which takes its name from Dalruhadhain, the old royal name of the place, and was founded in 1824 by Charles Colvill, grandfather of the present managing partner, Charles Colvill Greenlees. Some few years ago Messrs. David Colvill & Co. considerably enlarged the establishment, and made important additions to the plant and appliances, so that the work now covers nearly three acres of ground.

On entering the courtyard we ascended a staircase, which brought us to the Distillery offices, where after a short interview with the principal partner we made a tour of the buildings under the guidance of the Manager. We first inspected the three Barley Lofts and four Malt-barns, which are built of stone and well lighted. The former are capable of holding 5,000 quarters of grain ; the latter are of the following measurements, Nos. 1 and 2 are 100 feet by 31, No. 3 is 90 feet by 32, and No. 4 is 90 feet by 36. Three of the Steeps in these buildings will wet eight tons and the other six at one time. Connected with the Maltings are two capital Kilns, each about 33 feet square, and floored with Bridgwater tiles ; Peat only is used in drying the Malt.

We then passed on to the Mill which contains the usual machinery, then the grist-loft, and the usual Hopper for feeding the Tun,—from thence to the Mash House, a roomy building, which contains the heating coppers and a large Mash Tun capable of mashing 2,000 bushels at one time ; also the Underback placed below the Tun.

The coolers, which are of iron and of large size, are placed in the open, so that they cool the Worts rapidly. We next entered the Tun Room and inspected the seven Washbacks, passing from there to the Still-House, which contains three Pot Stills, holding 2,750, 1,886, and 850 gallons respectively. The Wash Charger is placed on an elevation, but the three Receivers are sunk into the floor.

Adjoining this House there is a Spirit Store, which contains a Vat holding 1050 gallons, and in close proximity a 7-horse power steam engine and boiler, the latter 20 feet long and 7 feet in diameter.

Our guide then directed us to the five Bonded Warehouses, which are distributed about the premises, the largest of them measures 130 feet long by 60 broad, and the whole contain nearly 3,000 casks. Inside the enclosure there are two wells, 9 feet from the surface, containing natural springs of the greatest purity, and used principally for reducing purposes. Most of the work in the Distillery is done by gravitation ; and there are sixteen men employed. The Whisky is Campbeltown Malt and is sold chiefly in London, the west coast of Scotland, and the Colonies.

Annual output 112,000 gallons.

No. 20.

Lochead Distillery, Campbeltown.

PROPRIETORS, W. TAYLOR & COMPANY.

CAMPBELTOWN is a pleasant place in summer for those who rejoice in a boundless sea, plenty of boating, fishing and golfing. Before visiting Lochead we drove out to the Salt Pans five miles distant, a favourite resort of the Campbeltonians who visit it in crowds during the summer months, and which possesses a golfing ground, said to be the best and most extensive in Scotland. At the time of our visit a party of Oxford students were playing a match with the Club, among whom we descried many of our friends the Distillers who are noted champions at the game. We returned home very unwillingly, being loth to leave the animating scene, passing on our way many familiar faces bound for the spot we had left behind. On reaching the Hotel we found our luncheon waiting, and all three of us fell to with a hearty good will. We weie comfortably entertained at the White Hart during our stay, and both the landlord and his good wife did everything in their power to render our visit both comfortable and agreeable. Their horses and traps were the best we had used during our tour, and would be a credit to any city hiring establishment. After our meal, we walked to Lochead, another of the few old-fashioned Distilleries, remnants of the romantic smuggling days. It is built on the banks of the Lochead Burn and close to the Kinloch Park, and was there erected in 1824. As you enter the enclosure you observe an air of antiquity round and about you. There is a small swift stream running through the works into the sea, and a large burn outside. What was once a cluster of old houses and an ancient mill, with doubtless several illicit stills, is now a licensed Distillery; and time has indeed dealt leniently with its old stone walls and fences. The establishment has now absorbed the whole four corners of a block covering two and a half acres of ground.

The four old-fashioned Barley Lofts, or as they used to call them Granaries, are situated at the south-east end of the work. There are four Malt Floors with three Steeps; two Kilns, with the patent German tile flooring, where peat only is used in the drying, good Malt Stores and Mill Room, and the Mash Tun is said to be the largest in Campbeltown. There is also a ten horse power steam engine, a very large Boiler, steam pump, eight Washbacks each holding 8,000 gallons, a Wash Charger and two Pot Stills heated by steam holding 3,300 and 1,800 gallons respectively; two Receivers each containing 1,600 gallons, and three Heaters. The Coolers are in the open, and stretch right across the burn; there is also a Morton's refrigerator. Adjoining the Granaries there is a capital Spirit Store with a Vat of 2,000 gallons capacity. There are also five Warehouses capable of stowing some 3,000 casks.

The Whisky made here is Campbeltown Malt, and finds a market chiefly in Glasgow. The annual output is 111,000 gallons.

The Chief Excise Officer is Mr. Hammett.

No. 21.

Glen Nevis Distillery, Campbeltown.

PROPRIETORS, D. MACCALLUM & CO.

NEARLY every morning it was our delight to stroll down to the quay, and watch the early boats leave the landing stage. Steam navigation is of incalculable benefit to Campbeltown, there being no railway within 80 miles; also to the Highlander, as by it he can send his fat cattle and produce to Glasgow and other markets. Although Argyleshire is of such an immense extent, it happens that there is not a single dwelling place more than 10 miles from the sea, and scarcely a loch, bay or inlet but holds daily or weekly communication with Glasgow. A wonderful change has been made by the steamboat traffic in the Highlands during the last thirty years not only has it raised the value of land 40 per cent. and encouraged the farmers to fatten their stock, which they would never otherwise think of doing, but it has enabled them to improve their arable land, and with the extra profits to buy luxuries to which they were hitherto strangers, and thus communicated to them sentiments of taste and refinement; and we were surprised to see evidence of this in several farm houses we visited. What a transition has this same steam communication effected! The farmer of Laggan or the Highlander who spends his life on the Kintyre Hills, can descend in the morning from his lovely home, and setting his foot on board a steamboat at some neighbouring pier or jetty, suddenly finds himself in company with tourists from all parts of the world, and he who slept last night in the blue mists of the mountains, the next, is traversing the gas lighted streets of Glasgow or Edinburgh. The town clock striking ten recalls us from these musings to duty and our appointment at Glen Nevis whither we now bend our steps.

This Distillery is quite a new work, and was built in the year 1877. It is situated under the brow of the Gallow Hill, facing the main road, and commands fine views of the bay and hill-sides. The buildings, rectangular in shape, enclose a spacious yard, covering two acres, and have a frontage of 440 feet. The Distillery has a commanding appearance, and is both modern in style and arrangement, containing all the new improvements of the present day. The Warehouses, Barley Stores, and Kilns run parallel with the road. The latter are constructed on the close furnace principle, with a wire netting floor, so that the peat smoke can permeate the barley and give it the aroma so characteristic of the Campbeltown Whisky; the Kilns are capable of working ninety quarters of barley in each, every four days. Adjoining the Kilns are the Malting Stores and Mill for grinding the malt prior to mashing. In the Distillery proper there is a large Mash-tun with the improved patent revolving machinery; a capital Engine of eight horse-power, and a Steam Boiler 22 feet long by 7 feet in diameter; and a centrifugal pump for driving the grains

and sparge water to a cistern in the exterior of the building, thus enabling the firm to mash more frequently. There is also an Underback, a Worts Receiver, and a Morton's Refrigerator of large capacity and cooling power; six Washbacks, each holding 6,000 gallons, for fermenting the worts; a Jackback, Wash Charger, Low Wines and Feints Receivers, and a Spirit Receiver to which is attached an indicator whereby the Revenue is secured, and the inspector prevented from having the charging and discharge cocks of this vessel open at the same time. The Low Wines and Feints Chargers act as feeders to the Stills. The Wash Still, a fine copper vessel, beautifully bright, clean and highly polished, has a capacity of 3,200 gallons; and the Low Wines Still 2,200 gallons. To them are of course attached the usual Worms for condensing. Adjoining the Distillery there is a large Spirit Store containing a Vat of 1,920 gallons capacity: here the casks are filled before being placed in the Warehouses, of which there are two, one a two-decker building, capable of storing 4,000 casks, the other capable of holding 1,000 casks.

There is an excellent Cooperage for repairs and stowage of empties; also a commodious Manager's House within the yard, which makes the establishment complete in every respect. The water used in this Distillery is brought from Crosshill Loch, a mile distant, out of the heart of Ben Ghoillan, the highest mountain in the district.

There are twelve persons employed on the premises; the Whisky made is Campbeltown Malt, and is sold principally in London, Glasgow, and the Colonies. The annual output is 100,000 gallons. The Whisky is shipped from the quay, a quarter of a mile distant.

The Chief Excise Officer is Mr. O'Connor.

No. 22.

Kinloch Distillery, Campbeltown.

PROPRIETORS, LAMB, COLVILL & CO.

AFTER living at Campbeltown a week we began to feel quite at home, our daily perambulations in the "spiritual town" had brought us in contact with many of the distillers, who by their courtesy, kindness and hospitality, contributed to our comfort and pleasure, and rendered our prolonged stay most agreeable. On our way from the "White Hart" to Kinloch Park we passed the venerable cross of Campbeltown, the chief object of interest in the place. It is situated in the middle of Main Street and consists of a very handsome pillar of hard blue granite, richly ornamented with sculptured foliage. Tradition says that it is a relic from the wreck of the 360 crosses which the Synod of Argyll, in 1560, commanded should be cast into the sea, and that it was transported from Iona by stealth. It stands nearly eleven feet high, on an octagon pedestal of six steps, and bears a Latin inscription, above which there is a chalice and an open book. On the right of the cross stand the Town Buildings, the steeple of which is ninety feet high; over the portico entrance are the town arms and underneath the significant motto, "*Ignavis precibus fortuna repugnat*," fortune spurns slothful prayers. Leaving the Town Hall we proceeded to our destination by way of the New Quay, where we witnessed large cargoes of barley being transferred from the steamers to the distillers' carts. As we crossed the park the surface was so thickly covered with fishing nets, laid out to dry, that we had to pick our way by a longer round to reach the establishment.

The Kinloch Distillery was commenced in the year 1823 by Mr. Dunlop's father, who assumed other partners, and started work under the co-partnery of Lamb, Colvill & Co., by whom the business has been carried on up to the present time; the firm now being the oldest established in the district. For a long time previous to that period the premises had been used as Malt Houses, for the purpose of supplying malt to the numerous smugglers who carried on their business in the country round about, and from whose products arose the far-famed Campbeltown Whisky now so well known in the market. It is a fine old work covering two acres of ground, with a frontage to Kinloch Park of over 400 feet and a depth to Longrow of 240 feet. It is quite close to the loch and harbour, and the continual movement on the water of fishing boats and steamers, together with the bustle and traffic on the wharf, gives this Distillery more life and animation than any of the others. The premises have been greatly enlarged during the past few years, and new utensils and modern machinery added. On entering the establishment the managing partner, Mr. James Dunlop, received us and courteously conducted us over the premises. We first visited the three Barley Stores, which contain metal Steeps, and the three Malting Floors, all of which are concreted, and afterwards ascended a stair to the floor of the Malt Kilns, three in number, two of which are floored with tiles and the other with wire cloth, all of them are heated with peat in enclosed furnaces. We next proceeded to inspect the Mill House and Stores, the latter is over the Mash Tun, and contains the usual feeding hopper for that vessel. Descending a flight of steps we came to the Mash House, a conveniently arranged building which contains a Mash Tun, 14 feet in diameter and 5 feet deep, with the patent revolving stirring gear therein, also two large heating coppers and the Underback. Crossing this apartment we entered the Tun Room, wherein are placed eight Washbacks, each holding 7,400 gallons, the switchers being driven by steam. On an elevation there is the Wash Charger, which holds 5,224 gallons, and a Low-wines and Feints Charger of 3,458 content. Retracing our steps to the courtyard we came to the Still House, a neat and very spacious building, where we were shown three Pot Stills, two heated by furnaces, the other by steam, holding respectively 2,900, 1,800, and 1,700 gallons. There are also three Receivers on an elevation, holding respectively 1,860, 1,781, and 1,425 gallons. We then visited the Spirit Store, which contains a Vat holding 2,292 gallons, passing on our way the Coolers and a Morton's Refrigerator. Mr. Dunlop next directed our steps to the Warehouses, four in number, which occupy one side of the block, and are of the following dimensions:—No. 1 is 100 feet long and 32 wide; No. 2 is 80 feet long and 100 feet wide; No. 3 is 70 feet long and 200 feet wide, and the whole contained at the time of our visit 2,461 casks, but they are capable of containing more than 3,000 casks. Near the Mash House there is a fine 12-horse power engine and a steam boiler, 20 feet long by 6 feet in diameter, and two large Worm-tubs. The water comes from the Crosshill Loch, and there is also excellent water obtainable from a deep well on the premises. Fourteen persons are employed in the Distillery, and the Chief Excise Officer is Mr. Thos. Pike. There are excellent offices for clerks, managers and excise, and we may here remark that important additions and improvements are being made to the works, the firm having recently acquired the adjoining land.

The make is Campbeltown Malt, and the annual output is 97,000 gallons; sold principally in Ayrshire, Glasgow and London.

But let the kirk-folk ring their bells,
Let's sing about our noble sel's;
We'll cry nae jads frae heathen hills
    To help, or roose us,
But browster wives and whisky stills,
    They are the muses.

Your friendship, sir, I winna quat it
And if ye mak' objections at it,
Then han' in nieve some day we'll knot it,
    And witness take,
And when wi' usquebae we've wat it,
    It winna break.

BURNS'S POEMS.

No. 23.

Burnside Distillery, Campbeltown.

PROPRIETORS, MCMURCHY, RALSTON & CO.

MANAGING PARTNER, JAMES W. GREENLEES.

WE joined a coaching party the next morning and drove to Glenlussa, five miles north of Campbeltown, through which, on its way to Kilbrannon Sound, runs the Ardlussa river. This glen has been famous from time immemorial for the strength, beauty, and intelligence of its inhabitants. The appearance and manly bearing of a company of volunteers raised in Glenlussa attracts the admiration of all beholders at Campbeltown, when they visit that town for their weekly drill, and we could not help regretting that this handsome body of men did not form a portion of Her Majesty's regular army. On our way we passed through well cultivated lands, where very fine barley is grown, and could perceive in the distant valleys other well tilled farms and smiling homesteads of equal promise. On its way back to the hotel the coach dropped us near Burnside. It is the only Distillery in Campbeltown that is actually in the country, being planted on the grassy slopes of Bengullien, and about half a mile from the centre of the town. Before commencing our duties we climbed a small portion of the mountain, from whence we obtained the finest view of the district we had yet seen.

The Distillery, which covers nearly two acres of ground, is built in the form of an oblong quadrangle, with several outlying buildings. It was built in the year 1825 by the grandfather of one of the present partners, and is solidly built and conveniently arranged. One of the Malt Barns is a very spacious building, and was used as a banqueting-hall and ball-room when the present Duke of Argyll came of age. Besides this there are three other Malt Barns and two large Granaries. Adjoining the Malt Barns are three Kilns, all floored with perforated tiles and heated with peat and blind coal. In close proximity there is a Mill and Stores and the Mash-house, which contains a Mash-tun, 14 feet in diameter and 5 feet deep, together with an Underback and a Morton's Refrigerator. The Tun-room is a neat and clean apartment, and contains six fermenting Tuns, each containing 5,500 gallons, also a Wash Charger 6,500 gallons. In the Still-house there are two Pot Stills, holding 3,000 and 1,250 gallons respectively, three Receivers, the usual Chargers and a Steam Pump. Near by there is a 15-horse power Steam Engine, and a Boiler 20 feet long by 7 in diameter. Ranged round the quadrangle are nine Warehouses with zinc roofs, all well lighted and ventilated, which contained 3,000 casks at the time of our visit. Seventeen men are employed in the establishment. The make is Campbeltown Malt, and the annual output is 96,000 gallons. The Whisky is sold principally in London and Glasgow.

No. 24.

Glengyle Distillery, Campbeltown.

PROPRIETORS, WM. MITCHELL & CO.

MANAGING PARTNER, WM. MITCHELL.

AFTER breakfast the next morning we left the inn and got on the Distillery track again, this time bound for Glengyle. As we were proceeding leisurely up Longrow the occupant of a passing carriage hailed us, and on nearer acquaintance proved to be our old friend, Mr. John Ross. At his courteous invitation we joined him in a visit to the Provost and other Distillers, who like him were interested in the compilation of the book on which we were engaged, and assisted us materially in the object of our visit. After making an appointment to visit both his Distilleries in a few days, we left Mr. Ross to pursue his drive homewards, and continued our journey to Glengyle. On our arrival we found much to our chagrin that Mr. Mitchell was away from home, hence our visit was brief and our information concerning this Distillery necessarily somewhat scant. However the Brewer kindly proffered his services which we gladly accepted, and at once commenced our inspection of the place.

This Distillery is situate in Glebe Street, about one mile from the wharf, in the suburbs of Campbeltown. In front of the works there is a fine view of cultured gardens, cultivated fields, and hill slopes whose tops are covered with heather. The works were built in the year 1873 by the present proprietors. It is a neat and compact place, covering upwards of two acres of ground, and all the buildings are spacious and clean. There is a fine Barley Loft, two Malt Barns with Steeps; a Kiln, with wire cloth flooring, in which peat only is used for drying; a good Mill-house and Stores, a Mash Tun, 12 feet by 5, with patent revolving machinery, a 10-horse power Steam Engine, a Boiler 30 feet long and 9 feet in diameter; two Pot Stills, one containing 3,100 gallons, and the other 1,860 gallons; three Receivers holding respectively 2,500, 1,200, and 1,128 gallons, and three Warehouses holding 2,000 casks.

There is a Morton's Refrigerator and a Force Pump. The Wash Charger holds 4,700 gallons, and there are six Wash Backs, each containing 6,600 gallons. A Spirit Store capable of holding 30 pun., and Vat containing 2,120 gallons; and the water used comes from the Crosshill Loch. Fourteen men are employed on the premises. The annual output is 90,000 gallons.

The Chief Excise Officer is Mr. James Douglas.

Gi'e him strong drink until he wink
  That's sinking in despair;
And liquor guid to fire his bluid,
  That's prest wi' grief and care;
There let him bouse, and deep carouse
  Wi' bumpers flowing o'er,
Till he forgets his loves or debts,
  And minds his griefs no more.

LOCHRUAN DISTILLERY

No. 25.

Lochruan Distillery, Campbeltown.

PROPRIETORS, THE LOCHRUAN DISTILLERY COMPANY.

MANAGING PARTNER, JOHN MCKERSIE.

THIS Distillery derives its name from a loch embedded amidst the hills two miles north-east from the town. The term "Lochruan" means the red loch, "rua" being the Gaelic word for red, and to anyone who has visited the locality when the beautiful autumnal tints of the heather are mirrored on the placid water, the appropriateness of the name is at once apparent. We found it a weird, romantic place, and not easily accessible. Upon one side there is a great black hill, which seems to frown upon you, even in the sunshine. Upon the other there towers a hill more variegated in aspect, while the extremities are bounded by somewhat lower but rugged ground. The loch, emanating chiefly from springs, is very deep. Old legends say it is bottomless, and that at eventide it is haunted by beautiful spirits, who by their incantations on the waters freed for a year from all bodily ailments the first mortal who thereafter chanced to partake of the consecrated stream. This distilled dew of the mountains, clear as crystal and refreshing as the nectar of the gods, freely circulates over the northern portion of the town, conferring a boon and a blessing wherever it flows.

The Lochruan Distillery is situated at the base of the hills leading up to the loch. It was built in the year 1835, and about twenty years ago came into the hands of the present proprietors, by whom it was extended and improved. It is about three hundred yards from Campbeltown Quay, and close to Kinloch Park. It commands a side view of the bay, and covers nearly two acres of ground. The works consist of two large Granaries, four Malt-barns, each 86 feet by 27 feet; two good-sized Kilns, each 36 feet by 27 feet, with tiled floors, where peat only is used in the drying, mill house and stores; a Mash-tun, 16 feet in diameter by $4\frac{1}{2}$ feet deep, with patent revolving machinery, a 16-horse power steam engine, and a boiler 20 feet by $6\frac{1}{2}$ feet in diameter. In the Tun-room, which is 58 feet long, 30 wide, and 34 high, and lighted by ten windows, there are seven Washbacks, each containing 6,708 gallons; two Wash Chargers, two heaters, and a large Morton's Refrigerator. The Still and Mash House is a lofty building, measuring 70 feet by 28 feet, with paved floor and whitewashed walls, and contains three old Pot Stills, holding 3,245, 1,835, and 1,785 gallons respectively, three Receivers, a patent safe, and a steam pump. Above the roof of the adjoining building there is a cooler, and next door a Spirit Store with a vat which holds 1,900 gallons. Distributed about the premises are five large Warehouses, containing at the time of our visit over 2,000 casks. The Whisky is Campbeltown Malt, and the annual output is 85,000 gallons.

The Lochruan Whisky owes its reputation to the peculiar excellence of the water, and the care exercised in the manufacture. The Whisky is sold principally in London, Glasgow, and the Colonies. There are twelve persons employed in the works. The chief officer of Excise is Mr. L. M. MacDonald.

No. 26.

Albyn Distillery, Campbeltown.

MESSRS. WILLIAM M'KERSIE & CO.

THIS Distillery is situated in Millknowe, in the suburbs of Campbeltown. From the gateway there is a delightful view of Bengoillean and the woods of Lime Craigs, the property of the Duke of Argyle. It was built in the year 1830 by the father of the present proprietors, on lines similar to the other works built about that time. There is a good look out from the front, and the eye takes in a wide range of hill and loch scenery. It stands about one mile from the wharf, and covers one and a half acres of ground.

The works consist of two Granaries, four Malt Barns with the usual steeps, and two capital Kilns with perforated tile flooring. Peat only, which is supplied in large quantities from the Hebrides, is used in the drying. There is a good Mill House and Stores; also a 14-foot diameter Mash Tun with revolving machinery; a fourteen horse-power steam engine; a large boiler, 24 feet long and 8 feet in diameter; six Wash Backs, each capable of holding 5,000 gallons; Low Wines and Wash Charger; three Pot Stills, one having a capacity of 2,500 gallons, another 1,650, and the third 580 gallons; Receivers, two Heaters, two old-fashioned Coolers, Spirit Store, Vat, and five large Warehouses, capable of storing 2,000 casks; Cooperage, &c.

The Water used comes from the Crosshills Loch. The Distillery is worked chiefly by manual labour, and there are eleven persons employed. The chief Excise officer is Mr. J. McDougall.

The Whisky is Highland Malt, and is sold chiefly in Glasgow, Ayrshire, and London.

The annual output is 85,000 gallons.

No. 27.

Scotia Distillery, Campbeltown.

PROPRIETORS, STEWART, GALBRAITH & CO.

EARLY next day we were again astir and started for the Scotia Distillery. The morning gave promise of a very hot day, which fortunately for us was fulfilled. We walked by way of the sea-shore and Kinloch Park, on our way encountering many hardy fish women, with sunburnt faces, selling fresh herrings which glistened like silver in the sunshine. Campbeltown is a great fishing station, and numbers are employed in this occupation and the manufacture of nets. After leaving Kinloch Park we reached the romantic and historical neighbourhood of Parliament Square; here in the year 503, Fergus, the first king of Scotland, built his Parliament House, where the affairs of Scotland were administered till 843. Tradition says that the Stone of Destiny, upon which the sovereigns of Scotland were crowned, originally came from this spot and was subsequently removed from Scone by Edward I. to Westminster Abbey.

The Distillery is situated at the end of a subway in High Street, and seems to have hidden itself away out of sight, as if the art of making Whisky, at that time, was bound to be kept a dark secret. It was built by the present firm in the year 1832, covers a little over two acres of ground, and has been several times enlarged to meet the requirements of an increasing business. At first sight it presents a somewhat straggling and old-fashioned appearance; nevertheless, the additions have been made as convenient as possible by means of gangways and other approaches, and it is a Distillery that can be easily worked.

On one side of the yard are three Barley Lofts, one of them holding 1,500 quarters of barley; beneath are three Malt Barns, one of which is 300 feet long, and in which are the usual Steeps. These Malt Barns are connected with the Kilns by means of a quaint old-fashioned wooden bridge across the yard. There are three Kilns floored with perforated tiles, and heated with peat mixed with a little blind coal. Contiguous is the Mill House and the Grist Loft; and in the adjacent Mash House there is a Mash Tun, 12 feet in diameter and 5 feet deep. The Tun Room contains the six Washbacks each of a content of 4,306 gallons. In the Distilling House there are three Pot Stills containing 1,640, 850 and 520 gallons respectively; also three Receivers, and on an elevation the Wash Chargers which command the Stills. The Coolers which are in the open possess fans which are driven by steam. The Steam Engine is 8-horse power, and the Boiler is 20 feet long and 7 feet in diameter. Across the yard is the Spirit Store, and there are seven Warehouses containing 1,700 casks.

The water used in the Distillery comes from the Crosshill Loch, but in addition there are two wells bored down to the rock 80 feet deep, which yield a never failing supply of clear water.

The Whisky is Campbeltown Malt, and the annual output is 85,000 gallons.

No. 28.

Rieclachan Distillery, Campbeltown.

PROPRIETORS, WYLIE, MITCHELL & CO.

MANAGING PARTNER, MR. H. MITCHELL.

WE finished up the afternoon by a visit to the Rieclachan Distillery which is situated at the head of Longrow, the principal street in Campbeltown, a district sacred to the memory of smugglers and their doings.

From the remotest days of antiquity distilling was carried on in the neighbourhood of the Distillery, if not on the very same spot. In the year 1815 there was only one legal Distillery in Campbeltown, but nine years after several others were erected, all on the plan of the Old Pot Still or Smuggler's Kettle, Rieclachan being among the number.

The Distillery is a fine old place, and was built in the year 1825 by the grandfather of the present managing partner. It is distinctly one of the old "Sma Still" works; but from time to time additions have been made, as the demand for the Whisky increased, so that it is gradually losing its old romantic touch of age; nevertheless, until it is pulled down and rebuilt (which would be a pity) it will always retain its primitive appearance. It covers an acre of ground, and is half a mile from the pier-head.

The Establishment is approached by a short lane, and entered by an old-fashioned pair of gates, which were evidently made to shut in the secrets of the Distillery from the outside world, and as there is no other possible entrance, without scaling the buildings, the secret of making old malt whisky has been well kept.

The work consists of two very large Barley Stores, two Malt Barns 170 feet long and 42 feet wide, and two Steeps; a Kiln, with wire flooring, said to be the largest in the town; a Mill-house and Stores. The Mash Tun is 10 feet in diameter and a little over 4 feet deep. There are seven Washbacks each holding 5,000 gallons, two Pot Stills each 2,139 and 1,600 content gallons respectively; three Receivers, holding respectively 2,362, 1,150 and 680 gallons; a capital 14-horse power Engine, and a Boiler 22 feet long by 7 feet in diameter. The offices used by the manager and Excise gentlemen face the entrance gates and are conveniently arranged for communication with every department. On one side there is a capital Cooperage and Cask shed, and opposite, a neat dwelling for the maltman and gatekeeper. The water comes from Crosshill Loch. There are three Warehouses containing 1,100 casks. The Whisky is Campbeltown Malt, and the annual output is 70,000 gallons.

Ten persons are employed on the premises. Chief Excise Officer, Mr. R. Wallace.

No. 29.

Glenside Distillery, Campbeltown.

PROPRIETORS, GLENSIDE DISTILLERY COMPANY.

MANAGING PARTNER, MR. J. ORR.

JUST as we were starting to visit the establishment which heads this chapter, our worthy landlord offered to drive us to see Saddell Castle, a place intimately connected with Campbeltown in former times, and standing in a district which used to be a favorite haunt of the smugglers. We accepted his offer and in ten minutes were bowling through the town at a great pace. The road is somewhat uninteresting, and was sadly wanting in trees to shelter us from the sun's rays, nevertheless, we were delighted with the old castle. It is built on a rock north-east of Campbeltown. McDonald or "Righ Fiongal," who resided here, was a great despot, tradition says that he knew the use of gunpowder, and for sport, to keep himself in practice, would shoot people with his long gun. He was also a terrible Don Juan, and if he fancied a married woman, would take her away from her husband, whom he would either imprison or kill. McDonald was also a very strong man. One day three Irish gentlemen came to visit him, and after entertaining them he put them to sleep in one of his barns. Next morning he got up early to salute them, but found them asleep with their necks bare, the temptation was too strong for him, and wishing to test his strength of arm he drew his sword and cut off their heads. Such playful conduct would hardly be tolerated in these days. On returning we drove direct to the Glenside, a district sacred to the memory of Burns, for there, almost close to the Distillery, formerly resided his "Mary," of whom he wrote,

"For dear to me as light and life
Was my sweet Highland Mary."

Her father was a sailor in a revenue cutter stationed at Campbeltown, and principally resided in a little cottage facing the bay.

"I ha'e sworn by the heavens to be true,
And sae may the heavens forget me
When I forget my vow."

The Distillery was built in the year 1830, and is about a mile from the harbour. The water is brought into the works by a conduit direct from the Aucholochie Loch at the back of the Distillery, and there is a well of splendid water within the enclosure.

The establishment covers two acres of ground and consists of an irregular section of buildings, which are all enclosed and entered by an arched gateway. It is almost as old fashioned as its neighbours, both as regards its appearance and internal arrangements. During the last three years many improvements have been made, but nothing short of pulling the place down, and rebuilding it, could ever give it the appearance of a modern Distillery, and, as the manager remarked, any such alterations would not improve the Whisky or increase the sale.

After paying our respects to Mr. Orr one of the partners and inspecting his quaint little office over the gateway, we commenced our tour of the buildings at the Barley Lofts which are three in number and capable of holding 2,000 quarters of grain. Adjacent are four Malt Barns with the usual Steeps which are connected with three Kilns, each of which is floored with tiles and heated by peat. We next visited the Mill which contains a pair of Malt Cylinders and the Grist Loft. We then descended by a stair to the Mash House, a neat whitewashed building which contains a large heating copper and a circular Mash Tun possessing the patent revolving stirring gear, also a metal Underback.

GLENSIDE DISTILLERY.

On leaving this place we noticed a capital 12-horse power engine and a steam boiler, 24 feet long by 6 feet in diameter, also an old fashioned fan cooler over the roof of one of the houses, and a Morton's Refrigerator. We were now conducted to the Tun Room, a heavy looking apartment corresponding with the Still House, which contains four Washbacks each holding 8,000 gallons. Passing through a doorway we came to the Still House which contains a Wash Still 2,483 gallons and a Spirit Still 1,372 gallons capacity respectively, both are of the Old Pot kind; also three Receivers and Chargers and the Safe. Adjoining this building there is a Spirit Store, Cooperage, and Carpenter's Shop. We then bent our steps to the Warehouses, five in number, all of which are dry and well ventilated and contained 1,600 casks at the time of our visit.

Twelve persons are employed on the works and the Barley used comes principally from Stirlingshire. The make is Campbeltown Malt and the annual output is 70,000 gallons, principally sold in London, Liverpool and Glasgow.

No. 30.

Longrow Distillery, Campbeltown.

PROPRIETORS, JOHN ROSS & CO.

SUNDAY in Campbeltown is carried to its Jewish length, and is quite a day of gloom and penance. The churches and chapels, which are scattered all over the town, are crowded with well dressed and staid looking people, and everybody carries a pious look on that day. Neither music nor whistling is allowed in either the houses or streets, and the landlady of the hotel was quite shocked at our proposing to play some sacred music on the piano. We might have expected this, as it is said that there are nearly as many places of worship as distilleries in the town. After church we walked out to Kilkerran churchyard, one of the most picturesque burying places we have ever seen. It lies at the foot of Bengoillean; the name means, cell of St. Kiarin, who was the tutor of St. Columba. He lived in a cave on this road, and built a church. It is said that St. Patrick converted St Kiarin and gave him a copy of the Four Gospels, and later on transformed his name into Columbahill, which signifies "the dove of the church." This good man planted churches all over the Peninsula, and after converting the Scots, settled in Iona, where he founded a Mission College. Returning by Shore Street and Bolgam Street, we paid a visit to the Drill Hall, wherein some religious service was being held, and back to our hotel in time for tea. The next morning we resumed our labours, and commenced at the Longrow Distillery. The street from whence it takes its name is the most important in Campbeltown, and contains three Distilleries. The first we came to was the one which heads this chapter. It covers two acres of ground, and was built in the year 1824 by Mr. John Ross, who is said to be the oldest living Distiller in Scotland. He is 85 years of age, and is apparently a hale and hearty old gentleman. We found him most hospitable and courteous, and were highly amused at his wit and racy anecdotes. Close by the work stands the United Presbyterian Church, possessing a lofty tower, surmounted by a handsome and massive cupola, which was built mostly at the expense of Mr. Ross, and this spiritual watch tower seems benignly to look down on the great work being carried on below. The establishment is so built in by the houses and shops in Longrow that it would be difficult for a stranger to find it. To reach it we entered a covered archway under the houses, which opened up into a courtyard, round which the Distillery buildings are ranged. They are old fashioned and of various styles of architecture. We first inspected the two barley lofts and three malt barns. They are neat buildings, but the roofs are low pitched. At the end there are two Kilns floored with tiles, wherein the furnaces are heated with peat and blind coal. Passing through the Mill and grist loft, we came to the Mash House, an old-fashioned building containing a heating copper, Mash-tun, and Underback. From there we went to the Tun Room, where are placed six Wash Backs, a Morton's Refrigerator, and the Wash Charger. The Still House is one of the quaintest buildings we have seen, and contains two Pot Stills of the smuggler's pattern, heated by furnaces, three Receivers and Chargers, a small sampling safe, and a steam engine which grinds the mill. Retracing our steps, we reached the three Warehouses, one of which is 130 feet long; they hold about 600 casks. There is a Spirit Store which contains a vat, and the usual casking apparatus; also offices for the distilling and Excise clerks. The water used comes from the Crosshill Loch and a spring rising from a deep well on the premises.

The make is Campbeltown Malt, and the annual output is 40,000 gallons.

Since writing this account of Longrow, we regret to say that Mr. Ross has joined the great majority, and the business is now being carried on by William and James Greenlees.

No. 31.

Kintyre Distillery, Campbeltown.

PROPRIETORS, JOHN ROSS & CO.

HAVING the afternoon to spare we devoted it to visiting the Kintyre Distillery, which also is a part of the Longrow business. It is situated in Lochend, a district black with Distilleries, and was built a few years later than Longrow, hence it is on a more modern principle and less scattered. It covers, however, about the same acreage of ground, but the buildings are of higher elevation. This establishment is very compact and easily managed, and consists of two Barley Lofts, three Malt Barns with the usual Steeps, a Mill House and Stores; two Kilns both floored with the old fashioned perforated tiles and heated with peat and blind coal; a fine Mash Tun, with the patent revolving machinery; an 8-horse power steam engine, a boiler 20 feet by $6\frac{1}{2}$ in diameter; and six Washbacks.

The Still House is a capital building and contains three Pot Stills heated by furnaces, three Receivers, and a Sampling Safe. There is also a Cooperage, and five Warehouses, one holding 500 casks.

The water used for condensing purposes is from a well, and there is also a further supply from the Loch away up the hills, for mashing purposes.

The Whisky is Campbeltown Malt, and is of the same quality as Longrow. We tasted some eight years old and were highly pleased with it.

Annual output is 67,000 gallons. Mr. Brick is the chief Excise Officer.

"Sages their solemn e'en may steek, And raise a philosophic reek
And physically causes seek. In clime and season.
But tell me whisky's name in Greek. I'll tell the reason.
Scotland, my auld respected mither! though whiles ye moistify your leather
Till whare ye sit on 'craps o' heather, Ye tine your dam
Freedom and whisky gang thegither!—Tak off your dram!"

BURNS.

No. 32.

Campbeltown Distillery, Longrow.

PROPRIETORS, THE CAMPBELTOWN DISTILLERY COMPANY.

THIS Distillery was erected in the year 1815 by John Mactaggart, great grandfather of Mr. Daniel Mactaggart, the Procurator Fiscal of Campbeltown, and is an old-fashioned work according to the present ideas of distilling, but when it was first built it was a great advance on the "Smuggler's Kettle."

On passing through a pair of ancient gates and turning to the left, the visitor comes upon a veritable "smuggler's work," so ancient is its appearance and tumble-down look.

The quality of its brew is said to have inspired Burns to sing, when he visited his Mary at Campbeltown,

"Oh! Willie brew'd a peck o' maut,
An Rob a' Allan cam' to pree;
Three blyther hearts, that lee long night,
Ye wad na find in Christendie.
We are na fou, we're nae that fou,
But just a drappie in our e'e;
The cock may craw, the day may daw,
And aye we'll taste the Whasky O."

The Distillery has undergone some changes since it was first erected, and some additions and machinery have since been added, nevertheless, nothing can take from the place its "old-world look" and ancient appearance.

The following is a very brief description of the place; there are two Barley Lofts, two Malt Barns and a medium sized Kiln, floored with the old English perforated tiles, and also an ancient Mill and Mill Stores. The Mash Tun (with revolving machinery) has a capacity of 4,000 gallons, it is 13 feet in diameter and 4½ feet deep. There is a steam engine of 14 horse power and a steam boiler 17½ feet long by 4½ in diameter, the five Washbacks hold 3,000 gallons each, and there are also two old "Sma Pot Stills," each holding 1,400 and 960 gallons respectively; the three Receivers are of the following capacity:—Spirit Receiver, 360 gallons; Feints Receiver, 730 gallons; and Low-wines Receiver, 800 gallons; two of them sunk into the ground, the other raised up from the floor.

The Spirit Store is a nice little building, and the Spirit Vat therein holds 1,351 gallons. The Coolers are in the open, and there is a large Morton's Refrigerator. The four Warehouses contained, at the time of our visit, 1,300 casks of Whisky, some of them very aged; the water used in this Distillery is brought from the Crosshill Loch. Peat only is used in drying the malt, nearly all manual labour is used in this establishment, and they work on the old system.

The Whisky, which is Campbeltown Malt, is sold principally in Glasgow and Ayrshire, and the annual output is 60,000 gallons.

The works are about a quarter of a mile from the quay.

The Chief Excise Officer is Mr. Joseph Wilson.

No. 33.

Argyll Distillery, Campbeltown.

PROPRIETOR, ROBERT GREENLEES, TRADING AS COLVILL, GREENLEES & CO.

THIS Distillery is situated in Longrow Street, on the north side of the town. It is a clean compact little work, and, although built as far back as 1844, it boasts of most of the improvements of modern times. The works cover an acre of ground, and are approached through a neat gateway; within the enclosure there are offices for the distillery and Excise gentlemen, and the various buildings, which mostly communicate one with another, are arranged round the yard.

There is a spacious Barley Store, a Malt Barn, 120 feet long by 28 feet wide, with the usual Steeps; a capital Kiln with tiled floor, where peat only is used in the drying; Mill Stores and Mill. An 8-horse power Engine, with a Boiler 18 feet long by 5 feet in diameter, supplies the motive power. The Mash Tun is 12 feet in diameter and 5 feet deep. There are five Washbacks, each containing 3,900 gallons; a Wash Charger, and a Low Wines and Feints Charger; two Pot Stills, one holding 1,070 gallons and the other 686 gallons; three Receivers, and two Heaters each holding 1,000 gallons. There are five Warehouses capable of holding 600 casks; a Spirit Store with Vat of 1,360 gallons capacity.

The water used in the Distillery is from the Loch, supplemented by the supply from a deep well on the premises. The Whisky made is Campbeltown Malt, and is sold chiefly in Glasgow and England. The annual output is 40,000 gallons.

No. 34.

Springside Distillery, Campbeltown.

PROPRIETORS, JOHN COLVILL & CO.

IN the afternoon we paid a brief visit to the Springside Distillery, the smallest work in Campbeltown. It consists of a scattered lot of buildings placed round a small yard, which were built in the year 1830 by the father of the present proprietor.

The Works consist of three small Granaries and Maltings, two Kilns floored with tiles and heated with peat, a Mill House and Stores. A Mashing and Distilling House, which contains a Mash Tun, 10 feet in diameter and $3\frac{1}{2}$ feet deep, Underback and heating Copper. In the Tun Room, we observed six Washbacks and a Wash Charger; and in the Still House two Pot Stills holding 1,205 and 394 gallons respectively, also the Receivers, Chargers and Safe. There are four bonded Warehouses which contained 600 casks, and a small Spirit Store. The water used for all purposes comes from the Crosshills Loch. The make is called Campbeltown Malt and the annual output is 30,000 gallons.

No. 35.

Ardbeg Distillery, Islay.

PROPRIETORS, McDOUGALL & Co.

RESIDENT MANAGING PARTNER, MR. COLIN HAY.

RESUMING our journey in pursuit of Distilleries, we left the vast Whisky centre, Campbeltown, at the early hour of six in the morning, bound for the port of Tarbert, to catch the boat to Islay. The air was crisp and the first few hours of the long drive chilly, but the morning sun soon filled our hearts with gladness, and we were enabled once again to enjoy the delightful scenery through which we passed and which has been described in a former chapter. Upon due arrival at West Tarbert we boarded the steamer bound for Port Ellen, a journey occupying some hours, yet withal rendered pleasant by weather that was all that could be desired. Tired and hungry after our long day we were glad to reach our destination, and immediately on landing proceeded to the "White Hart Inn" where for several days we took up our quarters, and found the accommodation excellent and the attendants obliging. The next morning we were early astir exploring the town and sea-shore, after which we partook of a substantial breakfast and started on our way to Ardbeg, distant four miles. The road mostly followed the coast line, but frequently a turn brought us almost to the water's edge. The shore is mostly rocky and dangerous, in many places huge masses of rock rise from the surface of the sea, forming tiny islets round and over which the swell rises and falls in impressive grandeur. Every now and then as we drove along, the scene assumed a new aspect; now we would come suddenly upon some little picturesque bay fringed with fantastic and peculiar shaped rocks, or ascending a gentle hill some inland view of green slopes and heather covered hills would reveal itself, which lent a happy contrast to the wild sea-girt shore. Nearly all the way we had in sight the opposite coast of Kintyre, and almost fancied we could distinguish the long coach road to Tarbert which we had traversed the day before. Journeying along we were continually reminded by the ruins of castles and churches that we were on one of the most historic islands of Scotland, in the land of romance and the home of the "Lords of the Isles," rendered classic by one of Sir Walter Scott's finest poems.

As we reached the top of a hill, a sudden view of beautiful Ardbeg, as seen in our illustration, presented itself to view and recalled our minds from romantic wanderings.

ARDBEG DISTILLERY.

The Ardbeg Distillery is situated on the south-east coast of the island, in a lonely spot on the very verge of the sea, and its isolation tends to heighten the romantic sense of its position. It was established in the year 1815, but long previous to that date it was a noted haunt of smugglers. For many years the supervisors had been searching for this nest of illicit traffickers without success; most of the band were known by sight, and endeavours had long been made to catch them when out in their boats. At length the spot where they carried on their nefarious practices was discovered, but the band was too strong for an open attack; however, one day, when the party were absent with a cargo of whisky, a raid was made and the place destroyed after a seizure of a large amount of the illicit spirit. As it was impossible to procure other vessels, and finding their occupation gone, the whole band was scattered, and most of them migrated to the Kintyre shores. The site of their operations was shortly after occupied by the founders of Ardbeg Distillery who chose it on account of the water, the chief characteristics of which are its softness and purity; it is obtained from Lochs Arinambeast and Uigidale.

The old Distillery of Ardbeg well deserves to be noticed, as it is one of the most interesting in the island; the buildings have no pretensions to taste and elegance, nevertheless they look picturesque and are substantially built. The walls enclose a very considerable extent of ground, a portion of which is not built upon, and, with the exception of the Distillery proper, the buildings are somewhat scattered and have the appearance of a Dutch settlement. At a distance of half a mile a fine quay has been built mostly at the expense of the firm where steamers call twice a week. The founders of this business were the McDougalls, of Ardbeg, the last survivor of whom, was Alexr. McDougall, whose name is still retained in the firm as being a good Highland representative name, although he died in 1853. He was well known among the members of the spirit trade in Glasgow about fifty years ago, and his integrity and straightforwardness of character gained him the entire confidence of his friends and customers. He was liberal and benevolent, while his clannishness was intense. This Highland virtue he prominently exhibited on a certain occasion, when he discovered in court that some unknown namesake was pronounced by the judge "Guilty" and sentence of a fine or imprisonment was imposed, Mr. McDougall interposed the statement "that it was impossible that a McDougall could do anything wrong" and therefore he would pay the fine!

In the olden days all the Islay Distilleries were small. Ardbeg fifty years ago was among the larger works and only made about 500 gallons per week, so that in the last half century it has increased tenfold, a proof that the Whisky is held in high appreciation by the public. On reaching the Distillery Mr. Hay received us most courteously and placed a guide at our disposal. We first visited the Malting Department, on the right of the enclosure, a short distance from the office. Ascending a staircase we found ourselves in the Granaries, which consist of five Barley Lofts, capable of storing nearly 3,000 quarters of grain. After walking through these spacious chambers we went down a flight of steps to the levels of the Maltings which are four in number, with brick floors and each possessing a brick and cement Steep capable of wetting fifty quarters at one time. Passing out at the northern door we came to the spacious Kilns attached to the Maltings, both are floored with hair cloth over wire netting. These drying floors are 14 feet above the fires, which consist of open *chauffeurs* wherein peat only is burned, which is dug from a hill two miles distant. The chief characteristic of the splendid peat used in Ardbeg is the absence of sulphur or other offensive mineral, the composition of the peat being purely vegetable deposit, not highly decomposed, some of the organisms being still traceable in the prepared peat. Adjacent to the Kilns are the Malt Deposits, the walls and floors of which are kept beautifully clean and much care is taken in the preservation of the malt previous to its being ground, as the maltman informed us that both dust and exposure to the air ruins good malt. When we went down stairs from the Malt Deposit we found ourselves in the courtyard again, and then ascending a flight of steps we reached the Grist Loft which is above the Mill, and contains the hopper which acts as a feeder to the Mash Tun. Following our guide we next visited the Mash House a capital building which contains the Mash Tun, a cast iron vessel 16 feet in diameter and 5½ deep, possessing the patent stirring rakes and draining plates. The grains are discharged from the Mash Tun by elevators; about one half of the draff is disposed of to the local farmers and the rest shipped to Larne and other Irish ports. Here also we were shown the two copper Boilers which supply the hot water to the Tun, also a cast iron Underback, two of Morton's Refrigerators and the customary appurtenances. Ascending a wide staircase we came to the staging of the Tun Room, a long gallery fitted up with the various pipes and pumping appliances, and in the middle, eight Washbacks, each with a capacity of 8,000 gallons. We then retraced our steps to the yard and entered the Still House, a spacious and ancient building, wherein we observed two "Old Pot Stills," a Wash Still containing 4,000 gallons, and a Spirit Still, 3,000 gallons. The Wash Charger is a handsome timber vessel placed on an elevation so as to command the Stills. Underneath are three Receivers, two Condensers, Pumps, etc. Following our guide we came to the Spirit Store, a neat building adjoining the Still House, containing a Vat which holds 6,000 gallons. Distributed about the premises are five Warehouses of large dimensions, all of them built with stone and roofed with slate; they contained 6,000 casks of Whisky at the time of our visit, and some idea of their proportions may be gathered from the fact that two of them are 228 feet long and 60 wide. Both steam and water power are available; and sixty persons are employed on the premises, for whom the proprietors have provided comfortable dwellings.

Mr. Colin Hay resides in a picturesque house on the property, which is built almost on the water's edge, and both he and his son are concerned in the management of the Distillery, while a practical distiller and brewer, Mr. John McMillan, has been in the employ of the Company at Ardbeg for the last thirty years. The make is Pure Islay Malt, and the annual output is 250,000 gallons, which is all taken up by the larger firms of wine and spirit merchants in Glasgow, Liverpool, and London. The firm are distillers from malt only, not dealers or merchants otherwise. Mr. Alex. W. Gray Buchanan, of Parkhill, Polmont, Stirlingshire, is the head of the firm.

Sole agents, Buchanan, Wilson & Co., 40, St. Vincent's Place, Glasgow.

No. 36.

Lagavulin Distillery, Islay.

PROPRIETORS, J. L. MACKIE & CO.

FROM Ardbeg our route homeward lay through the beautiful village of Lagganmhouillin or Lagavulin, "the Mill in the Valley," and no prettier or more romantic spot could have been chosen for a distillery. We trotted merrily along, the horse apparently knowing that its face was stable-ward, and the driver, evidently anticipating another "wee drappie" at our next halting place, occasionally broke out into song, but as it was in Gaelic we were none the wiser, and his command of the English language so limited, that he could not favour us with a translation. As we rounded a ridge of one of the hills we came in sight of the historical ruin of Dun-naomhaig Castle, which stands on a large peninsular rock, protected on the land side by a thick earthen mound opposite the village of Lagavulin. It is the place where Robert Bruce took refuge after his disastrous defeat by the Earl of Pembroke, and was also a stronghold to which the Lords of the Isles constantly retreated. There are remains of several such strongholds in Islay, the walls of some of them being 12 feet thick, and there is usually a gallery in the midst of the wall; one of those we visited had a stone-seat two feet high round the area.

The picturesque ruins of the principal castle and chapel where the Lords of the Isles resided in royal pomp, are on an islet in Loch Finlaggan, a lake three miles in circumference, and several traces are still to be seen on its shore of a pier and habitations used by their guards and men-at-arms. In former times a large stone was to be seen on which the MacDonalds stood when crowned King of the Isles by the Bishop of Argyle.

> "Where are thy pristine glories, Finlaggan!
> The voice of mirth has ceased to ring thy walls,
> Where Celtic lords and their fair ladies sang
> Their songs of joy in Great MacDonald's halls.
> And where true knights, the flower of chivalry,
> Oft met their chiefs in revelry—
> All, all are gone and left thee to repose,
> Since a new race and measures new arose."

Towards the head of Lochindaal on the same side of the Island, there are also vestiges of a similar pier and dwellings, where in olden times the MacDonalds had a body of 500 men to guard the shores of the loch, who were formed in two divisions, the first called Ceatharnaich was the principal one, and was composed of the very tallest and strongest of the islanders, of these a picked

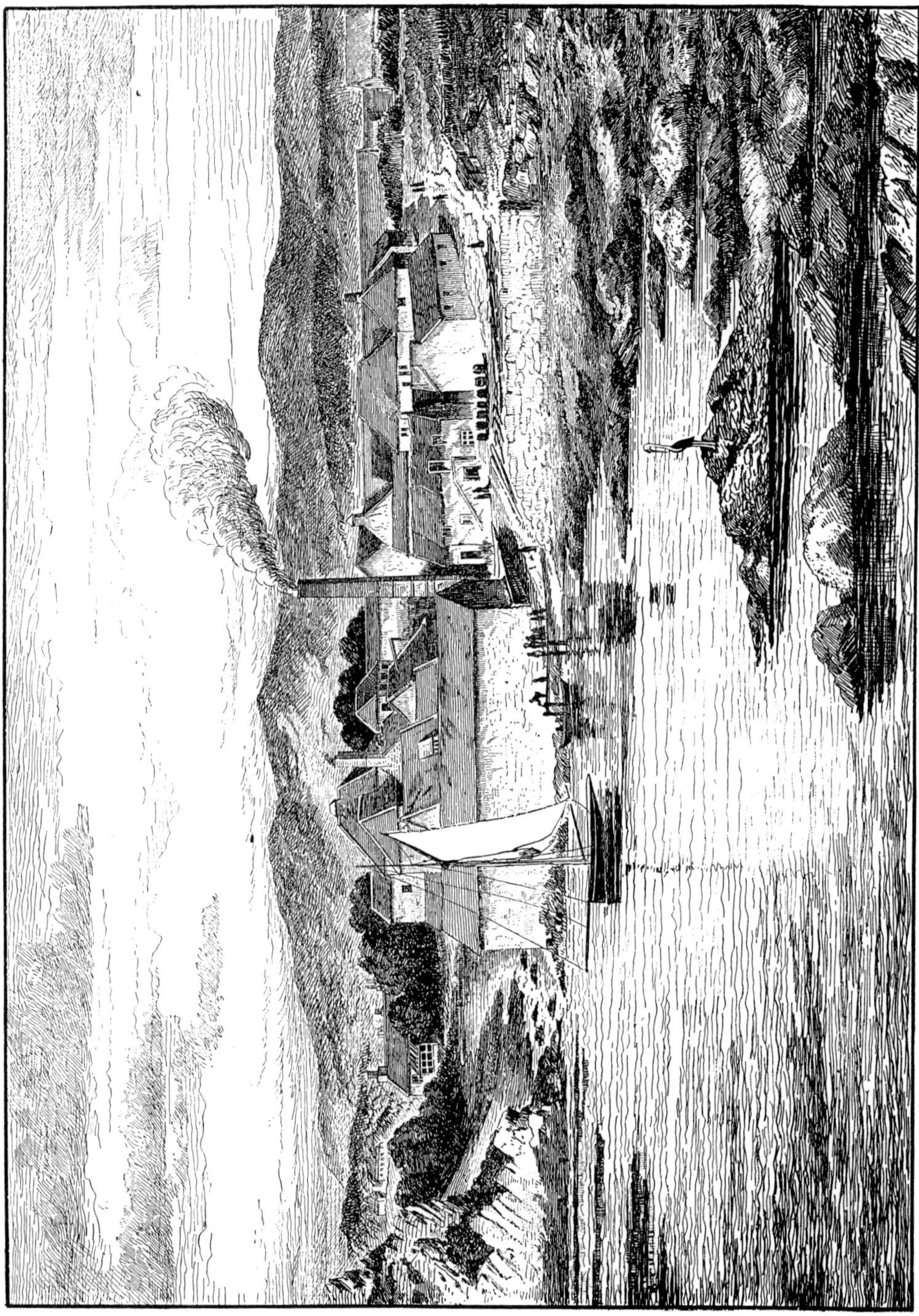

LAGAVULIN DISTILLERY.

body of sixteen, formed the body-guard of their lord, whose duty it was to attend him wherever he went, even in his rural walks and friendly visits; one of their number denominated Gille—"shiabadh-dealt" headed the band. This piece of honourable distinction was conferred upon him on account of his feet being of such enormous size and form as in his progress to shake the dew from the grass preparatory to its being trod by his master. These Buannachan, as they were called, enjoyed great privileges and were given lands, which rendered them particularly obnoxious to their countrymen. The last gang was destroyed in so ludicrous a manner, yet withal so sanguinary, that we cannot forbear relating the tale to our readers. The Buannachans were particularly distasteful to one Macphail in the Rhinns, whose occupation when not required to attend the Lord of the Isles on a foraying and slaughtering expedition, was that of a peaceful woodman. One day seeing the Gille—"shiabadh-dealt" and his comrades coming he set about splitting the trunk of a tree, in which he had partly succeeded by the time they had reached him. He requested his visitors to lend a hand which they willingly did. So ranging themselves eight on each side they took hold of the partially severed split, on their doing which the crafty Macphail removed the wedges which had kept open the split, which now closed on their fingers holding them hard and fast in this clever rustic man-trap. Macphail and his three sons then equipped themselves from the armour of their captives, and after compelling them to eat a lusty dinner, with fiendish cruelty beheaded every one of them and made their escape to Ireland.

Close to the Distillery, as if to throw round the establishment its spiritual protection, stands a quaint-looking church; the bell which summons the worshippers instead of being in the tower, is fixed on a cross-tree of pyramidical shape on the top of a neighbouring hill, so that its sound may reach the remotest parts of the parish. The clergyman's residence, like the church, is picturesquely situated beside a rocky inlet of the sea coast, and nearly opposite the castle before referred to. The country from Lagavulin to Port Ellen, three miles distant, presents a well cultivated and fertile aspect, and forms a striking and beautiful contrast to the rugged coast. On reaching the village we put the horse up and proceeded to inspect the Distillery.

The works are built at the head of a minature bay, around which rocks of fantastic shape rise abruptly from the sea; in some places detached masses have fallen in such a position that they rise from the sea like weird monsters of the deep, and by moonlight produce startling effects on the surface of the waters. Lagavulin is said to be one of the oldest distilleries in Islay, the business to a certain extent having been founded in 1742. At that period it consisted of ten small and separate smuggling bothys for the manufacture of "moonlight," which when working presented anything but a true picture of "still life," and were all subsequently absorbed into one establishment, the whole work not making more than a few thousand gallons per annum. The term "moonlight" used always to be applied to illicit Whisky in contradistinction to that which paid duty, which was termed "daylight." A century ago smuggling was the chief employment of the crofters and fishermen, more especially during the winter, and many were the encounters which took place between them and the Government officers. Up to the year 1821 smuggling was a lucrative trade in Islay, and large families were supported by it. In those days every smuggler could clear at least ten shillings a day, and keep a horse and cow. Early in the century the buildings were converted into a legal Distillery, and in the year 1835 they came into the possession of the present firm, who repaired the place and made considerable additions and improvements. During the past thirty years the works have been somewhat enlarged to meet the growing demand for the product, nevertheless the old character of the place has been preserved, and there is not a modern building to be seen, except one or two new Bonded Warehouses. The water used comes from the top of the hill of Solan, where there are two lochs, both brought into requisition, one for driving and the other for mashing. Our driver informed us that the Lagavulin water has a hundred falls before it reaches the Distillery, and that it travels over moss and peat lands all the way down, which is said to give the pronounced flavour to the Lagavulin Whisky. In the absence of Mr. Graham, the resident partner, the manager showed us over the works, and without his directions we should certainly have lost ourselves in the old place. The Maltings, which are arranged on one side of a long open court, are 150 feet long and 36 feet broad. The top floors, used for storing the barley, will hold 3,000 quarters, and underneath are the Malt-floors with stone Steeps. Attached to these buildings there is a Kiln, measuring 36 feet by 28 feet, floored with wire cloth, where only peat is used in drying the malt. A door-way from the Kiln floor leads direct into the Malt-deposit, a well-lighted room capable of holding 1,000 quarters. From this department the malt is sent by elevators to the Mill to be ground, from which place the pulverized malt is raised to the Grist-loft in the adjoining building. In this chamber there is a hopper into which the ground malt is tipped, and from whence it falls through the Mashing Machine direct into the Mash Tun below. We then followed our guide to the Mash and Distilling-house, a sombre building, which brings our memories back to the middle ages. It contains two Brewing tanks heated by steam, a metal Mash Tun, 18 feet in diameter and 5 feet deep, which possesses the usual revolving stirring rakes; a metal Underback, a Morton's Refrigerator, the Pumps, and in the roof a set of old fashioned Coolers. We next proceeded to the Tun-room, which contains seven Washbacks ranged round the wall, each holding 2,000 gallons and at an elevation a Wash Charger. The Still-house contains two old Pot Stills, heated by old fashioned furnaces; one of them is a Wash Still holding 1,200 gallons, inside of which is the revolving chain arrangement, and the other a Low-wines and Feints Still, holding 650 gallons. Here also are the usual Receivers, Chargers, and Safe. Crossing the roadway we next visited the Spirit Store, which contains a Vat holding 2,000 gallons, and the casking apparatus, where the spirit is weighed, branded, and sent to the Warehouses or under bond direct to the stores in Glasgow. From thence we bent our steps to the four large Warehouses, which contained at the time of our visit 4,000 casks of Whisky of various ages. There is a small cooperage, carpenter's shop, stores, stables, and cart-sheds on the premises.

The Whisky is mostly shipped from Port Ellen, but some of it is floated out to ships. The Distillery is under the entire management of Mr. J. C. Graham, the resident partner, who resides in a picturesque house opposite the works. The make is pure Islay Malt, and is principally sold in Glasgow, England, and the Colonies. The annual output is 75,000 gallons, and the make is held in high repute; we tasted some eight years old before starting, which was exceptionally fine. The make is largely used for blending purposes, but it is also sold as a single Whisky; there are only a few of the Scotch Distillers that turn out spirit for use as single Whiskies, and that made at Lagavulin can claim to be one of the most prominent.

No. 37.

Laphroaig Distillery, Islay.

PROPRIETORS, D. JOHNSTON & CO.

BEFORE starting for Bridgend, our next destination, we paid a brief visit to the Distillery which heads this chapter. It is one mile distant from Port Ellen, and situated on the road traversed the day before, and, like Lagavulin, is built on the margin of the sea. At a distance the establishment looked like a cluster of ruins, but on nearer inspection we found it to be a Distillery of a very old-fashioned type, and consisting of two ranges of low buildings standing at the edge of the little bay from whence it takes its name, and sheltered by huge rocks which project into the water. The sea view embraces a wide expanse of ocean, the Island of Gigha, and the Kintyre Coast. A pretty little burn, which rises in the hills, runs brawling over stones and bits of rock through the property, and then falls into the sea. The water of this burn is of excellent quality, and is used in the Distillery.

The Islay people are very hospitable. We had lunched at Ardbeg the day before, and at Laphroaig Mr. Johnston would not let us commence our labours until we had partaken of his hospitality.

This Distillery was built in the year 1820, and covers one and a half acres of ground. It comprises a large Barley-barn and Maltings, a Kiln, Mash House, Tun Room, Still House, and two Warehouses, all similar to Lagavulin, only on a smaller scale. In the Still House there are two old Pot Stills, Safe, two Receivers, Chargers, &c. There is also a small cooperage, good stables, cart sheds, and manager's house on the premises.

Peat only is used in the drying, and the Whisky is pure Islay Malt, the annual output being 23,000 gallons, all of which has for the last sixty years been supplied and sold by Messrs. Mackie & Co., of Glasgow.

We cannot forbear a brief allusion to the fact that all the Distilleries in Islay are built on the sea coast, but the Distillers maintain that the sea air has no effect whatever on the Whisky, and that the peculiarity of the Islay make arises principally from the flavour of the peat, dug in the island, and which is more strongly impregnated with moss than some other districts.

The Whisky made at Laphroaig is of exceptional character, being largely sought after for blending purposes, and is a thick and pungent spirit of a peculiar "peat reek" flavour. The small output renders it of high value in the market; and although the Distillery is of small dimensions, the proprietors would not attempt to disturb the present arrangements, as thereby the character of the Whisky might be entirely lost. The distilling of Whisky is greatly aided by circumstances that cannot be accounted for, and even the most experienced distillers are unable to change its character, which is largely influenced by accidents of locality, water, and position. No better instance of this can be given than the case of the Lagavulin and Laphroaig Distilleries, which, although situated within a short distance of one another, each produce Whisky of a distinct and varied type.

No. 38.

Port Ellen Distillery, Islay.

PROPRIETOR, JAMES RAMSAY.

BEFORE visiting the Distillery which is the subject of this brief chapter, we took a stroll along the shore to get a breath of the sea. Port Ellen possesses most delightful bathing sands, which would be much appreciated and visited if there were some lodging houses or cottages available, and the place were nearer Glasgow.

The lighthouse, at the opposite end of the bay from the Distillery, was erected in 1832, by the late Mr. W. F. Campbell of Islay, to the memory of his wife, Lady Ellinor, and is a conspicuous object from any part of the coast.

The Port Ellen Distillery is planted on the seashore, about half a mile from the village. The works cover three acres, and were built in the year 1825, but since that time several important additions have been made. In the absence of the manager, to whom we had letters of introduction, the distiller conducted us over the premises. We were first taken to the three spacious Barley Lofts, well lighted and ventilated, of the following dimensions, No. 1 is 100 feet long and 36 wide; No. 2, 110 feet by 52; No. 3, 135 feet by 30. The three Malting Floors are of the same size, each having the usual Steeps; in close proximity are two Kilns, floored with wire cloth, one 52 feet by 26, the other 36 feet square. A flight of steps leads into the Malt Store, off which is the Mill Room, containing a pair of malt rollers; and in the adjoining room is the Mash Tun, 14 feet in diameter by 5 feet deep, a Wash Charger containing 5,000 gallons, two heating tanks, etc.

From this department we proceeded to the Tun Room, which contains seven Fermenting-backs, of an average capacity of 7,000 gallons each. Passing from here we came to the Still House, containing two old Pot Stills, one holding 3,500 gallons and the other 2,100, also two Receivers, holding 1,400 and 1,600 gallons respectively. In a line with the Distillery are six handsome Warehouses, containing at the time of our visit 3,700 casks, holding 240,000 gallons of Whisky of different ages. We may here remark that only peat which is dug in the district is used in the drying, and the water comes from two lochs in the hills; the principal one used for distilling purposes is noted in the locality for its clearness and purity, the other is used for driving purposes. Elevators are used all over the works; there is a Cooperage and Seasoning House for casks, a fine Spirit Store, and one of Morton's Refrigerators. The Whisky is Islay Malt, and the annual output 140,000 gallons.

The following lines by a local wag, refer to the reputed litigious character of the crofters and small farmers in Islay.

"It's a very good Island to live in—
To spend, to lend, or to give in;
But to beg, or to borrow, or ask for one's own,
It's the very worst Island that ever was known."

No. 39.

Bowmore Distillery, Bowmore, Islay.

PROPRIETORS, W. & J. MUTTER.

WE found the coach drive from Port Ellen to Bowmore one of the most uninteresting that we had ever experienced. During the journey of four hours we saw but two or three habitations, and scarcely any trees ; in all our wanderings we have never travelled by such a dismal and lonely road. Fortunately we were a large party and a merry one, or we should have wearied of this dismal track long before we reached our destination. Sandy, our aged coachman, was a character, and drove us at about the rate of four miles an hour. We continually remonstrated with him, but to no purpose, and plied him with nips of Whisky to induce him to urge his steeds along, but no persuasions would induce him to trot his horses, except at those parts of the road where they were accustomed to increase their speed. Some of us walked many a mile, and were yet able to keep ahead of him.

Within a very short distance of our journey's end a most agreeable and surprising change came over the scene, and we found ourselves driving beneath trees whose thick branches met overhead, and passing through the well-cultivated policies and rural retreats, which form the aristocratic village of Bridgend. Presently the coach pulled up in front of a picturesque hotel rejoicing in the name of "Beul-an-ath," the best and only one of any importance in Islay, possessing gardens and grounds of most enchanting loveliness. The hotel was pretty full, but we were able to secure a comfortable bed, and made this place our headquarters for many days.

On the following morning having arranged with our host to provide us with a carriage during our stay, we drove to the Distillery which heads this chapter. A journey of three miles along the sandy shore of Lochindaal brought us to Bowmore, the capital of Islay, a town containing 800 inhabitants, and built on the face of a hill, at the top of which stands the parish church, a circular white-washed building with a spire.

The Bowmore Distillery covers nearly four acres of ground, and is built on a shelf of the sea coast ; the buildings are somewhat scattered, but all enclosed, and entrance is gained thereto through a gateway, from the high road, on the slopes of the hill. This establishment is said to be one of the oldest in the Island, having been founded early in the century by the Simsons, from whose hands it passed nearly fifty years ago to the father and uncle of the present proprietors, who carried on the business most successfully. At the time of their occupation, Bowmore was the only Distillery which was feued, the others being held on a

BOWMORE DISTILLERY.

tenancy, and it was not until several years afterwards that the other Distilleries in Islay became feus. At one time the old firm held the Jura Distillery, and for many years were very successful therewith, but the distance from the island, and the difficulty in reaching it in winter time, together with their own increasing business, induced them to give it up and confine their attention solely to Bowmore. The father of the present members of the firm was a scientific farmer, and along with his brother introduced many improvements in the mode of farming and modern implements used in husbandry. He grew the first crop of clover in the island, and was a noted cultivator of wheat and barley. As a landlord and neighbour, a benefactor to the poor and philanthropist, he was much beloved, and won the esteem of all classes. We were told a story of this gentleman, which betrays a marked characteristic of the Islay-men : When Mr. Mutter first came to the island, he was invited to dinner with Captain Walter Campbell. When the meal was over, the gallant Captain proceeded to give Mr. Mutter advice, and amongst other things warned him as a stranger not to accept a present from any of his neighbours ; "for if they send you a lamb they will expect a cow in return, therefore always refuse the gift, or pay for it."

In the year 1880 the Distillery came into the possession of their descendants, James and William Mutter, who have since then made great improvements and alterations in the works. It is a noticeable fact that all the Distillieries in Islay are built on the seaboard. The Distillers say that proximity to the sea favours the various processes of malting, brewing, and distilling. Bowmore Distillery is supplied with an unlimited quantity of splendid water from the Laggan, the best and largest river in the Island, and is favourably situated for the disposal and sale of the draff and pot ale, both most useful for cattle feeding, and a perfect boon in winter when fodder is scarce.

In the absence of the resident partner we were received by the manager, who conducted us over the premises, and first led the way to the Granaries and Maltings, which are placed on the lower slopes of the hill. No. 1 Barley Loft was the first we entered, which is 65 feet long and 18 feet broad holding 514 quarters. It occupies one end of a large square stone building, and underneath is a large Malting Floor measuring 60½ feet long by 58½ feet broad ; at the end built partly in a recess there is a Steep constructed with cement, 18 feet long, 10 broad and 4 feet deep, capable of wetting 420 bushels at one time, or an average quantity of 78 quarters per week. We next passed up some steps into the No. 1 Kiln, 65 feet long by 22½ feet broad, which is used for drying the Malt made on both Nos. 1 and 2 Malt floors. In this Kiln, which will dry 500 bushels at one time, we noticed that the old style of drying the malt is carried out, the floor being of hair cloth, and the malt dried from underneath by peats in four open iron *chauffeurs* placed in the Killogie, as the firing room is called. Descending by a flight of steps we came to the Deposit Room, a triangular shaped apartment, containing 392 quarters of malt.

At one end of this large chamber is the No. 2 Barley Loft and Malting, the former being 39½ feet long by 20½ feet broad, and holding 230 quarters of barley ; the latter 94½ feet by 19 feet, and possessing a Steep, 18½ feet long, 7½ feet broad, and 3½ feet deep, capable of wetting 320 bushels at one time, or an average of 360 quarters per week. Crossing the way we came to a long range of buildings also devoted to the storage of corn and malting purposes, having the No. 2 Kiln at the north end ; the Kiln is 41 feet long and 24½ feet broad—capable of drying 400 bushels at one time. Both Kilns possess the Louvre Ventilators, and are similarly arranged to those already described. The No. 3 Barley-loft is 100 feet long and 24½ feet broad, and will hold 1,184 quarters. Nos. 3 and 4 Malt floors are underneath. No. 3 is 100 feet long and 24 feet wide, and No. 4 is 94 feet long by 24½ feet wide, and has a Steep 23½ feet long, 5½ feet broad, and 3 feet deep, at its southern end capable of wetting 300 bushels at one time, or an average quantity of 56 quarters per week, and is so placed that it also serves the No. 3 floor. Following our guide we next visited No. 5 Malting, the floor of which is 104 feet long and 48 feet broad, over which is the No. 4 Barley loft, which holds 2,630 quarters, and possesses a Steep 38½ feet long, which will wet 504 bushels at one time, or 93 quarters per week. There are three Malt Deposit rooms, all of which communicate with the Kilns, and are contiguous to the Mill, to which we now repaired, wherein is placed the grinding machinery manufactured by J. Copeland & Co., of Glasgow, and a pair of malt rollers driven by steam power, capable of grinding 360 bushels of malt per hour, or 2,500 bushels a day. The ground malt is conveyed by elevators to the Grist-loft, so as to be ready for the next stage—namely, mashing. Ascending a staircase we found ourselves in the Grist-loft, 32 feet long, 27 feet broad, capable of holding 325 quarters of ground malt in bags. At the southern end of this range of buildings there are three hot-water coppers, holding together 8,767 gallons, all heated by fire, no steam being allowed into them either by coils or any other way. The boiling water from these vessels is conveyed to the Mashing-machine and Mash-tun through copper pipes. The manager-informed us that with the exception of the Mash-tun, Worts Receiver, and the two pumps in the Mash House, every pipe and vessel in connection with the making of the Whisky is of copper or wood.

Leaving this department, we crossed to the east side and entered the Mash House, a building 48 feet long by 35 feet wide, which contains a Mash-tun 17 feet in diameter by 6 feet deep, and said to be the largest in Islay, having a capacity of 1,050 bushels, or 8,487 gallons. The Grist-loft and Hopper is over this vessel, and on the floor above is fixed one of Miller's copper mashing machines, described elsewhere. The Draff is thrown out by hand through two apertures in the wall, and falls through a shoot direct into the Draff House, which can hold 3,000 bushels. The Underback, which is below the floor, is 15 feet long, 12 feet broad, and 4½ feet deep, holding 5,083 gallons. Alongside the Mash-tun we noticed one of Jeffries' Patent Centrifugal Pumps, which can throw 9,000 gallons an hour, used for pumping the sparges to the Coppers, and worts up to the Worts Receiver. There is also one of McPherson and Waddell's Wash Pumps. These powerful machines are capable of throwing 10,000 gallons an hour with only 64 revolutions per minute, while the centrifugal requires 960 revolutions a minute. Near to these pumps is a fine engine of 14-horse power, and in a room by itself a steam boiler 18 feet long and 4½ feet in diameter.

We next proceeded to the Underback Room which is at the northern end of the Mash House, and contains an Underback holding 5,083 gallons, which receives the worts from the Tun, and is also used for sparges, which are pumped from this dish to the Worts Receiver and Coppers. Through this room we passed into the new Tun Room, a lofty apartment facing the sea, 36½ feet long by 20 feet broad, in which are placed three Washbacks or Tuns, holding respectively 10,364, 10,389, and 10,340 gallons; mounting the platform which runs from end to end of this building, our guide directed our steps to the old Tun Room, 57 feet long by 17½ feet broad, on the same level, which contains six other Washbacks holding respectively 6,101, 5,973, 6,108, 6,171, 5,996, and 6,006 gallons; all the Backs are connected by copper pipes with the Worts Receiver, and are switched by hand. The refrigerators next claimed our attention, they are both by John Miller & Co., of Glasgow, and each of them is 14 feet long by 6 feet wide, capable of together cooling 6,000 gallons per hour. From the old Tun Room we entered the Still House, a light and roomy building, $64\frac{1}{2}$ feet long by 40 feet broad, which contains five Copper Stills, a Wash Charger, holding 7,897 gallons; also a Low-wines Charger, Low-wines Receiver, Low-wines and Spirit Pump, etc. The contents of the three Wash Stills are respectively 2,077, 2,200, and 2,400 gallons, and their charges, or working capacity, are 1,749, 1,978, and 1,863 gallons, and the Wash Charger which commands these Stills with a dip of $72\frac{7}{10}$ inches, holds 7,897 gallons. There are two Low-wines or Spirit Stills, holding respectively 1,400 and 1,210 gallons, and their actual working capacity is 1,053 and 923 gallons. The Low-wines Charger dips $46\frac{9}{10}$ inches, and is of 1,232 gallons content, and Low-wines and Feints Receiver dips $47\frac{9}{10}$ inches of 2,477 gallons contents. All the Stills are heated by fire and of a shape which the firm will not allow any deviation from, one of the Low-wines Stills having a double head and two worms, so far as we have seen, being

STILL HOUSE, BOWMORE DISTILLERY.

quite unique in this respect. The Wash Still chains are driven by a small over-shot water wheel; these chains are made of brass or gun metal, being a pattern of chain found in an old Still, demolished in the Brackla Distillery some years ago, by Mr. MacDougall, of John Miller & Co. In the outer courtyard, placed on solid masonry at a high elevation, are three Worm-tubs. The largest is $12\frac{3}{4}$

feet deep by 12 feet in diameter, and contains ten turns of Wash Still Worm, and nine of No. 1 Low-wines Still ; next to it is a new Worm-tub, oblong in shape, $17\frac{1}{4}$ feet long, $7\frac{1}{4}$ feet wide and 8 feet deep, having five double lengths and two single of copper worms, with flanges of gun metal. Adjoining this is a small Worm-tub, $6\frac{1}{4}$ feet in diameter at top, wider at bottom, and 10 feet deep, having thirteen coils of copper worm from the No. 1 Low-wines Still.

Standing against the walls of the Still House are two Copper Condensers, the Wash Still Condenser is $12\frac{1}{2}$ feet high and contains 121 copper tubes; that for the Low-wines is of the same height, but has only 91 tubes. These Condensers were the first in use in Islay, but when water is scarce they require more attention than the Worm-tubs. We next entered a long passage which leads to the Mash House, off which is the Spirit Receiver Room, $18\frac{1}{2}$ feet long by $10\frac{1}{2}$ feet broad, the Receiver placed therein is a timber vessel, having a dip of 60 inches, and contents 1,865 gallons. It possesses an indicator attached to the charging and discharging pipes, which permits of continuous working, as without this the fires would have to be drawn from the Stills until pumping was finished. We then retraced our steps to the outer court to reach the Spirit Store, it is nearly 62 feet long by 10 feet wide, and contains a Spirit Vat holding 2,354 gallons, and the casking and weighing apparatus.

Underneath the north end of the Old Maltings is the Cooperage consisting of two vaults, brick arched, each 40 feet long by 10 feet broad ; they were formerly the original and only Warehouses of Bowmore Distillery. Following our guide we next visited the bonded Warehouses ; No. 1 consists of two flats each measuring $112\frac{1}{2}$ feet by 48 feet ; the ground flat is cut out of the solid rock, and they are both dry and well ventilated. No. 2 is situated at the western end of the Kiln next the sea, and is 106 feet long by 21 feet broad ; it contained 150 puncheons and 200 hogsheads, equal to about 33,500 gallons.

The firm have also very extensive warehouse accommodation in the arches under the Central Station in Glasgow. As we passed along to the offices we observed an immense peat stack containing 1,200 loads, and a shed holding 1,000 tons of coal, both ready for winter's use. Lying at anchor was the s.s. "James Mutter," 145 tons, the property of the firm, used for the conveyance of Whisky to Glasgow, and for general traffic.

The water used at Bowmore Distillery comes from the Laggan River, and is conducted by a lade or water course nine miles in length, said to be the longest to any Distillery in Scotland, though, as the crow flies, the distance is not more than five miles, but the engineering difficulties met with were so great, owing to want of fall, that a very tortuous course had to be made. The Barley used is shipped from Inverness and Moray-shires.

The Whisky is pure Islay Malt, and the annual output is 200,000 gallons.

No. 40.

Lochindaal Distillery, Port Charlotte, Islay.

PROPRIETOR, J. B. SHERRIFF.

ON the other side of the loch, and nearly opposite Bowmore, is Lochindaal, and thither we first drove the next morning. It is six miles from the hotel, and situated in the heart of what is called the "Garden of Islay." Our way lay through the village of Bridgend, which is planted at the head of the loch and almost hidden by trees. The gardens of every house and cottage are well cultivated, and such a profusion of flowers we have never seen in any village in Scotland. The hawthorn, laburnums, and roses, literally filled the air with their fragrance, and the lawn-like meadows, the fresh green foliage of the beautiful trees, and the dog-roses in the hedges all reminded us of old England. As we crossed the ancient stone bridge we had a peep through the trees of a long stretch of the river wooded to its waters edge, where several of our companions at the hotel were busy fishing, and who supplied our table with some fine trout, the result of their day's sport. We next passed Islay House, which stands in an extensive park surrounded by fir plantations. Thousands of rhododendrons adorn this park massed together in deep rich colours or planted in patches and groups on the fringe of the woods. After passing Islay House the road skirted the loch for the rest of the journey. Lochindaal is really an arm of the sea, expanding into the Bay of Laggan, and terminating at the Point of Rhynns on the west, and the Maol-na-Ho on the east, where it forms the capacious Bay of Laggan. The cliffs on the Maol-na-Ho rise to a great height, and in one of them is a large cave called Sloc Mhaol Doraidh, of historical and smuggling fame, many a good cask of Whisky having been removed therefrom to the coasting ships. The nefarious and immoral trade of illicit distillation used to be carried on all over the island to a very great extent, and Whisky making was formerly, as now, the staple commodity of Islay. The steady and persistent discountenance which the illicit traffic received from the proprietors of the island in the early part of the present century, and the introduction of legal Distilleries, has well nigh put an end to smuggling. Along the route our driver pointed out several abandoned haunts of the smugglers.

As we drove along, the sea was smooth and calm as an inland lake ; but here, after a gale the Atlantic waves break in most magnificent array, and it is a sight never to be forgotten. We next passed Bruichladdich Distillery, which lies on the side of the road. Two miles further on we reached Port Charlotte, a village of little importance and interest except for the large Distillery owned by Mr. Sheriff, which employs a number of the labouring class, and gives some

LOCHINDAAL DISTILLERY, ISLAY.

little life to the locality. At the back of the Distillery the ground rises into hills, near the top of which are two beautiful lochs, the Garroch and Octomore, from whence the water supply to the Distillery is obtained. The works, which were built early in the century, cover about two acres of ground, and although old fashioned are very compact and conveniently arranged for the operations of the Distillery. We entered by a gateway which faces the sea; on the right are small offices and a residence for the Brewer, on the left the spacious Granaries and Malt Barns, and in the front the Distillery proper. The Kiln is floored with German wire cloth, the first we have seen in the island, and we were informed that it is very expensive. Peat only is used in drying the malt, fired in open *chauffeurs*. The old Mash-house, which is kept very clean and is white-washed, contains a circular Mash Tun, the Underback, and two heating Coppers. In the Tun-room there are eight Washbacks, with an average capacity of 10,000 gallons each. The Still-house, which is a neat building, well lighted, contains three old Pot Stills, and the usual Receivers and Chargers. On the opposite side of the road, on the sea shore, are several large bonded Warehouses, capable of holding 5,000 casks. The Whisky is pure Islay Malt, and part of it is shipped from Bruichladdich pier, the remainder floated out to the ships, ten casks being lashed together by iron pins and a chain called "dogs," and towed out by boatmen.

Mr. Miller is the general manager. The output in 1884-5 was 127,068 bulk gallons.

No. 41.

Bruichladdich Distillery, Islay.

PROPRIETORS, THE BRUICHLADDICH DISTILLERY COMPANY, LIMITED, ISLAY.

IN the afternoon we returned to Bridgend, calling at Bruichladdich on our way, as previously arranged. When we neared the Lighthouse, which is built on the margin of the sea, about a mile from Port Charlotte, we obtained a fine view of Islay House, called by the natives the White House, surrounded by its magnificent policies and stately woods, also the ridge of low hills on both sides of Lochindaal, which are cultivated in fine arable slopes almost to the edge of the sea. Day by day, as we get better acquainted with this fertile and interesting part of the island, we are convinced that it well deserves the appellation of the "Queen of the Hebrides." Bruichladdich is quite an aspiring and tastefully built village, and is planted on one of the finest and most healthy spots in Islay. The Distillery, which is two miles from Port Charlotte and six from Bridgend, was built in 1881, covers a little over two and a half acres of ground, and faces the sea It is a solid handsome structure in the form of a square, and entered through an archway, over which is a fine stone-built residence for the use of the partners when staying on the island.

Our inspection of this Distillery commenced at the Barley Lofts, two in number, both very spacious and airy, built above the Malting Floors, which in their turn are built over Bonded Warehouses, in one case of two storeys, and in the other of one. The barley, which is hoisted to these lofts in the usual manner, is thus conveniently placed for filling into the Steeps, which is effected by gravitation through iron shoots, which deliver it from different parts of the lofts.

We next visited the Malting Floors, which are laid with tiles, and connected with the Kiln by gangways, over which the malt, when ready for drying, is carried in bags. When dried it is placed in the Malt Deposit Room, situated immediately over the Mill House, and after being ground in the Mill, the ground Malt is conveyed by a long Elevator to the Grist Loft, which is in the Distillery buildings proper, and commands the Mash Tun, to which it is supplied through a Mashing Machine, in which the grist is mixed with hot water, thus obviating any dust rising in the Mash House, and facilitating the mashing process. The Mash House itself is a fine high room, containing a Mash Tun, 16½ feet in diameter by 6½ feet deep, the stirring gear of which, as indeed all the other machinery in this Distillery, is worked by a powerful steam engine, situated in the courtyard. There are also in this room two Brewing Tanks, an Underback, an intermediate Cooler, and a Morton's Refrigerator. The cooling of the worts in this machine is effected by cold water supplied from a large reservoir far up amongst

BRUICHLADDICH DISTILLERY, FROM THE SEA.

the hills, and from thence conducted in pipes, and is of sufficient pressure to rise to the Brewing Coppers, into which it flows at a high temperature, thus materially reducing the time and cost otherwise necessary to boil the water in these Coppers for mashing purposes. The worts, after passing through this refrigerator, run by gravitation to the Fermenting Backs, which consist of six large Tuns, situated in the adjoining Tun Room, each capable of fermenting 7,000 gallons; the fermentation completed, the Wash is pumped to the Wash Charger in the Still Room, and thence supplied to the Wash Still. In this Still Room, which is particularly cool and clean, all the firing of the Stills being done from the outside, there are two Stills, both heated by fire, capable of running over 3,000 gallons of spirit per week, besides the usual Feints and Low-wines Receivers and Chargers, and Spirit Receiver. From the Spirit Receiver the Whisky is run into a large vat in the Spirit Store and from this filled into casks for bonding.

The Distillery having been completed all at one time the buildings are more distinct and separate than in some of the other large works, where many additions have been made, the Malt Barns and Bonded Warehouses being entirely separate from the Kiln, Mill and Engine Room, as also from the Distillery buildings, thus insuring the greatest possible security against fire for the Whisky lying in Bond. Round the yard are six Warehouses, covering 30,000 square feet, all with good head room. The water used in the Distillery is brought from a reservoir in the hills, and is said to be of good quality. The make is Islay Malt, and is shipped to Glasgow by the steamers which leave the quay every Tuesday. Mr. Henry, the manager, resides on the premises. The annual output is 94,000 gallons.

No. 42.

Caol Ila Distillery, Islay.

PROPRIETORS, MESSRS. BULLOCH, LADE, & CO.

HOW pleasant is the process of exploration when performed in fine weather and in company with good companions. Our long day commenced with a stroll through the beautiful grounds of the Hotel and a climb up the steep hill in its rear. The haymakers were just commencing their work, and the air was laden with all the perfumes of early summer. It was a delicious morning, and as the light mists rolled away we could look out over the beautiful sea, from which the eye wandered to the gently undulating foreground, where patches of glittering green, and clumps of crimson rhododendrons guide the eye along the beautiful policies of Islay House. We felt that we could not leave the spot, but a signal from our coachman below compelled us to descend quickly, and mount the trim dog-cart for our drive of ten miles to Caol Ila. Away we go at a fine pace through the crisp air and glorious sunshine. The route lay through scenery of the most varied description; now we passed flourishing farmsteads and highly cultivated fields, then through tiny little villages nestling peacefully on the hillsides, while anon we catch glimpses from the hills, of lake and woodland. Ever since our residence upon the island we had been longing for a nearer view of the famous "Paps of Jura," and here they appeared before us, seeming to rise straight out of the sea, their base washed by the waters of the sound, which, looking so beautiful and yet so treacherous, rush between the two islands with a frightful rapidity. The Paps are generally enveloped in mist, but on this day their tops were seen distinctly, so bare, simple, and yet grand, in the clear atmosphere. On reaching Port Askaig we diverged from the highway into a mountain road. Here the driver directed our attention to an object about two miles away, which looked like a stump of a tree on a rock, but which he assured us was Caol Ila. On near acquaintance we discovered this to be the top of the chimney of the Distillery. After crossing a stream the route became more interesting; for miles

CAOL ILA DISTILLERY.

CAOL ILA DISTILLERY.

nothing met the eye but rolling hill slopes bare of bush or shrub, indented at a lower level with the loveliest little farmsteads, each surrounded with a few trees, all looking inexpressively homely and fertile, and then bursts upon our view an infinite expanse of sea, with Colonsay and other islands in the far distance. We soon came in sight of the Distillery lying directly beneath us, and we wonder for a moment how we are to get down to it. Our driver, however, knew the road well, for often had he been here before, and turning sharp to the right, we commenced the descent through a little hamlet of houses. But the way is so steep, and our nerves none of the best, that we insist upon doing the remainder of the descent on foot, much to the disgust of the driver, who muttered strange words in Gaelic. His remarks, however, are lost upon us, that language not having formed part of our education. As we descended the hill we paused now and then to gaze upon the far-stretching view before us, and to rest. Presently we found ourselves at the object of our search, and within a few yards of the sea. Caol Ila Distillery stands in the wildest and most picturesque locality we have seen. It is situated on the Sound of Islay, on the very verge of the sea, in a deep recess of the mountain, mostly cut out of the solid rock. The coast hereabouts is wild and broken, and detached pieces of rock lie here and there of such size that they form small islands.

Messrs. Bulloch, Lade & Co. have built a fine pier at which vessels can load or unload at any state of the tide, and besides the chartered vessels arriving with barley, &c., there are two of David MacBrayne's steamers calling here twice a week for Whisky. The buildings connected with the works are of solid construction and handsome appearance; they are all built of stone, hewn from the adjacent rocks.

The Distillery was built in the year 1846, and subsequently much extended and improved, and is arranged in the most modern style and possesses all the newest appliances used in the art of distilling. We had a letter of introduction to the manager, and were shown over the place by the brewer, whose explanations were most interesting. We were first conducted to the spacious Barns which are in close proximity to the landing stage. The barley is delivered on to the floors by means of a patent hydraulic hoist. The Barns are 120 feet long by 80 feet wide, the two lowest floors of which are used for malting purposes, and the two upper floors for storage of barley. Two cisterns are placed in the upper stories, of a steeping capacity of over 1,100 bushels; only the finest barley is used. There are two Kilns, one of which is about fifty feet square, and the other thirty-five feet, floored with hair-cloth, and the malt is dried with peat alone. Adjoining the Kilns, to the south of the premises, are three dried malt storage rooms, covering an area of 360 square yards. The Millroom is placed about the centre of the buildings on the ground floor, and contains a pair of friction rollers. After the malt is ground it is conveyed by means of elevators to the Grist Rooms above. These rooms have a storage accommodation for over 1,600 bushels of grist. The Mash-house and Still-house are combined and adjoin the Mill-room; it forms a very large square-built building which is beautifully kept and well lighted, and contains two brightly polished Stills and Spirit Safe, Spirits, Low-wines and Feints Receivers, Coppers for heating water, and Wash Charger. The Mash Tun is placed at one end of the building, over which is fixed a Patent Mashing Machine in which the grist and hot water mix together before reaching the Mash Tun, where it is again broken up and mixed afresh by the patent revolving metal rakes. The Mash Tun is of a mashing capacity of 500 bushels. The Underback is a large cast-iron vessel of almost equal size. A patent centrifugal pump connects this vessel and conveys the worts to the Wort Receiver situated in the Tun Room, which we next visited. This is a beautiful room and contains quite an array of Wash Backs, and a Patent Refrigerator. The Worm Tub adjoins the Still House and is a huge wooden vessel containing an endless variety of copper worms, supplied with cold water from the mountain stream. The Draff House faces the Sound of Islay, in close proximity to the wharf where the draff is stored previous to shipment. On the opposite side of the yard stands the Spirit Store, wherein are two huge Vats for collecting the Whisky previous to its being filled into casks. Our guide next directed us to the Duty Free Warehouses of which there are three, capable of holding nearly 2,000 casks.

The water used, said to be the finest in Islay, comes in the form of a crystal stream from a lovely lake called Torrabus, nestling among the mountains, over which ever and anon the fragrant breeze from the myrtle and blooming heather is wafted. This lake yields a never failing supply of this most essential factor in Distillation. We need not describe the suitable Cooperage and artisan shops, which are all perfect. The engine and steam boiler powers are highly efficient, and are evidently planned with a view to future extension. Comfortable dwellings have been provided for the employés, forming quite a little village in themselves, and we envied the healthy life of these men and their families.

The annual output is over 147,000 gallons, and the Whisky is sold in Scotland, England and the chief foreign markets, where the make speaks for itself. We understand that such is the demand for this favourite Whisky, that the orders much exceed the output, and have to be allocated amongst buyers at the commencement of each Distilling season.

There is a complete system of Hydrants with sets of hose and reel at all commanding points of the buildings. The Counting Houses form an imposing edifice fronting the Sound of Islay, the ground floor of which is occupied by the Inland Revenue officers, and the upper portion by the Manager and a staff of clerks. The Head Office of this Distillery is at 4, Bothwell Street, Glasgow, where all business is transacted.

We now bid farewell to this charming spot hoping that some future day will bring us an opportunity of a revisit to Caol Ila.

No. 43.

Bunnahabhain Distillery, Islay.

PROPRIETORS, THE ISLAY DISTILLERY COMPANY, LIMITED.

48, WEST NILE STREET, GLASGOW.

AFTER a short rest at Port Askaig, we drove to Bunnahabhain, three miles further on, over a winding mountain road, from which at various points and turns, most enchanting views were obtained. On the left nothing could be seen but rough hilly pasture, made picturesque by an occasional farmsteading or cottar's shieling, and by numerous herds of hardy Highland cattle—black, white, red and tawny, with fierce red eyes and enormous horns—which feed and sleep amongst the green brackens and purple heather on the hillside. Far below on the right runs the swift current of the Sound of Islay, which is here so rapid that a boat manned by four powerful Islesmen can make no headway against it. Beyond this silver streak is seen the west side of Jura, with its rugged hills of curious geological construction, while away to the north and west the island of Colonsay presents its well worn cliffs to receive the surly salutations of the wild Atlantic.

About a mile from the Distillery the rough hill road is joined by one which leads in serpentine curves downwards to the bay. This road was entirely constructed by the Company, and is as good as it was costly; but, although indispensable, the greater portion of it is not much used for heavy traffic, the extensive import and export being entirely by sea. The Company have several steamers constantly chartered for the purpose of carrying barley and coals, while Mr. MacBrayne's steamer "Islay," calls weekly with general stores, and loads Whisky for the return voyage. To enable the work of loading and discharging to be expeditiously performed, the Company have erected a commodious and handsome pier at a cost of about £3,500. It extends about 75 yards into the bay, built upon massive iron piles sunk deeply into the solid rock, and everything used in its construction is of the same metal. The depth of water is at all times sufficient to allow steamers to load and discharge on both sides of the pier.

Ten years ago there were but few Distilleries in Islay, but the increasing demand for this valuable make of Whisky for blending purposes, encouraged further enterprise in the extension of existing Distilleries and the erection of new ones. One of the most successful of these new ventures being the subject of our sketch.

The Bunnahabhain Distillery was built in the year 1881, and is situated on the bay of that name. At that time this portion of the island was bare,

BUNNAHABHAIN DISTILLERY.

and uninhabited, but the prosecution of the distilling industry has transformed it into a life-like and civilized colony. The works have a frontage towards the bay, and command a fine view of the opposite shore, and the celebrated "Paps of Jura." The Distillery proper is a fine pile of buildings in the form of a square, and quite enclosed. Entering by a noble gateway one forms an immediate sense of the compactness and systematical construction of the work. The southern wing is four storeys in height, the ground floor being occupied as a Warehouse, the second and third floors as Malt Barns, and the upper floor as a Grain Loft. The barley is raised to the Granary by means of Elevators driven by steam, and propelled by a screw working within a case, to any part of the Loft; the discharge being provided for by an adjustment of the openings of the case. The malt is likewise conveyed to the Kilns in a similar manner, and much waste of grain is thus prevented, as barrows are entirely dispensed with. We believe this is the only Distillery in Islay that has adopted this method of elevating the barley and loading the Kilns. At the eastern end of the Loft is the Steep, from which the moistened grain can be passed down to the Malt floors by simply raising some movable plates in the bottom. Two spacious Kilns occupy the angle of the building, and instead of the old fashioned close brick fire-places, they are furnished with open *chauffeurs*, from which the heated air ascends to the floor on which the malt is spread; this floor is of wire netting covered with hair-cloth. Nothing but peat is used in the Kilns, which is dug in the district, and is of exceptionally fine quality. A large quantity of this peat is always kept stored, so that only that which has become thoroughly matured is used, this is a very important consideration in drying the malt, as well-seasoned peat is free from the sulphurous matter which it contains when newly dug.

The western wing is of three storeys and contains Cooperage, Coal Shed, Mill Room, Malt Deposit, and Mash House. In the northern wing is situated the Engine House, Boilers and Still House; the latter a vast open building, containing the Cooler, into which the worts are forced by a centrifugal pump; the Refrigerator, one of Morton's best; the six Backs, or Fermenting Tuns each capable of containing 6,000 gallons; the Wash Charger of similar capacity; the Wash Still holding 6,000 gallons, and the Spirit Still, holding 3,000 gallons; and other necessary utensils. The Spirit Store adjoins the Still House. All the plant is of the newest and most approved description, and is erected on the gravitation system. The water is such as delights the heart of a Distiller, being of a soft peaty nature; it is obtained from a stream which is fed by Loch Staoinsha, and is collected in a concrete Reservoir some little distance from the works, being thence conveyed by pipes.

The Feu extends to fully 20 acres, and it has all been substantially fenced. Adjoining the works there are several large Warehouses, and commodious Offices; also Rooms for the Revenue Officers and the Company's Clerks. Neat villas have been erected on the rising ground in the rear of the Distillery for the Excise Officers, and two large ranges of houses provide ample accommodation for the workmen. A Reading Room and School Room have likewise, with praiseworthy liberality, been provided by the Company, and in the latter the children of the workmen receive an elementary education. There are fifty to seventy hands employed throughout the season.

The annual produce of Bunnahabhain Distillery is about 200,000 gallons and the registered Offices of the Company are in Glasgow.

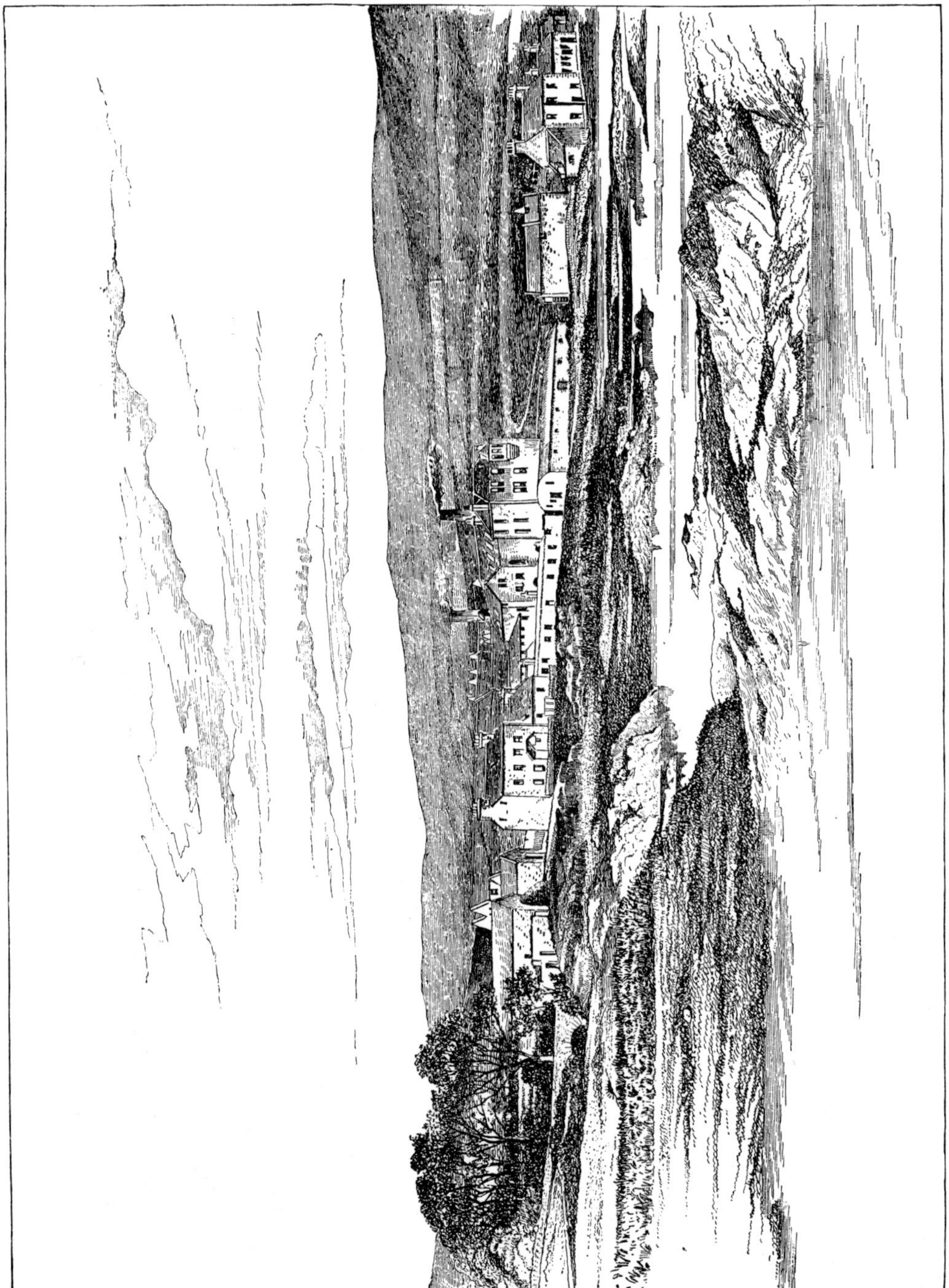

JURA DISTILLERY.

No. 44.

Jura Distillery, Island of Jura.

PROPRIETORS, JAMES FERGUSON & SONS.

FROM Tarbert we reached Jura by Mr. MacBrayne's steamer "Fingal," which leaves the mails every Monday. The route was for the most part the same as that traversed on our journey to Islay. The name of Jura recalls to our memories just such a lovely day as when, standing on the pier at Caol Ila, we first saw the island across the Islay Sound. The appearance of Jura from this position is very romantic, the mountains rising precipitately from the sea, some of them to the height of 2,500 feet above sea level. Three of these monster rocks are called "Paps of Jura," so named from their peculiar shape. Upon these majestic heights no trees strike root, and here and there beetling crags project, with no shadow to break their terrible ruggedness, whilst at their base are everywhere strewn gigantic boulders. The principal denizens of these weird rocks are eagles, red deer, and grouse. The Island of Jura is thirty miles long and seven broad, and contains a population of nearly a thousand persons. Its bays possess all the charms of Oban in miniature, and the mountain lochs team with trout. Craighouse, where the Distillery is planted, is on the eastern or habitable side of the island, and is the only place that can be called a village. It stands at the head of a small bay, and boasts of a handsome pier, which was erected by Messrs. James Ferguson & Sons. On landing we immediately proceeded to the Distillery, accompanied by Mr. Fraser, the courteous manager, who had met us at the boat. As there were yet several hours before sunset we took the opportunity of exploring the surroundings of the Distillery, and visited the Craig burn and waterfall. Then, at the suggestion of Mr. Fraser, we directed our steps to the three lochs, or watersheds, which feed the magnificent burn flowing past the Distillery. We ascended the hill at the back and found a path which ran along the banks of the burn, and although up hill and down dale, it proved a very pleasant ramble. The burn danced merrily over its rocky bed, making innumerable falls and cascades, and we were struck with the brightness and purity of the water. After an hour's toilsome ascent we reached the largest of the lochs, situated about three miles from the Distillery, and a magnificent view presented itself when we reached these heights. Looking above and below the scene embraced extremes of fertility and desolation: above, sterile rocks, over which clouds and mist hung which were sometimes lifted, and revealed tremendous masses of rock projecting from the lofty mountain above; below, well cultivated crofters' holdings and the rich verdure of the lower stretches of the mountain were revealed. Returning by another way we passed the two smaller lochs already referred to, abounding in trout preserved by the proprietors of the Distillery. It was now evening, but we were nearly home, and our path, if not well lighted was beautified by the soft light of the setting sun. On reaching the house which Mr. Ferguson had courteously placed at our disposal during our visit to the island, we found a meal ready, to which, after the long walk, we brought a good appetite. In Jura the inhabitants are beyond the reach of anything but dairy produce, potatoes and fish ; occasionally a mountain sheep is killed and divided among the community, but, as a rule, it is a question of a daily forage for a day's supply of food. We were, however, quite content with the repast provided. Rising early the next morning we proceeded to inspect the establishment. It is one of the handsomest we have seen, and from the bay looks more like a castle than a Distillery. It is the highest building on the island, and the most elevated portion forms the summer residence of the proprietors.

The works cover nearly three acres of ground, and are situated close to the pier, and a beautifully wooded glen. The Distilling and Mashing House consist of a lofty and solid stone block of buildings, which are visible for many miles round, and attached thereto are the old Maltings and Warehouses, which are built round a courtyard. The new Maltings are pitched higher up the slopes of the hill, but nevertheless they communicate with the other parts of the works. There is no steam engine on the premises, all the work being done by water and gravitation. The works are entirely enclosed by the buildings, and entrance thereto is obtained through a gateway facing the sea. The Distillery, which was established in the year 1810, came into the hands of Messrs. James Ferguson and Sons in the year 1875, who immediately set about its restoration, and have added new buildings, machinery, and appliances of the most modern description, at a cost of over £25,000 ; the establishment is now said to be one of the easiest worked Distilleries in the district.

The buildings have a frontage to the sea of some 500 feet, and are arranged in several sections, the central and lofty building already referred to being the Distillery proper. We first visited the No. 1 Maltings at the top of the hill, a granite structure consisting of three floors 138 feet long and 48 feet broad, the top floor of which is used for storing barley, and will hold 4,000 quarters. The middle floor, for malting, is paved with tiles, and the metal Steep connected therewith is placed on the upper floor, and wets 140 quarters at one time, discharging its contents from the bottom ; the lower floor is a Warehouse. At the north end there is a Kiln 48 feet square, floored with steel wire netting—Hermann's patent. It is lighted by six windows, possesses four patent ventilators, and has two entrances enclosed by double iron doors.

Passing on to the adjoining chamber, we found ourselves in the Malt Deposit, the top floor of a wing of the central and main building, an apartment 120 feet long, and so arranged that it is commanded by both Kilns. The Mill and Mash House are underneath. We next descended to the ground floor, and crossed a terrace to the No. 2 Maltings lower down ; they are of the same dimensions as the new Maltings already described, and originally formed part of the old Distillery. There is also another Malting of smaller dimensions, with a Warehouse below.

We were next taken to the Mill, which contains a pair of Malt Crushers, and from thence to the Grist Loft, in which there are two large Grist Hoppers, which feed the Mash-tun. Still descending, we then passed on to the Brewing House, a neat building 35 feet long by 25 feet broad, which contains a metal Mash-tun 20 feet in diameter by 5 feet deep, with stirring gear driven by the water-wheel ;

here also we observed two Heating Tanks, holding together 3,000 gallons, which supply hot water to a Mashing-machine, which mixes the grist before it reaches the Mash-tun. From the Tun the worts are pumped to a Receiver or Underback in the Tun Room, holding 8,000 gallons, and afterwards pass through the two Morton's Refrigerators fixed on a staging above, called the Cooler House. We should here add that the sparge and draff are pumped up to a second Mash-tun, where they are drained off into two Heating Tanks to be mixed with the next grist. The Tun Room, which forms part of the Still House, is at the eastern end, and is one of the loftiest houses we have yet seen; it is 60 feet high, 100 long, and 44 broad, and lighted by twelve windows. Therein are four Washbacks, each holding 13,000 gallons, and a Wash Charger of the same capacity, the latter so placed that it commands the Stills. Our attention was then directed to the three Pot Stills—one of them, a Wash Still, contains 6,650 gallons; the other two, which are Spirit Stills, hold 2,350 and 1,200 gallons respectively. On a second gallery we observed the Spirit Receiver, a handsome vessel holding 5,000 gallons, and the Low-wines and Feints Charger, holding 6,034 gallons, and the Safe. The wheel which drives the Still rummagers is 18 inches wide and 12 feet in diameter, and is placed below the Worm Tubs. The two latter vessels are elevated on brick piers 40 feet from the ground, and are supplied with water direct from the stream. Leaving the larger building, we turned to the left, and reached the Spirit Store, a new cement building 50 feet square, which contains a Vat holding 673 gallons, and the weighing apparatus, and afterwards inspected the four Warehouses, wherein the Whisky is stored. One of them is 165 feet by 150 feet broad, and the whole together will store 5,500 casks. At the time of our visit they held 3,504 casks, containing 232,000 gallons of Whisky of various ages. The Boiler House is contiguous to the Distilling House, and contains a steam boiler, 22 feet long and 5 feet in diameter, for heating water; there is only one pump on the premises. The Turbine water-wheel was erected by Messrs. Smith & Co., of Glasgow; it is of simple construction, and yet wonderful power, and capable of flooding the whole place in ten minutes. It is sunk just opposite an excavation in the burn called the smuggler's hole, lately filled up, the entrance to which is now covered with ferns. It is the very place where the smuggling founder of the Distillery, a century ago, for many years carried on his operations without discovery; and the tiny stream, tapped from the burn which ran through the centre of the cave, had to be stopped up by the present owners, when the hole was filled up. Opposite there is a fine Cooperage and carpenter's shop, also a cask shed. The manager, Mr. William Fraser, resides on the premises, and Mr. John Mulqueen, the Excise officer, dwells in a house built on the water's edge. The workmen's houses form the street of the village, and they have small plots of ground allotted to them by the Distillers, which are splendidly cultivated. The small farm attached to the Distillery is only twenty acres, but quite sufficient for the requirements of the fine cart horses and few beasts kept by the proprietors.

The Whisky is pure Highland Malt, and the annual output in 1884-85 was 60,339 gallons, 1885-86 65,000 gallons, but the works are capable of making 180,000 gallons.

We had just finished our tour of inspection when the steamer hove in sight, Mr. MacBrayne having permitted the captain to call for us. Bidding good-bye to our friends, we left Jura with regret, cherishing in our hearts the hope that we might return at some future day.

No. 45.

Glendarroch Distillery, Ardrishaig.

PROPRIETOR, WILLIAM GILLIES.

WE left Greenock on the morning of the 26th of July by the "Columba," one of Mr. David MacBrayne's swift passenger steamers, bound for the Distillery that heads this chapter. The boats on this route are fitted up with every imaginable convenience and contrivance for the comfort of passengers. On board there is a post office, with telegraph and money order departments; a daintily stocked fruit shop, bookstall, and a magnificent dining saloon. In addition to the "Columba" there is the "Iona" and "Grenadier," and one or other of these steamers takes this route daily throughout the year. The scenery on the journey is most picturesque and varied, and it would be difficult to find a more romantic district than that round about and on either side of the Kyles of Bute. The grand background of hills with shady vales nestling on their slopes, the beautiful deep waters of the lochs with their pretty sea-side retreats, combine to make this one of the most popular of Mr. MacBrayne's "summer tours."

ARDRISHAIG.

We reached Ardrishaig at one p.m., and after securing quarters at the hotel, made our way to Glendarroch, distant about half a mile. The Distillery is planted on the banks of the far-famed Crinan Canal, and is quite an object of curiosity to the thousands of tourists who, on board the celebrated little canal steamer "Linnet," pass by on their way to Oban. It is built at the foot of the Robber's Glen which runs upwards from the banks of the canal into the heart of the hills in the background; this glen was once the haunt of smugglers, and no more romantic spot could have been chosen for a Distillery. The Darroch, a burn which might almost be called a river, issues from the higher hills and flows through the glen, falling in its onward course over numerous rocks; reaching the grounds of Glendarroch it forms a lovely cascade falling seventy feet, and dashes over other rocks into a trout pool below; then, passing through a tunnel beneath the canal, it finds its way to the sea.

From the back walls of the Distillery the ground rises in the form of a steep thickly-wooded hill, where ferns and blue bells grow in rich luxuriance. We scrambled up the zig-zag path for about a quarter of a mile, frequently, to keep the path, having to stoop low under bending trees that had overgrown the track. Crossing the burn by a rustic bridge we climbed higher up the glen, where, amid trees of every shade of green and sylvan beauty, and the air filled with the rich perfume of hawthorn and lilacs rising from the luxuriant gardens below, one is lost in a scene of indescribable charm and beauty. Above are the higher hills covered with heather; below a vast stretch of the waters of the loch

DISTILLERY AND S.S. "LINNET," CRINAN CANAL, GLENDARROCH.

to the sea beyond. On the opposite side stands Kilmory Castle, with a background of mountains shading from green to purple, some parts thickly wooded, and the whole tinged with a roseate suffusion of the setting sun. This lovely wooded glen is a favourite resort of tourists and artists, but in olden days, as before stated, smugglers located themselves here, where, defying the law, they made a celebrated Whisky which was in great demand. Tradition says that there is a smuggler imprisoned in the heart of the hill, who is kept in durance vile by the avenging spirit of a revenue officer whose life he took. He is allowed to come forth once a year at midnight, on the anniversary of the day upon which the crime was committed, and should he then happen to meet the spirit of the comrade who betrayed him to the officers of the law, the spell would be broken and he released.

Proceeding on our way, every turn in the pathway brings out fresh views of the valley, and causes us to linger here far longer than the brief time appointed for our sojourn by our friends waiting below. It is a spot of enchantment, and no wonder that such a scene should excite us to enthusiasm when recalling those days spent at Ardrishaig. Descending the hill by another pathway we cross by stepping-stones over the Ard Burn which adds to the water supply of the Distillery. It runs from a loch three miles distant, higher up the hill, and we noticed that it was dammed up in several places where it is filtered over fine stones and gravel, eventually falling into a circular concreted reservoir on a level with the top of the works.

GLENDARROCH RESERVOIR.

The Glendarroch Distillery covers three acres of ground, and is solidly built of stone in the form of a quadrangle, with a frontage of 500 feet to the canal. We entered the enclosure through a gateway, which has a running door sliding to the right and left, and were courteously received by Mr. Hunter, the manager, who conducted us over the works. He informed us that the barley is brought to the Distillery by canal, and the vessels discharge it at the Granary doors. The water from the Achnagbreach Hill, before referred to, is used for distilling purposes, and that from the loch and Darroch Burn for driving power.

We first visited the Granary and Maltings, which are on the left of the quadrangle as you enter. They consist of a lofty two-storied building, measuring 131 feet by 48 feet, and at the western end there is a fine concrete Steep capable of wetting 66 quarters of barley at one time; a small part of the upper floor is also used for malting purposes, but the larger portion is for storing the barley, and is capable of holding 2,000 quarters of barley ; the grain is hoisted direct from the ships in the canal to the Barley Loft. At the end of this building there is a new Kiln, one of the finest we have seen in this part of Scotland, it is 51 feet square, floored with wire cloth, and heated with peats only, dug from the neighbouring moors. The malt is delivered by a steam hoist to the Kiln floor, which, when loaded, dries 1,000 bushels at one time. The dried malt is thrown through a shoot direct on to the floor of the Malt Deposit, the top floor of the adjoining building which forms the centre of the quadrangle, and facing the main entrance, it is 48 feet long by 40 feet broad, and the lower story is used for No. 3 Bonded Warehouse. Our guide next conducted us through a doorway direct on to the top floor of the Mill Building, which forms the Grist Loft, a chamber 50 feet by 30 feet, having a large hopper on one side. Underneath is the Mill which contains a pair of metal rollers driven by steam; here also is the engine department. The pulverized malt is lifted by elevators to the Grist hopper above, already referred to. As will be seen, the process of Whisky making in this establishment is mostly done by gravitation, and works round the quadrangle, ending in the Spirit Store.

Passing into the next building we find ourselves on the central platform of the Mash House, where there are two timber heating tanks, each holding 5,000 gallons. The first object that attracted our attention was a Steel's Mashing Machine, which is fed from the hopper in the Grist Loft. Descending to the ground floor we come to the Mash Tun, a vessel 17 feet in diameter and 6½ feet deep; enclosed within it there is a treble acting stirring gear driven by the water wheel. At our left, and under the floor, is the metal Underback, 11½ feet in diameter and 5½ deep, with a semi-circular opening guarded by a railing,

THE CRINAN CANAL, AT GLENDARROCH.

and underneath this vessel is the box of the Wort Pump, the only one in the premises, all else, besides pumping the worts, being done by gravitation.

The Draff from the Mash-tun falls through a sluice into a hopper below, and is removed by water power straight into the Draff House in the outer yard. The Mash House is a capital building 60 feet high, 39 feet broad, and 27 feet long.

All the old-fashioned coolers have long since been done away with, and the worts are now pumped up to a Miller's Refrigerator, fixed in the roof of the neighbouring building, and copper pipes run the worts direct from thence into the Fermenting Tuns. Ascending a staircase, we found ourselves in the Tun Room, some 10 feet above the level of the Mash-tun; it is 40 feet square, well lighted, and contains five Washbacks, averaging 5,500 gallons each; the switches therein are driven by a second water-wheel, to keep the liquor in motion during the process of fermentation. The floor underneath is occupied as No. 4 Warehouse.

We then passed through the Brewing Department and entered the Still House, considered by some to be a model of its kind. It is 65 feet long, 40 feet broad, and 60 feet high; its walls are painted white, and it is lighted by eleven large windows. At the eastern end, on a level with the bottom of the Washbacks, is the Wash Charger, a timber dish holding 6,000 gallons, to which the wash runs by gravitation. On the floor of the house are three "sma' Pot Stills," a Wash Still holding 4,726 gallons, and two Low-wines Stills; one of them holds 1,000 gallons, and the other 500. The Worm Tub is at the back of the house, and in close proximity to the Darroch. It is a fine timber vessel raised on piers, and fed by a continuous stream of cold water from the reservoir; it forms a conspicuous object from the canal, as will be seen in the illustration, and occasions many a question from tourists who are uninitiated in the mysteries of distillation, as to its use and purpose.

GLENDARROCH DISTILLERY.

We now ascended a flight of steps to a large gallery overlooking the canal and the beautiful Loch Fyne. Here there are placed two Feints Receivers, the No. 1 holding 1,571, and the No. 2, 1,549 gallons; also two Spirit Receivers, No. 1 holding 1,544, and No. 2, 500 gallons.

Besides the Safe and Sampling Safe, we noticed a portable fire engine and other appliances for the speedy extinguishment and prevention of fire. We were informed that Glendarroch is considered by the Excise authorities to be one of the most complete Distilleries in the district.

Following the course of the Whisky, we proceeded to the Spirit Store, a neat, light little building, which contains a Spirit Vat holding 3,248 gallons, and an Ullage Vat 231 gallons, the weighing apparatus, and an office for the Excise clerks. There are four large Warehouses, capable of containing 2,000 casks, and others at Waterloo Street, Glasgow, where also are to be found the Public Offices of the Distillery. Continuing our inspection of Glendarroch, we next visited the Engine Department; it contains a very handsome 25-horse power engine, and a steam boiler 31 feet long by $7\frac{1}{2}$ feet in diameter; and afterwards the Manager's and Excise offices; the former is over the Spirit Store, and the latter over No. 1 Warehouse. Glengilp House, the residence of a former proprietor of the Distillery, is now occupied by the manager, and the large old-fashioned garden, crowded with fruit trees and flowers, which stretches down to the canal banks, has been divided between that gentleman and the two Excise officers, Mr. Gillies having provided these latter with picturesque houses opening into same. In the park there are also eight houses for the workmen, each with a small plot of ground. The delightful meadows which skirt Glengilp House are in the occupation of Mr. Gillies, and produce unusually heavy crops of hay of fine quality.

GLENDARROCH WATERFALL.

At the back of the establishment, and convenient to the Kiln, is a large Peat Shed, containing upwards of 500 tons of peat ready for use. Near the Worm Tub, and facing the burn there is a large Cooperage, stables, and cart sheds.

The house of Glendarroch, which has lately been acquired by Mr. Gillies, and used by him as a summer residence, is on the other side of the waterfall. It stands in lovely grounds, and is almost hidden by trees; climbing over its walls and roof are roses of every variety, and hanging over the path which leads to it fuschia trees, 8 feet high, under which you walk, testify to the mildness of the climate in this district.

At the back of the estate rises a small park, from which delightful views can be obtained of the extensive and celebrated demesne of Auchindarroch, which immediately adjoins. It is a place of sequestered beauty unequalled in the district, and it skirts the canal for a considerable distance, forming a fringe of brushwood and trees festooned with honeysuckle and other trailing plants, familiar to all who have passed along this lovely route on their way to Oban and the north.

The Whisky made in the Glendarroch Distillery is pure Highland Malt, and the annual output is 80,000 gallons.

The sinking sun warned us that it was time to take our departure, so we stepped into the Distillery boat, and were quickly taken across the canal to our quarters on the opposite shore, where we donned our "war paint," and proceeded to the house of Glendarroch to enjoy the hospitality of its owner.

No. 46.

Oban Distillery, Oban.

PROPRIETOR, WALTER HIGGIN.

THE next afternoon we left Ardrishaig behind us and embarked on board the "Linnet," as pretty and comfortable a boat as sails on any canal in the kingdom. We steamed through the Crinan Canal, on which there are fifteen locks, and a delightful time we had. There were four of us, and how we all revelled in the glory of that summer day's procession; now we would alight from the boat and walk into the woods, or hasten forward and refresh ourselves with milk and wild strawberries, vended on the canal banks, or return to the boat to the next lock and smoke a cigar. It was quite easy to keep pace with the steamer, and most of our fellow passengers exercised themselves in this way.

After leaving the locks, the canal winds round the beautiful wooded ridge of Knapdale, and we are in the land of spells and witchcraft. Here, thirty-four years ago, the last *known* witch was burned. Start not, gentle reader, it was neither by the law nor Judge Lynch she suffered. She was a masculine kind of old woman, and said to have been tall and strong as most men. Sarah of the bog, as she was called, was extensively engaged in smuggling, and unlike Meg Merrilies, she had *not* borne twelve "buirdly sons and daughters," but had lived like Queen Bess—"in maiden meditation fancy free." To cover up her illicit traffic, she practised necromancy, and the inhabitants of the district being very superstitious, propitiated her good graces by providing peats, potatoes, and meal, and many instances of the belief in her powers and the manner in which she levied her contributions were related to us. But Sarah grew old, and having acquired the taste for stimulants amid the exciting scenes of her youth, like Neil Gow, she

"Dearly lo'ed the whisky, oh,"

and regularly dosed herself with the contents of her whisky keg. One night she drank too much, stumbled and fell into the fire, and when the house was next visited, the miserable creature was found with her head black and burned to a cinder.

At the next bend of the canal we came in sight of Kilmahumaig, or the tomb of St. Omaig, a bold promontory; and for a moment only, the small canonical mound called Dundonald, where tradition saith, the Lords of the Isles were wont to sit, in their periodical visits to Knapdale, to deliver judgment on offenders. And now the "Linnet" has reached Crinan, and the "Chevalier" Captain McMillan, lies at the wharf with her "blue peter" flying, indicating that all was ready for a start. As we stepped on board the welcome sound of the dinner-bell sent us all below to the dining saloon, where we found as sumptuous a repast as could be served at any hotel. When we reached the deck again the steamer was passing through some of the most interesting scenery on the route. It was such a perfect day that we found it difficult to leave the deck, even when pressed by our cheery companions Cruickshank and Cook, of Edinburgh, who occasionally dived down to the saloon to taste the drink of their country. We reached Oban at seven o'clock in the evening, taking the road up to our hotel by a route which passed the Distillery we had come to visit. The Craigard Hotel is pitched on the top of a rock, and the view therefrom is signally fine. It commands a sort of bird's eye view of the town and bay, and when we reached the terrace in front we stopped to gaze at the scene below. On the water all was life and gaiety as far as the eye could reach, and innumerable boats were seen studding the surface of the sea, and vessels of all descriptions and sizes from the light skiff to the biggest yacht; whilst the streets and promenade were crowded with people and enlivened with music.

The next morning we descended the hill by a pathway through the grounds of the hotel down to the sea, and from thence bent our steps to the Oban Distillery. It is a quaint old-fashioned work, and dates back prior to the existence of the town, having been built in the year 1794. The establishment covers two acres of ground, and is entered from the main street by a pair of timber gates. It was built by the family of Stevenson, the founders of the town of Oban, which previous to their advent was only a small fishing village. The Distillery consists of an oblong set of buildings, with three sectional annexes, which have been added by the present proprietor. He has also made vast improvements in the machinery and appliances, and built two new bonded Warehouses. We gained access to the establishment by an old-fashioned stair thrown across the basement cutting, which leads from the road to the clerks', manager's, and Distillery offices. These are all contiguous and mostly under one roof, and were formerly the residence of the Stevensons; a part of the sitting room was made to project over into the Still House, and we were shown the "peep-hole" door through which the proprietor could watch the progress of the work. We made the tour of inspection under the guidance of Mr. James Gordon. This gentleman is a nephew of the late Mr. Smith, of Cragganmore, and his father was the pioneer of distilling in the north, serving at one time as brewer and distiller to as many as seven Distilleries in the Glenlivet district, and taking each in turn. The Oban work is quite enclosed, and built under a rock, which rises 400 feet, and is festooned with creepers and ivy. The water supply is from two lochs in Ardconnel, one mile above Oban, the waters of which are collected from the peaty uplands, and are reputed to be of splendid quality.

We first bent our steps to the outer courtyard, on two sides of which, in the form of a triangle, are the Granaries and Malt-barns. They are built with stone, and, being nearly a century old, have a very ancient appearance. An outside stone staircase gives access to the two upper floors, which are used for storing the barley. The ground floors are concreted, and each possesses a stone Steep. At the end of the building there is a Kiln, which is 30 feet square, and is floored with wire cloth. It is heated with peats, enclosed in an old-fashioned brick furnace. The sides of this enclosure are very spacious, and are used for storing and drying the peat; there is besides on the hill, a large shed which contained sufficient for two years' consumption. On a level with the floor of the Kiln and communicating therewith is a Malt Deposit 50 feet long and 27 feet wide, capable of storing 400 quarters of malt. At this place the raw material changes its residence from one side of the quadrangle to the other, and a rustic timber bridge has been thrown across the way, over which the dried malt is wheeled to the Mill building attached to the Brewing House. The latter is two stories high, the basement containing the malt cylinders and mill machinery, driven by steam. The top flat is used as the Grist Loft, and contains a hopper, into which the pulverized malt is tipped before passing through the Mashing-machine. We next followed our guide through a narrow doorway, and found ourselves on a platform overlooking the Mash House, whereon are placed two antiquated timber Heating Coppers, holding together 2,000 gallons, and a sparger. Descending to the floor, we are shown the Mash-tun, a peculiar little metal vessel standing on the ground; it is 9 feet in diameter and 5½ feet deep, containing the usual stirring gear driven by steam. Mr. Gordon here drew our attention to a loft over head, where is placed the Worts Receiver, to which we ascended and obtained a view of the Coolers; they consist of an open shallow tank forming the inside roof of the Tun-room. From this receptacle the worts run by gravitation into the Washbacks. Descending a few steps, we then passed through an archway direct into the Tun Room, a building by itself, bearing indisputable marks of antiquity. It contains seven Washbacks, each holding 1,200 gallons. We next proceeded to the Still House, passing under a gallery on which is placed the Wash Charger, which holds 1,200 gallons, and the Worm Tub and Water supply, one of them of singular construction and position. It consists of a narrow timber trough or tank high up in the air, stretching right across the yard, and contains an enclosed pipe, leading direct from the lade through which runs a continuous stream to the worms, and passing out on the other side, the water is utilized to turn the rummager of the Wash Still. We had seen the Still House before from the distiller's parlour, but on entering it from the court, and observing its walls and roof, it presented the appearance of a monastic building. It contains two old Pot Stills, one a Wash Still holding 1,000 gallons, the other a Spirit Still holding 500 gallons, both heated by fire, and the rummagers therein driven by water from the Worm Tub. There is a platform running across the old building, on which are placed the Low-wines and Feints Charger and Safe, and in the adjoining chamber are the Receivers. Following our guide, we next entered the Spirit Store, which forms the basement of the offices, and was formerly the distiller's kitchen. It contains a Spirit Vat of 1,200 gallons content, and the casking appliances. Opposite there is a small Cooperage and cask shed; also a 10-horse power engine, which has been at work upwards of forty years, and shows no signs of decay; also a steam boiler, 14 feet long and 5 feet in diameter. Distributed about the premises are four Warehouses; two of them are newly built, and although not of large dimensions, are of great height and solid construction. That most recently finished is three stories high, and measures 60 feet by 30 feet, and will hold 60,000 gallons of Whisky. Lower down the hill there is a second building, also of three stories, 78 feet by 30 feet. These new Warehouses are fitted up with fixed gauntrees on every floor, the timber supports of which are most substantial, and run from the ground to the roof, so that they will bear any weight, and help to support the building; they are all arranged so that any cask can be removed without affecting its neighbour. The whole of the Warehouses together will store 3,500 casks.

The Whisky is not only pure Highland Malt, but a good self Whisky, and the annual output is 35,000 gallons.

No. 47.

Tobermory Distillery, Island of Mull.

PROPRIETORS, MACKILL BROS.

THE voyage from Oban to Tobermory in fine weather is one of the pleasantest imaginable; the scenery is described in many of the guide books, but none of them have ever done it justice. After passing the ruins of Aros Castle, we obtained a fine view of Benmore, 3,097 feet above sea level, the highest mountain in Mull, and for the next two hours we feasted our eyes on scenery of surpassing beauty. Steaming round the island of Calve, we entered the bay, at the head of which stands Tobermory, "the Well of our Lady St. Mary."

The Island of Mull is uneven and mountainous, but nevertheless the soil is deep and fertile, therefore better adapted for pasturage than Skye, to which island it bears great resemblance. It has, however, a very boisterous coast, a wet and stormy climate, and an unpromising and trackless surface, redeemed by a few sheltered spots here and there at the heads of bays or indents of the sea. In ancient times woods were so numerous in Mull as to be celebrated for their extent and beauty, but with the exception of Tobermory they have long since vanished. The mountains rise in terraces, by stages from the shore, the highest being Benmore, which we saw from the boat; the next, Benychat, 2,294 feet above sea level.

The town of Tobermory is encircled by high precipitous banks, above which the ground rises in a series of gentle sloping hills. There is a good steamboat quay, well served by Mr. MacBrayne's swift steamers from Glasgow and Oban. Formerly the communication was once a week, now it is daily throughout the year. The Island of Mull is generally mountainous and bare, but in the vicinity of Tobermory the scenery is very beautiful and romantic. To the left of the town is Drumfin, better known by the name of St. Mary's Lake, one of the most charming spots in the district, and Drumfin Castle, situated between two beautifully wooded hills. In close proximity is the celebrated St. Mary's Well, a spring of the purest water, dedicated ages ago to the Blessed Virgin, and there are many persons still living in Tobermory who not only venerate it, but still use its waters in preference to all other and nearer sources, for domestic purposes. Tobermory Bay is protected from the winds and waves by the island of Calve, which renders it one of the most secure havens on the coast; whilst for beauty of position and surroundings the little picturesque town, with its richly wooded shores, will compare favourably with Oban.

Sacheveril says of Tobermory: "Its sequestered beauty and indulgent shades resemble Italian scenery." We have never visited that sunny land;

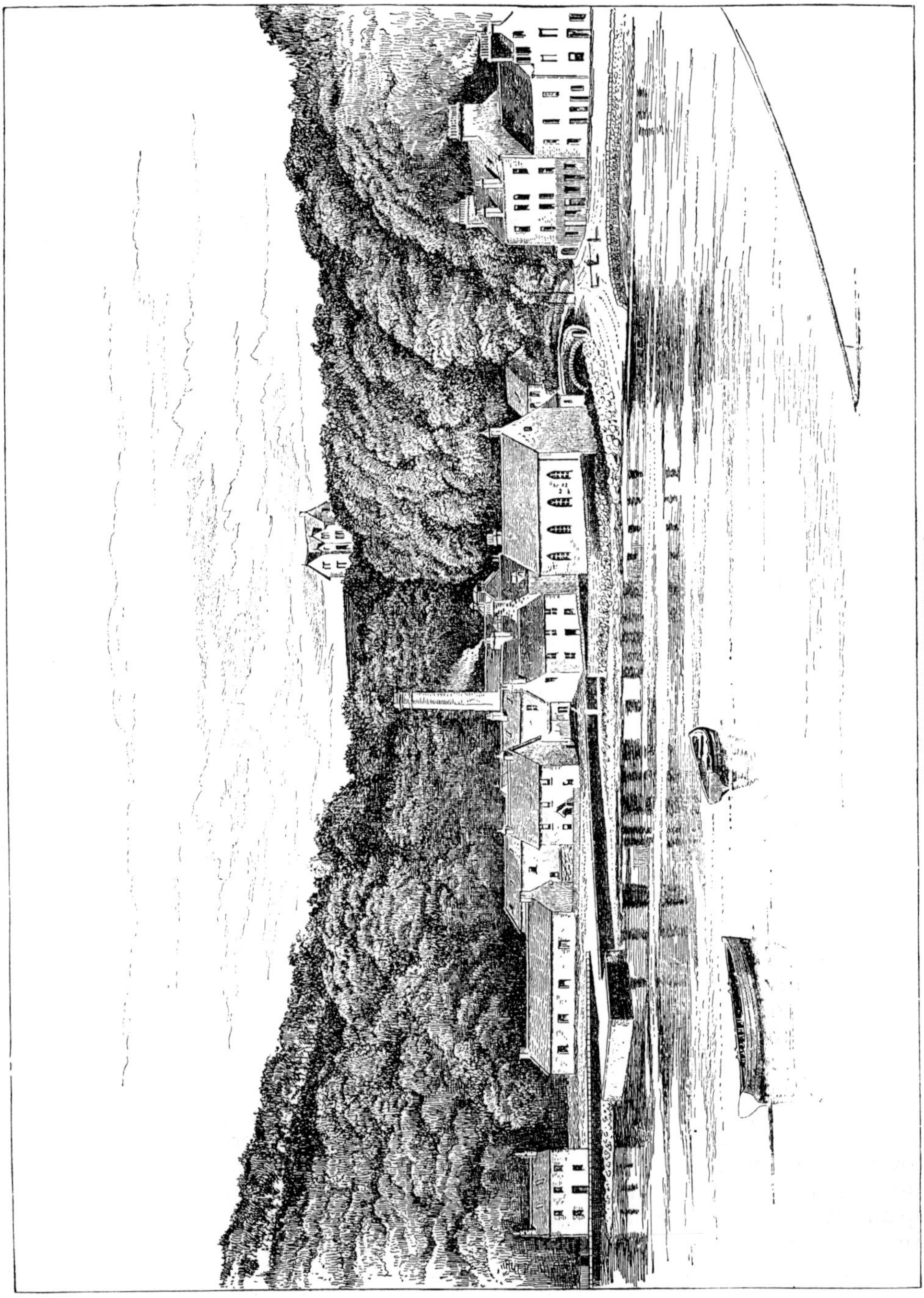

TOBERMORY DISTILLERY.

nevertheless we appreciated the glories of Tobermory, and wondered within ourselves that a place possessing such charms, fine hotel accommodation, and withal so come-at-able, should apparently be so neglected. As we steamed into the harbour the captain pointed out the spot, just below Drumfin, where the Spanish ship "Florida," one of the Invincible Armada, was sunk by an emissary of Queen Elizabeth. Many attempts have been made to raise the ship, all of which have been unsuccessful; but guns of brass and iron have been brought up, two of which are still to be seen at Dunstaffnage. The Distillery is planted at the head of the bay, and stands almost underneath a lofty and perpendicular rock. This hill is relieved by masses of the greenest foliage, which here and there seem to hold some fantastically shaped rock in their soft embrace, whilst at its base shrubs and ferns grow in wild confusion. On landing we committed our luggage to the care of an attendant from the Western Isles Hotel, and then proceeded direct to the Distillery. As usual, we commenced our observations with the water supply, which is literally inexhaustible, and comes from the burn called the "Tobermory river," flowing past the Distillery into the sea. It has its source in the celebrated Misnish Lochs, and in its downward progress tumbles over huge rocks, forming nearly twenty cascades of from twelve to twenty feet, culminating in a grand waterfall of nearly sixty feet, close to the walls of the Distillery, as seen in our illustration. The burn runs through a thickly wooded and deep glen, and ferns of almost every description grow to the water's edge. Just above the last cascade a stream from St. Mary's Well joins forces with the waters of the burn, and the addition of this water has given its present reputation to Mull Whisky.

The Distillery, which was established in 1823, covers two and a half acres of ground, and is built with stone in the form of a double triangle. There are two entrances, both by covered archways, one on the side of the steep hill near the waterfall, the other from the main road facing the sea. The Barley used is from Ross and Inverness-shires, shipped therefrom by Mr. MacBrayne's steamers, and carted up from the wharf by some of the finest Clydesdale horses on the island.

On reaching the Works, we introduced ourselves to Mr. Robert Simpson who acts as Manager and Distiller, and was trained to the business from boyhood. He conducted us first to the Granaries and Maltings, a crescent-shaped building, measuring 163 feet long by 24 broad, divided into three flats, all of which are entered by an old-fashioned outside stone staircase. The top flat is used for storing the barley, and holds a thousand quarters. The other two have concreted floors and are used for malting, each possesses a metal Steep capable of wetting 280 bushels at one time. At the south end of these Maltings is placed the Kiln, an elevated building 32 by 25 feet, floored with wire cloth and heated by peat, which is dug on the estate a short distance from the Works. The furnace in which the peats are fired is enclosed in sheet iron sloping to the drying floor above. Ascending a long and narrow staircase and crossing a passage, we came to the Malt Deposit, which consists of two spacious floors well lighted. A wing of this building forms the Mill, which contains the usual malt rollers driven by water-power. The pulverized malt is lifted by elevators from this chamber to the grist loft, and afterwards filled into sacks ready for use. After a short walk we turned up an alley enclosed by a high building, which brings us to the Mash House on the west side of the quadrangle, a building 72 feet by 28, where, placed on an elevated platform is the iron Mash-tun, 17 feet in diameter and 5 feet deep. Here our guide pointed out the Mashing Machine suspended over the Tun, and informed

TOBERMORY FALLS, IN FLOOD.

us that the sacks of grist already referred to were tipped into a hopper which feeds this Machine. The Mash Tun contains the usual stirring gear driven by water-power, and is capable of mashing 350 bushels at one time. There are two Brewing Tanks constructed with timber placed on brick piers, they each contain 3,365 gallons and are heated by steam. On the ground we observed an Underback with a timber cover, holding 3,000 gallons, from which the worts are pumped up to a Miller's Refrigerator, whence they run by gravitation to the Washbacks. Crossing a passage we now came to the Tun Room which is on a higher level than the Mash House. This Hall is 40 feet long, 20 broad and 30 high, built with stone and well lighted. Therein, and ranged along the wall, are four Wash-backs holding 7,384, 7,427, 7,381 and 7,347 gallons respectively, all of which are switched by water power. Passing out at the northern end we came to the Wash-charger which is placed on a brick pedestal twelve feet high, so as to command the Stills. We next bent our steps to the Distilling House and were there shown two "Old Pot Stills," the Wash Still holding 2,530 gallons, and the Spirit Still 1,710 gallons, the former heated by fire and the latter by steam. The Worm Tub is outside the Still House on an elevation, and fed direct from the Burn. Here we observed the two Water Wheels, one of them is very large, being twenty-five feet in diameter, the other is a much smaller one and used only for the Rummagers and Switchers. We returned to the Still House and ascended by some steps to a gallery loft at the east-end of the building where Mr. Simpson directed our attention to the Receivers and Chargers. They comprise a Low-wines Receiver and Charger of 1,200 gallons content, a Feint's Receiver and Charger, 1,200 gallons, and a Spirit Receiver holding 1,259 gallons; here also there is a Refrigerator of superior make, and the Spirit safe. We descended by another way and found ourselves at the second entrance gates having almost completed a circuit of the buildings. On the left of the gateway we entered the Spirit Store, a neat building, which contains the Spirit Vat holding 2,400 gallons and the Casking Apparatus. Next door is the Engine Department where we were shown a little five-horse power Engine for the Pumps, and a Boiler 24 feet long and 8 feet in diameter. All the grinding and mashing is done by the Water Wheel driven by the Tobermory River. The Buildings opposite consist of two Bonded Warehouses containing at present 2,000 casks of Whisky. Over the Main Entrance are situated the Partners' Offices, whilst those for the Manager, Clerks and the Excise are in the adjoining building.

On the premises there is a large Peat Shed, Cooperage and Carpenter's Shop. Twenty persons are employed in the Distillery and Mr. Ferguson is the chief Excise Officer. Messrs. Mackill Bros. are noted breeders of cattle, which consume a greater portion of the Burnt Ale and Draff on a large farm in the immediate neighbourhood.

The make is called "Mull Whisky"; it is pure Highland Malt, and the annual output (1885) was 62,000 gallons.

No. 48.

Talisker Distillery, Isle of Skye.

PROPRIETORS, RODERICK KEMP & CO.

AT Oban we put up again at the Craigard, decidedly a well-appointed hotel in every respect, and started the next morning for Skye by the steamship "Glencoe," which leaves the pier at 7 a.m., our route for the first part of the journey being the same as that to Tobermory. For weeks we had anticipated our voyage to Skye, and consequently were anxious about the weather; fortunately the sea was smooth, and although the atmosphere was hazy, it showed promise of a brilliant day.

After a hearty breakfast, which we partook of as soon as the boat left her moorings, we clambered to the upper deck, and found that the "Glencoe" was just passing Lismore Lighthouse, and was steaming amid mountain scenery of the grandest description in Scotland. As the mist dispersed, a picture presented itself to our view which we shall never forget. Whilst we gazed at the calm sweet blue of the sky, out came the sun pouring down its golden light over the scene, bringing out crag after crag in bold relief, and casting every kind of fantastic shadow.

Leaving the Island of Mull, we soon found ourselves on the waters of the Atlantic, and passing the Islands of Muck, Eigg, and Rum. As we approached the Skye Coast, the Cuchullin Hills appeared to view; and then our course for a brief time became less prosperous, in the shape of a summer shower, which sent everybody below; however, it lasted but half an hour, and by that time we were nearing the Bay of Scavaig, into which Loch Coruisk discharges itself. It was to visit this famous lake that our steamer had left its usual course, delaying the journey to Portree some two hours.

On entering Loch Scavaig, a scene of unexampled grandeur disclosed itself, and from the rocky shore there suddenly appeared a couple of large boats, manned by a sturdy set of Skyemen, dressed in handsome uniforms with Mr. McBrayne's badge on their caps and jerseys, who took us from the steamer to a projecting rock, which formed a natural landing stage. A five minutes' climb brought us to the margin of Coruisk, when a sight presented itself to our view that we shall never forget, and whose awful grandeur it would be impossible to describe.

It is a fresh-water lake nearly two miles long, from the sides of which rise naked and precipitous mountains, and for sterile desolation no spot in Europe can compare with this silent wilderness.

"A scene so wild, so rude as this,
Yet so sublime in barrenness,
Ne'er did my wandering footsteps press
Where'er they happ'd to roam."—SCOTT.

Re-embarking on the "Glencoe," we continued our voyage, and after rounding the Point of Sleat we sailed along for many hours amid scenery which on either side was as beautifully diversified as one could wish. With the exception of a couple of showers, we had a magnificent sail, although the wind and tide were both against us, and somewhat impeded our progress; but this we did not mind, as there was so much in the surroundings to delight the eye and occupy our attention. We were much indebted to Captain Baxter for his kind attention and interesting descriptions of the scenery through which we passed. After leaving the Island of Raasay, the steamer shot rapidly round a rocky point, and in a few minutes we found ourselves in the harbour of Portree, and were soon landed on the quay. A short walk up a steep hill overlooking the sea brought us to the Portree hotel, kept by Mr. D. McInnes, to which we had been recommended by our friends.

Early the next morning we started on our journey of discovery, and during the whole drive of nineteen miles from Portree to Carbost, we did not pass a single village. It would be difficult to describe this romantic, wild and mountainous island; the road for the first few miles being somewhat bleak, but afterwards becoming more interesting. Unfortunately the rain came down in torrents, and we had to don our waterproofs; when it ceased the Cuchullin Mountains appeared to our view, and the sight of their grandeur called forth our admiration, and fascinated us for the best part of our journey. This island is famous for rainy days, even in summer, and from experience we must confess that it comes down sometimes with a heaviness that washes away every particle of dust from your clothes, and pierces your mackintosh like duck-shot through a boat's sail.

The sun was shining again when we reached the Sligachan Hotel, and for the rest of the day the weather was brilliant. We put up our horse, and after resting him for an hour and fortifying ourselves with a substantial meal, proceeded on our way. This hotel stands at the head of the loch from which it takes it name, and is a favourite resort of tourists who wish to ascend the Cuchullin Hills. The hotel is the starting point for climbing Scuir-nan-Gillean the highest of the Cuchullin range, and is in the very midst of an assemblage of mountains, red and grey, and all of them bare from base to summit.

On leaving Sligachan we ascended a hill, and the road thereafter lay through a desolate valley of some six miles in extent, without any signs of habitation, except one or two shepherd's huts and a small shooting lodge. Our drive next took us round a considerable stretch of the noble Loch Harport, and views alternately occurred of hill and sea, which strongly appealed to our imagination. We had to ford two swift flowing streams. These rivulets after heavy rains become mountain torrents, and are sometimes not fordable for days together. At this point of the road we obtained a good view of the Distillery, about three miles distant, and the country began to assume a more cultivated and cheerful aspect; we soon passed a church and several cottages after that, and for the rest of the drive, everything looked more flourishing, and the fields exhibited fine crops of potatoes and turnips.

The Talisker Distillery stands at the foot of a beautiful hill, in the centre of the smiling village of Carbost, which, after the bare and rugged track we had passed through, was an agreeable change, and seemed quite a lively place. On the broad slopes of the hill, which were covered with crofters' holdings, husbandmen were busy tilling the soil; whilst at the Distillery below and the village which surrounds it, all was life and motion. Driving along we were struck with the picturesque situation of the Distillery, which stands on the very shore of Loch Harport, one of the most beautiful sea-lochs on this side of the island. To reach the works we crossed the bridge over the Carbost Burn, which supplies all the water used in the Distillery. This stream runs down the face of Stockveil Hill, a gentle slope six to seven hundred feet high, and which descends to the shore of Loch Harport; and like the opposite hill is of a delicious green, and quite refreshing after the barren mountains we had passed on our way. But to return to the Carbost Burn; this rivulet, like all the others in the Island, falls over a rocky bed and many small waterfalls before it reaches the sea. About 100 yards above the Distillery it is tapped, and a "Lade" carried therefrom along the Distillery property into the works, where it is used for distilling purposes, and for driving the machinery when steam power is not used. The farm and house of Talisker, from which the Distillery takes its name, is about six miles distant, and is situated in the parish of Bracadale on the other side of the hill.

The Distillery, which was erected in 1830, is beautifully situated, and covers two and a half acres of ground. The old part of the work is built in the form of a quadrangle, but such important additions have been made to it from time to time during the past nine years that the Distillery has almost lost its identity, and two-thirds of the whole property are of modern construction, and contain all the newest appliances and vessels known in the art of distilling. The new part consists of the Kiln, a Warehouse, Still House, and one of the Granaries. The old part is the Mash House, Spirit Store, and two of the Warehouses. Small steamers, or as they are here called "puffers," come up the loch to within fifty yards of the Granaries. These bring the barley and stores used in the works; and besides this, the "Hebridean" from Glasgow, a deep sea steamer, calls once a week. The barley is carted up to the Granaries from the boats, which are accessible at low tide, and is lifted to the various floors by old-fashioned hoists. Mr. Alexander Green, the Manager, received us, and directed us over the establishment.

We were admitted through a covered gateway into the quadrangle, and proceeded at once to the Granaries and Malt Barns, which are situated at the right hand corner. They are two in number, and, like the rest of the buildings, are constructed of stone.

One of them, the old building triangular in form, is 100 feet long, 40 wide, and two stories high, each floor being divided in the centre. No. 2 is a new building, and is 126 feet long by 31 broad; the top floors on both are used for storing grain, and each possesses a Steep. That in the new Granary is constructed with cement, 6 feet wide and 4 feet deep, and will wet 400 bushels of barley at one time.

The two Kilns adjoin each other, and are both connected with the Maltings. The old one is 24 feet by 20 feet; and the new one, which is of handsome elevation, is 28 feet by 25 feet. They are both floored with wire cloth, and heated by peat in open furnaces. The peats are brought from a moor about a mile distant from the Distillery.

We saw a number of hardy women busy digging and bringing home this fuel, where they stacked it in an open shed, 104 feet long, roofed with corrugated iron. But to return to the Kilns; both of them communicate with the Malt Deposit, which is one of the oldest buildings in the Distillery, and is connected with the Mill building by a hopper, which is on the same level as the Malt floor.

The Mill underneath contains a pair of Malt-rollers and the usual grinding machinery, driven by steam power. The pulverized malt is carried in sacks to the Mash-tun, which vessel is placed in the next building, a little old-fashioned place, now being newly roofed. This Tun is 14 feet in diameter and 5 feet deep, containing the usual stirring rakes, which are driven by steam. From this dish the Draff is shovelled out through an aperture in the wall to the Draff House outside, and from thence it is carted away by the farmers.

The Underback is in the basement of the next building; and passing along we noticed two timber Brewing Tanks, which supply hot water to the Mash-tun just described.

Our guide now conducted us to the Tun Room, which forms the south corner of the quadrangle, and adjoins the Mash House, wherein are six Washbacks. Descending from the staging of this house, we noticed one of Henderson's large-sized Refrigerators, and then passed through a doorway into a passage, where are situated the Excise offices and the mashman's rooms, both reached by an outside stone staircase, which leads into the courtyard.

Passing these apartments we descended a ladder, and found ourselves in the Still House, which occupies the left hand side of the court, and faces the bridge over the Burn, which we crossed to reach the Distillery. The Still House contains three Pot Stills; the Chargers, both of them timber vessels, are placed on a platform, which runs across the Still House. There are two Worm Tubs in connection with the Stills, both of them fed by running water direct from the Burn. In the receiving room besides the Safe, there are three Receivers, a Low Wines 355 gallons, Feints 450 gallons, and Spirit 526 gallons. Retracing our steps we now came to the Spirit Store, which opens into the public road and contains a Vat capable of holding 1,766 gallons. On the opposite side of the way, facing the sea, are two large newly built Warehouses, capable of holding 1,000 casks. There are three other warehouses on the premises of a similar capacity. On the same side of the road as the new Warehouses referred to there is a Manager's and Clerk's Office, also a neat Cooperage.

Inside the Distillery proper there is an Engine House, which contains a splendid horizontal engine of ten-horse power; a steam boiler, 20 feet long and 6 in diameter, also various pumps and other appliances.

Part of the employés live in houses on the property, and there is a fine newly built house occupied by the manager. The Chief Excise Officer, Mr. W. O'Brien, also lives in a neat house close by the Distillery.

The make is Highland Malt, and the average annual output for the three years ending April 1886, was a trifle over 40,000 gallons.

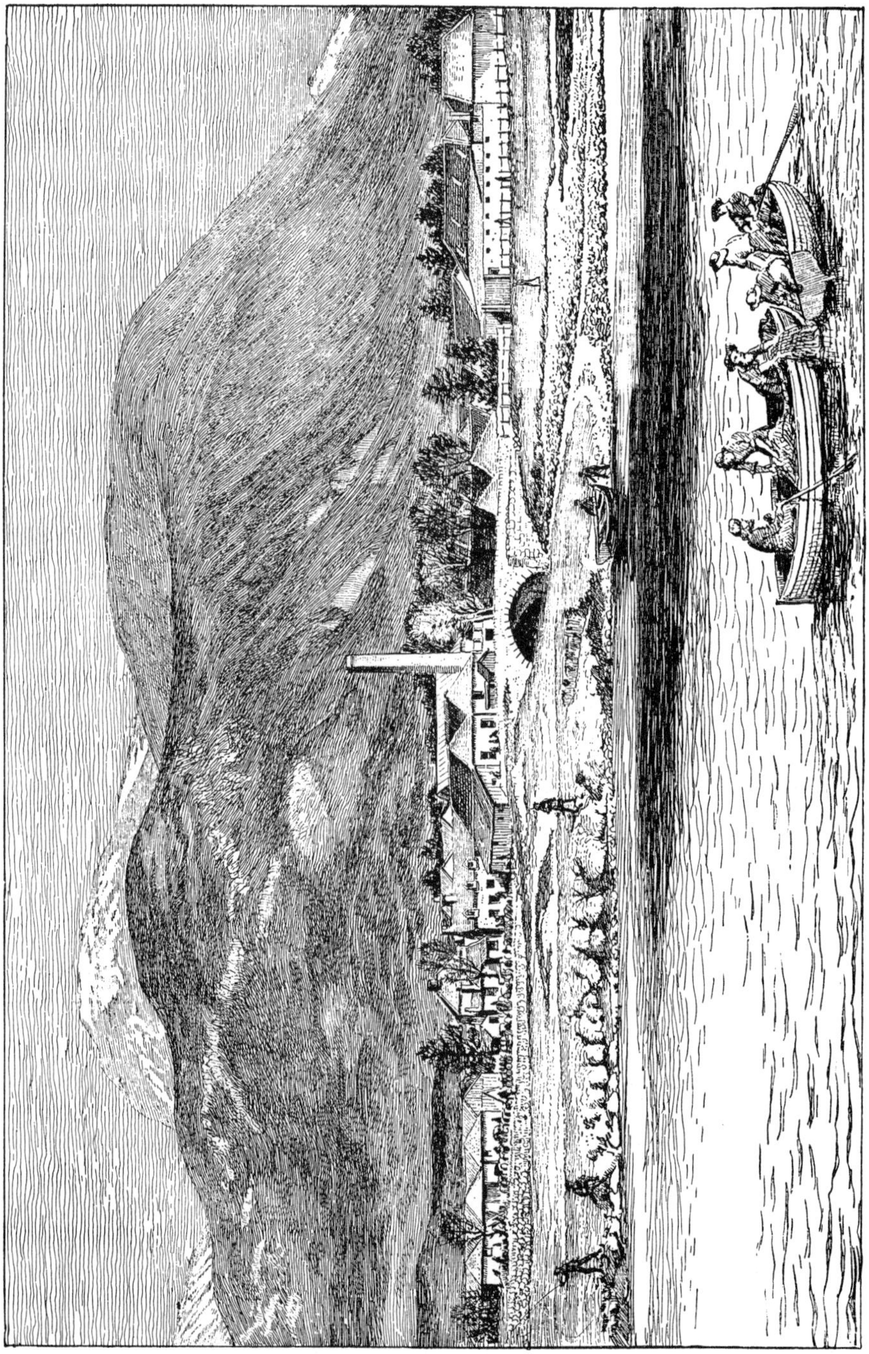

BEN NEVIS DISTILLERY.

No. 49.

Ben Nevis Distillery, Fort William, Invernesshire.

PROPRIETOR, DONALD P. McDONALD.

WE left Oban—the Charing Cross of the Highlands—by the morning steamer, and shall long remember the voyage from that place to Fort William. The sea was smooth, the sky clear, and the weather all that could be desired. There are surely few experiences to be found more delightful, than steaming through the romantic scenery of the Highland Lochs upon a fair morning in summer, under such conditions as now linger in our memory. As a matter of fact there are no better appointed steamers in the United Kingdom, than those belonging to Mr. David Macbrayne. Most of them have been specially built for tourist service, and admirably answer the requirements, and anticipate the wants, of the travelling pilgrim. Strolling upon the maindeck of the "Mountaineer" we had ample time to study the beauty of the scenery, as we steam along with that sense of freedom and exhilaration, which the modern invention of the railway train has struck out of the list of human enjoyments. Lochs Lomond, Etive, Katrine and Earn, full of historic fame and of world wide reputation, need only to be mentioned to recall to many the grandeur of the shady valleys and lofty sunlit hills; but the voyage from Oban to Fort William transcends them all. We have travelled many a highway at home and abroad, but can recall nothing so varied and lovely. Leaving Oban, and rounding the point upon which stand the ruins of Dunolly Castle, we entered Loch Linnhe, and the mighty mass of Ben Nevis, with its grey barren domes flushed with sunshine in the distance, burst upon our view. This grand eminence, the highest mountain in the United Kingdom, rises 4,406 feet above the level of the sea. It stands almost isolated, by two yawning ravines, from the adjoining lofty mountain ranges. Its base at one side is almost washed by the sea, and from any point of view its appearance is most imposing. The brow of this majestic mountain is generally encircled with an icy diadem, and its topmost furrows and chasms filled with snow. On the northern side of the summit there is a tremendous precipice, falling some 1,500 feet; and at the height of 1,700 feet from the base there is a wild tarn or mountain lake, whose dark waters look weird and terrible.

When free from its soft covering of clouds there is a grand view from the summit of Ben Nevis, and the spectator is astounded at the wild and strange sublimity of the scene, augmented by the depth of the surrounding precipices. Gazing over the horizon an ever-changing panorama meets the eye; now Ben Cruachin, Ben Lomond and other lofty mountains in the far distance are revealed, then for a time they will be hidden by banks of mist that sailing on the wind fill the rugged depths of chasms, black as night, and impenetrable to the eye and light of day. These again pass away and the awe-struck spectator finds himself amidst cloud and mountain scenery, the beauty and ever-changing complexion of which no words or pen can describe. On the summit of the mountain the Scotch Meteorological Society have erected an Observatory, having obtained a feu of an acre of ground from Mrs. Cameron Campbell of Monzie, the owner of that portion of the mountain, which is included in her estates of Fassifern and Calart. In establishing this National Observatory the object sought is to obtain a knowledge of atmospheric changes and disturbances, and from this source the value of forecasts of the weather over the British Isles is greatly enhanced, a detailed report from the Observatory appearing daily in the columns of the *Times*. All honour to the little band of observers, who, for weeks at a time, are cut off from intercourse with the outer world, save by the power of the electric wire; and who, in the cause of science, isolate themselves from the world, and suffer cold and privations, that they may keep hourly watch over the weather, and by the power of the telegraph flash the results to all parts of the United Kingdom.

But to return to Fort William. This place was formerly called Maryburgh and the Garrison of Inverlochy, from the ancient castle which still stands in solitary magnificence. The fort was one of the garrisons erected by Oliver Cromwell to overawe the Scotch, and was destroyed and re-erected by William III, from whom it receives its present name. It played an important part in the rebellions of 1715 and 1745, and was maintained as a garrison until 1864, when it was purchased from the Government by Mr. Campbell of Monzie. The dark tragedy of Glencoe is intimately connected with the history of Fort William, while it will be remembered that the MacDonalds figured as the victims of that awful massacre. On nearing our destination one of the first objects that strikes our view is the handsome new pier, built by Mr. McDonald on the property of the Ben Nevis Distilleries, for his fleet of steamers.

THE PIER, FORT WILLIAM.

On the landward part of the quay there is a neatly built block of houses occupied by the Distillery employés, and a row of warehouses for general supplies and stores for the works. The quay is entirely built of concrete, and was constructed by Mr. McDonald's workmen under his own superintendence.

On our arrival at the landing stage we proceeded to the West End Hotel for refreshment and rest. The next morning we drove to the Ben Nevis Distillery, situated south-east of Lochiel and two miles from the town. It takes its name from the gloomy mountain, its solitary companion, and was the first legal Distillery in the Lochaber district. Our way led over the river Nevis, past the battle-field, immortalized by Sir Walter Scott in his "Legend of Montrose," and by the ruins of the ancient and royal Inverlochy Castle which stands on Mr. McDonald's farm, a short distance from the Distillery.

Ben Nevis was built in the year 1825 by Mr. John McDonald, the father of the present proprietor, and, with the new Distillery on the banks of the Nevis, a little nearer the town, is the only Distillery within 50 miles. Mr. Donald P. McDonald, the present owner, descends from the Keppoch branch of the McDonalds, formerly one of the most powerful clans in the Highlands. His father, who was a man of great stature and noble physique, was familiarly called "Long John" to distinguish him from the many other Johns of his numerous clan. On looking up the records of this ancient and historic clan, we find that in 1745 the McDonalds nobly came to the assistance of "Bonnie Prince Charlie" and sent upwards of 2,000 men to fight for him, and the chief of the Keppochs was killed at the battle of Culloden. As we drove in at the gates of the Distillery we were struck with the picturesque appearance of the buildings, all of which are grouped about on a carpet of green, bordered with fir plantations, in striking contrast to the background of the mountain whose projections intrude themselves up to the walls of the Distillery. Forty years ago this establishment was on a very small scale, and the Whisky manufactured by "Long John" but little known and appreciated; now it is famous in all parts of the world. Then 200 gallons per week was about the average make; now it exceeds 3,000 gallons.

The first place we visited was the Malting House, a stone building of two floors, the upper one used for storing barley, and the lower as a withering floor, with a timber steep at the end filled by means of a trough running direct from the side of the stream. The Maltings proper, connected with this Distillery, are situated in the town, close to the harbour on Mr. McDonald's property, and are conveniently arranged for unloading the barley from the ships. At one end of the Maltings at the Distillery, is placed the Kiln, floored with wire cloth, heated with peat, and the furnaces enclosed with sheet iron. The malt is hoisted to the Kiln by an old fashioned windlass, and after being dried is carried across the yard and over the stream in sacks to the Malt deposit, which forms the roof of the building on the side of an acclivity, on a level with part of the yard, and which is over the Mash house. Here the Malt is dropped into a hopper and falls into the mill below, which contains a pair of Malt Rollers, driven by a turbine water-wheel, made by the Lowmoor Iron Company, Bradford, one of the first erected in Scotland for that purpose. The grist is elevated from here to an apartment over the Mash Tun, where it is tipped into a sluice, and run first through the Mashing machine, thence into the Mash Tun, which is 13 feet in diameter and 6 feet deep, holding 3000 gallons, and capable of mashing 200 bushels, and having the double action stirring gear. The Mash House is a substantial building 42 feet by 22. The three heating coppers, which supply the hot water to the Mash Tun, are in an adjoining building. Under the Mash Tun is placed the Underback, an iron vessel holding 2,500 gallons. From the Underback the Worts are pumped up by a centrifugal pump into the Worts

Cooler placed above, from whence they run over a set of Lawrence's upright refrigerators into a trough alongside the Tun Room into the six Washbacks, each of which contains 6,000 gallons. The Tun Room, 84 feet long and 24 feet wide, is a bright, cheerful and clean house, contiguous to the Still House and above the level of the Stills. The wash is pumped by another centrifugal pump into the Wash Charger, holding 6,000 gallons, placed on an elevation in the Still House, and the liquor now runs by gravitation into the Wash Still. Very few of the old Distilleries can boast of such a fine Still House as Ben Nevis possesses. It is 72 feet long and 27 feet wide, lofty, well lighted, and kept in perfect order. The Stills therein are all of the "sma'" pot kind and of the following capacities: the two Wash Stills, 1,000 and 800 gallons respectively, and the Spirit Stills, two 350, and one 500 gallons. In this House there is a capital little 6-horse power engine, and steam boiler 12 by 6, also two Low-wines and Feints Receivers, and two Spirit Receivers with indicators. The two Worm-tubs are outside the Still House. We walked across the top of these Receivers into the Safe Room, which contains a Main Safe and two Sampling Safes. Across the court and adjoining the Excise Office is the Spirit Store, wherein are two Spirit Vats holding 700 and 200 gallons respectively.

On another side of this court are the Smithy and Engineers' Shop, a Cooperage, Joiners' Shop and a Saw-mill. Ranged round the yard are Cart Sheds, Stables and Stores. Distributed about the premises are ten Warehouses entirely detached from the Distillery and from each other. No. 9 Warehouse is a large building, 126 by 108 feet, roofed with sheet iron, lighted by windows, and containing over 2,000 casks of Whisky placed in tiers on gauntrees from end to end of the building, with working avenues between. No. 10 is the newest and most recently built, 156 by 84 feet, of a similar construction, and contains 1,600 casks of Whisky. No. 8 is 124 by 78 feet, and the other seven Warehouses are somewhat smaller. The whole together contain 8,161 casks, holding 523,722 gallons. The original, and at that time only Warehouse belonging to the Distillery, is still to be seen, and is a picturesque old building. We now walked across the park to the farmsteading, which brings us to the old castle of Inverlochy, the stately and extensive old ruin before referred to. Mr. McDonald farms about 150 acres of arable land, and rents upwards of 5,000 acres of Ben Nevis mountain, whereon are about 2,000 sheep. The farm buildings are neatly arranged and contain nearly 200 head of cattle, which are fed with the grains from the old Distillery.

Thirty men are employed on the farm and the Distillery, for whom dwelling houses have been provided. There are three Excise Officers.

The Whisky is pure Highland Malt, and the annual output for the year 1884-5 was 152,798 gallons.

Urgent business at this time called us home, and our next visit to this district was in the winter, and in the following chapter we describe the new Distillery which Mr. McDonald has erected in close proximity to his old work.

No. 50.

Nevis Distillery, Fort William.

PROPRIETOR, DONALD P. McDONALD.

FROM Edinburgh to Oban, on a cold winter's day with the snow on the ground and sleet beating against the windows of the railway carriage is no joke, and a sail from Oban to Fort William, with the wind due east in mid-winter, requires some fortitude even if the weather is bright and the sky cloudless. We were well provided with warm wraps, and braved the piercing wind on the main deck of the "Mountaineer" in order to catch a view of the scenes which we had passed during the previous summer, now wrapped in their winter robes. It would be impossible for us adequately to describe the various pictures presented *en route*. The atmosphere was so clear that the snow-covered hills on either side seemed terribly close, and impressed us deeply with their grandeur and solitude. As we steamed along between these "ocean mountains," if we may so call them, the most remarkable and beautiful winter scenes came into view; now extraordinary ravines, their waterfalls frozen into huge solid hanging masses of quaint and fantastic devices; then some little bay or intersection of the coast fringed with dark pine trees, which seemed to stand out in bold relief from the white background of the mountain; anon a little hamlet, with its kirk nestling cosily on the mountain side, the whole forming a picture it would be impossible to describe. As we passed Appin we catch sight of Ben Nevis, the monarch of the mountains, and shall never forget its appearance on that day. As a rule, fogs, clouds, or a hazy state of the atmosphere often conceal certain portions of the grand mountain, and thus disturb the wonderful impression of the whole, but we were fortunate, and could see this gigantic mass almost from its base to its summit. Its near presence and supreme dignity, standing out, as it does, from the surrounding hills, awed us, and suggested the might and power of the Great Creator. As we looked on its heights and glimmering peaks, dark projections of rock peered out and broke up the spacious white mantle, whilst at the top the frozen snow glittered in the sunbeams, and contrasted brilliantly with the black masses beneath. We continued our journey and neared our destination, keeping this glorious prospect in view, our minds full of the wonders we had witnessed, and thankful that we had been permitted to gaze upon this stupendous work of creation, clothed in all its winter glory. Well might Mackellar break out into song and say:—

"Oh for a sight of Ben Nevis,
Methinks I see him now,
As the morning sunlight crimsoneth
The snow-wreath on his brow;
As he shakes away the shadows
His heart the sunshine thrills,
And he towers high and majestic
Amid a thousand hills.

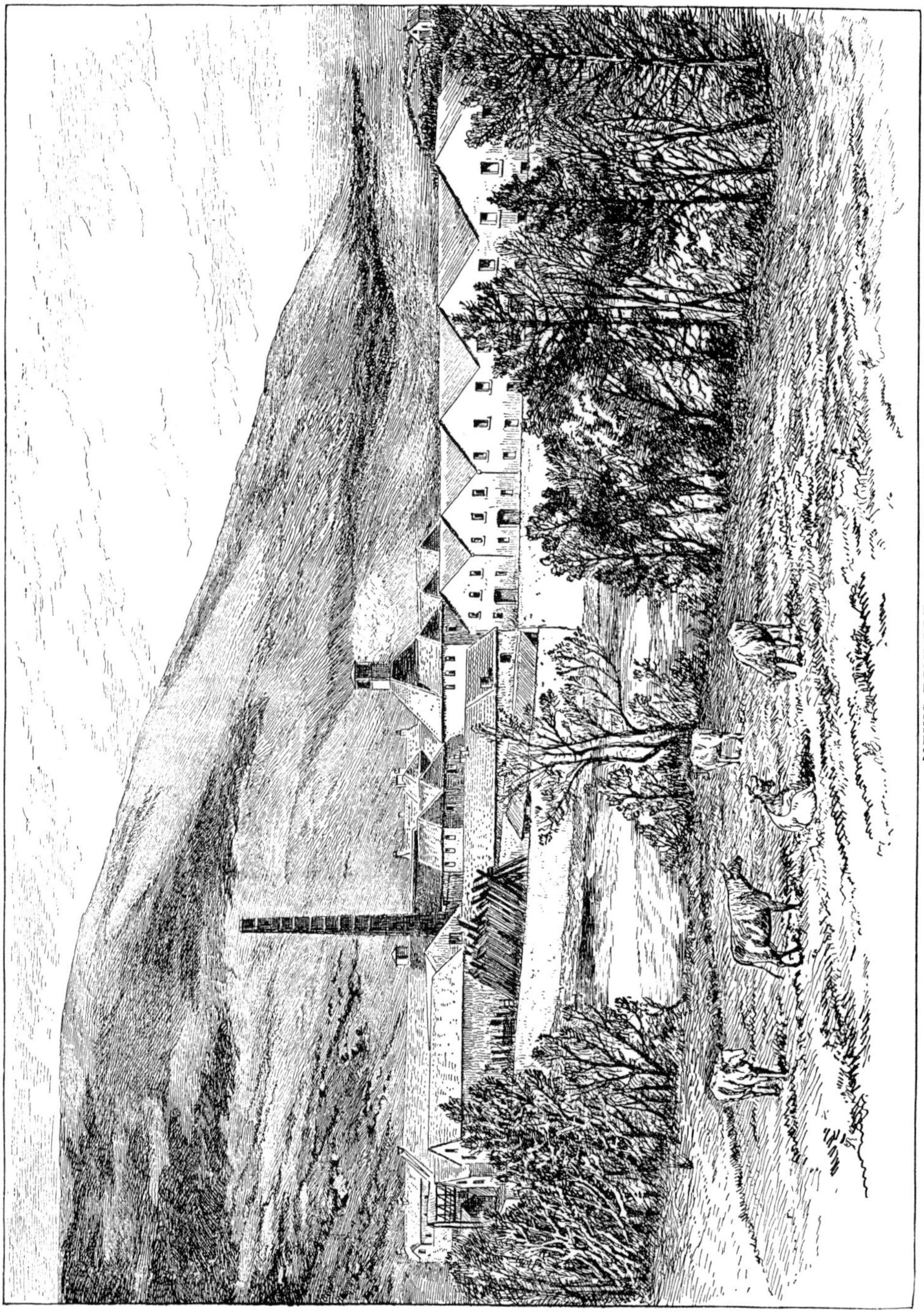

NEVIS DISTILLERY.

After passing Stroncreggan, we soon found ourselves at Fort William, welcomed by friends who had come down to the boat to meet and convey us to our destination.

Early next morning we set out to explore the Nevis Distillery Works, which are situated on the banks of the river Nevis, about half a mile from the town. They are approached from the turnpike road by a stone gateway, and consist of a double series of white concrete buildings, divided by a central avenue, and all communicating with each other by gangways and bridges. On the morning of our arrival the whole place looked like a busy village, and we were informed that some unusually heavy export orders had arrived, and deliveries by that day's steamer were most important. There was a foreign air about the whole proceedings; the dazzling whiteness of the concreted buildings, the numerous carts, gaily painted a crimson and green colour, laden with casks of Whisky, the big coopers with their leathern aprons, the noise of the blacksmiths' anvils, the Distillery clerks and excisemen running to and fro, reminded us of the champagne districts.

The Nevis Distillery is a modern work, and was built in the year 1878 by Mr. D. P. McDonald on the most approved plans, and under his own personal supervision. At the death of his father in the year 1856, the present proprietor succeeded to the business, which at that time was the only Distillery in the district. Ben Nevis was turning out about 200 gallons per week. In 1864 the trade had so much increased that the Distillery was enlarged from time to time, until its capacity reached 3,000 gallons per week. In 1878 it was found necessary to build a new work to meet the growing demand for "Long John's Dew of Ben Nevis"; hence a new Distillery was built in close proximity to the old one, on the banks of the river after which it is named. It contains all the newest improvements known in the art of distilling, and Mr. McDonald has here brought to bear his long experience and practical knowledge, in planning and erecting a model Distillery. The water used is the same as is supplied to the old Ben Nevis Works, and has its source at the top of the mountain from the spring now known as "Buchan's Well," which is the highest in the kingdom, and whose water has been celebrated for ages past in prose and song, more particularly when converted into the "Dew of Ben Nevis," and imbibed by mortals below. We have seen the analysis of this wonderful water, by Dr. Stevenson Macadam, who closes his remarks with these words:—"The freedom of the water from organic impurities may be observed from the general analysis. The water is therefore very pure, and I am decidedly of opinion that either for domestic purposes or distilling operations it is of the very best quality: cannot be surpassed, and is very seldom equalled in quality."

The Distillery buildings cover six acres of ground and are so arranged and connected with each other by gangways, bridges, and elevators, that the barley is developed into Whisky through the various stages by a continuous process of gravitation. On the right hand side as you enter there is a raised roadway, which leads to the top storey of the first series of maltings; at the door of this building the barley is shot out of the carts and distributed over the floors. It is a three-decker house, 160 feet long and 127 feet broad, with concrete floors. The ground and first floor are used for Malting, and the top storey for storing the barley, at the end of which are two lofty Kilns each measuring 30 feet square, and contiguous to same are three large Malt Deposits. At the beginning of the season of 1885 these Deposits contained 6,000 quarters of Malt made in the previous season, which was noted for the particularly fine quality of barley grown in the north-eastern counties. The dried Malt is filled into oval box barrows and wheeled from this department over a short foot-bridge into the Mill, which contains two handsome sets of cylinders for crushing the Malt.

Our guide now conducted us to the No. 2 Maltings across the roadway, the largest under one roof in the north of Scotland, measuring 151 feet long and 112 feet broad, consisting of an upper deck with an open space in the centre for lighting and ventilation, and for keeping the building cool for late season's malting Seven hundred quarters of barley are malted on the ground floors of these maltings weekly throughout the season. The upper deck or gallery before referred to covers two-thirds of the area of the whole house, and is capable of storing 5,000 quarters of barley. The ground or withering floor is of concrete, and is so capacious that 3,000 persons could be seated there with ease. At the west end of the building there is a double concrete steep which wets 200 quarters of barley at one time. The Kiln attached to this Malting is at the east end of the building, and is 40 feet square. It is floored with wire cloth, and heated with peat only, in Furnaces, which are enclosed hopper shape in sheet iron, concentrating the heat and causing a current of cold air to pass over the fire. The Malt is lifted to this Kiln by a patent American Elevator, which is so rapid in its movements that it loads the Kiln in twenty minutes. We next bent our steps to the Malt Stores, five in number, which communicate with the Mill before described by an iron bridge slung across the roadway, and from thence were conducted to the Grist Loft which is built directly over the Mash Tun. We then descended by a rather steep staircase into the Mash House. It is a lofty building forty-five feet by thirty-five and contains a circular iron Mash Tun twenty feet in diameter and six feet deep, also the Underback made of metal, twenty-four and a half feet long, seven feet broad and three feet deep. From the Mash Tun the grains are floated into a large iron drainer in the Draff House and the liquid returned into the Brewing Tanks, the grains left behind being used for cattle food. In the Mash House we were also shewn four Heating Tanks, with a total capacity of 25,000 gallons, a fine Engine by Tangye of twenty-five horse power, a Steam Pump, a Centrifugal Pump, and a Gwynne's Pump of ingenious design and great power. At the back of the Engine we noticed two capital Steam Boilers twenty feet long and six feet in diameter, and it may here be remarked that the two lofty chimney stacks form a landmark in the plain and are distinguishable many miles distant. The Worts Receiver covers a part of the roof of the Mash House and the liquor runs therefrom over three of Lawrence's Upright Condensers into the Wash Backs. We now retraced our steps a few yards, and came to the Tun Room, the lightest and cleanest we have seen in our travels. It is sixty-four feet long and thirty-five feet wide and contains eight handsome Wash Backs, two of which hold 17,000 gallons, and the other six 8,000 gallons respectively.

We now followed our guide to the Still House, a noble building, said to be as modern in style and construction as any in Scotland. At the northern end is placed, high up on a gallery, the Wash Charger, a timber vessel holding 7,000 gallons. The wash runs from the Fermenting Tuns straight into this vessel. We noticed that the seven Stills are all of the old "sma' pot kind," kept beautifully bright, and heated by furnaces. Two of them—the Wash Stills—have a capacity of 2,000 and 3,500 gallons respectively, and five Spirit Stills, two holding 450 gallons, two 500 gallons, and one 580 gallons. The wash runs by gravitation from the Charger into the Wash Still, and the imperfect spirit, on leaving the

Worm Tub, runs into the Spirit Stills to undergo a second and similar process of distillation, emerging therefrom a perfected spirit, and running direct through the

STILL-HOUSE, NEVIS DISTILLERY.

Safe into the Receiver. There are eight in all of these latter vessels placed at the end of the Still-house. On leaving this interesting department we wended our way to the Spirit Store, where the Whisky is casked, branded, and sent to the Bonded Stores. At this point we were introduced to Mr. McRae, the chief Excise officer, who courteously conducted us over the four Warehouses, which occupy the left wing of the Distillery. They are all solidly built of concrete, and roofed with corrugated iron, and for convenience, economy of space, light and ventilation, we commend them to the notice of distillers intending to build new warehouses. Mr. McDonald has fitted up every one of them with "gauntrees." These strong timber frames are erected in rows down the centre of the Warehouses for the support of the second, and, if necessary, a third tier of casks, so that not a single one rests on another, and each cask can be removed without disturbing the rest. We first entered the No. 1 Warehouse, the largest of the group. It is 231 feet long, 192 feet broad, and is a two-decker. Some idea of its size may be gathered from the following facts. There are 28 avenues in the building, with gauntrees on either side filled with casks, and to walk down them all you would cover 30 yards more than a mile. We now proceeded to inspect the No. 2 Warehouse, which comes next in size, being 165 feet long and 60 feet broad, and is similarly arranged to the one described. Nos. 3 and 4 are both of the same size and length as No. 2, but a little narrower. These warehouses combined contain at present 9,915 casks, the whole of which has been bought and paid for by customers.

As we pass through all the different departments we are struck with the neatness and order of all the buildings. Everything goes on like clockwork, and the workmen seem to take a pride in keeping all the vessels sweet, bright, and clean. To every department there is appointed a chief workman, who is under orders from the manager, whilst Mr. McDonald Jun., like a general of an army, controls the whole staff. The Still-men are justly proud of their Stills, and pointed out their perfections and brightness with as much pride as a sailor would the fittings of his ship. And as to the Brewers, their anxiety that we should peer down to the depths of some of the enormous Washbacks, down which they threw the light from the lamp, was positively amusing.

We now returned to the Distillery Offices to rest ourselves for a short time, after which our former guide conducted us to see the various industries pursued on the premises. The Joiners' Shop is fitted up with all the necessary appliances, including a turning lathe, &c., and it is a notable fact that the operatives in this department have done all the joinery work in building the new Distillery, also the Warehouses and Stores connected with the Harbour and Wharf, and a whole street of Workmen's Cottages. All the carts and lorries in both Distilleries and on the Farms have been made in the Wheelwrights' Shop, which adjoins the Smithy and Engineers' Shop. The Cooperage is an interesting department, and employs three skilled workmen and several subordinates on cask repairs. All the new casks are shipped from Glasgow, and placed in dry store sheds ready for use. The Stables and Cart Sheds are situated at the western end of the courtyard. A procession of twenty horses and carts are constantly going to and fro between the Distilleries and Harbour. The motive power is principally water, supplied by a turbine wheel, fed by the river Nevis, which is here some 70 feet wide, and whose waters are as clear as crystal. Steam power is supplemented when necessary. There are fire-plugs and hose all over the premises, and beside this two extincteurs of a modern pattern. Mr. McDonald owns two large peat moors, and has therefore an inexhaustible supply of this fuel. There are 200 workmen employed, for whom the proprietor has provided most comfortable, and, in some cases, most picturesque dwellings.

The make is pure Highland Malt Whisky, and the annual output in 1884-5 was 260,103 gallons.

"Here's a health to the land of the mountain and glen,
To the land of the lake and the river,
Where the wild thistle grows in her rude rocky den,
Proud Freedom's stern emblem for ever!
The land of the Claymore, the Kilt, and the Plaid,
The Bagpipe, the Bonnet, and Feather,
Let's join heart and hand upstanding in pride,
Here's the land of the bright blooming heather."

No. 51.

Highland Park Distillery, Kirkwall, Orkney.

PROPRIETORS, STUART & MACKAY.

ONCE more resuming our wanderings, we take train from London to Thurso, a tedious journey occupying a day and a half. On reaching Thurso we hastened to embark on board the mail steamer, "St. Olaf," which leaves Scrabster Pier soon after seven. The passage across the Pentland Firth is one of the roughest and usually most unpleasant in the British Isles. It is the channel which connects the two seas, and is never smooth. Here the unbroken flow of the Atlantic comes rolling in, and as it approaches the German Ocean the huge waves are dashed against the projecting headlands of Caithness and Orkney. Within a quarter of an hour after leaving the harbour we are in the thick of it. Soon we were buffetting and overtopping the waves, one moment in the air, and the next in a seething cauldron of enraged waters. Now we bounded over the waves, anon we charged at them, and were frequently drenched in a shower of spray after each shock. After two or three hours of this terrible treatment, we at last began to sail among the islands in smooth waters, and finally arrived at Scapa Pier about midnight. From the Pier to Kirkwall is a drive of two miles, and we thoroughly enjoyed it. There is no night in these regions during the summer months. It is light enough even at midnight to enable a person to read, and during our ride the lark and landrail kept up a constant chorus of music. Indeed, all nature seemed awake on this summer's night, which really was but a softer day, and the scene was one that will be remembered by us all when back again at our southern homes. On reaching the Castle Hotel, the buxom landlady was waiting to receive us, and presented each person with a nip of neat whisky and a ginger cake, according to custom.

Kirkwall is a much larger and more interesting place than we expected. Many of the houses have their gables towards the street, and are verging on antiquity. The first object that arrests the attention is the ancient and venerable Cathedral of St. Magnus, built in the 12th century, and one of the most complete architectural monuments of the time existing in Scotland. Its stately form rises above the town, and is seen on either side of the island very many miles distant. Not less interesting are the magnificent ruins of the Earl's and Bishop's Palaces, and picturesque narrow paved streets. The morning after our arrival we ascended the Wideford Hill, to take stock of the surrounding islands. Although only 721 feet above the level of the sea, it is the highest hill in the vicinity, and a breezy spot we found it. Here there is always a wind on the premises, and many an enthusiastic tourist, like one of our party, forgetting all else in the grandeur of the view stretched out before him, has thus doffed involuntarily to Æolus. Nothing is easier than to forget everything in the mere enjoyment of the sense of sight as we stand in such a novel position and with such an outlook. On either side stretched

HIGHLAND PARK DISTILLERY.

the sea, the sun pouring down its rays on an infinite expanse of water. From this eminence the whole archipelago is distinctly visible, and what a variety of tone and colour is presented by the surface of these islands. Some are dark heath covered; others with beautiful green fields, interspersed by many holms and skerries; whilst here and there are some, barren and black, encased as it were in a range of lofty precipices, which rise perpendicularly from the ocean, or even as in some places overhanging the surging waters. The Orkneys appear to us Cockneys to be quite out of the world, and each island a little sphere apart. Although only a few hours' sail from the mainland, they appear to be so isolated that each is complete and complacent in itself. The inhabitants are grave and reticent, but proud of their history and descent from the ancient Vikings.

As we descend the hill, our guide points out to us the Highland Park Distillery, about a mile distant, planted on the opposite slope. He is delighted when we tell him the object of our visit, the old man having been connected with the Highland Park half a century ago. From him we learn that the site whereon the Distillery now stands, was the place where the famous Magnus Eunson, carried on his operations. This man was the greatest and most accomplished smuggler in Orkney. By profession he was a U. P. Church Officer, and kept a stock of illicit whisky under the pulpit, but in reality he was a "*non Professing*" distiller. This godly person was accustomed to give out the psalms in a more unctuous manner than usual if the excise officers were in church, as he knew that he was suspected, and that a party of the revenue officers, taking advantage of his absence, might at that moment be searching his house. A singular story is told of this man. Hearing that the Church was to be searched for whisky by a new party of excisemen, Eunson had the kegs all removed to his house, placed in the middle of an empty room, and covered with a clean white cloth. As the officers approached after their unsuccessful search in the church, Eunson gathered all his people, including the maidservants, round the whisky, which, with its covering of white, under which a coffin lid had been placed, looked like a bier. Eunson knelt at the head with the Bible in his hand and the others with their psalm books. As the door opened they set up a wail for the dead, and Eunson made a sign to the officers that it was a death, and one of the attendants whispered "smallpox." Immediately the officer and his men made off as fast as they could, and left the smuggler for some time in peace. We have seen numerous stories in print of this clever smuggler and his band, but space will not permit us to reproduce them here.

It is a pleasant walk to Highland Park, and occupied us about a quarter of an hour. Mr. Milne is now the resident partner on the island, and, as he had only recently arrived in Orkney, he handed us over to Mr. James Ellis, the Manager, who conducted us over the Distillery. Before commencing our tour of inspection, we ascended the hill a few hundred yards above the establishment to see the water supply, as there is a peculiarity about it which led to the site being chosen by Magnus Eunson, and continued by his successors. Here there is no mountain stream or brawling rivulet; the water wells up from two springs at opposite angles of a small park, and is conveyed by aqueducts to two reservoirs, where the waters are mixed together and conveyed into the Distillery fifty yards distant. The whole of the works and the park above referred to are enclosed in a substantial stone wall, and the main entrance to the Distillery is from the high road from Kirkwall to Holm. The establishment covers three acres of ground, and is built in three terraces on the slopes of a hill. It faces Wideford Hill, and has Scapa Flow on its left and Kirkwall Bay on the right. Passing through a gateway we find ourselves in a large open court with a tree in the centre, the first we have seen in the island; hence it attracted our notice. Ascending the hill a short distance we come to the Granaries and Maltings, a V shaped stone building of two floors, at the apex is an old fashioned Kiln, which commands both sides of the structure. These two ranges are each one hundred feet long and twenty feet broad, and roofed with slates. We should here state that there is very little barley used here, which doubtless all connoisseurs of Highland Park Whisky know. The grain used is the old-fashioned "bere" grown in the neighbouring islands, dating back to the time of the Norwegians, and used at Campbeltown until the last twenty years. It is, of course, a species of barley, but a lighter grain. But to return to the Maltings. The top floors of each section are used for storing the bere, and will hold 2,000 quarters of grain. The lower, are used for Malting purposes, and have each a stone Steep capable of wetting twenty-five quarters at one time. These floors are of a compound mixture of clay and earth which keeps them continually moist. The Malt when properly developed is hoisted to the Kiln by an old fashioned windlass, and tipped on to a floor which is composed of flat metal plates, through which holes have been drilled out, of a primitive pattern.

We now ascended a movable stair to inspect this ancient Kiln, the outward appearance of which is that of a dungeon. It has walls over two feet thick and the building is about twenty-four feet square. The celebrated Orkney peats are the only fuel used in drying with the exception of a little heather hereafter referred to. On each side of this Kiln is an antique chamber now used as a Malt Deposit, each holding about five hundred quarters of dried Malt, where the Malt is filled into sacks and carried on the backs of stalwart Orcadians through the contiguous buildings, and across a drawbridge swung over the Mash Tun to the Mill building, where it is tipped into a hopper, and falls into the Mill below, which contains the usual malt cylinders driven by steam. The Pulverized Malt is raised from the mill floor by a windlass and shot into the hopper communicating with a Steel's Mashing Machine, where the grist becomes properly mixed with hot water and falls into the Tun below. The Mash House bears indications of great age and little or no restoration. It has an open roof and a boarded floor, and contains on a shelf stretching across the building, a Heating Copper (with a capacity of eight hundred gallons) the shape of a tea urn of the last century, also on the floor a circular iron Mash Tun ten and half feet in diameter and five feet deep, with the usual stirring gear, which is driven by steam, and the Under Back, holding three hundred gallons, which is of metal and is placed below the floor. As we stand on the bridge, which has been slung over the Mash Tun for our benefit, our heads are on a level with the open roof of the next building, and we see stretched out before us the Coolers, which are in two divisions, each of which measures thirty feet square, and both having the old fashioned revolving fans driven by steam. Descending from our perch we come to a stairway, at the bottom of which we found ourselves in a narrow passage, leading to the Tun Room or Back House. On passing through the doorway we step into a gloomy building of a triangular shape, which contains ten Wash Backs, each averaging 2,128 gallons contents, and all switched by hand props.

On leaving this department, a few steps down brings us to the Still House, paved with stone—the oldest part of the works, its exterior green with age, but inside cleanly with whitewash and paint. As we enter the building we pass under a low gallery, on which are placed the Wash Charger, holding 3,655 gallons, and the No. 2, Lowwines and Feints Receiver, holding four hundred gallons. Opposite the door by which we have entered, and standing back against the wall, are two old Pot Stills, of ancient pattern and design, one of them a Wash Still, holding 1,180 gallons, the other a Spirit Still of eight hundred and forty gallons, both heated by Furnaces. Under the gallery already referred to, there is a Spirit Receiver holding four hundred and thirty-five gallons, a No. 1, Lowwines and Spirit Receiver seven hundred and eleven gallons, and the safe. The pure Spirit is pumped from the Receiver into a Vat, which holds 1,627 gallons placed in the Spirit Store, an adjoining building.

Having done justice to the Still House, we now passed into the yard, and proceeded to inspect the two large Worm Tubs at the back of the Stills. On our way we noticed a peculiarly shaped timber building, which our guide informed us is called the " Heather House." Here heather is stored, which has been gathered in the month of July, when the blossom is fully set. It is carefully cut off near the root, and tied into small faggots of about a dozen branches. One or two of these faggots are used with the peat in drying the malt every time the fire is made up, and imparts a delicate flavour of its own to the malt, rendering Highland Park Whisky unlike any other made in the kingdom. To convince us of this, a few sprigs, well covered with dried blossoms, were thrown into an open *chauffeur* with a small quantity of peat, and we must confess that we detected a most pronounced odour, and quite different from the peat when used alone. We have only seen the heather used in three other distilleries in the whole kingdom. Opposite the Heather House is the old fashioned Water Wheel, and higher up the hill we come to the enormous Peat Sheds and Stacks, which together extend 400 feet up the slope, and contain some thousands of tons stored here for winter use. Descending on the other side of the Distillery proper, we come to the Excise and Brewers' Offices, Racking Store, and one of the large new Bonded Warehouses. It is 130 feet long, 42 feet broad, and both well lighted and dry. The other ten warehouses, which are distributed in the front and sides of the courtyard round the premises, are not quite so large. The whole of the eleven warehouses contained, at the time of our visit, 3,194 casks, holding 213,509 proof gallons.

In the Engine House, which is an annexe of the Mash House, we noticed a 12 horse-power horizontal engine, and a boiler 16 feet by 6 feet diameter. The Excise officers' houses, are beautifully situated, and command a view of the sea on either side of the island. At the left hand of the gateway there is a small detached building, which is used for the Distillery offices, and contains a private room for the resident partner. The burnt ale from the Distillery runs into a tank by the side of the public road, over which a pump has been fixed for the free use of the small farmers in the vicinity. Mr. Graham is the chief Excise officer, and there are fifteen persons employed in the Distillery.

The Whisky, which is pure Highland Malt, is sold principally in Scotland and England, whilst some of it is shipped to the Colonies.

The annual output is 50,000 gallons.

No. 52.

Scapa Distillery, Orkney.

PROPRIETORS, MACFARLANE & TOWNSEND.

THIS Distillery is the newest in the island, having only been completed in October, 1885. It is two miles from Kirkwall, and situated at the head of Scapa Bay. The country hereabouts is destitute of trees, but much of the land is under cultivation. So striking is the appearance of this treeless country, that a Yankee, who had arrived by the steamer during the night, exclaimed on getting out the next morning, that he had never seen such a "tarnation fine clearin'." But the beautiful sea-scape somewhat compensates for this loss, for sparkling in the bright sunshine are the white sails of ships, and boats manned by crews who know every creek on the coast, and whose voices can be heard singing the favourite "Orkney Boatman's Song:"—

"The foaming sea is dear to me,
It bears me on to thee, love!
And what care I though the spume-drift fly,
It speeds me on to thee, love!
The heart that's true ne'er dreads the view
Of stormy clouds or sea, love!
The curling wave may scare the slave,
It ne'er will scare the free, love!" etc.

A few yards from the Distillery are to be seen the remains of a "Broch," one of those numerous ancient buildings commonly called "Picts' houses." These Brochs are undoubtedly the most interesting class of Scottish antiquities. They were truncated round towers, built of large undressed stones, without mortar, and measured from 50 to 70 feet in external diameter, with a height of about 50 feet, having no outward opening but a low doorway. The walls were about 12 feet thick at the base, but at higher levels were hollow, having stairs and chambers in their thickness. These Brochs are ascribed to the early Celtic inhabitants, who built them for the purpose of affording shelter and safety. At Scapa, the foundations alone remain, and when first discovered, a considerable quantity of bone and stone implements were found therein, with a large number of ornamented clay vessels and a few Roman coins of the first century.

The Distillery is built on the Lingro Burn. The water supply is from springs and the Burn, from which it is carried a great distance in large iron pipes. On the Lingro is a large water-wheel for driving all the machinery, but should there happen to be an insufficient supply, the engine is available. The works consist of a block of buildings, covering one and a half acres of ground. At the entrance are three offices for the manager, clerks, and the Excise officers. The first building, as you approach on the left, is the Malting House, 80 feet long by 54 feet wide, the top floor of which is used as a Barley Store, having two cast iron water Steeps at one end, 3 feet deep, each capable of wetting 25 quarters of grain at one time. These Steeps discharge through traps or sluices on to the Malting Floor below, which is concreted and of same dimension as the barn above. Here the wet grain is spread out to grow in the usual manner, and is afterwards lifted by elevators to the Kiln.

We now crossed the way to the south of the Malting, and came to the Kiln, a detached building, 29 feet square, floored with the German sectional steel wire flooring; it is heated with peat in the ordinary manner. At the level of the drying floor is a gangway bridge, carried on iron beams to the neighbouring building, along which the malt is passed when dry to the Malt Deposit. On the floor over the Engine House is the Malt Mill, containing a pair of steel rollers, whilst above it is the Grist Loft. The grist is raised by elevators from this department to the hopper supplying the Mash-tun.

We next proceeded to the Still and Mashing House, a building 86 feet long and 29 feet broad, the portion devoted to the Stills and Mash House being one lofty storey; and the other part, for boiler, mill, and grist, arranged in three flats. We commenced our inspection at the Mash House, which contains a circular metal Mash-tun, 12 feet in diameter and 4 feet deep, into which the grist passes from a Steel's masher. It contains the steam or water-driven stirring gear, and on the bottom perforated draining plates, leaving the draff behind after the liquor is drained therefrom. The draff is afterwards subjected to a mechanical "sprinkler," so that the utmost is extracted from it. The worts run from the Mash-tun by gravitation into the Underback, an iron vessel holding 750 gallons, and flows therefrom through a Morton's Refrigerator, where it is cooled before being driven by a centrifugal pump into the fermenting vessels.

The Tun Room adjoins the Mash House and is a well-lighted and ventilated apartment. It contains four Washbacks, each with a capacity of 4,740 gallons, from which the Wash is pumped by another centrifugal pump into the Wash Charger, a timber vessel placed in the Still House and holding 4,000 gallons, from whence the Wash flows into the Wash Still holding 1,100 gallons, where the first process of distillation takes place, and the vapour which is now called Low-wines is passed through the Worm Tub, an outside tank 30 feet long, into the Low-wines Receivers, and thence it is pumped into the Low-wines and Feints Charger. The imperfect spirit is now run into the second or Low-wines Still, holding 700 gallons, to be re-distilled and undergo the same process. The pure spirit now runs through the safe into the Spirit Receiver, holding 1,500 gallons, and thence it is pumped by self-acting vertical pumps into a Vat which holds 1,500 gallons. The Stills are of the newest type and heated by steam instead of fire, and are both fitted with "collapse" valves, which allow air to enter in the event of a vacuum being formed. The Spirit Store adjoins the Still House and is a separate building 25 feet square. Here the Whisky is run out of the Vat into the casks and gauged before being sent to the Duty Free Store, a fine building on the right hand side of the entrance road. It is 84 feet long by 54 feet wide and roofed with corrugated iron. All the other buildings are slate roofed. We then retraced our steps to the Mill building, the basement floor of which constitutes the engine-house. It contains a horizontal engine of 8 horse power, a water-tank, a donkey-engine for feeding the boiler, and a steam boiler, 16 feet long by 5 feet diameter.

The Establishment is certainly one of the most complete little Distilleries in the Kingdom.

The Whisky produced is pure Highland Malt, the annual output is 40,000 gallons per annum.

The head office of the Distillery is at No. 48, St. Enoch's Square, Glasgow.

No. 53.

Stromness Distillery, Orkney.

PROPRIETORS, MACPHERSON BROS.

A TOUR to the Orkneys may strike a rash observer as unlikely to be fruitful or interesting, but let him just take the next steamer and spend a week on the Orcadian Islands, and he will not only cease to wonder, but regret that he has so long left unvisited these remote "Isles of the Sea." The early history of the Orkneys is as stirring and romantic as that of any country owning allegiance to Britain. From the earliest times the bold and daring deeds of the Vikings have been chronicled in the prose and poetry of many lands. The numerous acts of cruelty and conquest perpetrated by these northern sea-kings have so moulded the habits and formed the customs of their posterity, that to this day they betray their origin, in their lofty bearing, erect carriage, and simple faith in their ancient customs and folk lore. Every day during our stay in Orkney there was something new to see, and our three hours' drive from Kirkwall included more wonders than we had dreamt of, or could relate here.

We must not, however, omit to mention one or two curiosities of the journey After passing the celebrated Maes-Howe, or tumulus, like that described in a previous chapter, we came to the Standing Stones of Stennes; these antiquarian relics, whose fame is second to Stonehenge in repute as Druidical monuments, are situated on a peninsula in the midst of Loch Stennes. The Circle of Brogar (as they are called) is about 340 feet in diameter, round which the "Standing Stones" were originally planted, each averaging 18 feet high and 5 feet wide, and all placed at equal distances of 17 feet apart, and thirteen of these dumb sentinels are still standing.

We next came to the head of the Stennes Lake, which has a tidal communication with the sea, so narrow that it is spanned by a bridge, which our carriage passed over; and shortly after this we reached our destination, and arrived at the most northern point of our tour.

Stromness, so named from "Strom," a stream or current, and "nes," a promontory, is a seaport, and the town is unlike any other we have seen in Scotland. A good many of the houses, between the beach and the street, stand within high water-mark, and have little bulwarks, jetties and quays of their own, for their fishing operations, and unloading boats, etc. The bay is, in reality, a natural harbour, about a mile long and half a mile broad. There is a good pier, which is used by the mail boats and vessels starting for the Arctic regions, which sometimes call in here for shelter and provisions. The hero of Sir Walter Scott's "Pirate," John Gow, the "Captain Cleveland," was born on the Cairston Shore, Stromness, and we were shown the remains of Gows Garden, where his father's house formerly stood. He was commander of the "Revenge," 24 guns, and used to visit the town and give dancing parties to his friends, and before his true character was discovered engaged the affections of a beautiful and rich lady. He was finally captured in Edday and sent to London, where he was executed. It is said that the young lady whose affections he engaged, went to London to see him before his execution, but arriving too late she requested a sight of his corpse, and touching its hand formally resumed the troth plight, believing that her lover's ghost would not then haunt her should she bestow her hand upon another. The town consists of one paved street, about a mile long, so narrow and crooked that two vehicles cannot pass each other. At the north end is the quaint little Distillery we had come so far to see. It is planted at the foot of a steep hill, and was built in the year 1828 by Hector Munn, and covers about half an acre of ground. The water used for mashing and distilling comes from a burn, having its source in the hills rising between the Distillery and the celebrated Black Craig.

The following is a brief description of this, the most remote Distillery in the kingdom. It is built in the form of a parallelogram, and enclosed by substantial stone walls. There are three Barley Store Rooms, and two others for Malt. The Kiln is floored with metal plates, and heated in the usual way by a fire, wherein peat only is burned. In close proximity is the Mill, containing a pair of metal rollers for crushing the malt. In the Mill Store, which combines a Mash House, are the Heatings Copper and the Mash Tun, a vessel, 10 feet in diameter and 5 feet deep, with a large tank underneath it, used as an Underback. The Tun Room contains four Washbacks, each holding 2,200 gallons, fixed on solid blocks, a Wash Charger with a capacity of 1,100 gallons, and three Receivers suitable to the requirements of the above vessels.

The Distillery being situated on the side of a hill, no pump is required until the wort is run into the Wash Still. In the little old-fashioned Still House are to be seen two of the "sma' old Pot Stills," each holding 300 gallons. One of these, a veritable smuggler's Still of a peculiar shape, is the quaintest we have seen in our travels, and was formerly the property of a noted law evader; its body is shaped like a pumpkin, and is surmounted by a similarly shaped chamber one fourth the size, to prevent the goods boiling over, through which the neck passes to the head of the Still. On the floor of the house is placed an old-fashioned Low-wines and Feints Charger, a stumpy-looking vessel constructed of timber. This building is the oldest part of the Work, and consists of a vaulted chamber cut out of the solid rock, and was formerly used by the smugglers as their Still and Mashing House.

There are two Bonded Warehouses, containing, at present, nearly 300 casks of Whisky. The Malt is crushed by both water and steam power, the water-wheel being 9 feet in diameter. The steam-engine is of 12-horse power, and by means of shafts stretching all over the place, can be made to do almost all the work of the Distillery.

The Whisky, which is Highland Malt, is principally sold in Scotland, where there is a good demand for it, and the annual output is 7,000 gallons.

Mr. Samuel Watson is the Excise officer.

No. 54.

Pulteney Distillery, Wick.

PROPRIETORS, JAMES HENDERSON & CO.

WHEN we left Kirkwall the weather, although cold, was fine, but after we reached the outer islands the rain came down in torrents, and the sea was so rough that our voyage was prolonged nearly two hours. Fortunately, the weather cleared up a little before we arrived at Scrabster Pier, and right glad were we to reach the hotel, and rest ourselves after the stormy passage.

We rose with the lark next morning, and caught the early train to Wick, which place we reached before breakfast. It is a seaport town, and the name, which is of Scandinavian origin, signifies an opening or bay, which is quite descriptive of the situation of the town. Wick derives its chief importance from being the great emporium of the herring fishery of Scotland, and during the season from 800 to 1,000 boats may be seen leaving the bay.

On the south side of the bay stands the gloomy ruin of Auldwick Castle, said to have been built before the twelfth century, which serves as a landmark to mariners and is called "the Auld Man o' Wick," and, on the north side, "John o' Groats," which is about eighteen miles distant from the town. The coast is engirt with rocks, rising precipitously from the sea, which from the steamer look inaccessible; but here and there are to be found some curious little retreats for boats, hidden behind niches of projecting rocks. In one of these creeks, called Whalligoe, there is a fine cascade, which falls abruptly over the cliff, and to see this waterfall with the sun's rays upon it is a sight never to be forgotten.

The sea coast throughout Caithness is generally lofty and rugged, and presents scenery of the grandest description. The iron-bound precipices are cleft by innumerable "goes" or fissures, whose steep sides in the breeding season are covered with thousands of wild fowl. At their base, in many places, gloomy caves open out, and here and there shoot up the isolated pillars of rock called stacks, which impart a peculiar and striking feature to the scene. Some of them are hollowed into arches by the restless surge, which, when agitated by the gale, is ever and anon seen pouring through them with a rush of foam. One of the most remarkable of these stacks, called The Brough, is situated near the Auld Man o' Wick; this immense oval-shaped rock, which is about 300 feet high and 600 feet long, is perforated from end to end, the passage being so large and water so deep that a boat can easily pass through in fine weather, and in the centre of the passage is a large space with an opening through the top, which lights up the interior.

There are several lofty headlands along the coast, but the most celebrated are the Ord of Caithness, Holburn Head, and the Promontory of Duncan's Bay.

The Ord, so well known as a formidable pass between Sutherland and Caithness, is situated at the eastern boundary of the two counties. On the Sutherland side the headland is cleft into a huge ravine or gorge of great depth, running a long way up into the interior. The old road, along which the mail coach travelled in olden times, was the only practicable route into the country, and was a mere path or shelf along the outer edge of the promontory, without any protection from the precipice, so that it could not be passed with safety in a storm. Holburn Head, which is about three miles from Thurso, is a magnificent promontory. It runs out on the west side of the roadstead of Scrabster, and with its bold precipitous ridge, forms, as it were, a gigantic wall to protect it from the fury of the Atlantic. At the extremity of the headland there is an immense isolated rock, called the Clett, which adds considerably to its picturesque and striking appearance. The roadstead of Scrabster has been long famous as an anchorage, where a large number of vessels can ride safely at anchor during a storm. The most beautiful promontory on the coast is Duncan's Bay Head, which lies about a mile from John o' Groats. It is a semi-circular shape and about two miles in extent, the greater part of which is surrounded by the sea, and forms a continued precipice remarkable for its stupendous boldness, and the wild and striking appearance of the few chasms and goes by which it is indented.

The scenery inland is tame and bleak, and with the exception of one or two small plantations near the town, there is scarcely a tree visible for many miles. The town is divided by the Wick river, and that part on the south side, where the Distillery is planted, is called Pulteney Town. The works are built close to the shores of the German Ocean, and about one mile from the station; they are quadrangular in form, and cover nearly 3½ acres of ground.

Pulteney is the farthest north Distillery on the mainland of Scotland, and is one of the oldest Distilleries in the North, having been established in the year 1826 by the late Mr. James Henderson, by whose family it is still carried on. Previous to its erection, Mr. Henderson was the proprietor of a small Distillery further inland for a period of nearly thirty years, but on finding the demand for his "make" increasing, he determined to start a Distillery nearer the sea coast, which in those days was the only mode of transit to the south; the firm may, therefore, claim to have been Distillers from about the beginning of the century. Entering the establishment through a covered archway, we observed on the right the Maltings; they consist of three commodious and well ventilated Barley Lofts, capable of storing 2,500 quarters of grain; and two Malting Floors, also of large dimensions, each possessing Steeps of proportionate size, which will wet 25 quarters at one time. At the end of these buildings are the Kilns, floored with iron plates, and where peat only is used in drying the malt. Adjoining the Kilns are two large Malt Deposits, each capable of containing 4,500 bushels. We crossed to the other side of the square, where are situated all the buildings connected with the Distillery proper, and mounted a staircase which leads to the Mill, placed over the Mash House. The dried malt is carted there from the Kilns; the malt rollers will crush 250 bushels per hour. Two shoots from the Mill Room convey the ground malt direct to the Mash-tun. In the adjoining apartment we noticed two Heating Coppers, holding together 3,000 gallons, which vessels are both heated by steam. Descending to the ground floor, we came to the Mash House, a building used for brewing only, containing a Mash-tun, 12 feet in diameter and 5 feet deep, fitted with revolving rakes and draining plates; also the Underback, placed below the floor.

We then retraced our steps to the level of the Mill Floor, and passed through a doorway into the Tun Room, where there are four Washbacks, each with a capacity of 6,000 gallons. Crossing this floor, we found ourselves on a

PULTENEY DISTILLERY.

gallery overlooking the Still House, on which are placed the Wash Charger and two Low-wines and Feints Chargers. From this elevation we noticed below us three old Pot Stills; one of them the Wash Still, holding about 4,000 gallons, and the other two Spirit Stills, holding about 2,000 gallons, of the oldest pattern known, similar to the old smuggler's kettle, and are all heated by furnaces; here also are the Receivers, Safe and Sampling Safe, and Pumps.

Following our conductor, we passed the Manager's house and offices; also the Spirit Store, which is opposite, containing a Vat holding 2,500 gallons, and finally reached the Bonded Warehouses, of which there are eleven, capable of holding 3,000 casks; one of them is newly built, and consists of three floors, which will store 100,000 gallons of Whisky.

There is a large water-wheel at the back of the Still House, and two large Worm Tanks. The water used comes from the Loch of Hempriggs, distant three miles, and is said to be of that peaty flavour so much sought after by smugglers in bygone years; the barley used is from Moray and Ross-shires.

In the courtyard there are capital offices for the Distillery and Excise. Mr. George Todman is the principal officer on the premises.

The Whisky is pure Highland Malt, and the annual output is about 80,000 gallons, which is chiefly sold in the provincial towns of England and Scotland.

No. 55.

Gerston Distillery, Halkirk.

PROPRIETORS: THE GERSTON DISTILLERY COMPANY.

WE took Halkirk on our way from Pulteney to Brora. The country round Halkirk is flat but well cultivated, and it has a special attraction to the angler in the splendid fishings in its neighbourhood. The village is situated on the river Thurso, one of the best angling streams in the North of Scotland.

The Gerston Distillery is situated about half a mile from the village of Halkirk and one mile from the railway station. It is also within six miles of Thurso, from which town there is a regular service of steamers to all parts of the country. Owing to its position and construction the Distillery is a commanding feature in the landscape, and has been erected close to the site of the old Gerston Distillery, which enjoyed a reputation for the excellence of its Whisky, said to have been due to the quality of the water, the sole rights to which have been conserved to the new Company. The buildings and plant are constructed on the most approved principles, full advantage being taken of a natural fall on the site for getting everything worked on the gravitation system. On the highest part of the ground are erected the Malt Barns, with Grain Lofts over them, adjoining which is the Malt Kiln, so arranged as to be easily loaded and discharged, and by a simple contrivance the application of the hot air to the malt is under complete control. From the Kiln the malt passes into the Deposit Room, thence into the Hopper, which supplies it to the Mill; after being ground it is instantly elevated to the Grist Hopper, from whence it drops into the Mash Tun, and when the mashing is completed the grains drop through a sluice port into the Draff House, which is immediately under the Mash Tun.

From the Mash Tun the Worts pass into the Underbacks, and then flow by gravitation through the refrigerator into the Washbacks in the Tun Room, which adjoins the Still House. The Stills, which were manufactured by Willison & Co., are heated by steam from a large boiler placed at one end of the Still House. The latter vessel also supplies the steam for boiling the water in the Brewing Coppers in the Mash House; there is thus only one fire to stoke instead of four, the furnace being situated on the lowest level, close to the coal store. This arrangement effects a great saving of manual labour, and leaves the Mash and Still House beautifully clean.

The present proposed output is 2,000 gallons per week, or about 80,000 gallons per annum, but the Works have been so constructed that the output can, at little expense, be doubled if required. The whole buildings and internal fittings and plant have been carried out from the drawings and under the superintendence of Messrs. A. Maitland & Sons, architects, Tain.

No. 56.

Clynelish Distillery, Brora, Sutherlandshire.

TENANTS, GEORGE LAWSON & SONS.

LEAVING Georgemas Junction, we proceeded southwards down the Highland Railway to Brora. It was a three hours' journey, and a somewhat tedious one; but, with our faces towards Inverness and more civilized parts, we bore it with equanimity. The Clynelish Distillery is situated on the north side of the comparatively extensive plain which forms the mouth of Strath Brora. It is about one mile from the village of Brora, seventy-one from Wick, and ninety from Inverness, by the Highland Railway. Loch Brora, through which runs the excellent salmon stream of the same name, is about two miles to the west of the Distillery, and forms one of the principal attractions of the district to tourists and anglers.

In the early part of the present century the inhabitants of the county of Sutherland, who up to that time had lived in scattered hamlets in the interior, were, by the proprietors, moved down to the coast, where allotments were provided for them, and in 1819, with a view of affording a ready market for the grain produced on the newly cultivated land, the Marquis of Stafford, afterwards first Duke of Sutherland, founded the Distillery now under notice. The situation was chosen partly on account of the proximity of the Brora coal-field, but in the present day this is of no advantage, as the coal produced at this mine is of such poor quality that none of it is used at Clynelish. The Distillery has been in the hands of Mr. Lawson, the senior member of the firm, since 1846, and a new lease has recently been entered upon.

A few miles beyond Brora, stands Dunrobin Castle, the favourite seat of the Duke of Sutherland, which was founded in the year 1097 by Robert, Second Earl of Sutherland, whence its name, Dunrobin. It is one of the most princely palaces in the Kingdom, and all the modern additions have been built with white freestone from Bora, on the Duke's own property. The grand entrance tower is a prominent object from the railway, and is upwards of 100 feet high, the approaches therefrom and staircase being lined with polished Caen stone. Inside the Castle is arranged into suites of apartments, all containing a complete set of sitting and bed rooms, furnished most sumptuously. Each suite has its own peculiar style of decorations and colour, and named the Duke's, the Argyle, the Blantyre apartments, and those of other members of the family. The grand suite in front, and which face the German ocean, have been appropriated to Her Majesty, whose apartments are complctly separated from the rest of the Palace by a wide gallery. The sea frontage is over 300 feet, with bastions at the end, enclosing a paved terrace, from whence magnificent views, from Ben Wyvis, round by the Mountains of Inverness, Moray, and Aberdeenshire, and across the Firth almost to the Ord of Caithness, which is concealed from view by a projecting headland, can be obtained.

The buildings are in the form of a rectangular oblong, with two courtyards in the interior, and a fringe of buildings, consisting of warehouses, offices, &c., round the north and part of the east and west faces. They cover about two acres, are all roofed with slates, and have been put into a thorough state of repair. To the south is the yard for peats, which are cut from a moss about a quarter of a mile away, and from this moss is also drawn the water required for motive power. The water used in the Distillery is taken from a small stream, which originates in a loch, some miles distant amongst the hills. In its course it runs alternately over moss and gravel until within about a mile of the Distillery, when it enters a rocky gorge, and, tumbling over several falls, is caught at the foot of the hill in a substantial stone cistern, from which it is led to the Distillery in iron pipes.

There are three Granaries, capable of storing about 2,000 quarters of grain, and two Malt Barns, one with a stone, the other an iron Steep. The Kiln, which is a new erection, and in which nothing but peat is used, can dry 20 quarters at a time. The Malt Mill, as also the Worts and Wash Pumps and the Coolers, are driven by an over-shot water-wheel.

The Mash House is of large dimensions, and contains a Mash-tun, 13 feet in diameter and 3 feet 6 inches deep, two large Copper Boilers, also the Underback, and the Worts and Wash Pumps. In the Tun Room are four Washbacks, with an average capacity of 3,000 gallons, above which is the cooling floor. The two Stills, which have recently been put in, are both of the old pot type, and are heated by coal. In addition to them, the Still House contains the Wash and Low-wines Chargers, and Low-wines and Spirits Receivers ; also the Spirit Safe.

In the Spirit Store there is a vat of 900 gallons content, and the usual casking appliances. Distributed about the premises there are five large Warehouses, all built of stone and lime, with slate roofs, and capable of holding about 900 puncheons of Whisky. During the summer months the distilling operations cease in this establishment.

The Whisky made is Highland Malt, and the average annual output is nearly 20,000 gallons.

It is sent out duty paid to private customers all over the kingdom, and the demand for it in this way has become so great that the firm have for some years been obliged to refuse trade orders. This system entails the keeping a heavy stock of Whisky while it is maturing; and the whole of the extensive warehouse accommodation being required for this purpose, all offers to purchase in bond are declined and the whole stock is thus available for the ordinary business of the firm.

No. 57.

Balblair Distillery, Edderton, Ross-shire.

PROPRIETORS, ANDREW ROSS AND SON.

FROM Brora to Tain is a sabbath day's journey. The train crawled lazily along giving us ample opportunity to see the country; we were not sorry for this as the whole district was new to us, and the scenery in some parts most interesting and beautiful. We found a very comfortable hotel at Tain, which we made our headquarters for a couple of days. The town is a royal burgh, and is remarkably clean in appearance. It contains some handsome modern buildings and the court-house is really an elegant structure. Contiguous, and in striking contrast to the latter building, is an ancient tower, surmounted by a conical spire, which forms a conspicuous feature in the landscape.

The next morning we drove from our hotel, a distance of six miles, to the Balblair Distillery. It is situated about a mile from the station and a quarter of a mile from Dornoch Firth. We should have travelled by railway, but the trains are so infrequent that it was impossible to make use of them. Our route lay mostly through a fine agricultural district, and we had a good view of the sea nearly the whole way.

The Distillery was founded in the year 1790, and in the early part of the century was very small and old fashioned. About fifteen years since, Messrs. Ross & Son enlarged the works, removing the Maltings, Mashing, and Distilling Buildings higher up the slope of the hill, in order to get the benefit of gravitation in working the Distillery, and the old buildings at the bottom of the hill were then converted into Bonded Warehouses.

The barley is shovelled from the Maltings into the Kiln, and when dried is delivered to the Mill below in the same manner. After it is ground, the grist descends direct into the Mash-Tun, from whence the worts run into the Wash Backs, all by gravitation; the natural fall of the ground, having been so utilized that no pumps are necessary. The Wash runs into the Wash-Charger which commands the Stills and the Spirit descends in like manner to the Vat in the Spirit Store. As the internal arrangements and vessels are like the other Distilleries in the district, it is not worth while to recapitulate them.

All the streams in the district of Edderton are considered suitable for distilling purposes. There is also an inexhaustible supply of peat close by, Edderton being known as the "Parish of Peats." In former days the whole neighbourhood abounded in smuggling bothies, and was the scene of many a struggle between the revenue officers and smugglers.

The Whisky manufactured by Messrs. A. Ross and Son, is Pure Highland Malt, and the annual output is 50,000 gallons, which is sold principally in Glasgow, Leith and Aberdeen.

No. 58.

Glenmorangie Distillery, Tain, Ross-shire.

PROPRIETORS, MATHESON & CO.

FROM Balblair we drove to Glenmorangie, through a series of gentle uplands and well cultivated farm lands, calling on our way at the residence of Mr. Matheson, who received us courteously and entertained us hospitably. We then drove with him to the Distillery, some half-mile distant, which is certainly the most ancient and primitive we have seen, and now almost in ruins. It is splendidly situated on the margin of the Dornoch Firth, and the sad sea waves wash its foundations. The building dates back to 1738, and was formerly an old brewery, noted from Tain to Inverness for its fine ale.

"Let husky wheat the haughs adorn,
And aits set up their awnie horn,
And peas and beans at e'en or morn,
Perfume the plain.
Leeze me on thee, John Barleycorn,
Thou king o' grain!

"On thee aft Scotland chows her cood,
In souple scones, the wale o' food,
Or tumblin' in the boilin' flood
Wi' kail and beef.
But when thou pours thy strong heart's blood,
There thou shines chief."

BURNS.

In 1843 this old brewery was turned into a Distillery by William Matheson, and ever since has had to be renewed and repaired to keep it together. At the time of our visit, the proprietor was arranging to build a new Distillery on the same site. The water, which is of excellent quality, comes from the hills of Tarlogie, and is used both for driving the water-wheel and for distilling operations. As the old place is so soon to be pulled down, we need not describe the interior arrangements, except to say that only Pot Stills have been in use.

Peat of fine quality is dug in the district, and is the only fuel used in the establishment.

The Whisky is pure Highland Malt, and well known in the Scotch and English markets. The annual output is 20,000 gallons.

When the new Distillery is built, double the quantity will be turned out; meantime, Mr. Matheson informed us that he holds a large stock of not less than five years old Spirits, with which to supply his customers during the rebuilding of the Distillery.

No. 59.

Dalmore Distillery, Alness.

PROPRIETORS, MACKENZIE BROS.

WE took leave of Tain early in the morning, and proceeded on our way by the rail as far as the village of Alness, where there are two Distilleries—Dalmore and Teaninich. After leaving the highly cultivated district of Logie, the track runs through the stately policies of Balnagown Castle, and crosses the river by a very elegant bridge of 50 feet span. The banks of the Balnagown river, which are clothed on either side with the richest woods, have been reclaimed, and converted into a flower garden on a scale of magnificence unequalled in the north; whilst the castle, one of the most imposing and stately edifices in the district, combines all the appurtenances of feudal greatness with modern comfort.

We next came to Invergorden, an important town, pleasantly situated on the Cromarty Firth, which possesses a good harbour and a ferry across the Frith to the Black Isle. After this for some distance the railway skirts the grounds of Invergorden Castle, which are beautifully planted with American, Australian, and other choice shrubs, but the dense foliage prevents the castle being seen from the line. A few minutes afterwards the train slackened speed, and we arrived at the little station of Alness. Ten minutes' walk brought us to the thickly wooded hill overlooking the Dalmore Distillery, from whence we were struck with the beauty of the Cromarty Firth, which we had frequently noticed at a distance during our journey. On the other side of the Firth are to be seen hills covered with rich verdure; on this, wide-spreading woods and well cultivated lands. Although it was summer time, a pretty strong breeze was blowing, which gave the waters a lively and sparkling appearance. From this position we had a good view of the Distillery lying at our feet. It is favourably situated, having a branch line from the railway running into the premises, and sea communication almost at its doors; added to this, it is placed in the centre of a good barley-growing district, and there is an abundant supply of fine peats in the district. The Distillery has sole command of the river Alness, which issues from the beautiful Loch of Gildermory, close to Ben Wyvis, and which is of the finest quality for distilling purposes.

This establishment, which is about half a mile from the station, is mostly enclosed, and built in the form of a double quadrangle on the slope of a hill. On one side are the Malting Floors and Granaries, on the other is a long range of high buildings, and at a lower elevation a smaller row, which includes Offices, Warehouses, and Bonded Stores.

Dalmore was established in the year 1839, and since that time has been frequently enlarged to meet the growing demand for the Whisky therein manufactured. We entered the establishment by the large gates which face the sea, and then proceeded up some stone steps on the left to the public offices, where we were received by Mr. Mackenzie, who showed us over the Distillery. In the first courtyard we noticed several buildings, which included, besides the Distillery and Excise Offices, Racking and Bottling Stores, &c. From this place we passed through an opening into a second and larger yard, on the right hand of which is a Spirit Store and an office for the Manager, and on the left the Distillery proper. Proceeding up an incline we came to the Malting Barns, a stone building three stories high, 120 feet long, and 22 feet broad, the two top floors being used for storing barley, the bottom for malting, where is a Steep capable of wetting 50 quarters at one time.

In front of this building, and at a somewhat lower elevation, is another Malting House of larger dimensions, consisting of two floors, both being used for malting, and each possessing a Steep of the same capacity. At right angles there is a third house of four stories, three of which are used for storing barley and ground malt, and the remaining one is a Malting Floor, possessing a Steep which will wet 52 quarters at one time.

There is a lofty Kiln, 40 feet by 30 feet, floored with wire cloth, and heated by peats, capable of drying 50 quarters every 48 hours, which commands all the malt floors. In close proximity is the Malt Deposit, with two discharge shoots on to a lower floor. We next visited the Mill, which contains a pair of Malt Rollers, driven by a water-wheel. The malt is carried in sacks across to the Mill, which is over the Mash-tun.

Following our guide we now commenced our explorations of No. 1 Still and Mash House. This building is the largest of the range, and is of an old-fashioned type. Placed at the eastern end is the Mash Tun, a vessel 16½ feet in diameter by 5½ feet deep, holding 2,700 gallons, with the patent stirring gear enclosed therein driven by a water-wheel; also two copper heating tanks, one holding 3,000 gallons and the other 2,000 gallons. There is a large Underback below the Mash Tun, from whence the Worts are pumped up to the old-fashioned Coolers which have the revolving fans and a horizontal Refrigerator. Leaving this house for a short time, we proceeded to the two Tun Rooms adjoining, in which are placed eight Washbacks of a capacity of 5,000 gallons each. The Wash Charger, which holds 4,500 gallons, is placed near the top of the Stills. We then returned to the Still House and inspected the two Stills, one of them, the Wash Still, holds 3,500 gallons, and the other, a Spirit Still, 1,800 gallons. To reach the No. 2 Still House we passed through an archway underneath the burn. This Still House, like the other, is nearly 30 feet square, and also contains two old Pot Stills and a Wash Charger, of same dimensions as those described. We then crossed a gangway to the Receiving House, wherein is the Low-wines and Feints Charger holding 2,000 gallons, a Safe, Spirit Receiver holding 1,200 gallons, and two Low-wines and Feints Receivers. The Spirit Store, which adjoins the Cooperage, contains two Vats holding 860 gallons each, and the usual casking apparatus. Distributed about the premises are six large Bonded Warehouses.

The Whisky is pure Highland Malt, and the annual output is 80,000 gallons.

Messrs. Mackenzie Bros. farm a considerable extent of arable land, and grow large quantities of barley, besides breeding some noted Aberdeen Angus Polled cattle, and pedigreed Clydesdale horses.

No. 60.

Teaninich Distillery, Alness.

PROPRIETOR, J. MCGILCHRIST ROSS.

ON leaving Dalmore we proceeded to Teaninich situated on the other side of the river, to reach which we were obliged to return to the station and go through the rural village of Alness.

The surrounding country is naturally rich and fertile, and we were struck with the beauty of the corn-fields, ripe with golden-grain, and the verdant meadows in which cattle were placidly grazing.

" All the tree tops lie asleep,
Like green waves on the sea,
As still as in the ocean deep
The ocean woods may be;"

In the background were seen the huge projections of Ben Wyvis, whose summit was bathed in sunshine, and its slopes covered with peaceful farms and woodlands. Crossing the bridge we turned to the left and followed the course of the river, whose banks are overhung with trees of considerable size, the grateful shade of which we fully appreciated as we pursued our way to Teaninich.

The Distillery, which is beautifully situated on the margin of the sea, and about one and a half miles from the station, consists of several ranges of substantial buildings, which, together with the Manager's house, workmen's cottages, and farmsteading, give it the appearance of a small colony.

It was founded in the year 1800, and covers upwards of four acres of ground. The establishment is almost encircled by a broad belt of fir trees, and is only divided from the sea by a roadway.

In the absence of the Proprietor, the Manager showed us over the premises, and took us through the Maltings, Mash-house, Tun-room, and Still-house, all neat and well-arranged buildings. The Kilns are heated with peat, and the Stills are of the old Pot kind.

Teaninich is the only Distillery north of Inverness that is lighted by electricity; besides which it possesses telephonic communication with the Proprietor's residence and the quarters of the Excise Officers. There are several spacious bonded Warehouses distributed about the premises.

The make is pure Highland Malt, and the annual output is 80,000 gallons. We were informed that the actual sales for the year 1884 amounted to 74,000 gallons.

Teaninich is a very interesting place, and we much regretted that we had so little time at our disposal, as, after hastily inspecting the Distillery, we had to hurry to the station to catch a passing train to Dingwall.

No. 61.

Ben Wyvis Distillery, Dingwall, Ross-shire.

PROPRIETOR, D. G. ROSS.

ON Thursday evening we reached Dingwall, which lies nestled at the foot of Ben Wyvis and at the entrance to the beautiful Strathpeffer Valley. We strolled out next morning before breakfast to look at the town with its surroundings. It consists principally of one street, and possesses two remarkable buildings, the Court House, an ancient castellated edifice, and the Town House, a dignified looking building, which possesses a spire. In all our journeys, for the last few days, Ben Wyvis has always been the main feature in the landscape. It is 3,722 feet above the level of the sea, and is unlike any other mountain we have seen, being covered to the top with soft green sward, and its summit crowned with snow. It has never been free from snow but once in the memory of living man, and that was in September, 1826. In the old charter of Fowlis it is stated that the forest of Naish is held of the Crown, on condition of presenting at Court a snowball of three wains of snow gathered from the top of Ben Wyvis, on any day in the year on which it may be required. Dingwall is the nearest town to the celebrated watering-place of Strathpeffer, from which it is distant four miles. The drive through the fertile valley is one of the most beautiful in the district. Everywhere you are surrounded by soft landscapes, luxuriant beauty, and fine hill-screens, all overhung by Ben Wyvis, and enlivened by the lovely stream of Peffer. After breakfast we walked to the Distillery, which is only a quarter of a mile from the town and railway station. It is on the main road, facing the railway and the Cromarty Firth, and was built in 1879. Mr. David Mather, the manager, conducted us over the premises and explained to us the method of working the Distillery. The works, which are of imposing appearance and cover three acres of ground, are erected on terraces cut out of the face of a steep rocky hill some 200 feet high, and are arranged as follows. The Barley Barns are on the top, access to which is had by a road cut out of the hill and leading up from the main road, and on successive terraces are Malt Barns, Kiln, Malt Deposit Room, Mill Room, Mash House, Tun Room, Still House, etc., and on the level, Spirit Store, business and Excise offices. On the opposite side of the road, and connected by a siding with the railway, are placed the Bonded Warehouses, which form a conspicuous object as you pass along in the train. They consist of a range of buildings 300 feet long and 36 feet broad, and five stories high. The three top flats are devoted to the store of grain and the two lower floors as Bonded Warehouses. In close proximity is the Cask Shed, 100 feet long by 30 feet wide, roofed with iron, and adjoining is the coopery. On this side also there is a large Burnt Aie Tank, conveniently arranged for supplying the farmer's tanks, or casks, with this valuable cattle fattener.

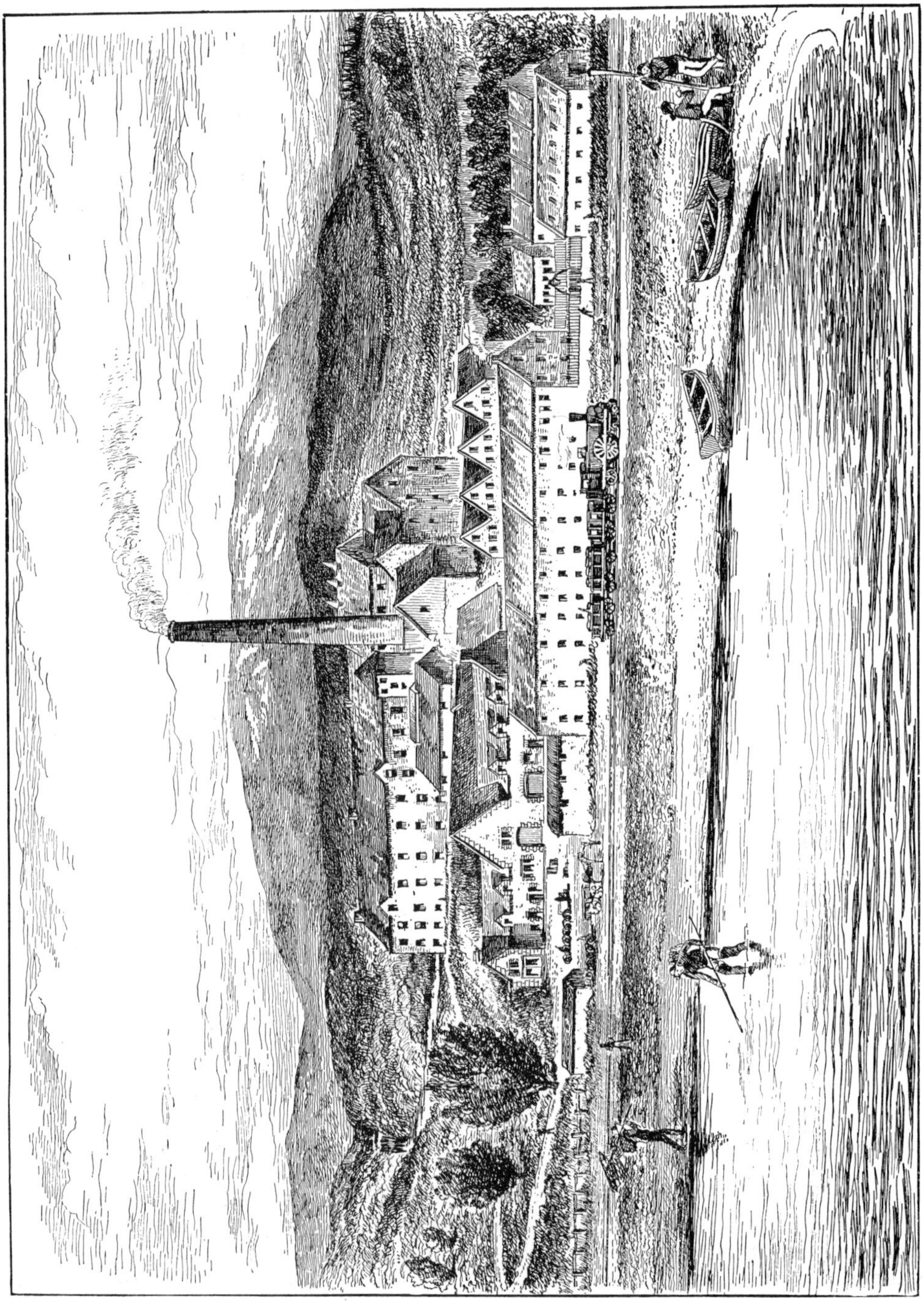

BEN WYVIS DISTILLERY.

The water used in the Distillery is brought through a conduit 3½ miles from Loch Ussie, and Dr. Stevenson Macadam reports favourably on its virtues.

The barley is carted to the Granaries by the road already referred to, and emptied into hoppers in the wall on to the floor, from whence it is sent by an elevator, and endless belt, to any part of the building. From the Grain Loft the barley is dropped through spouts into the Steeps, situated at the south ends of the malt Barns. When the malt has matured on the floors, which are of Portland cement concrete, it is raised by the afore-mentioned Grain Elevator, and, by means of a screw, distributed at the rate of 16 bushels per minute on the wire cloth floor of the Kiln. By a simple arrangement of air passages the supply of hot air to the malt is under complete control. From the Kiln the malt passes to the Malt Depôt, and thence into the Malt Hopper No. 1, a huge iron Receiver, capable of holding 1,000 bushels of malt, divided into two compartments of 500 bushels, being the quantity presently used at each mashing. From this hopper the malt passes through the Mill, and is instantly elevated by machinery into the Grist Hopper No. 2, which holds 1,000 bushels of grist, also divided into two compartments of 500 bushels. From this hopper it passes through a mashing machine into the Mash Tun, a vessel so excellently got up as to be worthy of special examination. From the Mash Tun the "wort" flows into the Underback, and when exhausted the Draff is also dropped into this vessel, from whence it slides through Sluice Ports on to the Draff loading bank. From the Underback, which holds 8,000 gallons, the "worts" runs by gravitation through a patent refrigerator into the Washbacks, which are calculated to ferment 13,000 gallons each. From the Backs it flows into the Wash Charger, and thence into the Wash Still. In thus following the liquid through its various transits we were struck with the absence of pumps. The vapour from the Wash Still is condensed in a tubular condenser, on the principle of the old-fashioned worms, but much more economical of water and space, and more rapid in its action. This condenser is kept sufficiently high to permit of the Low-wines being run through the Safe into its Receiver, and thence into the Spirit Still, all by gravitation. The spirit vapour is similarly condensed, and after passing through the Safe and Receiver it is run into the Spirit Store immediately underneath, where it is casked and rolled across the road, either into the railway trucks or into the Bonded Warehouses. The waste water from the condensers passes over a minature water-wheel, which drives the agitating gear of the Wash Still. With a view to economy of fuel the flues from the Stills are carried under the steam boiler before entering the stalk, and so important is this utilization of otherwise waste heat, that steam in the boiler is got up by this means alone. The steam boiler, which is of large dimensions, serves many important purposes. Besides supplying steam for both engines, and furnishing the means of rapidly cleansing the various utensils, it is utilized for boiling the water in the two large coppers in the Mash House. These coppers each contain 7,000 gallons of water, and a steam pipe introduced to each of them makes the contents boil in one hour and twenty minutes.

The Mash Tun is 18½ feet in diameter and 6¼ feet deep, and in the Tun Room there are four Washbacks, each holding 13,000 gallons, and a Wash Charger holding 12,000 gallons. Both the Stills are of the Pot kind, and the following are their capacities. The Wash 4,000 gallons and the Spirit 2,000 gallons. In the Engine Department we noticed a horizontal engine of 20-horse power, and a steam boiler 21 feet long and 7 feet in diameter.

The Whisky is Highland Malt, and the annual output is 160,000 gallons.

ORD DISTILLERY, BEAULY.

No. 62.

Ord Distillery, Beauly.

PROPRIETOR, ALEXANDER MACKENZIE.

ON leaving Dingwall by the early train, we soon found ourselves beyond the environs of the town, passing through a rich and undulating country, teeming with woods and plantations, and enjoying ever and anon glimpses of distant mountains, whose summits shot far up into the sky. Arriving at Beauly, we entered the carriage provided for us, and drove to the Distillery. Our way lay through the town and past the ruins of the ancient Priory, founded by John Bisset, of Lovat, which rears its venerable walls above the trees by which it is surrounded. Quitting the boundaries of the town, we soon came to the pretty demesne occupied by Mr. Mackenzie, to which is attached a large farm of 250 acres.

A short distance from this place is the romantic little chapel of "Cille Christ"—Christchurch—lately restored by a legacy of £1,000 left for the purpose by the late Frank Gillanders, of Newmore, who is buried therein. It was the scene of one of the most sanguinary deeds of Highland ferocity that history has recorded. It occurred as follows:—On a Sunday morning, in the sixteenth century, a numerous body of the Mackenzies were assembled at prayer within the walls of the old chapel, when they were surprised by a strong party of Glengarry men, bent on revenging the death of Angus, the son of their chief, who had been killed during a foray into the Mackenzies' country. Fastening up the doors, and placing his followers so as to prevent all possibility of escape, Allan, the chief, gave orders to set the building on fire. The miserable victims were without a single exception—man, woman, and child,—swallowed up by the devouring element, or massacred by the swords of the relentless Macdonalds; whilst a piper marched round the church playing a pibroch, until the shrieks of the Mackenzies were hushed in death. The Macdonalds did not, however, escape with impunity, for the funeral pile of their clansmen roused the whole tribe of the Mackenzies to vengeance, and they immediately started in pursuit, dividing their force into two bodies, one commanded by Murdoch, and the other by Alexander Mackenzie. The latter came upon a large party of the Macdonalds at the burn of Altsay, who were nearly all extirpated, whilst a still more severe retribution befel the other party, who were pursued to Inverness by Murdoch Mackenzie. They were overtaken and shut up in a wayside inn, where they had been carousing, which was set on fire, and the whole party, thirty-seven in number, perished by the same agonizing death that they had inflicted on the Mackenzies.

Proceeding, we soon reached the Moor, or Muir of Ord (celebrated for its periodical cattle markets), where are to be seen two curious and historic

"Standing Stones," which commemorate an ancient feat of arms, connected with the prophesied extinction of the clan of Mackenzie. That consummation, however, has not yet arrived; as one of the clan, the proprietor of the Ord Distillery, was our companion, and is busily engaged in the manufacture of a beverage daily imbibed by the descendants of those who foretold his clan's effacement.

Continuing our journey we soon passed over the railway, when quite a change of scenery presented itself, the hills all round being crowned with magnificent woods rising terrace upon terrace, with a fine background of mountains. The Distillery, which is erected on the slopes of a gentle hill, is quadrangular in form and compactly built. It is supplied with fine water from the Glen Oran and two lochs in the hills of Knockudas; and there are besides two reservoirs, one of them holding 500,000 gallons. The Oran rivulet, which proceeds from the glen, rattles along, close to the roofs of some of the buildings, and the quality of the water is said to be superior to any in the district.

Glen Oran has, for more than a century, been the favourite resort of smugglers, and even to this day they carry on their illicit business, and every now and then a bothy is unearthed. The site of the Distillery itself was a smuggler's bothy, early in the century, but it was not until the year 1838 that it was turned into a legal Distillery.

Under the guidance of Mr. Innes, the Brewer, we commenced our inspection of the Distillery from the top of the hill. Crossing a footbridge over the burn, we entered through a doorway into the top floor of the Maltings, arranged in two divisions, and measuring 250 feet long, with storage capacity for 3,000 quarters. Underneath are the Malting floors, of the same dimensions, each possessing a Steep capable of wetting 45 quarters at one time. Immediately adjoining there is a lofty Kiln, 24 feet square, which is floored with metal plates and heated with Dava peats. The Kiln floor is built at a considerable height above the furnace, in order that the heat may be distributed, and the Malt not scorched. In a large room, adjacent, is the Malt Deposit well lighted and spacious; the Malt descends therefrom, through a spout, into the Hopper placed over the Mill, which latter building contains a pair of Malt cylinders driven by a water-wheel. The crushed Malt is afterwards lifted by elevators to a large hopper, holding 1,200 bushels, situated over the centre of the Mash Tun. Contiguous to the Mill, in a recess of the adjoining building, are the two copper heating tanks, which hold 3,200 gallons, supplying hot water to the Tun.

We next visited the Mash House, a stone building 30 feet square, containing a Steel's Mashing Machine, and a metal Mash-tun, 18 feet in diameter, and 5 feet deep. From this dish, which is stirred by revolving gear, driven by water-power, the Worts flow into an Underback placed below the floor, holding 2,000 gallons, whence they are pumped up into a Receiver placed in the Cooler House. On leaving this vessel the Worts flow over a large Morton's Refrigerator into the Washbacks.

Ascending a few steps we passed under a gallery to the Tun-room, and were much struck with its appearance. It is a lofty paved building, 40 feet by 30 feet, with a platform at the end, whereon is placed the Wash Charger, a timber vessel holding 3,000 gallons, and a Low-wines and Feints Charger, 2,000 gallons. This large hall contains a range of eight Washbacks, splendid vessels, each holding 3,000 gallons. They are switched with props, and after due fermentation has taken place, the wash is pumped into the Charger which commands the Stills. As we descended from the gallery we took a peep through an open window at the two Condensers outside, consisting of upright cylinders, each of which contains over a hundred tubes. The Worm-tub is underneath, and so arranged that a channel from the burn constantly runs through it.

Our guide now led the way to the Still House, a large building of handsome elevation, containing two old Pot Stills: a Wash Still, holding 4,736 gallons, and a Spirit Still, 2,750 gallons. The wash runs by gravitation into the Wash Still, and after distillation has taken place by the product running through the Worm, the spirit flows into the Low-wines and Feints Receiver, a vessel holding 1,925 gallons; it is afterwards pumped up into the Low-wines and Feints Charger, whence it runs into the Spirit Still for re-distillation.

On leaving the Still, and again passing through the condensing worm, the pure spirit flows through the Safe into the Spirit Receiver, a timber vessel holding 1,900 gallons and is finally pumped into three Vats placed in the Spirit Store. The next objects that attracted our attention were eight Warehouses, the larger ones measuring 130 feet by 50 feet, the others 100 feet by 50 feet, mostly built of timber and brick, roofed with corrugated iron, and all conveniently arranged and well ventilated. One of them is built entirely of iron, quite a new departure in material for Bonded Warehouses, and highly recommended by Mr. Mackenzie. The whole contained, at the time of our visit, 174,000 gallons of Whisky of various ages. We tasted some 1882 make, and found it very agreeable to the palate.

Sages their solemn e'en may steek,
And raise a philosophic reek,
And physically causes seek,
In clime and season;
But tell me whisky's name in Greek,
I'll tell the reason.

Scotland, my auld, respected mither!
Tho' whiles ye moistify your leather,
Till whare ye sit, on craps o' heather
Ye tine your dam;
Freedom and whisky gang thegither!—
Tak' aff your dram!

Continuing our perambulations, we came to a courtyard, not previously visited, sheltered by the trees of the plantations which skirt the Distillery. Here we were shown the Spirit Store, Cooperage, Peat Sheds, and Heather House; like the proprietors of Highland Park and a few other Distillers, Mr. Mackenzie believes in the use of these blossoms with peat, in drying the malt. There is no engine on the premises, all the work being done by two large water-wheels.

Home-grown barley only is used, and the Whisky, which is pure Highland Malt, is sold principally in Leith and London, and exported to Singapore, South Africa and other colonies. The annual output is 80,000 gallons. Mr. A. Macdonald is the chief Excise officer.

We had now reached the gate at which our carriage awaited us, and taking leave of our courteous guide, we drove back to Beauly, there to join the train and proceed to Inverness.

No. 63.

Glen Albyn Distillery, Inverness.

PROPRIETORS, GREGORY & CO.

FROM Beauly to Inverness is a delightful half hour's journey. The track lies most of the way on the borders of Loch Beauly, which is but the inner portion of the Moray Firth. Travelling along a country so truly Highland, it is a source of unexpected pleasure to inhale the freshness of the sea breeze, and find the signs of maritime life so far inland. On our right are Alpine heaths and valleys, cultivated grounds and gentlemen's seats, hidden in masses of wood.

Everything has been done for Inverness that could be effected by wood and cultivation. The course of the noble river, which flows from the great lake six miles to the sea, and within a mile of the town, is divided into various branches by a series of islands, luxuriantly wooded, the surface of which is laid out in delightful and shady pleasure walks, and all are connected with each other and the mainland by chain bridges.

The river, on reaching the town, is crossed by two handsome bridges, and immediately afterwards falls into the Firth. Previous to 1745, Inverness was for generations the chief malting town in Scotland; the inhabitants almost enjoyed a monopoly, and supplied most of the northern counties and the Hebrides with malt; but unfortunately they made too much money by this occupation, which they spent upon the productions of numerous Breweries. Afterwards came the revolution, and the trade was swept away. Except two or three old Malt Kilns, and a couple of Breweries, all the rest fell into decay, and we were informed that Glen Albyn was built on the ruins of one of them. It was founded in the year 1846 as a Distillery by the late Provost Sutherland of Inverness. About twenty years afterwards it was turned into a Flour Mill. In 1884, Glen Albyn Distillery was rebuilt by the present proprietors. From the banks of the Caledonian Canal Basin, on which run the rails of the Highland Railway Company, we entered the Grain Lofts; the buildings consist of three flats, the upper two for storing Barley, the under being a Spirit Warehouse. Each flat measures 140 feet by 30 feet, and are well lighted. The Grain is transferred from these lofts by a Screw direct into the Steep placed in the building alongside the Granaries. This building consists of two flats, the upper one, having a concrete floor, used as a Malting House, the under flat, which connects with the ground floor of the first building, is also used as a Spirit Warehouse. Each of these flats, including a wing at right angles to the Kiln, measures 180 feet by 30 feet.

The Steep wets 40 quarters of Barley at one time, and is constructed with metal. After the Barley is duly vegetated it is raised by Elevators to the Kiln, which is 30 feet square, and can dry at one time 350 bushels. Here peats and coke are used in the drying, the former being got from Dava, on the Highland

Line, and are of fine quality. The Kiln has an open furnace, and to prevent any scorching of the Malt the floor is 30 feet above the fireplace.

The dried Malt is transferred to the two Deposits, forming the upper floors of a building over the archway, which are each 50 feet long and 30 feet broad, and capable of storing 6,000 bushels. The Malt Mill, which occupies one of the sides of the archway, is fitted up with the latest and most improved style of machinery for grinding, and the crushed Malt is conducted by Elevators into the hopper, above the Mashing Machine. When the slide therefrom is duly drawn, the process of mashing begins, and the Malt comes down, meeting the hot water, which is regulated in temperature by a thermometer being screwed into the hot-water pipe immediately before it joins the malt. The water and malt being thoroughly mixed by the Mashing Machine, falls into the Mash Tub, the size of which is 14 feet in diameter and 4½ feet deep. This dish is made of best heart larch-wood, and no stirring-gear is used, the whole being done by wooden oars, so that there is no contact of metal with the Worts.

The Mash House is 40 feet by 30 feet, and is a clean well-lighted apartment. The Mash Tub therein is raised about 7 feet from the ground, so that the Worts drain direct from it, through copper pipes, into a Morton's Refrigerator placed in the adjoining building, which apartment measures 18 feet by 21 feet. In this room the Worts and Wash Pumps are also placed. The Wort, when cooled, is pumped into the Backs in the Tun Room, which building is 40 feet by 27 feet, and contains three Backs, with "seats" for three more; each Back contains 4,640 gallons, switched by steam power. From the Backs, the liquor, which by the process of fermentation has now been converted into "Wash," is conveyed in copper pipes to the Wash Charger in the Distilling House. This latter building is 40 feet by 30 feet, and the Stills take up the whole height; but behind them, and on a level with their heads, there is a second flat, on which is placed the Spirit Receiver, Low-wines and Feints Receiver, and Wash Charger, also an enclosed office for the Brewer. There are two Pot Stills, the Wash Still, capable of charging 1,800 gallons, and the Low-wines Still, 1,500 gallons, both worked with fire in the usual way. The condensing Worms are of the latest and best approved style, each Still has from 300 feet to 400 feet of Worm pipes; these Worms, after the first few rounds, each branch into two smaller pipes, and, instead of being of the usual round form, are shaped like the letter D, having the flat side down. The reason for this is obvious, the spirit which at first rises in steam is condensed into liquid by the time it reaches these smaller pipes, and having to run on the *flat bottom* of these is spread over a much larger surface than if running in round pipes, and thereby gives a greater increase in the cooling power, which is a most important factor in the making of a good Whisky. The Stills, which were manufactured by Fleming, Bennet & McLaren, of Glasgow, are of the most improved and modern style. In the Distilling-house there is also a Low-wines Charger, holding 2,583 gallons, and a Spirit Receiver, with a capacity of 1,525 gallons. From this latter vessel, the Whisky is conducted in a pipe to the Vat in the Spirit Store, which holds 1,750 gallons. This Store is a separate building, 40 feet long and 27 feet wide, of two flats. It contains besides the Vat referred to a weighing beam, and all necessary utensils for filling, sampling, and weighing of casks before they are sent to the duty-free Warehouses. The second flat of this structure is occupied by Excise and Distiller's Offices, the latter being connected by telephone to the head offices in Inverness, which are about one and a half miles' distant.

The make is Highland Malt. and the annual output is 75,0C0 gallons.

No. 64.

Millburn Distillery, Inverness.

PROPRIETOR, GEORGE ROSE.

WHAT a lively and interesting place is Inverness. The constant influx of tourists, from all parts, and the ever increasing bustle, combine to invest it with light and life. On leaving the Station Hotel we ascended the Castle Hill, and from thence obtained a fine view of mountains and valleys, river and sea. After spending half an hour in this elevated position, we descended the hill by another way to the main street, where we chartered a cab and soon reached Millburn. The Distillery is about one mile from the town on the old Roman Road, which leads to Fort George, and it is situated under the brow of a steep hill, which faces the sea. It has a very handsome appearance, and is built principally of stone. The open cooperage, generally an unsightly building, is here beautified with enclosed trellis-work, painted a rich green. The Distillery was established in the year 1805, and rebuilt on a larger and more improved scale in 1876. Entering the gateway we crossed the Mill Burn, a pretty stream which rattles under the bridge on its way to the sea. On the right hand side of the enclosure, and at the back of the offices, we were shewn the Barley Lofts and Malting Floors, which consist of a range of buildings divided into several floors. The Steeps for wetting the barley are constructed with metal and fixed on the Barley Loft, discharging their contents underneath to the malting floors below. The Kiln is in close proximity, and peat only is used in drying the malt. The Distilling and Mash House is a spacious and lofty building, in the centre of the courtyard and facing the entrance gates. It contains a Heating Copper of 1,600 gallons content, and a metal Mash Tun with the usual revolving stirring gear. Leaving this department for awhile, our guide next conducted us to the Tun Room, on the other side of the yard, a clean and well-lighted building, which contains four Washbacks, each holding 4,000 gallons. We then retraced our steps to the larger building, which communicates with the various departments on either side. On a gallery we observed the Wash Charger, which holds 3,000 gallons, and a Refrigerator. Standing on the Floor are two old Pot Stills, and in close proximity is the Low-wines and Feints Charger, holding 1,300 gallons, a Low-wines and Feints Receiver of same capacity, and a Spirit Receiver of 1,200 gallons content. We next paid a visit to the Spirit Store, which contains two Vats, each holding 600 gallons, and the usual weighing and casking apparatus. From thence we directed our steps to the three spacious Bonded Warehouses and the Bottling Store. This last is a well-arranged department, fitted up with all necessary appliances and machinery.

In addition to the cooperage already referred to, there is a carpenter's shop, and capital offices for the distillery and Excise clerks. The Whisky manufactured is pure Highland Malt, and the annual output is 60,000 gallons.

No. 65.

Royal Brackla Distillery, Nairn.

PROPRIETORS, ROBERT FRASER & CO.

A SHORT railway journey from Inverness brought us to Nairn, one of the most charming sea-side resorts in the north, and called the Brighton of Scotland.

On our arrival we discovered, much to our chagrin, that the Royal Brackla Distillery was six miles distant, and that there was no way of reaching it but by hiring a carriage. We at once proceeded to the hotel, and were fortunate in securing an open landau and a good steed, which bowled us along through a most delightful country. After crossing the bridge which spans the river Nairn, our drive took us over hill terraces covered with pine woods, and along undulating lands as pastoral as an English scene. When we reached the Red Knock we had one of the finest landscape views at our feet that it is possible to witness. The Nairn steals along in its sinuous course, now slyly peeping round the corner of a belt of trees, then again a bit of it is seen between the hillocks, anon a stretch for a quarter of a mile, when it suddenly disappears, to reappear again, surprising us as often as possible. Barley fields stretched away for miles across the plain, in the centre of which we distinguished the Distillery, the object of our journey. As we neared the establishment our driver, an intelligent fellow, reminded us that we were on ground made classic by Shakespeare, in "Macbeth." The Cawdor Moss is just above the Distillery, and running through it is the famous Cawdor Burn, which, after passing through a deep rocky ravine beautifully wooded within the park surrounding the ancient castle of Cawdor, splashes past and flows into the Nairn. This burn, which supplies all the water to the Distillery, was in remote days used by the noted Tarrick and other smugglers, whose illicit stills abounded on its banks.

The Brackla Distillery was built in the year 1812, by Captain William Fraser, and consists of several ranges of old and new buildings, covering upwards of four acres of ground. On driving into the yard we were received by one of the partners, who, in the absence of the Manager, conducted us over the works.

We commenced as usual at the Barley Lofts, which are built over an enormous duty-free Warehouse. They are 140 feet long by 90 broad, and will hold 2,000 quarters. The barley is raised from the farmer's wagons to these floors by a friction hoist, where it is pitched into a moveable square hopper, so arranged that the grain is measured into the bushel as it passes through to the floor. It is next lifted by elevators into a screw-box by which it is conveyed to the Malt floors, and dropped by shoots into the required Steeps. The two Malt Barns adjoin the Granaries, and are 120 feet long by 45 broad. From these floors the malt is raised by another friction hoist to the Kiln, which is floored with metal plates and heated by peat. In the yard there are two enormous sheds filled with peat ready for the winter's use, dug from the neighbouring moor. We next crossed the Kiln floor to the malt deposit, a gallery 70 feet long and 54 wide, situated over the Mill building, and having in its centre a large fixed hopper, through which the malt is shovelled, to be ground between the malt cylinders below.

From this department the ground malt is sent by elevators and screws to another hopper, over the Tun Room, which feeds a patent Mashing Machine. Following our guide we soon found ourselves in the Mash-house, a lofty and spacious building, which contains a Mash Tun 17 feet in diameter and 6 feet deep, possessing the usual stirring gear and draining plates; also a metal Underback of somewhat less proportions. From the latter vessel the Worts are pumped up through a Morton's Refrigerator to the Worts receptacle, from thence they run into the Fermenting Tuns. A few steps across the paved court brought us to the Tun Room, a well-lighted apartment, both walls and ceiling being painted white, in which are placed eight Washbacks, each holding 5,000 gallons. The Switches therein, which are driven by machinery, move at a high and low speed, and, by the ingenious arrangement of a lever, each can be worked separately. From these vessels the Wash is pumped up into the Wash Charger, a handsome circular timber vessel, holding 7,000 gallons, fixed on a gallery in the Still House. Leaving this house we were next conducted to the Engine-house, which contains a little horizontal engine of 13 horse-power; also a donkey-engine for feeding the boiler, which works in conjunction with the water-wheel and the usual pumps; and a steam boiler, 20 feet long and 7 feet in diameter, for supplying hot water to the Mash Tun.

We next visited the Still House, a stone building of large proportions, which contains two old Pot Stills, partly heated by steam coils; a Wash Still, holding 4,700 gallons, and a Low-wines Still of 2,680 gallons capacity; also a Low-wines Receiver, holding 2,000 gallons, a Low-wines and Feints Charger, and a Spirit Receiver, which latter vessel is placed on the ground.

The Spirit Store, which is in close proximity, contains a Vat, holding 2,060 gallons, and the usual weighing apparatus. Our guide now led the way to the Bonded Warehouses, five in number, all substantial buildings. One of these is 272 feet long by 50 broad, with a span roof, and is divided into sections, so that Whisky of any age can be found at once. They contained at the time of our visit 2,000 casks. From thence we went to the Cooperage, and Duty-Paid Racking Store, the latter for the convenience of local customers.

The arrangements for extinguishing fire are very complete, consisting of a fire-hose and extincteurs distributed about the premises. The proprietors have provided a good house for the Manager, and convenient dwellings for the work-people. The Whisky is carted to the station six miles distant by a traction engine, which brings back coals from Nairn. It is necessary to have a large supply of this fuel, as it is not an uncommon occurrence in winter to be cut off from all communication by snow-drifts for a fortnight at a time. Attached to the Distillery there is a farm of 320 acres, mostly under barley cultivation. There are three ponds or reservoirs close to the works, and most picturesquely situated, shaded by willow trees and fed by the waters of the Cawdor Burn. In this latter stream are placed the coolers, a capital arrangement when the position of the Burn will permit.

Both water and steam power are used in the Brackla Distillery, and the barley consumed is all home-grown.

The make is pure Highland Malt, and the annual output is 70,000 gallons.

No. 66.

Glenburgie Distillery, near Forres.

PROPRIETORS, ALEXANDER FRASER & CO.

OFFICE, 219, HIGH STREET, ELGIN.

FORRES is the junction for the delightful Highland route from Inverness to Perth, which takes in the Pass of Killiecrankie and Blair Athole. It is four miles from Forres to the Glenburgie Distillery, which is situated in a valley, and is a short distance from a range of hills, from which can be seen Sutherlandshire, Caithness, and Ben Wyvis; indeed, this giant mountain can be seen any clear day along the coast for 70 miles. Glenburgie is a very ancient Distillery, and about as old fashioned as it is possible to conceive. It was founded in the year 1810 by the grandfather of the celebrated surgeon, Dr. Liston Paul, of London, and is said to be one of the oldest Distilleries in the north, having been steadily worked for over seventy years.

The Malt House is of an old-fashioned type, and built with stone. It is two stories high, the top being used for storing barley, with the usual Steep, and the ground floor for Malting. Connected with the building there is a small Kiln, floored with perforated bricks, and heated with peats brought from the celebrated peat deposits of the Dava and Dallas Moors. Adjoining is the Malt Deposit and Mill, the latter with the usual grinding machinery. At the end of the yard is the Still House, which contains the following vessels: a Mash-tun, 10 feet in diameter and 3½ feet deep, Heating Copper, Underback, Worts Receiver, Refrigerator, Spirits and Feints Receiver, Wash Charger, and two "sma'" Pot Stills, holding respectively 1,500 gallons and 800 gallons.

In the Fermenting Room there are five Washbacks, with an average capacity of 2,430 gallons each. Three new Bonded Warehouses have lately been added, and in proportion to the size of the works the Warehouse accommodation is extensive.

We may further add that, in addition to the beauty of its surroundings, this Distillery is situated in the centre of the finest barley growing district of the north. The water used is taken from local springs of great purity, whilst a small burn drives the water-wheel.

The Whisky is pure Highland Malt, and is said to be of fine quality. We were informed that the sales are principally confined to select wine merchants, and the annual output is about 24,000 gallons. The establishment is two miles from Kinloss Station. Messrs. Fraser & Co., the present proprietors, succeeded Charles Kay in the business.

MILTON DUFF DISTILLERY.

No. 67.

Milton Duff Distillery, Elgin.

PROPRIETORS, WILLIAM STUART & CO.

WE arrived betimes the next morning at Elgin, and at once made our way to the Gordon Arms, a well-known hostelry, patronized by the Duke of Edinburgh and other notables. After securing comfortable quarters for our intended abode for a few days, and refreshing ourselves with a substantial breakfast, we drove to Milton Duff. Our good host, Mr. Edgar, who does the principal posting in the district, and prides himself on his stud of horses, turned us out in fine style, and our high stepper started off at a rattling pace. Leaving the pleasant suburbs of Elgin, and crossing the bridge over the Lossie, our way lay through the richly cultivated plain of Pluscarden, called the "Garden of Scotland,' and justly celebrated for its growth of fine barley. At the head of the vale, in a secluded and beautifully wooded glen, stand the romantic ruins of Pluscarden Priory. This ancient monastic establishment, said to have been one of the richest in Scotland, was founded in 1230 by Alexander II., and the lands belonging thereto, which stretched almost to the borders of Rothes, included the site now occupied by the Milton Duff Distillery. The monks of Pluscarden, among other things, were adepts in the art of brewing fine ales, the quality of which was considered to be superior to any in Scotland. It was so good that it—

"Made the hearts of all rejoice, and filled
The abbey with unutterable bliss;
Raised their devotions to that pitch
That Heldon's hills echo'd their hallelujahs."

They brewed their ales and made their drinks from the waters of the Black Burn, a rivulet which descends from the mossy uplands of the Black Hills and runs through the plain, and which every storm converts into a torrent. Of this stream the following legend is told:—On a New Year's Day in the fifteenth century, an imposing ceremony occurred on the grounds where now stands Milton Duff. It was the occasion of blessing the waters of the Black Burn, previous to its being used by the Benedictine Monks of Pluscarden. Attended by his priors, palmers, and priests, an aged abbot proceeded to the banks of the stream, where, kneeling on a stone with hands outstretched to heaven, he invoked a blessing on its waters, and ever after the life-giving beverage distilled therefrom was christened "aqua vitæ," the rivulet being to this day held in high repute and veneration by the natives. We were shown the stone on which the abbot is said to have knelt; it bears an indistinct date, and is built into the wall of the Malt Mill.

Our driver was a clever, cheery individual, well up in the annals of the district, and as we proceeded on our way interested us very much. He asked, with a serious air, if we had heard of "Enoch Arden." On our replying in the affirmative, he informed us that this gentleman lived close by, and if we liked he would drive us there in ten minutes to see the house. We immediately assented, and soon found ourselves passing a rustic cottage, standing in a well cultivated garden. From an upper window a comely-looking matron was looking down upon her children below, and our driver informed us that she was Mrs. Arden No. 2. As we returned to the main road, the coachman related the story as follows:—"'Arden,' a married man, with no family, was in straitened circumstances, and leaving his wife behind, went to America to retrieve his fortunes. After a time, having prospered, he wrote for his wife to join him in his adopted country, but received no reply to his various communications. Time rolled on, and believing his wife to be dead, he married again, and had two or three children. After the lapse of a few years, on returning to his native country, accompanied by his wife and family, he found, to his surprise and distress, that his first wife was still living, but mourning for him as one dead. Now comes the strange part of the story of Enoch Arden reversed, Mrs, Arden No. 1 was overjoyed at seeing her husband again, and included in her embrace his second wife and her children; from that moment they all fraternized, and have been living together in perfect bliss ever since, to the horror of the parsons and the amazement of their neighbours. 'Arden' is said to be the only man in the country who is blessed with two wives!"

Our first halt was at the Old House of Milton Duff, occupied by Mr. Stuart, an ancient and picturesque building, dating back to the year 1640. Its grey walls are of immense thickness, and mostly covered with pear-trees, said to have been planted by the monks. After strolling through the pleasure and fruit-gardens, we entered the house to explore some of its hidden nooks and quaint apartments, and found it to be one of the most curious and interesting dwellings we have ever visited. We then returned to our carriage, having previously regaled ourselves with a nip of creamy Old Milton Duff Whisky, and then drove to the Distillery, a short distance further on. The appearance of Milton Duff is a complete contrast to the other Distilleries in the district. There is scarcely a building alike, and they are all, with one exception, detached.

The works, which now cover two acres of ground, were mostly rebuilt as far back as the year 1824, by Pearey and Bain; but previous to that time the site was occupied by the descendant of a band of smugglers, of whom many interesting tales are told. At one time there were as many as fifty illicit stills in the Glen of Pluscarden, and there are those living who remember some of them in operation. In this well-known establishment some of the oldest fads and methods are in use, and the ancient style of stills and utensils as carried on by the smugglers, have also been continued. These gentlemen, who were the pioneers of whisky making, well knew in what locality the best water was to be found, hence their choice of Pluscarden, and the erection of "sma' Stills" by the score on the banks of the Black Burn.

Our friend, Mr. Ross, the manager, conducted us over the premises, and first led the way to the Malt Barns, a triangular building, the top flat of one side being used for the storage of barley, and containing upwards of 2,000 quarters; the lower and remaining portions divided into three compartments which are used for malting purposes, and contain a concrete Steep. One side of this triangular building measures 160 feet, the other 130 feet; both are 30 feet wide. The Kiln is a very ancient structure, about 40 feet high and 28 feet square. It is floored with steel plates, and only Orkney peats are used for drying the malt. The Orkney peats are said to be the finest in the kingdom. In the adjoining sheds we saw two ship-loads of this valuable fuel, which Mr. Stuart had just imported from Edday, in Orkney, for the following winter's use.

The dried malt is pitched through an opening in the wall to the two Malt Deposits, which are placed at a slightly lower elevation, and when required the malt is dropped therefrom through a Sluice Hopper to the Mill below, which contains a pair of metal malt cylinders, driven by steam power, grinding 150 bushels every hour. Leaving this department we now crossed the yard to the Still House, which also combines a Mash House. This venerable building is at the left hand corner of the courtyard, and tradition says that it was the brew-house of the ancient monks. Some parts of the roof were so low that we had to stoop as we went along; at some places there were depressions of the floor, and our guide frequently said "mind the steps." Ascending a ricketty stone stair we

COURTYARD, MILTON DUFF DISTILLERY.

reached a gallery whereon is placed the grist hopper and a copper heating tank, which holds 1,600 gallons; the pulverized grist is brought over from the Grist Loft in sacks to this hopper, which conducts the ground malt to a Steel's Mashing Machine. Looking over this projecting gallery we see below us the Mash Tun, a metal vessel, 14 feet in diameter and 4 feet deep, wherein the worts are stirred with oars. The draff from the Mash Tun is thrown out to the pit by manual labour, and is used for feeding a number of fine cattle Climbing a short flight of steps we came to the Cooling Room, where is placed a Morton's Refrigerator and the Worts Receiver. This latter is an old-fashioned vessel made out of an old Mash Tun, which originally belonged to the smuggler-founder of the Distillery. The Worts are pumped up to this dish, and from thence flow over the Refrigerator to the Washbacks. We then passed through the gallery, and came to the stage in the Tun Room, a building 40 feet square, wherein are placed seven Washbacks, three of them holding 4,000 gallons, and the others 3,000. From the Backs the Wash is pumped into the Wash Charger, a square wooden vessel holding 3,500 gallons. We then retraced our steps to the Distilling House, where there were many things to awaken our interest, not only from the monastic associations of the place, but also from the quaintness and antiquity of the vessels in use. At the east end the roof is considerably higher, and here are placed two old Pot Stills of great age; one of them is a Wash Still, and holds 1,500 gallons, the other a Spirit Still, called the Low-wines, holds 1,200 gallons. The Wash runs by gravitation from the Charger to the Wash Still, and after distillation has taken place the process is twice repeated. This is certainly the most interesting part of the process, and if we had space and time, would describe fully how the Whisky at Milton Duff undergoes the operation of three distillations, and the old-fashioned way in which at various stages it is manipulated.

After lingering here much longer than our guide approved, we passed out into the open square, and were shown the Worm-tub connected with the Stills. It consists of a deep cement tank, 20 feet square, with a pathway round and a bridge across it, which contains upwards of 400 feet of worm coils. Standing on this bridge, we noticed two well-worn but solid timber vessels for supplying cold water to the Refrigerator, and the large water-wheel which drives the still chains. The waste water from this wheel also supplies a smaller one, which drives the saw mill machinery connected with the carpenters' shop. At a short distance is the open conduit, by which a part of the stream has been diverged from the Black Burn, and which here rushes madly on to join the latter before it reaches the Lossie. We now returned to the Still House, and ascended a step-ladder to the Charging and Receiver Loft, where are to be seen a Low-wines and Feints Charger holding 1,400 gallons, a Spirit Receiver, 1,200 gallons, a Low-wines and Feints Receiver, 600 gallons, and the Safe. Returning to the court, we continued our tour of the Distillery, and after passing the Spirit Store, entered the largest of the five Warehouses distributed about the premises; it is 240 feet long and 120 feet broad, very dry and well ventilated. All the Warehouses together held, at the time of our visit, 3,100 casks, containing 274,000 gallons of Whisky of various ages. They are, however, capable of holding another 1,000 casks. Adjoining the larger Warehouse is the Cooperage and Carpenters' Shop, before referred to; also the stables wherein were twelve horses, two of them magnificent animals, used only for carting Whisky to the station. Mr. Stuart's farm covers 200 acres, and at a short distance he owns a delightful shooting box on the river Lossie. The chief Excise officer is Mr. Bain, and ten men are employed, for whom Mr. Stuart has provided comfortable dwellings.

The Whisky, which is supplied to all parts of the world, is pure Highland Malt, and the annual output is 75,400 gallons.

No. 68.

Glen Lossie Distillery, Glenlivet District.

PROPRIETORS, J. DUFF & CO., ELGIN.

AN agreeable place is Elgin, clean and well built, with an unmistakeable air of antiquity about it, notwithstanding its new buildings and modern Town Hall. The Gordon Arms, where we stayed, is a venerable hotel, and quite in keeping with the appearance of the old cathedral city. It is a substantially built rambling old place and from time to time has been visited by many noble and royal personages, the last being H.R.H. the Duke of Edinburgh. In all our wanderings we had never slept in better rooms, received more attention, nor been more comfortable. John the waiter anticipated our every want and was quite hurt if we did not bring good appetites to the meals provided.

Before proceeding on our journey to Glen Lossie we drove round by the eastern end of the ecclesiastical city to inspect the ruins of its old cathedral, the glory of Elgin and long and justly styled "The Lanthorn of the North." The objects most conspicuous on our way were the Hill of Cullen, which rises from the plain, and forms a landmark to mariners, and the hills which enclose the Valley of Rothes, whose beautiful grassy slopes afford excellent sheep pasture.

The Distillery takes its name from the Lossie, which issues from a small loch in the parish of Dallas, and runs a course of 26 miles to the Moray Firth. This beautiful river winds along the town of Elgin where it is crossed by three bridges, and after running through well-cultivated fields and fertile pastures falls into the sea at Lossiemouth, six miles below Elgin, the port of that town.

The Establishment, which covers three acres of ground, is four miles from Elgin, and was built by and under the supervision of Mr. Duff, from his own plans. It stands at the foot of a fir-clad hill and consists of a double oblong range of buildings, and with the exception of the Distilling House (which is built of stone) is constructed entirely with cement, which, under the sunlight, as we descended the hill, looked beautifully white and clean. The work is carried on entirely by water power and gravitation. The Reservoir is about 200 yards distant and is supplied with water from the Mannoch Hills. There is also the Creich Spring in the hill, a quarter of a mile distant, which is brought in a conduit to a large covered cistern sunk into the sides of the hill, near the large water-wheel, which latter is fed by a lead from the Reservoir and does all the driving required.

After putting up our horse, Mr Ross, the manager, conducted us through the Distillery, and first led us by a raised road which is some 20 feet from the level, leading round to the back of the Granaries, and by which the barley is carted to the doors of the Barley Lofts. We first entered the No. 1 Barn which is the top floor of the building, 123 feet long by 54 feet broad, divided in the

GLEN LOSSIE DISTILLERY.

centre. At the end there is a large Steep sunk into the floor, at the bottom of which are sluices to let out the wet barley on to the floor below. It is capable of wetting 50 quarters at one time. To reach the Malt Barns beneath, we retraced our steps to the front of the establishment and ascended a stair. Like the floor above, they are divided, but cover a larger area, one of them being 135 feet and the other 108 feet long. From these Barns we visited the Kiln which is on the same level, and forms the gable of the first range of buildings. It is 26 feet square, floored with iron plates, and heated with peat brought from the Mannoch Hills, five miles distant, and shut off from the adjoining department by a pair of stout iron doors. Crossing the floor of the Kiln we emerged through the doorway into the Malt Deposit, a fine square chamber at the end of which is placed the Malt Hopper. Descending a steep flight of steps we reached the Mill Room below, which contains the usual malt rollers and machinery for crushing the malt. A few steps lower down brought us to the Mash House, a clean and lofty building containing an old-fashioned timber Mash Tun, 13 feet in diameter and 5 feet deep. As the Grist falls from the Mill Hopper it is directed into a Steel's Mashing Machine, over the Tun, which thoroughly mixes the pulverised malt with the hot water before it falls into the vessel. The Mash Tun is the only vessel in the Mash House except the Refrigerators, one of which was made by Morton and the other by Henderson. The Worts run by gravitation from the Tun into the Underback, a circular iron vessel placed under the floor of the next house. Our guide now led the way up to the Tun Room, to reach which we passed through the Still House and ascended a staircase. It is a large house, 80 feet long, and has a platform all round. It contains six Washbacks, each holding 3,000 gallons, and a Wash Charger, a timber vessel of similar capacity.

After inspecting this place we returned to the Still House, a spacious building (with concreted floor) which communicates with all the principal departments in the Distillery, and where, as in the Tun Room, neatness and order are everywhere remarkable. Our attention was first directed to the two large heating coppers, each holding 2,000 gallons, placed on the left of the doorway, which supply the hot water to the Mash-tun, and afterwards to the two handsome Old Pot Stills, both heated by furnaces. The Wash Still holds 1,765 and the Spirit Still 1,648 gallons. Placed near these vessels there is a Low-wines and Feints Receiver, and a Spirit Receiver, a safe and sampling safe, &c. Following our guide we now returned to the courtyard and visited the Spirit Store, wherein is a Vat of 1,200 gallons content; then to the Racking Store, and afterwards to the five Warehouses, which are all built on a terrace above the level of the roadway and form a handsome group of buildings, together they held 4,000 casks of Whisky at the time of our visit. In close proximity there is a capital Cooperage and Cask Shed, also large peat stores, stacked away for winter's use. We next proceeded to the Offices of the Distillery and Excise, both of which are conveniently arranged; afterwards we crossed the public road to the neat farm-steading, where Mr. Duff has 50 head of cattle which are fattened on the draff and spent-wash of the Distillery. On the bank above the works there is a pretty villa, occupied by Mr. Jones, the principal Excise officer. The employés on the Farm and Distillery, numbering twenty, have dwellings provided for them in the little hamlet opposite.

The Whisky is Highland Malt, and the annual output is 90,000 gallons.

Mr. John Hopkins is a partner in the Distillery, and the firm of John Hopkins & Co., London and Glasgow, have the sole sale of the make.

No. 69.

Linkwood Distillery, Elgin.

PROPRIETOR, WILLIAM BROWN.

THE next morning we drove out to Linkwood, distant about two miles. Our way lay along a pleasant country road, amid smiling hedgerows and hay-fields. The Distillery is embosomed in woods, hence its name, and was rebuilt in 1873 by the present proprietor.

Mr. George McBain, the manager, conducted us over the premises, and directed our steps first of all to the Granaries. They are stone built, of two floors, the upper portion being divided into three Barley Lofts. One of them is 100 feet long by 21 feet broad, and capable of holding 1,200 quarters. Underneath are two Malting Barns, measuring 130 and 100 feet long respectively, each is 21 feet broad, and at either end are the Steeps, capable of wetting 30 quarters at one time. In close proximity is the Kiln, a neat building, 25 feet square, floored with wire cloth, and heated with peat. To reach this floor we climbed two pairs of stairs, and found ourselves on a level with the Malt Deposit, which takes up the entire roof of one of the Barley Barns, and communicates direct with the Kiln. We next descended to the first landing and came to the Mill, which is an elevated chamber, in the lofty Mash House, and contains one pair of Malt Cylinders. The ground malt falls from thence through a Steel's Mashing Machine into the Tun below.

The Mash House is a well-lighted stone building with paved floor. It is 48 feet long and 24 feet broad, and contains a Mash Tun, 12 feet in diameter and $3\frac{1}{2}$ feet deep. The Heating Copper, holding 1,000 gallons, which supplies the Tun with hot water, as well as the Underback, are also in this house. The latter is a timber vessel, holding 600 gallons, and is sunk in the floor below. The worts are pumped from the Underback to the Coolers, which cover the roofs of the Tun Room, Spirit Store, and Coal Shed.

We then passed into the Tun Room, which is the same height and dimensions as the Mash House, and contains five Washbacks, each holding 3,200 gallons; and at the end a Yeast Store. Continuing our progress we came to the Still House, which is in the centre of the block, and is a lofty and light apartment. Here on a gallery is the Wash Charger, Low-wines and Feints Charger, and Receiver, and on the ground-level two Pot Stills; the Wash Still holding 2,000 gallons, and the Spirit Still 1,850 gallons, heated by open furnaces, and the Safe and Spirit Receiver.

We next bent our steps to the central court, where is placed the Spirit Store, containing a Vat with a capacity of 1,850 gallons; and three large Bonded Warehouses, holding together 2,000 casks; also a Racking Store, Manager's and Public Offices, and the Excise Offices.

The water used for mashing is brought from the Black Hills, six miles distant. At the back of the Distillery are the Cart Sheds, Stabling, &c., also the Burnt Ale Tank.

The Whisky is Highland Malt, and the annual output is 50,000 gallons.

No. 70.

Glen Grant Glenlivet Distillery.

PROPRIETORS, J. & J. GRANT, ROTHES, MORAYSHIRE.

WE next set out for Rothes. The route traversed was not so interesting at first, but became more so as we pursued our way; indeed, on emerging from the hills and entering the valley it became suddenly beautiful, and we found ourselves in sight of the village, nestling in its cosy nook of the lovely valley of the Spey. For beauty of position nothing that we have seen can excel the situation of Rothes. It is quite engirt by mountain ranges that lend grandeur to the view on all sides. The lofty Benrinnes and Benaigen look down on it from beyond the river; woods clamber up the sides of Benaigen almost to its top, whilst to the right and left lower hills, alike clothed in their robes of greenery, are charmingly interspersed with cultivated fields down to the bottom of the valley. Rothes is a village of considerable size. It has 1,400 inhabitants, two churches, good hotels and shops, and no less than three Distilleries—Glen Grant, Glen Rothes, and Glen Spey. A busy place it has always been. In former times, when there were no railways, its trade depended largely on its proximity to Garmouth, which, until the harbours of Lossiemouth and Burghead were built, was the principal seaport for the valleys of the Spey and its tributaries. Coals and articles of general merchandise were imported at Garmouth, carted ten or twelve miles to Rothes, and thence distributed over a wide district of country. The central position of Rothes—not far from the sea on the one hand, and close to the inland valleys and Highland mountains on the other, while near also to the famous barley-growing plains of Moray—led to its being selected by the Messrs. Grant, in 1840, for their Distillery. They found a most convenient site for the new establishment by the side of the Glen Grant Burn, which flowed down from the hills through a most picturesque ravine, supplied capital water for mashing, and gave in addition all the motive power required for driving machinery, until the Distillery was so much enlarged that steam had to be added.

Just as we steamed into Rothes Station we caught sight of the handsome residence of Major Grant, now the sole partner of the firm of J. & J. Grant, and proprietor of Glen Grant Distillery. It is the oldest Distillery in Rothes, and for more than thirty years was the only one. It stands on the western slope of the hill, commanding a view of the whole of the magnificent scenery we have just been describing—a view that is perhaps unrivalled in Scotland. Benaigen, directly opposite, rises to a height of 1,600 feet above the sea; Benrinnes, away to the right, rises to very nearly 2,800 feet. The Spey washing

GLEN GRANT DISTILLERY.

the feet of these mountains, next to the Tay in volume among the rivers of Scotland, is the swiftest flowing and one of the best salmon rivers in the kingdom.

The Grants are one of the oldest and most powerful clans of the Highlands. Their chiefs have owned Strathspey for six centuries, and have come down in unbroken line for about thirty generations. The principal mansion of the chiefs of the clan is Castle Grant, in the very centre of Strathspey, some twenty miles up the valley from Rothes town, and came into their possession since the present century began. Glen Grant Distillery was built in the year 1840 by the uncle and father of its present proprietor, Major James Grant, who, in addition to being an energetic and excellent man of business, is a well-known sportsman and disciple of Isaac Walton. At first the establishment was on a small scale, but, as the demand for this Whisky increased, additions were made from time to time, until the Distillery has outgrown all the other Distilleries around it. The buildings cover about three acres of ground, but the property connected with the works has an area of upwards of 20 acres. There are two plantations on one side, and some beautifully laid out orchards on the other side of the burn; whilst the background consists of a series of hills.

The barley, most of which is grown in the fine county of Moray, is received at the doors of the Granaries, and conveyed by elevators to the different barley-lofts. Two of the Granaries are splendid three-decker buildings, of solid stone, and slate roofed; the ground floors are concreted for Malting, each having a stone Steep with the usual draining arrangements.

The No. 3 buildings, used for the same purpose, are larger, but not quite so long. Contiguous is the Kiln, 58½ feet long by 20 feet wide, with wire flooring, heated by peat and coke in two open *chauffeurs*. It is capable of drying 50 quarters in 24 hours. The Malt Deposit adjoins the Kiln, at a lower elevation. The malt falls through a shoot, of some five feet in length, direct to the Malt Deposit, which holds about 3,000 bushels, and thence to the Mill underneath, where it passes through a powerful set of rollers or crushers. After the Malt is ground it falls by gravitation into the Hopper over the Mash House, through the Mashing Machine into the Tun below, which has the usual rotary stirring gear. This Mash Tun is a circular vessel, 18 feet in diameter, 5 feet deep. The Worts are drained off from this vessel by three huge cocks into the Underback, which has a capacity of 1,200 gallons. After this the Worts are pumped up into the Receiver, contiguous to the Tun Room. They then go through a Morton's Refrigerator, thence by gravitation to the Washbacks of which there are eight, each containing 7,000 gallons. The Worts rise from the bottom of these vessels, and as soon as they reach the proper temperature a certain proportion of yeast is added. Fermentation then takes place, and as the froth

GLEN GRANT DISTILLERY (Courtyard).

rises, revolving switchers, driven by a small steam-engine, break it up and prevent it from overflowing. Now commences the interesting part of the process The liquor changes its name and is called wash, and is run off through close copper pipes into the Jackback, a timber vessel let into the floor of the Mash House. From the Jackback the wash is pumped into the Wash Charger, which holds 6,000 gallons, whence it runs by gravitation into two Wash Stills, holding 5,000 gallons and 2,500 gallons respectively. A small water-wheel, propelled by the waste water from the Worm Tub, turns the rummagers in the Wash Stills, all of which are of the Old Pot kind. These rummagers prevent the sediment of the Wash from settling down to the bottom of the Stills, while preventing at same time the danger of the Stills being burned.

GLEN GRANT DISTILLERY (Exterior of Still House).

We noticed a purifier attached to the head of each Still, consisting of a copper vessel with a water basin at the top, which effectually prevents anything but the purest steam from passing, all impurities being sent back into the Still.

There are above the Stills, on an elevated gallery, two upright condensers. From the Wash Stills the spirit goes through the condensing worms, which coil through a concrete tank, 24 feet long and 8 feet deep. The water in this tank is supplied from a constant stream brought from an aqueduct erected on the side of the hill above the Distillery. There is also another Worm Tub, a huge square vessel, lower down, supplied from the same source. From the Worm the spirit flows through the Safe into the Low-wines and Feints Receiver, whence it is pumped up into the Low-wines and Feints Charger above; whence again it flows into the two Spirit Stills, each holding 2,500 gallons and 1,600 gallons. The same process is repeated as before described, except that the pure spirit, after passing through the Safe, falls into the Spirit Receiver, which is in the Running Room. Of course the reader will understand that the impure, or Feints Spirits, go back into the Still to be re-distilled. From the Receiver the Whisky is pumped into a Vat in the Spirit Store which nolds 2,500 gallons.

We may here remark that the Still House is a most substantial building, with iron roof, and girders of the same material. The heaters, or coppers, holding 6,000 gallons and 4,500 gallons respectively, are heated by steam. In the boiler-house we noticed two boilers, 18 feet long by 5 feet in diameter, each possessing steam-domes. In the engine-house are two fine engines, one horizontal of 14 horse-power, the other one a vertical of 24 horse-power, for driving a dynamo, the electric light being laid all over the premises, for the first time in any manufacturing place in the North of Scotland; it is also laid over the whole of Major Grant's residence. The chimney-shaft is 100 feet high, but looks dwarfed by the background of the steep wooded hill, twenty yards distant. There are thirteen Warehouses on the premises, of enormous size, five of them having two floors, and several of them being 211 feet long and 31 feet wide. They are all stone buildings, and slated. Some idea of their size may be obtained by the fact that they contained over 500,000 gallons of Whisky, nearly all of which lies to the order of customers.

The arrangements for prevention of fire are very complete, and consist of hydrants, with water supply, and hose to carry same all over the premises, assisted by a portable fire-engine which is kept on the works. Capital offices for the Managing Brewer, Clerks, and Excise Officers, have been provided.

The following industries are to be found on the premises—a Cooperage, Smithy, Carpentry, and Engineers and Fitters' shop, &c., whilst in the yard, at the back of the Distillery, we saw large stacks of peat, sufficient for two winters' consumption, and stacks of ice, for summer use, covered with sawdust and thatched with straw. There is fine stabling for eight horses, and a capital farm-steading, where large numbers of cattle are fed on the draff and spent wash.

The water, used for distilling, is brought some miles from a mountain spring, and the Glen Grant burn supplies the driving power supplemented by the engines.

The make is pure Highland Malt, and the distilling power is 4,500 gallons per week, or 234,000 gallons a year. The output for 1883-4 was 172,917 gallons; for 1884-5, 140,370 gallons. The Whisky is sold principally in England, Scotland, and the Colonies, and commands a high price in the market, alike for use by itself and for blending.

"WHISKY."

Thou clears the head o' doited Lear;
Thou cheers the heart o' drooping Care;
Thou strings the nerves o' Labour sair,
At's weary toil;
Thou even brightens dark Despair
Wi' gloomy smile.

Oh whisky! soul o' plays an' pranks!
Accept a Bardie's gratefu' thanks!
When wanting thee, what tuneless cranks
Are my poor verses!
Thou comes——they rattle i' their ranks
At ither's a—!

No. 71.

Glen Rothes Distillery, Glenlivet District.

PROPRIETORS, W. GRANT & CO.

THE next day we again visited Rothes, proceeding by the same route. The first part of the journey was tame and uninteresting, but after a short time we left this behind us, and the country assumed a hilly aspect. When our train neared Rothes, the beauties of the valley became more apparent than on the previous day, as the atmosphere was clearer. Our eyes were enchanted with the picturesque and smiling grandeur of the valley; the steep wooded hills presented one vast expanse of foliage of various shades and tints, and scarcely a barren spot or boulder was visible on the mountain side to mar the peaceful aspect of the scene; while the Spey, the most rapid and capricious of all the rivers in Scotland, ploughed its way between cliffs of gravel and rocks, the sides of which were arrayed in a robe of greenery and the haughs above covered with trembling birches.

On leaving the station we proceeded through the town to the Distillery, which is about 500 yards distant. The principal trade of Rothes is Whisky-making, for which the water from the neighbouring hills seems peculiarly adapted. When trade is brisk and the three Distilleries in Rothes are in full work 350,000 gallons are manufactured in course of a year; while little short of a million gallons are stored in the Bonded Warehouses at the Distilleries.

Glen Rothes is situated a short way up the Glen, formed by the Burn of Rothes, which flows from the Mannoch Hills, and which supplies the water required in the manufacture of the Whisky, as well as the motive power for the machinery. The water is soft, and of that brown tinge so common in Highland streams, but also clear and bright. For supplying the Worm Tub for cooling the spirits in course of distillation, and other purposes, spring water is brought in pipes a distance of two miles.

On the side of the hill, on a level with the top of the Still House, a huge Worm Tub has been erected, 33 feet square and 12 feet deep, constructed with cement, a favorite material in this establishment.

The Distillery, which was erected in the year 1878, is built entirely of stone, and the whole establishment, except the new Bonds on the north side of the stream, is enclosed. We entered by a pair of handsome gates, and made our way direct to the office of Mr. Robert Dick, the resident partner. This gentleman received us courteously and introduced us to his manager, Mr. J. B. Henderson, who conducted us over the premises.

Our first visit was paid to the Malt Barns and Granaries, a building three stories high. The first is 151 feet long and 30 feet broad, and the second

GLEN ROTHES DISTILLERY.

$158\frac{1}{2}$ feet by $25\frac{1}{2}$ feet; the top floors are used as grain-lofts, and will hold 3,000 quarters of barley, the bottom floor, which has stone Steeps, is used for malting. There is also another building similarly arranged, but of larger proportions, which measures $158\frac{1}{2}$ feet by $26\frac{1}{2}$ feet. The barley is raised to the several floors by elevators. The Kiln which is attached to these Maltings gives a handsome finish to the block of buildings. It is floored with wire-cloth and heated by peats. We next crossed the Kiln-floor to reach the Malt-deposits, two large apartments well lighted and holding 7,000 bushels. In the floor is fixed a sluice or shoot through which the malt falls into the Mill below, to enter which we descended a step-ladder. It contains the usual pair of metal cylinders.

The pulverised malt is lifted from the bin to the hopper, which is over the Mash Tun. This hopper is of unusual size and will hold 1,000 bushels of malt. Our guide now led the way to the Brewing-house, a clean apartment, some 50 feet square and 40 feet high, which contains a metal Mash Tun, $15\frac{1}{2}$ feet in diameter and 4 feet deep, with a Steel's Mashing Machine through which the grist runs with the hot water and gets thoroughly mixed before reaching the Tun. It contains also a revolving stirring-gear driven by the water-wheel, and the usual draining plates at the bottom.

The Underback is beneath the Mash Tun, and measures 6 feet by 3 feet. The worts are pumped up from this metal vessel into the Worts Receiver, a timber dish placed on an elevation, from whence they pass through a Morton's

Refrigerator, erected on a gallery outside the Mash House, and then run direct into the Tuns.

We then retraced our steps and entered the Tun-room, another granite structure of large dimensions; here were pointed out to us six Washbacks or Tuns, each holding 6,400 gallons, which unlike some others we have seen are filled from the bottom. As soon as the worts begin to flow therein, yeast is put in from the top, and by this means a proper fermentation is maintained. After fermentation has taken place the wash flows into a metal vessel called a Jack-back, which is sunk in the floor of the Tun-room, from whence it is pumped into the Wash Charger, a timber vessel holding 5,309 gallons.

Passing through an opposite door we reached the Still House, a lofty building with concreted floor, daily deluged with water. It contains two Old Pot Stills, the Wash Still holding 3,000 gallons, and a Spirit Still holding 2,500 gallons, also a Wash Charger which commands the Wash Still. Running through the Worm-tub the product now falls into the Low-wines and Feints Receiver from whence it is pumped up into the Low-wines and Feints Charger, a vessel holding 2,800 gallons, where it is ready for a second operation as follows: First it flows into the Spirit Still, having lost in its onward progress about two-thirds of its volume, then through the Worm-tub and afterwards through the Safe into the Spirit Receiver holding 2,163 gallons. We should here add that on leaving the Still the Feints or Fore-shot runs back into the Low-wines and Feints Receiver, containing 1,440 gallons, for re-distillation. The Spirit is pumped from the Receiver into a Vat, which holds 2,227 gallons, placed on a gallery in the Spirit Store across the way.

As a rule, in this Distillery the pure Spirit is filled from this Vat into the casks, in which it remains from Saturday to Monday before being weighed and removed, which is an advantage to the customer.

The Warehouses, as will be seen from the illustration, are mostly on the north side of the stream, and newly built with concrete; they are five in number and will hold some 3,000 casks, and at the time of our visit they contained 247,351 gallons.

We noticed a large stock of Peats in the sheds; and there is a capital Cooperage. The arrangements for extinguishing fire consist of fire-plugs, hose, and extincteurs.

Three Excise Officers are occupied in the Distillery, the principal being Mr. Wilson. The Whisky is pure Highland Malt, entitled to be called "Glen Rothes Glenlivet," and when blended with other makes in the district "Blended Glenlivet."

The annual output is 80,000 gallons, but the Works are capable of producing 132,000 gallons.

"Gie him strong drink until he wink,
That's sinking in despair;
An' liquor guid to fire his bluid,
That's prest wi' grief and care;
Here let him bouse, an' deep carouse
Wi' bumpers flowing o'er,
Till he forgets his loves or debts,
An' minds his griefs no more."

No. 72.

Glen Spey Distillery, Rothes.

Proprietors, James Stuart & Co.

OUR next halting place was Glen Spey, the newest Distillery in the district. It is built just underneath the hill on which stands the ruins of the Castle of Rothes, the ancient seat of the noble family of Leslies, Earls of Rothes.

We commenced our tour of the Distillery, which stands at the opening to the glen, and close by the Rothes Burn. The buildings, erected in the form of a quadrangle, are of modern design and handsome appearance, and cover about two acres of ground. We first inspected the Malting, a large building on the left side of the square, which consists of two floors, each divided into three compartments, the top used for Barley Barns, with concreted Steep, and the bottom for Malting; at the end there is a large Kiln, floored with wire cloth, and heated by peat. Adjoining is the Malt Store, through which we passed to reach the Mill, a neat apartment, containing the malt rollers and grinding machinery.

We next crossed over to the Still House, at the top of the quadrangle, a splendid building, which combines a Mash House, and contains a circular Mash-tun, with the revolving stirring gear, the Heating Coppers, and a Morton's Refrigerator; also at the other end two old Pot Stills, with a capacity of 2,400 and 1,300 gallons respectively. In close proximity is the Tun Room, which contains six Washbacks, each holding 4,500 gallons. The Spirit Store and large Bonded Warehouses are distributed round the quadrangle.

The Whisky is Highland Malt, and the annual output is 60,000 gallons.

No. 73.

Macallan Distillery, Rothes, Elgin.

Proprietors, James Stuart & Co.

FROM Glen Spey we drove to the above Distillery, which belongs to the same proprietors. This old-fashioned establishment is situated in the hilly district above the Spey, and is one mile from Dandaleith Station. It was established in the year 1824, and its internal arrangements are similar to the other Spey-side Distilleries. The Whisky is Highland Malt, and the product, like that of Glen Spey, mostly finds its way to the English market. The annual output is about 40,000 gallons.

No. 74.

Aberlour-Glenlivet Distillery, Aberlour, Banffshire.

PROPRIETOR, JAMES FLEMING, JUN.

WE left Elgin by the night train for Keith, where we found excellent quarters at the Gordon Arms, one of those rare old-fashioned hostelries, which are fast passing away. Mr. Barclay, the jolly landlord, received us on our arrival, and made us exceedingly comfortable, during our fortnight's sojourn at his house. The next morning we again entered the train, this time bound for beautiful Craigellachie. From Keith the track strikes off abruptly to the left, alongside the river Isla, into a picturesque country of woods and stream, where the undulations of the ground have necessitated short tunnels and deep cuttings. We had here at intervals such pictures of rocky ridges, wooded plantations, miniature waterfalls, river and mountain, that it all seemed like magic, and when we finally emerged from the last intersection, suddenly found ourselves at our destination. Craigellachie is a good hiring station, and it is well for travellers to know this, otherwise they may have to retrace their steps for many a long mile before they can procure a horse and vehicle ; so few of these railway stations in the Highlands possess hiring accommodation. On our arrival we secured a stout horse and trap from Charlie Stuart, the proprietor of the hiring establishment, who personally coached us to Aberlour. It was a lovely day, and we started off in high spirits. After passing through the village of Craigellachie, we came in sight of the magnificent iron bridge, which crosses the Spey, near its junction with the Fiddich River. The bridge springs from a rock on the western side of the Spey, and is of 160 feet span. The road of access to the bridge is most picturesque, being cut out of the face of the solid rock, amid scattered firs of the impending mountain. For two miles the course of the river is very beautiful, and in some parts the road overhangs the boiling stream. We were quite sorry to diverge from this path, but we had come to our journey's end, for on our left, hidden among the trees, lay the Distillery, the object of our visit. Aberlour is a charming village, at the foot of Benrinnes. This grand mountain is 2,765 feet above the level of the sea, and from its summit ten counties, from Caithness to Perth, are visible. On the east shoulder there is a spring, which develops into a small pond, and near it, we were shown a cave which James an Tuam, or James of the Hill, a noted freebooter, made one of his coverts. The water from this receptacle runs down

ABERLOUR-GLENLIVET DISTILLERY.

the mountain side, and, before reaching Aberlour, forms a beautiful cascade, called the Lynn of Ruthrie. It has a fall of 30 feet, broken in its descent by a projecting rock, and is received into a gloomy pool below. Above the fall the rocks are covered with trees, which reverberate the sound of the water, and greatly contribute to the interest of the scene. The Burn from the pool is now called the Lour, and runs rapidly to the Spey. The Spey is, in volume of water and extent of basin drained by it, the second river in Scotland. It rises in Badenoch, about six miles from Loch Laggan, and flows for about 100 miles. After flowing for about a mile from the source it expands into Loch Spey, after leaving which it flows eastward to the sea, receiving in its progress the Marky, the Calder, and a number of smaller streams. It takes rank, as a salmon river, next to the Tay and the Tweed.

The Aberlour-Glenlivet Distillery, distant about a quarter of a mile below the waterfall, is built on the banks of the Lour, about 300 yards from its confluence with the noble river Spey, which here rushes northwards to the Moray Firth, and a like distance from the Aberlour Station of the Great North of Scotland Railway. The work, a perfect model Distillery, was rebuilt in the year 1880, and covers two acres of ground. It consists of a triangular block of stone buildings, of neat appearance, and conveniently arranged for the various processes of distillation. Our guide, Mr. R. Gauld, the Brewer, first took us to the Malt Barn, a handsome building, 121 feet long and 40 feet deep, at the end of which are two concrete Steeps, capable of wetting 70 quarters of Barley at one time. Ascending a stone stair we came to two Grain Lofts, one above the other, capable of holding together 3,000 quarters of barley. At the angle of this building is the Kiln, measuring 25 feet square and floored with wire cloth. It is heated by peat in open *chauffeurs*. A doorway from the floor of this building lead us down 10 feet to the Malt Deposit, below which, at a depth of 13 feet, is the Mill Room, containing a pair of Malt Rollers, driven by water. This apartment is 30 feet square and 13 feet high. The malt is passed to the Mill through a hatch in the floor, to a hopper over the cylinders, which pulverize the malt. After being ground, the grist passes into another hopper over the Mash Tun in the room below.

The Mash and Still Houses are about 50 feet long by 30 feet broad, and contain an iron Mash-tun, 12 feet in diameter and 4 feet deep, possessing the usual stirring gear. On passing through the hopper referred to, the ground malt falls into the Steel's Mashing Machine, which mixes it thoroughly with the hot water before it falls into the Tun below. The wash is cooled by being pumped up through a pipe 200 feet long, which is immersed in the Worm Tank, which is the only Cooler. We then ascended a staircase to a lofty apartment, called the Tun Room, over the Mash House, where the floor is concreted, and which contains five Washbacks, each holding 4,000 gallons. The liquid, after fermentation, runs by gravitation into the Wash Charger and from it to the Wash Still, which has a capacity of 1,600 gallons, thence into the Low-wines and Feints receiver, from whence the immature spirit runs by gravitation into the Spirit Still, holding 1,200 gallons, and after that process it runs as a pure spirit through the Safe into the Spirit Receiver. All these latter vessels are in the upper flat of the Still House, and both Stills are of the old Pot kind.

The plan of the cooling is novel. The Worm Tank is formed of concrete, 50 feet long by 6 feet wide and 3 feet deep, divided by a partition along the centre, a continuous body of water capable of, and used for, turning two wheels, rushes along the one side and back the other, over the worms, proving the simplest and most effectual condensing method we have met with.

The lower flat of the Still House is sunk 10 feet on the side opposite the Copper and Stills, so that the coals are emptied from the cart through a shoot and landed beside the furnaces without any further labour; here there is accommodation for holding 50 tons of coal.

The next compartment is the Spirit Store, where there is a Vat containing 1,750 gallons, which receives the spirit from the Stills. Here the Whisky is casked, branded, and sent into the Bonded Warehouses, two in number, roofed with corrugated iron, and built with stone. One of these Warehouses is of three spans, each 40 feet wide and 100 feet long. The other is a two-decker, 80 feet by 40 feet, and there were 2,000 casks of Whisky of various ages stored in these Warehouses.

There is no steam power in this Distillery, the continuous flow of water being sufficient to drive all the machinery, which includes grinding, mashing, elevating, steering, and pumping. Several industries are carried on. We visited one or two of them, notably the Cooperage and Cask Sheds, spacious buildings, neatly arranged and possessing the necessary appliances for sweetening and repairing. Adjoining is the carpenter's shop and smithy, and across the yard the stables and cart sheds. Near the entrance there is a small office for the Distiller, and another for the Excise. The Manager resides in a neat house adjoining the barns.

The Whisky is pure Highland Malt, and the annual output is 80,000 gallons, which is sold principally in England and Scotland.

The chief Excise officer is Mr. F. J. Ivinson.

No. 75.

Dail-Uaine Distillery, Carron, Strathspey, Glenlivet District.

PROPRIETORS: MACKENZIE & Co.

WE arrived early in the morning at the Spey-side Junction, so as to have a long day at Dail-Uaine. The carriage which we had ordered from Stuart, by wire, was waiting our arrival, and the weather was simply the perfection of a summer's day. The drive to Carron takes us round a considerable stretch of the noble river Spey, and, as anticipated, we found much enjoyment in the journey. Our horse was a good one, and we started on the swing of a good round trot. Proceeding along, we catch exquisite glimpses of the river; now it is hidden by hillocks, anon by thickets of foliage. How the road winds! what hills we ascend and descend, what peeps amid the trees of the tortuous course of the beautiful stream, with its banks strewn with boulders, or in other places lawns sloping to the water's edge. Gazing from this Eden-like valley to the horizon, we see, on all sides, picturesque outsteppings of mountains and hills; most conspicuous of them all being Benrinnes, along whose broad base we drive all the way to Dail-Uaine. As we leave Aberlour the road begins to ascend, and presently we gain the level of the first height, which overlooks one of the most beautiful reaches of the Spey. Continuing our progress up the acclivity, we come to one spot where we would fain have lingered for hours. Here the whole glory of the scenery below suddenly burst upon us, and new points of beauty presented themselves. Words can convey but a feeble idea of the enchanting loveliness of Strathspey as it is now opened before us enclosed in its frame of hanging woods. As we diverge from the main road leading towards the Glenlivet Distillery, we get our first glimpse of Dail-Uaine, nestling in one of the most beautiful little glens in Scotland. We now begin to descend into the valley through some of the beauties we have already described. Never was there such a soft, bright landscape of luxuriant green, of clustering foliage, and verdant banks of wild flowers, ferns and grasses. The whole scene is dainty enough for a fairy's palace, and we do not wonder at the choice of the ancient Queen, who, during the wars between the Danes and Scotch, selected Dail-Uaine as a resting place, and pitched her tents there as she journeyed to join her husband after the battle of Mortlach. As we continue our descent beneath trees whose tops meet, and pass glades and nooks, brilliant in a glory of gorse, our driver points out on the opposite hill, above the Distillery, an old-fashioned mansion, the residence

DAIL-UAINE DISTILLERY.

of the proprietor of the Distillery. Here dwelt for a time the celebrated Mrs. Grant, of Carron, the authoress of "Roy's Wife of Aldivalloch," which was composed in that very house. It was in this locality that James Grant, known as James-an-Tuan, or "James of the hills" the noted freebooter and outlaw had his principal stronghold, and engaged in many a fierce conflict with the lairds of Ballindalloch.

A short distance up the glen, by the side of one of the burns, there dwelt in olden times a nest of bold smugglers, and the ruins of one of their so-called bothies was pointed out to us on the Distillery premises. A popular legend has it that the midnight wanderer may yet see evidences of their craft, and that the darker the night and the wilder the weather the more likely is he to stumble across the haunted bothy, which is situated in a rocky cavern in a ravine through which rushes one of the Dail-Uaine Burns. There the Still-fires are seen weirdly sparkling like eyes of diamonds, and the ghosts of the departed smugglers busy at their ancient avocations. This discovery was made one winter's night by a shepherd, who took shelter in a cleft of the rock from the bleak winds and drifting snow, but he declined to say if he tasted the ghostly spirit. Some are rude enough to hint that a stiff glass of Dail-Uaine inspired the vision ; far, however, be it from us to doubt the worthy shepherd.

Reaching the foot of the hill, the first building that attracts our attention is the pretty double-fronted villa occupied by Mr. Parrott, the chief Excise Officer in the Distillery. It is built of stone and is a charming little bijou place, with its garden sloping down to the water's edge. In close proximity there is a handsome range of newly-built Bonded Warehouses, separated from the establishment by the Carron Burn. As we drive over the bridge and get a view into the Distillery, what a sudden contrast presents itself to our view. Outside all is quiet and the stillness of death reigns ; inside it is all life, bustle, and activity, and the establishment a little world of industry in itself. In this retired spot, far removed from noisy cities and prying eyes, surrounded by all that is beautiful and lovely in nature, is carried on the mystery of John Barleycorn,—his death, burial, and resurrection. No wonder with these surroundings that the pure spirit emerging from such an Eden should be appreciated by mortals all the world over.

Dail-Uaine, is built on the banks of the Carron Burn, a stream which is fed from three other rivulets, all emanating from the heights of Benrinnes, and falling over the mossy uplands of that mountain. One of these burns was our companion for some distance and was brawling and gurgling all the way down the hill. The establishment is situated at the top of the glen at the head of a wooded ravine, and quite protected from harsh winds by the surrounding mountains. The private road through the Distillery skirts a steep acclivity wooded to its very top, and on the opposite side of the valley rise lofty hills covered with birches and backed by Benrinnes, whose massive projections intrude themselves into the Distillery grounds. As we proceed we pass successively the newly-built Warehouses, Excise Offices, and Malting Stores, after which our driver pulls up at the office door, where we receive a hearty welcome from the proprietor in the good old Highland style. Unfortunately for us, Mr. Mackenzie is just starting for London. However, before bidding us good-bye, he introduces us to Mr. John Lorimer, his manager, who from that moment takes us in tow and pilots us through the buildings.

The Distillery, which is three miles from Aberlour, covers five acres of ground, and attached to it there is a farm of a hundred acres. The work was

DAIL.UAINE DISTILLERY.

founded early in the present century, and during that time has been the property of the family of one of the present proprietors. Within the last few years nearly the whole of the Distillery has been rebuilt on a larger and more modern style, and the work now contains all the latest improvements in the art of distilling. The main buildings form a quadrangle, and there are three outer sections, all built of solid granite, and of handsome elevation. We were first taken to the No. 1 Malt Barns, which form a wing of the central building. It is two stories high, 183 feet long and 40 feet wide. The top floor is used for barley, and will hold 2,000 quarters, and the lower for malting purposes. It has a concreted floor, and contains two metal Steeps, each of which is capable of wetting 50 quarters of barley at one time. From here we were conducted to another building, designated the Old Malting, at the back of the new Granaries in course of construction. It is built in the form of the letter L, and is 160 feet long and 18 feet broad. The barley, which is grown in Morayshire, is delivered at the Granaries in carts, and dropped into the hoppers, at the bottom of which there is a continuous screw, which delivers the grain to the elevators, depositing it at any part of the buildings required. We may here remark that one of the new patent screening machines is in use at this Distillery. We were surprised to learn that even home-grown barley sometimes contains foreign objects, such as small stones, bits of metal, seeds, &c., which, without the use of this machine, would remain with the barley and spoil the flavour of the Whisky. The malt, when properly grown, is lifted from the floors to the Kiln by an elevator, and dropped on to the drying floor; a double set of swing iron doors give admittance, and we found ourselves in a building some 30 feet square, with an open roof and floored with perforated iron plates. Under this floor are two open furnaces, where peat only is used for drying the malt; between them and the drying floor there is a space of twenty-five feet. From the drying floor the walls rise eight feet, and then the roof, which is of the steepest pitch in Scotland, rises to a height of thirty feet. This gives the Kiln its tower-like appearance. It is considered that height is of great advantage where peats are used solely, as it gives the malt a delicate aroma, without having to use coke to prevent the flavour being too pronounced. We were taken to the peat sheds, where we saw two thousand yards of two-year-old peats ready for immediate use. One shed is situated on a height above the Distillery, connected with those below by means of a large enclosed timber shoot, through which the peats are discharged as required.

Returning to the second landing of the Maltings, we come to the Malt Deposit, running at right angles with the two Malt Barns. This department, which is 60 feet long and 24 feet broad, is divided off into a number of large bins, and malt is conveyed from the Kiln to these bins by a continuous band. Descending a few steps we come to a second Malt Store, similarly binned, and containing an automatic machine for weighing the malt before it goes to the Mill Hopper. This machine also registers the quantity passing through it; and our guide here drew attention to a suspended machine, through which, on passing from the elevators, the malt is relieved of the "cummins" and all extraneous matter, so that nothing passes on to the Mill except the malt pure and simple.

Through a hatch-door our guide suddenly disappears, but at our exclamations as quickly reappears. He is for taking a short cut to the Mill, and now produces a light to guide our steps. Emerging from the gloom of this passage we find ourselves in the Mill building. The Mill, which contains a set of Malt Cylinders, is here fixed on the ground, in order that the machinery may be quite firm and steady, thus grinding the malt better. This building is 40 feet high, and the pulverized malt is lifted by elevators to a stage in the roof, in front of an opening in the wall of the next building, wherein are four of the largest Grist Hoppers we have seen in the north of Scotland. In order to inspect them, we ascend two long flights of stairs and cross a plank bridge stretching over their yawning mouths. Depending from the wall is a moveable and jointed sluice, which is attached to the spout of the elevator, and diverts the grist into whichever Hopper required; each of these Hoppers holds 500 bushels of grist. We now followed our guide down another staircase, which brings us to the Distillery proper. It is the main central building, 80 feet square, well lighted and stone paved. Here, at the east end, we come across our old friends, the Grist Hoppers, looking like inverted pyramids, connected with a Steel's Mashing Machine, which, unlike others we have seen, is composed of solid brass. The ground malt, on passing through this machine, becomes well mixed with hot water before it falls into the Mash Tun below. This latter dish is a circular iron vessel, 17 feet in diameter and 6 feet deep, with a small foot gallery placed round it. The interior contains the usual stirring gear, which is driven by either steam or water power. In connection with this vessel there is an Underback, an open circular concrete tank, the top of which is level with the paved floor. On a projecting shelf, in close proximity to the Tun, are the two Heating Tanks, which supply it with hot water. They contain together 8,000 gallons. From the Underback the Worts are pumped into a Worts Receiver holding 3,000 gallons, placed on a loft over the water-wheel, from which vessel they run through a Morton's Refrigerator in an adjoining department. We may here remark that the brewer takes great pride in the cleanliness of this Distillery, and informed us that every part is sluiced down twice a day. To enable this to be done effectually, an iron water-pipe is fixed all round the Mash House, Tun Room, and Distillery, and on every side there are two-inch water hose depending therefrom.

We now leave the Still House for a short time to follow the process, and pass through a stone archway to the Tun Room, a triangular building adjoining. It contains eight Washbacks, each with a capacity of 5,000 gallons, and all switched by water-power. As we retrace our steps to the Still House we notice a square metal vessel, supported on iron pillars, which we are informed is the Wash Charger, and contains 8,000 gallons, and is the receptacle to which the liquor, after due fermentation, is pumped from the Washbacks. At the north end of this building are three old Pot Stills, all heated with furnaces and of the following capacities: the Wash Still, 1,500 gallons, and the two Spirit Stills, each 700 gallons. Messrs. Mackenzie prefer small Stills to large ones, being convinced from long experience that they make better whisky; the old smuggler's motto being "the smaller the still, the finer the product." Outside, and on the western side of the building, there are three Worm Tubs, constructed of timber, and, when compared to their near relatives the Stills, of large size, but necessarily so, as everything depends upon the spirit being properly condensed. In order to follow the product into its happy hunting-grounds we now passed on to the ball or running-room at one corner of the Still House. Here we observed a handsome brass safe with plate-glass sides, some ten feet long, which we were informed was designed by the resident partner. Through this machine the spirit runs from the Worms into the Spirit Receivers, and we should here note that it has a false bottom, in which are enclosed filters for the low wines and feints, which pass through it. At this end of the Still House we observed on a raised floor the Low-wines and Feints Receiver holding 1,000 gallons, and the Spirit Receiver of same capacity, this latter being a handsome dish constructed of solid oak, and polished. Returning to the main court we take a peep into the Spirit Store, where there are vats holding 1,300 and 1,600 gallons respectively, and the usual scales and appliances for casking the Whisky under the supervision of the Excise. Distributed about the premises are seven Bonded Warehouses, all built of solid granite, and one of them measuring 180 feet long by 66 feet wide and three stories high. They are capable of storing 6,000 casks.

The Cooperage and Cask Sheds, which cover nearly a quarter of an acre, are well arranged, and three men are constantly employed therein. Adjoining, are the Carpenter's and Painter's shops and the Smithy.

Our guide now led the way to the engine department, which contains a horizontal engine of 10-horse power, a steam boiler 20 feet long and 6 in diameter, a centrifugal pump for wash, and an auxiliary one in case of a breakdown, also a Worts and Spirit and Low-wines Pump. We noticed also a neat little contrivance whereby the waste water from the Worm Tub is made to drive the Low-wines and Spirit Pumps, also the rummagers in the Wash Still and Wash Charger.

The arrangements for extinguishing fire on the premises are very complete; a moveable iron drum, some 3 feet in diameter with 50 feet of hose, is kept in the principal building, and in a few moments is attached to the numerous plugs in the walls or roadway, and the pressure is so great that the water reaches the highest building. In addition to this there are the hose depending from the walls, already referred to.

There is telephonic communication between the Distillery office and Carron Station, and arrangements are now being made to bring a tramway into the Distillery premises from a siding on the Great North of Scotland Railway, which passes within a few hundred yards of the Distillery.

The Whisky made at Dail-Uaine is pure Highland Malt, and is sold principally in England and abroad. The annual output is 160,000 gallons.

Before taking our departure, at the suggestion of the Manager, we ascended an eminence, from which can be seen, almost in a circle, no less than seven other Distilleries:—The Glenlivet, Glenfarclas, Cragganmore, Cardow, Benrinnes, Aberlour and Macallan, forming most of the celebrated Speyside Distilleries, Glen Rothes, Glen Spey, Glen Grant and Mortlach being hidden from our view by hills and woods.

On returning we find our coachman impatient and anxious, so, after quaffing a drop of the nectar, for which the Distillery is famous, we trot merrily back in the cool of the evening to Craiggellachie and arrive just in time to catch our train.

"Here's a health to the land of the mountain and glen,
To the land of the lake and the river,
Where the wild thistle grows in her rude rocky den,
Proud Freedom's stern emblem for ever!
The land of the Claymore, the Kilt, and the Plaid,
The Bagpipe, the Bonnet, and Feather,
Let's join heart and hand upstanding in pride,
Here's the land of the bright blooming heather."

CRAGGANMORE DISTILLERY.

No. 76.

Cragganmore Distillery, Glenlivet, by Ballindalloch.

PROPRIETOR, JOHN SMITH.

WE next set out for Cragganmore, leaving Carron soon after breakfast. For two hours our road lay through varied scenery under a changeful sky, and it was not until we reached the far-famed grounds of Ballindalloch that the sun shone out brightly. About two miles from Cragganmore we diverged from the main road and began to descend into the valley; we passed the palatial entrance to the castle of Ballindalloch, and immediately afterwards crossed the bridge over the river Aven, a fine stream, which takes rank as the third in Scotland, for salmon fishing. We then drove past the quiet rustic village and grand policies of Ballindalloch. From this point we descended a steep hill which leads to the Distillery. Cragganmore is situated in the heart of a mountain district, and close by the river Spey. The beauty of the Spey valley is enhanced by the contrast it offers to the wild and rugged scenery around it. The surrounding slopes are adorned with graceful birches, and the irregularities of the hills give endless variety to the scene and enhance its grandeur. At the foot of the hill we passed the Ballindalloch railway station, then crossed the bridge, rather a dangerous one, over the burn, and in ten minutes arrived at our destination. The Cragganmore Distillery was built in the year 1869, by Mr. John Smith, and covers three acres of ground. It faces the river Spey; and the hill of Cragganmore, 1,600 feet above the sea-level, rises at the back. The water supply is from the Craggan Burn, which flows through the property, and drives both water-wheels. The establishment consists of a series of outlying old-fashioned buildings, and are none of them enclosed.

Mr. William Smith, the son of the proprietor, is the manager of the works, and showed us over the place. We commenced our inspection at the Granaries, which are situated on the slope of the hill. The No. 1 Granary is a two-decker building, 300 feet long, the top is used as a Barley Barn, and will hold 3,000 quarters of grain. The bottom floor, which is concreted, is for malting, and has a metal Steep which will wet 36 quarters at one time. At the right angle is another Granary, exactly similar, but a few feet smaller, holding 2,500 quarters of grain, and the Steep in this malting is of the same size and capacity as No. 1. We then crossed a grass plot to a smaller Barley Barn, underneath which is a Bonded Warehouse, and from these we were conducted to the Malt Kiln, placed at the apex of the two Granaries. It is a stone building, 30 feet square, floored with perforated iron plates, and heated with peat in open furnaces; the malt is lifted to the floor of the Kiln by elevators. At this point our guide took us to see the peat stacks and sheds, the latter 100 feet long, where were stored some hundreds of tons of this valuable fuel. He informed us that the peats are left to dry for a year on the peat moss, and are afterwards carted a distance of three miles to the Distillery, where they are stored for three years before being used. Adjoining the Kiln, but at a lower level, is the Malt Deposit, and underneath it the Mill, the latter contains a pair of metal cylinders driven by steam and water The pulverised malt is measured into bags, and tipped over into the Mash-tun which is on the ground level a few feet from the doorway. The Still House and Mash House form one building, and are at the south side of the quadrangle adjoining the kiln and mill building. Here is placed the metal Mash-tun, 16 feet by 4½ feet, and possessing the usual stirring gear, driven by steam; underneath is the Underback, 10 feet in diameter and 5 feet deep. From this receptacle the worts are pumped up to the Morton's Refrigerator, and from thence run into the Backs. The Tun Room, a dark and old-fashioned apartment, contains six Washbacks, each holding 2,500 gallons, switched with props in the ancient style. From these fermenting Backs the wash is pumped into the Wash Charger in the Still House, a circular timber vessel, supported on iron columns. On the opposite side of the wall, and facing this Charger, are placed two old Pot Stills, one of them a Wash Still, holding 2,000 gallons, and the other a Spirit Still, holding 1,250 gallons. We then passed from the Still House into the Receiving and Ball Room, which contains a Low-wines and Feints Receiver holding 800 gallons, the Safe, Sampling Safe, &c. This Ball Room is a low pitched chamber, and is the remaining and only portion of a smuggling bothy, which was not demolished when the Distillery was built. Mr. Smith informed us that a few years previous to the erection of this Distillery, there were as many as 200 illicit Distilleries at work in the Glenlivet district.

We next retraced our steps to the inner court and visited the Spirit Store, which adjoins the Distillery and Excise Offices. The Spirit Vat therein contains 1,448 gallons. Distributed round this yard, and in the roadway, are eight Bonded Warehouses. One of them has been recently erected, and is constructed to hold 2,000 casks. It is a two-decker building, fitted up with hoisting apparatus and well ventilated. The others, although very old buildings, are exceptionally dry, and the whole eight warehouses contained 234,000 gallons of Whisky at the time of our visit.

Adjoining the No. 1 Warehouse there is a large Cooperage and Store Sheds, and on the rising ground at the back of same (about 50 yards distant) stands the detached residence of the proprietor, and from his garden is obtained a bird's-eye view of the whole work. In close proximity there is a pretty villa, erected by the proprietor for the occupation of Mr. M. Gill, the principal Excise officer. Mr. Wm. Smith, in addition to his appointment of Manager, rents the adjoining Lagmore farm, of 125 acres, and his father, the proprietor of the works, rents other two farms, together 336 acres, and is noted for his breed of cattle.

The Whisky is pure Highland Malt, and the annual output is 90,000 gallons, all purchased by Messrs. James Watson & Co., Scotch Whisky Merchants, Dundee, ever since the Distillery has been established. They first introduced it to the market, and to them its success is mainly owing.

It is with regret that we have to add that, since the above report was written, Mr. John Smith has died. His son, in connection with his uncle, is now carrying on the business.

No. 77.

Cardow Distillery, Knockando.

PROPRIETRESS, MRS. E. CUMMING.

OUR next start in the afternoon was for Cardow, an old established and famous Distillery, situated on the North side of the Spey. On our way we halted for a few minutes at Dail-Uaine, and then commenced our long drive in the opposite direction. The first part of the road skirted Mr. Mackenzie's farm, we then crossed the Spey by an iron bridge, and in a short time reached the road that leads to Cardow. Our progress from the valley of the Spey was by a gradual ascent through birch plantations, which at times seemed almost to overhang the river; soon, however, the scene changed and we were driving through a wild and desolate district, which continued until we came to the Distillery.

Cardow is 4½ miles from Carron, which is the nearest railway station. We were very glad to arrive at our destination, the keen mountain air and sharp exercise had given us a mighty appetite, which was soon allayed by the well-known hospitality of Mrs. Cumming, the proprietress of the Distillery. Cardow was established as a licensed Distillery in 1824, previous to which date illicit distillation was carried on both there and in other places in the neighbourhood.

The establishment was originally built on the farm of Cardow, without any title to the buildings, beyond the currency of the lease, which periodically expired at the end of every 19 years. When we saw it, the buildings were of the most straggling and primitive description, and although water power existed, a great part of the work was done by manual labour. It is wonderful how long this state of things continued, considering the successful business that was carried on for so many years. Previous to the time of our visit a feu had been obtained to a piece of ground in close proximity to the old work, and an entirely new Distillery had just been built on the most approved plan, and with all the latest improvements and appliances.

The modern Distillery, a handsome pile of buildings, is capable of turning out 60,000 gallons of Whisky annually, and we were informed that the new "make" had been submitted to competent judges, who pronounced it to be similar in character to that made at the old Distillery, which is of the thickest and richest description, and admirably adapted for blending purposes. Our guide told us that a single gallon of it is sufficient to cover ten gallons of plain spirit, and that it commands a high price in the market.

As the old Distillery will shortly be demolished, we need not describe it, but proceed to give a few particulars of the new work. The Malt Barn, which is light and lofty, measures 116½ feet long by 30 feet wide inside walls, and has two Grain Lofts above. Adjoining is the Kiln, 25 feet square, floored with German V wire, and fired with peat. The Mill and the Malt Deposit are both the same size, and measure 32 feet by 25 feet, containing the usual malt rollers and mill machinery, driven by a water-wheel 18 feet in diameter. Adjacent is a building of handsome elevation, which combines a Mash and Still House, measuring 40 feet by 25 feet. The Mash Tun is 12 feet in diameter and 5 feet deep, with the usual stirring gear and draining plates. Under the floor is the Underback, holding 500 gallons, and the Worts are pumped up therefrom to a Miller's Refrigerator, 25 feet by 12 feet, placed in the Cooling Room. Next door is the Tun Room, an apartment 38 feet long, by 25 feet broad, which contains six Washbacks, each holding 4.000 gallons ; and a Wash Charger, in the loft, which holds 3,216 gallons, and commands the Stills. We then returned to the Still House, where there are two old Pot Stills, heated by furnaces. The Wash Still holds 2,010 gallons, and the Spirit Still 1,600 gallons. The Rummagers in the Wash Still are driven by a small water-wheel 4 feet in diameter. Outside of this house there is a cement Worm Tub, 30 feet by 12 feet, fed from springs in the neighbourhood. Off the Still House is the Ball Room, measuring 25 feet long by 15 feet broad, which contains a Low-wines and Feints Receiver and Charger, holding 1,829 gallons, a Spirit Receiver, 1,702 gallons ; also a Safe and Sampling Safe. Adjoining is the Racking Store, 25 feet by 15 feet, wherein is a Vat which holds 500 gallons, and a Cooperage. Across the court there is a handsome Bonded Warehouse of two floors, 120 feet long and 30 feet broad, fitted up with gauntrees in modern style, and well ventilated The peats used are brought from the Mannoch Hill, three miles distant, and stored in a lofty shed 100 feet long and 30 feet broad ; adjoining which are the Coal Deposits, Oil Stores, and Tool Shed The water is brought from the Mannoch Hill through two miles of pipes into the heart of the Distillery

The Whisky is sold principally in Leith, and the annual output is expected to be about 40,000 gallons. In the old work the annual output was 25,000 gallons.

No. 78.

Glenfarclas Glenlivet Distillery, Ballindalloch, Banff.

PROPRIETORS, J. & J. GRANT.

OUR journey to Glenfarclas was a longer affair than we expected, for what seems near in mountain scenery may be, after all, a very long way off. Beautiful the prospect certainly was not; for without the soft magic of green hills, woodlands, and the river meandering in the verdant meadow, no scene can deserve the qualification; nevertheless, if unlovely, all was strange, gigantic, and sublime. It was a most peculiar day, a languid sunshine pervaded the hazy atmosphere, creating a vagueness in the landscape. The mist stole in and out the crags and buttresses of Benrinnes, and every now and then, when it lifted, the higher peaks were just visible, like tiny black islands, against which the misty billows rose and fell. We were fascinated by this weird sight, as, with the exception of the distant views of the valley of the Spey, there was nothing else to claim our attention on this lonely waste. We could see Glenfarclas for miles before we reached it, standing isolated at the base of Benrinnes. So unlike is it to a Distillery, that without the tall chimney stack we should have taken it for a scattered farm-holding.

Glenfarclas was established in the year 1836, and the buildings cover three acres of ground. After resting a short time, we began our inspection of the establishment at the Barley Barn, which is situated on the left-hand side of the Office, and is capable of holding 1,200 to 1,500 quarters of barley. Contiguous is the Malt Barn, 200 feet long by 15 feet wide, possessing a Steep capable of wetting 50 quarters of barley at one time. At the end of these buildings stands the Kiln, which is floored with wire cloth and heated with peat, and is connected with the Malt Deposit and Mill.

On the east side of the Kiln is the Brewing House, containing a Mash Tun capable of mashing about 100 to 120 bushels, and an Underback. Passing through this House, we come to the Tun Room, wherein are six Washbacks, and over these, on a large flat in the roof, are the Coolers for cooling the worts. Opposite the Brewing House is the Still House, containing a Wash Still and Low-wines Still—both of the old Pot kind. After leaving this house, we inspected the seven Warehouses, which are all situated on the west and south sides of the Distillery, which, at the time of our visit, contained 2,000 casks. In the court-yard there is a Cooperage, Cart Sheds, and Stables. The water used comes from several springs on Benrinnes, and the make is pure Highland Malt, the annual output being 50,000 gallons.

No. 79.

Benrinnes Distillery, Glenlivet, Banffshire.

PROPRIETOR, DAVID EDWARD.

EARLY next morning we left Keith for our day's journey to Benrinnes. On arriving at Craiggellachie Junction, we again procured a dog-cart from Stewart's Livery Stables, the proprietor himself being our coachman. For a good part of the way our route was the same as the day previous ; first along by the Spey, then through Aberlour, and afterwards up the beautiful mountain road. But soon the trees cease, and we are manifestly attaining a considerable elevation. Here, as we look back, we get a view of all the beauties we have left behind, and feel almost sorry that we have so soon exchanged it for the mighty hills, with their apparel of gloom and shade. These sudden and great changes in Highland scenery are very exciting, and leave impressions on the mind not easily effaced. We afterwards traversed this route in the depth of winter with the snow lying deeply on the ground, and marvelled at the vivid green of the fir trees in the valley, and the distances revealed by the clear cold atmosphere of the mountain heights. The road ascends very gradually at first, but afterwards on leaving Aberlour, it becomes very steep, and here we get a fine view of Benrinnes. The Distillery is planted on its eastern side 1,030 feet above the level of the sea, and no more weird or desolate place could be chosen. The founders selected the site on account of the water, which rises from springs on the summit of the mountain, and can be seen on a clear day some miles distant, sparkling over the prominent rocks on its downward course, passing over mossy banks and gravel, which perfectly filters it before it reaches the Distillery. The front of the Distillery commands a view of an unbroken expanse of moor and hill, with scarcely a tree or hedge to break the monotony, and it was not difficult to imagine the loneliness of winter in these latitudes.

As we drove into the yard, we noticed that the workmen were busy re building the Maltings, on a modern scale, with stone quarried in the district. On alighting from our carriage we at once adjourned to the office to refresh ourselves with a little of the Benrinnes Malt Extract to remove the dust from our throats after our long drive in the sun. The works were built in the year 1835, and from that time to the present have been continually altered and enlarged. Our first visit was paid to the new Maltings referred to. They are two in number, and 170 feet long by 30 feet wide, and each consists of three floors, the top being devoted to the storage of barley, and the lower for malting, each of the latter floors containing a stone Steep, capable of wetting

40 quarters of barley at one time. The Kiln, which is a new building of lofty elevation in the form of a tower, is placed at the end of these Maltings, and is floored with German steel wire flooring, and heated with peat only, which is dug in close proximity to the Distillery. The malt is brought by elevators to the top of the Kiln, which is shut off from the adjacent buildings by double iron doors.

We now descended to the adjoining building, wherein is the Malt Mill, containing a pair of malt rollers for crushing the malt. The pulverized malt is raised from here by elevators to the Grist Loft above, from whence it is tipped into the Hopper above the Tun. This loft is exactly under the malt deposit, so that the dried malt falls direct into the mill hopper. The heating copper, holding 2,000 gallons, which supplies hot water to the Mash Tun, is placed in the Still house. Through a doorway, on the ground level we come to the Mash House, a triangular building, which contains a circular Mash Tun, 12 feet in diameter, and 5 feet deep, which possesses the patent stirring rakes driven by water power.

In connection with the Mash Tun there is a Steel's Patent Mashing or Mixing Machine, and the vessel contains the usual draining plates at the bottom. The undershot water wheel, which drives the stirring rakes, switches, &c., is under this house.

The Underback is below the Mash Tun, and is a metal vessel, 4 feet wide and 2 feet deep. Fixed on a gallery in the Still House we noticed the Wash Charger, a handsome new square metal vessel containing 3,000 gallons.

The Tun room is differently arranged from the others in the district, being placed at the top of the buildings and floored with solid concrete. It is light and lofty, and contains five Washbacks, each holding 4,000 gallons. Built over the staircase, which leads to the Tun room is one of Hodgson & Stewart's Refrigerators, also a fine worts Receiver, holding 1,000 gallons. The four-inch Worts Pump is driven by water power. It is the only pump in connection with the Distillery.

Our guide now conducted us to the Still House, which contains two old Pot Stills, the Wash Still holding 1,080, and the Low-wines 1,004 gallons, also a Low-wines and Feints Receiver (a timber vessel holding 1,815 gallons), a Charger and a metal spirit Receiver, the latter holding 1,815 gallons. We should here note that the Distiller believes in using only small Stills to produce a rich thick Whisky. The Worm Tub connected with the Stills consists of a square concrete tank built at the back of the Still house, and close to the chimney from the Furnace Stills. This shaft or chimney is 63 feet high.

We now bent our steps to the Spirit Store and Warehouses. The former building contains two vats, one holding 526 and the other 1,500 gallons. There are seven Bonded Warehouses, two of them two decker buildings. another of one floor only, and the whole containing 1,700 casks of Whisky of various ages.

The Brewer, Mr. A. Mackintosh (late of Kirkliston), conducted us through the place, and explained the various stages of Whisky making.

This Distillery works on through the summer, the high elevation allowing malt to sprout and produce as well in summer as in winter.

The make is Highland Malt Whisky, and the annual output is 50,000 gallons.

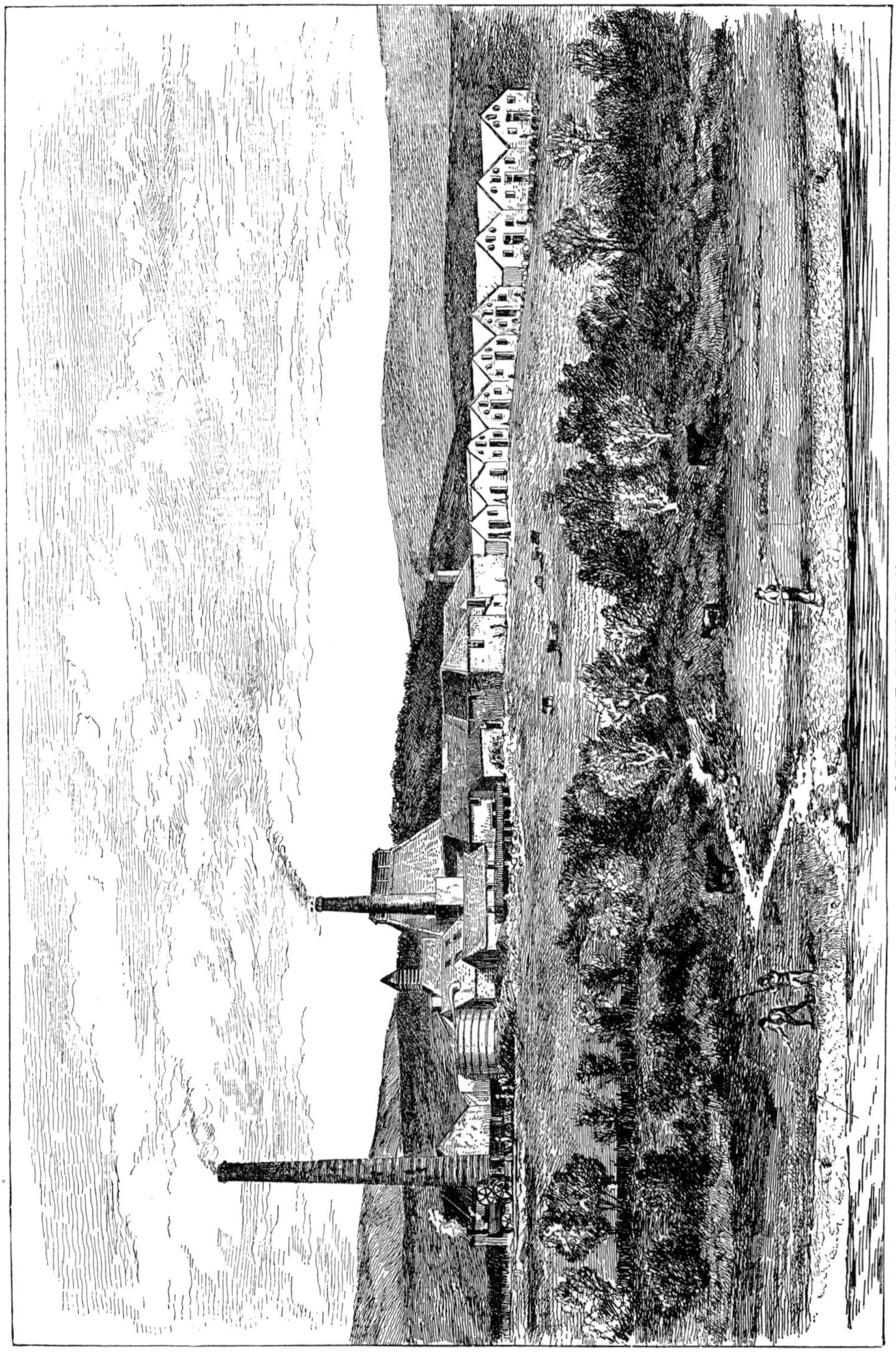

GLENLIVET DISTILLERY.

No. 80.

Glenlivet Distillery, Glenlivet, Inveraven, Banffshire.

PROPRIETORS, G. & J. G. SMITH.

WE shall never forget our ride of twenty miles to Glenlivet on a bright spring day. We proceeded by the Spey side, one of the most rapid and beautiful rivers in Scotland, through the plantations and copses of Ballindalloch, up mountain roads, across highland moors, and past old Benrinnes, standing out like a mighty giant against the clear sky, the scene changing at every turn of the road like a bit of fairyland, until at last we came in sight of Glenlivet. The Distillery planted on its slopes has a background of distant mountains, grim and bare to their very summits, and we wished for the pencil of an artist to enable us to transfer to canvas this scene of majestic grandeur. The whole district of Glenlivet is rich in historical memories. Here, on the banks of a mountain stream, was the battlefield on which in 1594 the Royal Army, under the Earl of Huntly, defeated the forces of the Covenanters under the Duke of Argyle. The position which the latter occupied on the side of the hill gave him an immense advantage over his opponents, who, by reason of the mossiness of the ground and the open pits from which turf had been dug, were at a disadvantage; notwithstanding which Huntly advanced, and a bloody battle ensued, each party fighting with equal bravery. During the contest the Earl of Huntly's horse was shot under him, and he was in imminent danger; but another was immediately procured, and the contest renewed with so much vigour that Huntly drove the Covenanters' army from the field, and would have pursued them, but the hills were too steep for his cavalry. On the side of Argyle five hundred men and several nobles were killed. The Earl of Huntly's losses were trifling in comparison, fourteen gentlemen, including the Earl of Errol, were killed, and a considerable number of persons wounded. At the conclusion of the battle the conquerors returned thanks to God on the field for the victory they had won.

The parish of Glenlivet extends to a distance of nine miles, and the entire population does not exceed a thousand persons, who are mainly Roman Catholics, this part of the country never having entirely succumbed to the Protestant wave. It is a wildly highland region, with mountains on

GLENLIVET DISTILLERY, BONDED WAREHOUSES.

all sides, that are intersected here and there with rills and burns. The Livet runs for a course of nine miles through the district to the river Aven. The hills in the immediate vicinity of the Distillery are called the Braes of Glenlivet, and the water used in the works comes from springs in the mountains 1,200 feet above the level of the Distillery.

This neighbourhood has always been famous for its Whisky. Formerly smuggling houses were scattered on every rill, all over the mountain glens, and at that time the smugglers used to lash the kegs of spirit on their backs, and take them all the way to Aberdeen and Perth for disposal. Now all is changed, and in the year 1824 a legal Distillery was built by the father of the present proprietor, who was a man of great moral courage and physical strength. So great was the opposition of the smugglers to his settlement in the district that for a long time until they were dispersed he had to carry firearms for his protection; hence he commenced work under great difficulties, but his indomitable perseverance overcame all obstacles in the end, and his efforts were crowned with such success that "Smith's Glenlivet" has become a household word, and the Whisky is appreciated in every country. From 50 gallons per week the output speedily increased to 1,500, until in 1859 a new and larger Distillery was built, and the output now exceeds 4,000 gallons per week.

The works are planted on the slopes of the mountain, 840 feet above the level of the sea, and cover nearly five acres of ground. There is not a village or town anywhere near the place; the nearest railway station is about seven miles distant—a more lonely spot in winter, or a more delightful one in summer, could not be found for those who like quietude and rest. Truly it is very far away from the "madding crowd." The hospitable proprietor is a true highlander, and not only entertained us and our driver, but invited us to spend our next vacation with him, and have some days grouse shooting on a fine moor of about 10,000 acres, which he rents from His Grace the Duke of Richmond and Gordon and Lady Seafield.

The Distillery has a frontage of 800 feet, and is built in the form of a triangle. The barley is carted from Ballindalloch Station, a distance of seven miles, in the return carts which take down the Whisky to the rail, and for this purpose Major Smith keeps numerous teams of magnificent horses; we passed as many as sixteen during our drive up to the Distillery. The barley is hoisted to the two granary floors, which are capable of holding 3,000 quarters of barley, from whence it descends to the three Stone Steeps, capable of wetting 55 quarters of barley in each. Here it rests from forty to sixty hours. The water is then drained off by means of false bottoms, and the steeped barley is thrown out on to the malting floors, which consist of three splendid apartments, floored with concrete, and together capable of working about 2,500 bushels per week. The dimensions of these malting floors embrace an area of 15,000 square feet. The malt men turn over this wet barley at intervals according to the state of the weather, until it is properly germinated; when this process is satisfactorily completed, the sprouted barley is removed to the Kiln by means of elevators. The Kiln is a lofty building, being 80 feet long by 28 feet, floored with perforated tiles and fired principally with peat, which is of fine quality and dug in the district. From this department the dried malt is removed to the stores adjoining, from whence it is dropped through a hopper into the Malt Mill, where it is crushed through a pair of metal rollers. The grist or pulverized malt is now elevated to the Grist Loft, a spacious apartment above the Mash Tun, and the ground malt now begins its important work by first of all passing through a Steel's Patent Mashing Machine (before described), and from thence descends into the Mash Tun, a circular vessel 14 feet 6 inches in diameter and 4½ feet deep, which contains the double-action stirring rakes, where water with an average temperature of 155 degrees is first added, followed by two similar processes at increasing temperature. The wort is now drawn off into the Underback, from which vessel it is pumped to a tank which commands a Morton's Refrigerator, where it is naturally cooled until it becomes about 74 degrees Fahrenheit, and runs into the Washbacks, of which there are ten holding 3,700 gallons and other two 7,000 each, where the yeast is added, and fermentation commences at once, and continues for about forty-eight hours, more or less.

The liquor is now called wash, and descends by gravitation into the Wash Charger, from whence it is pumped into the Wash Still, holding about 3,700 gallons, which contains in its interior the old-fashioned revolving chain arrangement for stirring the wash, so as to prevent it from burning. From this Still the spirit goes into the Worm or Condensers, two large tanks placed outside, continuously renewed with mountain water, which is conducted underground from the springs before referred to. These Worms are circular tubes of 14 inches in diameter, decreasing to about 4½ inches at the bottom.

From the Worm the spirit passes through the safe, an instrument for testing, locked up and under the charge of the Excise gentlemen, who from the time the wash enters the Still, henceforth have their eye upon it, and every vessel is by them securely locked.

From the safe the spirit falls into the low-wines Receiver, from whence it is pumped up into the low wines and feints Charger, holding 3,000 gallons. It is now run into the low wines and feints Still, holding 750 gallons, and for a second time undergoes the same process as from the wash Still. The pure spirit is now pumped into a large vat placed in the Spirit Store, a contiguous building, where it is filled into casks, weighed, branded, and sent into the Warehouses.

We were now conducted to the Engine House, which contains a twelve horse-power horizontal engine and a large tubular steam boiler; to the coopery, engineers, carpenters, and painters' shops, the smithy, stores, and cart sheds; and last, not least, to the magnificent stabling, which at the time of our visit contained thirty horses.

Attached to the Distillery is a capital farm-steading, in which there are about forty cows, one-half of them of the fashionable pure-bred polled breed, and the other mostly pure-birth short-horned; also other feeding cattle, in all about 120 head, which consume the draff and spent wash of the Distillery, much to their own satisfaction and profit to the proprietor.

About fifty men are employed on the establishment, for whose comfort excellent cottages, bothies, dormitories, and farm kitchens have been provided.

There are four Excise officers on the premises; the chief, Mr. Hogan, is a thoroughly practical and scientific gentleman. The Stills are all of the old-fashioned Pot kind, and the Whisky, which is pure Highland Malt, is shipped to all parts of the world. The annual output is nearly 200,000 gallons.

No. 81.

Balmenach Distillery, Glenlivet District, Strathspey.

PROPRIETOR, JOHN MCGREGOR.

OUR next halting place was Cromdale, and although the Carron Station had been open for more than twenty years, we were the only persons who had ever booked to Cromdale first class, the number of our tickets, which were faded with age, commencing at ought.

Soon after leaving the Station we passed the magnificent policies of Ballindalloch, and then commenced on either side of the track, a great variety of scenery, mountain, hill and river alternating for many miles. The railway runs almost alongside the River Spey, and the hills, which rise from its banks, are for a considerable distance clothed with forests of pine, larch and oak. An hour's travelling brought us to Cromdale Station, where we had no difficulty in finding the path to the Distillery, as it is the most conspicuous object in the "Haughs of Cromdale," and can be seen many miles distant.

Our way was along the Cromdale Burn, and as we proceeded, the range of the Cromdale Hills, some seven or eight miles long, stretched out before us. In days gone by these acclivities were the favourite haunts of smugglers, who chose the locality on account of the numerous hill-streams, whose waters are of fine quality and highly suitable for distilling purposes. At our request, when we reached the Distillery, Mr. McGregor, Jun., took us to see the various haunts of the smugglers, who in days gone by were pretty numerous in the district, and whose romantic history has been the subject of many adventurous tales.

He first directed us to the double-arched cavern, dug deep into the hill, fifty yards from the Distillery, in which at one time a noted band of smugglers carried on their operations, but it has since been demolished. It possessed an underground spring, wherein the little coil of worm, which condensed the precious spirit, was laid, and at a lower level it dripped into a receiver, made out of an earthern jar some two feet high, with a wooden lid thereon. The little copper Still stood on a furnace made with the loose stones that had fallen from the rock behind, and the Mash-tun had originally been a wash-tub. The place was totally dark, and no light was ever permitted except that which came from the furnace fire. One night the Revenue Officers made a raid on the place, and knowing the desperate men they had to deal with, were all well armed. On their arrival they crept stealthily through the narrow entrance to the cave, following the informer, who knew the place well. Meanwhile the smugglers, unconscious of the close proximity of their enemies, were scattered about the cavern, some sleeping, others smoking, and one or two looking after the distilling operations. One of their number opened the furnace door to replenish the fire, and the momentary flash of light revealed to his comrade the figures of the officers stealing upon them. With great presence of mind he instantly unhooked the pipe which connected the furnace with a concealed chimney in the roof, and then fired off his pistol at the nearest enemy. The noise alarmed the gang who escaped from the cave, under cover of the dense smoke emitted from the open furnace. The officers were dumbfounded, and almost choked, but the informer quickly replaced the chimney-pipe, and as soon as the smoke had dispersed, the officers lighted their lamps from the furnace fire, and proceeded to demolish the place. They broke up the Still, Worm, and vessels, kicked the debris and loose stone into the well, annexed a few kegs of Whisky, and departed with one of their comrades slightly wounded. This scare broke up and scattered the notorious gang, and since that time there has been very little smuggling in this district.

BALMENACH DISTILLERY, FROM THE NORTH.

Within two hundred yards of Balmenach, Mr. McGregor showed us another place which, a century ago, was a smuggler's bothy, and one of the largest of its kind in the famous Glenlivet district.

The Distillery was established in the year 1824, by James McGregor, father of the present proprietor. From time to time, as the demand for the Whisky increased, various additions have been made to the establishment, until it now covers three acres of ground. It is not enclosed, and consists of a range of buildings, grouped in the form of a letter T, with the exception of the Warehouses, which are built on the banks of the stream. A tramway is about to be laid from the Distillery to the Cromdale Station, a distance of one mile, which will bring up the barley to the doors of the Granaries, and also deliver the Whisky to the railway. Under the guidance of Mr. Dunbar, the Manager, we began our tour of inspection at the principal Maltings. They are built with stone, two stories high, and are the most uniform of the group, measuring 120 feet by 34 feet. We ascended by an outside stone stair to the top storey, which is used for storing Barley, and holds 1,000 quarters; and then retraced our steps to reach the ground floor, as there is no internal communication, the barley falling through sluice holes into the Steeps. This place is divided, each division possessing a stone Steep, capable of wetting eighteen quarters at one time. On leaving this building our path led for a few minutes along the carriage-way, and at length opened on to the banks of the Cromdale Burn, facing which is a second Malting, of somewhat less dimensions and capacity, which we entered by a low doorway. It is a sombre place, but nevertheless suitable for the purpose, and barley can be malted in it all through the summer. We next passed up a rugged and narrow alley, which led into an enclosed yard, on one side of which, attached to the old smuggler's Distillery, there is a third Malting, a quaint little place, with an old-fashioned stone Steep. Returning to the main roadway we came to the Kiln, which is placed at the end of the first Malting visited, and which has recently been enlarged. It is 25 feet square, floored with iron plates and heated entirely by peat in open furnaces. When the malt has properly vegetated, it is raised by Elevators to the Kiln floor, and after it is dried falls through a shoot on the side of the wall, direct into the Malt Deposit, an adjoining apartment over the Mill. On leaving the Deposit Room we descended by a wooden enclosed staircase to the ground floor of the Mill building, which contains a pair of metal malt rollers, and the usual grinding machinery, driven by water power, and from thence ascended to the Grist Loft over the Mash Tun, to which the pulverised malt has been lifted by Elevators, and there stored ready for brewing operations. On our way downstairs our guide pointed out the Coolers, which run along the roofs of the Tun Room, and possess the old-fashioned revolving fans for cooling the surface of the worts. We soon reached the Brewing House, thirty feet square, and nothing could be more primitive than this place; the chief object is the Mash Tun, an old-fashioned timber vessel, 14 feet in diameter and 4 feet deep, in which oars are used to stir up the mash, which has previously passed through a Steel's Mashing Machine, worked by a water-wheel. At the side of this place there is a large heating copper, and beneath the floor the Underback, also of timber, holding 500 gallons, from which the worts are pumped to the Coolers by an ordinary pump, the only one on the premises, all the work being done by gravitation. We next visited the No. 1 Tun Room, to reach which we descended some steps cut out of the solid rock. It is a gloomy structure, containing seven Washbacks, holding 2,300 gallons each. Passing through an archway we entered a second and similar building of smaller dimensions, which contains other three Backs of same capacity, and all of them are switched with wooden props to keep down the fermentation. From this last-mentioned apartment we went through a narrow opening on to a gallery, and found ourselves in the Still House, on a level with the heads of the Stills, and by our side a Wash Charger, a clean timber vessel, holding 2,300 gallons. Looking down from this gallery we note that, like all other parts of this establishment, the building and its contents are of the most antiquated type. Never did we see such picturesque old Pot Stills and vessels as are to be seen in this ancient Distillery, and we were assured by

Mr. McGregor that for no consideration would he change a single thing, as he attributes the quality of his Whisky to his vessels, almost as much as he does to the splendid mountain water, so much prized by his ancestors. The Stills which are placed on the rocky floor of the house, consist of a Wash Still, holding 3,000 gallons, and a Spirit Still 2,000 gallons ; the rummagers of both being driven by a small water-wheel, supplied from the overflow of the Worm Tub outside, which latter vessel is of timber 22 feet long, and is placed partly over the Still House. Leaving the gallery we crossed a staging to the Ball Room, which contains the Low-wines and Feints Receiver, holding 1,400 gallons, a Spirit Receiver, 550 gallons, and the Spirit Safe.

Underneath this chamber is the Spirit Store, wherein is a Spirit Vat, holding 800 gallons, a Racking Store and the Brewer's Office. Descending by a step-ladder we made our way through the Still House to the Cooperage and Cask Shed, and afterwards crossed the road to inspect the two Bonded Warehouses. One of them is said to be the largest in the north of Scotland. It is built of iron, on stone foundations, 340 feet long by 60 feet wide, and contained at the time of our visit 3,000 casks, holding 241,326 gallons, dating from 1876, but when filled it is capable of containing double that quantity.

We tasted some 1873 Whisky and found it prime, and far superior in our opinion to old Brandy. Some of this Whisky was supplied, by desire, to the proprietor of the Gairloch Hotel, Lochmaree, in 1878, for the special use of Her Majesty the Queen, and her suite.

In the roof of this same building, by an ingenious contrivance, there is a smaller Warehouse, 54 feet by 36 feet, standing on piers, reached from a doorway on the high ground outside. This building was the first iron Warehouse licensed by the Excise Authorities, and the proprietor had to overcome great obstacles, and make many alterations before he succeeded in obtaining the license.

Attached to the Distillery there is a farm of twelve hundred acres, and Mr. McGregor owns a 1,000 sheep and 100 head of cattle. The Draff House is at the back of the works, in close proximity to the farmsteading, and the burnt ale is pumped up to a large wooden tank, and from thence runs some little distance into the cattle-yard.

The peat in the district is of fine quality, and this fuel only is used in drying the malt; it is dug in the Burnside Moss, at the foot of Cromdale Hill. Our guide next took us to see the water supply, brought from the Watersheds of Cromdale, two of the principal ones having been annexed for the Distillery reservoirs; besides these, there are the Cromdale and the Smugglers' Burns, both of excellent quality.

On the property, just above the larger stream, there is a neat dwelling-house, occupied by the Manager; and scattered about at the base of the Hills, and in the Glen, there are cottages with little gardens attached, for the employés.

The Whisky is sold principally in England, Scotland and the Colonies, where it is of some reputation ; it is rich and highly flavoured, much used for blending, and largely appreciated as a self Whisky. The make is pure Highland Malt, and the annual output is 90,000 gallons.

No. 82.

Milton Distillery, Keith.

PROPRIETORS, WILLIAM LONGMORE & CO., LIMITED.

THIS being our last day at Keith, we devoted the morning to a ramble through the old and new town. Old Keith is a place of great antiquity, and dates back at least 675 years. It has been the scene of many a sanguinary conflict and romantic episode, and epitomises the whole history of the district. In the old churchyard, on the bank which overhangs the river Isla, was fought in the year 1646 the celebrated battle between Montrose and Baillie, which proved so fatal to the fortunes of the latter. This quiet and impressive spot was on several other occasions the arena of deeds of war and bloodshed. Five years afterwards, Montrose appeared in the same place under sadly altered circumstances, as a captive instead of a conqueror, having been betrayed by a former adherent, MacLeod of Assynt, and was there compelled to listen to the sermon of a preacher, who insulted the fallen general and disgraced his cloth by his bitter and bigoted vituperations.

" Come hither, Evan Cameron !
  Come, stand beside my knee—
I hear the river roaring down
  Towards the wintery sea.
There's shouting on the mountain-side,
  There's war within the blast—
Old faces look upon me,
  Old forms go trooping past :
I hear the pibroch wailing,
  Amid the din of fight,
And my dim spirit wakes again
  Upon the verge of night.

" 'Twas I that led the Highland host
  Through wild Lochaber's snows,
What time the plaided clans came down
  To battle with Montrose.
I've told ye how the Southrons fell
  Beneath the broad claymore,
And how we smote the Campbell clan
  By Inverlochy's shore ;
I've told thee how we swept Dundee,
  And tamed the Lindsay's pride;
But never have I told ye yet
  How the great Marquis died !

"A traitor sold him to his foes—
O, deed of deathless shame!
I charge thee, boy, if e'er thou meet
With one of Assynt's name—
Be it upon the mountain's side,
Or yet within the glen,
Stand he in martial gear alone,
Or backed by armèd men—
Face him, as thou would'st face the man
Who wronged thy sire's renown;
Remember of what blood thou art,
And strike the caitiff down!"

AYTOUN'S LAYS.

After keeping Montrose a prisoner in the Castle of Ardvrack for a short time, Macleod of Assynt removed him to Edinburgh, where the noble soldier, of whom it was said that "*he was a man of the most lofty and elevated soul, and of the most unshaken constancy and resolution that the age had produced,*" suffered death on the 21st of March, 1650. On his way to death through the streets of Edinburgh, the gazing stock of the multitude heaped ignominy on his devoted head The cart stopped at Argyle House, where the Lord Lorn, with his new wife, sat on a balcony, joyful spectators of the scene.

In 1667, another event of a stirring and warlike character occurred in Keith, by the visit of Peter Roy Macgregor, a predecessor of the celebrated and more humane Rob Roy, who, at this time, was only nine years of age. On arriving at Keith, Peter and his band commenced to levy toll, or blackmail, on every family in the parish, but a parishioner alarmed the neighbourhood by ringing the church bell, causing the inhabitants to assemble in great numbers in the churchyard, including the lairds of Auchoynanie and Glengerroch. These brave sons of Strathisla, headed by the lairds, now prepared to receive Roy and his band, who by this time were marching over the "Auld Brig" on to the churchyard, headed by their piper. A well-aimed shot from the churchyard soon silenced the piper and put an end to his music. One of his companions gave his body a kick and sent it over the bridge into the stream, and the pipes, by the convulsive pressure of the dying man, continued to screech out his requiem, until both were silenced in the waters of the Isla. They continued their march, when a general and vigorous engagement took place. The Laird of Glengerroch singled out Roy and they were speedily engaged hand to hand in single combat, resulting in the Highlander being severely wounded. Roy's lieutenant now came to his assistance and to cover his chief's escape. In the encounter which followed, Glengerroch cut off the Highlander's hand, which only hung by a piece of the skin. The Highlander contemplated the mutilated limb for a moment or two, and, tearing it away, cast the bloody hand against the west gable of the church at a considerable height. The freebooters seeing the day going against them, retreated, but next morning Roy was found, and taken to Edinburgh, where he was tried and executed.

We ascended the hill to Fife Keith, and from that point had a delightful view of the two bridges, the old town, parish church, and the hill of Mulderie. After this we bent our steps to the Catholic Chapel, built in 1832, which contains the famous altar picture given by Charles X., King of France, and said to be worth a very large sum. It represents the incredulity of St. Thomas, and the faithful worshippers here may well be proud of their treasure.

The most notable building in Keith is the Longmore Hall, where the sheriff holds his court, and in which all the public meetings and entertainments are held. It is a handsome structure, and was the munificent gift of the late Mr. William Longmore, proprietor of the Milton Distillery, who gave it, with the grounds attached, to the town of Keith. Mr. Longmore was a public benefactor, and his memory is highly venerated in his native town.

The Milton Distillery is about half a mile from the town and railway station, and covers about four acres of ground. It is bounded by the river Isla, which rises at Loch Park, Drummuir, seven miles distant, and falls over a small cascade just before it reaches the works. On our journey from Rothes the railway traversed this loch. It is a mile long, and situated at the foot of a steep but beautifully wooded hill. The surface is dotted with pretty little islands and covered with rare water-fowl. The position of the Distillery is most romantic; a wood-crowned hill overtops it on one side, whilst the opposite side of the valley is ornamented with pretty villas, whose grounds stretch down to the water's edge, and the old kirk on another hill looks serenely into the busy establishment below.

The river is crossed by a rustic foot-bridge, and all the Distillery buildings have an old-world look, suggestively characteristic of the long established character of the works, which are approached from the main road to Keith by a carriage drive, and, with the exception of the new Warehouses, are all enclosed. The Distillery was established in the year 1786; originally a small work, it has from time to time been considerably enlarged, and under the superintendence of the present managing partner most of the newest appliances have been added, and the premises remodelled, so that the Distillery is quite comparable with the recently built Distilleries on Speyside, in modern improvements, whilst possessing the charm of age few others have.

Our steps were first directed to the Barley Lofts, which are four in number, situated at the rear of the buildings, and capable of holding 4,000 quarters of barley. From thence we were conducted by Mr. McCurrach, the distiller, to the No. 1 Malt Barn. This building, which is in the form of the letter L, is 102 feet long by 63 feet wide, and possesses a large stone Steep. No. 2 Barn is of the same shape and dimensions, and has a concrete Steep. Each of these Maltings holds 1,000 quarters. The Malt Barrows for wheeling the Malt to the Kilns are a peculiar feature of this establishment. They are so ingeniously arranged, that by pressing a lever the back falls down and the Malt discharged wherever required. The Kiln is on the same level as the malting floors. It is 55 feet by 30 feet, and floored with steel plates. Peat is chiefly used in drying the Malt which partly comes from Bogbain Moss, the remainder being shipped from Orkney. We saw some stacks of this fuel 60 feet long and 30 feet high.

Adjoining the Kiln is the malt deposit, a stone building of two floors, holding 1,000 quarters of malt. At a lower level is the Mill, in which are placed a set of malt rollers, which grind 40 quarters per hour. From this place the grist is hoisted by elevators to the Grist-loft, which contains in the centre floor five distinct hoppers, all of which feed one central hopper over the middle of the Mash Tun, by which the grist descends through the Mashing Machine into the Tun below. This vessel is 18 feet in diameter and 5½ feet deep, fitted with the patent revolving stirring gear.

On iron columns outside the Still-house is placed the large iron tank, which supplies the Mash Tun with hot water. It is heated by exhaust steam from the engine. The worts are pumped up from the Mash Tun by a centrifugal pump into the Worts Receiver, fixed on an outside shelf, from which they run through a refrigerator, and from thence on to the fermenting backs. Our way now lay through an archway up some stone steps into the Tun Room to another fine apartment, wherein are placed six backs, or fermenting tuns, each with an average capacity of 8,000 gallons. The switching rakes in these vessels for keeping down the fermentation are driven by steam. We then ascended to the roof of the Still House, where the Wash Charger, holding 8,000 gallons, is so placed as to command the Stills. Retracing our steps we entered the Still-house, a fine square building, kept, like all the premises, beautifully clean. Here are two handsome Pot Stills, of the old-fashioned make, with a capacity of 2,000 and 5,000 gallons respectively ; also the Mash Tun before described ; two large heating coppers, each with a capacity of 6,000 gallons, and the pumps.

MILTON DISTILLERY, KEITH, SOUTH END.

In the Wash Still the liquor takes its first degree, so to speak, and the vapour becomes spirit. It then runs through the worm in the Worm Tub, a spacious reservoir, some 60 feet square, built of concrete, in the bed of which are laid the worm pipes. This reservoir is constructed on rising ground, above the level of the Distillery, hence the spirit runs by gravitation through the safe into the Low-wines and Feints Receiver, and is pumped from this vessel into the Low-wines and Feints Charger, holding 2,000 gallons, which is placed on a gallery in the Still House, so as to command the Spirit Still. Here the imperfect spirit undergoes the same process as before, and emerges from the worm a perfected spirit, passing through Condenser No. 2, in the Still House, to which water is raised from a spring, which, in the hottest day in summer, is icy cold, thus allowing distillation to be carried on at a time when most other works are obliged to stop. It then descends through the safe into the Spirit Receiver, which holds 1,400 gallons, from which it is pumped into the Vat, in the Spirit Store, holding 2,000 gallons. Our polite guide next conducted us to the Bonded Stores, which are distributed about the premises, and consist of eleven spacious and well-ventilated Warehouses, containing, at the time of our visit, 4,034 casks, holding 300,000 gallons of Whisky, in all stages of maturation.

Dispersed about the premises are engineers' and carpenters' shops, cooperage, cart sheds, and stables. Twenty men are employed on the premises. At the extreme end of the works are the general clerks', excise, and partners' offices, comprising a neat Gothic building, overhanging the river, and commanding a fine view of the valley through which the Isla passes.

MILTON DISTILLERY, KEITH, NORTH END.

The water used in distilling comes from the Broomhill Spring, rising in the hill above the works. We visited the reservoir, wherein it is collected, said to be haunted nightly by the fays and fairies. The water is so bright and clear that a pebble we dropped into it seemed magnified into a huge crystal boulder. After the water leaves this receptacle, it is mixed with a small quantity of that from the Isla. The original proprietors had great faith in the efficacy of this marriage of the elements, and the old custom is continued to this day. This operation gives the name of "Strathisla Whisky" to the make of this Distillery, which we need scarcely say is pure Highland Malt.

The annual output is 90,000 gallons, which is principally sold in England and the colonies. Messrs. Longmore and Co., Limited, have also an extensive Scotch trade.

MORTLACH DISTILLERY.

No. 83.

Mortlach Distillery, Glenlivet, Dufftown, Banffshire.

PROPRIETOR, GEORGE COWIE.

ON leaving Keith, the railroad pursues its course through a beautiful hilly country, clothed with rich and variegated foliage, passing over several mountain streams, whose waters run in furious haste to join the larger river. On our way we passed Lochpark, a small but deep lake, confined by two almost perpendicular hills; this loch emits the parent head-stream of the Isla, and the railway runs for a mile along the banks of the loch. When we arrived at Dufftown Station, we were informed that the village and the Distillery were some considerable distance away, so we hired the only vehicle, an antiquated machine, deficient in springs and requiring renewals in several places. The horse was, however, a good one, and in less than half an hour we found ourselves at our destination, very little the worse for the jolting.

Dufftown is a quaint village, almost aspiring to be a town, and stands close to Mortlach Church. As you enter the village, the chief building that attracts your attention is the gaol, which stands in the centre of the square, and you fail to understand why the best position in the place should be appropriated to so large and unsightly a building.

The village is screened by Benrinnes, and there are two beautiful glens in the vicinity, Glenfiddich and Dullan. The former is one of the loveliest straths in Scotland, and the latter contains some fine bits of scenery, including the "Giant's Chair" on the river Dullan, with the pretty little cascade called the "Linen Apron," with its surrounding drapery of waving foliage. At the south of the village are Coryhabbie Hill and Cook's Cairn, whose summits look down into Glenlivet.

Mortlach Church and churchyard are famous as having been the scene, in the year 1010, of the great battle between Malcolm II. and the Danes, resulting in the defeat of the latter.

The Mortlach Distillery was built in the year 1823, and consists of an irregular pile of buildings on the right and left of the principal gateway. The Barley Lofts are 360 feet, and the Maltings 300 feet long, with a Kiln floored with metal plates, and where peat only is used in drying the malt.

On one side of the enclosure is the Mill building, which contains a pair of metal rollers, and to which is attached the Mash House, over which is the Grist Loft. In close proximity is the Back House and Still House; the latter contains several Pot Stills. There is a capital range of five Warehouses, which contained 2,000 casks of Whisky at the time of our visit. The water used in distilling comes from the Conval Hills and the famed Priest Well, and is of excellent quality. That used for driving purposes comes from the same source.

The Whisky is Highland Malt, and the annual output is 85,000 gallons.

No. 84.

Inchgower Distillery, Fochabers.

PROPRIETORS, ALEXANDER WILSON & CO.

WE started off for Inchgower on a bright summer morning with an Italian sky over our heads. All along the route, noble woods crept up and covered the lofty hills. Hedges, rejoicing in a wealth of foliage and blossom, divided the cultivated lands, and in the valley below, numerous water courses sparkled in the sun light. When we reached Fochabers Station we found our carriage awaiting the arrival of the train, so off we started under a broiling sun. The heat was so intense that the cottagers remained in the shadow of their homes and the husbandmen sought the shadiest places in which to rest. Driving along we soon reached some thick plantations and came to a rippling burn, murmuring among the young fir trees, whilst below, the valley of the Spey lay mapped out at our feet, and the river, now a roaring stream, winding through the wooded hills and rocky cuttings, rolled in furious haste to reach the sea. Immediately in front of us stretched out for miles in all their glory and beauty the densely wooded policies of Gordon Castle, and behind us rose Benaigen and the rugged and massive hills of Benrinnes. We were now in the midst of scenes which no pen could justly describe or pencil delineate, but which have left traces on our memories never to be forgotten. After crossing the new bridge over the Spey, which has replaced the old one, washed away in the floods of 1829, we reached the beautiful and picturesque village of Fochabers, environed by the deer park and woods of Gordon Castle. Leaving the grateful shade of the lofty trees, which for a mile or two overhang the road, a wider range of country opened before us. Cultivated fields clothed the slopes of the hills which reached the roadside, and a glorious and expansive view of the sea and the hills of Sutherlandshire across the Moray Firth, was obtained. Proceeding along we passed broad acres of goldening grain, studded over with gaudy corn flowers and ornamented with lines of beautiful trees. Here and there were patches of wild flowers, growing in the rose-covered hedges, the yellow, blue and white cups of these humble blossoms upturned to the sun. As we rattled along through this rich and fertile country, we now and then caught sight of a village or hamlet and presently, on our left, the famous Bin Hill of Cullen, some miles distant, standing out in bold relief from a background of blue sky. At the next turn of the road the Distillery came into view and the Letter Burn, which runs through the meadow land of the plain and past Inchgower. As we drive along our coachman points out a farmhouse on the high ground, opposite the Distillery, where lived McPherson, a noted smuggler, who for many years evaded the law, but was at last captured with several kegs of whisky in his possession, which he was carrying in his cart, concealed in trusses of straw, to the sea-shore. He was heavily fined and in default of payment imprisoned. The fine would have been remitted had he revealed to the judge the Still from whence it was procured. As a matter of fact it was the product of an illicit Still at Aultmoor Glen, at the back of the Bin Hill, a regular smuggler's haunt, and these men used the same water as that now in use at the Distillery.

The Still was worked in a cavity in the hill side, the entrance to which was covered up with turf and heather, and might be passed a hundred times and yet never be seen. It was an accident which disclosed the secret. Some Highland cattle were being driven home, when one of them strayed from the track and putting its foot in a hole displaced a large piece of turf, disclosing to the eyes of the farmer, who was up to every dodge of the smugglers, McPherson's well-kept secret and the means of securing the offered reward. On reaching home he communicated with the revenue officers, who proceeded to the place, dismantled the Still and vessels, broke up the Worm, and brought away several kegs of whisky. McPherson and his associates, having heard of their approach, took to their boats and escaped.

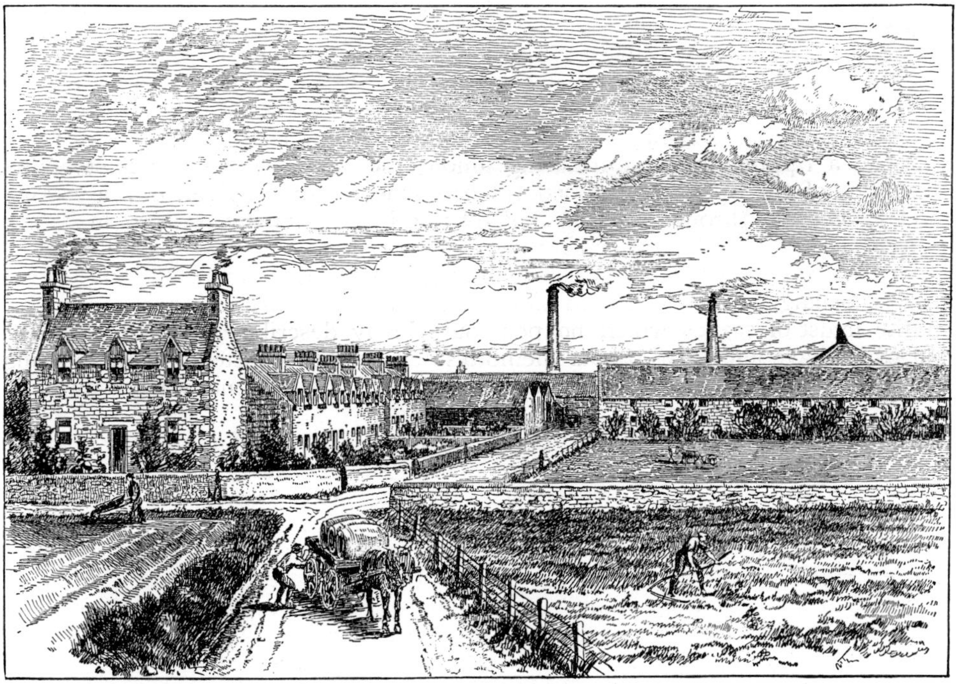

INCHGOWER DISTILLERY, FRONT VIEW.

Our carriage then diverged from the public way down a private road which led to Inchgower. After passing the picturesque house on the left, occupied by the Brewer and Manager, and the eight model workmen's cottages, designed and built by Mr. Wilson, we drove through a pair of timber gates direct into the large quadrangle, where we were received by Mr. Wilson, to whom we made known the object of our visit.

The Distillery, which lies in the parish of Rathven, four miles from Gordon Castle and five from Fochabers, is of handsome elevation, and the buildings, which are of stone, and slated, are erected in the form of an oblong quadrangle, and cover nearly four acres of ground. It has a frontage of 454 feet to the highway, and 500 feet to the sea, the ends being 145 feet. The original business was established at the Tochieneal Distillery, in the year 1822, by Alexander Wilson, the grand-uncle of the present proprietor, who there carried on most successfully the manufacture of the Whisky for which his name is famous.

A VIEW OF LETTER BURN (From Craigmin Bridge, One Mile from the Distillery).

In the year 1871 the present handsome Distillery, Inchgower, was built, and the business of Tochieneal removed there. It is a modern work, and is fitted up with all the latest improvements of machinery and vessels. Inchgower is situated in the heart of the finest barley-growing district in Scotland, and the water supply is from the Letter Burn, which runs from the uplands over huge peat mosses and flows past the Distillery into the sea, and also the water of Aultmoor, both of superior quality.

The manager, Mr. John Gallow, escorted us round the work and explained the various operations. We commenced at the Maltings, two-storied buildings, which form the right side of the quadrangle. They are 400 feet long and 26 feet wide, with open roofs, and lighted by forty-five windows. The top floor is the Granary and will hold 3,000 quarters of barley. Following our guide we next inspected the Malting Floors underneath, which are in three divisions, Nos. 1 and 2, 100 feet long, have each a stone Steep wetting 30 quarters of barley at one time, and No. 3, 150 feet long, wetting 45 quarters. Crossing to the opposite side of the quadrangle we came to the Kiln, a tower-like structure, 50 feet high, to the floor of which the malt is sent by elevators driven by steam-power. Peat is the only fuel used in the open furnaces for drying the malt, and the floor above is laid with metal plates. The dried malt is conveyed from the Kiln floor, through a sluice, into the Malt Deposits adjoining, one of the most convenient places for the purpose we have as yet seen. It is divided or binned off into six compartments for convenience sake, also to keep the malt dry and clean ; very little light is allowed to penetrate, and the air is excluded as much as possible. These compartments hold together upwards of 6,000 bushels of malt, and there is a Feeding Hopper, in the centre of the floor, for the Mill below. Continuing our progress through the Mill building, which contained a pair of malt rollers and grinding machinery, we came to the Grist Loft, a neat little chamber, where the

INCHGOWER DISTILLERY, FROM THE WEST.

pulverized malt is stored ready for use, and when required is projected by a screw to the Hopper over the Mash-tun.

We next inspected the Engine-house which contains a 10-horse power engine, which does all the work of the Distillery, also a steam boiler, 18 feet long by 5 feet in diameter, and a centrifugal and other pumps. The two chimney-stacks are 60 feet and 50 feet high, respectively. Ascending some stone steps, from the courtyard, we entered a noble building which forms the Mash House, Tun Room, and Still House. The section devoted to mashing is 65 feet long and 24 feet broad; the two metal brewing tanks, heated by steam, hold 2,500 gallons, and are built into a recess, underneath which is the Draff House. In the building there is a Steel's Mashing Machine and a metal Mash-tun 11½ feet in diameter and 5 feet deep, with the usual draining plates and stirring gear enclosed. Underneath the Tun is placed the Underback, from which vessel the worts are pumped up to the Coolers, forming the roof of the Tun Room, and possess a double set of old-fashioned fans. Passing through an archway we next came to the Tun Room division, which contains six Washbacks, two holding 4,500 gallons and four 2,500 gallons each. From these fermenting Tuns the wash is pumped up to the Wash Charger placed on a platform over the Stills. Returning once more to the quadrangle we entered by a stone porch into the Distilling division. This part of the house has a lofty and church-like appearance. It is 60 feet long by 24 feet wide, lighted by stained windows, quite a suitable habitation for the perfection of the barley into a perfect spirit. Here we were shown two Old Pot

Stills, consisting of a Wash Still, holding 2,900 gallons, and a Spirit Still 1,700 gallons. A small water-wheel, driven by the waste from the Worm Tub, drives the Still chains.

In the front of these vessels there is space sufficient to seat a small congregation of spectators to witness the progress of the work and spiritual mission carried on within its boundaries. Against the wall, at the end of the building, there is placed a grandfather's clock, a relic of the old Tochieneal Distillery, which keeps time better than any other clock on the premises. On the floor at the opposite end of the Still House are placed a Low-wines and Feints Receiver, holding 2,200 gallons, a Spirit Receiver, 1,500 gallons, and a Spirit Safe. For cleanliness and neatness this Distillery will vie with any of the modern Distilleries of the north.

We next bent our steps to the Worm Tub, a deep concrete vessel, 40 feet square, supplied with water from the Letter Burn, and afterwards to the Spirit Store, which contains a vat holding 2,500 gallons, and the usual weighing and casking apparatus. In a line with this building there is a Cooperage and Carpenter's Shop, quite a department in themselves, containing a steam saw and other machinery and appliances. All the Washbacks and timber vessels were

INCHGOWER DISTILLERY, COURTYARD.

made on the premises by skilled workmen. Continuing our inspection, we visited the Smithy, a little work of itself; the smith with brawny arms was there, but the chestnut tree was wanting. At the western end of the quadrangle there is, besides the duty-paid Racking Store and Inland Revenue Offices, a Cask Shed and the public offices of the Distillery. Opposite the Still house are the Bonded

Warehouses, forming a range of buildings, 100 feet long by 80 feet broad, divided into three sections and holding 2,000 casks. At the back of the Distillery we noticed two large peat sheds, each containing about 400 loads of peat, also capital cart-sheds and fine stabling premises for six horses.

Connected with the Distillery there is a farm of 200 acres, and a model farm-steading arranged on new sanitary principles. Upwards of 100 head of black-polled cattle, nearly 200 sheep, and a quantity of pigs, all bred on the farm, are fed with the burnt ale and draff, conveyed by gravitation from the Distillery to the farm buildings. We noticed that most of the workmen were middle-aged or elderly, and of a superior class, and were informed that most of them came from the Old Distillery, and had been with the firm all their lives. Mr. J. Bayley is the principal Excise Officer, and there are upwards of 20 persons employed on the premises. The make, which is pure Highland Malt, is a single as well as a blending Whisky, and is sold principally in England and exported to the Colonies. It is considered clean and mellow to the palate and much appreciated by connoisseurs. The annual output is 62,000 gallons, the bulk of which is generally sold before it is manufactured. After fulfilling our duties at the Works we accepted Mr. Wilson's invitation to dinner. His house is a charming country retreat, embosomed in trees and surrounded by lawns and gardens. We thoroughly enjoyed the Highland hospitality, and we would gladly have accepted his pressing invitation to stay a night; but alas, business and duty called us to the South, and we, who would fain have lingered many a day, parted from our host with regret, only to wish that another opportunity might be afforded us of renewing these enjoyments.

When we returned the sun was lingering among the hills, and the hum of the insects, together with the chirping of crickets, made pleasant companionship during our homeward journey to Fochabers.

No. 85.

Glenglassaugh Distillery, Portsoy.

PROPRIETORS, GLENGLASSAUGH DISTILLERY COMPANY.

FROM Keith to Glenglassaugh is nearly an hour's journey through a rich and well cultivated country. Within two miles of our destination we came to Portsoy, a charming little seaport town, beautifully situated and rapidly rising into notoriety. After this the track runs through plains laden with most luxuriant crops, which delighted our eyes and gladdened our hearts; farmhouses were scattered here and there, surrounded by ample barns and stabling, all betokening the easy circumstances of the farmers, and on our right the beautiful sea stretched out as far as the eye could reach. We have noticed in our travels that all the northern Distilleries are planted in the country, either on the sea shore or by the mountain side, and seldom in towns or cities, and have asked the reason of the Distillers, who generally reply, "We must have plenty of water power and good water, so we select the banks of a quickly-flowing stream. Then, again, we use home-grown barley, and only peat of the finest quality for drying the malt; also, we believe that a good climate and pure air are indispensable in the production of a delicate spirit like Whisky."

A pleasant walk of ten minutes from the station through the Glenglassaugh property brought us to the ruins of an ancient mill, built over a lofty brick archway, through which we passed to the Distillery, close by.

The Glenglassaugh Distillery, which is about half a mile from the station, was established in the year 1875. It is built on the slopes of a steep hill close to the sea, from which it is screened by a sand hill. All the work is accomplished by gravitation and water power, and the buildings, which are handsome and substantially built, contain all the new appliances and vessels as in other modern Distilleries. The Glassaugh river, which rises in the Knock Hills, flows through a strip of woodlands, which we crossed by the railway, and from thence through the establishment into the sea. Its waters are considered very pure and suitable for distilling purposes, and it was for this reason that the work was located in the Glassaugh Glen.

We were conducted over the premises by Mr. Mathieson, the principal manager, and first inspected the Malt House, a three-decker stone building, 106 feet long by 45 feet broad. A part of the top floor is used for storing barley, and will hold 500 quarters; the other two flats are Malting Floors, and each possesses a Steep, 9 feet deep and the width of the floor. We next crossed a large open space to the Granaries, a very handsome range of buildings, 123 feet long by 40 feet broad, and, like the others, well lighted. We ascended an outside stone staircase to reach the top floor, which, like those underneath, is used only for storing barley, and all together hold 3,000 quarters. The basement of this house, which is a Bonded Store, is dry and well ventilated. The Kiln forms the gable end of the Granary, and, as the buildings are all on the slope, the barley is wheeled direct on to the Kiln floor. The Kiln, which is 30 feet square, is of modern construction, open roofed, floored with German wire cloth, and fired with peat only in open *chauffeurs;* it divides the Granaries from the Malt Deposit. To reach the latter we retraced our steps to the hillside, and ascending a staircase found ourselves in a chamber, 30 feet by 26 feet, over the end of the Mash House. A wooden trough from the side of the Kiln conveys the dried malt to this floor. Underneath is the Mill Room, 15 feet square, partitioned off from the Mash House, which contains a pair of malt rollers and the grinding machinery, driven by a water-wheel. The pulverized malt is raised by elevators to the large hopper in the Grist Loft. Continuing our progress, we next entered the Brewing House, which also combines the Tun Room, and is a noble gallery, 84 feet long by 43 feet broad. From the roof depends a Steel's Patent Mashing Machine, which is fed from the Grist Hopper already referred to, and on one side there are two Heating Coppers, holding 2,000 gallons. The Mash-tun is 14 feet in diameter by 4 feet deep, with the usual stirring machinery and draining plates therein. Over the Tun is a Machine, an ingenious invention, for sparging the grains after the worts have been drained off. Sunk into the concrete floor is the Underback, a large open vessel, from whence the worts are pumped up through a copper pipe, which runs outside the building a distance of 90 feet, to the open Coolers in the roof of the Tun Room, which are arranged on the old-fashioned fan principle, and measure 43 feet by 30 feet. There is only one pump on the premises. On leaving the Coolers, we once more descended into the Mash House, through which we passed into the Tun Room, a large hall, against the walls of which are ranged five Washbacks, each holding 4,500 gallons. Continuing our descent, we passed through the Yeast House on to the gallery of the Still House, which is 20 feet from the floor, and contains the Wash Charger, holding 4,500 gallons; also a Low-wines and Feints Receiver, Spirit Receiver, and the Safe. The Still House is a modern edifice, and is fitted up with all the latest improvements; it contains a Wash Still, heated by a furnace, holding 4,000 gallons, also a Spirit Still, heated by a furnace, holding 2,000 gallons, &c.

On the next terrace below, on the banks of the stream, is the Spirit Store, 35 feet long by 20 feet, and with the two large Bonded Warehouses, are at the lowest level of the Distillery. One of these Bonds is 160 feet long by 80 feet broad, the other is not quite so large; there are four of them altogether. Near by we observed five large peat stacks, containing together upwards of 400 tons, which is dug from the Crombie Moss, two miles above Glenbarry; also a Carpenter's Shop, Cooperage, and Cask Shed. The Manager resides in a stone-built modern villa, and there is also a row of neat cottages on the property for the workmen. Besides these, there are two handsome dwelling houses, with large gardens at the main entrance, occupied by Mr. Tolmie and another Excise gentleman.

The Worm Tub is a square timber vessel, fed by the dam, which is above the tallest building in the establishment, and flows along a conduit at the back of the Brewing and Distilling House, and then falls over a water-wheel of immense proportions, which does all the driving in the Distillery.

The property covers 17 acres, and there is in addition a farm of 80 acres, which grows some of the finest barley in the district. The Whisky is pure Highland Malt, and the annual output is 80,000 gallons, and is said to be steadily gaining favour in the market.

No. 86

Banff Distillery, Banff.

PROPRIETOR, JAMES SIMPSON.

WE felt somewhat sorry to leave Keith, as our daily excursions to the Speyside had been most enjoyable, and our good host of the Gordon Arms had made us so comfortable. We proceeded by train to Banff through a rich agricultural district, and put up at an hotel whose name we wish to forget, where everything was bare and comfortless. Banff has attractions rarely equalled, rejoices in a fine seaboard, and is the most fashionable seaport in the north of Scotland. It is also environed by a superb park, and possesses a splendid river.

The old town of Banff has a good many interesting features. It dates from the time of Malcolm IV., and the old castle, of which there are not many stones left to tell the tale, has been the scene of many a deed of daring by the Earls of Buchan, Seafield, and others, who have left their names on the pages of Scotland's history.

The Distillery which heads this chapter is situated at the Mill of Banff, about one mile from the town, and near the Moray Firth. It has a special siding on the Great North of Scotland Railway, called "Boyndie Siding." This gives great facility for the heavy portion of the business.

The work was originally established in the year 1824, immediately after the passing of the Distillery Act of that date, which relieved Distillers from many vexatious trammels and unwise regulations to which the trade had previously been subjected.

In 1863 the Distillery was built on a new site, where the business has since been conducted on a more extensive scale than formerly. In the year 1877 the Distillery proper was burned down, and afterwards rebuilt on a more modern and commodious plan.

The Lofts can store nearly 5,000 quarters of barley, and the Malthouses are conveniently arranged with respect to these buildings and the Kiln. Contiguous is the Mill building, Grist Loft, Mash House, Tun Room, and Distillery.

The process of manufacture is the same as those already described in the Highlands.

The Still House contains three old Pot Stills, one Wash Still, and two Low-wines Stills. Water is brought by gravitation to the top of the houses; and the first Worm Tub is on a level with the heads of the Stills. Both steam and water power are available for driving the elevators, mashing, pumping, and all the work of the Distillery.

The Whisky is Highland Malt, and the annual output is nearly 200,000 gallons.

No. 87.

Glendronach Distillery, Huntly.

PROPRIETORS, GLENDRONACH DISTILLERY COMPANY.

THE next morning our host of the Insch Hotel provided us with a good horse and trap, and off we started over the hills for the far-famed Glendronach Distillery. It was a very tedious journey, and the country through which we passed bleak and uninteresting. On reaching the vicinity of the Distillery the scene suddenly changed, and before us were the delightful woods of the Bognie Estate and the demesne of Glendronach. Shortly afterwards the Parish and Episcopal Churches, with their respective Manse and Parsonage, came to view. Near to these there is a magnificent Public Hall, gifted to the parish by the late Mr. Scott, the former tenant of Glendronach.

On driving up the avenue the first thing that attracted our attention was the charming House of Glendronach, next the Distillery, itself embosomed in lofty trees, in the branches of which there is an extensive rookery. It is considered fortunate to have a colony of these birds over a Distillery, as they are said to bring good luck, and, strange to say, there is no instance on record where this has not been the case.

The route to Glendronach, either by Huntly (the nearest railway station) or by Turriff, is as lovely as the one we traversed was desolate. If we had gone by Turriff we should have passed through the picturesque valley of the Deveron, the banks of which river are covered with country seats.

Glendronach is planted in the Valley of Forgue, and the hills at the front and back are called the Foreman and Coulsalmond range. The Dronah Burn, which runs over rich beds of peat and mossy uplands, runs through the Works, and not only supplies all the motive power, but is also used for distilling purposes. This stream is of great reputation in the district, and its water, although tinged with a golden brown, is pale enough to delight the heart of a distiller, and is also bright and perfectly clear. The Distillery, built in the form of a square, covers four acres of ground, and was established in the year 1826 by James Allardyce and others.

We commenced our inspection of this quaint and picturesque place at the Malt Barns, Mr. Walker, the Acting-Manager, being our guide. The No. 1 Building is three-storied, the top being devoted to the storage of barley, holding 1,000 quarters, and the two under floors, which are concreted, for malting, each possessing a metal Steep capable of wetting 250 bushels.

In close proximity is the No. 2 Malt Barn, of somewhat smaller size, of two floors only, the top used for barley, the bottom for malting. From these floors the malt is carried on the backs of the malt-men to a Deposit Room, from whence it is raised direct to the Kiln, a building 25 feet square, floored with iron plates, heated by peat fired in open furnaces, placed a good distance from the floor to prevent the malt being scorched.

Following our guide, we next visited the Malt Deposit, from whence we descended to the Mill, which contains a pair of metal malt rollers, the machinery being driven by a water-wheel 11 feet in diameter. After that we went to the Grist Loft, which is in an adjoining building and over the Mash House.

This latter building is about 40 feet square and contains a metal Mash-tun, which is stirred with oars, underneath which is the Underback holding 3,400 gallons. Near the Tun are the coolers, with the old-fashioned revolving fan arrangement. Continuing our progress, we came to the Tun Room, a well-lighted and spacious apartment, wherein are placed four Washbacks, holding 4,500 gallons each, and a Wash-charger holding 3,309 gallons, &c. From this building we went outside and turned to the left a few yards, and then reached the Still House, which is about 50 feet square, and is the oldest part of the Works. It contains two old Pot-stills, heated by furnaces, one of them, a Wash-still, holds 1,500 gallons; the other, a Spirit-still, 1,200 gallons; also two Low-wines and Feints Receivers, and a Spirit Receiver. Next door is the Spirit Store, wherein is a Vat holding 1,584 gallons, and across the way, in the centre of the Court, a Cooperage and Cask Shed. On our way thither we noticed two Worm-tubs, which are placed at a lower level than the burn, by which source they are constantly fed with water. There are two water-wheels on the premises, no steam power being used.

Following our guide, we bent our steps to the six Bonded Warehouses. One of these is celebrated for maturing the Whisky in two or three years (equal to five in the others), owing to a peculiarity of the atmosphere; another is a newly-built stone Warehouse of large dimensions, holding upwards of 1,000 casks.

On leaving this Department, we crossed the burn by an ancient bridge into a large court, consisting of Stables for four cart horses, byre for 28 head of cattle, large Piggeries, and a Thrashing Mill. We then returned to Glendronach House, where, earlier in the day, we had taken lunch, and were conducted to the spacious drawing room to view the fine collection of medals and silver plate, awards for prize cattle to the late Mr. Scott, who was one of the most celebrated breeders of prize animals in the country. We were exceedingly interested in these valuable trophies, never before having seen so many in a private house.

The Glendronach make is pure Highland Malt, and held in high repute both in England and Scotland; we tasted some 1878, which was very much like liqueur brandy. The annual output is 55,000 gallons.

Since our visit to this Distillery, its former proprietor, Mr. Walter Scott, has died, and the property has passed into the hands of the "Glendronach Distillery Company," who have retained the services of Mr. C. Grant, who acted as manager to Mr. Scott for upwards of eleven years. The Offices of the Company are at 45, Quality Street, Leith.

No. 88.

Benachie Distillery, by Insch, Aberdeenshire.

PROPRIETORS, CALLANDER & GRAHAM.

IT would puzzle you to find a more desolate drive than that from Glendronach to Benachie Distillery. The mountain road is one of the bleakest and most lonely we have traversed. We saw no signs of a habitation for many miles, neither did we pass a single person or vehicle. It was with a sense of relief that we approached the Benachie Distillery, and came in sight of the little river Jordan, which flows through the property. The establishment takes its name from the Bennochie Mountain, which rises between Alford and Garioch, and is 1,442 feet above the level of the sea, and whose chief peculiarity is its bold peaks, which give it a remarkably imposing aspect. The Distillery was founded in the year 1824, by a pious distiller, who called it Jericho; we were not told if he also gave the name of Jordan to the pretty little river. If there is anything in a name, the spirit distilled from such a source should be of the best. Some of the old inhabitants of the district attribute sacred properties to the stream, and the Distiller informed us that its waters are of excellent quality and most suitable for mashing. The present proprietors, on assuming the property, changed the name of the Distillery to Benachie, and it has been known by that title ever since. As you enter the works the buildings are ranged on either side of the yard, and slope down to the stream.

The first places we entered were the two Malt Barns, each of which is 140 feet long and 25 feet broad, consisting of two floors, the top used for the storage of barley, the lower for malting, and the Steeps, which are of concrete and iron, are placed at each end of the barns. From the Barley Loft we passed through a doorway into the Kiln, an apartment floored with perforated iron plates, and measuring about 24 feet square, where peat only is used in drying. There is any amount of this valuable fuel dug in the district, of very fine quality.

At a lower elevation is the Malt Store, which consists of two lofts, into which the malt is conveyed by shoots from the Kiln Floor; underneath is the Mill Room, which contains a pair of iron malt-rollers, driven by water power. From the Mill the ground malt is conveyed to the Mashing Hopper, situated in the Mashing House further down the hill, and placed above the Mash-tun. Thither we next bent our steps. It is a neat little house and contains the Mash-tun, an iron vessel, 12 feet in diameter and 4 feet deep, with the revolving stirring gear, driven also by water power. Below the Mash-tun is the iron Underback, from whence the Worts are pumped up into the Coolers at the top of the building, and extending over the whole area of the adjoining Tun Room. The Worts, when cooled, are run into the several Washbacks, which are four in number, containing about 3,000 gallons each. The Tun Room is conveniently arranged, and is contiguous to the Still House, which is situated at the foot of the hill, and contains, besides the Wash, and Low-wines, and Feints Chargers, two Old Pot Stills and their respective Receivers. The Stills hold 1,400 gallons and 706 gallons respectively. Here also is the Safe, which is in connection with the Worm Tub, outside the Still House.

The Spirit Store adjoins the last-mentioned building, and contains a Spirit Vat holding 1,100 gallons, and all the necessary appliances for filling and weighing the casks of Whisky.

We were now conducted to the four Warehouses, which contained, at the time of our visit, 400 casks, holding 23,000 gallons of Whisky. The firm are also building a new Warehouse, which, when completed, will be larger than all the four combined.

We noticed a small Cooperage and Smith's shop, adjoining the offices, also cartsheds and stables.

The district is noted for its fine barley, and the proprietors have no need to go from home to buy the raw material. The make is Highland Malt, and the annual output is 25,000 gallons. When the enlargement of the premises is completed the firm will be able to turn out 40,000 to 50,000 gallons.

No. 89.

Glenadon Distillery, Old Deer, Aberdeenshire.

PROPRIETORS, GEO. J. WILSON & CO.

ON our way to Peterhead we stopped at the pretty village of Old Deer, to inspect its little Distillery. The village is pleasantly situated in a plain, on the south banks of the Deer river. The surrounding country is ornamented with woods and plantations, and there are heath-covered ridges in all directions. Near the village are to be seen the ruins of the Abbey of Deer, built in the thirteenth century by the good Earl of Buchan, for some monks of the Cistercian order; from the appearance of the remains it must have been a very extensive building. There are also, in the vicinity, four Druidical temples, that at Biffie being the most conspicuous, and an object of great interest to antiquarians

The Lowlands of Aberdeenshire are good grain-growing districts, hence the establishment of Distilleries and Breweries in this neighbourhood. The Glenadon Distillery was built in the year 1845, by Messrs. Milne & Co., the former proprietors of the Biffie Brewery close by. It is a nice little compact work, but too small for us to enter into detail, suffice it to say, that the water used comes from the Biffie springs, in a glen some 200 feet above the level of the Distillery, and that home-grown barley only is used. The Whisky is pure Malt, and the annual output is 12,000 gallons. In addition to the Distillery, Messrs. Geo. J. Wilson and Co. are now also the owners of the Biffie Brewery.

No. 90.

Glenugie Distillery, Peterhead.

PROPRIETOR, SIMON FORBES.

LEAVING Glenaden, we continued our journey to Peterhead, the largest town in the district of Buchan. It stands upon a peninsula projecting into the German Ocean, and forming the most easterly point of Scotland. It is a town of considerable antiquity, having been founded in the year 1593, when the number of its inhabitants amounted only to 56. Now, however, it boasts of a population of 12,000, which becomes nearly doubled during the herring fishing, an industry which is prosecuted with greater spirit at Peterhead than at any other town in Scotland. The maritime advantages it possesses have also enabled it for many years to send more vessels to the Greenland and Davis Straits seal and whale fisheries than any other town in Great Britain. The two noble harbours which adorn it, known as the North and South Harbours, were built after plans by the celebrated engineers, Telford and Smeaton. The town itself is built of Peterhead granite, a material now of world-wide fame, and unequalled for building purposes. Many historical memories attach to the place, and the house can still be pointed out where the Pretender resided for a short time and privately received his friends in the year 1715.

Leaving Peterhead by the Aberdeen road, and passing on the left the grand natural site chosen for the national harbour of refuge, directly in front of which is the well-known lighthouse of Buchaness, standing on a lofty rock, and further into the interior the distant hills sink into mountain ranges. The scenery around us was not very interesting, being merely hilly, but the glorious ocean fully compensated us, for the seascape here is one of the finest in Britain. After a good mile's journey we left the high road, and descending a hill soon found ourselves entering the gates of the establishment, and making the acquaintance of the courteous Proprietor.

The Distillery is situated at the foot of a hill, and near to the sea shore. It was built in the year 1875, in a modern style, on three sides of a square, and was acquired by the present proprietor about three years ago, who has made very considerable improvements and additions to the plant, and the increasing demand for the Whisky will necessitate very soon the erection of a new Warehouse and Maltings. The buildings cover four acres, but the site laid off for the works is nearly double that in extent, consequently ample provision has been made for further additions when the necessity arises.

The barley used at this Distillery is principally grown in the Buchan district which is, as is well known, of fine quality, and very suitable for

GLENUGIE DISTILLERY.

malting purposes. The principal Maltings and Warehouses consist of a building of three stories, 100 feet long and 100 feet wide, built of granite and slated, the lower flat being used as Bonded Stores, the second as Maltings, and the upper as a Grain Store, capable of holding 3,000 quarters. The barley to be malted is placed in a concrete Steep, situated on the upper flat, capable of holding 60 quarters at a time, and after being steeped is discharged by two doors in the bottom of the Steep into the Malting Floor below, thus effecting a great saving in manual labour from the usual practice of throwing the barley over the side of the vessel with shovels. There is another Malting House on the north side of the square, adjacent to the Kiln, with three separate floors, having a concrete Steep in each, capable of malting in all 60 quarters at a time. The Kiln is a lofty building, being 25 feet high and 30 feet square, and floored with cast iron punched plates. It is heated with peats from a large *chauffeur* below, and can dry 30 quarters of malt in less than 24 hours. The peats used are of excellent quality, and are to be found in great abundance about five miles distant from the works. There was a supply on the premises, consisting of three large stacks, sufficient for two seasons.

We next descended to the Malt Deposit Room, which joins the Kiln at a lower elevation. The malt falls through a shoot, some 10 feet in length, into the Malt Deposit Room, which holds over 5,000 bushels, and thence to the Mill underneath, where it passes through two powerful rollers. After it is ground, it is conveyed by means of elevators to the Malt Hopper, which is placed over the Mash-tun. It then passes through the Mashing Machine into the Mash-tun, which is a cast iron vessel, 15 feet in diameter and 6 feet deep, fitted up with internal stirring rakes, and capable of mashing 400 bushels at one time. The worts from this vessel are drained off through the usual perforated false bottom and by orifices inserted in the sides into the Underback below, which is situated on the ground floor, and has a capacity of 800 gallons. It is then conveyed by means of two pumps, worked by steam power, to the Wort Receiver, a square shallow vessel, erected above the Washbacks. From this they pass through a Morton's Refrigerator into the Washbacks, of which there are four, each of a capacity of 9,500 gallons. Yeast is then added to the worts and after fermentation has begun the liquor is known by the name of wash. There are switchers fitted in the Washbacks, propelled by steam, which are called into play when fermentation is very vigorous, to break up the froth and prevent the liquor from overflowing. After fermentation has ceased, the wash is run by gravitation into the Wash Charger, and thence to the Wash Still. The former vessel is a metal one of considerable size, being capable of holding 9,000 gallons. Both the Wash and Low-wines or Spirit Stills are of the old Pot kind, the former holding 5,360 gallons, and the latter 2,860 gallons. In connection with the Wash Still we noticed a Horizontal Condenser of a very modern design, having 200 tubes in it, the other one for the Spirit Still being of the ordinary upright kind, with 50 tubes. The distillate from the Wash Still, after passing through the Condenser, enters the worm, where it is re-condensed and cooled, thence through the Spirit Safe into the Low-wines and Feints Receiver, a metal vessel, holding 2,500 gallons. The worms form a continuous coil of copper piping, placed in a large metal tank outside, 22 feet long and 4 feet deep, and has a constant stream of water flowing through it. The spill or overflow water from this tank passes over a small water-wheel underneath, which drives the rummager in the Wash Still. The rummager serves to keep the sediment in the Wash Still afloat, as were it allowed to settle down on the bottom, there would be a danger of the Still being burned. We also noticed an important contrivance on the air cocks of the Stills, for the prevention of a collapse or explosion, comprising a frame round the cocks, which have solid heads, so that the lever or handle employed for opening the discharge cocks cannot be got off the former without necessarily opening it. This we would recommend to all who have not yet adopted it.

The spirit produced from the first distillation is imperfect, and is denominated "Low-wines." It is collected in the vessel termed the Low-wines and Feints Receiver, which also serves as a Charger. From this vessel it flows into the Spirit Still, and the same process as that which the wash undergoes is repeated, the only difference being, that the impure portions, which are denominated "Feints," after coming into the Safe are directed to the Low-wines and Feints Receiver, and the pure spirit to the Spirit Receiver, which is situated in the Running Room. From the Receiver it is pumped to the Vat in the Spirit Store, where it is filled into casks and removed to the Warehouses. Both these vessels are large, the former holding 2,000 gallons and the latter 4,400 gallons. We may mention that the present warehouse accommodation is equal to 150,000 gallons, and at our visit there were nearly 80,000 gallons, most of which belonged to customers. Adjacent to the Spirit Store is the Weigh House and Racking Store, all of which are below the Malt Deposit. The Mash and Still House is very commodious and well ventilated, and we do not exaggerate when we say that the arrangements for carrying on this department are of the most complete kind we have yet seen, and in fact, the opinion of one of Her Majesty's Inspectors, from Somerset House, on the occasion of a visit some years ago, was, that in this respect, Glenugie was one of the best Distilleries in the north of Scotland. The Heating Tanks hold about 4,000 gallons each, and are heated by steam. They are placed at a high elevation, thus affording great pressure for the Mashing Machine—a matter, it will be admitted, of no little importance. There is a horizontal engine of 12-horse power, besides a donkey-engine of 2-horse power, which is used for pumping worts, also water, through a hose, for the thorough cleansing of the Washbacks and other vessels, and as a fire extinguisher. The steam boiler is 16 feet long and 6 feet in diameter, with patent feed injector attached, and the chimney shaft, which serves for both boiler and Stills, is 100 feet high. There is a cooperage, joiner's, engineer's, and fitter's shop on the premises, also stabling for five horses, with hay-loft and cart-sheds attached.

Splendid houses have been provided for the Excise Officers, also offices for both them and the manager, clerks, &c., and houses for the manager and the principal workmen.

The water used in the manufacture of the Whisky has its source in the mossy moorlands, from three to four miles from the works. It is of excellent quality being soft and pure, and was pronounced by Professor Brazier, F.C.S., of the Aberdeen University, who analyzed it, to be admirably adapted for distilling purposes.

The make is Highland Malt, and is sold in England, and Scotland, and the Colonies. It commands a good price, and being a Whisky that matures rapidly is very suitable for blending purposes. The present output is about 90,000 gallons, but this could be considerably increased if desired.

No. 91.

Glengarioch Distillery, Old Meldrum, Aberdeenshire.

PROPRIETORS, J. F. THOMSON & Co.

IT is a pleasant journey of 18 miles, on the Great North of Scotland Railway, from Aberdeen to Old Meldrum, a place both interesting and historical. The Distillery takes its name from the celebrated valley of the Garioch, called the Granary of Aberdeenshire, which begins at Old Meldrum, and extends for upwards of 20 miles. It is a fertile, highly cultivated, and well sheltered valley, bounded on all sides by a range of hills, which command extensive views of the Foremartine and Buchan districts, and the lofty Bennochie.

On the summit of the Barra Hill, which is 600 feet in height above the sea level, and about one mile from the Glengarioch Distillery, are to be seen the remains of a camp, of circular form, with three ditches, called "Cummins' Camp," which probably belonged to the Danes before the Cummins took possession of it. They were a numerous and warlike race, and originally owned a greater part of the Buchan and surrounding district, and were disaffected to King Robert Bruce, who, after he had fought and won the battle of Inverury, marched his troops against the Cummins, stormed their camp, and put them to flight. It is said that the celebrated "Thomas de Longueville," the companion of Wallace, was killed in this battle, and in the churchyard there is shown a rough-hewn statue in stone, which is said to be his effigy.

Old Meldrum is a market town, and boasts of a town hall, surmounted with a spire ; but its streets, although they contain a number of good houses, are very irregularly built.

The Distillery, the subject of our sketch, was founded in the year 1797, by Ingram, Lamb & Co., and renewed at various times from that date to 1840, when it came into the possession of John Manson & Co., who subsequently sold it to J. F. Thomson & Co., of Leith, the present proprietors. The work is under the practical supervision of Joseph F. Thomson, one of the partners, who resides on the property. It covers one and a half acres of ground, and is situated in the valley of the Garioch.

The works are enclosed, and consist of two Maltings, fine stone buildings, 100 feet long and 60 feet broad, of two floors each, the top used for storing the barley, which is all grown in the neighbourhood, and the ground floors for malting purposes. The Steeps are placed at each end of the Barley Lofts ; one of them is composed of concrete, the other iron. Adjoining this department is the Kiln, built of the same materials as the Maltings, floored with perforated iron plates, and heated with peat. From the Kiln you descend a few steps into the Malt Store, which is in direct communication with the Mill, a neat little building, containing a pair of malt rollers. After the malt has been crushed, it is sent up by elevators into the Grist Loft, weighed and measured into bags of five bushels, and delivered through the Mashing Machine into the Mash-tun, which is placed at one end of the Still House. It is a metal vessel, 14 feet in diameter and 3½ feet deep, having the usual stirring gear. The Underback, which is sunk into the floor below the Tun, is capable of holding 3,000 gallons. From the Underback the worts are pumped up into the old-fashioned Coolers, which cover the roof of the Tun Room, and have the revolving fans in the centre. On leaving the Coolers, the worts run by gravitation into the five Washbacks, each holding 3,000 gallons, and placed in the Tun Room underneath.

The liquor here changes its name, and is called wash, and is now pumped by a double-action pump up to the Wash Charger, a vessel constructed of oak, placed on a gallery in the Charging Room at back of the Still House, so as to command the Stills. The Still House, a newly-erected structure, is of modern arrangement, and contains a Wash Still, holding 1,900 gallons, and a Low-wines Still, holding 1,500 gallons; also the Safe and the usual Receivers. Outside this building is a fine Worm Tub, an oblong vessel, 40 feet long and 5 feet deep, constructed of timber. On the opposite side of the way, adjoining the Maltings, is a capital Spirit Store, containing a Vat holding 1,400 gallons, into which the spirit is pumped from the Receiver by a manual pump.

There are three Bonded Warehouses, which contained about a thousand casks of Whisky, and the firm are now building another new Warehouse for the requirements of their customers. The new building will consist of three floors; the top for a Granary, the second a Malting, and the ground floor a Bonded Store. On the premises are conveniently arranged offices for the Distillery and Excise clerks, a private office for the partners, workshops, and general stores. Twelve men are employed on the works, and the peat used in drying the malt is dug in the district. We may also mention that all the machinery and pumps on the premises are driven by an 8-horse power steam engine. The water for mashing, washing, &c., is also heated by steam being ejected into the copper from the boiler, which supplies steam for the engine. The water used comes from the Percock Hill, on the beautiful estate belonging to Meldrum House. It is of fine quality, and most suitable for distillery operations.

The make is pure Malt Whisky, and the annual output is 50,000 gallons. It is sold principally in Edinburgh, Leith, Glasgow and London.

No. 92.

Bon Accord Distillery, Aberdeen.

PROPRIETORS, THE BON ACCORD DISTILLERY COMPANY, LIMITED.

WE arrived at Aberdeen, the "City of Bon Accord," very early in the day, having started from Insch by the first train. We made our way direct to the Imperial Hotel, and were delighted with the quarters we had chosen. After breakfast we strolled forth to explore the Granite City, or, as it has been aptly termed, the "Silver City by the Sea," and were struck with its cleanly and beautiful appearance. All the buildings are erected with solid blocks of greyish white granite, and most of them are of handsome elevation. Aberdeen ranks next to Edinburgh and Glasgow in point of importance, and is the capital of the north of Scotland. It stands between the rivers Dee and Don, the former being crossed by four bridges, one of them a stone bridge of seven arches, built in the sixteenth century by Bishops Elphinstone and Dunbar. Union Street, which is a mile long, is without doubt the most attractive part of the city, and contains some beautiful shops and magnificent buildings. Part of the street is carried over a ravine by means of a granite bridge, consisting of one arch of 130 feet span, 44 feet in breadth and 50 feet above the surface of the ground below, and we were informed that it cost upwards of £13,000. Near this bridge we noticed a bronze statue of Prince Albert, by Marochetti. The chief attraction, however, is the Municipal Buildings, situated at the eastern end of Union Street. It is one of the largest and most imposing granite buildings in Scotland, and its most striking feature is the tower which rises to the height of 190 feet, from which we had a fine view of the City stretched out like a panorama. There are many places of interest in this City, notably King's College, founded in 1494, a stately fabric. Marischal College, founded in 1593, was united to King's College in 1859. Aberdeen has for ages past been the seat of learning and culture, and its various libraries contain a rich mine of literature. Having occupied a couple of hours in our explorations, we returned to our hotel to equip ourselves with the necessary papers and introduction for our visit to the Bon Accord Distillery, resolving to complete our tour of the City the next day.

Our route to the Distillery was through the noble market buildings, up Union Street, and along the Bon Accord Terrace. Here we turned sharply to the right, and descended a steep hill into Union Glen, the most prominent object before us, on the opposite slope, being the Distillery. There is a lively rivulet running past the works called the Ferry Hill Burn, but its waters are not used in the works, and it is allowed to pursue the course of its own sweet will unmolested into the river Dee.

Bon Accord—"good agreement"—was the watchword of the Scotch on that wintry night in the old churchyard, when the English were attacked by the townspeople in the time of Wallace. Without this password they would not have been able to distinguish friends from foes.

The Distillery dates back to the year 1785, when it was an old brewery, and supplied the notables of that period with its famous "stingo." It adjoins the property of the old Union Glen Distillery, built in the year 1820, and which was dismantled in 1855, the Stills and other vessels being purchased by the former proprietor of Bon Accord Distillery. In the year 1876 the whole of the Bon Accord property was acquired by the present limited company, who made extensive alterations and improvements to it; but early in 1885 all the old buildings, except the No. 4 Granary and No. 2 Malt Barns, were burnt to the ground, and, as an evidence of the enterprise of this company and the diligence of the contractor, we feel bound to state that the whole Distillery, with the exception of the ancient buildings referred to, was rebuilt on a larger and more modern style, fitted up and furnished in eleven months.

The Distillery, built of solid granite, is of handsome elevation, and covers nearly three acres of ground. The work consists of a quadrangular block of buildings, with a projecting wing on the left at the back of the new offices and board room. We were admitted to the spiritual precincts through a postern gate, and found ourselves in a covered roadway or court, 140 feet long and 16 feet wide, which leads to all the departments of the establishment. We made our tour of inspection under the guidance of Mr. John Thomson, the manager of the Distillery, who explained to us the arrangements and *modus operandi* as we went along. We were struck with the neatness and order displayed in every department, and the ingenuity which had contrived the arrangement and position of the vessels. Our guide first led the way to the Barley Lofts and Maltings, so that we might follow the process from the beginning. These Maltings are built on the steep part of the hill, and a roadway through an outer yard on the same property has been constructed to the doors of the Barley Lofts, so that the grain can be tipped direct on to the floor without the use of hoists or elevators. We began to ascend the moment we left the covered roadway, and gradually passed round by means of staircases to the south-east angle of the Work, where are the Nos. 1 and 2 Maltings, built in the shape of the letter L, and which form the wing of the Distillery before referred to. One of these buildings, which is designated as the No. 1 Granary and Maltings, is 154 feet long and 49 broad. It is a lofty structure, and is divided into three floors, each of which is well lighted and supported by massive iron columns. The top story is the Granary, and some idea of its size and capacity may be ascertained by the fact that it will hold 5,000 quarters of barley. At its northern end there are two Steeps, each capable of wetting 60 quarters at one time. These metal Steeps are sunk into the floor, and their contents discharged on to the lower floor by the simple contrivance of a lever screw, which raises the sluices from the bottom. This Malting Floor is concreted, and of same dimensions as the Granary above. The third or basement floor is a Bonded Warehouse. We now paid a visit to the No. 2 Granary, which communicates with the others, but is not quite so large. Here there is a Cock-loft in the roof 128 feet long and 19½ broad, holding 2,000 quarters of barley, whilst the Granary floor underneath, which is of the same length, but 40 feet broad, will hold 3,000 quarters of grain. Under this floor there are two Warehouses of same dimensions. Before leaving this section of the Works our guide conducted us to the platform on the roof to see the huge Water-Tank, which covers part of the No. 2 Granary, and holds 45,000 gallons. We may here state that the Company possess a well about 100 feet deep, which cost £3,000 to sink, and it is that water which is pumped up to this tank. Where we stand is the highest point of the Distillery, and the prospect, although not extensive, is interesting, embracing on one side the city, with its monuments and stately buildings, the harbour and the German Ocean; and on the other, the Strawberry Bank, crowned by Bon Accord Terrace; and at the back, the grounds of Willowbank.

We now descended to the ground level, and crossed the roadway to the other Granary Building which forms a portion of the old work erected in 1788 and spared by the late fire. It is a three story structure, 108 feet long and 19 broad. The top holds 1,000 quarters of barley, the second is a concreted Malting, whilst the basement forms the No. 4 Bond. Adjoining the main building and at the end of the new Maltings there is a lofty Kiln, 36 feet square and 65 feet high, floored with metal plates, heated with peats from Orkney and shut off from the other buildings by a double set of swing iron doors. Exactly opposite and at the end of the old Maltings, and forming a part of the central block, is another Kiln of similar size and dimensions, the intervening space between the two being filled up by the Malt Deposit Room, said to be one of the largest in the north of Scotland; it is 65 feet long by 33 wide and 16 feet high, holds 1,200 quarters and is filled from either or both of the Kilns. We now descended by a stair to the Malt Mill, which contains a pair of metal rollers, and is fed from a chamber above, which communicates with the Malt deposit through a doorway shut off by a pair of fire-proof doors. On the same floor as the Mill is the Engine House, containing a capital horizontal Steam Engine of 30 horse power, which, with a small donkey engine, used for pumping water to the boiler and driving the chains in the Stills, etc., is the only motive power on the premises, so much being accomplished by gravitation. At the right hand we now pass through a doorway into the Mash House, 34 feet by 27 and 30 feet high, entirely devoted to the brewing department. As we pass along Mr. Thomson described to us how the ground Malt is lifted by the elevators to the Grist Chamber above, and we climb a stair to have a peep into the hopper which fills the mouth of the Steel's Mashing Machine, where the hot water joins the grist and never leaves its company again until they both become etherealised, and start on their voyage to minister to the enjoyment of mankind. But to return to the Mash House; on an iron bridge above the Tun are two heating tanks with a capacity together of 11,000 gallons, and underneath, in the centre of the floor, is the Mash Tun, a circular iron vessel 17½ feet in diameter and 6 feet deep, containing the usual drawing plates and stirring gear, the draff from which is pumped into the Grains Receiver and can be dropped from there, either into the courtyard or into the farmers' carts. The Underback, which is constructed of metal, is under the Mash Tun and holds 4,000 gallons. From that receptacle the worts are pumped by a centrifugal pump to the Worts Receiver holding 3,000 gallons, which rests on three iron beams over the court-way, and from whence the worts run through a Morton's Refrigerator into the fermenting tuns. We now entered the Back-house, a stone structure 50 feet long, 36 wide and 30 high, possessing a double staging floor constructed with stout pine laths. It contains six Washbacks, each holding 10,000 gallons, the switches of which are driven by steam. The basement of this large building is used for cleaning, steaming, and storing casks, and the floor is concreted. We now leave the covered way and pass through an open court into the Boiler House, which contains a steam boiler 26 feet long and 7 feet in diameter, over which is placed the Wash Charger holding 10,000 gallons. This is rather a good arrangement, as the wash gets warm before running into the Stills. We were now conducted through a doorway into the next building, which is the Still-house. It is 65 feet long, 36 wide, and 30 high, and contains four pot Stills, two of them being wash and two spirit Stills. The former contain each 3,600 gallons, and the latter 2,036 gallons each, all heated by open furnaces. The Worm Tub forms the roof of the boiler house, and is constructed on a new principle. It consists of a deep iron tank, 62 feet long and 20 broad, wherein are coiled four distinct worms, the peculiarity of which consists of the liquor being divided into 16 separate parts, in the centre of the worm, and after running over a hundred feet in this way, is again collected and conducted in one pipe to the spirit Receiver. This worm tank is copiously supplied with cold water through a perforated pipe extending along the bottom the whole length of the tank, and the heated water is taken off the top by an overflow pipe at each end of the tank. On a gallery at the end of the Still-house is placed the safe, also a Low-wines and Feints Receiver, holding 3,412 gallons, and a Spirit Receiver 3,440 gallons.

We now returned to the covered court and visited the Spirit Store—a neat apartment 50 feet long, 33 wide, and 12 high, containing a Vat which holds 5,000 gallons, and receives the spirit from the Receiver by gravitation. From there we passed on to the Bottling Store, which is at the side of the main entrance, and is 30 feet long, 27 wide, and 15 high, well lighted and floored with cement. The Manager informed us that the Company only bottle for export, and ship same under bond, the brand being the well-known "Cock-o'-the-North." A representation of the game-cock, forming a part of the Registered Trade Mark of the Company, has for upwards of a century adorned the parapet of the main entrance to the Distillery. The four large Bonded Warehouses already referred to, are capable of storing upwards of 8,000 casks, and are all well lighted and ventilated. There is a Cooperage in the outer yard, and good Store Sheds. Over twenty men are employed on the premises, and there are three Excise Officers.

The Whisky is fine Malt, and the Distillery is capable of producing over 300,000 gallons annually, which entitles "Bon-Accord" to rank as one of the largest Highland Malt Distilleries in Scotland.

No. 93.

Devanha Distillery, Aberdeen.

PROPRIETORS, WM. BLACK & CO.

ON entering the City of Aberdeen by the railway from the south, the attention is at once attracted by the Devanah Distillery, which, seen from the lofty bridge, has a very imposing appearance. It is situated on the banks of the beautiful river Dee, within two miles of its confluence with the German Ocean, and nearly a mile distant from Aberdeen. The works, which have a frontage to the river of some 500 feet, are built principally of granite, and separated from the Dee by a splendid esplanade, which has been recently constructed, and cost the city £95,000.

DEVANHA DISTILLERY.

This Distillery, which was established many years ago, consists of two quadrangles, the main buildings of both abutting on the railway.

Mr. Flockhart, the general manager, showed us over the place. We commenced at the south buildings facing the river, which are enclosed in a courtyard. Passing through a gateway, we ascended an outside stone staircase to the top floor, which is one of the Barley Barns, and is 150 feet long by 50 feet broad; thence through an archway, shut off by a double pair of iron doors, into the left-hand angle of the building. This floor is 120 feet long and 60 feet broad, and the two Granaries are capable of holding 10,000 quarters of grain. The barley is lifted by an enclosed hoist outside the building, the wheel of which is attached to a wire rope stretching 200 yards over the roof to the steam-engine in the Distillery. The two floors underneath the first building we entered are concreted and used for malting purposes; they possess two Steeps, each capable of wetting sixty quarters at a time. The basement of this building is used as a Bonded Warehouse. Under the Granary floor of the left angle are three other floors, all Bonded Warehouses. From the Maltings we passed into the Kiln, a lofty, building nearly 80 feet high and 36 feet square; it is floored with perforated iron plates, and peat, with a small admixture of coke, is used in the drying. The malt is raised by elevators to the Kiln floor. In the same building are three Malt Stores, immediately connected with the Kiln, capable of holding together 2,000 quarters. Under these stores there is a large shed filled with peat.

We next returned to the esplanade, and entered by a postern door into the Distillery proper. After inspecting the duty-paid Racking Store just inside the court, we mounted a stair to the balcony, which runs along in front of the Excise and Distillery offices. This balcony, which is reached at the other end by stone steps, overhangs the Worm Tub, which is stretched out before the office windows, like a small lake, and is nearly 100 feet long, in which are laid several hundred feet of worm coils. As we stood at the end of this terrace or balcony, we obtained a fine view of the river and its picturesque surroundings. But to return to the process, the malt is brought from the Malt Deposit direct to the Mill in the enclosure, which place we next visited, where it is pulverized between a set of Malt-rollers, after which the grist is raised by elevators to the Hopper in the Refrigerator room, and from thence screwed away into a smaller receptacle over the Mash House. In this room, besides two of Miller's Refrigerators, there are two Worts Receivers and a large Heating Copper, and on our way down we passed other two Heating Coppers, supported on iron columns, and commanding the Mash-tuns below. When we reached the ground level we were taken to see the two separate Brewing Houses, each containing a Mash-tun, and no other vessel. The No. 1 vessel is 10½ feet in diameter and 5 feet deep, and No. 2 ditto is 12 feet in diameter and 5 feet deep, each having connected therewith a Steel's Mashing Machine and the usual stirring gear. Our guide then conducted us down some stone steps to the two chambers underneath, each of which contains an Underback, holding 1,900 gallons, and made out of the former Mash-tuns, which did duty in this Distillery at the time of its foundation. From this stone chamber the worts are pumped up to the top of the building into the Refrigerators, and from thence by gravitation they run into the Washbacks. There are a couple of Tun Rooms in this establishment, wherein are placed fourteen Washbacks, each holding 4,000 gallons.

Continuing our progress, we inspected the Engine House, which contains a 25-horse power horizontal engine and a steam boiler and pumps. At the end of an open path we come to the new Still House, a large and lofty building, concreted and well lighted. Here, on a gallery, is placed the Wash Charger, which commands the Stills, and holds 4,500 gallons. There are two Pot Stills—the Wash Still, which holds 3,300 gallons, and the Spirit Still, 2,800 gallons, a Low-wines and Feints Receiver, a Spirit Receiver, and the Safe. At the back of the Still House, enclosed by the high embankment of the railway, is the Spirit Store, wherein is a vat holding 6,000 gallons; the small paved yard in front is covered with empty casks, waiting to be filled. Distributed about the premises are four Bonded Warehouses.

We then retraced our way to the main entrance, and our guide conducted us to an old building which had escaped our notice, and adjoins the Brewer's residence. It is the old Distilling House, erected many years ago, and still used by the firm. It contains two Pot Stills of very ancient pattern; one of them, a Wash Still, holds 2,315 gallons; the other, a Spirit Still holds 1,338 gallons, a Wash Charger, and two Receivers of similar capacity as the Stills; also the Safe and Sampling Safe, &c.

Adjoining this building there is a Carpenter's Shop, Cooperage, &c. Fire plugs are fixed all over the premises, and hand buckets on the floors, which are always filled ready for use in case of fire.

There are fine springs on the premises, but the water used in mashing comes from the City Waterworks, and the condensing water is pumped up from the Dee.

The Whisky made is from Malt only, and the annual output is 220,000 gallons.

The Bonded Stores can hold 6,000 hogsheads of Whisky, and are considered by the Excise some of the finest and best arranged Warehouses in the country.

Now but and ben the change-house fills,
  Wi' yill-caup commentators;
Here's crying out for bakes and grills,
  And there the pint-stoup clatters;
While thick and thrang, and loud and lang,
  Wi' logic and wi' scripture,
They raise a din, that in the end
  Is like to breed a rupture
    O' wrath that day.

Leeze me on drink, it gi'es us mair
  Than either school or college:
It kindles wit, it waukens lair,
  It pangs us fou o' knowledge.
Be't whisky gill, or penny weep,
  Or ony stronger potion,
It never fails, on drinkin' deep,
  To kittle up our notion
    By night or day.

The lads an' lasses, blythly bent
  To mind baith saul and body,
Sit round the table weel content,
  An' steer about the toddy.
On this ane's and on that ane's look,
  They're makin' observations;
While some are cozie i' the neuk,
  And formin' assignations
    To meet some day.

BURNS.

No. 94.

Strathdee Distillery, Aberdeen.

PROPRIETORS, HENRY OGG AND COMPANY.

THE next day we drove to Strathdee, about a mile from the Imperial Hotel. Our route was through the western suburb, the finest part of Aberdeen, which we need hardly say is one of the prettiest cities in the Kingdom. Strathdee Distillery is situated on the Deeside or Balmoral Road, in the valley of the Dee. The Works, which are mostly of the old-fashioned low-roofed character, cover a large space of ground. The Distillery was built in 1821 by Mr. Henry Ogg, father of the present proprietor.

Previous to the year 1820 the whisky consumed in Scotland was almost entirely made by Highland smugglers, who distilled it in bothies in the glens among the hills. The Upper Dee and the Upper Don were noted for the production of illicit whisky. The evasion of the Excise Laws was not generally looked upon as immoral in those days. The popular sympathy with the smuggler in his warfare with the gauger is shown in the ballads and songs of the day, and notably in the poems of Burns, who laments his own degradation in having "turned a gauger." In Aberdeenshire the trade was conducted by the smugglers with great boldness. There was many a battle or running fight between them and the officers, in which the casualties were sometimes serious and occasionally fatal. The whisky was brought down from the mountains, usually during the night, on the pack-saddles of ponies or small horses, in single file, to the number of six or a dozen, the halter of the second being tied to the crupper of the first and the third to the second, and so on. The owner usually rode the first horse, and his friends scouted behind and before to give warning of danger from either direction. Sometimes the whisky was captured, and sometimes the smugglers escaped with their booty.

To remedy these evils the Government resolved, about the year 1820, to encourage distilling under legal authority, and the erection of Distilleries was suggested to the brewers of the period. Strathdee, one of the first Distilleries in Aberdeenshire, was erected by Mr. Ogg, the principal partner of the Ferryhill Brewery, and about the same time the Devanha Distillery was established by the owners of the brewery of that name.

When Strathdee was built, the out-put was from about 15,000 to 25,000 gallons. About thirty years ago the Works were rebuilt on a much larger scale; and they do not, at first sight, look very much like a modern Distillery—it is only when you enter the Still House that you are assured of the fact by seeing the old Pot Stills at work. The motive power is steam, but water can be made available if required.

The buildings are enclosed in a large yard, entered by a gateway from the main road. We commenced our inspection at the Grain Lofts, which are on the left-hand side as you enter, and are together 150 feet long by 40 feet wide, and capable of containing 1,200 quarters of barley. The Malting House is a two-decker building, divided into two compartments, and there are large concrete Steeps on three of these floors. The malt is elevated from the floors direct on to the Kiln, which adjoins this building. It is 30 feet square, floored with wire cloth, and heated with peat and coke. The Malt Deposit adjoins the Kiln, into which the malt, when dried, is transferred by means of a Shoot, and in close proximity is the Mill, which consists of a pair of huge Rollers, and placed immediately under the Mill Room. When the malt has been crushed by these Rollers it is raised by an Elevator, and passes into a hopper above, communicating with the Mash Tun. We then descended by a stair into the principal building, which is large and divided on the ground floor into three compartments. In the east division of this building is the Still House, and on the floor over the Still House the Brew House. Here our guide pointed out to us the Mash Tun, a large vessel, with stirring gear driven by steam and drained by iron plates. Near the Mash Tun we saw two large heating Coppers, where the water for brewing is brought up to the proper heat. The Underback, which is a metal vessel, is placed under the Mash Tun. The Worts are drained off from the Mash Tun into the Underback, and from it are run into large iron Coolers, supported on iron beams, which cover the whole of the western division of the building. The Fermenting Tuns are placed in the lower floors of the building immediately below the Coolers, and into these Backs the Worts are run when of the proper temperature.

From the Fermenting Backs the Worts are pumped into the Chargers, which are placed in a separate building behind the Still House, but communicating with it. The Low-wines, as well as the Wash-chargers, are in this building, and from these both the Wash and the Low-wines are run by gravitation into the Stills.

After leaving the Mash or Brew House, we examined the Tun Room, where there are five Washbacks, each holding 2,830 gallons.

In the Still House there are three old Pot Stills, two being Wash Stills, one holding 2,150 and the other 2,544 gallons respectively, and a Spirit Still of the capacity of 1,770 gallons. The Worm Tub consists of a spacious open concrete tank sunk in the ground. It adjoins the Still House, and through it runs the Manofield Burn. The copper pipes in which the Low-wines and Spirits are cooled are sunk in this tank. Attached to each Still there is a Condensing Column or Refrigerator, in which the hot vapour is condensed before it reaches the cooling copper pipes, and from these the Low-wines and Spirits, when cold, are led into their respective receivers.

We then crossed the yard to the Spirit Store, which adjoins the large Bonded Warehouses. It is a neat building and contains a Vat which holds 3,300 gallons. The Warehouses are extensive, dry, and well ventilated. At the time of our visit they contained 1,026 casks or 73,196 gallons of Whisky of various ages. There is a spacious Racking and Bottling Store, as Messrs. Ogg and Company do a large case trade. The water used for general purposes is from the Manofield Burn, but that used for distilling purposes comes from the same source as the city water supply.

The Whisky is Highland Malt, and the annual output is from 45,000 to 55,000 proof gallons. It is principally sold in Leith, London, and Liverpool.

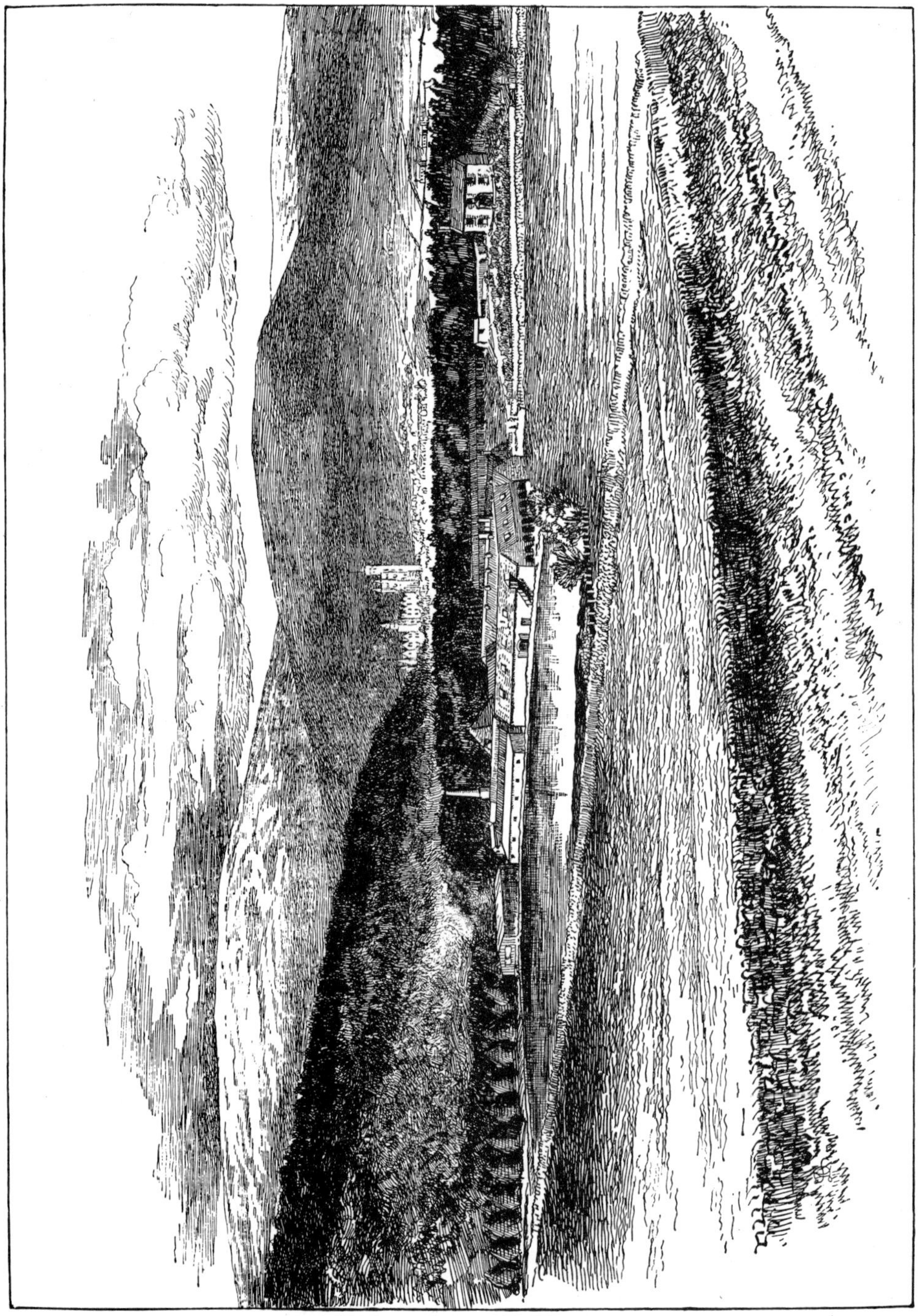

ROYAL LOCHNAGAR DISTILLERY.

No. 95.

Royal Lochnagar Distillery, Balmoral.

PROPRIETOR, HENRY F. BEGG.

WE left Aberdeen at a very early hour on the morning of our visit to the Royal Lochnagar Distillery, as the coach to Braemar leaves Ballater on the arrival of the first train. The railway runs along the valley of the Dee, or Deeside, as it is popularly designated, one of the most celebrated tourist routes to Balmoral. On our way we passed the Catholic College of Blair, about six miles from Aberdeen, which contains the renowned portraits of Queen Mary and Cardinal Beaton. After this the route becomes delightfully picturesque, and we pass Drum Castle, the House of Durris, and many other notable and historic places. At Banchory the Dee is joined by the Feugh, a dark and angry-looking stream; in the distance can be seen the hills among which its waters rise, and anon the summits of Caer Loch, 1,890 feet, and Cloch-na-ben, 1,963 feet above sea level; the latter with a vast projecting hump, looking like a huge wart upon its brow. On reaching Aboyne the rail runs due west on the property of the Marquis of Huntly, and fine views of wide stretches of forest land, picturesquely broken with rocks, are obtained. Passing through a tunnel, a more open range of country opens out, the monotony of which is relieved by distant hills and the fine background of Lochnagar mountain, the monarch of the district, bending in a gracefully waving outline; it rises about 3,800 feet above sea level. Close by is Ballatrich, the farmhouse where Byron, when about eight years of age, stayed after an attack of the scarlet fever. He has described Lochnagar as one of the most sublime and picturesque amongst our "Caledonian Alps." Its appearance is of a dusky hue, but the summit is the seat of eternal snow. The impression made upon his poetic mind by the lovely scenery of this district is shown in his lines to the mountain, the last stanza of which runs—

> Years have roll'd on, Loch na Garr, since I left you,
>   Years must elapse ere I tread you again:
> Nature of verdure and flow'rs has bereft you,
>   Yet still are you dearer than Albion's plain.
> England! thy beauties are tame and domestic
>   To one who has roved o'er the mountains afar:
> Oh for the crags that are wild and majestic!
>   The steep frowning glories of dark Loch na Garr!

Again in "The Island," written a year or two before his death, he breaks out in poetic admiration of this Highland Monarch, and from the period of his stay in the district he dates his love of mountainous countries, the glories and beauties of which he describes in many a verse such as he alone could frame. The ascent of Lochnagar can be made from Braemar, Crathie, or Ballater; from the latter place it is a little over twelve miles. Once at the top, the traveller is amply repaid for the toilsome ascent.

Upon arrival at Ballater, the first thing to be done is to secure a seat on the coach, and if the box seat can be obtained it is lucky, for the drive to Balmoral from start to finish is superb, and upon a fine day the scene presented to the eye is one not easily forgotten. A short way before coming upon Her Majesty's Highland home we obtained an excellent view of another and far more ancient royal abode, namely, Abergeldie Castle. This picturesque old building, with its quaint architecture, its turrets and bartizans, is situated quite close to the Dee on the south side of the river, and is always viewed with interest. Abergeldie has been in the possession of the Gordon family for at least four centuries, and while, as mentioned, the seat is entitled to be called a royal residence, it does not belong to the Crown, the Queen holding the castle only on lease, and devoting it to the accommodation of distinguished visitors. Here it was that the Duchess of Kent, mother of Her Majesty, used to reside, finding it a charming summer home. Here also, during some past years, Eugenie, ex-Empress of France, the lonely relict of the Third Napoleon, through the gracious consideration of the Sovereign of England, found a fitting retreat when stricken with the great sorrow of her widowhood, the lamented death in Zululand of her beloved son, the Prince Imperial. Eugenie was the object of the deepest respect in the upper strath of Dee, and when out driving never failed to acknowledge from her carriage the lifted hat or bonnet of the humblest wayfarer. Abergeldie Castle is the residence of Their Royal Highnesses the Prince and Princess of Wales when they pay their autumn visit to the Aberdeenshire highlands. As we approached Crathie the lovely vale of Balmoral lay spread out before us, bordered all round with magnificent woods and almost encircled with majestic mountains; this lovely spot forms a picture said to be unrivalled in Europe. Here is the chosen retreat from the cares of state of our beloved Queen, and it would be difficult to find a more beautiful spot. On one side a wooded haugh slopes gently down from Craig Gowan's shaggy side to the margin of the river Dee, on the borders of which the noble castle is built; on the other are ranged battlements of hills with glimpses of magnificent scenery, while eastward is to be seen the Rock of Oaks and the pine-covered hills of Invercauld. As the eye returns to the point first noticed, it is glad to rest on the soft foliage of the "birks of Craig Gowan," and one can fully endorse Black's opinion that in all Scotland there is no region in which the sublime and beautiful are more harmoniously blended. Balmoral is a fine property, comprising upwards of ten thousand acres, more than a thousand of which are under wood, and in addition there is a deer forest of upwards of thirty thousand acres.

Leaving the coach and bidding good-bye to its occupants, we crossed the beautiful suspension bridge which leads to the grand entrance to Balmoral, and turning to the left begin the ascent of the steep hill which leads to the Royal Lochnagar Distillery. The road is beautifully wooded, and half way up we pause to rest.

The Distillery was built in the year 1825 by one John Robertson of Crathie, an old smuggler, and it came into the hands of Mr. John Begg in the year 1845. It is situated within a mile of Balmoral Castle, and the late

Mr. John Begg held a lease of the property under Her Majesty the Queen; there is no Distillery within fifty miles round, therefore its isolation gives it a distinctive character. It was first visited by Her Majesty and His Royal Highness the Prince Consort on the 12th September 1848, and by Their Royal Highnesses the Prince and Princess of Wales on the 15th September 1863, and we were informed that the Whisky made at the Distillery has been supplied to the Royal Palaces and Court for the past thirty-six years.

At the decease of Mr. John Begg in the year 1882, the Distillery came into the hands of his son, Mr. Henry Farquharson Begg, the present proprietor. The Distillery, with the farm attached thereto, covers one hundred and thirty acres of ground, and lies at the foot of the mountain from which it takes its name. The works consist of a series of oblong buildings, mostly detached, and none of which are enclosed. At the back there is a fine reservoir, in which is collected the water of a spring which, rising in the mountain, runs down its sides in the form of a burn, collecting numerous other little streams in its onward progress over heather and peat mosses.

Our guide first conducted us to the Malt Barns, of which there are three, triangular in shape, and averaging from 60 to 90 feet in length by 30 to 40 feet wide; they are two-deckers and together hold 2,700 quarters of barley. We then crossed the way to the Malting House, a peculiar old building with stone floor peculiarly adapted for malting purposes; it is 105 feet long by 64 feet broad, and possesses an ancient stone Steep capable of wetting thirty quarters of barley at one time. Here also are two other Granaries of large dimensions, capable of holding 3,000 quarters of barley. In conjunction with these buildings is one of the quaintest Kilns we have seen, 30 feet square, floored with wire cloth and heated with peats burned in open *chauffeurs*. The neighbouring moors supply good peats, and we noticed a fine lofty shed filled with dry peats sufficient for several years supply.

Leaving the open court we next came to the Distillery proper, which forms the central building of the group, and first entered the Mill which contains a pair of steel malt crushers. The Grist Loft is above, to reach which we ascended an outside ladder and found ourselves in a low pitched chamber, which on account of its difficulty of approach would have made a good hiding place in olden times; the grist is removed from this floor by manual labour. Returning to the main building we passed two huge Heating Tanks, and then came to the Mash House, which forms a part of the upper floor of the Still House, and through which the Still Heads protrude to the Worms. The Mash Tun is 10 feet in diameter and 4 feet deep, and connected therewith is a Steel's Mashing Machine, and a set of revolving stirring rakes driven by a water-wheel. The Underback is in close proximity and near the doorway at a lower elevation. Over the roof of the Mashing Department are placed the Coolers 54 feet long and 27 feet wide, up to which the worts are pumped from the Underback, and they possess the old-fashioned fan arrangement driven by water power. In the next building which is called the Tun Room, we observed five Washbacks, each with a capacity of 800 gallons, and on a loft above is the Wash Charger, a timber vessel holding 2,000 gallons. The Still House is a neat stone building and contains two old "Pot Stills," the Wash Still holding 1,362 gallons, and the Spirit Still 899 gallons. The Worm Tub connected with these vessels is a square iron dish supplied with a constant stream of water from the "Craignagall Dam" or Reservoir. At the end of the Still House are placed the

Low-wines and Feints Charger, Spirit Receivers and Safe. In close proximity is a Spirit Store which adjoins the duty-paid racking store. Mr. Donald Stewart, the Excise Officer, was introduced to us and conducted us to the two duty-free Warehouses, where we tasted some remarkably fine old Whisky, and thus refreshed completed our tour of inspection. We then visited the Distillery and Excise Offices, the latter a rustic edifice, standing in the beautiful garden attached to Mr. Begg's house. From thence we proceeded to the Brewer's neat little residence, and afterwards inspected the cottages occupied by the employés, of whom there are twenty. There is no steam power on the premises, all the driving being done by water-wheels.

LOCHNAGAR DISTILLERY WAREHOUSES, ABERDEEN.

In the adjacent farmsteading are a hundred head of fine cattle, which consume the draff and spent wash. The farm lands which stretch almost to Abergeldie, the house already referred to, of His Royal Highness the Prince of Wales, produce splendid barley and other grain. The Bonded Warehouses at Lochnagar are small, as the greater part of the Whisky manufactured there is bonded in the eight Lochnagar Warehouses on the quay at Aberdeen, where also are handsome offices and large Bottling Stores. These buildings stand on the site of the once well-known "Cowie's Brewery," and cost, including excavations, vaulting, &c., close upon £8,000.

The Whisky which is pure Highland Malt is sold principally in the United Kingdom, and the annual output in 1884-5 was 65,000 gallons.

No. 96.

Royal Glenury Distillery, Stonehaven, Kincardineshire.

PROPRIETOR, WM. RITCHIE.

WE made a brief halt at Stonehaven to see the Glenury Distillery, and visit the celebrated ruins for which the town is famous. Who has not heard of Dunnotter Castle, which forms one of the most majestic ruins in Scotland. We drove direct to it from the station, and were amply repaid for our trouble. It is situated on the site of a stupendous perpendicular rock, 160 feet high, which projects into the sea, and is almost separated from the land by a deep chasm, forming a natural fosse. The castle consists of a series of stately towers, and other buildings; and before the advent of artillery was quite impregnable. We drove back by way of the town to the Distillery, which is planted on the banks of the Cowie, and takes its name from the Glen-Urie, through which the river passes on its way to the sea. After crossing the Cowie we ascended a gentle acclivity, and reached Glenury by a road cut through the face of a sandy hill, which on one side shelters the establishment.

The situation of the Distillery is most picturesque, the lofty railway viaduct, which crosses the glen, adding beauty to the scene. It is a mile from the town, station, and sea shore. The Works, which cover three and a half acres of ground, consist of several ranges of stone buildings; the central block contains the Distilling and Brewing houses, and the outer ones the Granaries, Maltings, and Warehouses.

The Glenury Distillery was founded about the year 1836 by Captain Barclay, the well-known champion pedestrian, who walked a thousand miles in a thousand hours. He carried on a most successful business, and afterwards disposed of it to Mr. William Ritchie, the present proprietor, who has since made many additions and improvements in the place, and increased the annual output considerably.

Mr. John Watt, the manager, first conducted us to the Granaries and Maltings which stand in a delightful old-fashioned garden, and in some places the river almost washes the walls. The No. 1 and No. 2 Maltings are neat stone buildings of four flats, two of them appropriated for barley storage, the others for Malting Floors, these last are concreted and have metal Steeps. The No. 3 Granary building is divided from the No. 1 and No. 2 by the Kilns and Excise Offices, and is not quite so lofty, having only three floors, two for barley, and the bottom a Malting Floor with a metal Steep. Served by these Maltings are two Kilns, both connected by an overhead bridge, across which the malt is wheeled; the floors are of wire cloth and the furnaces are fired with peat. On the level of the Kiln Floor is the Malt Deposit, and adjoining is the Mill, above which is the Grist Loft. A water cistern stretches over the pathway from the roof of the Mill House to the Still House, and holds 50,000 gallons of water, which is pumped up from the river. Another bridge forms the communication between the Grist Loft and Mash House, over which the ground malt is conveyed direct into the Tun. Following our guide we entered the Mash House, a spacious apartment containing a metal Mash-tun 17 feet in diameter, possessing the usual stirring gear and draining plates. On a gallery we observed two boiling coppers with a capacity of 6,000 gallons, and sunk into the pavement outside are the two Underbacks. The worts are pumped up to two old-fashioned fan coolers in the roof of the Back House, in which the fans are driven by a water-wheel. Ascending two pairs of stairs we reached the top staging of the Back House, wherein are five Washbacks, each holding 6,000 gallons, switched by water power. This house is 90 feet long and 30 feet wide. We next retraced our steps to the courtyard, and came to the Still House, passing on our way a fine Worts and Wash Pump, driven by water power. This building is 54 feet square, and contains a Wash Charger holding 7,000 gallons, and a Low-wines and Feints Charger 3,000 gallons, both new vessels, and placed on a platform supported by iron pillars. On the floor of the house are two Old Pot Stills, one of them a Wash Still, holds 4,000 gallons, the other a Spirit Still of 3,000 gallons, also a Low-wines and Feints Receiver, and Spirit Receiver, the former holding 2,500 gallons, the latter 3,000 gallons, and a Spirit Safe.

Attached to the Spirit Still there is a brass Charging Gauge, an ingenious device for preventing accidents whilst the Still is being charged. The Worm Tub consists of a huge cement tank 80 feet long and 12 feet wide, wherein are laid 900 feet of copper worm; all the water used in the Distillery runs through this receptacle from the aqueduct above, turning a large water-wheel, which drives all the motive power in the place. On leaving the water tank we paid a brief visit to the Spirit Store, containing a vat holding 4,000 gallons, and to the five Warehouses, capable of holding nearly 10,000 casks. There is also a large new warehouse of two stories, in the town, of 120 feet square, in four sections, which contained 350,000 gallons at the time of our visit.

In the Distillery yard there is a Racking Store, also a Cooperage, over which is a carpenter's shop containing an engine, made by a workman in the place, for driving three turning lathes and two sawing machines; also a joiners' and engineers' shop. Home-grown barley only is used; the district being celebrated for the fine quality of the barley. There are three Excise Officers, besides the Supervisor, Mr. H. Thompson. The make is Highland Malt, and the annual output is about 132,000 gallons.

No. 97.

Fettercairn Distillery, near Laurencekirk.

PROPRIETOR, DAVID DURIE

WE stayed all night at the cosy little inn at Stonehaven Station, and next morning started early for Laurencekirk. The Fettercairn Distillery is six miles from the station, and is situated at the foot of the Grampians, where "our fathers fed their flocks" and smugglers made the Whisky. It was the head-quarters of these latter gentlemen, and many a racy tale is told by the villagers of their daring and boldness. The drive for some few miles is not very pretty, but as you approach the village it becomes more interesting, and the driver delights to tell you not only that it is a very historic place, but that our Gracious Queen some years ago actually stayed one night in the village on her way from Balmoral down Glen Esk, returning by the Cairn road. Balmoral is forty miles from Fettercairn, and the drive for rugged grandeur and wild scenery is equal to any in the north of Scotland.

In the village of Fettercairn stands a curious octagonal pillar, surmounting a circular mass of masonry in the form of a flight of steps, bearing the insignia of the Earl of Middleton. It is believed to have been the cross of the extinct town of Kincardine, and bears the date of 1670. On one side there is an iron rivet, to which the old Scottish tool of punishment, the "jougs," was formerly suspended.

About a mile from the village is the estate of Fasque, with its grand castellated mansion, built in 1809 by Sir Alexander Ramsay, surrounded by its own beautiful woods, and well worth a visit. To the lovers of tragedy and romance the whole district is intensely interesting, and it would not be possible to mention in these pages one-half of what we were told, as it would form a book of itself. However, we cannot pass by the ruins of Fenella's Castle without referring to the tragic event that occurred therein. This castle, which stands on an eminence near Fettercairn, was the scene of the murder of Kenneth III., King of Scotland. He ascended the throne in the year 970, and occasionally resided at a castle about a mile distant on the east side of the village. The king excited the deadly hatred of the royal lady, Fenella, daughter of the proud Earl of Angus, for having legally put to death her son, Crathilenthus. She invited him to the castle, where she had prepared an "infernal machine," which consisted of a brass statue, which threw out arrows when a golden apple was taken from its hand. It stood in a handsome apartment, surrounded by rich drapery and curious sculptures Under pretext of amusing the king with this curiosity, she conducted him to the apartment, and courteously invited him to take the apple. The king, amused with the idea, did so, when instantly he was pierced with arrows and mortally wounded. The attendants, on coming for their royal master, could not gain admittance to the castle, from whence the assassin had already fled. However, they forced open the doors, and found to their horror and consternation the king weltering in his blood. So much for a woman's vengeance.

But to return to the Distillery. It was originally established two miles higher up the mountain, in the heart of a smuggling district, on the slopes of the "Cairn-o'-Mount," one of the Grampian hills, over which the public road passes to Deeside, Balmoral, and the north Highlands. In 1824 a new Distillery was built on a much larger scale at Fettercairn, and the old work was abandoned. It is situated near the Esk, a river noted for its charming scenery and heavy takes of salmon. The water used for distilling operations and driving power comes from the top of the Grampians, and is of superior quality.

The following is a brief description of the work, which covers about two acres of ground.

As you enter the gateway, the first buildings that attract your attention are the Maltings, constructed of stone and slated; they are 120 feet long and 21 feet broad, and of two stories. The top is used for grain, and contains a Steep made with stone. The bottom floor is used for malting, and adjoins the Kiln, which is floored with metal plates and heated with peat and coke. We next ascended to the Malt Deposit, a neat apartment over the Mill, in the floor of which there is a sluice trap, through which the malt falls into the Mill below, which consists of a strong pair of metal rollers, driven by water power. In close proximity is the Mash House, a well-lighted building, which contains the Heating Coppers and an iron Mash-tun, 10 feet in diameter and 4 feet deep; also the Underback, sunk into the floor below, holding 2,000 gallons. We then bent our steps to the Tun Room, which is joined to the Brewing House. It is 50 feet long and 22 feet broad, and contains five Washbacks, each holding 40,000 gallons, and on a loft above the Wash Charger, which commands the Stills. Through a doorway we came to the Still House, a lofty building, 60 feet long and 25 feet broad, wherein are two old Pot Stills, as follows: a Wash Still, holding 2,000 gallons, and a Low-wines, 1,400 gallons. The Worm Tub is placed outside the Still House, and the Coolers, which consist of a metal trough, are placed in the bed of the running stream, which drives the machinery. In the Running Room, besides the usual Safe and Sampling Apparatus, are two Receivers.

The Spirit Store is opposite the Still House, and contains a vat which holds 1,100 gallons, and near this building there is a small Cooperage, a carpenter's shop, and smithy.

Distributed about the premises are five Warehouses, containing 60,000 gallons of Whisky of various ages.

The Whisky, which is Highland Malt, is sold principally in Glasgow and Leith, and the annual output is 85,000 gallons.

Mr. H. Thomson is the chief Excise officer.

No. 98.

Brechin Distillery, Brechin, County of Forfar.

PROPRIETORS, GUTHRIE, MARTIN & CO.

THE journey from Dundee to Brechin was a pleasant one, and our fellow passengers very agreeable. One of them, a fine stalwart young Scotchman, amused us much; he maintained that Burns was right when he said "Freedom and Whisky gang thegither," and that Bonnie Scotland with her culture, industries, and ambition, was a proof of it. We reluctantly left this party at Brig o'Dun Junction, and after a short time arrived at Brechin, the object of our journey. A ten minutes walk over the hill brought us to Messrs. Guthrie, Martin, & Co.'s Distillery, which is situated in the parish of Brechin, about half a mile from the railway station. It is half a mile from the river South Esk, and four from the celebrated bridge of Dun, a district sacred to the memory of the Great Reformer, Sir John Erskine. To the west of Brechin, a busy manufacturing town, on a rock overhanging the river, stands Brechin Castle, the seat of the Earl of Dalhousie; the site of an old fort, where the Scots made so brave a stand and stout resistance to Edward I. of England, making, by their doughty deeds of warfare and heroism, many a page of history.

The Distillery was built in the year 1820. Previous to its erection, Brechin and the neighbouring towns were supplied with Whisky made in the northern Grampians by smugglers, who carried it from thence in kegs slung across the backs of their ponies. The originators of the firm were Messrs. David, John, and Alexander Guthrie, brothers of the late eminent divine Dr. Thomas Guthrie, and the present proprietors are descendants of the same family.

The Whisky is Highland Malt, and the water used in its manufacture is conveyed in pipes from the Grampian mountains, and the peats employed in drying the malt come from the same source. The district around Brechin being highly cultivated, barley of the finest quality is grown and carted by the farmers into the lofts of the Distillery, where nothing but the very best barley is malted. The annual output is 100,000 gallons.

Though the buildings of the Still House and Malt Barns are old, the internal arrangements are of modern description, and in every case where machinery can be used in place of manual labour advantage is taken.

The spirit is distilled in the old-fashioned Pot Stills, and condensed in Worms laid in the bed of the Den Burn which runs through the works. The Warehouses for the storing of Spirits are as fine as any in the north. One, built a few years ago, and which contains 100,000 gallons, is 200 feet long by 50 feet broad.

Besides supplying wholesale houses with Whisky, Messrs. Guthrie, Martin, and Co. are also large holders of very old spirits, which they keep to meet the demands of their Duty-paid trade.

No. 99.

Glencadam Distillery, Brechin, County of Forfar.

PROPRIETORS, THE GLENCADAM DISTILLERY CO.

ON leaving Brechin, we bent our steps to Glencadam Distillery, situated in the cleft of an undulating hill, about half a mile from the town, and the same distance from the delightful river Esk. Brechin is rich in historical memories. Long ago it was a walled-in city, with a handsome cathedral, erected about 1150, dedicated to St. Ninian. The present parish church occupies the west end of the building, and the ruins are very interesting. For a long period during the Middle Ages, Brechin was the seat of piety and culture, and many a mitred bishop and sandalled monk has here taught learning and fine arts hand in hand with his religion. Here, alas! also was the scene of much sanguinary strife, and many a battle has been lost and won under the grey towers of its castle.

In 1452 the Earls of Huntly and Crawford fought a great battle, when the latter was defeated. In 1572 Sir Adam Gordon surprised a number of the King's soldiers, and cut off the whole party. All is now changed, and Brechin has become a peaceful, thriving, busy manufacturing town, and not the least element in its commercial operations are its Distilleries.

The following is a brief outline of the Glencadam Distillery, which was built at the beginning of the century, and covers two acres of ground.

It is supplied with fine water from Moorfoot Loch, giving abundance of the pure stream for driving and mashing purposes.

The barley, which is all grown in the district, is carted by the farmers direct to the Granaries, of which there are two, capable of holding 1,000 quarters.

The Malt Barns are two in number, and when the grain is properly germinated it is removed to the Kiln, which is floored with German wire cloth. Peat only is used in the drying. From thence the malt is carried to the Malt Stores, where it is dropped through shoots into the malt rollers, and the grist is then conveyed to the Mash-tun, a vessel containing 800 bushels, with the usual stirring rakes. The liquor is then drawn off into the Underback, and after it is cooled in the regular way it goes into the five Washbacks, each holding 1,200 gallons. After fermentation has taken place, it is pumped to the Wash Stills, and afterwards run into the Low-wines Receiver; thence to the Low-wines and Feints Charger, containing 1,000 gallons, then to the two Stills, which are of the old Pot kind, and afterwards into the Spirit Receiver, descending thence to the Spirit Stores into a vat, from whence it is drawn off into casks, weighed, branded, and warehoused. In the courtyard there is a 10-horse power gas engine and a fine boiler for heating water.

The six Warehouses will contain 3,000 casks of Whisky, which is Highland Malt, and the annual output is 40,000 gallons. Eight persons are employed in the works, and the product is chiefly sold in Glasgow and neighbourhood.

No. 100.

Isla Distillery, Perth.

PROPRIETOR, JOHN FORBES.

"What's to do?
Shall we go see the reliques of this town?
I pray you let us satisfy our eyes
With the memorials, and the things of fame,
That do renown this city."—*Twelfth Night.*

PERTH, which is more a City of the past than the present, is most romantically situated on the banks of the Tay. It was once as famous for its architectural riches, as it has always been for the unrivalled beauty of its position, and well does it deserve the flattering appellation of the "Fair City."

On leaving our hotel we crossed the river by the handsome bridge, from the centre of which we obtained a grand prospect of the broad and smiling valley of the Tay, the City of Perth, the rugged chain of the Grampians, and the majestic hill of Kinnoull. It was near the site of this bridge that the Roman army of invasion, under Agricola, stood entranced by the matchless view, which so forcibly reminded his tired legionaries of their own sunny Italy that they burst forth with the exclamation "Ecce Tiber! Ecce Campus Martius."

"'Behold the Tiber!' the vain Romans cried,
Viewing the ample Tay from Baiglie's side;
But where's the Scot that would the vaunt repay,
And hail the puny Tiber for the Tay."

We found the Distillery, the object of our quest, about 300 yards from the bridge, and planted on the front of a hill facing the Tay. It consists of a series of stone buildings erected round a quadrangle, covering one and a half acres of ground. Under the guidance of the manager we commenced our tour of inspection from the upper roadway at the back of the works, where we found ourselves on a level with the Granary Floors, two in number.

In the floor at the end of each of these, there are circular openings through which the barley is dropped into the Steeps below. Descending a staircase we reached the Malt Barns, the back windows of which look out on the pretty gardens attached to the proprietor's house. The Steeps are composed of brick and cement, but the floor is made with a composition, which, although hard, is slightly moist, thus enabling the Distiller to malt all the year round. Passing along a narrow passage we ascended by an outside stone staircase to the Kiln Floor, which is composed of perforated sheet iron. The building is 22 feet square; peat only being used in the drying. In the roof there is a capital contrivance, which consists of a "Conductor," leading into an exhaust fan, which removes the damp from the surface of the malt, on the Kiln Floor. After examining this machine with the deepest interest, we proceeded to inspect the Malt Stores, which consist of three separate enclosed Malt Deposits, where the malt is kept from the air and light as much as possible. From this department we crossed a timber bridge over the quadrangle, into the Mill, which contains a pair of metal rollers and usual machinery; from thence we went through the Grist Loft, where there is a Hopper for feeding a Steel's Mashing Machine, and also two Heating Tanks, holding together 3,500 gallons.

Afterwards we passed to the Mash House, an apartment 50 feet square, with paved floor. It contains a Mash-tun 13 feet in diameter and 5 feet deep, stirred with oars, and an Underback of similar proportions. Leaving this house for a few minutes we entered the Tun Room, where there are four Washbacks, each with a capacity of 4,000 gallons; and over the roof, a set of open coolers with a revolving fan therein. The worts, before running into these Coolers, pass through a Drum Refrigerator, like those in use at Messrs. Barclay & Perkins' Brewery. Off the Tun Room we noticed a small chamber, wherein is placed the Wash Charger holding 8,000 gallons.

Retracing our steps we came to the Still House, where there are four Pot Stills, two of them Wash Stills, holding 700 gallons; the others, Spirit Stills, holding 600 and 350 gallons respectively. At the back of these Stills are three Worm Tubs, supplied with water from a small stream, which runs through the Distillery, and is used for no other purpose. The water from the Tay is used for brewing, and is pumped up from the river to a cistern at the highest point of the works. Following our guide we inspected the Receiver Room, containing a Low-wines Receiver, 500 gallons; Feints Receiver, 500 gallons; and a Spirit Receiver, 700 gallons; also the Spirit Safe.

The next place we visited was the Engine Department, where there are two engines, one of two, the other seven-horse power, a steam boiler and the usual pumps. Across the court there is a Spirit Store, with a Vat holding 1,000 gallons, a Cooperage, Excise, and Distillery Offices.

The buildings are lighted by the Bower light, the first we have seen in Scotland, and which is considered to be only second to electric light. We were next conducted over the four Bonded Warehouses, which are spacious and well ventilated, and contained together upwards of 1,000 casks.

The annual output is 30,000 gallons.

No. 101.

Blair Athol Distillery, Pitlochrie.

PROPRIETORS, P. MACKENZIE & CO.

FROM Perth to Pitlochrie is a railway journey not excelled, if equalled in Scotland for variety and beauty of scenery. We passed Birnam woods and other scenes made famous by Shakespeare in the tragedy of "Macbeth," and with bonnie Dunkeld on our right we fairly entered the vale of Athole. Sir Walter Scott has described the county of Perth as the most varied and beautiful province in Scotland, and the vale of Athole is undoubtedly one of the loveliest portions of it.

We put up for the night at the splendid hotel owned by Mr. Fisher, capable of entertaining 150 guests, and which in summer is crowded to overflowing. The next morning we drove to the Blair Athol Distillery, which is situated on the main road at the south end of the village of Pitlochrie, where we were received by the polite manager, Mr. Thompson, who conducted us over the works.

This Distillery was established in 1826 by Mr. Conachar, said to be one of the descendants of the chivalrous young Conachar, who was the early companion and admirer of Catherine Glover, the Fair Maid of Perth. Be that as it may, Mr. Conachar and his family carried on the Distillery until it was taken over by Messrs. P. Mackenzie & Co. a few years ago, since which time it has been considerably enlarged and improved. The works now cover about two and a half acres, and consist of two large Granaries, each with concrete Steeps, two Malt floors, and Kiln, all adjoining and arranged on the principle of saving labour. The machinery and plant in the Still House are of the most modern and approved description, consisting of copper Stills, iron Mash-tun and Underback, Refrigerator, Washbacks, Spirit Receiver, &c., all nearly new, and capable of turning out 1,500 gallons of Whisky per week. The Bonded Warehouses are five in number, and are capable of storing from 80,000 to 100,000 gallons.

The manager informed us that Messrs. Mackenzie buy none but the finest quality of barley, and the malt is dried with peat brought from Orkney. The water used comes direct from Ben Vrackie, and is of the purest description, sparkling and clear as crystal.

The Whisky produced in the vale of Athole has been famous from time immemorial, and Pitlochrie was celebrated for its Usquebaugh long before Excise locks and bars were ever heard of. Doubtless it was the mellow barley bree from the caverns of Ben Vrackie that warmed the hearts and strengthened the arms of the Highlanders at Killiecrankie, and which enabled them to rout the Southerners from the pass.

The make is Highland Malt, which is sold principally in Scotland and North of England. The annual output is about 60,000 gallons.

No. 102.

Edradour Distillery, Pitlochry.

PROPRIETOR, JOHN McINTOSH.

JOURNEYING to Inverness by the Highland Railway from Perth, the traveller will probably pay a visit to beautiful Dunkeld, but if he can spare the time he will do well to stop a few days at Pitlochry, where he will find himself in a place equally delightful, and in the centre of some of the most charming scenery in the Highlands. If he is an angler there is salmon fishing to his heart's content, and several trout streams in addition. We stayed at "Fisher's," one of the most comfortable and elegant hotels in the district. It possesses a banqueting hall, capable of seating 300 persons, with some fine suites of rooms attached, all of which look out on to lovely gardens and grounds. Attached to the hotel is an extensive livery establishment, where there is a good selection of both horses and vehicles. Mr. Fisher, jun., manager of the hotel farm, and son of the proprietor, drove us to Edradour, and entertained us by the way with a description of the places we passed. It is a half-hour's journey over the hills, from the top of which we had fine views of the valley, including Pitlochry village, the Hydropathic Establishment, country seats, and a spreading country as far as the eye could reach. The Distillery, which was built in 1837, is situated at the foot of a steep hill on the road side, and consists of a few ancient buildings not unlike a farmstead, past which flows one of the most rampant and brawling streams in the district. On either side of this river, heather in rich abundance hangs from the banks and jutting corners of the rocks, and there is water power sufficient to drive several water-wheels. The works consist of a Barley Barn, Malting House, and Mill, all in one building. The Mash Tun has a capacity of 1,000 gallons, and there are four Washbacks holding the same quantity. The Still House is across the yard, and contains a Wash Still and a Low-wines Still, the former holding 740 and the latter 420 gallons. There are three Warehouses, a Spirit Store and small cask shed, and at the end of the yard a cart-shed, stable, and some outhouses.

The Whisky is Highland Malt, and the annual out-put is 6,600 gallons. Mr. McIntosh rents the Distillery from the Duke of Athole, whose delightful estate of Blair Athole is in the next parish, and contains many noted waterfalls. Before leaving the district we visited some of them, and also the celebrated Pass of Killiecrankie. The cascades are of great interest and variety, the water running over the rocks from one dark basin or linn to another, succeeded by more considerable waterfalls from twelve to thirty-five feet high, and over several of these chasms bridges have been thrown.

No. 103.

Auchnagie Distillery, Ballinluig, near Pitlochry.

PROPRIETOR, P. DAWSON.

FROM Pitlochry lovers of nature and of wild and picturesque scenery may make plenty of excursions. It is encompassed on every side by hills and mountains, and there are charming walks in the neighbourhood. Our worthy landlord, Mr. Fisher, again provided us with a smart horse and trap, and drove us at a swift rate to Tullymet. Our road was direct through the village, past the delightful grounds of the Hydropathic and the Blair Athol Distillery, and then along the valley road towards Tullymet. The whole of this beautiful Strath Tay is one continued scene of the beauty of nature in its simplest, wildest, and most imposing character. In some parts it is only wooded on one side, but the variety, richness, and stillness of the whole—the fragrant birches, graceful hazels, rolling hills of the greenest verdure, and back ground of mountains, all form some of the richest pictures on which the eye could wish to gaze. In olden times it was customary for every traveller to stop at Moulinearn, a place just above the junction of the Tay and Tummel, to refresh himself with a glass of "Athole Brose," a celebrated local compound of whisky and honey. The natives have a high opinion of it, but we must confess to a preference for the whisky by itself or with a small addition of the crystal stream from the hills. After passing through the village we left the "birchin" bowers of Tullymet behind, and came in sight of the Distillery, which was erected in 1812, and is situated in a somewhat desolate position in the centre of some farm lands, and at a distance looked like a small, old-fashioned farmsteading.

The Rivers Garry and Tummel abound in salmon, and there are, besides, half-a-dozen streamlets running in all directions, full of trout.

At the time of our visit the works had ceased operations, as the weather was too hot for malting. The Distillery consists of a Barley Loft, Maltings, Still and Mash House, and a few other buildings, including Spirit Store and Warehouse accommodation for 40,000 gallons.

The water used comes from the Auchnagie Hills, and the make is Highland Malt. Only peats brought from Loch Broom are used in drying the malt.

One exciseman is employed at the Distillery, who informed us that he leads quite a pastoral life here, and spends his summer days in his garden and little farm-yard.

The annual output is 19,000 gallons; but 24,000 gallons can be made.

No. 104.

Grandtully Distillery, Aberfeldy.

PROPRIETORS, THOMSON & SON.

ONCE more we embarked on board the train, this time bound for Inverness by the Highland Line, one of the loveliest railway tours in Scotland. We broke our journey at Ballinluig Junction just to run up the branch line and see the famous little Distillery of Grandtully, at Aberfeldy, the smallest in the United Kingdom. The railway track runs through alternations of valley and along hill sides, and crosses the beautiful Rivers Tummell and Tay. We got off the train at Grandtully Station, where we hired a vehicle at the village inn, and drove to the Distillery, three miles distant. Although the weather was cold, the sun shone brightly, and we had a most enjoyable drive. The way leads through a most romantic district, and we were literally engirt by mountains. We had the Tay on our right the whole length of the journey; it is the chief salmon river of Scotland, and for natural beauty and historic events connected with the many castles and places of interest on its banks, takes precedence of all others. A prettier drive can hardly be conceived in summer time, the road for the most part of the way being carried through plantations, over gentle acclivities, with the swift-rushing Tay, some 300 feet wide, at our feet, past the fine old Castle of Grandtully, immortalized by Sir Walter Scott, and always the majestic hills before us, covered with snow and the sun glittering on their frozen summits.

In olden days the whole of this district abounded with smugglers' bothies. Our loquacious driver was the grandson of a notorious smuggler, and pointed out to us as we passed, a farm-house perched on the top of a hill, which was the scene of the smuggler's nefarious practices. On the face of this hill, and just under the farm-house kitchen, was a spacious cave, entered by a small opening made by a dried-up water-course. This they blocked up with stones and pieces of rock, leaving an opening of a few inches wide for the water to trickle through from a spring, which they diverted from the other side of the hill, and brought through the cave. They then burrowed an entrance from a distant thicket, for ingress and egress, and carried a flue from the furnaces some seventy yards underground to the farm-house chimney. Here for years they made the whisky, whilst their confederate lived in the farm-house pretending to till the land, but always on guard. In an evil day for them, one of their number, out of revenge, peached to the revenue officers, who made a raid upon the place in the middle of the night, broke up the still, tubs, and worm, and took away a few kegs of whisky. Three only of the smugglers were at work at the time, who

it falls through a spout into the Hopper, and is crushed by a pair of fine metal Malt Rollers, driven by a water-wheel. When the grist has been collected into bags it is wheeled across the roadway on to a wooden gallery over the Mash Tun. It may here be remarked that the Still House combines also the Mash House, Running and Receiving Room ; that the inner workings of the Distillery are of the oldest fashion, plan, and type, and of the same character as in vogue half a century since. Here are no new fads, appliances, or patents, but, like the buildings, the vessels are all of the ancient pattern.

The sacks of grist are emptied through a sluice into the Mash Tun. This vessel is 14 feet in diameter and 5 feet deep, with revolving stirring rakes. From this the worts run into the Worts Cistern, from thence into Morton's Refrigerator, afterwards into the Underback, and then pumped into the Wash-backs. But these last-mentioned vessels are placed on a stone parapet overhanging the river.

We then passed through a doorway into the No. 1 Backhouse, which contains eight Washbacks, holding about 2,400 gallons each. The No. 2 Backhouse adjoins this building and contains two large Washbacks, each of them having a capacity of about 5,000 gallons. The wash is pumped up from these vessels into the Wash Charger, placed at an elevation outside the Still House, so as to command the Stills. It has a capacity of 4,500 gallons, and stands alongside the metal Worm Tub, which is fed from the swiftly-flowing stream.

We next returned to the Mash House, and were shown two Pot Stills of the old shape and form. The Wash Still holds 2,500 gallons and the Spirit Still 1,700. Another overshot water-wheel works these Stills and drives the stirring gear in the Mash Tuns. Water is the only motive power in this establishment, and truly there is plenty of it everywhere. The river torrent rushes so impetuously over the hugh boulders that we could hardly hear ourselves speak.

Returning by way of a narrow and rocky path on the water's edge, we arrived at the Bonded Warehouses, some of them very spacious. There are five altogether, including those under the Granaries. A little further on is a large dwelling house, in the occupation of one of the Excise officers, facing the main road, the basement of which is on a level with the Distillery, and is used as a Racking Store. The Spirit Store is a building of itself, and contains a Vat of 2,200 gallons. The Peat Shed adjoins the Kiln, and there is stored of this valuable fuel about 300 tons ready for use.

The chimney stack is 120 feet high, the top of which came into view as soon as we turned into the glen. It is used for the furnaces in connection with the Stills and Boilers only. We noticed one of Wallace's Multitubular Boilers in the Still House. It is used for heating the water which supplies the large Brewing Copper over the Mash Tun.

Good offices have been provided for the three Excise gentlemen, of whom Mr. P. Cunningham is the supervisor. There is also a General Clerks' and Brewer's Office.

The Whisky, which is sold in Glasgow and Leith, also England and Ireland, is pure Malt, and largely used by bottling firms. The annual output is 90,000 gallons.

No. 107.

Glenochil Distillery, by Stirling.

PROPRIETORS, THE DISTILLERS COMPANY, LIMITED.

REGISTERED OFFICE, 12, TORPHICHEN STREET, EDINBURGH.

MANAGING DIRECTORS OF THIS DISTILLERY: MCNAB BROS.

WE left Crieff on Saturday night, and travelled direct to the Bridge of Allan to rest ourselves until Monday in that quiet and lovely retreat. We were favoured with most glorious weather, and shall never forget our brief sojourn in this favourite resort.

We rose early next morning, and after quaffing a goblet of the celebrated mineral waters from the Airthrey Wells, dispensed by a charming Scottish lassie in most bewitching attire, we ascended the heights above the Hydropathic and were amply repaid for our toil. The view that opened out before us was surprisingly beautiful. It embraced Stirling with its fine old castle, backed by a distant range of mountains; Wallace's Monument, built on a rocky acclivity, with its pedestal almost hidden in the dense foliage of the hill on which it stands; and the sinuous windings of the Forth, discernible almost to Edinburgh. The grand Ochil Hills with their intersections of cliff and wood stretching out as far as the eye could reach, and beneath our feet, a vast panorama of beauty unmatched in the kingdom; little wonder that the fire burned in the heart of our companion, the McQueen Barr, a native of the place, and that the blood rushed faster through his veins as he proudly asked, if it were possible to obtain such another view in all the British Isles.

After gazing for some time on the prospect before us, we descended by another route from that by which we had ascended, and kept along on the face of the hill to the left, and then zig-zagged our way downwards until we joined the road along which we had passed in the morning. On this side of the hill we caught sight of Dunblane, and had a beautiful view of the Allan river, which flows through one of the most picturesque bits of scenery it is possible to imagine. Along the whole valley it is framed by the variegated ornaments of wood, rock and hill slopes, till lost to sight, but "to memory dear." We started early the next morning to visit the Glenochil Distillery, which is the largest in the Clackmannan district, and were favoured with a continuance of the same delightful weather.

We were a merry party, including the McQueen Barr, and our route lay amid scenery both mountainous and pastoral. On one side stretched a valley with waving cornfields and rich plantations heavy with foliage, and on the other the Ochil Hills, some of them rising in their grandeur to a height of 2,000 feet above the level of the sea; from the heart of these hills flows the water that feeds the Glenochil Distillery. It is called the Balquhan Burn, a very small stream at its source, but gathering strength as it flows along, breaking into numerous waterfalls, some of them falling forty feet, passing its way down a delightful ravine, it finally flows over the Menstrie moss at the foot of the hills, and thence into the works.

The Distillery, which is the oldest in the district, having been established in 1746, is four miles from Tillicoultry on the banks of the Devon; five from Stirling and the Bridge of Allan, and thirteen from the celebrated Rumbling Bridge. The Works cover ten acres of ground, and all the buildings are large and lofty. The tall chimney stacks are the most notable objects in the plain, and were discernible for some miles before we arrived at the establishment.

The proprietors have, during the past forty years, as their business increased, made important additions and alterations to the Works, and a business has been built up second to none in the district. The Distillery is entered through an old-fashioned gateway leading into a courtyard, wherein are ranged on one side the partners and general clerks' offices, and on the other the house of the acting manager. Beyond this another opening leads into the works proper. After making ourselves known to Mr. McNab, he handed us over to the acting manager, Mr. Wm. Leal, who conducted us through the place and explained to us the working of the Distillery.

Our steps were first directed to the huge Grain Stores, lofty buildings eleven in number, each 120 feet long by 80 feet broad. In front of these Stores is a railway siding direct from the main line to Alloa, which brings the trucks laden with grain to the doors, where their contents are emptied into a hopper, and delivered to the top floors of the Stores by elevators. From thence the grain is conveyed by a continuous screw along the roof of the building for nearly a quarter of a mile, into whichever Store is desired; in this way 1,000 quarters can be emptied daily. Contiguous to the Stores is the hot air Kiln, capable of drying two hundred quarters in 24 hours, from whence the dried grain is conveyed by screws and trap doors and received into an elevator, from which it is transmitted by other continuous screws to the Mill stones, where it is pulverised into flour and again passed by screws and elevators to the Mashing department, where it is collected and weighed into bags of 168 lbs. each. These are afterwards emptied into the Mash Tun, a large vessel 20 feet in diameter and 12 feet deep, having the patent revolving stirring gear inside. The liquor from this vessel is now let down on the malt in the Mash Tun below, which is of the enormous measurement of 30 feet in diameter and 7 feet deep, with the usual revolving stirring gear. From here it is drawn off by cranes into the two Underbacks, each 12 feet by 24 feet, and 4 feet deep, and then pumped up by centrifugal pumps to the Cooling Machines, and to three of Morton's largest Refrigerators, where it is cooled to the required temperature prior to fermentation. The Wash is now put into the Fermenting Tuns, of which there are a great number placed in an extensive building, where it goes through the process of fermentation.

The carbonic acid gas given off during this process is highly dangerous to the workmen in the lower part of the Tun Room, the gas being much heavier than ordinary air. The building, however, is freely ventilated, and the men only remain a brief time when washing out the building and watching the process.

After the fermentation is complete the liquor is transferred through closed pipes into the Wash Charger, a vessel containing upwards of 30,000 gallons, and from thence into the Coffey's Patent Stills, which differ from the old Pot Stilling in that they are more economical, and are capable of making a purer spirit. The fusel oil, which forms a proportion of every kind of grain, is by this process completely separated from the spirit and collected into a vessel specially designed for that purpose, and emptied at the end of a period. It may here be mentioned that the oil is a valuable commodity, being used, not only for illuminating and chemical purposes, but, after undergoing a patent process of rectification, is converted into a most useful medicine.

The hot spirit in passing from the Still near the top goes to the Condenser, is cooled in the usual way, and afterwards runs into the two Spirit Receivers, each holding about 5,000 bulk gallons. Here the charge is taken, and the Spirits are pumped into the vats, placed in the Spirit Stores, where it is run into Casks, branded and sent into the Warehouses, of which there are seven covering about three acres of ground and all under one roof. They have a very imposing appearance from the road, and are so arranged that carts can drive down the various avenues and deposit or fetch away the Whisky.

We next retraced our steps to the Malting department, where there are three Barley Stores, conveniently arranged buildings each 120 feet long by 60 feet broad. The Barley is carried to each floor by a powerful hoist and dropped through sluices on to the three malting floors. In close proximity is the Malt Kiln, 24 feet by 45, a lofty apartment and floored with perforated steel plates.

The Malt Stores are of great depth. Here when the Malt is taken from the Kiln, it is laid until the building is full, and then put into another Store of the same size until that is filled, so that whilst the contents of the one is maturing, the other one is in use.

We then proceeded to the Mill, a capacious building of several stories, which contains seven pairs of stones for crushing the dried grain and pulverising the Malt.

Our guide next led the way to the Engine department, which contains six engines from 5 to 50-horse power, and six steam boilers about 24 feet long by 7 feet in diameter.

The Company manufacture an enormous quantity of what is called German Yeast, considered superior to that manufactured on the Continent, and which commands a good price in the market.

Within the works there is a large Cooperage for the repair of casks, also carpenters, engineers and blacksmiths' shops. Upward of 100 persons are employed in the Distillery, and there are seven Excise Officers on the premises.

The Whisky made at this establishment is pure Grain and is said to be of superior quality, and the annual output is nearly 1,000,000 gallons.

No. 108.

Cambus Distillery, Clackmannanshire.

PROPRIETORS, THE DISTILLERS' COMPANY, LIMITED.

REGISTERED OFFICE, 12, TORPHICHEN STREET, EDINBURGH.

MANAGER OF THIS DISTILLERY, THOMAS ARCHIBALD.

WE wish that we were able to present to our readers some few pictures of the lovely scenery through which we were daily passing; nothing could well exceed the beauty of these Ochil Hills. As we passed in the train from the Bridge of Allan to Cambus, the sun, hitherto obscured, suddenly shone forth, pouring down its golden light upon the scene, bringing out in bold relief each crag and pinnacle, and casting fantastic shadows on the wooded slopes below, relieving the former of their wild ruggedness, and rendering to the latter an air of peaceful repose. For once we could not regret that our locomotion was slow, and that the train stopped at every station, otherwise we might have lost the view of the Wallace Monument, standing on a crag 560 feet above the level of the plain, the Links of the Forth, and the swelling hills each with their rich groupings of scenery, intersected here and there with farmhouses, skirted or enclosed by woods. Just before arriving at the station we crossed the Devon, a river of sparkling beauty immortalized by Burns, which, wending its course through a district most romantic, falls into the Forth hard by the Cambus Distillery.

This Distillery was founded in the year 1806 by John Moubray, grandfather of one of the Directors of the Company. Previous to that date it had been an ancient Mill, some parts of the ruins of which are still to be seen. Originally a small work, it has now grown to enormous dimensions, and in the year 1877 it was, with five others, annexed by the Distillers' Company, Limited. Since the formation of the Company, this Distillery has been under the management of Mr. Thomas Archibald.

The buildings are spread over fully eight acres of ground, and are everywhere intersected by the railway, with sidings to all the principal Warehouses. Although most of the grain is brought by rail, a large quantity is landed at the public wharf, the magnificent river Forth being within a few yards of the Distillery. The carts from the wharf and the railway wagons drop the grain into a Hopper placed in the centre of the "six foot way,"

CAMBUS DISTILLERY.

from whence it is delivered by elevators and screws, the latter running along the roofs of all the buildings to the different Lofts. There are also underground screws connected with the various Grain Stores which return the corn to the elevators.

CAMBUS DISTILLERY—Continuous Screw over Roofs.

We first directed our steps to the seven Grain Stores, handsome two-storied buildings, capable of holding 8,000 quarters of grain. At the rear of these buildings are two Corn Kilns, one of which is floored with iron plates, and the other with wire flooring. On our way thither we passed a huge compressed dreg-sediment shed and spent Wash Tank, opening on the public road, where farmers attend daily to fetch it away. The Mill buildings are attached to the Kilns, and contain six pairs of stones. On an upper floor are the Grist Lofts, so arranged as to command the Mash Tuns; they are large and commodious buildings. Here also we noticed many hundreds of filled sacks of 168 lbs. weight ready for use. The Grist in this establishment is twice ground, in order to get it fine.

A few steps down brought us into another apartment, where we were shown four Brewing Tanks of immense size, three of wood and the remainder iron. We then were shown the Mash-house, which contains two Maize Tuns sunk in the floor, timber vessels 20 feet in diameter and 11 feet deep; a circular iron Malt Mash Tun, 27 feet in diameter and 7 feet deep, all having the revolving rakes. Here also is the Underback, which has a capacity of 3,200 gallons. The Worts are here pumped into the Wort Receivers, holding 11,572 gallons; they then pass through the Morton's Refrigerator and the cooling pipes, which are laid in the bed of the river Devon.

Passing under a covered archway, we next were taken to the Tun Room, a spacious apartment, in which the fumes from the boiling Worts were almost overpowering. Here are seventeen Wash-backs, each with an average capacity of 22,142 gallons. On the top of this building we were shown a Draff Receiver, so arranged that the maize dregs can be drained therein, falling into a second and similar tank, from whence, almost in a dry state, it falls through shoots into railway trucks and farmers' carts, each standing on Steelyards, where they can weigh the exact quantity wanted. Alongside the Water-wheel House entrance, across the lade, is a large building fitted up with machinery for making German Yeast, where about two tons can be produced weekly, but at the time of our visit this department was silent.

On the opposite side of the yard is the No. 1 Still-house, where are the two Wash Chargers, having a capacity of 30,589 gallons and 31,310 gallons respectively. Here also are six powerful pumps, consisting of two water, a wash, hot feints and wash-heater pumps. Our guide pointed out a patent wash-heater, invented by Mr. Moubray, the late proprietor, consisting of a series of zig-zag pipes and worms, fixed in an upright frame, through which the Worts are made hot before passing to the Coffey's Patent Still. By this patent the power of the Still is increased to the extent of producing one-fourth more gallons of spirits per hour.

No. 2 Still-house contains the Coffey's Patent Still, for a description of which see the chapter on Glenochil Distillery. The Spirit from this Still flows through the Safe at the rate of 250 gallons per hour. The Safe is placed in the Running Room, where also are two Spirit Receivers, one holding 3,020 gallons and the other 1,694. Below the clerk's office is the Spirit Store, which contains two Vats with a capacity of 6,699 gallons, into which the Spirit flows after passing through the Safe. Adjoining is the Racking Store for blending, a neat building conveniently arranged for the Bonded Stores.

Crossing the yard the Engine-house is reached, where there are four handsome Engines, with a combined horse-power of 105, and six Boilers, 20 feet long by 7 feet in diameter. We next proceeded to inspect the Maltings; those near the wharf are square stone buildings of three floors, the top a Barley-loft, the second a Malting-floor with Steeps, and the basement one of the Bonded Warehouses. The Malt Kiln is on a level with the second flat. It is floored with iron plates, and heated from beneath by two open furnaces. The other Maltings form one of the boundary walls to the Distillery, and are only entered from the main road; enormous buildings 150 feet square, having two Barley-lofts and a Malt-barn, with usual Steep. Adjacent is the Kiln, the same as the one before described.

Distributed about the premises are six Warehouses; one of them, just newly built near the station, covers an acre of ground, and is of two stories elevation. The whole Warehouses contained on the 12th of January, 1886, 17,002 casks, holding 1,365,287 gallons of Whisky of various ages since 1865. These Warehouses are capable of storing 2,000,000 gallons.

Like Glenochil, the following trades are represented in the establishment—coppersmiths', engineers', and carpenters' shops, a good cooperage, stables for five horses, and cart sheds. Sixty men are employed upon the premises. Part of the Distillery is now being remodelled, and a new Still House is being built, having as its roof a handsome cast-iron tank, 29 feet by 27 feet by 4 feet deep, carried by eight strong malleable iron rolled girders; the contract has been secured by Mr. R. G. Abercrombie, Broad Street Engine Works, Alloa.

The Brewer and Distiller is Mr. P. Murray, and there are seven Excise officers on the premises, Mr. Maslin being the principal, and George Ferguson, Esq., the supervisor.

The annual output is 900,000 gallons.

The chief driving power is steam, in conjunction with a huge Water Wheel. The two chimney shafts, which can be seen for many miles before you reach Cambus, are 90 and 150 feet high respectively. The beautiful river Devon, before described, supplies all the water used in the Distillery.

No. 109.

Carsebridge Distillery, Alloa.

PROPRIETORS, THE DISTILLERS' COMPANY, LIMITED.

REGISTERED OFFICE: 12, TORPHICHEN STREET, EDINBURGH.

MANAGING DIRECTOR OF THIS DISTILLERY, COLONEL BALD HARVEY.

A LONG night's rest in our comfortable quarters at the Bridge of Allan, and a delightful drive of some eight miles through a splendid country, greatly refreshed us after our toil and fatigue on the previous day at the Cambus Distillery. Our route lay through charmingly diversified scenery; Dunmyat, a grand projecting mass of the Ochils, 1,350 feet above sea level, overhangs the road, and here and there we caught sight of the waters of the Forth creeping serpent-like towards the sea. We stopped a short time at Alloa to see that busy "brewing town," and visit the celebrated Alloa Tower embedded in trees, and which marks the residence of the ancient family of Mar. The old Castle was built in 1300, but the whole of it, with exception of the tower, was burnt down in the year 1800. The walls of this old relic of the past are 11 feet thick, and from its summit, although standing in the plain, nine counties can be seen. In the distance appear the gigantic Benledi and Ben Lomond lifting their heads to the sky; nearer, Stirling with its Castle, and Wallace's Monument; whilst beneath is the gradually expanding Forth. All around is a panorama of changing beauty, and one is lost in wonder and admiration at the beauties of nature thus spread out before the eye.

The Carsebridge Distillery is about a mile from Alloa, and was originally, built as a Malt Distillery about the year 1799, by John Bald, of Carsebridge, who gave it over to his eldest son, Robert Bald. He, in the year 1845, disposed of it to his brother, the late John Bald, for several years resident at Monzie Castle, Perthshire. The name of the firm previous to the transfer to the Distillers' Company, Limited, was John Bald & Co., the partners being the above-mentioned John Bald, and his nephew, Colonel Bald Harvey, of Tormaukin, Perthshire, now Director-Manager. About thirty-five years ago the Distillery was changed into one for raw Grain, and has since been gradually enlarged to its present size. Strange to say, at the time of its transfer, as though to mark the event, a colony of rooks came and set up an establishment in the big trees which adorn and overhang the Distillery, and there built up a rookery of considerable dimensions. At the time of our visit they were very busy, and holding a noisy parliament. The odours of whisky in the air had evidently

CARSEBRIDGE DISTILLERY.

loosened their tongues, and done them "much good." The works are very extensive, and cover altogether ten acres of ground. They have a frontage of 800 feet on either side of the roadway, and the buildings are admirably constructed to facilitate each consecutive process in the manufacture of Whisky.

The grain is shipped to Alloa Harbour, where on the wharf, the Company have two powerful portable steam cranes, which hoist it from the ships into covered carts or boxes. The grain is weighed at the ship's side and deposited into these boxes, which are carefully locked before starting them off to the Distillery. Arrived there the corn clerk unlocks them with his duplicate key, and the grain is then discharged into hoppers. Each of these carts holds five quarters of grain.

We were first conducted to the south side of the works to the two Granaries, fine two-storied buildings, 200 feet long and 60 feet wide, containing at the time of our visit 7,000 quarters of grain. Adjacent there is a similar building of somewhat smaller dimensions, capable of holding 5,000 quarters. The lower floors of these buildings are devoted to malting purposes, and there is a Kiln attached to each building for drying the malt. They are spacious apartments, floored with wire cloth and perforated plates, and heated by open furnaces and hot air. On the north side again is another Grain Store, 100 feet long and 40 feet broad, and a Barley Loft of same dimensions, to which are attached two Dry Corn Kilns, floored with steel plates and heated with hot air. In addition, and on the same side of the works, there is a patent Kiln by Armstrong, of Belfast, enclosed in a building of handsome architectural proportions 70 feet high.

We were next conducted to the three Mill buildings, which contain thirteen pairs of stones. Here the maize and other grain is pulverized, weighed into bags of 168 lbs., and placed on an outside covered gallery convenient to the Mash-tuns. Through a doorway and down a few steps, the Mash House, a large and conveniently arranged place, is reached. It contains six fine brewing tanks, some of which are square and composed of iron, the others, circular, are of wood. Two have a capacity 20,000, two 15,000, and the other two 10,000 gallons. In this department there are also three Maize Mash-tuns and three Grain Mash-tuns; the former being circular timber vessels all enclosed; the latter circular iron vessels 27 feet in diameter and 8 feet deep, all possessing the double-action revolving stirring gear. Among the latest additions to this department is a fine cast-iron Mash Tun, 26 feet in diameter and 8¼ feet deep. It is made of larger sized plates than usual, and the seating consists of seven malleable iron-rolled girders, set on substantial stone walls; the space between the latter being wide enough to allow of the free admission of carts to receive the draff. The false bottom is closely fitted, and being placed farther above the bottom than usual, a very free and clean drain is obtained. The stirring-gear, which is of the usual description, is driven from an overhead shaft. The maker of the Tun is Mr. R. G. Abercrombie, Broad Street Engine Works, Alloa.

We then proceeded to the next department, and on our way passed through a place which put us in mind of the stage well at a theatre, so closely was it intersected with pipes, sluices, and a network of machinery. The Tun Room is divided into three sections. In it are ranged, like opposing armies, twenty fine Washbacks, of imposing size and capacity, as the following figures will testify. One will contain 40,000, four 20,000, seven 30,000, and thirteen 10,000 gallons, each with the usual switching apparatus.

We next crossed the yard and proceeded to the Distillery proper. The two

Still Houses comprise a tower of handsome elevation, which, roofed with a water cistern in case of fire below, rears its head far above all the other buildings. In it are two elegant Coffey's patent Stills, each shut off from the other by means of iron doors. The Wash Charger in No. 1 Still House is sunk into the ground, and some idea of its size may be gathered from the fact that it covers the whole floor of the building, which is eighty feet square. On a gallery above are four circular refrigerators, and beneath this is a fine horizontal engine for driving two sets of three-throw pumps, to pump the wash to the Stills, and a double-action plunger pump used for the same purpose. Adjoining the Stills and parted off with an iron door is a small fire-proof house, containing three upright copper vessels for the reception and retention of the fusel oil, which is sold to manufacturing chemists, who, by rectification, and a patent process, obtain from it a valuable product used in the manufacture of a patent quinine.

We were next conducted to the Engine Department, an important feature of this Distillery. It contains a fine compound beam engine of 160 indicated horse power, which drives eight pairs of mill-stones; a second which drives the elevators; a third for pumping water into the boilers, and several others for the pumps and other various work. Altogether in and about the premises there are 14 engines, combining in all 400-horse power. The eight boilers have double flues, and are 25 feet long by eight feet in diameter; and in addition to those already described there are two other sets of three-throw pumps.

The two chimney stacks are 140 and 100 feet high respectively, the former, which has a Starling Box attached half-way up, being quite a landmark in the district. Near the gateway, on the north side of the works, is the Spirit Store, a spacious building which contains four Spirit Vats, having a capacity of 12,000, 5,494, 3,262, and 2,164 gallons respectively. Here also are two Water Vats of purest water for reducing purposes, and a patent cooling apparatus, wherein the spirit runs by gravitation from the vats through zig-zag worms, and is quickly rendered cold.

On the opposite side of the court-yard is the Cooperage, wherein six men are constantly employed, and which contains a fine circular saw, driven by steam power; adjoining are engineers' and carpenters' shops and stores.

The arrangements for contending against fire are most complete in this Distillery; the tanks over the Still Houses we have already referred to. There are, further, no less than 44 water plugs, with hose fittings, a Shand and Mason's fire engine, and a trained fire brigade of 40 men, each having his special duty and post assigned to him.

We next crossed the roadway to the south side of the establishment; here there is a large Malt Store, Cart Sheds, Stabling for 13 horses, Loose Boxes and other buildings; also a fine range of offices, consisting of sampling room, private rooms for the Managing Director and the Sub-Manager, Clerks' Offices, Lavatories, &c. Distributed about the premises are twelve large bonded Warehouses. The total grain storage on the premises is 25,000 quarters. One hundred and fifty men are employed, for some of whom dwellings have been provided by the Company.

The water used comes from the Gartmorn Dam, a large artificial reservoir of about one mile in diameter, situated about a mile distant from the Distillery.

The Whisky made is pure Grain, and the annual output varies from 1,400,000 to 1,700,000 gallons.

No. 110.

Glenfoyle Distillery, near Stirling.

PROPRIETORS, JAMES CALDER & CO.

FROM Carsebridge we proceeded by railway to Stirling, and from thence re-booked for Gargunnock, the nearest station to Glenfoyle. The Distillery is only a short distance from the station and village. On presenting our credentials to Mr. Bryce, the Manager, we were conducted through the establishment. It was built in 1826, by Messrs. A. Chrystal and John McNee, and came into the hands of Mr. Calder in the year 1880, since which time it has been considerably enlarged. We first visited the Maltings, a substantial brick building, 180 feet long, and 24 feet wide, two stories high. The top is a barley loft, and the ground floor, which has a Steep, is used for making the malt. Attached to the building there is a Kiln, 24 feet square, floored with metal plates, and capable of drying 30 bushels at one time. Adjacent is the Malt Store, 36 feet by 24 feet ; a gangway therefrom across the roadway leads into the Mill Building, containing a pair of malt rollers, driven by steam power.

Following our guide, we entered the Brewing House, and were shown an ancient heating copper, with furnace underneath, and a Mash-tun 14 feet in diameter and 6 feet deep, capable of mashing 719 bushels at one time. At the side, and under the level of the Mash-tun, is placed the Underback, which holds 537 gallons. Connected with this house is the Tun Room, which contains six Wash-backs, four of which average 2,466 gallons content, the other two 1,869 gallons. On a platform above, we noticed the Wash-charger, a timber vessel, with a capacity of 2,233 gallons. In the Still House are two old Pot Stills, a Wash Still, holding 1,050 gallons, and a Spirit Still, 650 gallons ; also two Low-wines and Feints Chargers, holding respectively 620 and 546 gallons ; also a Low-wines and Feints Receiver, 676 gallons, a Spirit-receiver, 582 gallons, and the safe. The coolers are in the roof of the Mash House, and possess the ancient fan arrangement. We were next taken to the Engine House, where there is a steam boiler, 16 feet long by 5 diameter, and an eight-horse power steam engine ; afterwards to the Bonded Warehouses, at the end of the works. There are four of them, one, recently erected, measures 80 feet by 60 feet ; together they contained at the time of our visit 772 casks, holding, 56,170 gallons. Adjoining is the Manager's, Clerks', and Excise Offices, also the Spirit Store, which contains a vat holding 595 gallons.

The water used for distilling and reducing is brought from the Campsie Fells, through closed pipes into the Distillery.

The Whisky is pure Malt, and the annual output is 30,000 gallons.

No. 111.

Glenguin Distillery, Old Killearn.

PROPRIETORS, LANG BROS.

ON leaving Glenfoyle we proceeded by rail to Old Killearn passing on our way through a lovely country. The Distillery is situated at the base of Dungoyne, and just below a romantic waterfall 50 feet in height, which supplies all the water used in the works.

We walked from the station to Glenguin, a distance of half-a-mile, and at once proceeded to inspect the Distillery, under the guidance of the Manager. It was built in the year 1833, covers about two acres of ground, and consists of a Granary, 150 feet long, and three Malt Barns, each capable of working 100 quarters at one time, with usual Steeps. From these buildings our guide conducted us to the Kiln, 24 feet square, floored with wire cloth, where coke and peat are burned in drying the malt; next crossing a gangway we came to the Malt-deposit and Mill, the latter containing a pair of malt rollers and the grinding machinery. On leaving this place we entered the Mash House, and were shown a Mash-tun holding 2,200 gallons, and fitted with revolving stirring gear; also an Underback, placed on the floor of the house, holding 800 gallons, and in close proximity one of Miller's Patent Refrigerators. We were next taken to the Tun Room, a neat white-washed building, wherein are placed six Washbacks, five holding 2,000 gallons each, and one 3,500 gallons; at an elevation is the Wash-charger, containing 3,500 gallons. Passing through a doorway we came to the Still House, which contains two old Pot Stills, a Wash Still holding 1,210 gallons, and a Spirit Still 850 gallons; on a platform are placed a Low Wines Receiver, containing 600 gallons, a Low Wines and Feints Charger, of similar capacity, and a Spirit Receiver, holding 800 gallons. The Worm-tubs are placed in the open on the hill-side, and fed with water from the Burn. We may here mention that the Spirits are distilled three times by the various processes of working in this Distillery. A short distance from the Still House is the Spirit Store, which contains a vat holding 945 gallons; and next door an Engine House, wherein is a 12-horse power engine, and a steam boiler 18 feet long by 6 feet in diameter. Crossing the main road, we inspected the four bonded Warehouses, capable of holding together 2,000 casks; one of them recently erected is 80 feet long by 60 feet broad. There is a capital house for the manager on the works, excise and clerks' offices, etc., nine persons being employed in the establishment.

The make, which is principally sold in Glasgow and London, is pure Malt, and the annual output is 45,000 gallons.

No. 112.

The Caledonian Distillery, Edinburgh.

PROPRIETORS, THE DISTILLERS' COMPANY, LIMITED.
Registered Office: 12, TORPICHEN STREET, EDINBURGH.
Secretary: E. F. DUDGEON.

OUR tour in the north, which had been such a source of pleasure to us, was now virtually at an end, and we left Stirling with some feeling of regret. The journey to Edinburgh was short when compared with the distances we had traversed. Recently our "spiritual wanderings" had been among the heather, valley, and mountain; we were now again to visit city distilleries of such magnitude that a dozen of those lately described could be crowded into one of these establishments. It was a lovely day, and as we approached the noble and ancient metropolis of Scotland, the hills in the back-ground revealed to us a combination of glories now wreathed in green-clad garments—anon rugged and broken, sometimes lifting their heads to the clouds with a sombre reverence, at others shaded by still higher crags in a mass of ever-changing witchery—and later on as we drove along Princes Street, and noted the scenic groupings of monuments, the stately Castle, and noble surroundings of this city of tragedy and romance, we were thrilled with wonder and delight, and called to mind some lines we had seen:

"Grand auld city, decked in splendour,
On the rocky heights that rise,
Scotia's guardian and defender,
Tow'ring upwards to the skies.
Fair Edina—fair remain!
Scotia's proud auld darling mither;
Where 's a street to match our ain
Princes Street in sunny weather?"

On the morning after our arrival we paid a visit to the Caledonian Distillery. It is situated at the west end of the city, and in a neighbourhood sacred to the memory of Sir Walter Scott, who lived for many years on the estate of Dalry Manor, six hundred yards from the Distillery. Sir Walter Scott was born in Edinburgh, where he received his instruction and learning, but the better part of his education was gathered here and there through all Scotland—in huts and halls, from ancient battle fields, Highland chieftains, Border reevers, and the rudest ballads—no mind ever fed on more varied elements or turned them to better use. Dalry Road, where he last resided with his daughter, is in close proximity to the Distillery, and the whole locality is full of interesting reminiscences of this great man.

From the main road we diverged down a turning in close proximity to the Haymarket Station, at the end of which the whole pile of buildings connected with the works stretched out before us. Arriving at the gateway, after producing our credentials, we were admitted within.

The Caledonian Distillery covers $7\frac{1}{4}$ acres of ground, and was built in the year 1855 by Messrs. Menzies & Co., who transferred it to the Distillers' Company, Limited, in the year 1884. It is the second largest Grain Distillery in the United Kingdom, and in all respects it may be called the model Distillery of Europe, as it contains every improvement of machinery and new patent known in distilling, and fully justifies this appellation. It has also the advantage of two lines of railway right through the works (the Caledonian and the North British). The grain is delivered in bulk-covered waggons with sluice flap bottoms (the only ones of the kind we have seen in Scotland), each holding 50 quarters of grain. Arriving at the grain department the attendant unbolts the trap, and the grain falls into a sluice in the middle of the six-foot way into a continuous screw, which almost in an instant sends it to the elevators (50 feet distant) carrying

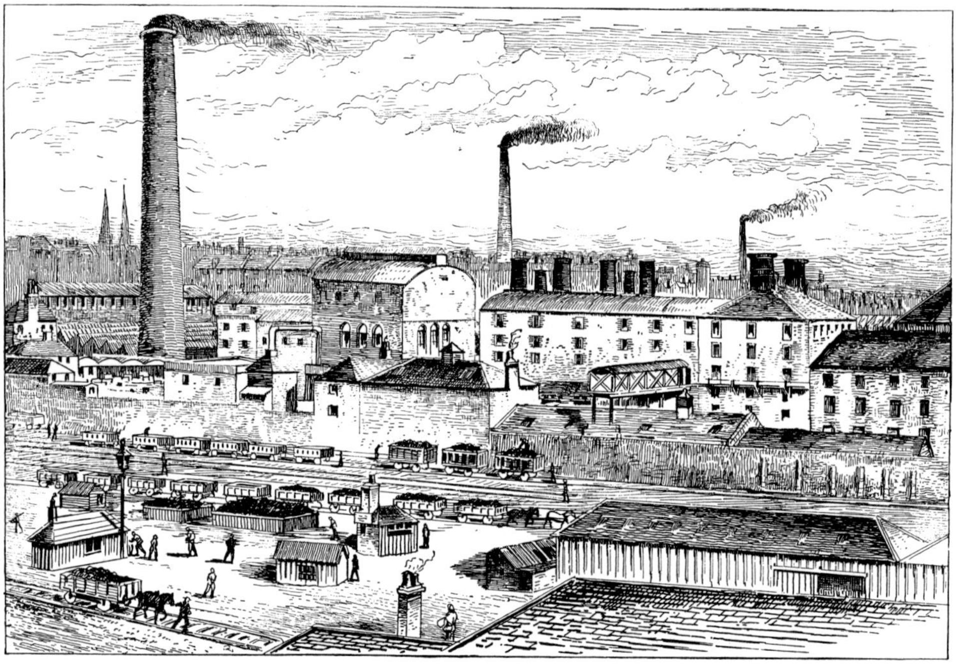

CALEDONIAN DISTILLERY, EAST END.

it up to the top floors, and delivering it by the screws, to the various grain departments—thus almost doing away with manual labour. These screws are wonderful contrivances, and consist of an endless screw the shape of a corkscrew with steel flanges, which is *enclosed* in a box, or trough, a foot square. The end of the screw is turned by steam power, and as the grain descends into the machinery it is screwed away any distance, and stopped in its onward progress by a very simple contrivance, at any floor or department required.

There are fourteen Grain Stores holding together over 15,000 quarters of grain, and we noticed that some of the barns were so full that the doors had burst open with the weight. The divisional departments of the Grain Stores where the tackle goes through, and the fans for steam drying are concerned, are all floored with iron plates. The four Kilns hold collectively 1,100 quarters. From the Kilns the grain is removed by the screws to the two Mills, which contain eight pairs of stones and a set of rollers for bruising the grain. Here the pulverised grain is weighed into bags of 224 and 182 lbs. and dropped through the sluices into two large Mash-tuns below, measuring 28½ feet in diameter and 7 feet deep, each holding 26,000 gallons. The stirring gear, though ponderous from its size, works with a rapid, easy movement. There are likewise three pulping vessels for Indian Corn, where the grain is boiled before dropping it into the Mash-tuns, to be mixed with the malt and other grain. The Mash-tuns are in a house specially erected for the purpose, and the draff is lifted from the building by elevators and delivered straight into the railway trucks, a train laden with same being despatched from the works every twelve hours. From

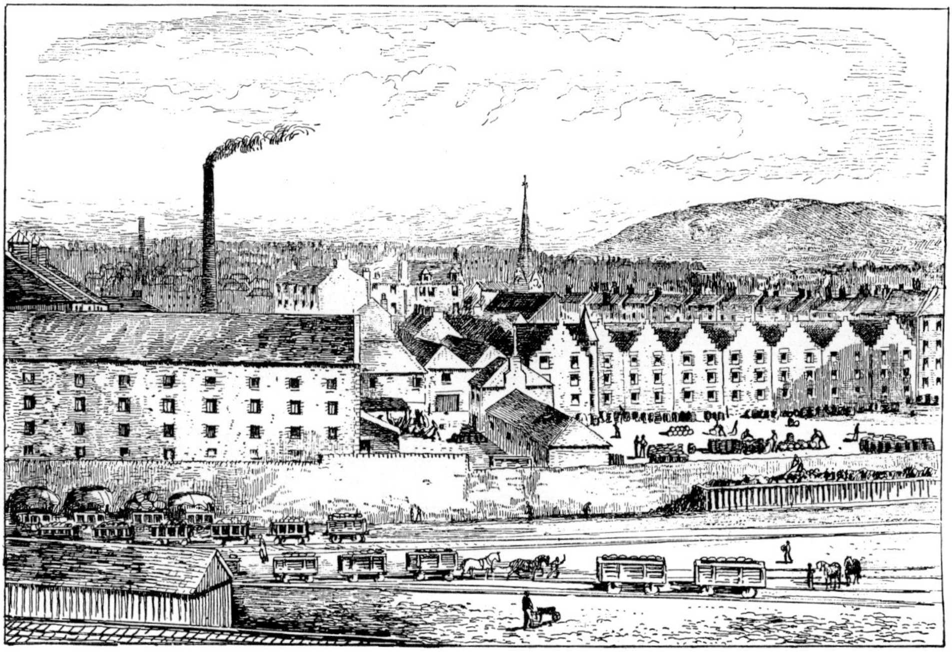

CALEDONIAN DISTILLERY, WEST END.

the Mash-tuns the liquor travels by gravitation to the Underback, which holds 6,000 gallons. We may here remark that there are two sets of Brahma Pumps, a Cooler, and six Morton's Patent Refrigerators. We next proceeded to the Back-house, where are eleven Washbacks of the following capacity:—nine of them contain 53,000 gallons, and two of them 43,000 gallons each, also two Wash Chargers holding together about 100,000 gallons, and two intermediate Wash Chargers of the same capacity. From this department the liquor is pumped into a Coffey's Patent Still, said to be the largest in Europe; thence through the safe at the rate of 1,000 gallons per hour into the six Receivers. From here the pure spirit flows into the five spirit vats in the Spirit Stores, where it is casked in the usual way and delivered into the Warehouses, which are six in number—enormous buildings covering three acres of ground. One of them, a new lofty Gothic structure, is a notable object from the railway as you approach the Haymarket Station. Most of these Warehouses are two and three-deckers, having hydraulic lifts. No. 1 Warehouse contained 8,000 casks of Whisky, and No. 2 about 10,000.

At the extreme end of the works is the Malting Department, the Main Barley Loft being connected with the Grain Department by an outside gallery. It is a lofty building 172 feet long by 76 feet broad, and contains 3,000 quarters of barley, which is delivered by the screws into the two Steeps, 34 feet square and 3½ feet deep, each holding 160 quarters. The grain falls from the steeps above into the couch below, and is distributed by manual labour over the seven Malt Barns, mostly 172 feet long by 76 feet broad. There are two Malt Deposits, each holding 3,000 quarters. The two Malt Kilns are 110 feet long by 52 feet wide, and are capable of drying 900 quarters of malt weekly. Our guide then conducted us to the Still House, a fine building containing three Pot Stills, 16,000, 9,000, and 5,000 gallons content respectively, four Feints Receivers, also a large Carter's Rectifying Still capable of holding 4,000 gallons, from which the spirit runs through a patent safe at the rate of 200 gallons per hour.

The steam power is on an extensive scale in this establishment, there being seven powerful engines from 10 to 150 horse power, and eleven boilers each 30 feet long, and 7½ feet in diameter.

The Cooperage is a large department, and the ground in front reminded us of the Burton Breweries, for there are many thousands of casks waiting their turns to be filled. There is a smiths', joiners' and coppersmiths' shop, together with buildings for general stores, also saw-mills and hydraulic pumps.

The water used comes from the Union Canal, and is of fine quality. The make is Grain Whisky, and the annual output of the Distillery is a little over 2,000,000 gallons.

There are 220 persons employed in the Establishment, and eleven Excise gentlemen on the premises, the chief being Mr. Halley.

The works are close to the Haymarket Station, and would amply repay the tourist a visit.

" Edina ! Scotia's darling seat !
All hail thy palaces and tow'rs,
Where once beneath a monarch's feet
Sat Legislation's sov'reign pow'rs !
From marking wildly-scatter'd flow'rs,
As on the banks of Ayr I stray'd,
And singing, lone, the ling'ring hours,
I shelter in thy honour'd shade.

" There, watching high the least alarms,
Thy rough, rude fortress gleams afar ;
Like some bold vet'ran, grey in arms,
And mark'd with many a seamy scar ;
The pond'rous wall and massy bar,
Grim-rising o'er the rugged rock ;
Have oft withstood assailing war,
And oft repell'd th' invader's shock.

" With awe-struck thought and pitying tears,
I view that noble, stately dome,
Where Scotia's kings of other years,
Fam'd heroes ! had their royal home :
Alas, how chang'd the times to come !
Their Royal name low in the dust !
Their hapless race wild-wand'ring roam,
Tho' rigid law cries out, 'twas just ! "

BURNS.

No. 113.

Edinburgh Distillery, Sciennes Street, Edinburgh.

PROPRIETORS, ANDREW USHER & CO.

THE next day we paid a visit to the old town, and were more or less interested in the ancient character of its buildings, churches and fine old castle. After seeing all in that way that we wished and had planned to visit, we at length found our way to Sciennes Street, wherein stands the Distillery, the subject of our sketch. The very name of Sciennes calls to memory the days of Mary Queen of Scots—suggestive of romance and history. In this street, in the year 1512, Lady Jane Seton founded the Dominican Convent of St. Katherine, and her house was the popular resort of all the pious and holy notables of the day. The husband of Lady Jane was slain at the battle of Flodden; as also was his brother, the Earl of Bothwell. Thereafter she remained a widow, and, after her son had attained his majority, became the first Prioress of the Convent she had founded. So blameless were the lives of the nuns of St. Katherine, that at the Reformation they were excepted from the general denunciation of that time. Lady Seton lived until she was seventy years of age, and was buried in Seton Church, by the side of her husband. Sciennes Hill House is said to be the house where Sir Walter Scott, at the age of seventeen, was introduced to Robbie Burns.

The neighbourhood of the Edinburgh Distillery has always been the location of the malt and brewing business. In 1510, the Burgh Records state that three acres of the Burgh Muir (now the Meadows) were let to build thereon Malt Barns, and that servants were to be hired for the making of malt betwixt the 30th of April and Michaelmas, and failing to do that, the lessees were to pay £40 fine and a penalty of £5 per acre. On the fields adjoining the Distillery James IV., mustered the largest army that ever marched against England, consisting of 100,000 men. These fields, together with the loch, which is now filled up, are called the Meadows or Borough Loch, and are laid out as public gardens and promenades. Opposite, and about one mile from the Distillery, stands the gigantic rock, "Arthur's Seat," lifting its rugged head high above all the surroundings. It seems so close that you never lose sight of its crags, cliffs, and buttresses, looking the very embodiment of grandeur and repose. The Distillery was established in 1849. Previous to that it was one of the most celebrated breweries in the old town, and we have seen a tablet in the wall bearing date 1430.

The Granaries and Maltings, &c., are situated at St. Leonards, and consequently the proprietors have the benefit of two lines of railway past the premises. The following are a few particulars of same:—The Granaries contained 2,000 quarters of Barley, and the Malt Barns are of the same capacity, with Steeps of a proportionate size. There are traps in the Steeps through which the barley is dropped on to the Malting Floor, and a very unique contrivance is used for distributing it over the floors. From end to end, and at intervals of 6 or 8 feet, "travellers" are affixed to the roof, on which baskets, holding 15 to 25 bushels of grain, are suspended by iron handles, having a little wheel in the centre. When the baskets are filled, the slightest impetus will start or stop them wherever the grain is required to be distributed. When the malt has passed through the Kiln, which is floored with wire flooring, it is dropped into the Malt Stores by means of a slanting trough, some 6 feet wide, from whence it is carted to the Distillery Malt Stores, and from thence it descends to the Mill and through the Crushing Rollers. From this department a short gangway communicates with the Mash House, a clean building with a concrete floor, unlike any other we have seen in Scotland. The grist is wheeled across the bridge, and dropped direct into the Mash Tun below, a beautifully clean vessel, 18¼ feet in diameter and 5 feet deep, with the patent stirring gear. From here the liquor descends by gravitation into the Underback, a cast metal vessel, 8 feet square and 3½ feet deep. From the Underback a Centrifugal Pump sends the wort into the Cooler, a large vessel, 26 feet long and 6 feet deep, afterwards to a Morton's Refrigerator. From here the liquor descends to the thirteen Washbacks, each having a capacity of about 2,700 gallons. From these vessels the wort is pumped into the Wash Charger, a wooden vessel, with a capacity of 2,785 gallons, from thence it descends to the Wash Still, holding 3,200 gallons; afterwards through the Worm above, and then to No. 1 Low-wines and Feints Receiver, and again from there into the Low-wines Still, holding 2,170 gallons. It may here be remarked as a special feature of this establishment, that all the copper vessels are kept as bright as the fittings on a man-of-war, and the wooden and other vessels are the perfection of cleanliness. From the Low-wines Still the spirit ascends to the Cooler and Refrigerator, thence to the Spirit Vat in the Spirit Store, where the Whisky is weighed and casked, and from here it is carted to the Warehouses at St. Leonards.

There are three Brewing Tanks, square and oval vessels of large capacity, a 20-horse power Engine, and two steam Boilers, each 18 feet long by 8 feet in diameter. At the end of the buildings there is a good Cooperage (where four men are employed) for storage and repairs.

The precautions against fire are very complete, every floor being supplied with water-pipes, hose, and extincteurs.

The Distillery is lighted throughout with the electric light, it being the second Distillery in Scotland to adopt that method of lighting. There is also telephonic communication with the offices in Nicolson Street and St. Leonards.

Good offices have been provided for the Excise gentlemen and the manager.

The water used in the Distillery comes from the Pentland Hills. The Whisky is pure Malt, and the annual output is 132,000 gallons.

Twenty-five persons are employed in the Distillery. The chief Excise officer is Mr. J. Mackintosh.

No. 114.

Dean Distillery, Edinburgh.

PROPRIETOR, JAMES JOHNSTONE.

YESTERDAY we explored the Old Town, this morning we did Princes Street, the squares and public gardens, finishing up the afternoon by visiting the Dean Distillery. It is about 100 yards from Randolph Crescent, and 1½ miles from the Waverley Station. The Dean Bridge, after which the Distillery is named, spans the ravine of the water of Leith, and was built after designs by Telford. It is 447 feet long, 39 feet wide and 106 feet high, and consists of four arches, 96 feet in span. This bridge commands a superb view down the Valley of Fifeshire, and the prospect to the east is most picturesque and romantic. Beneath us is seen the water of Leith rolling over deep beds of shelving rock, its banks for a considerable distance overhung with woods and terraces. At the bottom of the ravine is St. Bernard's Well, covered by an open structure, erected in 1790 by Lord Gardenstone. It is in the form of a Doric Temple, and composed of a rude basement, from which arise a number of columns that support a canopy under which is a statue of the goddess Hygeia. St. Bernard's is a medicinal spring of similar quality and property as the springs of Moffat and Harrogate, and is held in high repute for its curative powers.

The Distillery is on the western side, almost under one of the arches of Dean Bridge; to reach it we descended the face of a steep hill, and in ten minutes found ourselves in front of a range of buildings erected on the solid rock, rising abruptly from the water of Leith.

The works, which were formerly corn mills, are of ancient date; as we discovered, from a charter in the archives of the city, that David I. conferred them on the Canons of Holyrood, but later on, in the seventeenth century, they came into possession of the Edinburgh Bakers' Corporation, an old-fashioned Guild enjoying special privileges. In the year 1881 the premises came into the possession of Mr. Johnstone, who converted them into a Distillery.

Mr. W. McConnachie, the manager, conducted us through the works, which cover 1½ acres of ground, and explained the arrangements. The Barley Lofts are 140 feet long and 30 feet broad, and there are five Malting Floors of the same dimensions. Adjacent is the Kiln, 35 feet square, floored with perforated tiles, which communicates with the Malt Deposit, a lofty building, holding 18,000 quarters of malt. We ascended a circular stone staircase, and entered first the Mill Buildings, which are thus arranged—the top floor is occupied by the Mill, which consists of a pair of metal rollers for crushing the malt; the next floor below is the Grist Loft, and below this is the Mash House, and adjoining the Tun Room, over which are two very large water Cisterns, holding

6,000 gallons. The Mash Tun is 20 feet in diameter, and 6 feet deep, possessing the usual stirring rakes. The two Brewing Tanks have each a capacity of 5,000 gallons, and the Underback is on the same level in the next buildings. In the Back Room we observed five handsome Washbacks, each holding 9,000 gallons; the Wash Charger, which holds 7,000 gallons, is fixed on a gallery over the Stills. It will, therefore, be noticed that all the work in this establishment is carried on by gravitation. We were next conducted to the Still House, which contains two old Pot Stills, viz., a Wash Still, holding 4,789 gallons, and a Spirit Still, 3,004 gallons, two Low-wines and Feints Chargers, and one Spirit Receiver. The Running Room is also on the same level, and contains, besides the Safe, a Morton's Refrigerator and two patent Condensers.

The Spirit Store is next door to the last described places, and contains a Vat holding 2,600 gallons. We then retraced our steps and came to the Engine House, which contains a 15 horse-power Engine, centrifugal Pump for the wash, and a steam Boiler, 28 feet long and 6 feet in diameter. The chimney stack is on the other side of the river, and the flue is carried across the stream on a bridge exactly over the waterfall. Still following our polite guide, we entered seven Bonded Warehouses, all built in the solid rock, wherein were 2,500 casks of Whisky, of various ages. Most of these Warehouses are two deckers, and all are very dry. Adjacent are a small Cooperage, Offices, Stables, Peat Sheds, and Clerks' Office. The city water, which is of excellent quality, is used for every purpose, even cooling.

The Whisky is pure Malt, and the average annual output is about 73,000 gallons; the Whisky is sold principally in the district and the North of England. The chief Excise officer is Mr. J. M. Brewster.

Before returning to the "Balmoral" we paid a visit to the imposing monument erected to the memory of Sir Walter Scott. It is built in Princes Street, opposite St. David Street, and the design was furnished by a humble self-taught artist, George Mickle Kemp, who unfortunately was drowned in the canal during the course of its erection. It is an open monumental spire of Gothic architecture, and consists of a platform on the top of a flight of steps, which supports a pedestal on which is placed a statue of the illustrious Scotchman, sculptured by John Steele, from a block of white Carrara marble. The minstrel is represented in a sitting posture, with his favourite dog Maida lying at his feet. The height of this magnificent monument is 200½ feet from the level of Princes Street, and the top gallery is reached by a flight of 287 steps, from whence we obtained an exceeding fine view of the city and surrounding country.

No. 115.

Auchtermuchty Distillery, Auchtermuchty.

PROPRIETOR, ALEXANDER BONTHRONE.

TO reach this queerly named place, we crossed over to Burntisland by the early boat, and from thence journeyed by rail to Auchtermuchty. Our course lay along the coast, which here rises from the water's edge to lofty rugged rocks, here and there broken by side gulfs and miniature bays. After we passed Kirkcaldy we lost sight of the beautiful and busy waters of the Forth, and the country began to assume a character that bespoke a fertile soil and a high state of cultivation. The country slopes gently down from the Ochils to the River Eden, but the East Lomond forms the finest object in the surrounding landscape. It is a regular and beautiful mountain, 1,650 feet high, with a cairn on the top. As we proceed along we see in the distance Falkland Palace, where the Royal Family of Scotland resided up to the time of Charles II. It was this palace that the famous Rob Roy garrisoned in 1615 with a party of Macgregors, when he laid the whole district under contribution. As we diverge from the main line the track is through a rich and well-cultivated plain, but towards the north it rises to hills which are covered with heath, and through this plain runs the Eden—

"Where flows the cool, unsullied stream,
Deep sheltered from the scorching beam."

The Ochil and Lomond Hills were in former times the resort of smugglers, both male and female, and Mr. Bonthrone's brother, as late as the year 1828, supplied them with malt, which was carted by night to the foot of the hills, and fetched away by the smugglers under cover of the darkness. The celebrated "Lady Miller," a most daring and masculine woman also kept an illicit still in these hills, and for a great many years evaded the law. Mr. Bonthrone was well acquainted with her, and told us some stirring tales of her doings.

Auchtermuchty is 15 miles north of Kirkcaldy, and is a quaint, picturesque little town. The following humourous lines have been ascribed to James V.:—

"In Auchtermuchty dwelt a man—
An husband, as I heard it tauld—
Quha weil could tipple out a can,
And nowther luvit hunger nor cauld."

The Distillery, which was founded in the year 1829, is situated in the small town of Auchtermuchty, about half a mile from the railway station. It is built in the solid rock in front of a tributary of the river Eden, which stream comes from Lochmill and runs through the town. It took nearly two years to blast and cut out the rock, and 3,000 loads of stone were removed by the excavators. With the exception of the Distillery proper, the buildings, more especially the Maltings, are somewhat scattered, and cover about 2½ acres. The Distillery has been in the hands of the Bonthrones, father and son, for nearly a century. The present proprietor is reputed to be the oldest distiller in Scotland, and, although well advanced in years, he was, at the time of our visit, both hale and vigorous, and able to attend to his business. It was in the year 1829 that he first began to make whisky, and made about 3,000 gallons the first year, since which time the output has greatly increased and many additions have been made to the works.

Mr. Bonthrone is assisted in the Distillery by his two sons, who have been trained to the business, and understand the art of distilling in all its branches.

In connection with the water supply, we noticed a very ingenious contrivance. Mr. Bonthrone has tapped the celebrated Lovers' Pool, just above the Distillery, and had it conveyed through an aqueduct along a ledge of the rock at the back of the Distillery at such an elevation as to command the water vessels. It is splendid water, and as pure and sparkling as crystal.

Mr. Bonthrone, jun., was our guide, and took us first of all to the four Barley Lofts which are scattered about the property, the largest measuring 90 feet by 28 feet, and holding together 1,000 quarters of barley. The four Malt Floors are of brick and concrete, and each possesses a stone Steep and Kiln, the latter floored with old-fashioned plates and heated with Orkney peats. One of the Malt Barns is several feet below the roadway, and the floor is on the solid rock; it can, therefore, be worked all the year round. We then crossed the roadway to the Mill, which is contiguous to the Malt Deposit, and underneath which there is a large water-wheel several feet below the burn, which drives the Mill and mashing machinery. There is also a second wheel, not quite so large, which drives the worts from the Mash Tun to the Coolers, pumps the wash from the Backs to the Charger, sends the low-wines and feints from the Receiver to the Still, and drives the fans for cooling the worts. The third wheel is smaller, and is only used for driving the chains in the Wash Still. We may here remark that there is no other motive power used in this Distillery but water, of which there is an unlimited supply. Passing through a passage we found ourselves in the Mash House, which contains a heating Copper holding 2,000 gallons, and a Mash Tun, 11 feet in diameter and $4\frac{1}{4}$ feet deep, also, at a lower level, the Underback, of a similar capacity. We then ascended a few steps into the Tun Room, which contains six Washbacks, each with a capacity of 2,000 gallons, and on an elevation above the Tuns, a Wash Charger, holding 2,000 gallons. We then retraced our steps to the Brewing House, at the end of which are placed two old Pot Stills of a mediæval pattern, both of great age and in a good state of preservation. The Wash Still, which holds 960 gallons, is nearly a century old, and the Spirit Still contains 460 gallons. This last was purchased from a smuggler 60 years ago. Mr. Bonthrone informed us that he would not exchange these Stills for fifty of the newest patterns each twice the weight and capacity, and that he attributed the quality of the Whisky to the water and these old Stills. The Worm Tub is an iron vessel, 20 feet long and 6 feet deep, which is placed in a recess cut out of the solid rock. In the next building there are the usual Chargers, Receivers, and Sampling Safe, and in close proximity the Spirit Store. The five duty Warehouses are placed on the roadside, and convenient for carting to the station. They contained 600 casks of Whisky of various ages, all of which was sold. Mr. Bonthrone informed us that five merchants take all he makes, and that the annual output is 20,000 gallons.

The Whisky is pure Malt, and is all sold at Leith, London, and Glasgow.

No. 116.

Cameron Bridge Distillery, Windygates, Fifeshire.

PROPRIETORS, THE DISTILLERS COMPANY, LIMITED.

REGISTERED OFFICE, 12, TORPICHEN STREET, EDINBURGH.

MANAGING DIRECTOR OF THIS DISTILLERY, HUGH V. HAIG.

AT Thornton Junction we changed carriages, and a journey of about ten minutes on the Leven and East of Fife Railway, brought us to this famed Distillery. The station is so closely allied to the works that it forms part of the estate; in fact the railway cuts the establishment into two parts which are connected with each other by means of an iron bridge.

Cameron Bridge, situated in the most beautiful part of the Shire, is a place of great interest. On the south bank of the Leven about a mile from the Distillery, there is an old baronial hall called Balgonie. It stands 40 feet above the level of the stream in thickly wooded grounds and charming plantations. Kennoway, a mile and a half from the works, is a delightful place situated at the head of a romantic glen, the sides of which are rocky and precipitous, containing numerous caves, the haunts of smugglers and marauders of a bygone age. Many a tale of daring and bold adventure is told by the inhabitants, and it is said that at one time some revenue officers were blind-folded and taken into the caves, where they were compelled to swear that they had been inside, but had seen nothing illicit.

Near to these caverns is to be seen "The Maiden Castle" which has a subterranean passage running to the old tower of Brunton on which many a novel has been founded. It was in Kennoway village that Archbishop Sharpe passed the night previous to his being waylaid and massacred on Magus Moor while on his way to St. Andrews. Another most interesting place in the vicinity is the house of Balfour which contains the portrait of the beautiful "Mary Bethune" one of the four Marys of Mary Queen of Scots so frequently referred to in Sir Walter Scott's novels. The celebrated John Knox is said to have passed a night in one of the caves before referred to, which to this day bears his name.

The Distillery is under the management of Mr. Hugh V. Haig, son of the late John Haig, who worked Cameron Bridge Distillery from 1824,

CAMERON BRIDGE DISTILLERY.

until 1877 when it was merged into the Distillers Company, Limited. Prior to Mr. John Haig's accession, Mr. John Edington and Mr. Robert Haig, of Lochrin Distillery, for many years carried on this Distillery. It may not be out of place here to mention that the present Director at the Cameron Bridge, represents the sixth successive generation who have been engaged in the work of Distillation. The first "Continuous Distillation Still"—which is fully described by Morewood in his work on Inebriating Liquors, published in 1838—was an invention of Mr. Robert Stein, cousin of the Haigs, and there is an apparatus after his plan still working on the premises, and to it is due the flavour of the "Malt Spirit," made at this Distillery.

The actual buildings cover about 14 acres, and the Bonded Warehouses are capable of stowing 3,000,000 gallons. Another feature of Cameron Bridge, peculiarly its own, is the water power: four large Wheels drive almost everything in the works, and as there are sluices at Loch Leven twelve miles off that are kept down in winter, a regular and constant supply of water is obtained. The corn and grain is brought into the establishment by covered vans, and discharged into Hoppers, whence it is carried by means of screws and elevators to any portion of the Grain Stores. The principal Granaries consist of two large blocks of buildings, four stories high, each 150 feet long by 60 feet broad, for grain of all descriptions. The two top floors in each building will hold 6,000 quarters of grain. The two lower floors are used, one for a barley-floor, the other for malting, and are of the same capacity. The malting-floor possesses two steeps, one of which holds 190 quarters. From this department the grain is sent by screws to the three hot-air Kilns, each capable of drying 90 quarters in four hours. The air is driven through a series of tubes and heated up by the exhaust steam from the engine. In addition to these there are three Malt Kilns capable of drying 250 quarters. Contiguous to these Kilns are the two Dried Grain Stores, of large capacity, each holding 1,700 quarters.

We were next conducted to the Mill building, a spacious structure of three floors, containing six pairs of stones, and connected with which there is a most ingeniously contrived grist sifting apparatus, formed by a number of square wire sieves through which the grist falls; the coarse which remains behind is afterwards sent back by machinery to be re-ground. From here the grist is sent by elevators and screws into the Grist Lofts, which are conveniently placed above the Mash House. The pulverized grain next falls through Hoppers and Spouts direct into the Mash Tuns below.

Through a spacious doorway we next proceeded to the Mash House wherein are two large maize Mash Tuns, handsome enclosed timber vessels, the staves of which are made of pitch pine six inches thick. There is also a large malt Mash Tun 30 feet in diameter and 9 feet deep, with draining plates and double-acting stirring gear. On one side of this building we noticed the following, a draff scraping machine, eight sets of three-throw pumps, five of them for water the rest for worts, and a metal Underback from which the worts are pumped up to four Morton's Refrigerators fixed on an elevated gallery. Beneath this are two Wash Chargers, and on the ground level a fine "old Pot Still," ancient in years as well as old in name, and held in high repute by the Distiller. We were also shown an ingenious contrivance for heating the water used for feeding the boiler; it is worked by spent heat from the boilers, and consists of an arrangement of tubes and scrapers whereby cold water can be quickly raised to boiling point before passing into the boilers. Unlike some of the Distilleries, here the four heating-tanks, each holding 12,000 gallons, are wooden vessels. Over this building there is a huge Spent-Tank into which the draff is pumped up from the Mash Tun by a steam pump capable of throwing 60,000 gallons per hour. This Draff-Tank has a false bottom similar to the Mash Tun, by means of which the liquor is drained off to several other tanks provided with spouts to take it direct into the farmers' carts.

We next proceeded to the Back House, a well lighted and iron roofed building containing twelve Wash Backs each having a capacity of 25,000 gallons, and two large Wash Chargers. Up a few steps and through a doorway we arrived at the No. 1 Still House wherein are two Coffey's patent Stills, handsome machines, with their copper tubes brilliantly polished, and the whole machinery clean as a new pin. Number 2 Still House contains two of Stein's Patent Steam Stills. Number 3, which is a Pot Still House, contains an old Pot Still, the sampling safe and a patent condenser. All these houses are shut off from each other and protected by double iron doors. The roofs of the Still Houses consist of huge water tanks for use in case of fire, and are tapped by pipes running right and left through the buildings, with fire plugs attached on every floor. In the Receiver-house are three spirit Receivers. Across the yard is a fine Spirit Store containing three Vats of a similar capacity to the Receivers. The extensive Bonded Warehouses cover several acres, and are ten in number.

We then crossed the grounds to the Cooperage which is quite a little work in itself. In summer time there are some thousands of casks under the spreading branches of the noble trees which adorn the grounds of the Distillery. Besides a Saw mill, there is quite a small village of industries such as engineers' and coppersmiths' shops, a brass foundry for casting, joiners' shops, &c. At one corner of the premises are the Gas Works; the Company make their own gas and supply the Railway Station as well. There are railway sidings direct into all parts of the works, bringing coals to the furnaces, and grain to the granary floors. On the south side are the offices and three of the large Bonded Stores, whilst on the north are the Granaries, Maltings, Still-house and other Bonded Warehouses.

In the spacious engine house are five engines each about 20-horse power, and adjacent, six boilers 29 feet long by 8 feet in diameter. The four water wheels before referred to, are on the branch of the river which here forms a triangle. Over one of the streams are erected two large spent-wash Tanks each holding 36,000 gallons; in addition, there is a large concreted pond used for the same purpose. Both the wash and the draff find a ready sale among the local farmers; the former is strained and put into sacks the same as at the Caledonian Distillery.

Near the works, and standing in a small park, is a handsome building which we at first took for a Church, but on enquiry we learned that it was the "Yeast House," erected by the Company for the manufacture of French Yeast, a large quantity of which finds its way to Glasgow and London, where its fine quality is much appreciated, and yields a large revenue. The three huge chimney stacks which rise from the works are of an average height of 150 feet.

The Whisky made here is said to have no rival in the world. There are several kinds manufactured, first patent "Grain Whisky," second "Pot Still Irish," third "Silent Malt," and fourth "Flavoured Malt." The annual output is 1,300,000 gallons, but this could be increased if necessary.

No. 117.

Auchtertool Distillery, by Kirkcaldy, Fifeshire.

PROPRIETOR, WALTER BARTHOLOMEW.

THERE is a cordiality and absence of ceremony about Scotch hospitality which we always thought very delightful. It is hospitality not measured by the quantity of meat and drink set before you, characterized by a total absence of all affectation, with a desire to welcome you and contribute to your happiness which, in our experience, does not altogether accord with the character for gravity and reticence sometimes attributed to the race. We, though passing guests, were generally treated like old friends, and made free of the house, horses, and vehicles.

On arriving at Kirkcaldy, we went immediately to Mr. Bartholomew's residence, and were welcomed in the usual Highland manner. Kirkcaldy Bay is one of the finest we have seen anywhere. It has the magnificent Forth in front and the beautifully wooded parks and pleasure grounds of Rath and Dunnikeir in the background. On a bold eminence, at the east end of the harbour, stand the ruins of the Castle of Ravenscraig, which was given to the Earl of St. Clair of Orkney by James III., in 1470, when the earl resigned the title.

Kirkcaldy is a busy manufacturing town and a royal burgh. Unfortunately, we had not much time to explore this interesting and historic place, as our trap was waiting, so we at once started for Auchtertool, a distance of four miles, being driven by our worthy host, who knows well how to manage the ribbons. We had a high-spirited horse, and bowled along at a splendid pace through a most delightful country. For several miles our drive was all up hill, and when we reached the Auchtertool church the view was surpassingly grand, embracing a fine view of the sea, which included the Isle of May, Bass Rock and North Berwick, the three Lomonds, and the Cullaloe Hills. On reaching the top of the hill, the Distillery lay directly below us, with its white and brown buildings looking like a small colonial settlement. Entering the covered archway, we drove down the short roadway to the office, and commenced our inspection.

There is something decidedly quaint and striking in this Distillery. It consists of a number of irregular buildings, connected with one another and disposed in the form of a hollow square, with a Kiln at one end rising a little above the rest of the buildings. Just outside and across the road are the new Maltings, to which we shall refer later on. The Auchtertool Distillery covers four acres of ground, and was founded as a Brewery in the year 1650. In the 18th century it was noted through Fifeshire for its excellent brew, and had its praises sung by the local poets. In 1845 this ancient establishment was turned into a Distillery, and, in the quality of its new beverage, has continued the reputation of the production from these works. The estate which adjoins is farmed by large holders of land, and fine crops of barley are raised thereon, which is

AUCHTERTOOL DISTILLERY.

used in the Distillery, supplemented with the produce of neighbouring farms. Agricultural operations in this district are in a very advanced state, and the country is famous for its fine barley and wheat.

The works contain three large Barley Lofts, with Steeps at each end. One of them is very large, and capable of drying 100 quarters at one time. Underneath these Lofts are the Malting Floors, all of them concreted. Connected with this building are three Kilns, floored with iron plates, and peat only is used therein to dry the malt. These Kilns being slightly elevated above the next building, which contains the two Malt Deposits, the dried malt falls through a shoot, and no manual labour is required. We were next taken to the Mill Building, which is close to the Malt Deposits, and contains a fine set of Malt Rollers. After it is ground the pulverized malt is raised by elevators to the Loft above, where it is weighed into bags of 200 cwt. ready for use. These sacks are afterwards tipped into the hopper of a Steel's Mashing Machine, through which the grist passes into the Mash Tun.

We then descended a staircase into the Brewing Department, where is to be seen the Mash Tun, 18 feet in diameter by 5 feet deep, with the patent stirring gear, and the iron Underback, which receives the worts from the Tun. The two heaters which supply hot water to the Mash Tun are copper vessels, and are placed on one side of this house, and the Coolers, which are on the old-fashioned principle, cover the roof. The worts are pumped from the Underback into the fermenting vessels. We then followed our guide up another stair-ladder into the Back House, an apartment entirely devoted to the fermenting process. Here we were shown eight Washbacks, or Fermenting Tuns, each having a capacity of 2,780 gallons. The revolving switches therein, for keeping down the fermentation, are driven by steam power. The worts, after this process, change their name into wash, and we followed it into the Still House, a very old-fashioned building. Here the wash is received into the Wash Charger, into which it runs by gravitation. This vessel is of timber, and is placed above the Stills on an elevated platform. Both the Stills are of the old pot kind, and of the following capacity:—The Wash Still 2,500 gallons, and the Spirit Still 1,360 gallons. Distributed about in this house are to be seen the Feints Charger and Feints Receiver, the Low-wines Receiver, Spirit Receiver, and the safe and sampling apparatus. We next crossed the yard to the Spirit Store, passing on our way the Worm Tub and Refrigerators. In this Store there is a vat which holds 2,000 gallons, also the casking apparatus. Following our guide we took a peep at the nine Warehouses, which are scattered round the establishment. Some of them are very spacious, and they are all well ventilated. At the time of our visit they contained 2,275 casks of Whisky and were not full; as a matter of fact, they will hold, if necessary, 6,000 casks. A special feature in this Distillery is the Cooperage, a huge warehouse used in the olden days of the brewing, as a store. It is now converted into a cask shed, and contained at least a thousand empty sherry casks waiting to be filled, and in the adjoining building the coopers, looking very picturesque in their leather aprons, were busy purifying, sweetening, and repairing casks. We just looked in at the smithy and carpenters' shops, and then crossed over to the stabling and cart-sheds, where we were shown seven cart-horses, magnificent creatures, well adapted for carting the loads of Whisky down to Kirkcaldy Station.

We next paid a visit to the new Maltings, recently erected on a slope of the hill in front of the Distillery. They are 178 feet long and 60 feet wide, and, with the buildings adjacent, cover an acre of ground. The top floor is used as a Barley Store, and contained, at the time of our visit, 1,800 quarters of home-grown barley, but they can store 6,000 quarters. The Malting Floors are underneath, and at the end there is an enormous stone Steep. At the end of the building there is a handsome tower, which forms the Kiln. It is very lofty, measures 48 feet by 33 feet, and is floored with perforated iron plates. The Malt Deposit is on a lower floor in the next building, and so arranged that the dried malt falls therein by gravitation. On the opposite side of the enclosure there is a capital Draff House and Spent Wash Tank, conveniently arranged for sale and delivery to the farmers. The dreg and wash are conveyed through pipes under the roadway, from the Distillery to this receptacle. In the courtyard were four large stacks of peat, piled as high as the buildings. Mr. Bartholomew has provided comfortable dwellings for all his employés, and excellent residences for the Excise officers, of whom there are three, the chief being Mr. A. W. Ping. The Whisky made at Auchtertool is pure Malt, and the annual output is 86,000 gallons. It is principally sold in England and Scotland.

As we drove along home, the last lingering rays of the setting sun were falling on the russet coverings of the trees, and the hills, which now began to darken the horizon, were flushed by the sunset, and before we reached home the sea, which now almost appeared at our feet, was enveloped in mist.

We rattled along in high spirits, enjoying the drive, and regretting that we should not have the same pleasure for many a long day.

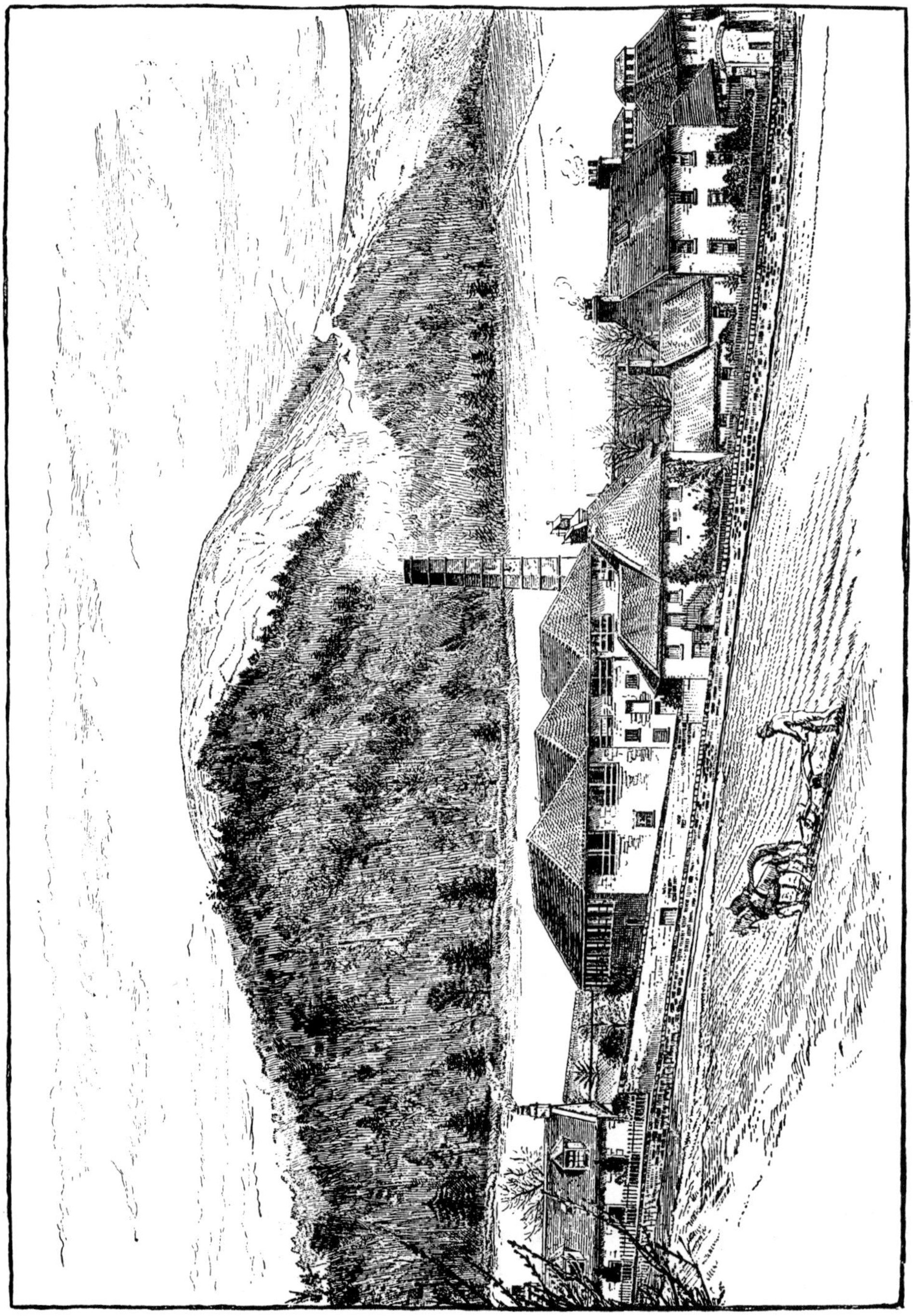

UPPER END OF THE GRANGE DISTILLERY, BURNTISLAND.

No. 118.

The Grange Distillery, Burntisland.

PROPRIETORS, W. YOUNG & Co.

ONCE more we left the "Balmoral" for a sail across the Forth to Burntisland, a place we had frequently passed through, but never explored; it is a royal burgh and seaport town on the waters of the Firth of Forth. In olden times a great trade was done from here with Holland. There are good docks, and it is the largest coal-exporting port in Scotland. It is situated on the Fife coast, directly opposite Granton, and was at one time called Wester Kinghorn, being a part of the barony of Kinghorn, but the union of these two towns was dissolved by James VI., who gave Burntisland the privileges of a royal burgh. As the steamer approaches the harbour you notice the beautiful appearance of Burntisland, with its fine plains and lofty rising ground behind; but these are not its chief attractions—they consist principally in its natural beauties, with rocks on the one side and sands, beautifully firm and level, on the other, and hills rising in the background. Burntisland is rich in historic reminiscences; midway between the town and Kinghorn is the ivy mantled stone, which marks the spot where, in 1286, King Alexander III. met his death. At the west end of the town is situated Rossend Castle, which occupies a prominent position. It was erected in the year 1119 by the Abbots of Dumfermline, and is delightfully picturesque. It was so built that some of its numerous windows catch sunshine every instant of its duration throughout the year. Cromwell, the Vandal and despoiler, resided here during the occupation of the country by his troops. It was at this castle that the beautiful Queen Mary loved to rest and secure a temporary respite from the affairs of the State. We must not omit to mention the Church, which dates back to 1592. This old building contains some very antique carving, and it was here that, in 1601, James VI. met the General Assembly of the Church of Scotland. The weather, we are told, was very stormy at the time, and as he could not get over to Edinburgh, he made the Assembly come to him, in order that he might oblige them, by re-swearing, to adhere to the Solemn League and Covenant. After leaving the church, we made our way, in company with our companions, two choice spirits, to the house of a friend, who had persuaded us to stay with him for a few days.

We had a pleasant time of it, as it was our good fortune to be the guests of Mr. P. H. Cameron, of Colinswell, a genuine Scotchman, and an author of some repute, who entertained us right royally, and whose house we quitted most reluctantly to resume our wanderings in the realms of spirit-land. By a strange coincidence we ascertained that our present abode was formerly the residence of one of the Messrs. Young, son of the founder of the establishment which heads this chapter.

Colinswell is a lovely old-fashioned place, possessing gardens well stocked with fruit trees and laid out in terraces, which stretch down to the sea shore. Such a wealth of blossom and fruit we have never before seen in any garden. As we sauntered on the terrace after dinner, admiring the gardens with their floral wealth, and gazed across the Forth to beautiful Edinburgh and its surroundings, the music of an organ stole upon us, and we found ourselves compelled to stop and listen to Sullivan's "Lost Chord," played by one of our number, who had slipped away unseen to the music-room, to try his 'prenticed hand on the grand old organ, which is one of the many treasures the house contains. From the higher terrace at the back of the house we obtained fine inland views, the most noticeable object being The Grange Distillery, about half-a-mile distant, situated at the foot of Binn Hill, a steep woodland acclivity, some 600 feet above the level of the sea.

To the Distillery we bent our steps next morning, and were deeply interested in this ancient work. Although, on a near inspection, we found that the buildings possess an old-world look, they are most conveniently arranged internally, the proprietors having brought to bear considerable ingenuity and experience in their re-arrangement, and the Distillery will now compare favourably with any work of its size in the Kingdom.

The Grange Distillery has been in existence 100 years, having been established in 1786 by the grandfather of the present proprietor. It possesses a fine water supply; that used for mashing comes from a loch belonging to the Distillery on the top of Dunearn Hill, in the neighbourhood, some 800 feet above sea level, and is pure soft water free from any contaminations, and is conveyed through a copper pipe nearly a mile in length direct to the Distillery. The condensing water comes from a burn which rises among the hills to the north and west and runs through the works, over which supply there is a servitude. The ground enclosed covers over six acres, and is all built upon. The buildings are of stone with tiled roofs, except the Still House, which has a roof of iron. The Distillery forms three separate ranges of buildings along the valley. The brewer, Mr. H. Thompson, who resides in a charming, old-fashioned house on the premises, was our guide, and conducted us first of all to the five Granaries and Maltings, all of which are three-decked buildings. The Maltings or Growing Floors are concreted, and the Steeps built of iron and stone. We commenced our inspection at the No. 1 Building, which stands beside the entrance gates of the Distillery, and passed on through the series of floors, which communicate by a gangway bridge, to the Kilns. While crossing one of these bridges we had a magnificent view of the Forth, with Arthur's Seat and Carlton Hill in the back, ground. The Maltings have a storage capacity of 3,500 quarters of malt and 4,500 quarters of barley, with a malting power of 400 quarters per week. The barley is purchased principally from the farmers in the district, who deliver at the door of the Granaries. We noticed that the Kilns were more lofty than some we had seen; they have open roofs, are floored with iron plates and heated with peat and coke in open *chauffeurs*. From this department we crossed the yard to the second range of buildings, and were first shown the Mill Building, which consists of three floors, and contains in the Mill two pairs of Malt Rollers, which pulverize the malt at the rate of about 25 quarters per hour. The Grist Loft is underneath, and the grist is conveyed by Elevators and Screws to the Hopper and Mashing Machine over the Mash Tun. We next made our way to the Mash House, a well-ventilated building, containing a Mash Tun, 22 feet in diameter and 7 feet deep, capable of mashing 100 quarters at a time, and possessing the usual revolving stirring gear. The draff from the Mash Tun is removed by elevators and screws to the farmers' carts, this valuable commodity being in great demand for feeding cattle. On a stone gallery in this house are placed three fine Heating Coppers of the shape of an orange, heated by steam, and holding together, 20,000 gallons. We then ascended a few steps and found ourselves in a lofty apartment, called the Tun Room, which contains ten Fermenting Backs, with a working capacity of 6,000 gallons each. The Wash Charger, having a capacity of 6,500 gallons, is placed on an iron gallery next to the Still House, so as to command the Stills, and is built of metal, instead of wood, as in most places. Our guide then conducted us to the Still House, an entirely new building, well lighted and ventilated, arranged on the most modern principle and fireproof. It contains two old Pot Stills, by Fleming and McLaren, of Glasgow, of 4,000 and 2,400 gallons, cubic content; the Still power is capable of producing 6,000 to 7,000 gallons per week. In this house are also placed the following vessels :—the Low-wines and Feints Charger, holding 3,000 gallons, and the Low-wines Receiver 3,000; also a Safe with sampling apparatus. There are two large circular tubs at the rear of this building, with condensing worms. The Spirit Receiver Room adjoins, and contains a Spirit Receiver and Feints Receiver. Nearly all the work in this Distillery is done by gravitation. We noticed that the Coolers, assisted by a large Refrigerator, cover the entire roof of both the adjoining Granaries. This is an excellent arrangement, and is frequently adopted; but we have often wondered in our travels why distillers do not put all their vessels which contain hot and cold water on the roofs of buildings, as besides making use of the room taken up on the ground, they have water ready to flood the buildings always at hand in case of fire; the plan is frequently adopted in Ireland. Attached to the Still House is the Engine Department, and our attention was directed to a fine new steam engine, by J. Brown, of Kirkcaldy, which drives the Still chains, and pumps the low-wines, feints and spirits to their respective chargers. The two steam boilers measure 23 by 6½ each. Adjacent to the Still House is the Spirit Store, which contains a vat holding 3,895 gallons. The fire arrangements are most complete, extincteurs and stop-cocks are placed on every floor, whilst the hose commands every building. At one end of the courtyard there is a smithy, a joiner's shop, and a capital cooperage, also stables, cart-sheds, and stores. The gas-works are quite detached and are most complete. Messrs. Young & Co. make all the gas used on the premises and in the houses adjacent occupied by the managers, clerks, and Excise gentlemen.

We next retraced our steps to the lower part of the enclosure, where are ranged 19 Bonded Warehouses, having a storage capacity of 650,000 gallons. Some of these buildings are new, they are all well ventilated, and on the ground floor. There is a capital arrangement in this Distillery for collecting all the foulage into a settling tank, and running it therefrom through a pipe into the sea.

The old-fashioned mansion, formerly the residence of the proprietor of the Distillery, has now been turned into fine offices for the clerks, managers and principals.

The Whisky is a fine Lowland Malt, and the annual ordinary output of about 200,000 gallons is within the capacity of the work, as 260,000 gallons have been made under pressure of orders. All the produce is sold in Scotland, England, India, and the Colonies. There are six Excise officers on the premises and a supervisor, Mr. S. T. Kinsman.

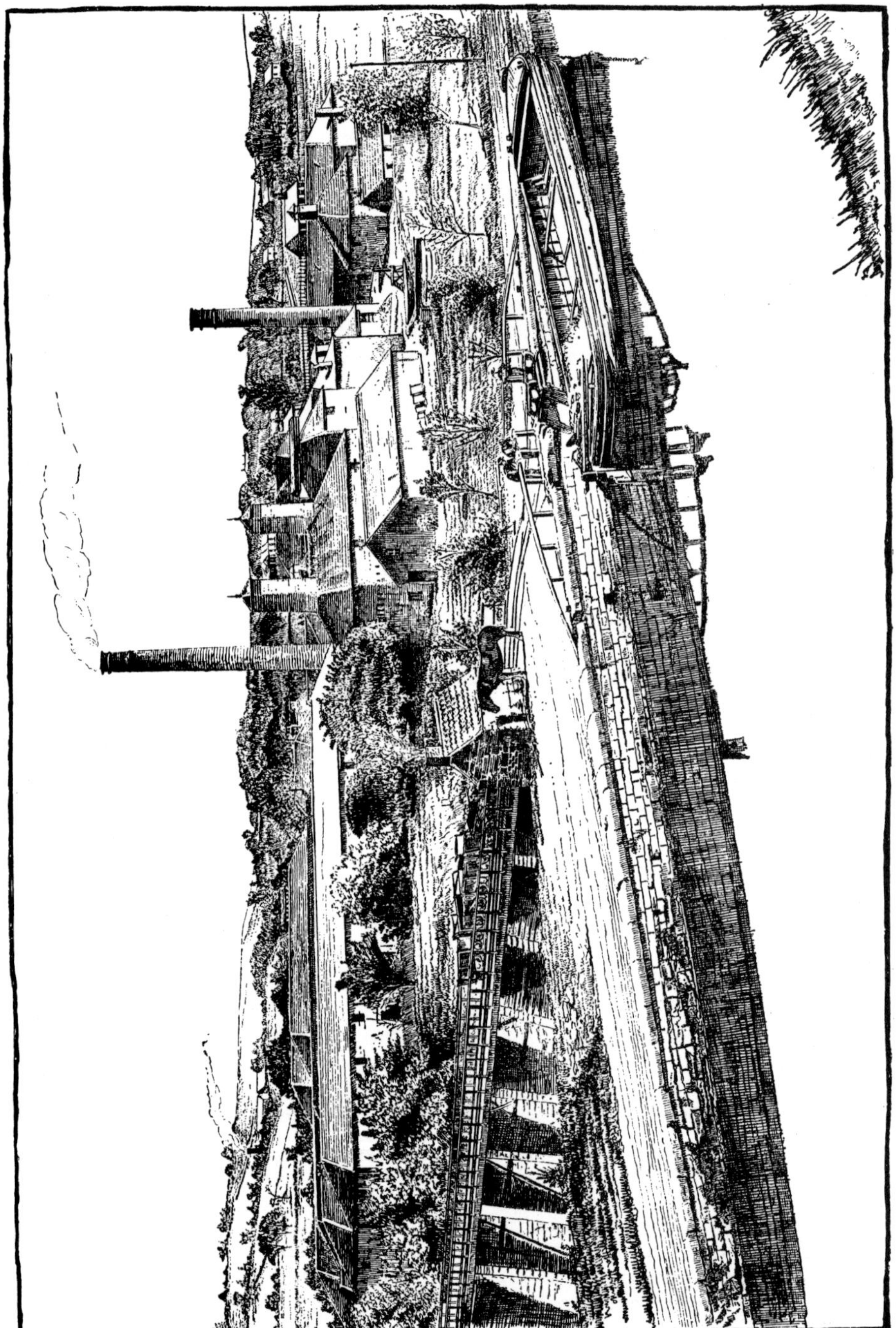

BANKIER DISTILLERY.

No. 110

Bankier Distillery, near Denny.

TRADING AS "BANKIER DISTILLERY COMPANY."

PROPRIETOR, JAMES RISK.

OUR last expedition was by steamboat; to-day we journeyed by rail, starting early that we might have time to explore the neighbourhood of Denny and the surroundings of the Bankier Distillery. The scenery through which we passed, after leaving Linlithgow, was very interesting. Pretty hills enclose pleasant looking valleys, and the meadow lands and plantations were as gay with wild flowers as a bit of tapestry. As we proceeded, the landscape appeared even more pastoral: little streams ripple in and out through the waving corn fields, and the soft beauty is much enhanced by the distant back-ground of verdant hills. There were times in the history of Scotland when this now peaceful district was the scene of carnage and strife, but happily "the sword has been changed for the ploughshare, and the spear into a pruning-hook." Castlecarey, one mile distant, is the nearest station to the Distillery. This place was an ancient fortress on the line of Antonius' wall. The fort is nearly effaced, and we saw nothing but a few remains of a keep or fosse. The Roman Wall runs through Castlecary, for many miles parallel with the remarkable river Carron, which runs a course of fourteen miles through this district, falling into the Forth at Grangemouth. There are many waterfalls on this river, the finest being called Auchintilly "linn spout," this cascade is well worth a visit. The Carron is certainly the most historic river in Scotland; when the Roman Empire was in its glory this river formed the boundary of its conquest in Britain. Many a bloody battle has been fought on its banks, but it has now ceased to roll its stream to the din of arms, and lends its aid to trade and manufactures, supplying not only the paper mills and printing works of Denny and district, but also the great reservoir of the Carron Iron Works, the most extensive iron foundry in Europe. Macneil, a native poet of this county, expresses himself thus:—

"Round Carron's streams, O classic name!
Whar Fingal fought, and ay ow'rcame,
Whar Ossian wak'd, wi' kindling flame,
His heaven-taught lays;
And sang his Oscar's deathless fame
At Duin, na bais!"

On leaving the train we walked to the Distillery, as there was no sign of a vehicle of any kind, or place where a machine could be hired. Our way lay alongside the railway track for half a mile, and then diverged into a country road, here and there overshadowed by trees. The Distillery is planted on the banks of the Forth and Clyde Canal, which at this point has a beautiful and picturesque appearance. The Canal runs through a glen forming a part of the Netherwood Estate, and in some parts the richly-wooded plantations slope down to the water's edge. At its extreme end the valley is crossed by a noble railway viaduct of great length and height, which adds to the beauty of the view.

The Bankier Distillery was built in the year 1828, by Daniel Macfarlane, of Paisley, but previous to that time it was a noted corn mill. The buildings are of stone, handsome in appearance, and cover six acres of ground. They are built on the slopes of a hill, at the bottom of which runs the Bonny River; whilst at a higher elevation, and cutting the left wing of the establishment into two parts, rolls along the Doups Stream, which turns the overshot water wheels and supplies all the tanks. It rises in the Lower Grampians, and is of excellent quality for mashing purposes. The premises, which are all arranged with intersections of roadways, mostly communicate with each other, and have all the appearance of a country Distillery, both as regards space and surroundings.

As you cross the Canal by the lock-bridge you get a splendid view of Bankier, and a busy scene it is, with the carts going to and fro from the wharf and the continued movement inside the works. The wharf is in close proximity to the western gates of the Distillery, and is the landing place for the barley which comes from Aberdeen and Forfar shires.

We first inspected the two Maltings, each of which is lighted by twenty-four windows. One of these Maltings is 200 feet long, by 60 feet broad; the other is not quite so large. The top floors of both buildings are used for storing the barley, and each holds about 4,000 quarters. Our attention was called to the Steeps, which are of cast iron, sunk into the floor, supported underneath by massive iron columns, and are most ingeniously arranged. After the water has been drained off, a circular sluice is raised from the bottom by a lever, and lets out the wetted barley on to the couch below. One of these Maltings is a two-decker and the other a three-decker. All the lower floors are concreted and used as withering or malting floors.

We next crossed a footbridge over the stream, which connects the Maltings with the two Kilns and Malt Stores. The former are 40 feet square, and adjoin the latter buildings. A rustic-looking covered outside passage, from end to end of these buildings, on the side of the stream, forms the means of communication through which the malt is wheeled to the Kilns.

We were afterwards conducted to the third and smaller Maltings on the opposite side of the yard, which, like the others, are built of stone and similarly arranged. They comprise a barley Store, with Steep, and underneath a malting floor; the Kiln, which is 24 feet square, forms a wing of the building. All the Kilns are floored with wire cloth, and are heated with peat in open *chauffeurs*. The dried malt is conveyed by screws to the Mill building, which is in the centre of the courtyard and adjoins the Brewing House. The mill rollers therein are driven by the water wheel, supplemented by steam power when necessary. From the Mill the pulverised malt is sent by elevators direct into the grist loft, which is over the Mash House.

The Still House and Mash House are under one roof, and form the central and most conspicuous building of the establishment. They are built of stone, in the form of a triangle, and measure 100 feet by 60 feet. On one side of this house, in the mashing department, are placed two cast-iron heating tanks: one of them is 16 feet long, $10\frac{1}{2}$ feet broad, and 9 feet deep; and the other is 16 feet long, 9 feet broad, and 9 feet deep. The Mash Tun is an iron vessel, 22 feet in diameter and 6 feet deep; it possesses the double action stirring gear, which revolves by steam-power. Below this vessel there is a screw, which conveys the grains direct to the Draff House in the yard, ready for the farmers to cart it away. Beneath the floor of the Brewing House is placed the Underback, a vessel 27 feet long, 6 feet wide, and 5 feet deep, which receives the worts from the Mash Tun. All the vessels are beautifully clean, and painted a warm red colour. Close by is the three-throw pump, which is used for pumping the worts into the Washbacks. We then left this building for awhile to follow the process, and were taken to the Back House. This is a very spacious, well-lighted and ventilated room, 50 feet long, by 55 feet broad and 35 feet high, containing 5 Washbacks, of 12,000 gallons capacity each. These have all the most modern fittings of steam piping, &c., for equalising the temperature of the room and cleansing purposes. Above, suspended on iron beams, we observed a large Morton's Refrigerator and cooling tank, with Yeast Room adjoining. We then retraced our steps to the Still House, to see what becomes of the liquor from the tuns, which is now called wash. On our arrival we mounted a central platform, which divides the building, and forms a partial division between the Brew House and Still House. Here is placed the Wash Charger, which holds 4,500 gallons. The wash flows from the tuns into this vessel by gravitation, and the Charger is placed at a sufficient altitude to command the Stills, as thither is the next destination of the wash. On this platform is also placed the Low Wines and Feints Charger, containing 3,000 gallons, and underneath the five Receivers. From this elevation we had a good view of the busy scene below. On our right are the mashmen, busy at their brewing operations; on the left the stillmen actively engaged in feeding the furnaces, polishing the brasswork, or watching and testing the running spirit in the glass safe; and we can but note with admiration the order which prevails, and the quiet and intelligent manner in which the workmen perform their duties.

The Stills are of the "Old Pot Kind," of the following capacities: the Wash Still, 6,551 gallons, No. 1, Low-wines, 1,975, and the No. 2 Low-wines, 1,895 gallons. One of them, a steam-jacketed Still, was supplied by Willison, of Alloa, and is fitted with the automatic anti-collapse valve. On the side of the west wall is a low-wines and feints pump and a spirit pump. We then left this interesting department and made our way a few yards up the hill to the Spirit-store, which contains a Vat holding 4,000 gallons and the necessary casking appliances. From thence we proceeded to the seven Warehouses, which are all detached and built on the higher ground above the Distillery. These spacious Warehouses are built of stone and roofed with slates, and together are capable of storing 4,500 casks. They contained at the time of our visit a little over 200,000 gallons of whisky of various ages, some dating back to 1874. Two of these Warehouses measure 100 feet by 60 feet.

Opposite these buildings, and at the back of the Still House are two cooperages, one for repairs and the other for cleaning and sweetening purposes. In the latter department we noticed the coopers purifying and cleansing the casks by a very simple method. Steam and hot-water pipes are laid on from the boilers, to which are attached double-jointed tubes. The hot-water pipe is first used, and afterwards the steam-pipe is inserted into the bung-hole of the casks. Thus they are thoroughly steamed and sweetened.

Extensive alterations and improvements are being carried on, including re-arrangement of Tun Room, erection of a range of new Tuns, a new cast-iron Wash Charger, with Centrifugal Pump for filling same. The engineering part of the work is in the hands of Mr. R. G. Abercrombie, of Alloa.

We then retraced our steps down the hill and paid a visit to the Engine House, which contains a handsome steam engine and two steam boilers, the latter 28 feet long by 8 feet in diameter. The two chimney stacks measure respectively 100 feet and 75 feet in height. At the foot of the hill, and near the bridge which crosses the Bonny Water, is placed the Gasometer and Gas House, as the firm make all the gas that is consumed on the premises. In close proximity is the Smithy, Engineers' Shop, Store House, Stables, and Cart-sheds. On the canal side of the yard there is a huge Peat-shed, filled with peats dug in the Cumbernauld Moors.

As a protection against fire, water pipes are laid over the premises, to the plugs of which can be attached a set of fire hose, worked by a pump from the water-wheel. The most prominent objects in the yard facing the canal are the two Spent-wash Tanks, of an enormous size, conveniently placed for the farmers' carts; the Draff House is also contiguous. On the left side of the Distillery, and quite apart from the works, is built a model Piggery. It is a quadrangular building, with the pig-styes in the central court, all of which are numbered. One hundred pigs are kept here and fed on the grains and spent wash of the Distillery. They form a very profitable receptacle for the disposal of the draff unsold to the dairymen.

We next crossed the Doups stream, and, by a short cut, found ourselves at the Distillery offices, which are newly built and very complete. Those for the use of the firm are fitted up in a handsome and substantial style, the walls and ceilings being richly panelled in oak. On the turnpike road, facing the eastern gate of the works, there is a pretty rustic cottage, occupied by the manager, and at a short distance therefrom are the workmen's dwellings.

About a quarter of a mile to the back of the Distillery, higher up the hill, as shown in the etching, is Bankier House, the residence of Mr. Risk, which stands on the borders of a miniature lake, on which swans gracefully move to and fro. The grounds surrounding the house are prettily planted and laid out, and from the front terrace we obtained a delightful view of the valley beneath and the "Hill of the Oaks."

The Whisky distilled at Bankier is now made on North Highland principles, and, although the Distillery is situated in the Lowlands of Scotland, the quality of the spirit appeared to us to be of a most pronounced and excellent Highland style of Whisky. The annual output is 150,000 gallons, the works are, however, capable of producing 180,000 gallons if required.

No. 120.

Rosebank Distillery, Falkirk, Stirlingshire.

PROPRIETOR, R. W. RANKINE.

FROM Edinburgh to Falkirk is a railway journey of about 40 minutes. We started early in the morning and spent the best part of the day at this interesting Distillery, Rosebank is one mile from Falkirk, and half a mile from the River Carron, and is built on the banks of the Forth and Clyde Canal. It is not so isolated as many of the Distilleries are, being placed by the main road, on which there is a constant stream of traffic, and also fronting the canal, where boats and steamers are continually passing to and fro. The policies of Bantaskine are adjacent to the works, and form a lovely wooded background to the Distillery, while on the left the grounds of Rosebank House, with their fine old elm trees, in which rooks have built their nests, add materially to the picture.

The water used for distilling percolates from the Bantaskine grounds to the Distillery, and from thence runs by a tunnel underneath the canal to the Maltings on the other side. The site of this Distillery was chosen on account of the inexhaustible supply of water; it was the first, and is yet, the only Distillery in the immediate district. The celebrated brewers, Messrs. James Aitken & Co., Falkirk, previous to the year 1851, carted this water to their works for brewing purposes. The Glenburnie rivulet, a tributary of the Carron, running at the foot of the Maltings, supplies all the water necessary for the undershot water-wheel, which is used for pumping the water to the tanks.

The works have been connected in some way with distilling for nearly a century, for, in the year 1798, the statistical records inform us that a Distillery was carried on by the Messrs. Stark Brothers at that date. The portion now occupied by the Distillery proper was formerly a Malting, but in 1840 Mr. James Rankine, the father of the present proprietor, commenced operations therein as a distiller. Five years after that date the buildings were considerably enlarged, and later on, in the year 1864, they were entirely rebuilt in a modern form by the present owner. The whole property connected with the Distillery covers five acres of ground, three of which are devoted to the works, and the remainder form the grounds and gardens of Rosebank House, one of the residences of Mr. Rankine. The establishment comprises two distinct ranges of buildings divided by the canal. On one side are placed the Maltings, covering upwards of an acre of ground, and occupying the site of the original Camelon Distillery, a work which was all pulled down in 1865, except one of the buildings, now used as a small Malting, and of antique structure.

To reach these Maltings, which are built in the shape of a triangle, we crossed the swing-bridge over the canal and entered the enclosure by the lower gateway, and were conducted, first of all, to the No. 1 Barley Loft, which, approached by a handsome outside staircase some 20 feet high, forms the top floor of a solid stone and brick building, each floor being supported by iron columns, and the interior staircases fixed on pulleys, which, by a simple contrivance, can be lifted up or down at pleasure. This Barley Loft holds 3,000 quarters of grain, and is 320 feet long by 50 feet broad. It is on a level with a roadway made by the proprietor, brought down from the upper gateway, so as to enable the farmers to deliver the barley direct on to the floor. The Malting Floor is underneath, and is of the same dimensions and paved with concrete. There are two large iron Steeps, capable of wetting 160 quarters at a time, and on the upper floor is a water tank, capable of holding upwards of 10,000 gallons, for the purpose of supplying the Steeps. Adjacent to this building is the Kiln, 43 feet high, 55 feet long and 45 feet broad, floored with wire cloth and closed off with fireproof doors; the furnaces are enclosed with iron sheets, the same as at Benmore Distillery. Peat is mostly used for the drying, and there is a good moss ground within four miles, where sufficient fuel can always be obtained to supply the kiln fires,

Our guide next conducted us to the Malt deposit, which is a building the same size as the Kiln, and consists of two floors, well lighted, the inner walls being lined to the roof with red timber to keep the malt dry. The beams of this and *all the buildings* are sandwiched with red timber and plates of iron bolted through. The malt is shot from the Kiln to this department by two sluices, and is here sacked and carted over the way to the Distillery buildings. Under the Malt Store is the peat shed, beneath the floor of which is sunk a cemented brick-built tank, where the spring water is collected and from whence it is pumped up to the tank, on a level with the barley loft before described, by a donkey pump driven by the water-wheel. The remnants of the old Distillery, as we have said, consist of a small Malting, in close proximity, which has been remodelled in the style of the new one, and contains a barley loft, one Steep, two malt floors, a Kiln, and Malt Store, the latter lined with red timber. This building, which is on a lower slope of the hill, near the gateway we first entered, is of three stories, and communicates with the larger Maltings from the upper floor, which is on a level with the ground floor of the principal Malting, and is reached by an elevated gangway. Inside these premises there is a capital dwelling-house for one of the principal maltmen.

We then recrossed the Canal to the Distillery proper. The buildings cover one-and-a-half acres of ground and face the Canal. They are close to the wharf, from whence a boat goes every day to Glasgow. We entered an enclosed courtyard, with the handsome newly-built offices and a range of Warehouses to the right and left. On the right also are the Mill buildings, sheds, &c., and opposite, the Mash House, Still House, Warehouses, and the Excise Offices.

We first visited the Mill, to reach which we had to mount a staircase. It forms a building of two floors over one of the interior archways, and contains a pair of malt rollers. From this point we noticed that a large water cistern was fitted into the roof of the Boiler House. The three iron Brewing Tanks for heating the water, containing 1,500 gallons each, are placed on iron pillars in the Still House, and are of the most solid construction. We then entered the Mash House, a brick building some 30 feet square, lighted with six windows, with walls of a dazzling whiteness. It contains a circular iron Mash Tun, 16 feet in diameter and 6½ feet deep, with the usual Mashing Machine and double-acting stirring gear. The draff is shovelled out of the Mash Tun into a paved court beneath, and carted away by the farmers. Below, in the same house, is the Underback, which contains 2,000 gallons, from whence the worts are pumped to the No. 1 Coolers, placed over the Brewing Tanks in the Still House, from whence they run by gravitation to the No. 2 Coolers in the Tun Room. Then we crossed over to the Tun Room, which is an equally light and cleanly building. In it are eight Washbacks, each with a capacity of 3,500 gallons, wherein the switches are all driven by steam, also a fine Morton's Refrigerator, said to be the second one erected in Scotland in any Distillery. The discharge pipes from the Washbacks are all made of copper, an unusual thing in a Distillery, with stop-cocks of solid brass ; the Coolers are fixed in a gallery above, half the size of the building. We then descended a few steps and came to the Still House, which contains three Pot Stills of the old-fashioned type, two of them containing 3,000 and the other 1,500 gallons. This House is a large and lofty building, being upwards of 40 feet high and 70 feet square, having an open ventilated roof. It contains, besides the Stills, a fine "crank overhead Engine" of 28 h.p., two Feints, one Spirit, and one Low-wines Receivers, two double-action Plunger Pumps for worts and water, and two others for pumping low-wines, feints, and spirits, also a centrifugal Pump for pumping Wash into the Wash Chargers. On a gallery herein is the Wash Charger and Low-wines and Feints Charger. The Sampling Safe is on a platform commanding the Receivers. To the Bonded Warehouses we next proceeded. No. 1 is 108 feet long by 78 feet broad, divided into two sections and is three stories high. Nos. 2, 3 and 4 are all under one roof. One of them is 156 feet long and 34 feet wide. The other two are 81 feet by 66 feet. No. 5 is of three stories, and similar in size to No. 1. In the No. 2 Bond, there are two Vats for blending purposes, used for vatted Whisky for the trade, they contain 2,064 and 1,214 gallons respectively. The Racking Store for the use of the local trade is next to No. 1 Warehouse. The Bonded Warehouses are capable of storing about 500,000 gallons.

The Spirit Store is opposite, and adjoins the Warehouses ; it has a door on each side so as to command same. The Vat therein contains 3,000 gallons. We noticed three fine circular Worm Tubs elevated on brick butts, and so placed as to be commanded by the Stills. The chimney-shaft is 150 feet high, and so arranged that the two flues enter on both sides, it being lined with an inner casing of brickwork to a height of 30 feet. In the engine department there is a Galloway's double-flued boiler, 30 feet by 7 feet.

The arrangements for extinguishing fire are very complete, there being three extincteurs and fire hose and plugs about the premises. There is a capital cooperage, and on the public road, adjoining the Maltings, are workmen's houses, the property of Mr. Rankine. The new offices, already referred to, contain private offices, brewers' and manager's and general clerks' offices. The excise offices are over the cooperage.

In the roadway there is a capital weighing machine, with an office attached for checking the barley and coals brought into the Distillery.

The whisky produced in this establishment is pure Malt. The annual output is 123,000 gallons, and is principally disposed of in Edinburgh and Glasgow. There are three excise officers employed—viz., Mr. Gavin Russell, Mr. William Bastard, and an assistant ; the two former having been upwards of thirteen years in the Distillery.

No. 121.

Bo'ness Distillery, Linlithgow.

PROPRIETORS, J. CALDER & CO.

TO reach Bo'ness from Edinburgh we changed carriages at Manuel, which station is in the parish of Munavonside, one of the most diversified and beautiful districts in the county. Immediately on leaving Manuel, we crossed the River Avon, and had a glance—all too brief—of the lovely Avondale, a pretty wooded glen, through which the river flows over huge boulders, each one of them making a miniature waterfall. Our train emerging from the cutting skirted the Forth to Bo'ness, the journey altogether being accomplished in rather less than an hour.

We were somewhat disappointed with Borrowstounness—or Bo'ness, as it is now called—as the collieries and iron works entirely spoil the look of the place. It is a seaport town, three miles from Linlithgow, on a low peninsula washed by the Forth. A century ago it was one of the most thriving towns on the east coast, and ranked as the third port in Scotland, but when the junction of the Forth and Clyde was effected by the canal at Grangemouth, the last-mentioned place became the chief town of commerce, and was afterwards turned into a separate port. Notwithstanding this, Bo'ness is still a place of some importance, on account of its extensive ironworks, earthenware manufactories, chemical and manure works, and last, but not least, the large Distillery which heads this chapter.

The Distillery, which is about half-a-mile from the station and harbour, covers about four acres of ground, and is situated under the brow of a rocky hill, called the "Pans Braes," indeed, the road at the back of the works, and some of the buildings are cut out of the solid rock. The establishment was founded in the year 1830 by Mr. A. Vannan, and in 1873 it came into the hands of Mr. Calder, the present proprietor. At that time it was a Malt Distillery, but in 1876 it was considerably enlarged and converted into a Grain Distillery. The works, which have a frontage to the main road and the Forth of some 700 feet, are of an oblong shape and all enclosed. We entered by a gateway, which has a sliding or running door, and which also gives admittance to the railway wagons, there being a siding direct from the harbour and the North British Railway into and through all the works. On the right-hand side as you enter are the new offices for the clerks, managers and Excise officers, and further on the new Grain Stores, Maltings, and Warehouses in course of erection, which, when finished, will be the largest in the district, constituting a solid block of granite buildings, 240 feet long and 150 feet broad.

Our guide first conducted us to the Grain Stores, at the extreme end of the courtyard, where railway wagons were delivering the grain into a large outside Hopper, from whence it is raised by Elevators direct to all parts of the buildings. There are two Kilns adjacent, one of them, a handsome new and lofty structure, 33 feet long by 45 feet wide, floored with iron plates; the other is not so lofty, and measures 31 feet by 26 feet. The grain is spread over these floors for drying at a depth of 2 feet. We then crossed the roadway to the Mill Building, which consists of four floors and contains seven pairs of stones, five for crushing maize and the other two for malt, etc. From here we proceeded to the Grist Lofts, of which there are three; the top is devoted to maize, the second for ground barley, and the third for malt. At the back of this building, in the open, are placed three Heating Tanks, one holding 7,000 gallons and the other two 8,000 gallons respectively.

Adjoining the Mill is the Mash House, where are to be seen three huge maize Mash Tuns, capable of mashing 30 tons of grist at one time. In the next house there is a circular metal Mash Tun, 25 feet in diameter and 7 feet deep. All the Tuns are provided with the revolving stirring gear, driven by steam. We then ascended a few steps, and found ourselves in the first Tun Room, a lofty apartment, 90 feet long and 50 feet broad, in which stand eight Washbacks, or Fermenting Tuns, each with a capacity of 13,000 gallons. Through a doorway we reached No. 2 Tun Room, which contains other six Washbacks, each holding 6,000 gallons. Over the roof of the first house we noticed four of Morton's Refrigerators and a Worts Receiver, holding 4,000 gallons. The worts run by gravitation from these vessels into the Washbacks. Abutting on to the Brewing Houses, or Tun Rooms, is an ancient building, which looks like a church ruin, and where formerly the "Sma' Pot Still" Whisky was made. It is now being demolished to make room for the important extension of the Tun Rooms. In the basement of the Back House are two Centrifugal Pumps and a Donkey Engine of 20-horse power, for pumping the worts up from the Mash Tun into the Coolers, and here also is placed the Underback, which holds 4,000 gallons.

We were next conducted to the Still House; it is a stone building 80 feet square, and contains a fine Coffey's Patent Still, with all the usual connections. On one side are two Wash Chargers, each holding 13,000 gallons, from whence the wash is pumped up to the Still. At a higher elevation, and near to the top of the Still, are two timber Worm tubs, oblong in shape and plentifully supplied with water; also a safe and sampling safe. On a lower gallery are placed the two Spirit Receivers, holding 2,276 and 2,285 gallons respectively, and the Ether Receiver holding 136 gallons. This last mentioned vessel receives the impure spirit thrown off in evaporation, whilst on the landing-stage above the Wash Charger are the hot and cold feints Receivers, the hot holding 1,000 and the cold 1,150 gallons; also a hot feints condenser and a large copper "oil-trap," which receives the feints and fusel oil thrown off from the Still, and separates them, the oil remaining behind and the feints being pumped up to the Still for rectification.

We next came to the Spirit Store, a conveniently arranged building underneath one of the Grain lofts. It contains two Vats, holding 4,578 and 4,988 gallons respectively. On the opposite side of the way is the draining tank fixed on the top of a lofty tower, under which the railway wagons run to receive the draff whilst the liquor is drained back into the Mash House. The draff is pumped direct from the Mash tuns to this tank, a distance of 500 yards.

Under the principal Tun Room is the patent Yeast House, where a large and remunerative business is carried on. Here the yeast from the fermenting backs is collected into three tanks. Afterwards these yeast skimmings are pumped into an accordion-shaped iron press—a German patent—containing twelve leaves or intersections, which are covered inside with linen cloth of various textures, forming separate divisions, through which the yeast is driven by great pressure. The dough-like material which exudes from the last intersection, is then collected and passed through a fine sieve, whilst the liquid expressed or squeezed therefrom runs into a tank. The yeast material left in the sieve, which looks like flour cakes, is afterwards weighed out in 7, 14, and 28 lbs., and pressed into conical bags and shipped off to England and Germany.

Adjoining the Mash House is the engine department, which contains a horizontal engine of 50-horse power; two others of 9-horse power; six steam-boilers, 20 feet long and 7 feet in diameter; and nine pumps, one of them being a three-throw pump, for pumping wash to the Still. Adjacent are the Stores and Cooperage, as also the stables, cartsheds and other buildings. Outside the gates and on the opposite side of the main road are two Bonded Warehouses, 150 feet long and 120 feet broad, containing 5,000 casks of whisky. At the side of these premises are two enormous tanks for spent wash. Here the liquor is drained off and pumped by an engine kept for the purpose to a higher tank, from which the farmers take it away. The dreg which remains behind is packed into bags and sold to the dairymen, and some of it is shipped to Ireland. The manager's house, formerly occupied by the distiller, is a picturesque place, with pretty gardens, &c., and adjoins the works. Of late many important additions have been made to the plant and buildings, including new malt Kilns, grain stores, and grain distributing machinery. The grain stores are on the "Bin" principle, and the machinery for filling and discharging them has been designed and constructed by Mr. R. G. Abercrombie, Alloa, who has brought the work to a very successful issue, notwithstanding the fact that the rather scattered positions of the various buildings (caused by peculiarities of the ground), necessitated a good many special contrivances, involving many novel details, in the various elevators, screws, and shoots. The distribution of the grain is done on the "gravitation" system, the elevators delivering it at a height from which it descends by gravity, through iron shoots to the various buildings, no screws being used except in conveying grain from the "Bins" to the elevators. Forty men are employed in the Distillery, and five excise officers, the supervisor being Mr. Wm. Ross.

The make is pure Grain Whisky, and is sold principally in Scotland. The annual output is 870,000 gallons.

No. 122.

St. Magdalene Distillery, Linlithgow.

PROPRIETORS, A. & J. DAWSON.

AS we left the Waverley Station for Linlithgow, we thought with regret that our pleasant sojourn in "dear old Edinburgh" would soon be over. The run of seventeen miles was accomplished in half an hour, and as the train steamed into the station we passed the extensive Distillery which was the object of our visit. On alighting, we found that we had an hour or two to spare before our appointment at the Distillery. Linlithgow is a dull, sleepy place, and it is difficult to believe that it is a royal burgh, and was once a seat of Royalty. It is, however, rich in splendid ruins and historic remains, which more than compensate for its dullness.

We proceeded to the Royal Palace, one of the most extensive and stately ruins in Scotland, standing on peninsular ground, and engirt by a pretty loch. One of our companions—an artist—being well acquainted with the Palace, proffered his services as guide, and gave us the history of this venerable place. It was the favourite residence of several kings, and the birthplace of Mary Queen of Scots. We were shown the room in which, on the 7th of December, 1542, she was born. As we passed through the banqueting-hall, state apartments, chapel, and suite of rooms once devoted to the use of the beautiful queen, we pictured to ourselves the stately processions of courtiers, noble ladies, and servitors, who daily trod these corridors and gave life and light to a place now so cold and dead.

We ascended one of the towers, from which the whole country round and the town beneath could be seen, but as the wind was high and the position dangerous, we quickly descended, and shortly afterwards left with regret this monument of a bygone age.

> "Thy vanished floors have bent to mailèd feet,
> Warm firelight slanted thro' those windows, blind;
> And thro' those chambers echoed voices sweet,
> Which now are haunted by the unhappy wind."

We then wended our way to the Distillery, to commence our inspection of that establishment. At one time there were as many as five distilleries in Linlithgow. One of the oldest was the Bulzion, which was in existence before the middle of the last century. Soon after, Mr. Dawson, who owned a Distillery in the Carse of Falkirk, erected another at Bonnytoun, Linlithgow. Shortly after this, and to oppose the Bulzion Distillery, one Sebastian Henderson feued the lands of St. Magdalene's Cross from the Countess of Dalhousie and built

St. Magdalene Distillery. Ultimately it was purchased by Mr. Dawson, who removed to it from Bonnytoun, and now the works are so extensive that they cover the site of both Distilleries. The works comprise nearly four acres, but the ground in connection therewith extends to other six acres, and they have a frontage to the railway of six hundred feet. The Distillery buildings are all enclosed and built with stone. They are entered from the Edinburgh Road by a large gateway, and at the back there is another gate, close to the wharf on the canal, which is only used for canal traffic. The picturesque old dwelling-house in front of the establishment, formerly the residence of one of the original proprietors, has been turned into offices, for the use of the partners, managers, head brewers and excise officers. On our arrival, Mr. Alexander Kerr, the courteous manager, took us in hand, and first of all directed our steps to the west Maltings, which are on the right-hand side of the entrance. These lofty buildings are 124 feet long, 75 feet broad, and five stories high. The top floor is used as a grain loft; under this there are two malting floors, and the first floor and basement are duty-free Warehouses. In the grain loft, at the time of our visit, there were about 4,000 quarters of barley. A gas engine of two-horse power supplies the motive power for hoisting the barley to this floor. An outside gangway on the level of the lower malting floor gives entrance to these departments. On the barley floor there is a Steep capable of wetting 130 quarters at one time, sunk in the floor, so that the workmen can tip the barley in without lifting it. It is supplied with water from a reservoir in a field on the south side of the canal, where the ground rises rapidly, and also, if desired, from a tank on the roof of the west Maltings; in fact, at pleasure, or if necessary, the water can be made to circulate round the works. The Kiln attached to these Maltings is 60 feet long by 37 feet wide, and is floored with wire cloth and heated by two furnaces; 1,300 bushels of malt can be dried off at a time. The fuel used is a mixture of peat and coke, in stated proportions. The peat is obtained from the moors above Falkirk and round Slammannan.

Our guide then conducted us to the east Maltings, on the left-hand side of the entrance. They are smaller than those already described, but the buildings are four stories in height and have two entrances, one near the canal and the other from the inner court. The large staircase at this point, owing to the sloping nature of the ground, is six stories in height, and the tank already referred to surmounts the roof. From the platform adjoining we had a glorious view of the surrounding country, which included Bonnytoun House and policies, the residence of the widow of the late Provost Dawson, one of the proprietors of the Distillery. But, to return to our subject, these Maltings are similar to those on the west side, having a grain loft and two malting floors, but only one duty-free warehouse underneath. In this loft there were 1,500 quarters of barley at the time of our visit, and the Steep is capable of wetting 85 quarters at one time. The Kiln is 37 feet by 36 feet, and is also floored with wire cloth, and dries off 850 bushels of malt at one time. From this Kiln the malt is conveyed to the deposit by a travelling belt. Notwithstanding the extent of the Maltings, they cannot keep pace with the mashing; so that it is necessary to keep on malting during the summer months in order to have a stock of malt—about 30,000 bushels—on hand at the commencement of the distilling season. At times they mash 3,600 bushels per week, but when we visited the Distillery they were mashing only 3,400. A third Kiln is only used for the drying of barley.

The Mill is situated near the entrance gateway, between the engine room and Mash House, and contains two malt rollers driven by steam. The pulverised malt is carried up by elevators to the upper flat, thence into bags to make up the various mashes or grists. The hopper over the Mash Tun is immediately adjoining, and the Malt Deposit is on the same floor.

Our guide then took us to the Mash House,—a clean, spacious, and lofty building, situated to the east of the Mill, which contains a Mash Tun 21 feet in diameter and 6 feet deep, possessing the double-acting stirring rakes, propelled by steam power. On one side of this building are metal heaters, which supply the Tun with hot water, whilst the Underback is below the surface of the floor. A centrifugal pump throws the worts therefrom to the coolers above, from whence they flow through a Morton's refrigerator into the Washbacks, or fermenting tuns, as they are called.

Adjoining the Mash House on an out-side iron gallery, over which the coolers already referred to form the roof, is a fine draining tank connected by pipes with the heaters, so built and arranged that carts can draw underneath to receive and take away the draff. In close proximity is a smaller tank similarly placed for retaining the washings of the vessels, and the draff so collected is also sold.

We then wended our way to the Tun Room or Back House, which contains 14 Washbacks, each with a capacity of 6,500 gallons; a donkey engine drives the switchers in these fermenting vessels, and is also used for pumping water to the tank formerly mentioned. We next return to the brewing department and came to the Still House,—a building 60 feet by 27 feet and built of stone. The first vessel pointed out was the Wash Charger, placed at a high elevation to command the Stills, and capable of containing 9,000 gallons. Our attention was next directed to the five old Pot Stills as follows: two Wash Stills holding 3,500 and 4,881 gallons respectively; three Low Wines Stills, holding 1,500, 1,867, and 2,676 gallons respectively; also a Low Wines and Feints Charger, holding 3,000 gallons. There is an overshot water wheel in this house, which drives the stirring gear in the Wash Stills. We may here mention that the three Worm Tubs in connection with this important department are fixed on stone and brick seats in the courtyard outside.

We next passed from the Still House to the Ball room, as it is called, where are to be seen the Safe and sampling apparatus, a Low Wines Receiver, a Feints Receiver, and two Spirit Receivers. Here also is placed another donkey engine for pumping the wash, low wines, and feints and spirits to their different vessels. Following our leader we then crossed the yard to the Spirit Store, a neat building fitted up with casking appliances, and containing a Vat holding 2,300 gallons. From thence we proceeded to the Warehouses, which in this establishment are on a most extensive scale and cover a large space. There are nineteen in all, and as already indicated in our description of the Maltings, a number of them are on the west side and a number on the east. The west range contains eleven distinct Warehouses; the east range seven. Those in each range are all intercommunicating, so that only one entrance door is necessary—a great convenience to the Excise gentlemen, whose office is just outside the door of the west range. On the wall hangs an index board of the divisions and sub-divisions of the Warehouses, and a moveable indicator thereon shows the section where the warehouse-keepers are at work, so that they can be found at any time.

These Warehouses, although some of them are of two floors, are apparently on the ground floor, the building of which they form the basement being on the side of a hill. The tramways are very ingeniously arranged, and must be seen to be appreciated; they fit any size of cask, and the inclines are so gradual that they slide along with ease. There is some very old Whisky stored in these bonds; we saw a number of casks branded 1875 and 1877, and a few still older. Altogether there were 7,500 casks here, and each cask is registered in a book and can be found immediately when required. We must not omit to mention that another Bonded Warehouse has been recently built of enormous proportions on the other side of the railway; it is of brick, and has a slated roof and, we understand, it is about to be enlarged.

The racking Store is at one corner of the premises and is a neat building; contiguous is a large shed for storing casks, and a cooperage; also a joiner's and smith's shop, and peat sheds. For bringing in coal and coke the company have a wharf of their own on the Union Canal, which runs along at the back of the Distillery, and the railway is in front of the works.

All the arrangements for prevention of fire are very complete. Coils of hose are kept in different parts of the works ready for instant use. There is also a manual fire engine, and in the Mill there is a small hand engine, while buckets filled with water are distributed at various points. A trained brigade, who are exercised weekly, complete the arrangements.

The engine department consists of a handsome beam engine of 20-horse power, two donkey engines, and a steam boiler 20 feet long by 7 in diameter. Adjacent are the two chimney stacks, one of which is 120 feet high. There is an inexhaustible supply of water, consisting firstly of that drawn from the canal, used for condensing purposes, driving the water wheel, and for supplying steam; secondly, a noted spring; thirdly, an artesian well 300 feet deep, and a spring situated near the top of the hill, these two last being used for brewing purposes. Forty men are employed on the premises, and there are four Excise officers, the chief being Messrs. Allice and Macfarlane Robertson.

The Whisky is pure Malt. We were informed that the company make nearly 7,000 gallons per week, and the average annual output is 200,000 gallons, but it has been as high as 225,000 gallons. It is sold principally in England and Scotland.

"Of all the palaces so fair
Built for the Royal dwelling
In Scotland, far beyond compare
Linlithgow is excelling.
And in its park in jovial June
How sweet the merry linnet's tune,
How blithe the blackbird's lay!
The wild buck bells from ferny brake,
The coot dives merry on the lake;
The saddest heart might pleasure take
To see all nature gay."

"*Marmion.*"

No. 123.

Kirkliston Distillery, West Lothian.

PROPRIETORS, THE DISTILLERS' COMPANY, LIMITED.
REGISTERED OFFICE: 12, TORPHICHEN STREET, EDINBURGH.
MANAGING DIRECTOR OF THIS DISTILLERY, ROBERT STEWART.

TO reach this Distillery we took the early train from the Waverley Station, and in half-an-hour found ourselves at Kirkliston. It is a pretty village about eight miles from Edinburgh, situated on the river Almond, which flows by the Distillery before passing through Kirkliston. We paid a visit to the Church, which is said to be one of the oldest in Scotland. This historical edifice has been made classical by Sir Walter Scott, in his tale of "The Bride of Lammermoor"; here in the family vault of the Earls of Stair, lies interred the unfortunate Janet Dalrymple, the original of his Lucy Ashton.

From the higher ground of the churchyard we had a striking view of the surrounding country, embracing the estate of Newliston, with its pleasure grounds, formerly the property of the Earl of Stair. This demesne is quite a curiosity in its way, the Earl of Stair having arranged it in wooded groupings and clumps of trees, in resemblance of the army of the British troops on the eve of the battle of Dettingen. The shrubberies and trees are trimmed and kept as neat as were any of the soldiers in Queen Anne's Army. About two miles distant from the church is Niddry Castle, the asylum for a time of Mary Queen of Scots when fleeing from Lochleven Castle. In another direction can be seen the hill where King Edward rested his troops on his way to Bannockburn, and further on, the Fife coast, with the Ochil Hills in the background.

We then turned our steps towards the Distillery, situated at the foot of the hill just outside the village, and here caught sight of the river Almond. At a short distance above the works the river has high sloping banks and picturesque surroundings, but as it nears Kirkliston it becomes somewhat tame and uninteresting. This Distillery, which covers twelve acres of ground, was in existence at the end of the last century, and in 1825 was much enlarged and improved. The works were formerly the property of Messrs. John Stewart and Co., who purchased them in the year 1855 from Messrs. Buchan & Co. At that time the Distillery turned out about 2,000 gallons a week, but now, at a push, it has made 20,000 gallons in the same time. In 1878 it was acquired by the Distillers' Company, Limited, Mr. Stewart remaining Managing Director, assisted by his son, Mr. J. C. Stewart, who acts as his Sub-Manager. The water used in the Distillery is brought from two sources, Craigmaiellen and the Humbie burns, and is collected into two reservoirs above the works. One of them, the Humbie reservoir, covers eight acres, and the other, the Kirkliston, two acres.

There is a railway siding direct into the works, and the grain wagons are emptied at the door of the principal warehouse into a semi-circular iron tank. From this deposit it is sent by a double set of elevators to the different stores. The elevators are enclosed in box tunnels some three feet deep, and are carried over the roofs of the buildings and across the courtyards; during our progress through the works we never lost sight of these vehicles, which extend diagonally right across the Distillery.

Mr. Wilson, the works manager, directed us through the buildings, and we commenced our survey at the Maltings and Grain Stores. No. 1 is a stone building 240 feet long and two stories high; the ground floor, used for malting purposes, contains a steep 40 feet long and 10 feet wide, and has a large Kiln and Malt Store at the end; the top floor is used for Barley and Maize. Nos. 2

KIRKLISTON DISTILLERY, WEST END.

and 3 are similar buildings with the exception that they are not quite so large, and are commanded by a Kiln 30 feet square, floored with wire cloth and heated by peat in open *chauffeurs*.

We next crossed the courtyard to Nos. 4 and 5 Malt Barns with stone Steeps, each commanded by No. 3 Kiln which is similar to the others, but is 42 feet by 24 feet. No. 6 is a smaller and detached Malting, with a neat little Kiln, whilst Nos. 7 and 8 are very old-fashioned, and about half the size of Nos. 2 and 3.

We then retraced our steps and came to the Brewing House, adjoining the Still House, wherein are five Brewing Tanks, each with a capacity of from 12 to 20 thousand gallons. Contiguous to this is the Mill building, which contains five pairs of stones; attached to this is the Grist Loft.

Our steps were next directed to No. 1 Mash House, which, besides the Mash-tun, contains a turbine wheel, for driving the Mill, of about 25-horse power. Thence to No. 2 Mash House, a fine building wherein are placed a Maize Mash-tun 24 feet in diameter and 8 feet deep, and the No. 2 Underback, which is sunk below the level of the Mash tun. The Worts Receiver is placed on the side of No. 3 Kiln, which is on a high elevation, and from which the Worts run a great distance through copper pipes placed in the bed of the mill lead, thus reducing them to the proper temperature for fermentation.

We then entered the Tun-rooms, two fine apartments containing 14 Wash-backs, averaging 18,000 gallons each. In a recess over No. 6 Washback are two of Miller's Refrigerators. At a short distance are also three Wash Chargers with a capacity of 41,880, 16,700 and 1,678 gallons respectively.

KIRKLISTON DISTILLERY, EAST END.

Communicating with this building by an elevated bridge across the roadway is a new building called the Draff and Dreg House. On the top floor is placed a large circular tank holding 22,000 gallons through the bottom of which the Draff, or grain refuse, is dropped into carts or waggons below.

Some years ago the greater part of this refuse used to flow into the river Almond, but Mr. Stewart, desirous to avoid polluting the stream, built two very large storage tanks into which it now runs. It is there allowed to settle, and the liquid portion is pumped to the sea at South Queensferry, through a pipe which runs along the North British Railway branch line to Queensferry, and for which permission was obtained by Act of Parliament. The solid matter is sold for feeding stock, and is found to be very good for cattle and pigs. A large number of the latter are kept at the Distillery—between four and five hundred—and the Company have taken first prizes at the Highland Society's and other large Agricultural Shows in Scotland. They have at present a very fine breed of Berkshires.

Recrossing the road the Still House next claimed our attention. It is a splendid building 40 feet high and 80 feet square, with a division down the centre. At the entrance to the first compartment is the No. 1 Maize Mash-tun, and a little further on the No. 3 Maize Mash-tun, close to which is a huge enclosed water-wheel, supplied from the reservoirs on the hill, for pumping water, feints, and spirits. The Running Safe is here for the Malt Whisky, also four Feints, and four Spirit receivers. The second division contains six Pot Stills, holding 5,600, 8,000, 2,740, 1,861, 1,550, and 1,800 gallons respectively; six sets of three-throw pumps for pumping Wash, Feints, &c.; a little wash pump engine, and six sets of Willison's Upright Condensers, and a Worm Tub of a most primitive pattern.

The Low Wines and Feints Chargers are in this building, and in a brick recess we saw three peculiar vessels connected with the Coffey's Patent Still; they are cylindrical shaped vessels and are used, one for hot Feints, and the other two for extracting fusel oil. The patent Still House is a lofty building and adjoins the Pot Still department. It contains a powerful Coffey's Patent Still capable of distilling 3,500 gallons of wash per hour.

We then crossed the road and came to the duty-paid Racking Store, a neat brick building wherein are three Vats holding 649, 869, and 2,004 gallons respectively; adjoining this is the Spirit Store, wherein are two Vats, containing 9,640 and 9,651 gallons respectively. At the head of this inner court is placed one of the two Excise Offices, the other being alongside the Works Manager's Office. There are six Excise Officers engaged on the premises, and Mr. Henderson is the supervisor.

The six huge Bonded Stores are fine buildings and are distributed about the works. They contained at the time of our visit 8,955 casks, containing a total of 800,781 gallons of Whisky, some of which was very old.

In the main roadway there is an extensive Cooperage, Joiners' Shops, Stables, Cart Sheds, and the new Dreg House before referred to. Here also is a stationary Fire Engine, with 15 Fire Plugs.

Around the central courtyard are grouped the following buildings: a Yeast House, Engineers' and Fitters' Shop, Store Room, Gas House, Brewer's Office, and the Engine and Boiler House. There are 13 Engines, one of 80, one of 35, ten of 10 each, and one of 6-horse power. There are six Boilers 30 feet long by 7 feet in diameter.

On the hill overlooking the works there is a pretty brick-built residence for the Works Manager. The ancient and picturesque residence of a former proprietor stands in a pretty old-fashioned garden; it has now been turned into Clerks' and Directors' Offices.

The Company own large Stores and Warehouses at Queensferry, distant about three miles. They occupy about two acres, and the Bottling Stores about one acre of ground. The stock of Spirits in these Warehouses is about 200,000 gallons.

The Whisky made in the Kirkliston Distillery is both Malt and Grain, and has a good reputation in the market. The annual output is 700,000 gallons

No. 124.

Glenmavis Distillery, Bathgate, Linlithgowshire.

PROPRIETOR, JOHN MCNAB.

WE made an early start on Saturday morning for Bathgate. It is a thriving town, about twenty miles from Edinburgh, with a population of about 4,000 inhabitants. The church is a fine structure and is of some historic interest, Malcolm IV. presented it, with the surrounding lands, to the monks of Holyrood. The town also lays claim to considerable antiquity. It was given by Robert Bruce to "Walter," the celebrated high sheriff of Scotland, as the dowry of his daughter, Lady Margery. Walter himself died here. Glenmavis Distillery is built at the foot of the little glen, from whence it derives its name, and is adjacent to the beautiful grounds of Balbardie. From any point, the views of the surrounding country are most charming and English-like in their undulations. Above the works the Burn ripples through a little wooded valley, and the plantations extend close to the back of the Distillery. At the time of our visit, the water was falling in such abundance through the conduit, that the overflow formed several miniature waterfalls in its descent to the water-wheel.

Glenmavis is a picturesque and delightfully old-fashioned Distillery. It was founded about the year 1800, and in 1831 came into the occupation of the present proprietor. It is one mile from the railway station, and covers about three acres of ground. At a little elevation on the right is the pretty residence of the Distiller, standing in its own grounds which abut on the Distillery property. The establishment is built in three sections, the central and principal range being the Still House, Mill, Mash House, and Tun Room, all built on the slope of the hill.

We were first conducted to the Barley Lofts, consisting of the two top floors of a three-decker building, 80 feet long and 24 feet wide, the bottom being the Malting Floor, and concreted, with the usual Steep. There are also other four Barley Lofts, a large malting and a Bonded Warehouse in the town of Bathgate. Through a doorway we passed into the Malt Deposit, an apartment 20 feet square, to which is attached the Kiln, a solid stone building 28 feet square, floored with wire cloth and heated by furnaces. Our guide next led the way to the Mill, at the other end of the buildings, half way up the hill.

The dry malt is carted up to the Malt Deposit, which is on the top floor of the mill building, and to reach which we had to climb a rustic outside staircase. Here the malt is dropped through a Hopper into the Mill below, containing a pair of stones and a set of malt rollers. The ground malt is sent by elevators direct into the Hopper over the Mash-tun, in the adjoining house, a very old-fashioned building, which contains two heaters, copper vessels, heated by steam, holding respectively 3,300 and 3,900 gallons; a circular Mash-tun, 16 feet in diameter and 6 feet deep, with the usual double acting stirring rakes, also the No. 1 Underback, which consists of a shallow open tank 25 feet square, where the worts are drained before running into No. 2 Underback, similarly constructed, of the same dimensions, and placed outside the building. The worts now run by gravitation into the large Fan Cooler, which covers the whole roof of the Tun Room, and from thence descend into the six Washbacks, which are made of timber, and hold 4,400 gallons each. The switching-rods therein are turned by hand.

Through a doorway we descended some steps and found ourselves in a building some 70 feet square, the upper portion of which is devoted to the Wash Charger, &c., and the lower to a Cooperage. Here we observed several men neatly repairing and hooping casks, and others sweetening or purifying them, as it is highly necessary that they should be perfectly sweet before being filled with a delicate spirit like Malt Whisky.

Our intelligent guide, Mr. Joseph Halliday, who has been in the service of the Distiller upwards of thirty years, conducted us to the Still House, a lofty tower-like building. On one side is placed the Intermediate Charger, which commands the Still and holds 1,200 gallons. It receives the wash from the Charger, which is placed in the roof of the Cooperage. In close proximity to this vessel is the Hot Feints Charger, &c., over which, on a gallery some 20 feet high, are placed a Cold Feints Receiver, a Spirit Receiver, and a McNaughton's Refrigerator. But the central figure of all is a handsome Coffey's Patent Malt Still, erected in the year 1855, the first we had seen, which makes Malt Whisky at the rate of 2,000 gallons every twenty-two hours. In this Still there is no fusel oil, it being all absorbed in the manufacture, and helps not only to mature, but to preserve to the spirit the aroma of the malt.

We then retraced our steps to the higher part of the hill and were shown the Spirit Store, which contains a Spirit Vat, holding 2,011 gallons, in direct communication with the Still House. Here the spirit is racked into casks, weighed and branded by the Excise gentlemen, and sent into the different Warehouses. Following our guide we came to No. 1 Bond, which occupies the basement floor of the Distillery and Excise Offices, thence to three others at different parts of the premises. The whole of these Warehouses, including the one in the town, are capable of holding say 2,000 casks. At the time they contained 1,500 casks of whisky of various ages.

The Draff House, Sludge Tanks, and Yeast House, are under the Mash House and Tun Room. Mr. McNab has about 65 head of cattle, which are fed and fattened on the draff and spent wash.

Adjacent to the works are conveniently arranged cart-sheds, and stabling for seven horses. Sixteen persons are employed in the establishment, and there are usually three Excise Officers, the chief being Mr. Metcalf.

The water used for all purposes in the Distillery comes from the distant hills, and is collected into two reservoirs, one on the top of Castle Hill, the other at Sunnyside. There is also a burn running down Glenmavis. With the exception of the pumps in the Still House, all the motive power is water, driven by a overshot water-wheel.

The Whisky, which is pure Malt, is principally sold in Scotland and England, and shipped to many parts of the Colonies. The annual output is 80,000 gallons.

No. 125.

The Glen Kinchie Distillery, Pencaitland.

PROPRIETORS, GLEN KINCHIE DISTILLERY COMPANY, LIMITED.

IT was a "blast o' Januar' win" that greeted us as we started from the Balmoral Hotel, Edinburgh, to visit this Distillery. We have seen "the modern Athens" under every aspect, and in all kinds of weather, and we must confess to a preference for the summer time, although in its winter garb of ice and snow it is far more beautiful than any other city in the kingdom. But its winter winds are not to be forgotten; Princes Street with a strong north-easter blowing gaily down the broad valley catching one at every turn calls up memories none too pleasant.

We were a well-assorted company of three—Mr. Hannan, the principal partner of the Distillery; Gordon Fraser, an artist friend, and the writer, in a comfortable carriage, and as we drove along the Regent Road, past the Calton Hill on our left, with Holyrood and Arthur's Seat on our right, historic associations intermingled with our high spirits and prepared us for a thorough enjoyment of the bracing drive.

We passed through Piershill, otherwise known as Jock's Lodge, the chief cavalry depôt of Scotland, Portobello, the Brighton of Scotland, and Musselburgh, said by its natives to be the most ancient of Scottish burghs.

"Musselburgh was a burgh when Edinburgh was nane,
And Musselburgh 'll be a burgh when Edinburgh 's gaen."

Leaving Musselburgh we passed on our right the battle-field of Pinkie, on our left the Links, the seat of Edinburgh golfers and the head-quarters of Scotch horse-racing, and soon reached Tranent, immediately to the left of which is Prestonpans, where the famous battle was fought between Sir John Cope and Bonnie Prince Charlie, which nearly changed the current of British history. Hitherto our road had skirted the Firth of Forth, but now we turned to our right and struck up through the inland part of East Lothian, which county has been termed the agricultural garden of Scotland, and passing Winton Castle and Salton Hall, the latter the residence of the Fletcher family, descendants of the patriot Fletcher, author of the famous saying, "Give me to make the songs of a nation, and others may make its laws," and through Pencaitland, a pretty little village lying in a valley of the Tyne, we came upon the brow of the hill overlooking the Distillery, which is so closely hidden in the glen that we were almost upon it ere we saw it.

The Distillery is situated in the centre of the Glen of the Kinchie, a tributary of the river Tyne, from which it derives its name, in the midst of scenery which may not be wild and romantic, such as we have seen in the North, but nevertheless possessing a quiet beauty of its own.

Immediately to the south are the Lammermoor Hills, the highest point towering to about 2,000 feet, from the lower slopes of which a rich alluvial country stretches to the Firth of Forth, and it is entirely from this district that the barley for the Distillery is supplied. On both sides of the works the ground is freely interspersed with trees, which were covered with a fringe of snow, and gave a graceful beauty to the surroundings, wanting in wilder landscapes.

GLEN KINCHIE DISTILLERY FROM THE HILL.

The natural situation of this Distillery has been taken full advantage of by the proprietors. To the left of the entrance gate is one of the large Bonded Warehouses—of which there are two, the other being situated on the right of the gate—and at the back of this extending its entire length is the Barley Loft, immediately at the foot of the hill overhanging the Distillery, in which is stored the barley to be used in the manufacture of the whisky. On the top of this hill are placed two large Hoppers, into which the barley is emptied from the carts, and runs down shoots of about 100 feet in length to the Lofts, these are fitted with an overhead railway, fastened on beams, on which the carriers—large baskets suspended on wheels,—run along and carry the barley to any place required. This railway is continued to the

Steeps in the Malting House, a large two-storied building separated from the Barley Loft by a wide courtyard, across, on what may be termed, a suspension bridge, having on each side a reversed inclined plane. The carriers, filled with barley in the loft, are shot right across the courtyard to the Steeps, where they are emptied, and returned on the reverse plane to the Loft, to be again filled, and so on. The Malting Floors are also fitted with the same overhead railways, which convey the barley,—changed to malt by germination, to a large Elevator, which lifts and deposits it in the centre of a large Kiln with a wire-cloth floor, where it is properly dried, and then it is shot direct into the Malt Deposits which lie alongside on a lower level. At the end of the deposits is the Grinding Room, on the same level, and into this the grist, as the malt is now technically termed, is easily conveyed when required for grinding, previous to the mashing process.

The Mash House is attached to the Grinding Room, and the ground malt is lifted to the Grist Hopper by elevators, worked by an engine placed in the Grinding Room, from which it falls into the large Mash Tun, just below it, where it is stirred by rakes driven by an engine specially used for this purpose. After standing the necessary time the infusion is drawn off and passed over a Refrigerator alongside, into the Underback, from which it is lifted by a powerful steam-pump to the fermenting tuns in the Tun Room, where the process of fermentation goes on. When this is completed, the wash, as it is now called, is run into the Wash Charger, situated in the same room, and this supplies the Stills, of which there are two, of the kind known as Old Pot Stills, where by distillation, the wash is changed into whisky, and the process is completed; and at this point we saw what we had seen nowhere else,—after the spirit is extracted from the wash, there is a very large residue known as *dreg*, which in towns is very largely used for cattle-feeding purposes but in remote districts is practically useless, and requires to be disposed of in some way; it cannot be emptied into the stream, for the riparian proprietors would object, so it is lifted by a steam-pump to a tank 500 yards from the distillery, and 70 feet above it, and used by the neighbouring farmer to irrigate his fields, and he is highly pleased with the result.

It will be seen from our description that each part fits into the other, and that the arrangements are such that manual labour is reduced to a minimum. Every facility was afforded us to examine everything, and in addition to the perfectness of the general plan, we were much struck with the absolute cleanliness which prevailed.

The annual output of this distillery is about 76,000 gallons of fine Malt Whisky.

By the time our inspection was completed darkness had set in, so we could see nothing of the country through which we passed on our way home, which was by the inland route *viâ* Dalkeith. There was a heavy snowstorm, but as we were comfortable inside our carriage, it added zest to our enjoyment, and with the champagne air of the Highlands of the Lothians, conduced to a pleasant night's sleep, the fitting sequel to an interesting and enjoyable day.

No. 126.

Bladnoch Distillery, Wigtown.

PROPRIETOR, CHARLES McCLELLAND.

AT length the hour came when we were to quit Edinburgh ; a few toasts were drank to the hope of meeting again, and we took farewell of those kind friends with whom we had passed so many pleasant hours. It was at the railway station that we exchanged our last adieu, and as we looked back out of the carriage window we saw our friends waving us a prosperous journey.

> " Fareweel, Edinburgh, and a' your daughters fair ;
> Your Palace in the sheltered glen, your Castle in the air,
> Your rocky brows, your grassy knowes, and eke your mountain bauld ;
> Were I to tell your beauties a', my tale would ne'er be tauld.
>
> "Now, fareweel, Edinburgh, where happy we hae been ;
> Fareweel, Edinburgh, Caledonia's Queen ;
> Prosperity to Edinburgh in every risin' sun,
> And blessin's be on Edinburgh till time its race has run."
>
> *Author of " Caller Herrin."*

As we left the "Modern Athens" we felt regret that our pleasant tour was so near its end, and that in a few days (after we had visited the four Southern Distilleries) we should be leaving Bonnie Scotland, and travelling in less interesting places.

The carriage was too crowded for us to indulge long in these reflections, for we were a snugly dovetailed party, thirteen Christian souls occupying the space allotted to eight ; fortunately, good humour prevailed, and our discomfort only lasted the distance of three or four stations. The route traversed was through scenery as diversified as it is possible to imagine, sometimes pastoral, then wild, and at Dumfries, and for many miles beyond, it combined all the luxuriant beauty of the Lowlands with some of the grandeur of the Highlands. Thereafter the country became more rugged and desolate, nothing being seen but a vast expanse of moor, broken with rocks and boulders. It was night when we arrived at Wigtown, and after the weary journey of ten hours, we were glad to reach the hotel, and seek the rest and refreshment we so much needed.

On the following morning, before starting on our duties, we explored the town, which presents a fine appearance from the railway and sea, being perched on an eminence. Wigtown is well arranged, and contains a beautiful central square, laid out in flower gardens, tennis courts, and promenades. Strange to say, this burghal ornament, unique of its kind in Scotland, was once the refuse and dust heap of the town.

We took a carriage from the hotel and drove to Bladnoch, distant about a mile beyond the suburbs. The Distillery is situated at the head of the village, from which it takes its name, and on the banks of the river Bladnoch, which is here a fine stream. The Establishment consists of a square pile of buildings, erected round a court-yard, and was founded in the year 1817 by John and Thomas McClelland, father and uncle of the present proprietor. In 1878, the Distillery was enlarged and modernised, and now covers two acres of ground, and there are other 50 acres attached, which are farmed by the proprietor. The water used in the works comes from a mill-dam, which is supplied from the upper reaches of the river, and the overshot water wheel does all the driving power.

We first visited the Malting House, mostly a stone building, 118 feet long by 28 feet broad, with slated roof, the wood-work being painted red; it has three floors, the ground floor for malting, and the top stories for barley, each possessing a stone steep. There are besides, two other barns, 95 by 32 feet, similarly arranged. At the right and left angles of the court there are Kilns, both loaded by hoists, floored with perforated iron plates and heated with peats. On the top floor of the intermediate building there is a capital Malt Deposit on a level with the Kilns, and underneath it is the Mill and Grist Loft. Returning to the quadrangle, we next visited the Mash House, a well lighted building, 40 feet square, containing two heating coppers, holding together 5,700 gallons, and a Mash-tun 16 feet in diameter and $5\frac{1}{2}$ feet deep, with stirring gear. Sunk in the bed of the water-course is the Underback, holding 3,000 gallons, which is considered a good arrangement for cooling the Worts.

Ascending a few steps from the yard we reached the Back House, where are placed against the wall, six Washbacks, two of them holding 6,000 gallons, and four 3,500 gallons; also a Miller's Refrigerator, and the Wash Charger containing 3,500 gallons, to which the Worts are pumped by a centrifugal pump. Following our guide we next came to the Still House, the oldest part of the Establishment, and containing three Old Pot Stills, consisting of a Wash Still, 13,000 gallons, and two Low-wines Stills, each of 400 gallons content. After this we went to the Receiving Room, which contains three Low-wines and Feints Receivers, the Spirit Safe, and a Spirit Receiver holding 400 gallons. Outside there are three Worm-tubs fed from the river, and adjacent a Spirit Store, containing a vat holding 530 gallons, and the Excise and Distillery Offices. There are four Bonded Warehouses ranged round a second court-yard, holding 805 casks containing 80,700 gallons.

The peat shed is quite a handsome erection, being supported on iron columns, with slated roof. In the main courtyard there is a small cooperage and cask shed.

The make is pure Malt, and the annual output 51,000 gallons.

No. 127.

Annandale Distillery, Annan, Dumfriesshire.

PROPRIETORS, JOHN S. GARDNER & SON.

AFTER resting and refreshing ourselves at Dumfries, we resumed our journey southwards, and made our next stoppage at Annan, the capital of Annandale. It stands on the high road from Dumfries to Carlisle, is a royal burgh, and one of the cleanest and pleasantest towns we have seen in the Lowlands.

Annandale, from whence the distillery takes its name, is really the valley of the river Annan, commonly called the How of Annandale, and one of the most garden-like districts in Scotland. The soft bright landscape of luxuriant green, of clustering foliage, of rich verdant pastures, gives to this valley the appearance of English scenery. The river Annan, which rises in the Hartfell mountains, runs a course of thirty miles through this valley into the Solway Firth. We drove 1½ miles from the hotel to the Distillery, along a pretty country road, from which we diverged down a private carriage-way, crossing a bridge over the Annan Burn, and found ourselves at the gates of the works.

The Distillery is a short distance from the Annan, and is picturesquely situated, being embosomed by trees. It is built in a solid square, with a small central court, and entered by a pair of sliding gates. The firm derives its supply of water for distilling purposes from the Middleby Burn, high amongst the hills, which is the property of the town of Annan; but the water used for driving the turbine wheel, &c., comes from a swiftly-flowing stream above the works.

The Distillery was formerly in the occupation of Mr. George Donald, an excise officer, who built it in the year 1830, and resided there for forty years. In 1883, Mr. J. S. Gardner, of Liverpool, leased the property, cleared the buildings of all the old-fashioned machinery, and then re-arranged the whole place, putting in new plant, and all modern appliances used in distilling.

Mr. Gardner is the son of a former Mayor of Liverpool. At his father's death he retired from business with ample means, but, being a man of active mind and untiring industry all through life, he found he could not be happy without employment, and when the Distillery and property of Warmanbie were in the market, he leased them and found just the occupation to suit him.

We spent a pleasant afternoon on this little estate. Mr. Gardner himself was our guide, and conducted us first of all over the farm buildings at the back of the works, higher up on the slopes of the hill. It is quite a model farmstead, the cowsheds, piggeries, and stables being ranged round a square yard; and we saw upwards of twenty fine head of cattle almost ready for the butcher, and a considerable number of pigs, all fed from the draff or grains from the Distillery. Here also are superior stables for harness horses, carriage and harness house, &c.

On the hill just above the work is the residence of Mr. Gardner, standing in its own grounds, and in close proximity to the works. Passing into the Distillery, we were first taken to the Maltings for storing barley, and two withering floors underneath, with a steep at each end. These buildings are of solid stone.

The malt is raised by elevators to the Kiln at the end of the Maltings, which is floored with wire cloth and heated with peat. We next ascended a stair to the top story of the adjoining building, which forms the Mill Room, and contains a pair of malt rollers, underneath which is the Grist Loft—-a floor some five feet above the level of the Mash Tun, in the adjoining house. *En route* to the Mashing department, we passed two copper heating-tanks, with open furnaces facing the yard. A spout or enclosed wooden trough conveys the pulverized malt into the Mash Tun—a circular iron vessel, holding 3,200 gallons. The house in which it is placed is spacious, well-lighted, and of superior construction. The worts are drained off from the Tun, and the liquid is pumped into the Worts Receiver.

The Underback is, as usual, placed on the ground of this building. The Distillery proper is a large house, arranged on three terraces or steps on the side of the hill, all under one roof. The top terrace is devoted to the Washbacks—new vessels four in number, each holding 3,600 gallons. On the next terrace is placed the Wash Charger—a fine vessel holding 2,800 gallons, also the various Receivers, &c., and on the lowest floor are the Stills, all of the old pot kind.

In the Still House is placed the safe, where the running safe is exposed to view in a glass case, kept locked by the excise, and under certain conditions it can be tested. The spirit flows through this safe into the Receiver in the Still House, and from thence it is pumped into the spirit vat in the Spirit Store.

We noticed three old-fashioned worm tubs outside the Still House, and adjoining the latter building an engine-house, wherein is a capital little 12 h.p. engine to supplement the water power if necessary.

Opposite the Distillery, over the stream, are two bonded Warehouses.

The whisky is pure Malt, and the annual output is 28,000 gallons.

No. 128.

Langholm Distillery, Langholm.

PROPRIETOR, ARTHUR CONNELL.

ON leaving Annan we made for Carlisle, where we put up for a few days at the "Crown and Mitre," a noted old-fashioned hostelry, where we have always found good entertainment and reasonable charges.

Next day we set out for Langholm, passing through a fine stretch of country, which, when we reached Eskdale, became singularly beautiful. On either side, the hills rising from the banks of the Esk are richly wooded, and the noble river winds in and out among the slopes that close it in. Langholm is planted in one of the sweetest landscapes in Scotland; the old part of the town is on the east bank of the Esk, and the new part on the west.

In olden days it was famous for possessing an iron instrument called the Branks, made to fit upon the head of a shrewish female, and projecting a sharp spike into her mouth, effectually silencing the organ of speech. Husbands afflicted with scolding wives led them through the town thus decorated, and tradition affirms that this discipline never failed to effect a complete reformation. We drove first of all to the Langholm Distillery; Glentarras, the next object of our visit, being some miles further on.

Our way lay by the river-side through the recesses of the valley, and whether we looked up or down, new points of beauty continually revealed themselves.

The luxuriant woods, overlooked by romantic elevations, were crowned with every variety of colour, whilst the river presented new features of interest at every turn of the road; at one time we would see it careering amid rocks and stones, at another gliding steadily along in its course to the sea.

"It seems like Eden's angel-peopled vale,
So bright the skies, so soft the river's flow;
Such music floats upon the scented gale;
The very air seems sleepily to blow,
And choicest flowers enamel ev'ry dale."

The Distillery is built on a rock which projects into the River Esk, and from any point has an extremely picturesque appearance. It is built of solid masonry, and faces the high road, the waters of the river washing by its walls. Since its foundation, in 1765, few alterations have been made in the place, and it is easy of belief that Whisky was made therein before any of the present generation were born. The establishment has been in the hands of the present proprietor, Mr. Arthur Connell and his family, for upwards of sixty years, whilst the manager, Mr. Campbell, has been connected with it for more than that period.

On entering the Offices we were informed by the manager that there were neither Barns nor Malting Houses to visit, the malt being all supplied by Messrs. Bernard & Co., the eminent maltsters of Haddingtonshire. We first visited the Malt Store, a neat stone building, 50 feet square, situated nearly in the centre of the block, and, although possessing a gloomy interior, is a most suitable place for the purpose.

Underneath is the Mill, which contains a pair of Malt Rollers and machinery driven by water-power. We next inspected the Mashing and Still House combined, forming one building, an old-fashioned place with paved floor, all the vessels being quite in keeping with it. This house contains two heating Coppers for hot water, each holding 1,000 gallons, a Mash Tun, 13 feet in diameter and 5 feet deep, an Underback of similar dimensions, and on the distilling side a Henderson and Turnbull's Refrigerator. Passing through a doorway we came to the Tun Room, which contains several timber Washbacks, and a Wash Charger, holding 8,000 gallons.

Retracing our steps to the Still House, we observed three old Pot Stills, of ancient type, consisting of a Wash Still, holding 1,800 gallons, and two Spirit Stills, containing respectively 586 and 316 gallons. On our way to the Receiver Department we passed a small cooperage and cask shed, and then came to a rocky projection over the river, from whence we had a complete view of the water arrangements in the Distillery, and besides, the view embraced a part of the town of Langholm and the wooded banks of the river opposite, which presented an array of tints and shades in green and brown that would have delighted the heart of a painter, and given him a lesson in colouring not easily forgotten. This department contains a Low-wines and Feints Charger, Spirit Receiver, and Safe. Across the way is the Spirit Store, another quaint building, which has a Vat, of 998 gallons content. Following Mr. Campbell, we proceeded to inspect a few of the twenty Warehouses, which contained at the time of our visit 121,300 gallons of Whisky, dating from 1876.

The three Worm Tubs are built on stone piers over the river, the water being pumped up by a huge water-wheel. The motive power in the Distillery is entirely water, a portion of the river having been diverted through a channel cut out of the solid rock. The water used for brewing purposes is brought from a noted spring in Whitawell Hill, 1½ miles distant.

The make is pure Malt, and the aged Manager informed us that there is annually made a certain quantity of Birch Whisky, which his father taught him the secret of making. The Malt Whisky is used for blending, being somewhat rich and silent in flavour ; it is also sold as a self whisky, and disposed of principally in England. The annual output is 46,000 gallons.

No. 129.

Glentarras Distillery, Langholm.

PROPRIETORS, GLENTARRAS DISTILLERY COMPANY.

LEAVING the river Esk, and pursuing our way up the steep hill, which leads from the valley we soon find ourselves in the uplands, with a view of hill, valley, and river not easily described. As we drive along, a charming glimpse is afforded of the Distillery, peeping out from the clustering foliage looking quite picturesque in the distance, while far below runs the beautiful river Tarras looking like a band of dead gold along the course of the glen. From the high road we descend a steep path into the valley and diverge to the left alongside the river. Supreme quiet reigns in this lovely glen, only broken by the rippling river or the noise of the water wheel. There is a wealth of greenery all round and the rich copses stretch up to the very walls of the Distillery. As we jog along it is difficult to believe that with such surroundings, and in such a quiet retreat, we are in the immediate vicinity of a busy industry. When nearing the entrance to the works, the driver points out the Manager's residence, which is at the far end of the property. It is a picturesque cottage standing on a little island formed by two little rivulets, which entirely cut it off from the Distillery.

Glentarras was built in the year 1839, by Mr. J. Kennedy, a Scotchman, and in 1872 it came into the hands of the present Company.

The beautiful river Tarras runs in front of the works, and the whole of the Distillery was built from stones or boulders taken from its rocky bed. The establishment consists of a long row of buildings with a projection at one end, and with the workmen's cottages and manager's house covers some four acres of ground. The nearest passenger station is Langholm, four miles distant, but the Company have a siding on the line about a mile distant. The water used in the Distillery, is the Gaulsike water, which falls over the windstone rock and runs by a conduit through a ravine in the rocks behind the Distillery.

Mr. Joseph Twentyman, the manager, conducted us through the place, and first led the way to the Maltings and Granaries, a three storied building, 219 feet by 38 wide, the top being used for the storage of the barley, the middle floor for malting, with the usual steep, and the bottom floor as a bonded warehouse. Adjoining are two Kilns, floored with wire cloth, whilst beyond is a malt store and the mill, the latter containing a pair of malt rollers. We now returned to the open space in front of the river and came to the Mash-house, at the end of which is a steam boiler 20 feet long and 5½ feet in diameter, which supplies hot water to the two heating coppers, each of which holds 6,000 gallons. On a terrace of this building is placed a Mash Tun, 17 feet in diameter and 6½ feet deep. Immediately underneath, and by a clever arrangement, is the Draff House, so arranged that by lifting the sluices the grains fall direct into the farmers' carts beneath. We now passed along a stone passage on a lower level and came to the Underback, an open vessel, 27 feet long and 8 feet wide holding 2,300 gallons. Our guide now led the way across a plank bridge to the cooling and water wheel house, where is to be seen a Miller's Refrigerator, through which the worts run to the jack-back, a square iron vessel holding 2,000 gallons, at the side of which is the overshot water wheel 20 feet in diameter. In this apartment we noticed also a large timber Receiver, which collects all the spent wash in the place. We now take a few steps up the hill and come to the Tun Room, a lofty apartment, 68 feet long by 38 broad, solely used for fermenting operations, wherein are eight Wash-Backs, each holding 8,000 gallons. On the wall there is a rotary pump driven by the water wheel, which pumps the wash to the Charger. We now climb a few more steps to a house used for the Wash Charger and its basement for a cooperage. The Wash Charger, which holds 14,000 gallons, is an unusually tall vessel, rearing its head high up into the roof, whilst at its base are strewn casks in every stage of cleansing, purification and reparation. From this point we begin to descend the hill again, and on entering a doorway find ourselves at the top of the Still House, and looking down upon the heads of the four Pot Stills, a wash holding 5,440, spirit 1,225, do. 600, and a feints Still 1,000 gallons. On the next landing below us is placed the low wines and feints Receiver holding 1,200 gallons, and at the bottom of the stair two other receivers of a similar capacity, the safe and the spirit Receiver holding 1,000 gallons. Here also is a smaller water wheel, which drives the chains in the Stills. The manager now conducted us across a gangway to the Worm Tub, 50 feet deep, which, though apparently in the Still House, is let into an excavation in the side of the rock which overtops the Distillery. Descending the hill to the river side we come to the six large bonded Warehouses, which are thoroughly ventilated and very dry. They contained 200,000 gallons of Whisky at the time of our visit. The Spirit Store is conveniently arranged for these Warehouses, and close by the Excise offices.

Within a few yards there is a row of workmen's cottages, and residences for the Excise gentlemen.

The Whisky is highly and richly flavored Malt, and sold principally in London.

The annual output is 75,000 gallons.

After quaffing a glass of the ten-year old product of Glentarras, we bade adieu to Mr. Twentyman, and commenced our journey homewards. On reaching Carlisle, we found, much to our delight, that arrangements had been made for us to proceed to Dublin, *viâ* Greenock, before visiting Liverpool, as we had intended; so bidding good-bye to our friends, we started by the next train, full of anticipation and ready for new experiences in the Emerald Isle.

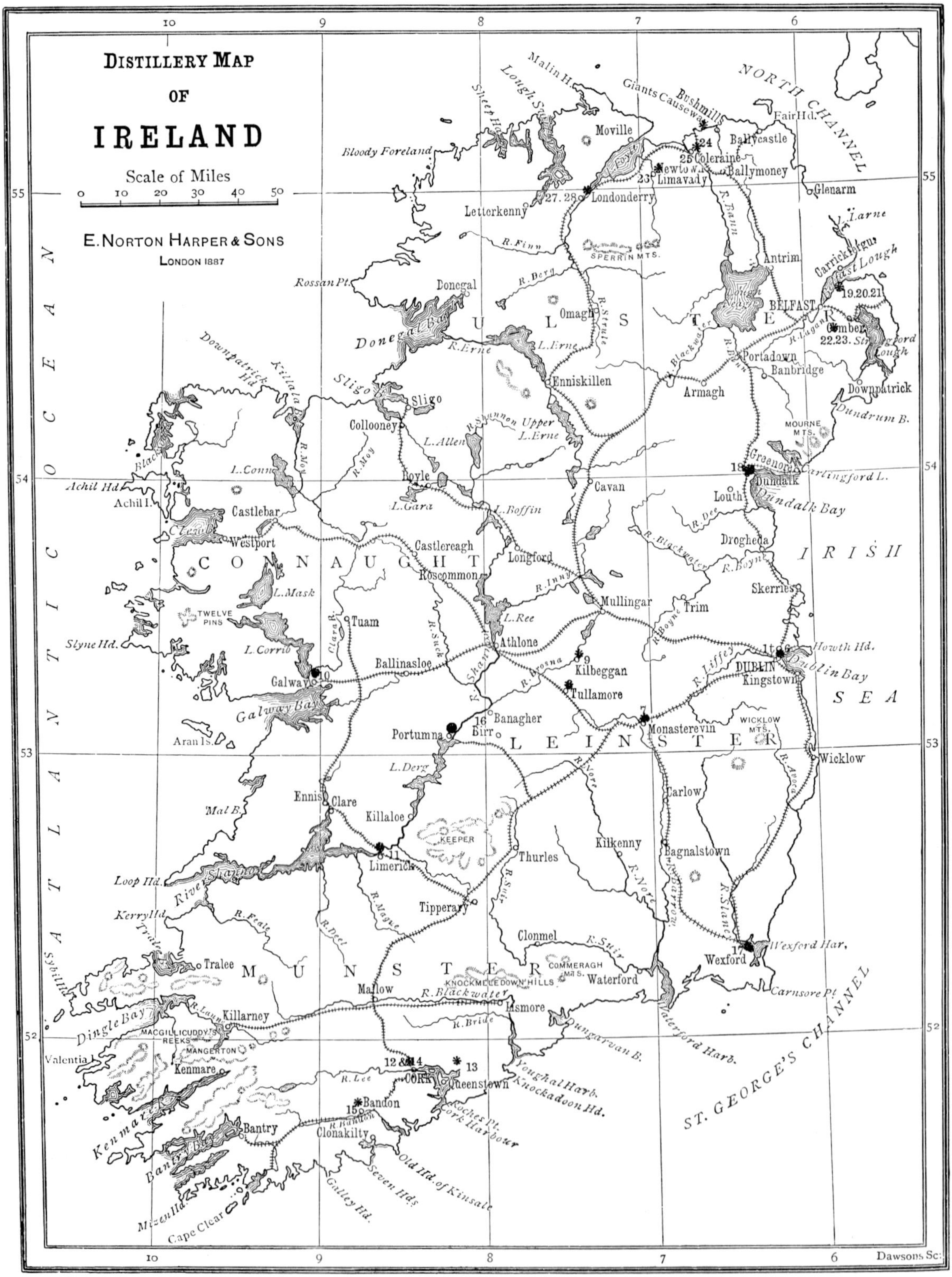
DISTILLERY MAP
OF
IRELAND
Scale of Miles
0 10 20 30 40 50
E. NORTON HARPER & SONS
LONDON 1887
NORTH CHANNEL
ATLANTIC OCEAN
IRISH SEA
ST. GEORGE'S CHANNEL
ULSTER
CONNAUGHT
LEINSTER
MUNSTER
Malin H.
Giants Causeway
Bushmills
Fair Hd.
Ballycastle
Moville
Bloody Foreland
24
25 Coleraine
Ballymoney
23 Limavady
Glenarm
27.28 Londonderry
Letterkenny
L. Larne
R. Finn
SPERRIN MTS.
Antrim
Carrickfergus
19.20.21
Rossan Pt.
Donegal
Omagh
BELFAST
Comber
22.23.
Donegal Bay
R. Erne
L. Erne
Portadown
Banbridge
Downpatrick Hd.
Killala B.
Sligo
Enniskillen
Armagh
Downpatrick
Collooney
L. Allen
Upper L. Erne
Dundrum B.
MOURNE MTS.
L. Conn
Boyle
18
Greenore
Dundalk
Carlingford L.
Achil Hd.
Achil I.
Castlebar
L. Gara
Cavan
L. Boffin
Louth
Dundalk Bay
Westport
Castlereagh
Longford
Drogheda
Roscommon
Skerries
L. Mask
Mullingar
TWELVE PINS
Tuam
L. Ree
Trim
Slyne Hd.
L. Corrib
Athlone
9
Kilbeggan
Howth Hd.
1
6
DUBLIN
Kingstown
Dublin Bay
10
Galway
Ballinasloe
Tullamore
Galway Bay
7
Monasterevin
WICKLOW MTS.
16 Banagher
Birr
Portumna
Aran Is.
Wicklow
L. Derg
Carlow
Mal B.
Ennis
Clare
Killaloe
KEEPER
Kilkenny
Bagnalstown
Thurles
11
Limerick
Loop Hd.
River Shannon
Tipperary
Kerry Hd.
R. Feale
Clonmel
R. Suir
17
Wexford
Wexford Har.
Tralee
COMMERAGH MTS.
KNOCKMELEDOWN HILLS
Waterford
Mallow
R. Blackwater
Lismore
Carnsore Pt.
Killarney
Dingle Bay
MACGILLICUDDY'S REEKS
MANGERTON
Valentia I.
Dungarvan B.
Waterford Harb.
12 & 14
13
CORK
Queenstown
Kenmare
Youghal Harb.
Knockadoon Hd.
R. Lee
15
Bandon
Roches Pt.
Cork Harbour
Bantry
Clonakilty
Kenmare
Bantry B.
Old Hd. of Kinsale
Seven Hds.
Galley Hd.
Mizen Hd.
Cape Clear
Dawsons Sc.

INDEX TO DISTILLERIES ON MAP OF IRELAND.

No. on Map.	NAME OF DISTILLERY.	WHERE SITUATED.	NAME OF PROPRIETORS.	No. of Page.
1	BOW STREET ...	*Dublin*	JOHN JAMESON & SON	353
2	JOHN'S LANE ...	,, ...	SIR JOHN POWER & SON	357
3	THOMAS STREET	,, ...	GEORGE ROE & CO., LIMITED ...	365
4	MARROWBONE LANE	,, ...	WM. JAMESON & CO.	369
5	JONES ROAD ...	,, ...	THE DUBLIN WHISKY DISTILLERY COMPANY, LIMITED	375
6	PHŒNIX PARK ...	,, ...	THE DISTILLERS' COMPANY, LIMITED	379
7	MONASTEREVAN	*Monasterevan* ...	CASSIDY & CO.	383
8	TULLAMORE ...	*Tullamore*	BERNARD DALY	387
9	BRUSNA	*Kilbeggan*	JOHN LOCKE & CO.	391
10	NUN'S ISLAND ...	*Galway*	H. S. PERSEE	395
11	LIMERICK	*Limerick*	ARCHIBALD WALKER	399
12	NORTH MALL ...	*Cork*	THE CORK DISTILLERIES' CO., LIMTD.	405
13	MIDLETON ...	*Midleton*	,, ,, ,, ,, ,,	409
14	GLEN	*Cork*	THE GLEN DISTILLERY COMPANY ...	412
15	BANDON	*Bandon*	ALLMAN & CO.	415
16	BIRR	*Parsonstown* ...	W. & J. WALLACE	419
17	BISHOP'S WATER	*Wexford*	NICHOLAS DEVEREUX & CO.	420
18	DUNDALK	*Dundalk*	MALCOLM BROWN & CO.	423
19	ROYAL IRISH DISTILLERIES	*Belfast*	DUNVILLE & CO., LIMITED	426
20	THE IRISH DISTILLERIES	,, ...	THE IRISH DISTILLERIES, LIMITED	428
21	AVONIEL	,, ...	WILLIAM HIGGINS	430
22	COMBER, UPPER	*Comber*	COMBER DISTILLERIES' COMPANY ...	430
23	COMBER, LOWER	,, ...	,, ,, ,, ...	431
24	BUSHMILLS ...	*Bushmills*	THE BUSHMILLS OLD DISTILLERY COMPANY, LIMITED	432
25	COLERAINE ...	*Coleraine*	R. A. TAYLOR	434
26	LIMAVADY... ...	*Limavady*	YOUNG, KING & CO., LIMITED ...	438
27	ABBEY STREET ...	*Londonderry* ...	A. A. WATT	440
28	WATERSIDE ...	,, ...	,, ...	442

BOW STREET DISTILLERY, DUBLIN.

No. 1.

Bow Street Distillery, Dublin.

PROPRIETORS, JOHN JAMESON & SON.

WE left Glasgow on our voyage to Dublin in somewhat boisterous weather, and were agreeably surprised on reaching Greenock to find the sea calm and the atmosphere clear. As we steamed slowly from the landing stage, the rays of the setting sun illumined the hills, giving to the banks of the Clyde a more than usually striking appearance. On nearing the sea, our voyage became still more interesting and pleasant, the clearness of the night enabling us to see with great distinctness the various islands and bold headlands of the coast, which during our course were successively passed. As soon as the outline of these had faded away, the twilight melted and blended into the soft darkness of a summer's night, and we appeared to sail straight out into the horizon. Just before turning into our berths our boat shot past Ailsa Crag, a huge insular rock which rises in mid-ocean, and is literally covered during the summer months with Solan geese and other sea birds. This mass of trap-rock has an altitude of 1100 feet from sea level to its apex, and is tenanted by goats and rabbits. It is accessible on the north-east side, and then only in very favourable weather. We had an excellent passage without the usual discomforts of a night journey, and by 5 o'clock the next morning were on deck again, watching the shadows as they fled away at the approach of the sun.

It was indeed a lovely sight that greeted us as we steamed into the bay; stretched out before us, as far as the eye could reach, were the Dublin Mountains, whose verdant slopes were covered with a mottling of gold and silver, cast by the rays of the brilliant morning sun. Nearing the shore we could distinguish at the base of the hills, villages and gardens of rich foliage, all lying commingled together, making up a picture that it would be difficult to describe. On the sea, the waves, which sparkled in the sunlight, were just sufficiently agitated to make the movement of the vessel enjoyable, and the ocean was here and there dotted with white sails flitting across its surface, all helping to complete the harmony of the scene.

Soon after passing the Hill of Howth, on which there is a splendid lighthouse, we entered the River Liffey, and found ourselves rapidly approaching the Irish Capital. On arrival at the North Wall we disembarked, when we beheld a sight which caused us much merriment. Jaunting cars rattled up to the wharf one after the other, their drivers arrayed in an assortment of garments from every old clothes shop in the kingdom. Corpulent men with garments so small that no efforts could bring together, and thin men with attire so large, that two or three could be embraced in their covering. These "jehus" are as sharp as needles; we were amused to see their quickness in singling out new comers with soft hearts, offering to drive them to all sorts of distant places for the smallest of fares. We secured one of the best of the shabby looking cars, and although the horse was somewhat gone in the legs, he rattled us along so fast that some of us had to hold on to the straps, to prevent being pitched into the dusty street, and we were quite thankful to reach the Gresham Hotel and dismiss our vehicle. Before we left the "Charmin' City" we got quite attached to these rollicking drivers, and preferred outside cars to any other mode of conveyance. We were up betimes the next morning, and once more tried our luck on an outside car. After driving through the principal streets, and taking a peep at some of the public buildings, we turned our horse's head towards Bow Street Distillery, visiting on our way the celebrated church of St. Michan's, which is in close proximity to Messrs. John Jameson & Son's Establishment. In olden times this district was a pleasant suburb, and St. Michan's one of the few churches on the north side of the Liffey. Close by this classic edifice dwelt for some time the great Handel, and it was upon the organ at St. Michan's that he first played the oratorio of "The Messiah." After inspecting the Church we directed our steps to the vaults. For ages travellers like ourselves have visited them, to be assured by ocular demonstration that their hidden wonders actually exist. We descended from the churchyard by some stone steps, at the bottom of which we found ourselves in a subterraneous passage, on both sides of which are stone recesses of various dimensions, containing many hundreds of bodies.

These vaults have for centuries been a subject of curiosity and philosophic research on account of the extraordinary antiseptic power they possess; bodies deposited there many hundred years ago are still in such a state of preservation that their features are easily discernible, and the bones and skin, which are of a dark colour, are quite perfect. We noticed that the coffins had in most cases mouldered away, and there was not the least smell discernible either from the old bodies, or those more recently entombed. The walls, roof, and atmosphere of these vaults are perfectly dry, the floor is always carpeted with a thick covering of dust, and the ceiling festooned with heavy curtain-like cobwebs, which it is believed receive and absorb the moisture as it ascends from the bodies; in addition, the walls and floor are composed of a stone said to be peculiar for its resistance of moisture. In some of the recesses, the bodies, which are all at full length, are placed one upon another almost to the roof, like so many piles of merchandise, in others, strewed on the floor. It did not seem like death to us, and the scene lacked the awful solitariness of the grave. One of our party raised the arms and legs of a body on which the flesh still clung; we were also shown the skull of a man who had been beheaded, its eyes covered with the piece of crape used at his execution. The open mouth of another body disclosed a false tooth attached to the others by a band of gold, which shone as brightly as on the day it was affixed. In one vault we saw the remains of a person who died at the advanced age of one hundred and eleven years, and the body, which has rested in this mansion of death for a century, is as completely preserved as though it had been embalmed, although not a remnant of the coffin now remains. Here also are two other bodies in even a better state of preservation, which were deposited in the vaults a hundred and fifteen years ago. We also noticed that the floral wreaths on coffins placed during the past year were still in good condition. Having completed our inspection of these venerable relics of mortality we returned to the light of day, and resumed our journey to the Distillery, some 200 yards distant.

The Bow Street Distillery, which is one of the oldest in Ireland, having been established about the year 1780, covers upwards of five acres of ground, and is a quarter of a mile from the Four Courts, and about half a mile from Sackville Street, credited with being the broadest street in Europe. The water used in the Distillery is obtained from two deep wells on the premises, noted from time immemorial for its quality, purity and suitability for distillation purposes.

The works originally belonged to an aristocratic trio, consisting of an Honourable, a Baronet, and a General, and it was from these gentlemen that the grandfather of the present proprietors purchased the works at the beginning of this century. During the past forty years they have been considerably increased, and partly rebuilt, while nearly every department has been supplied with new and improved machinery. Passing under the archway, we found ourselves in an extensive oblong court, where a very busy scene presented itself—workmen were hurrying to and fro, carts laden with Whisky were leaving the Stores, and casks of all sizes were strewn about the place. It was with difficulty that we picked our way through it all and reached the offices, which consist of a spacious suite of apartments for the partners, Distillery clerks, and revenue officers. We were conducted over the extensive works by the Manager, and commenced our inspection at the Barley Stores and Maltings. The first building entered was a lofty four-story structure, each floor measuring 126 feet by 48 feet; the top used for barley, and the two underneath, which possess the usual steeps, are for malting purposes. Attached to these is a large Kiln, 48 feet by 60 feet; this lofty building is the very perfection of cleanliness, the walls being painted a light drab colour, and the pillars bright scarlet. It is heated by four furnaces, and the floor above is laid with perforated Chester tiles. Our guide informed us that at Drogheda Messrs. John Jameson & Son have other three large Maltings and two Kilns on a more extensive scale than these.

Resuming our inspection, we were next conducted through the ten large Corn Lofts, three of which measure 96 by 84 feet; three, 126 by 60 feet; three, 92 feet square; and one, 225 by 48 feet. From these Lofts we ascended a long flight of steps to the two Corn Kilns, painted in the same style, and with open roofs, as the Malt Kilns already described. One of them is 38 by 35 feet, the other 47 by 28 feet. The grain is raised to all the floors by means of a hoist, but the dried Barley is sent by elevators from the Kilns to the Mill. This latter next claimed our attention, and is quite a little work in itself, the building having been divided off into Machinery and Mill Room, Hopper and Grist Lofts, and four large Grist Rooms. The Mill contains the ponderous grinding machinery, and four pairs of millstones.

The process of making Irish Whisky now commences in heating four coppers, having attemporating coils, each holding 36,000 gallons of barley water and weak wort. Six shoots convey the grist to the two Mash Tuns, each measuring 36 feet in diameter and 8 feet deep, with revolving rake shafts. The false bottom of the Tun is first of all covered with hot liquor, and the grist descends gradually with the water until it is full. From this vessel the wort runs into the two Underbacks, large metal vessels 14 feet in diameter by 8 feet deep; from thence it is pumped to the coolers, of which there are four sets high up in the open air, two sets of Miller's patent horizontal refrigerators, and six boxes of vertical copper pipes in iron cases 4 feet square and 13 feet deep.

The grains are pumped into large tanks, shot into a grain hole, and disposed of to farmers and dairymen ; the spent wash is also sold to these people after the spirit has been extracted from it.

On leaving the Mash House we entered the Tun Room, where there are ten Washbacks, clean wooden vessels, each holding 35,000 gallons ; afterwards to the Still House, one of the oldest buildings in the works, which contains the Wash Charger, Stills, and other vessels. When the brewing period is passed, the wash is conveyed into the Wash Charger, which has a capacity of 40,000 gallons, from here the wash descends by gravitation to the two Wash Stills, each holding 24,000 gallons. These Stills, in addition to fire, are heated by steam coils.

From these vessels the spirit, or low wines, ascends to the Worm Tubs (there are two, each fitted with two copper worms) through which the spirit passes, and thence through the Safe to the Low Wines Receiver. The Safe is 20 feet long, and most unique in its construction ; it was designed by Mr. Lockhart, the late Brewer in the establishment. From the Low Wines Receiver the vapour is pumped into the Low Wines Stills, which have a capacity of 14,500 and 13,000 gallons respectively. From here it ascends and descends as before to the Feints and Spirit Receiver, and from this vessel the spirit is pumped into one of the Vats (there are three, holding 17,000 gallons) there to be reduced as required, casked, weighed, branded, and sent to the Warehouses. The Feints are pumped back again into the Low Wines Still to be redistilled. All the Stills are Pot Stills, and were made by Messrs. Miller & Co. It may here be remarked that the Warehouses belonging to the Distillery usually contain about 25,000 casks of Whisky.

On the other side of the Still House is the Canpit Room, where there are five Receivers, two of them Low Wines, two Feints, and one Spirit. The Racking Store, a good substantial building, contains 6,000 gallons of duty-paid Whisky of various ages, for the convenience of customers.

On the Works are also to be found the following industries: a Smithy, Cooperage and Saw Mills, Engineers', Carpenters', Painters', and Coppersmiths' Shops. The firm make all their own carts and waggons, repair the machinery, and construct their own buildings. Every modern appliance of machinery is to be seen in active operation.

The Engine Department is an important one in this establishment. It contains two fine engines, one 35 and the other 16-horse power; four boilers 20 feet by 8 feet, 30 feet by 8 feet, 36 feet by 8 feet, and 38 feet by 8 feet diameter respectively; and in a building 94 feet square we noticed a vast store of coal ready for use, which, we were informed, amounted to 1,400 tons.

There are ten sets of three-throw metal pumps on the premises, and a fine handsome brass three-throw spirit pump.

Three hundred men are employed on the works, and it is a notable fact that the operatives are never turned away except for misconduct. We noticed many hale and hearty old men ; one old veteran was over eighty-six years of age.

The Chimney Stack is a fine structure. It was built in the year in which the Queen was born.

On the works are comfortable quarters for the managers and subordinates, and capital offices for carrying on the business of the Distillery and the Excise. There are eight excise officers employed on the premises and at the Warehouses.

The annual output of this famous Distillery is about 1,000,000 gallons.

No. 2.

John's Lane Distillery, Dublin.

PROPRIETORS, SIR JOHN POWER & SON.

OUR next day's expedition was to John's Lane Distillery, which is situated a short distance from Christchurch Cathedral. Soon after starting we had our first experience of an Irish shower, and received on our devoted heads some portion of the heavy libations poured on "Ould Ireland," which make her fields so marvellously green; they made us look ruefully blue. Fortunately it did not last long, and by the time we reached our destination the sun shone brightly. The Distillery, the subject of the following sketch, is a large work and reaches from Thomas Street to the Quay. It was founded upwards of a century ago by Mr. James Power, the great grandfather of the present proprietors, who owned the noted hostelry from which the mail coaches started for the north and west of the island.

In the year 1791 this hostelry was converted into a small Distillery, making about 6,000 gallons annually, its chief motive power being a horse mill. But it did not long remain at that small output. The founder was a man of energy and enterprise, and year by year, as his business increased, he continued to extend the Distillery. Since 1871 the whole place has been rebuilt in a handsome and modern style, and every known appliance in the art of distilling added thereto. The establishment now covers six-and-a-quarter acres of ground, and the offices, which abut on the busy thoroughfare of Thomas Street, form a neat and substantial frontage to it.

After making ourselves and the object of our visit known to Messrs. James and Thomas Power, the present partners, we were conducted upstairs to their private office and shown some relics and ancient documents relating to the founder of the Distillery, which greatly interested us. After inspecting these we were introduced to the Manager of the Works, who conducted us through the place and explained the *modus operandi* from the beginning. Passing through the lofty and spacious public offices, we crossed a paved court and entered the noble block of buildings devoted to the storage of grain. They are five stories high, well lighted, and measure 192 feet long by 100 feet broad; the front part of three of them being divided off into corn receiving rooms, each division measuring 85 feet by 45 feet. The barley is carted to the Distillery by the farmers, and lifted by hydraulic hoists to the receiving rooms. At the entrance to this department there is an enclosed office, with glass roof and sides, in which sits the corn-sampling clerk; a portion of each delivery is handed to him for comparison with the samples of the purchase, which hang in bags upon a frame on the wall. If the sample is not up to the mark he refuses delivery, and reports the fact

JOHN'S LANE DISTILLERY, DUBLIN.

through the telephone to the corn-buyer's office. So scrupulously particular is this firm as to quality, that all contracts are void if the delivery is not exact to sample. From the corn receiving department, the corn runs into the two patent cleaning machines placed at a lower level, which are of very clever contrivance, made by Vangelder and Apsiun, 1, Goree Piazza, Liverpool. The visitor would be surprised to see how every particle of foreign matter is eliminated from the corn. We saw pieces of metal, nails, buttons, bits of granite, and small seeds, which had been abstracted from the corn during the process; the small corn is also separated from the bulk, and is used for feeding young horses. From these machines the corn is dropped into a shoot on the ground floor, and sent from thence by elevators to the required lofts, where it is spread out on the floors 2 feet deep to become seasoned, and afterwards is sent through continuous screws to the different departments as required. We noticed that the elevators were all enclosed in cast metal frames, fixed in plates, so as to be easily removed if necessary, and not in timber as in most other places; this arrangement has the further advantage of being fire-proof. Ascending a series of open staircases which run through the floors of the five grain floors, we took stock of these spacious apartments. They are beautifully clean and well ventilated, and contained at the time of our visit 3,000 tons of grain. From this point we began in earnest to attend the death, burial, and resurrection of John Barleycorn. The first process of the manufacture of Whisky now begins, by the corn being sent from these floors to the two Kilns adjoining, whither we next bent our steps. These Kilns are indeed elegant buildings, each measuring 57 feet by 30 feet, with open groined roofs, lined with wood and stained oak, like small English parish churches, in fact far superior to many we have seen. Iron doors shut off these Kilns, which are heated by open furnaces, and floored with the patent perforated Worcester tiles. Retracing our steps to the ground floor, we next visited the Mill Room, a substantial and solid structure, which contains one of Turnbull's ponderous machines of from 60 to 70 tons weight, and seven pairs of mill stones, driven by a steam engine of 460-horse power, and grinding upwards of 1,500 barrels every twenty-four hours. The dried corn is sent to this building from the Kiln by elevators of the same kind as those before referred to. From the Mill the grist is elevated and passed through two large tubes across the yard to the meal loft. We found this loft a larger apartment than that generally used for the purpose, being 88 feet long, 35 feet wide, and 20 feet high.

REFRIGERATOR.

STILL HOUSE, JOHN'S LANE DISTILLERY.

Crossing a gangway over the yard, we stepped on to the top of the Brewing Coppers, which are protected by an iron floor screen, which runs along over the whole of them. These vessels are so large that they occupy a house to themselves, and all of them are heated by furnaces. Descending by an iron ladder, we reached the ground level and entered the Brewing House, which is under the Meal Loft. It contains two Mash-tuns, each 33 feet in diameter and 7½ feet deep, possessing the usual stirring gear, and each capable of mashing 35 tons daily. The false bottoms of these Mash-tuns are composed of perforated iron plates, 3 feet by 2 feet, each numbered and ingeniously arranged in order. The worts drain from this vessel into the Underback, from which receptacle one of Drysdale and Co.'s three-throw pumps sends them into the Worts Receiver, a handsome metal vessel, placed under cover, holding 25,000 gallons, from whence they flow through the Refrigerators into the Wash-backs. From the Brewing House we crossed the pathway to the Back House, a building of great height, 140 feet long by 44 feet broad, which adjoins the Still House. Entering the centre door we saw at a glance the proportions of the enormous Wash-backs ranged along its walls; they are circular timber vessels, eight in number, and each vessel holds 38,000 gallons. The platform is composed of ribbed wood, and kept as white and clean as a new pin. The wash is pumped from these backs to the Wash Charger, which is placed at an elevation in the Still House, and contains 34,000 gallons.

A noble-looking building is the Still House. It is 68 feet long, 66 feet wide, and 57 feet high, containing five Pot Stills, all kept as bright and clean as burnished gold; the wash flows by gravitation to the two Wash Stills, each holding 25,000 gallons, and said to be the largest Pot Stills ever made. The product from these stills called "Low Wines" is pumped up to the Low Wines and Feints Receiver and Charger, both of which hold 10,000 gallons each; passing from thence into the Low Wines Stills, each holding about 20,000 gallons, and afterwards to the Feints or Spirit Stills, each of the same capacity, where, by the various distillations, the spirit becomes perfected Whisky. At one end of this house there are five Spirit Receivers, each with an average capacity of 7,000 gallons.

On the north side of the yard, connected with the Still House, there are three circular wrought iron worm tubs, the only iron ones we have seen; they are 30 feet high and 20 feet in diameter, and contain a compilation of copper coils, ranging from 13 inches in diameter, in which the spirit is condensed. The Can Pit Room is opposite the Still House, and only separated by a narrow passage. In former days cans were placed in the pit underneath the Receivers to catch the spirit, hence the name of Can Pit. In this room we were shown the safe, a very handsome and elaborate instrument, 20 feet long, composed of solid mahogany and brass, the most ingeniously-arranged one we have ever seen; it was

THE SAMPLING SAFE.

designed by Mr. Henry Angus, the late distiller in this establishment. Following the progress of the Whisky, we next visited the Spirit Store, a lofty apartment, where there are three vats to receive it, of an average capacity of 3,500 gallons each. Here the spirit is reduced with water to an average strength of 25 over proof. It is then filled into casks, weighed, and taken account of by the excise, before being sent to the different Warehouses. Of these there are seventeen in the Distillery, which contained at the time of our visit, upwards of 12,000 casks. At the suggestion of our guide, we proceeded to visit these spacious bonds by way of the cask track, an incline tram rail, some 300 feet in length, on which the filled casks glide down to the Warehouses. The path opened into a long avenue of casks, waiting their turn to be deposited in the various bonds. Arriving at the end, a large opening appeared, and we were asked to step on a platform, when "hey, presto," we descended to the depths below, but not into darkness, as we expected, but to a well-lighted chamber, some 200 feet by 80 feet, filled with casks of Whisky of various ages.

This Warehouse consists of four floors, all equally well filled. On ascending to the ground level, we visited No. 12 Warehouse, which is 120 feet long by 80 feet, a dry and well-ventilated bond; the other fifteen we did not enter. The firm have splendid bonds at Westland Row and The City Markets; we drove down to see them both, and were amply repaid for the trouble.

The Warehouses at Westland Row occupy the basement or arches of the new station, and are over 500 feet long by upwards of 300 feet broad, from one central avenue numerous arches branch to the right, and all the casks are placed on the ground. There is a Warehouse Manager's Office at the entrance, and like the other bonds, it is connected by telephone with the Head office. We next visited the Warehouses underneath the New City Markets; they are 353 feet long and 226 feet wide, consisting of brick arches, supported on rolled iron beams, perfectly ventilated, and lighted by large area windows, lined with white enamel brick, and in addition to which fresh air is constantly introduced into the centre of the Warehouses, and diffused by shoots to every part, so that the temperature, both in summer and winter, is carefully arranged; we noticed thermometers on the walls of every division, which have the constant attention of the warehouse clerk in charge.

On returning to the Distillery, we proceeded to the Engine Department, at this establishment a special feature, one of the members of the firm being a practical engineer. The following is a brief description of same.

In No. 1 Engine Room there is a compound beam-engine, working a pressure of 80 lbs., and developing to 400 effective horse power; it was erected in 1879, by Turnbull, Grant and Jack, of Glasgow. No. 2 Engine Room is a handsome lofty apartment, with a polished floor, and contains a beautiful horizontal engine, by Courtney Stevens, of Dublin, which was exhibited in the Dublin Exhibition of 1882. No. 3 Engine Room contains a remarkable little ancient warrior, being an engine of upwards of forty years of age, and still doing its daily work with all the vigour of youth. It works day and night without stopping, except for cleaning purposes, and the proprietors say that they would not change it for the best engine in Ireland of the same power. No. 4 Engine Room contains a 30-horse power engine, used principally for the saw mills and the engineers' and fitters' shops.

Last, but not by any means the least, comes the No. 5 Engine House, lately erected, which is well worth a visit. It is built with Athy stock and

Staffordshire bricks, with chiselled granite base, granite window sills; the windows are 13 feet high and 5 feet wide, filled by one sheet of plate glass. Inside it is lined with enamelled bricks from floor to ceiling, and the interior of the roof with pitch pine, panelled. In the wall, set in granite, there is a splendid double-faced clock, visible day and night from inside and outside.

The engine bed consists of huge granite blocks, the bed itself costing £800. It would be impossible for us to describe the engine technically, so we therefore adopt the engineer's graphic description. "It is a compound beam engine of 250-horse power (manufactured by Messrs. Turnbull, Grant and Jack, of Glasgow), with box bed-frame and entablature, supported on six polished columns, having the cylinders attached to the walking beam on opposite side of the main centre. The high pressure cylinder is 22 inches diameter and 1 foot 9 inches stroke, fitted with an automatic cut-off valve-gear, regulating the speed of engine by the amount of cut off. The low-pressure cylinder is 26 inches diameter and 3 feet 6 inches stroke. Both are steam jacketed and fitted with pistons, having Jack's patent automatic packing, which gives both a vertical and side adjustment to the packing rings. The crank shaft, crank, connecting rod, and valve gear are all of wrought iron, and the walking beam, piston rods, and crank pin of Siemen's steel." The power for driving the Mash Tuns and Pump gear is transmitted by ropes direct from the crank shaft, which gives a very smooth and easy drive. All departments which this engine works are connected by electric bells, this being also the case with the other engines of this firm. At the end of the Engine Room there is a pit, about 30 feet deep and 6 feet by 9 feet wide, the bottom of which is floored with black and white encaustic tiles; this pit contains a Centrifugal Pump for pumping spent wash. This pump being below all other vessels in the concern, they can be emptied by it in case of accident to the other pumps. Following our guide, we next visited the Boiler House, where there are several Boilers, 35 feet long and 7 feet in diameter; afterwards to the Saw Mill, Carpenters', Engineers', Fitters', and Coppersmiths; Shops. The chimney stacks are 95 feet and 120 feet high respectively, and are of ornate design.

The model Stables, which attract many visitors who are fond of equine pursuits, next claimed our attention. They were built under the immediate superintendence of one of the partners, who is a noted breeder of shire horses. The Stall Stable is built of enamelled bricks and has an ornamental open roof, the sides of each stall being lined with close fibre matting and paved with blue Staffordshire bricks. From the lofts at the side are corn sluices running down to the manger, by touching a button one bait of corn only is delivered at a time. Adjoining these Stables is the Harness Room, containing the usual Weighing Machine and other appliances. On the other side are three loose Boxes, and across the court a Horse Hospital, or "Sick Boxes," built of enamelled bricks, same as the stables, and paved with blue Staffordshire bricks. The Coach House and other buildings complete this department.

The Offices before-mentioned are very complete, and combine Excise and Clerks' Offices, Waiting Rooms, Luncheon Hall, Sampling Room, private offices for each of the two partners, Telegraphic and Telephonic Rooms, Lavatories, &c.

There are twenty-five clerks and two hundred and fifty workmen employed on the premises. The water used in this Distillery is principally from the "Vartry," hereafter described in another chapter. Some of the old-fashioned customers of this firm still send with their orders two empty casks—one to be filled with whisky, and the other with water from a special tap on the premises, with which they reduce their whisky on its arrival at its destination, thus uniting once more the same natures so rudely separated by the Still!

The Distillery, altogether, is about as complete a work as it is possible to find anywhere; being built on a hill, and running down from the main street to the quay, it thus has the advantage of natural gravitation.

The annual output is 900,000 gallons. The chief Excise officers are Messrs. Jarr, Davy, Lees, Royston, and Smith.

On completing our tour of inspection over the Distillery, we accepted the hospitality of the partners, and did ample justice to a substantial luncheon. We had previously sampled the firm's make of 1885, which we thought good and most useful, either as a blending or single whisky. The old make, which we drank with our luncheon, was delicious, and finer than anything we had hitherto tasted. It was as perfect in flavour, and as pronounced in the ancient aroma of Irish Whisky so dear to the hearts of connoisseurs, as one could possibly desire, and we found a small flask of it very useful afterwards on our travels.

As the frontispiece to this volume, we give an etching of a curious old portrait of the founder of the firm, which hangs in the private room of the senior partner. It is quaintly and beautifully worked in coloured silks, the face being painted by hand on ivory. It is said to be an excellent likeness of this famous pioneer of the Irish Whisky trade, and our artist has succeeded in catching the portrait with true fidelity.

It may be interesting here to note that it was Sir John Power, the first Baronet, who laid the first stone of the O'Connell National Monument. We were shown the massive silver trowel with which he performed the ceremony, and upon which the following is engraved:—

"This Trowel was used by Sir John Power, Bart., of Roebuck, co. Dublin, 23rd Sept., 1854, on laying the first stone of the National Monument to the Liberator of Catholic Ireland—O'Connell.

"'His victory in a glorious strife
To feeling, faith, and freedom dear,
Cost not one patriotic life,
A wound, an outrage, or a tear.'

"Presented by the O'Connell Monument Committee."

No. 3.

Thomas Street Distillery, Dublin.

PROPRIETORS, GEORGE ROE & CO., LIMITED.

THIS Distillery is situated on the south side of the River Liffey, and nearly opposite the main buildings of Messrs. Guinness & Co.'s Brewery. The entrance to the establishment is most striking, and unlike any other Distilleries we have seen, reminding us of some of the chateaux in France, with their ivy-covered walls and flower beds. The locality in which it is situated is sacred to the memory of several Irish patriots, it having been the scene of many a battle and much strife, from the early time of the Danish occupation down to the rebellion of '98. It was in that year, and close to the Distillery, that Lord Edward Fitzgerald was arrested on a charge of high treason, shortly after an engagement with the red-coats, at which he was wounded, and soon afterwards died in prison.

Dublin is remarkable in that it contains two cathedrals—St. Patrick's and Christ Church, or the Blessed Trinity. Christ Church Cathedral was built A.D. 1038, by Sitricus, the son of Amlave, King of the Ostmen, of Dublin and Dunan, the first Ostman bishop, who was buried in the choir of the Cathedral at the right hand side of the altar, A.D. 1074. Christ Church, which stands in the centre of the city, was originally built on a range of arches, erected by the deans as stores for merchandise, and in those vaults St. Patrick first appealed to the inhabitants on behalf of the Christian religion. It was then called the Cathedral of the Holy Trinity, and was erected for secular canons; but in the year of our Lord 1163, those canons were changed for others from Flanders, by Lawrence O'Toole, archbishop of Dublin. Lawrence was the son of Maurice O'Toole, Prince of Imaly, and was consecrated in the Cathedral of Christ Church. The choir, steeple, and two chapels were all built at the joint expense of archbishop Lawrence, Richard Strongbow, and others. In 1283 the steeple, chapter house, and cloisters were destroyed by fire, together with one side of the street called Skinner's Row; but the citizens, with commendable piety, subscribed for the restoration of the Cathedral before their own houses were repaired. For centuries the Cathedral was the scene of many famous events. In 1395 four Irish Kings received the honour of knighthood at the hands of Richard II. of England, and in 1450 a Parliament was held in the church by King Henry VI. Thirty-seven years after Lambert Simmell, the imposter, was crowned by the title of Edward VI., with a crown borrowed from a statue of the Blessed Virgin. In the year of our Lord 1559, Thomas, Earl of Sussex, Governor of Ireland, held his Parliament in a room of the cathedral.

Before its restoration, it was so disfigured by buttresses built up against the side walls, and altogether was in such a ruinous condition, that only sufficient remained to indicate its former stateliness.

The old Mill, which rises from the centre of the Distillery, which has been left standing as a distinguishing feature and a relic of the past, is a land-mark for many miles round. It is of solid construction, some 70 feet wide at its base, and rises to the great height of 150 feet. Crowning its summit is a vast cupola, surmounted by a brazen figure of Ireland's patron saint, mitre and crozier in hand. In the olden times this Wind-mill used to supply the entire motive power for the Distillery. The racket courts of the old Marshalsea used to adjoin, and now form part of, the Distillery, and the rollicking debtors—say old roysterers—like boys at school, used frequently to send their tennis balls flying into the Distillery premises, with the object of arousing the sympathies of their neighbours, but we fear with little effect.

The Thomas Street Distillery was purchased by the late Mr. Peter Roe in the year 1757. At that time it was quite a small concern, but every few years, as his trade increased, the proprietor kept building and making additions, while within the last twenty years alone his successors have expended upwards of £70,000 on the works. Mr. Henry Roe, the late proprietor of the Distillery, in which, although he has given up the active management, he still holds a large interest, is a man of princely liberality, and Dublin may well be proud of the man who, at a cost of £220,000, restored Christ Church Cathedral, and has thus left behind him an enduring monument, which, as long as the fabric lasts, will bear witness to his noble deed. The Distillery is now in the hands of a limited Company, under the personal management of one of the Directors, who has a practical knowledge of the business, and devotes his entire time to its conduct.

The following is a brief description of this undertaking:—The factors contract to deliver the corn direct into the Grain Lofts, which communicate with the Kilns, and are capable of holding upwards of 100,000 barrels of grain. After the grain is dried, it is dropped through slides into the Dry Grain Deposit Room, and from thence is conveyed by belts into the Grain Store. These belts are the invention of Sir Wm. Armstrong, whose name is associated with warlike implements, rather than such peaceful apparatus and appliances. When the grain is cooled it is once more started on its journey, and passes by elevators to the Mill, which contains eight pairs of stones, capable of grinding 1,500 barrels daily. The meal then passes by continuous screws to the Grist Loft, where it is weighed into bags ready for mashing, and dropped into the three Mash Tuns below, the largest of which being 36 feet in diameter and 7½ feet deep. From here the liquor is drained into Coolers, and sent through the Morton's Refrigerators, of which there are five, into the Fermenting Vats, of which there are sixteen, each with a capacity of 40,000 gallons. From these Washbacks the wash is pumped up into a Wash Charger, a large wooden vessel, holding 40,000 gallons; from here it goes by gravitation into the Wash Stills, each having a capacity of 20,000 gallons, and, after undergoing three distillations, the spirit is pumped into the Vats in the Racking Stores, which holds 11,784 and 11,901 gallons respectively. Here the spirit is reduced to 25 over proof, and racked into puncheons or casks, weighed, branded, and sent to the Warehouse.

The Still Houses contain eight Pot Stills—there are no patent Stills on the premises—holding from 12,000 to 20,000 gallons respectively. There are five powerful engines averaging from 16 to 30 nominal horse power; one of them is a Siddely and Mackay Dee Engine for reducing water some twenty degrees for worting purposes in summer, the only one in use in Dublin; all the engines are models of brightness and cleanliness. There are seven boilers 30 feet long by 8 feet in diameter, and four sets of three-throw pumps; also a powerful brass pump in the Still House.

The Storage Warehouses, one of which is over 360 feet long, are capable of holding 23,000 casks, representing upwards of 1,250,000 gallons; but this is only a part of the storage capacity connected with this Distillery, for the Company own large Warehouses and vaults at Mount Brown and elsewhere capable of containing 6,000 casks. The Company also have at Mount Brown large maltings, capable of making 16,000 barrels of malt per annum. The Kilns and Maltings at this place are most complete in their arrangements, and cover nearly as much ground as the Distillery at Thomas Street.

The works at Thomas Street cover in all seventeen acres, and extend to the Quay, crossing two streets in their progress, and it is possible to enter the buildings on the left-hand entrance in Thomas Street, and by means of bridges and gangways to keep almost under cover till you find yourself again at Thomas Street, having completed the circuit of this fine work. There is upwards of a mile of belting enclosed in a two-feet square case, in addition to an almost equal length of continuous screws for conveying the grain into the various departments. The principal Chimney Stack is a fine structure, 120 feet high; it was finished in the year 1868, having been built entirely by the workmen employed on the premises, who completed the work in less than two years. Besides this fine structure, there are three other Chimney Stacks in different parts of the works.

The Cask Loft, for storage of empty casks, is the largest in Ireland, covering an area of 200 square feet, and would contain 6,000 casks. There are steam lifts to raise the casks to the Store, and from thence is an ingeniously planned inclined bridge across the road, some 50 feet long, down which the casks roll in the Racking Store. The Cooperage is a work of itself, covering nearly an acre of ground; here are to be seen casks in every stage of their existence, fifteen to eighteen men being continually employed in their manufacture, repairing, purifying, &c. The Stable and Cart Houses adjoin the Cooperage, and cover an equal area; here also are Smiths', Engineers', Fitters', and Carpenters' Shops. Two hundred hands are employed at the Distillery.

The water used comes from the Vartry and the Grand Canal.

The Whisky is Dublin Pot Still of the finest quality. The annual output has reached in some seasons the enormous quantity of nearly 2,000,000 gallons. Like that of the other Dublin Distilleries, however, it has been reduced considerably during the past few seasons. The Whisky is shipped to all parts of the world, the foreign exports being more particularly to Canada, the United States, and Australia, and is well known and appreciated everywhere.

MARROWBONE LANE DISTILLERY, DUBLIN.

No. 4.

Marrowbone Lane Distillery, Dublin.

PROPRIETORS, WILLIAM JAMESON & CO.

THE next day we devoted to a visit to Marrowbone Lane Distillery, which is situated in the suburbs of Dublin, close by the beautiful Grand Canal, which from this point presents a straight vista of water, with overhanging trees, nearly a mile in extent, until the whole is lost in a background of foliage and hills. On the other side there is a fine view of Dublin and the Wicklow Mountains, with the celebrated chimney shaft of the Ballycorus Lead Mines, which has a flue running up the side of the mountain a mile in length, the upcast of which stands out like a skeleton giant, and forms a prominent feature in the view. Here, also, is Katty Gallaher's Hill, of local romantic history; she, waiting for her lover who never came, was transformed into a hill, and remains an everlasting picture of blighted hope. This hill now forms the boundary of the Lead Works, which extend over about 70 acres.

Marrowbone Lane is not far from the scene of the rising under T. A. Emmet in 1803, and an ancestor of the present proprietor was dining in his house—now used as the offices of the Distillery—when it commenced, and heard the first shots, and cries of the wounded; and it was on that day that Lord Kilwaden was dragged from his carriage and murdered in the streets. A desperate battle afterwards ensued, and Emmet was taken prisoner; and this gifted and eloquent orator, who pleaded his own and his country's cause with such fervour and pathos, that he drew tears from the eyes of his judges, was executed in Thomas Street, on the very spot where the battle had been fought. The water used in the Marrowbone Lane Distillery comes from the Vartry, and the high level of the Grand Canal. The former a lively, dashing little river, rises from the southern base of the Great Sugar Loaf, a mountain 1,650 feet above the level of the sea, opposite to which is the Small Sugar Loaf, and the lovely valley lying between the two is called the "sweetest valley" in Ireland. From the summit of these mountains is to be viewed one of the finest panoramic views in Europe, embracing the lovely and thickly-wooded Dargle, and inland scenes of surpassing beauty; Bray, Dalkey, and all the coast places, including "the Charming City" itself; whilst the sea view takes in Howth, Ireland's Eye, and an infinite expanse of ocean. The river Vartry flows through the high moorland district which stretches from the Sugar Loaf to Roundwood, and in its progress over mossy falls and between banks of heather, it receives all the smaller mountain streams, till it falls over a ledge of rock into the Devil's Glen, through which it brawls over rocky beds, rushing and foaming among the huge boulders that impede its progress, adding

MASH HOUSE, MARROWBONE LANE DISTILLERY.

materially to the beauty of that wild romantic spot. The celebrated Guinness's Stout is brewed from the Vartry water, and Messrs. Wm. Jameson & Co.'s Whisky is made from the same source. On analysis it has been found that the Vartry water possesses special powers for dissolving vegetable matter, whilst it retains all the vegetable aroma so necessary for extracting the virtues from the malt.

The ancestors of the present firm purchased this Distillery about the year 1779; it was then a very small undertaking, making less than 30,000 gallons yearly, but as the product grew in reputation, so the buildings increased. To meet the demand for their Whisky, the present spirited proprietors enlarged the work and increased the plant at an outlay of £100,000, and the buildings now

CORN LOFT, MARROWBONE LANE DISTILLERY.

cover upwards of fourteen acres of ground. The following is a brief description of this extensive Distillery: At the very top of the buildings there is a fine green Corn Loft, light and airy, measuring 111 feet long by 100 feet broad, capable of holding 30,000 barrels; the two Kilns, each measuring 66 feet by 36 feet, with wire flooring are so arranged that the green corn comes in by upper doors, raised 12 feet from the floor, whilst a second series of doors, on a level with the Kiln floor, enable the dried grain to be conveyed direct into the two dry Corn Lofts, which are of the same large dimensions as the green Corn Loft. When the corn in this department is quite cooled, it is sent by elevators and screws into the grinding Mill, which turns out 150 tons of ground corn every twenty-four hours. Before passing to the Mill, the grain goes through the cleaning apparatus, in the hoppers of which are placed strong magnets, 3 feet long, which attract and retain metal objects, &c., and there is an elastic contrivance which most ingeniously sweeps these objects from the magnets into a bag at the side, and we were surprised to see how soon it was filled with bits of nail, steel, &c., which had been subtracted from the grain. These foreign objects, if allowed to remain, not only injure the Mills, but totally destroy the flavour of the Whisky; it is well known to Distillers that an inch or two of steel would spoil a whole mash. The Mill Room contains thirteen pairs of stones, and from this department the grist is lifted by elevators and thrown into lofts, 78 feet square, above the Mash Tuns. There is a peculiarity about

BACK COURTYARD, MARROWBONE LANE DISTILLERY.

these lofts somewhat difficult to describe; they are built and supported on the same principle as a suspension bridge, with iron girders across to prevent the necessity of pillars or supports in the Mash House below. In the Mash House are to be seen two Mash Tuns said to be the largest in the United Kingdom, each having a capacity of upwards of 100,000 gallons; sixteen spouts depending from the ceiling distribute the grist into the Mash Tuns, each, of course, being provided with the ponderous stirring rakes, &c. From these vessels the liquor passes into two large Underbacks; from thence it is pumped by three-throw pumps through the Morton's Refrigerator into the thirteen Washbacks, or fermenting vessels, some of which contain 100,000 imperial gallons; in fact, two or three of them are large enough to hold a two-storied villa, with a garden path round it included. From these Washbacks the fermented worts are pumped into a Wash Charger out on the roof, and therefore above the level of the Stills; thence they run into the Wash Stills in the usual course. There are four Old Pot Stills—no other kind being in use—with a capacity of 18,000, 12,000, 11,000, and 9,000 gallons respectively. From the Spirit Still the perfected spirit descends into an enormous Vat in the Spirit Stores, which holds 19,076 gallons. There are nine Bonded Warehouses, capable of storing 35,000 casks; they contained at the time of our visit 21,000. The Warehouses are not only well ventilated, but are particularly dry, both important adjuncts to the preservation and maturation of the spirit. The "Out" Warehouses of this firm, four in number, are situated in Liverpool Yard, North Wall, in the immediate vicinity of the shipping of the Port, and of the Goods' Terminus of every railway entering Dublin, with one exception; in these Warehouses are constantly stored nearly 7,000 casks, maturing for the firm and their customers, and they have been most carefully attended to as regards temperature and ventilation.

The Cooperage of this Distillery is on a large scale, and is quite a work of itself, covering nearly an acre of ground, and employing thirty men in making, repairing, hooping, and cleansing the casks. The following briefly describes the Engine Department: Four engines are used—an old one, 75 years in use, of 40-horse power, still works well; there is a new horizontal engine of 50-horse power; and also a smaller one put up in the year the battle of Waterloo was fought; these all do the principal work of the place. There are five steam boilers, two 36 feet long, and three 30 feet long; all 8 feet in diameter. There are five Chimney Stacks on the premises, varying from 80 to 110 feet in height.

Throughout the premises there is a complete system of fire-extinguishing apparatus; in all departments are iron mains, to which are attached leathern hose, by which means a fire can be almost immediately extinguished, the delay of attaching hose being completely avoided.

Carpenters', Painters', Engineers', and Smithy Shops are all to be found on the works. The Stables, &c., are situated in a large square yard, about the size of a cavalry barrack, comprising fourteen stalls with harness room, two hospitals, and coach house; there are also fine lofts for feeding stores, capable of containing twelve months' consumption. Two hundred persons are employed in the various departments of the Distillery.

The make is known as "Dublin Whisky," and the annual output is about 900,000 gallons; it is principally shipped to Melbourne, Sydney, Dominion of Canada, British India, The United States, West India, &c. The Excise officers are Mr. Stone, Supervisor, and Mr. Eyres and Mr. Mason.

"Whisky, drink divine,
Why should drivellers bore us
With the praise of wine,
Whilst we've thee before us?
Were it not a shame,
Whilst we gaily fling thee
To our lips of flame,
If we could not sing thee?"

JONES ROAD DISTILLERY, DUBLIN.

No. 5.

Jones Road Distillery, Dublin.

PROPRIETORS, THE DUBLIN WHISKY DISTILLERY COMPANY, LIMITED.

THIS Distillery is situated on the historic river Tolka, in one of the most picturesque suburbs of Dublin, and close to the estuary of Clontarf. From any point it commands fine views of Howth. a peninsula of considerable extent, which from its height and situation has been considered not unlike Vesuvius, in the Bay of Naples ; it is the most prominent feature in the scenery of the north side of the City, and contains, besides an ancient castle that has been spoiled by modern restoration and whitewash, a very interesting abbey ruin which contains many curious tombs ; it was founded in 1228, and is situated close to the sea in the quaint little town of Howth. The beautiful plains of Clontarf stretch from Howth to the Distillery, and the whole country round is rich in historic memories; here, within a hundred yards of the Distillery gates was wrought out the grandest chapter in Ireland's history, and the Danish power in Ireland crushed for ever by King Brian Boromhe, who, in the year 1014, with his powerful native princes and chieftains, fought and totally defeated the Danes on the plains of Clontarf. The Danish Commander commenced the battle early on Good Friday morning, and the venerable King Brian—he was eighty-eight years old—addressing his army, held aloft in his left hand a crucifix, and wielding his good broad-sword in his right, called upon them through the mercies of Christ who had died for them upon that holy day, to summon up their utmost strength and extirpate for ever the base confederate pirates before them. The battle lasted all through the day, and the Irish totally defeated and routed the Danes ; but alas ! the triumph of the conquerors was dimmed by the death of their grand old king, and also that of his son, the lion-hearted Mortogh (who performed prodigies of valour), his brave nephew, many princes and nobles, and eleven thousand of his valiant soldiers.

The river Tolka flows through the grounds of the Distillery, pursuing its course to the sea, distant but a few hundred yards; it rises high up beyond the valley of the Tolka, and its water is used for driving power only. There is a fine well on the premises one hundred feet deep, but the water used for distilling purposes is brought through a mile of pipe from the high level of the Royal Canal; no other distilling firms other than Messrs. John Jameson & Son and the Dublin Whisky Distillery Company have access to this water.

The following is a brief description of this the most modern of the Distilleries in Dublin ; it was commenced on the 22nd day of July, in the year 1872, and on the 22nd day of July, 1873, the Company were mashing; thus showing what Irish enterprise is capable of doing. The Distillery buildings are a fine stately work in red brick, some sixty-five feet high; at a distance the place looks like some public building, the architect having given it that character. The chimney stack, one hundred and thirty-five feet high, is also built of red brick, handsomely designed, and of great ornamentation; it rears its proud head from the centre of the courtyard in front of the gateway, and at a distance looks like a monument built to commemorate the virtues of some dead hero. The Distillery is partly surrounded by water, and is approached by a picturesque bridge; just before passing the works the river falls over a fine weir or waterfall.

The grain is received from the factors and farmers under a verandah or covered siding, and dropped into a cylinder on the sub-ground floor, from whence it is elevated to the different lofts and kilns, and depositing where required by means of continuous screws. There are five large corn lofts, elegantly lighted and ventilated, contiguous to which are two spacious Kilns, floored with perforated iron plates. The Malt Deposit is a spacious apartment, and adjoins the Mill, which contains eight pairs of stones, and the usual grinding machinery. Shut off from the Mill, by two sets of fireproof doors, is the Grist Loft, capable of holding 4,000 quarters, and underneath is the Mash House, where are two large Mash Tuns with the usual stirring gear, capable of working together or separately; each Tun has the new covers and curtain enclosures to prevent the loss of the fine grist. In close proximity hereto the Brewer has a capital office with glazed sides, enabling him at all times to see the whole of the operations in this important department. In the Tun Room there are eight Washbacks, and the usual number of Wash Chargers. The three Spent Wash Tanks are away in the court-yard, conveniently arranged for dairymen and farmers. In the building, under the Mash Tuns, which are supported by two colossal stone piers and iron girders, there is on the left-hand side a forest of pumps, which to the uninitiated look most perplexing, but the brewer assured us that he knew every one of them as well as an organist would know his stops and pedals. At the other side of this apartment there is a huge metal Underback and a double-acting "plunger pump"—supplied by Pearn & Co. of Manchester—acknowledged to be the finest specimen of hydraulic machinery in any Distillery in Dublin, being capable of raising 1,000 gallons of water per minute.

There are two powerful engines, one of them working up to 100-horse power, and three boilers 30 feet long by 8 feet in diameter; over these boilers are placed the four brewing tanks. There is a Leffel Turbine Wheel, the only one in use in any Distillery in Ireland, fixed in the middle of the stream, with a water power equal to 50-horse power; the shafting of the large engine is attached to this wheel. The roofs of the whole pile of buildings, which are all in one block, are, with one exception, quite flat, and entirely covered with tanks of water, the size of small lakes, some of them holding 100,000 gallons; and it may here be mentioned that there is a continuous stream of water constantly running through the whole of the iron columns which support the buildings, so that in case of fire they would not collapse. The whole arrangements for extinguishing fire are very perfect, water and hose being laid on to every floor, whilst depending from the walls are fire buckets and patent apparatus.

The Still House, or Distillery proper, is upwards of 60 feet high, with a double tier of wide iron galleries like those in the Crystal Palace at Sydenham. This building contains four "Old Pot Stills" on the ground floor, and on the first gallery there is an excellent Safe and Sampling Safe, Spirit Receivers, &c.; on another gallery up in the roof are the Coolers, and four of Morton's Refrigerators, and on the outside, communicating with this gallery, there are two Worm Tubs 28 feet square and 15 feet deep. Gazing down below from the upper gallery at all the arrangements and ingenuity displayed, we were compelled to acknowledge that a master mind and skilful hand had planned this great work. Across one of the galleries, through brick arches, we perceived the intermediate Charger erected in the roof of the next department. On ascending the Stage or Observatory of this building, we had such a delightful view of the City and surrounding country as to amply repay for the toil and climb of ladders and staircase; it consisted of distant views of cornfields; river and sea almost beneath our feet; Holy Cross College with its beautiful grounds; Clonliff College, where lie the remains of the venerated Cardinal Cullen; Glasnevin Cemetery, with O'Connell's Monument, and last, but not least, the Dublin Mountains, forming a background to the grand old City. The large Maltings connected with this Distillery are situated in Russell Place and Cork Street, and the Midland Railway is only a short distance off. There are four Warehouses, one a two-decker building, also a fine Spirit Store. The Cooperage, Stables, Cart Sheds, Smiths' and Carpenters' Shops, are at the back of the works, whilst there is a handsome terrace of offices containing Sampling Rooms, Board Room, Private Offices, Printing Room, Clerks' and Excise Offices, &c. The Company are about building other large Duty-Free Warehouses on an adjoining estate which they have recently acquired.

It may here be mentioned that the six Directors, whose names we give below, are business men, and have devoted themselves to the development of this business. The product made is of the highest class of Dublin make; only the best corn is used, and the distiller is a practical and experienced man. The Distillery is worked entirely by gravitation, the machinery is of the most modern style, and only "Old Pot Stills" are used.

The annual output is 560,000 gallons, but the Company could make nearly 800,000 gallons if required. The Whisky is sent to England, and is also shipped to India and the Colonies.

The Directors are Mr. George John Alexander, Mr. Mathew H. Chamberlaine, Mr. James Costello, Mr. William H. Maturin, and Mr. O. T. Allingham.

PHŒNIX PARK DISTILLERY, DUBLIN.

No. 6.

Phoenix Park Distillery, Dublin.

PROPRIETORS, THE DISTILLERS' COMPANY, LIMITED.

Head Office: 11, TORPICHEN STREET, EDINBURGH.

Manager of this Distillery: JOHN A. HAIG.

WE had reserved this, our last day in Dublin City, for our excursion to the Phœnix Park Distillery. We were favoured with most brilliant weather, and our drive through the Park was most enjoyable. It is the finest and most extensive public park in the United Kingdom, and embraces an area of 1,760 acres, giving a circuit of over seven miles. It was formerly part of the monastery grounds of St. John of Jerusalem, is finely diversified with woodland and undulating ground, and well stocked with deer. It was first laid down by King Charles II. in 1662, who was in possession of the lands of Kilmainham, surrendered to him by the Knight Prior of St. John of Jerusalem. Shortly afterwards, by command of his Majesty, James Duke of Ormond purchased the adjoining lands of Chapel-izod and Newtown, in order to extend the park. At that time it extended on both sides of the Liffey; but being so much exposed to trespassers, Sir John Temple, a far-seeing and shrewd man, undertook, on condition of being paid two hundred pounds out of the King's Treasury, to enclose the whole of that part on the north side of the river, and a grant was also made to him of all the excluded lands. Of late years it has received a terrible notoriety from the foul murder of Lord Frederick Cavendish and Mr. Burke, under circumstances of brutality never surpassed, the details of which must be strong in the memory of all. In the centre of the main drive there stands a fluted Corinthian pillar about fifty feet high, surmounted with a figure of a Phœnix in her burning nest. It was erected in the year 1747 by the celebrated Earl of Chesterfield, when Lord Lieutenant of Ireland, who did much to improve and beautify the Park. This column the proprietors of the Phœnix Park Distillery have adopted as an effective trade mark. The Park, however, takes its name from a corruption of Gaelic *Fion-uise* (fair water); so called from a spring at one time resorted to as a chalybeate spa.

We drove by the lower road to the little old-fashioned, but romantic, village of Chapel-izod, supposed to have derived its name from La Belle Isode, a daughter of one of the ancient Irish Kings, who had a chapel here. The village is chiefly remarkable for the beautiful scenery in its vicinity, especially along the banks of the Liffey towards Lucan, and for the extensive strawberry beds which are spread over the northern slope of the vale, a distance of nearly two miles.

The Distillery is situated on the banks of the Liffey, which runs through the property, and was established in the year 1878; previous to that date the premises had been used as a spinning-mill, and being very lofty and extensive, were easily converted into a Distillery. There is a steam tramway running past the works, which gives easy access to Dublin, which is distant about four miles. The Liffey at Chapel-izod is a beautiful clear stream, and quite unlike the Liffey at Dublin City. Its banks are finely diversified and display sylvan scenes of great beauty; skirting the demesne of Woodland they are covered with trees for more than a mile. Not far distant from the Distillery is the Salmon Leap, the lowest rapid on the Liffey; it is reached through the grounds of Westown, where the river enters a narrow ravine, through which it rushes among the rocks that impede its progress. About the middle of this ravine it throws its water over a wide broken ledge of rocks; at all times it is a beautiful sight, but when the river is swollen its magnificence is greatly heightened. The works cover five acres, and when the new Maltings, now in course of construction, are completed, will exceed six acres. The establishment is entered from the main road, through a handsome gateway, and the buildings are built in the form of a square. The offices are on the right, and are reached by a short stair; they contain, besides the general clerks' offices, private rooms for the manager.

After making ourselves known, we were furnished with a guide, who first took us to the Grain Stores, which consist of a range of buildings, 90 feet long and 42 feet wide, wherein are nine lofts capable of storing 12,000 quarters of barley, oats, &c., to which are attached three Kilns where the grain is dried by hot air. We next bent our steps across the close to the Maltings, which are 110 feet long and 60 feet wide, and consist of three floors; but there are larger Malt Houses in course of construction at the rear of the premises, covering an acre of ground, which, besides being modern in appearance, have a fine lofty Kiln floored with new iron patent flooring. On returning to the Grain buildings we were shown the machinery by which the dried grain is removed to the Mill. It consists of two wide continuous belts, traversing the whole extent of the buildings, and it is wonderful to see that not a single grain of barley is lost in its onward progress. We next passed on to the Mill building, which is a lofty brick structure containing five pairs of stones. The belt delivers the grain into a hopper over this Mill, and after being crushed, the grist is weighed into bags and deposited on the grist loft adjoining, ready for use; this loft is 90 feet long by 42 feet wide. The Mash House is under the grist loft; therefore, the hoppers into which the sacks are emptied command the Mash Tuns. These are circular vessels, 30 feet in diameter and 9 feet deep, containing the usual stirring gear and draining plates. The Heaters supply the hot water to these vessels, and are placed above them. From the Mash Tun the worts descend into the two Underbacks, placed under the floor; whilst the grains which are left behind are pumped into a huge tank, and afterwards sold to the dairymen in the neighbourhood.

We next ascended a stone staircase and found ourselves in a spacious apartment, 140 feet square, called the Back Loft. It contains twelve Washbacks, each with a capacity of 18,000 gallons; the worts are pumped up from the Underbacks, through a Morton's Refrigerator and coolers, into these twelve vessels by means of a three-throw pump, at the rate of 10,000 gallons an hour. From the Backs the fermented worts, which are now called wash, run into the two Wash Chargers, which are of a similar capacity, and so arranged that they command the Still, which holds 18,000 gallons, where it is distilled and condensed; thence it runs into the Low-wines and Feints Receiver, and is again subjected to a similar distilling process.

The Still House is a fine building, and fitted with every appliance. It contains four Pot Stills, holding 5,000, 11,000, 12,000, and 18,000 gallons respectively, all of them heated by furnaces. There is no steam power on the premises, the Liffey supplying all the motive power required, by means of a water-wheel, which stretches right across the river, and is said to be the largest in the kingdom, measuring 70 feet in breadth and 18 feet in diameter. We next proceeded to the Receiving Room, which contains, besides the Safe, ten Receivers. Contiguous to this department is the Spirit Store, containing two vats holding 16,000 gallons each. Retracing our steps, and passing the two Morton's Refrigerators and two large Worm Tubs, we crossed the court to the Bonded Warehouses, which are six in number; two with two floors, other two with three floors, and the remaining two with four—holding in all 16,000 casks. Adjoining is a Racking Store and Cooperage, also a smithy and carpenters' shop.

MILL WHEEL.

The Distillery is lighted by incandescent lamps; they have been recently installed, and give every satisfaction, not only saving money but insure greater security from fire. The electricity is supplied by an Ellwell-Parker dynamo, and the water-wheel supplies the motive power. In addition there are accumulators for storing the electricity, which are capable of supplying light to the works for six hours continuously without the use of the dynamo. With all the new improvements and machinery for saving labour, this Distillery, although the smallest, is the most modern of any of the Distilleries owned by the Distillers' Company, Limited. The machinery supplied to the new Malt House being the most perfect mechanism for lifting and moving grain that has, up to the present time, been invented.

Sixty persons are employed on the premises, and seven Excise officers, the chief of whom is Mr. W. Armstrong.

The water used for distilling purposes is brought from the upper reaches of the river through a closed pipe.

The make is called Dublin Whisky, and the annual output is 350,000 gallons, which find a market chiefly in London and the Colonies.

MONASTEREVAN DISTILLERY.

No. 7.

Monasterevan Distillery, Monasterevan, co. Kildare.

PROPRIETOR, JAMES CASSIDY.

WE left Dublin by an early train, which enabled us to spend five or six hours at Monasterevan on our way to Tullamore. It was a delightful day, and we were quite glad to quit for a time the busy haunts of men, and all their ways and works, and exchange them for green fields, flowering banks, and nature's wild beauty.

After leaving the suburbs of the "Charmin' City," our way lay through scenes of gentle beauty, intermingled here and there with wooded knolls and plantations. Afterwards for many miles it was less interesting. As we approached our destination, the extensive woodlands of Moore Abbey, which cover the greater part of the hill lying to the south of Monasterevan came into view, and we were soon in the midst of pastoral scenes and pictures of country life, which filled us with admiration. Moore Abbey is the seat of the Marquis of Drogheda, and it is the most interesting feature in the scenery for many miles. The noble mansion is a modern structure built on the site of an old and celebrated Franciscan Abbey. It stands near the town, and on the banks of the Barrow, which runs for two miles through the park. The demesne stretches up to the boundary walls of the Distillery, and in some places the stately trees thereon overshadow the buildings; indeed, the thick woods, sloping verdure, and running streams in the park add much to the picturesque appearance of the Distillery. The town takes its name from Moore Abbey, a monastery founded by St. Abben, who granted it the privilege of "Sanctuary." History informs us that in the seventh century, on his festival day (Dec. 22nd), St. Evin, a successor of St. Abben, placed therein a number of monks from South Munster, and brought with him a consecrated bell, which was used by the tribe of the Eoganachts to swear upon on solemn trials, and which was held in such high veneration that it was always in the charge of an hereditary chief. At the general suppression of monasteries Moore Abbey was granted to Lord Dudley, and afterwards it came into the family of the present Marquis.

Having somewhat digressed, for which we apologize, we now return to the object of our journey. Reaching the station, we walked through the town and had no difficulty in finding the object of our visit. The Distillery, which is its most striking feature, covers ten acres of ground, and has a frontage to the main road of 293 feet. We entered by a picturesque ivy-covered stone archway, and found ourselves inside an oblong quadrangle, with several inner courts issuing therefrom. After making ourselves known to Mr. Cassidy, we proceeded to his private office to obtain the necessary information as to the foundation of the works, and found by investigation, that the Distillery was built by the grandfather of the present proprietor in the year 1784, and a few years after was partly burnt down and rebuilt again, since which time many additions have been made. The old buildings are very picturesque, and the newer ones have been erected in a style to harmonise with the earlier portions of the works. The water used for brewing purposes comes from the celebrated "White Springs" of Borraderra, famed for its purity and sparkling appearance. A tributary of the Barrow which runs through the grounds has been diverted into a natural pond behind the Maltings, and in its bed are laid the cooling pipes. Under the guidance of Mr. Cassidy, we commenced our tour of the establishment at the corn buyers' office, which is approached from the high road and adjoins the Distillery offices. It is a stone-paved apartment, where the barley is sampled and, if purchased from the farmer, is parcelled, numbered, and the price and quantity registered in a book. The road which extends along the front of, and runs through the works, is called "Dublin Street," and twice a week in the season it is thronged with farmers and others, and, when we were there, presented quite the animated appearance of "Mark Lane" on a small scale, the roadway from end to end being strewn with corn. The stray fowls and ducks come here from the village, and have a high time of it after the market is over. When the corn is delivered to the receiving Warehouse, the checking clerk compares it with the sample, sees every sack weighed, and makes out the credit note for the farmer, who exchanges same for cash in the Distillery office. From the scales the sacks are emptied into the wells of the Elevators, and then lifted to the Corn Stores.

FARMERS' CARTS (Monasterevan Distillery).

Before visiting these, we passed through a doorway into the water tower at the back, where there is a large water-wheel that works the elevators, etc.

The Corn Store building, which holds 3,000 barrels, is five stories high, 60 feet long and 48 feet wide, lofty and well lighted. On these floors workmen were busy distributing the corn as it arrived from the shoots of the elevator. Leaving this department, we passed through the two Kilns, neat buildings, each 32 feet high and 42 feet square, floored with Worcester perforated tiles, underneath which are the old-fashioned open furnaces. At the time of our visit a number of little lads, without shoes and stockings, were busy pricking the holes of the tiles to unstop them, a process which has to be repeated three times a year to secure perfect ventilation. From the Kilns the dried grain is dropped through shoots into the Elevator and conveyed to the several dried Corn Lofts which adjoin this building, where it is spread out to the depth of 5 feet, and when required sent direct to the Mill. To the latter place we next bent our steps and were shown three pairs of Mill-stones and a set of Malt Rollers. The grist and ground malt descend from their respective hoppers into the Meal-room below which contains the Copper House, a tower-like building 80 feet square.

Following the process, we inspected the heating tanks and then passed into the Mash-house. It is a building quite unique in style and design, and certainly unlike any other Mash-house in the kingdom. It is constructed in the shape of a bee-hive, and at one time, during the erection of its conical roof, the workmen all left, fearing it would fall upon them before the key-stone was placed. The interior of this singular building is painted white and picked out in bright scarlet of chaste design. The Mash-tun, which is 40 feet in diameter and 9 feet deep, with usual stirring gear, is the only vessel in the house, except the Underback or Worts Tank below the paved floor. Mounting half-a-dozen steps, we promenaded the gallery round the top of the Mash-tun, 5 feet wide, and took a peep at the inside of this large vessel. A powerful three-throw Pump delivers the worts from the Underback to the Coolers above, and also those laid in the bed of the pond. We next visited the Tun-room, a lofty gallery which stands on a hewn stone foundation, the roof of which is appropriated entirely to the Coolers already referred to. Ranged along the wall are six large timber Washbacks, each capable of holding 24,000 gallons. After fermentation has ceased in these vessels, the liquor, which is now called wash, is pumped up to the Wash Charger holding 26,000 gallons by a single Pump, from whence it runs by gravitation into the Wash Still. On emerging from this house, our attention was called to the great elevation and size of the water tank, which supplies all the water-power of the establishment. We entered the Still-house by the eastern end and found ourselves in a fine building, roofed with corrugated iron 55 feet high and 50 feet square. On one side are placed the Old Pot Stills, comprising a Wash Still 26,000 gallons content, and a Spirit Still 5,600 gallons content. The Worm Tub, connected with these Stills, is placed on pillars 50 feet high in the court-yard, and contains 250 tons of water; from the Worm the spirit runs through the Safe into the Spirit Receiver in the Can-pit Room; here also are the Low-wines and Feints Receivers and Chargers. From the Receiver the pure spirit, which has undergone two distillations, is pumped into the three Spirit Vats, placed in the Spirit Store, where we followed it. We found the workmen busy racking off the spirit into casks; when filled, they are weighed and marked under the superintendence of the Excise, and then sent to the Duty-free Warehouse.

At the suggestion of Mr. Cassidy we visited some of the Warehouses, of which there are seventeen in all, containing, at the time of our visit, 7,210 casks of Whisky. They are all built of stone, dry and well ventilated, and are built round a courtyard, having together a frontage in the quadrangle of 800 feet. Crossing the yard we came to the Grain Tank, which is erected over the Engine House, where the grains are pumped from the Mash Kieve. A spout, depending from its side, serves to convey the grains into the farmers' carts. In close proximity there is a similar arrangement for the spent wash, which is collected into a metal tank, 120 feet long by 14 feet deep, and disposed of in the same way. We passed through the Engine House, where there is an engine of 30-horse power, and two steam boilers, 35 feet long by 8 feet in diameter, and came to the Cooperage, which consists of several buildings, wherein we saw nine coopers at work, some of them manufacturing and others repairing casks, which we saw in their various stages from stave to barrel. In our perigrinations we observed a duty-paid Racking Store, which contained, at the time of our inspection, 3,000 gallons of duty-paid Whisky for the convenience of local customers, and at each end of the court, a steam crane for hoisting both full and empty casks into the floats. The chimney shaft, which rises from the back of the Boiler House, is built in the old-fashioned style of one chimney inside the other, so as to equalise the draught.

Returning to the general offices by another way, we inspected the Carpenters', Smiths' and Engineers' Shops, Sheds, and Cart Houses; these last are roofed with corrugated iron. We next visited the Stables, which are very extensive, and contained thirty horses of a superior class, Mr. Cassidy being celebrated throughout the district for his fine breed of horses. The establishment is lighted throughout with gas, the proprietor having some time since erected a gasometer and built gas-works on the property. Within the boundary-walls of the Distillery there is a commodious house for the brewer and other officials. The proprietor's residence, a two-storied mansion, built in the Italian style, is within sight of the Distillery. It stands in a small park, bounded by pretty plantations, attached to which there is a grass farm.

Monasterevan is a very compact Distillery, and is easily worked. From the manager down to the smallest boy, every *employé* takes an interest in his work, and, although upwards of seventy persons are employed, it is a rare thing for any one of them to disturb the harmony of the community, or to be reprimanded.

The Whisky manufactured is of exactly the same character as the celebrated Dublin make, and the annual output is 203,000.

We tasted some of the "make," six years old, and considered it a fat, creamy Whisky, suitable both for blending and to use as a self spirit. Mr. Cassidy sells all he makes in the locality, except about 40,000 gallons to Messrs. Twiss and Browning for export, and a few thousand gallons to a Bristol firm. Three Excise officers are in attendance at the Distillery, Mr. J. Ryan being the chief.

Having completed our inspection of the Distillery and Corn Stores, we proceeded, in company with Mr. Cassidy, to the Maltings, which are situated near the railway station. They are built of stone, in one range of over 200 feet square, and hold 4,000 barrels of corn, whilst the Kiln at the end gives a handsome finish to the whole.

No. 8.

Tullamore Distillery, Tullamore, King's County.

PROPRIETOR, BERNARD DALY.

LEAVING the interesting town of Monasterevan, and the kind hospitality of Mr. Cassidy, we once more entered the train, this time for Tullamore, where, on arrival, we were just in time to see a National Demonstration. A procession, headed by a band of music, came in sight, followed by a rickety jaunting car, drawn by a venerable horse, rather groggy on his legs. The animal's harness was decorated with sprigs of evergreen, while on the car, under an arbour of the same, sat a middle-aged lady, with a pleasant air of jollity on her face, who, we were informed, was an evicted martyr, just released from prison. She was followed by hundreds of nondescript vehicles, and a great crowd of sympathisers. Whilst the first band was playing "Wearin' o' the Green," the second, which brought up the rear, gave us "God bless Ould Ireland," and although we hailed from the land of the Saxon, "We were not afraid." Indeed we enjoyed the fun immensely, and got mixed up with the crowd, feeling quite content for the time being to quaff Daly's Whisky, so freely offered us, and were almost induced to join their ranks.

The weather was bright and sunny, so we took a drive to see the beautiful environs of the thriving town of Tullamore, and later on to visit the Distillery which we had come so far to see. It is situated in the heart of the town, on the banks of the river Clondagh, and with its buildings and grounds covers about ten acres. It was founded in the year 1829, by Mr. Michael Molloy, uncle to the present proprietor. Being planted in the midst of a fine agricultural district, the Distillery has the advantage of being supplied with home-grown corn of the finest quality. There is an unfailing supply of water from the celebrated Lough, which feeds the Grand Canal, brought from a great distance direct into the Distillery.

In olden times the town of Tullamore was called Kilbride, but it was destroyed by fire, and rebuilt by the Earl of Charleville, whose beautiful estate comes right up to the town. Afterwards it was called by its present name, and later on it was the terminus of the Grand Canal, before it was extended to Shannon Harbour, which caused it to increase rapidly in prosperity and population. The town is the chief market for all kinds of agricultural produce from a large extent of surrounding country, and contains, beside the Distillery, a tobacco manufactory and several other industries. It is an assize town, and its county court-house is a fine building, in the Grecian style; near to it is the county gaol, a castellated building. The demesne of Charleville is an estate of great natural beauty and richly wooded; the mansion has all the appearance of an English baronial castle. In the park, which is beautifully laid out, there are two pretty lakes, the largest of which is studded with islands. The river Clondagh, which runs through and under the Distillery, drives a huge water-wheel which supplies the motive power. It passes through the Policies of Charleville, where, running through a deep glen overhung with trees, it forms several fine cascades, adding to the natural beauty of the park.

Not far distant from Tullamore Distillery are to be seen the ruins of a castle, built in 1326, and there are besides three small square castles of very ancient date. The district also contains several fine chalybeate springs, whose virtues were appreciated in ancient times, but are not now in use for medicinal purposes.

But to return to our subject. The Distillery came into the hands of the present proprietor some thirty years ago, having been bequeathed to him by his uncle, and since that time Mr. Daly has not only improved and considerably extended the work, but has added new machinery and all the recently invented appliances used in distilling. The Whisky made is of the same class and make as manufactured by the noted Dublin houses, and it is not only sold and appreciated in the district, but is supplied in large quantities to England and the colonies. At the front of the Distillery, facing the main street, there is a fine residence, formerly an old manor house, occupied by Mr. Daly, when he is in Tullamore. This gentleman, however, has a fine estate at Hazelbrook, Terenure, near Dublin, where he usually resides, and where we hope to spend a few days during the ensuing summer.

The Distillery is superintended by Mr. Bernard Daly's son, Mr. B. Mara, his nephew, and Mr. Charles Comyn, his son-in-law, but the general management is under the control of Mr. Daniel Williams.

The farmers deliver the corn to the Granaries, of which there are eight, capable of holding 60,000 barrels of grain. One of the stores has three lofts, each being 120 feet square, and capable of holding 10,000 barrels of corn. After being run through the self-acting cleaning machines, the grain is sent by elevators into four Kilns, each with open roof, and floored with patent wire flooring. These Kilns are capable of drying 1,000 barrels in each per week. The Dry Corn Lofts are attached to the Kilns.

The Mill Building contains eight pairs of stones, and the two Meal Lofts are over the two Mash Tuns, which are 24 feet in diameter and 8 feet deep, each capable of mashing 1,000 barrels weekly, so that Mr. Daly uses up 2,000 barrels, as he works a period every week. There are five sets of ponderous three-throw Pumps, and four of Morton's Refrigerators.

In the Back House there are ten Washbacks, each with a capacity of 16,000 gallons, and in the yard which commands the Stills, a Wash Charger, a fine metal vessel, holding 17,000 gallons.

Built on stone pillars, over the river, are to be seen, three Worm Tubs, very handsome vessels.

The Still House is a fine open building, containing four old Pot Stills (there are no others on the premises). The following is their capacity:

Two Wash Stills, each holding	. . .	16,000 gallons.
A Low Wines Still	,, ...	5,500 ,,
Spirit Still	,, ...	10,500 ,,

and it may be here noted that the Whisky in this establishment undergoes three distillations.

In the Running Room there is a fine Safe and Sampling Safe, a Spirit Receiver, holding 4,000 gallons, and Low Wines and Feints Receivers, capable of holding 30,000 gallons.

The Spirit Store is adjoining, and contains a Vat, holding 8,000 gallons, where the Whisky is reduced to 25 o.p., casked, branded, and delivered into the Warehouses, of which there are eleven large buildings, covering nearly five acres of ground, and containing at the time of our visit 900,000 gallons of Whisky, of various ages, principally in butts and hogsheads.

The Malting is a large department. There are four Barns, capable of malting 30,000 barrels, if necessary, with four Steeps and four large Malt Kilns, floored with perforated tiles.

The Coal Yard holds 5,000 tons. Mr. Daly charters a ship, and the coal is brought in barges by the Grand Canal to the Distillery.

In the Yard are two Chimney Stacks, that for the stilling being 108 feet high, and the other, for boiling, 60 feet high.

The Grains House and Spent Wash Tanks are conveniently arranged for the farmers to fetch away without going into the Distillery.

The following is a list of the industries pursued inside the establishment. A millwright and fitter's shop, with steam lathe and other appliances, carpenter's shop, cooperage, &c., and it may be mentioned that a resident certificated engineer resides in a capital house on the premises, who is capable of making and fitting an engine if required. There are three very fine engines, one of them 200-horse power, and four boilers, 30 feet by 7 feet in diameter, and there are four large heating tanks, for brewing by steam.

The Whisky is Old Pot Still, and is sold all over Ireland, but principally in Dublin, whilst a large quantity goes to Liverpool, London, and Australia. We tasted some eight years old, which was so good that it reminded us of Moore's lines :

"Never was philter found with such power
To charm and bewilder, as this we are quaffing,
The magic began, when in autumn's rich hour,
As a harvest of gold in the fields it stood laughing,
There having by nature's enchantment been fill'd
With the balm and the bloom of the kindliest weather.
This wonderful juice from its core was distilled,
To enliven such hearts as are here brought together.
And though, perhaps—but breathe it to no one—
Like caldrons the witch brews at midnight so awful,
In secret this philter was first taught to flow on,
Yet—'tisn't less potent for being unlawful.
What, though it may taste of the smoke of that flame,
Which in silence extracted its virtue forbidden—
Fill up—there's a fire in some hearts I could name,
Which may work too its charm, though now lawless and hidden.
So drink of the cup—for oh there's a spell in
Its every drop 'gainst the ills of mortality :
Talk of the cordial that sparkled for Helen,
Her cup was a fiction, but this is a reality."

On the right-hand side of the main entrance are the clerks' and general offices, and on the left those for the seven Excise gentlemen.

We were informed that no malt is purchased for this Distillery, as it is all made on the premises. The works are within ten minutes' walk from the railway station. One hundred persons are employed, and the annual output is 270,000 gallons.

BRUSNA DISTILLERY.

No. 9.

Brusna Distillery, Kilbeggan.

PROPRIETORS, JOHN LOCKE & CO.

EARLY the next day we left our little boycotted hotel at Tullamore, and proceeded to Kilbeggan, a drive of some eight miles. Our "turn out" would have afforded much amusement to some of our English friends, could they have seen us riding to our avocations that morning. The car, which looked like a large wine-case on wheels, was springless and sadly in need of a coat of paint; the horse was but a framework for a new edition, his tail being but a relic of the past, consisting of the stump and about half a dozen long hairs. Upon our remarking on the condition of the poor creature's caudal appendage, our jarvey exclaimed, "Shure yer honour, its a bit out of repair now, but its been a foine tail in its day." On nearing the bridge over the canal we came upon a crowd of persons evidently enjoying themselves, and remembering our experiences of the previous day, we bade our driver stop for a few minutes that we might witness the fun. To the music of a fiddle and a banjo, two Irish lads, regular "broths of boys," were dancing and shouting, and at times their movements were so infectious that some of the crowd joined in with them. An Irishman is always ready to fall into a jig, and the sound of music will generally set him off. Even our steed commenced prancing, and the six hairs in his tail were violently agitated, and kept swishing after the flies that, perhaps, were joining in the dance on his lean flanks. But we had business before us, and soon parted from the revellers, having first parted with some silver, being unable to refuse the blarney appeals of these rustic musicians.

After leaving Tullamore the road lay through a pastoral country, and finely-wooded estates, Within three miles of Kilbeggan we came to Durrow Abbey, the seat of the Earl of Norbury, whose ancestor was the notorious hanging Irish judge of the same name. The late Earl was murdered in the Park, in the open day, by a yet undiscovered assassin, and since then the noble mansion has scarcely ever been inhabited by the family. We drove through the thickly-wooded demesne, and soon came to the picturesque ruins of the Abbey, founded by St. Columb in 546, and the Church of Durrow, both of which adjoin the grounds of the mansion. They are situated in a most secluded spot, and the graveyard attached contains many ancient monuments, and a curiously sculptured cross, with scriptural devices thereon, which is supposed to have been brought from Iona by St. Columb, and is of a different kind of stone to any found in the neighbourhood. Near the church is a holy well dedicated to that saint. In 1186 Hugh de Lacey, while superintending the erection of a castle on the ruins of the Abbey, was killed by one of the labourers, a pious Catholic, who, indignant at the profanation of the sacred spot, struck off his master's head whilst he was stooping down to give directions.

We returned to the high road by another way, through the private grounds and along the edge of slopes, whose verdant soil was covered with the richest carpet of variegated mosses and wild flowers, canopied here and there with the spreading branches of luxuriant trees, everywhere inviting us to shelter and repose. You cannot travel many miles in this locality without passing some holy emblem or little chapel by the wayside, for the peasants hereabouts are fast and firm Catholics; and we have even seen, in some of the little hotels where we stayed, crucifixes and coloured pictures in the lobbies and passages.

A few miles further on we came to Kilbeggan, made interesting by Charles Lever, the novelist, who resided here, and many of the scenes and characters in his books are drawn from the district; notably "Con Cregan" and "Knight of Gwynne." The town is a famous and historic old place, situated about 45 miles from Dublin, on the coach road between that city and Galway. At the end of its main street, overlooking the Brusna Distillery, we came to the church, which stands in a picturesque graveyard crowded with curious old tombs. This ancient edifice occupies the site of a monastery founded by St. Becan, the contemporary of St. Columb, in the year 600; which, falling into decay, was rebuilt in the eleventh century by the family of Dalton, who dedicated it to the Blessed Virgin, and placed therein a band of Cistercian monks. After its dissolution, the monastery and its possessions were granted to the Lambart family, when a part of the monastery was enlarged, and a square tower added to it, and the building transformed into a parish church. As we descended the hill to the Distillery, our driver pointed out the place where, during the disturbances of '98, a party of the insurgents were defeated, after an obstinate resistance, by Colonel Blake, at the head of his Northumberland Militia; some of the rebels were hung in the town, and the others sent away as prisoners. The notable "Brothers Shears," who figured in the Dublin disturbances, and were afterwards executed at Newgate, came from Kilbeggan. Driving along, an extensive view presented itself: for several miles the valley of the Brosna displayed a very ocean of billowy hills, softly folded one upon another, with here and there plantations, pasture lands, and cultivated fields, through which the river flowed, looking like a silver ribbon—the whole a typical picture of the Emerald Isle. The Brosna is one of the feeders to the Grand Canal, a branch of which comes up to the town. We crossed this river, to reach the Distillery, by an old stone bridge, from the centre of which we obtained a good view of the establishment we had come to visit. In the Distillery grounds the river divides itself into two streams, forming a pretty little island of about an acre in extent, which has been utilized by one of the partners, and added to the grounds attached to his private residence.

A rustic bridge has been thrown across to the island, which is laid out in lawns, flower beds, and shady walks, and has in its centre a handsome stone fountain, always playing, supplied with water from the upper reaches of the river. Along the valley in olden times many smugglers were wont to locate, who gave a great deal of trouble to the Excise officers. At Mabrista, a secluded nook near the Distillery, formerly lived one "Mooney," who carried on his nefarious practices under the very nose of the revenue people. On one occasion a raid was about to be made upon him; Mooney, seeing in the distance the officers coming, called out to his wife to hide the three kegs of whisky in the garret. The ready-witted woman placed them in the middle of the floor, and then brought up her feather bed, which she ripped open, and completely covered the kegs. After searching all the rest of the house, the captain of the party entered the garret, and seeing nothing but a huge heap of feathers, called to his men that there was nothing in the d——d old cockloft but feathers, and it was useless to spoil their clothes by removing them.

The Brusna Distillery is said to be the oldest in Ireland, having been founded in the year 1750. It covers nearly five acres of ground, and the adjoining lands extending for half-a-mile on the river side, are also owned by John Edward and James H. Locke. Both these young men are practical distillers, and it is owing to their enterprise that the business has increased and the output been more than doubled during the last ten years. To do this they have, from time to time, made considerable additions to the old work—adding new machinery and modern appliances, still retaining, where practicable, the ancient ones, so as not to interfere with their old-fashioned Pot Stills, Mashing Vessels, and method of drying malt. The establishment, which is entirely enclosed, has a frontage to the main road of 150 feet, and entered by an archway, the clerks' and Excise offices being built therein. It stands on the banks of the river from which it derives its name, and the water for both driving and mashing comes from that stream. There is such an abundant and continuous supply, that at the time of our visit Messrs. Locke & Co. were arranging to use it for an electric light power in the premises. Having plenty of time, we first rambled through the old place with the partners, and afterwards commenced our duties by inspecting the Maltings, which are all built opposite the Distillery proper. They are light and well-ventilated buildings of five floors, capable of holding 10,000 barrels of corn. When we were there the yard at the back was crowded with farmers' carts, laden with barley put up in home-made flax sacks of a primitive shape and nearly 6 feet in length. After inspection by the corn-buyer, the barley is hoisted to the different floors and there spread out to a depth of 3 feet, from whence, as required, it is made to fall through traps on to the Malting Floors below, each of which possesses a stone Steep. The firm make all their own malt, being of opinion that they can manufacture a finer quality than can be purchased.

We next ascended a staircase, and found ourselves on a level with the Kiln floors, both laid with wire cloth and heated by open furnaces. On leaving the Kilns, we entered the Dry Malt Stores, consisting of a three-storied stone building with slated roof, capable of storing 4,000 barrels. We then proceeded to the Raw Grain Warehouses, which will hold 15,000 barrels of barley, to which is attached a Drying Corn Kiln, floored with Worcester perforated tiles, which seem to be in great favour with the Irish distillers. After having seen all that was of interest on this side of the way, we resumed the path from which we had deviated when we left the Distillery and entered the Mill building, a solid looking structure, containing six pairs of Mill Stones and a powerful set of Malt Rollers. Following our guide, we came to the Grist Room, a lofty chamber, 130 feet long, to which the grist is delivered by elevators. Previous to reaching the Mash House, we inspected the Brewing Tanks, which are each fitted with attemperating coils, and placed at an elevation to command the Mash Tun. In the Brewing House we observed two Mash Tuns, each with a capacity of 12,000 gallons, fitted with a double-action stirring gear; the two Underbacks of timber, which hold 5,000 gallons each, are placed on the paved floor of the house, and were made on the premises. Pursuing our investigations, we next visited the Tun Room, a large apartment, containing eight Washbacks, each holding from

10,000 to 14,000 gallons, also constructed by Messrs. Locke's workmen. After inspecting the Coolers, we crossed over to the Still House, a venerable building, whose outward appearance is altogether different from those we have recently visited. The first object which arrested our attention was the Wash Charger, a cast-iron vessel, placed on a gallery, holding 17,000 gallons; next the four old Pot Stills (by Miller & Co., Dublin), comprising a Wash Still, holding 10,320 gallons and 8,436 gallons; a Spirit Still, 6,170 gallons, and another 6,080 gallons. In these Stills are the revolving chains; we looked inside one that had served them for years, which was bright as a copper kettle. We have had frequent occasion to remark in the course of our lengthened tour that certain fads or customs were in use at some of the Distilleries, perhaps not very important in themselves, yet they give a character to the Whisky. Here, for instance, the same method of distillation is adopted that was used by the founders of the Distillery.

Proceeding up a few steps, we came to the Can-pit Room, situated at the rear of the Still House, which contains, besides the Safe, a Low-wines and Feints Charger, also a Feints and Spirit Receiver, holding respectively 8,000 and 4,000 gallons. Adjacent is the Spirit Store, containing the usual Spirit Vat and Casking apparatus; also a duty-paid Spirit Store, which usually contains from 25 to 30 puncheons of spirits of various ages to suit the requirements of local customers.

Passing through the quadrangle, we reached the two large Bonded Stores, excellent buildings, well ventilated, and which contained at the time of our visit over 2,000 casks of Whisky. A short distance from these Warehouses there is a large detached building, six stories high, which, until recently, was used for making the "patent oatmeal," but the increasing demand for their "make" led Messrs. Locke & Co. to abandon that business, and it is now used for Corn Stores.

Returning by another way, we passed the Spent Wash Tanks, one of them, a metal vessel, holding 14,000 gallons, erected by Ross and Walpole, of Dublin; also two new Worm Tubs, by Strong and Sons, of Dublin; one of them is on a high stone archway, the other covers the roof of the Still House. Here also we saw the Boiler House, containing a steam boiler, 32 feet long by 8 feet diameter, a Carpenters' Shop, Smithy, and Cask Shed. In the yard there is stabling for ten horses, a Cart Shed, and several cattle byres.

Seventy men are employed on the premises, the aged and infirm always being pensioned off or assisted. The make is "Old Pot Still," and principally sold in Dublin, England, and the Colonies. It is both a self and blending Whisky, and the annual output (1885—1886) was 157,200 gallons. The plant is, however, capable of making over 200,000 gallons.

Messrs. Reidy and Byrne are the chief Excise officers.

"POTEEN, GOOD LUCK TO YE, DEAR."

"They talk of the Romans of ould,
Whom, they say, in their own times were frisky;
But, trust me, to keep out the could,
The Romans at home here like whisky.
Shure, it warms both the head and the heart,
Its the soul of all readin' and writin',
It teaches both science and art,
And disposes for love or for fightin'.
Oh! poteen, good luck to ye, dear."

CHARLES LEVER.

No. 10.

Nun's Island Distillery, Galway.

PROPRIETOR, H. S. PERSSE.

IT was very early when we started from Tullamore for Galway. The morning was one of enchanting loveliness, and, as it afterwards turned out, too bright to last. Insects on leaf and flower were busy in the coolness of the morning, the rivulets rippled musically along amid the creepers and ferns, and the brilliant sun threw his rays on the many-hued foliage of the trees, the whole presenting a rare picture of summer beauty.

> "Sweet day! so cool, so calm, so bright,
> The bridal of the earth and sky;
> The dews shall weep thy fall to-night,
> For thou must die."
>
> HERBERT.

We were travelling through the so-called discontented country, but could see no signs of the agitators; the peasantry that we noticed at the railway stations, or from the carriage windows, looked neither ferocious nor turbulent; on the contrary, they looked merry and contented amidst their poverty and distress. The genuine Irish peasant is full of gentleness and affection, and although sometimes indolent, is generous, frank, and hospitable. We have seen them pass suddenly from the wildest and most extravagant gaiety, to a brief melancholy that is very touching, at other times displaying an impetuous courage that nothing could arrest; and it is well known that they are passionately fond of their home and country. As we passed along, we could not help noticing that their dwellings and little farm buildings were dreadfully out of repair and fast falling into decay, and it was quite evident that they were not let out on repairing leases. There was a motley crowd outside the principal stations as we passed along, and at one of these, where we changed carriages, we noticed a number of poor people, but no outward signs of a Nationalist amongst them; the many-vestured gossipers were happy enough telling stories and relating local scandal. The whole group composed a fertile study for lovers of the novel and picturesque. Most of them were dressed in garments which had evidently reposed in the obscurity of an old clothes' shop. One man had an ancient ragged-tail coat, far too small for him, the cuffs reaching just below the elbows; another a frock coat, the tails of which touched the ground; and it was very amusing to see how proud he was of this latter feature. A bright-eyed looking fellow was very happy in the possession of a soldier's faded tunic, and a pair of fustian knee-breeches in the last stage of consumption. Our first stoppage was at Athlone, built on both sides of the river Shannon, a garrison town, and considered one of the most important military positions in

NUN'S ISLAND DISTILLERY.

the Kingdom. We next passed Ballinasloe, celebrated for its annual fair for cattle, sheep, and horses, to which buyers from all parts of the Kingdom and the Continent resort. At Athenry we broke our journey for an hour to visit this old place, which was once a celebrated ecclesiastical city, but now a town of ruins. Whilst inspecting the remains of the old castle the weather changed, and we were glad to take shelter in the railway station. There is a branch line from Athenry to Tuam, and we regretted afterwards that we did not go up to see "the most splendid Catholic cathedral in Ireland." Resuming our journey, in less than an hour we arrived at our destination. As you approach Galway, "City of the Tribes," the general aspect is wild and gloomy, and the eye is seldom relieved by trees or landscape. The monotony is broken only by sterile hills, and the grass makes its way with difficulty through the stony surface. On arriving at the hotel we changed our damp garments, and fortified ourselves with a draught from the Nun's Island Stills to keep out the cold. Galway is situated most advantageously at the head of the Bay, and is built on both sides of a river issuing from Lough Corrib, which is crossed by two bridges. It is arranged on the plan of a Spanish town, many of the old houses being quadrangular, with an open court and arched gateway. In the Middle Ages Galway did a great trade with Spain, and many Spanish merchants settled there. Some of the houses they built still exist. We visited one of them, and found that it had been divided into small tenements, and was inhabited by several families.

Galway will always be memorable for the event which took place therein during 1493. James Fitzstephen Lynch was a wine merchant, and sent his only son to Spain with a purse of gold to purchase a cargo of wine. The son spent the money in riotous living, and purchased the wine on credit, bringing back with him in the ship the son of the wine-grower to visit his father and receive the money for the cargo. On the voyage young Lynch had the lad killed by his seamen, and swore them to secrecy with bribes. Some years afterwards, one of the seamen dying, disclosed to the father of Lynch, who was now a Judge, the history of the murder. Judge Lynch immediately had his son arrested and brought to trial, when he himself sentenced him to death. To prevent an intended rescue, this more than Roman father hanged his son from a window of his own house, under which we saw carved a skull and cross-bones in memory of the tragic event.

During the reign of Henry VIII. Galway supplied nearly the whole of the Kingdom with wine, for which purpose they had most extensive vaults at Athboy, the ruins of which, however, are still to be seen. The trade has declined, and the wine is no longer imported to Galway, but the manufacture of Whisky has now taken its place. Lough Corrib discharges its mighty volume of water through Galway in a foaming torrent, that would turn all the mills in Manchester. Alas! it is turned to little account, except for working the water-wheels of the Distillery and two or three flour-mills. This river is crossed, as we have mentioned before, by two bridges, and is as clear and rapid as the Rhone. It supplies all the water used in the works we were visiting, and about to describe.

The Nun's Island Distillery was established at the beginning of the century, and is the only Distillery in Connaught. It was purchased from the Encumbered Estates Court in the year 1840, by the father of the present proprietor, who considerably enlarged and improved it. Prior to that date, from 1815 to the period mentioned, it belonged to the Joyce family. During Mr. Persse senior's occupation, he turned the Distillery into a woollen factory, and it quickly became noted for its excellent friezes, but when the trade in this article declined, and Mr. Persse's lease of the Newcastle Distillery expired, he restored the works at Nun's Island to their original business, and carried on all his distillery operations there. The Distillery is planted on the centre of a small island, formed by the fork of the River Corrib, and is reached by a bridge from the main road. We entered by a stone gateway into a large triangular courtyard, round which are ranged a series of buildings. As you enter the yard the first object that strikes the eye is a large circular tank, elevated on stout iron columns, painted a bright scarlet, and which can be seen above the stone walls from the outside of the premises. We first visited the Maltings and Corn Stores, two lofty stone buildings on the right-hand side; five floors therein are devoted to the storage of corn and two for malting purposes, these latter have cement floors. Attached to this building, and up a few steps, is the Kiln, a lofty apartment, 40 feet square, whilst the Malt Deposit is at the rear of the general offices, and is an ingeniously constructed place, being almost hermetically sealed to prevent the action of the air. We then entered the Stone Loft, which is the top floor of the Mill building, where the malt and dried corn is pulverized through six pairs of stones, driven by a water-wheel. The ground floor of this building is used for taking in the barley from the farmer's carts; also the mill machinery. Adjoining is the Grist Loft, 145 feet by 43 feet; it is placed underneath the two Corn Lofts. We were then conducted to the Brew House, next door, an elegant building, and quite equal to any we have seen in Ireland. It contains two Mash Tuns, 27 feet in diameter and 8 feet deep, with the improved mashing gear driven by water power. Under the floor of this room are two Underbacks of a proportionate size, from which the worts are pumped up to the Coolers on the roof. Passing through a doorway on the right we came to the Back House, wherein are placed thirteen Washbacks, each holding about 18,000 gallons, and switched by machinery.

The Wash Charger is outside this building, and commands the Stills. It is a fine vessel and holds 16,000 gallons. Connected with the Back House is the Still House, a neat and well-lighted building, which contains a Wash Still, holding 16,000 gallons, Spirit Still 10,000 gallons and a Low-wines Still 6,000 gallons; also five Receivers of various capacities, and the Safe and Sampling Safe. The Worm Tub is in the open, and consists of a metal tank, 42 feet long, 18 feet wide and 10½ feet deep. Our guide conducted us to the river side and showed us a set of cooling pipes laid in the bed of the stream, and communicating by a series of pipes with the Distillery buildings.

Retracing our steps we visited the Spirit Store, conveniently arranged, and which contains a Vat, which holds 12,000 gallons, and from thence to the five Warehouses which are distributed over the premises. At the time of our visit they contained 5,000 casks of Whisky. Adjoining the Maltings there is a capital Smithy, Joiners' and Painters' Shops, etc.; and, at the end of the yard, Cart Sheds, Stables, and Store Houses. On the left, as you enter the gateway, are the Offices for the Distillery and Excise officers, the former contain private rooms for the Principal and Manager, and general clerks' offices.

For the prevention of fire, hose and pipes are laid all over the premises, there being an inexhaustible supply of water on all sides.

The make is called Galway Whisky, and the output is 10,000 gallons, 25 o.p., weekly, or annually about 400,000 gallons.

No. 11.

Limerick Distillery, Limerick.

PROPRIETOR, ARCHIBALD WALKER.

FROM Galway to Limerick was one of the most tedious journeys we had experienced during our lengthened stay in Ireland. The train proceeded for a greater part of the way at a snail's pace, through an uninteresting track, and to make matters worse, the railway guard kept the train waiting at several stations whilst he imparted the latest political news and local gossip to the stationmaster and his clerk. Fortunately, on nearing our destination, the scene changed, and we were travelling more rapidly through a pleasant country, along which the magnificent waters of the Shannon rolled on their way to the sea. This river is not only the *largest* river in Ireland, but of any other island on the globe; it waters eleven counties, and is 254 miles in length.

Soon the steeples and towers of Limerick came into view, and shortly afterwards we reached the station, where we found an omnibus from the hotel waiting for us, to which we speedily transferred ourselves and luggage. After dinner we sauntered forth in the cool of the evening to take stock of our surroundings, and view the famous places connected with this historic city.

In the tenth century the Danes took possession of Limerick and the adjacent islands in the Shannon; one of them, the most important, is exactly opposite the Distillery, as seen in the illustration. Most of these Danish Sea Kings were ferocious fellows, as cruel as they were brave. One of them, King Tergesius, was a terrible monarch, and ground the poor Irish to the dust. After subduing Malachy, King of Meath, the tyrant treated that prince with great indignity, but as events turned out, King Tergesius caught in Malachy a tartar, who served him out with more than poetical justice. Tergesius demanded the beautiful princess, daughter of Malachy, for his mistress, together with fifteen of the greatest beauties of Meath for his harem. Malachy dared not disobey the order, and sent his daughter, by night, to conceal her disgrace, accompanied by fifteen young heroes, dressed in female garb. On being ushered into the presence of the Danish King, the feminine attire was thrown off, and fifteen swords were presented to the tyrant's breast, as dowries with the maiden. The king was instantly bound a prisoner and his guards put to death, the castle gates were then opened to Malachy, who, with his soldiers, was waiting outside, and not a Dane was left alive, except the king himself, who, after a brief imprisonment, was drowned.

The history of the Old City of Limerick, for many centuries, is full of romance and tragical events; it is the only city that has never been taken by the

LIMERICK DISTILLERY.

English. It is called the "City of the Violated Treaty," from the following event: General Ginckle invested it in the year 1691, and after six weeks, failing of success, negotiations for a treaty were set on foot, amicable intercourse was established, and articles of capitulation signed, the garrisons were to march out with the honours of war, the Roman Catholics of the kingdom were to enjoy every privilege of King Charles the Second's time, and a parliament was to be summoned in Ireland. Alas, these stipulations were not fulfilled, and King William's successor enacted far more oppressive laws. This violation of a solemn treaty has hung as a curse on England for nearly two centuries. What miseries, rebellions, cruelties, and midnight murders might have been prevented by these concessions of civil and religious rights; and Ireland to-day would have been a loyal and happy country.

We visited some of the chapels, which were well attended by devout worshippers, male and female, presenting a striking contrast to the week-day services of the English churches, where one only sees, at most, a few women. After which we strolled along the river, and then returned to our hotel.

The next morning we drove to the Distillery, by way of the Thomond Bridge and along the banks of the Shannon. On our arrival we were received by the Manager with a hearty welcome, and conducted over every part of the establishment.

This fine old Distillery is planted on the banks of the Shannon, and just outside the walls of the city. Its origin dates from the beginning of the century, and it stands within a few hundred yards of the "Treaty Stone," and the celebrated Thomond Bridge, one of the six bridges that cross the river.

The works and buildings cover upwards of six acres, and are built on a very convenient plan, so as to work principally by gravitation, and there is an inexhaustible supply of water for every purpose. We commenced our inspection at the Maltings and Barley-lofts, which form a large building 203 feet long by 103 feet broad, and are of the shape and appearance of an old baronial castle, having two small inner courtyards, each of which is reached by a stone archway.

The Lofts used for the grain adjoin the Maltings, and are 110 feet long by 90 feet broad; they are situated over a large bonded Warehouse, and a powerful little engine hoists the grain to these floors at the rate of ten barrels a minute. The two Malting Floors, which have three spacious stone Steeps, are connected with four Kilns, two of them are in the centre, and one at each end of the building, two are floored with perforated Worcester tiles, the others with wire cloth, and all of them are heated by open furnaces. The Maltings are connected with each other on both floors by two spacious galleries, so that we were under cover the whole time. On our way to the Mill we passed through the Brewhouse, 80 feet long, which contains the four large brewing tanks, tuns, &c. The Mill is a spacious and lofty building, 50 feet long and 30 feet broad, divided into two separate departments, one for the grinding of grain, and the other for malt, the former contains four pairs of Stones and the latter two; the engine used in the Mill is a fine one of 30-horse power, and when necessary can be connected with another of the same size, which drives the machinery of the Distillery. In both Mills the grist and ground malt are carried by a double set of elevators and hoppers to the upper floors of the Mill, thence along a bridge into the Grist-loft over the Mash-house, to which place we next bent our steps. It is a handsome building, and contains two large Mash-tuns, with usual stirring gear and draining plates. The Underback in connection with these vessels is placed on the floor of the Pump-room, which adjoins the Brewing-house. Ascending a flight of steps we inspected the coolers, which form a part of the roof of the Mash-house, and also the capacious water tanks, placed on the roofs of the adjoining buildings, and therefore at a higher altitude than the Refrigerators.

At the suggestion of our guide, we climbed to a platform elevated over the tanks, where we gained a splendid view of the Clare Mountains, the counties of Limerick and Tipperary, the windings of the river Shannon, the City side of Thomond Bridge, including the picturesque King John's Castle, now used as barracks, and the island opposite, where a party of cavalry were exercising. Returning to the main building, we came to the Cooling-room, which contains four Refrigerators of the best and most modern pattern, also two cylindrical Condensers, like those at Messrs. John Jameson & Son's. From the outside landing we observed the Worm Tub of the Wash Stills, a vessel 48 feet long, which contains nine copper coils. It is in the open air, near the top of the Stills, and adjoins the Safe-room, to which place we next proceeded. It contains the usual Safe, Sampling Safe, and other appliances. From thence we went to the Pump Room, containing five sets of three-throw pumps, three used for worts and cold water, two for feints and one for feeding the boilers with hot water. At the end of the building we came to the Back House, a spacious open-roofed gallery, which contains five Wash-backs, each containing 30,000 gallons, with space left for other two in course of construction. The Wash-chargers are constructed of timber, and the Intermediate-charger of metal, all conveniently placed and of a capacity sufficient for the requirements of the work. Here our attention was called to the convenient arrangements for extinguishing fire—fire cocks and hose being distributed in every part of the Distillery, and ground boxes with hydrants placed along the numerous courts, these being all connected with the water tanks on the top of the building. A fire engine is also kept permanently on the premises. Crossing the square, we next entered the Still House, a lofty well-lighted structure, which contains three copper Pot Stills; one, the Wash Still, is placed near the steam boilers, the other two, in which the final operations are conducted, are situated near the two principal engine houses; they have open furnaces underneath, and possess all the latest improvements.

One of the last-mentioned Stills was constructed in 1885, for the manufacture of real Irish Whisky, and may be regarded as a model Still, embracing every improvement, which has suggested itself to its renowned builders, John Miller and Co., of Dublin, during their long experience. In close proximity are the Low Wines and Feints Chargers, and the various Receivers, all well grouped and conveniently placed as regards the different Stills. The floor under the Brewing Tanks is reserved for the grains or draff, whither it is conveyed from the Mash Tuns by means of a broad canvas belt, working upon rollers. After inspecting these, we crossed over to the Spirit Store, a building of neat elevation, 80 feet long by 60 feet broad, across the end of which a gallery has been erected for two large Spirit Vats. On the floor are the various appliances for casking and weighing the Whisky, previous to its being placed in the Warehouses.

A few yards' progress brought us to a range of four large bonded Stores, well ventilated and very dry. The brewer is accommodated with a capital dwelling house within the enclosure, also the resident engineer. We next inspected the General and Excise offices, and then took a peep at the Engine House, which contains four steam engines, two of them of 30-horse power and the others of somewhat less power; also six steam boilers of various capacities and dimensions, and from thence visited the Carpenters', Engineers', Coppersmiths', and Brassfitters' Shops ; all of them average 45 feet square, and are fitted up with every necessary appliance. Upwards of seventy persons are employed on the premises, many of whom have been attached to the place a number of years.

At the invitation of the Manager, we paid a visit to his house, a picturesque old mansion, communicating with the offices, and formerly occupied by the proprietor. It deserves some mention, not only for its size and antiquity, but for the beauty of its position, built as it is on the very margin of the river. The bay window of one of the drawing-rooms overhangs the stream, and commands a view that could not be surpassed from any house in Ireland ; comprehending the city of Limerick, the river and shipping, King's Island, where the artillery and cavalry daily exercise, sailing and fishing boats under the very window, and many other pictures too numerous to mention. After tasting the "make," we visited the garden, luxuriant in vegetables and flowers, and from thence to the stables and cartsheds, which are on an extensive scale, and finally to the Cooperage.

The Whisky made in this Distillery is of good reputation and full bodied, and is said to possess rapidly maturing qualities. It is designated "Pot Still Real Irish Whisky," and is sold all over the three kingdoms, and the annual output is 300,000 gallons. The principal Excise officer is Mr. Thomas Austin.

On leaving the Distillery, we completed our tour of the city before returning to our hotel, having arranged to start for Cork by an early train. In almost every town and city we have visited we have found that there is a church dedicated to Ireland's patron saint, and Limerick is no exception to the rule.

Swift personifies St. Patrick as follows :—

"Thee, happy Island, Pallas call'd her own,
When haughty Britain was a land unknown ;
From thee with pride the Caledonians trace
The glorious founder of their kingly race.
Thy martial sons, whom now they dare despise,
Did once their land subdue and civilize.
Their dress, their language, and the Scottish name,
Confess the soil from whence the victors came.
Well may they boast that ancient blood which runs
Within their veins, who are thy younger sons.

* * * * *

Britain, by thee we fell, ungrateful Isle,
Not by thy valour, but superior guile.
Britain, confess with shame this land of mine,
First taught thee human knowledge and divine ;
My prelates and my students sent from hence,
Made your sons converts both to God and sense."

WATERCOURSE DISTILLERY.

MIDLETON DISTILLERY.

NORTH MALL DISTILLERY.

No. 12.

North Mall Distillery, Cork.

PROPRIETORS, THE CORK DISTILLERIES' COMPANY, LIMITED.

CONTINUING our Distillery pilgrimage, we duly arrived at Cork, surnamed the "Beautiful City," the capital of the county, and charmingly situated on the River Lee.

The poet Spenser thus describes the river :—

"The spreading Lee, that like an island fayre,
Encloseth Corke with his divided flood."

On reaching the station we at once made for the Imperial Hotel, where we took up our quarters for a few days. After refreshing the inner man, we chartered a car and drove round to see the city. Cork is associated with the earliest history of Ireland, and is celebrated in romance and song. It was the abode of St. Finbar, who founded the cathedral church, and to whom, in the early days of his mission, such numbers of disciples flocked from all parts of the country, that the desert on which the cathedral stood soon became a noted city.

For more than 300 years the Danes repeatedly plundered the place and desolated its religious houses. In the year 1080 the city was destroyed by lightning, but was shortly afterwards rebuilt. Eight years later Dermot O'Brien, "the Violater," laid waste and plundered the town, carrying away with him the relics of St. Finbar, and from this time to the seventeenth century the history of this dear old city is full of incident.

In 1492 Perkin Warbeck, in his assumed character of Richard, Duke of York, landed here from Lisbon, and after a brief stay embarked for France. The mayor of the city, however, was hanged for countenancing the impostor. In the year 1568, during the absence of her husband, the Lord President of Munster, Lady Warham St. Leger, was besieged by the insurgents; and how the noble lady defended herself until Sir Henry Sidney's arrival from England with 400 men, is an interesting chapter of history.

Early next morning we made our way to the Distillery, which is situated in the suburbs of Cork. Passing along the main thoroughfare, we crossed a bridge and wandered beside the river, until we came to the North Mall Establishment. It is built on the banks of the Lee, and lies beneath the hollow of a rock, which is terraced with houses as far as the eye can reach. In the centre of the river there is an island, reached by a bridge, which has been utilised by the Company for workshops, coal and hay deposits, &c.

The Distillery buildings are erected on the site of the old Dominican Friary, called the Abbey of St. Mary of the Island, which was very extensive. They have a frontage of 684 feet, and were erected in 1779 by the father and uncle of the late Mr. Francis Wise, from whom the Company purchased the works, and who lately died worth three millions of money, besides possessing large estates in Cork and Kerry counties.

After presenting our credentials to the Manager, we were conducted over the place, and first visited the Corn Stores, which stretch along the whole of the higher ground of the works, and are reached by a roadway outside the boundary walls. They are stone buildings of several floors, and are capable of holding 30,000 barrels of barley, and nearly that quantity was then stored ready for winter's use. In this department the barley, before proceeding on its journey, is passed through a patent cleaning machine, like those previously described. Crossing these floors, we came to four spacious drying Kilns, of lofty and handsome elevation. When the barley has been properly dried in these Kilns, it is conveyed to the Grain Deposit rooms, and some idea of the size of these two apartments may be imagined, when we state that they contained 10,000 barrels, and there was room for more. The dried grain is sent by elevators from these floors to the Mill. Passing under an archway, we next found ourselves in the principal avenue, crossing which we came to the Mill building. It is five stories high, and built on arches over the stream, so as to enclose a water wheel, which is 25 feet in diameter, and drives six pairs of stones and all the ponderous machinery. The upper floors of the Mill are appropriated to meal rooms, &c. The grist is conveyed across a bridge over the roadway to the Grist Lofts, which are in the main building, whither we next bent our steps. They are spacious apartments, and conveniently situated for the Mash House. Descending a staircase, we found ourselves in the south gable of the brewing department, which contains two Mash Tuns, each with head cover and curtains, and measuring 30 feet in diameter and 8 ft. deep, with usual stirring gear and draining plates. The Underbacks are in the same house, also the Coppers for hot water. Emerging from the Mash House, we found ourselves in the Tun Room, in which are nine fermenting vats, holding from 30,000 to 45,000 gallons each.

The Wash descends from these vessels by gravitation to the Wash Charger, a handsome circular timber vessel, which holds 35,000 gallons, built over the stream, and is a prominent object from the other side of the river. The intermediate charger is in the Still House, and to that place we next paid a visit. It is a capacious and lofty building, with paved floor and well lighted. It contains three old Pot Stills (there are no other on the premises); the Wash Still has a capacity of 22,000 gallons, and the others 20,000 gallons and 16,000 gallons respectively.

We ascended a few steps from the floor, to inspect their respective Receivers and Chargers, and from this point we observed that the Still-men were so absorbed in their occupation that they hardly noticed us as we passed along. This house is interspersed with other vessels besides the Stills, and contains several powerful pumps and other machines. We made a special visit to the river, to see the cooling pipes, which are laid in the bed of the Lee. Watching this beautiful river, and hearing the bells chime out from a neighbouring steeple, we called to mind the following lines:—

"On this I ponder
Where'er I wander,
And thus grow fonder
  Sweet Cork of thee!
With thy bells of Shandon,
That sound so grand on
The pleasant waters
  Of the River Lee."

The Bells of Shandon.

From the river side we once more returned to the Distillery proper, passing on our way three capacious metal Worm Tubs connected with the Stills, and a Cooling House, where there are four of Morton's Patent Refrigerators. On entering the Can-pit Room our guide informed us that after the Spirit has undergone two distillations it runs through the Safe into the Spirit Receiver, placed in this apartment, which holds 8,000 gallons, from whence it is pumped into the Spirit Store. Turning to the right, at the end of the wall, we came to the latter place, and were shown three Spirit Vats of unusual proportions, each being of 7,000 gallons content. In this house the Spirit is reduced 25 o.p., casked, weighed, and then sent into the bonded Warehouses.

By passing through the Still House and another building, we reached the Warehouses much sooner than by going round the road. They are placed at the east end of the Distillery, and consist of eleven buildings, and it took us some time to inspect them all. They contained 7,210 puncheons of Whisky, of various ages; and it may be stated that there is another Warehouse, a three-decker building, which contained 3,000 butts.

On leaving these Warehouses we were taken to see the Maltings, which are a separate work, although connected with the Granaries before referred to. We entered them from the main road, and found them to consist of four spacious Malting Floors, with the usual Steeps, and at the end two Kilns, each of which is floored with Worcester tiles, and, like the rest of the works, kept beautifully clean; indeed, this is a marked feature of the whole Distillery.

Retracing our steps, we passed through the front entrance gate, and on turning to the right, found ourselves in the Engine Department, where there are two capital engines, by Rowan, of Belfast, of 60 and 40-horse power respectively, and six of Galloway's patent tubular boilers, 30 feet long by 8 feet in diameter, and eight sets of three-throw pumps. Formerly there were six chimney stacks on the premises, but, some few years since, in order to divert the smoke from the city, they were demolished and the Company, at a cost of £5,000, built the present handsome chimney stack, 160 feet high, into which they have diverted all the flues in the concern. Here also we noticed the arrangements for extinguishing fire, which consist of hydraulic pipes and hose, so placed in position that they reach every part of the buildings, and command the entire water force of the Distillery. Crossing the quadrangle, we next entered the Carpenters' Shop, where the Company make all their carts and floats; from thence to the Engineers' Shop, which possesses a fine lathe, driven by a donkey engine; and last, but not least, the Smithy, where we saw five stalwart Irishmen, with "their bared and brawny arms, making the welkin ring." Some of them were very handsome fellows, and would make capital soldiers. The Cooperage is an establishment of itself, and is within the enclosure. Here, besides being repaired and cleaned, the casks are manufactured, and we were much interested in the process. Crossing the bridge, we paid a visit to the island, already referred to, where the coal is stored. Each cargo averages from 230 to 250 tons. As the coal is landed it is stacked separately, in square solid piles, and the corners of these are whitewashed to prevent pilfering, and each labelled with the name of the vessel and date of delivery. Some idea may be formed of the magnitude of this stock, when we state that we saw 8,000 tons and the stacks covered half an acre of ground. On this island there are the other buildings before referred to. At the back of the Distillery, and by the riverside, the Company own many acres of beautifully-wooded grounds, a small portion of which has been appropriated for cottages, wherein the *employés* of the Distillery dwell.

The offices of the Company are in Morrison's Island, in the heart of the city. They consist of a handsome pile of buildings, containing general offices for twenty clerks, private ones for the Directors, and a commodious Board-room. Under the offices, and in a range of buildings at the back, the Company have large export Bottling Stores, and our guide informed us that they bottle nothing less than five-year old Whisky, with an average strength of 10 u.p. At the top of the grand staircase is placed the show-case used in the Philadelphia and Paris Exhibitions, in which are exhibited medals of award from Philadelphia, Paris, Sydney, and Cork Exhibitions, also samples of their make at Midleton and North Mall Distilleries. In the latter place there are 250 persons employed, and the Distillery is under the personal management of Mr. Maurice Murray and his son, Mr. Daly Murray, the local Managing Directors. For over a century the whisky made in this establishment has been popular in Cork and the neighbouring districts, but the name of Wise's Old Whisky is equally well known and imbibed all over Ireland, England, the Colonies and America.

A local bard, who was born and reared on the banks of the Lee, near the Distillery, thus sung of it:—

"Much I've heard about the Rhine
With vineyards gay and castles stately;
But those who think I care for wine
Or lofty towers, mistake me greatly:
A thousand times more dear to me
Is whisky by the silvery Lee."

The make at North Mall is called Wise's Cork Old Pot-Still Whisky, and the annual output is 510,000 gallons. As the Company have now concentrated all their works in Cork at the North Mall Distillery, and the capacity of both this and the Midleton Distillery have been more than doubled, the Green, Watercourse, and John Street Distilleries have been turned into Maltings, Corn Stores, and Warehouses. We paid a visit to them, as they were all within a mile or two distance.

The Watercourse Work is about 300 yards square, and contains three Granaries, which hold 40,000 barrels of barley; four Kilns, drying 450 barrels daily; a Steam Mill for grinding and Meal Stores, which are five stories high; seven Bonded Warehouses, which contained 6,000 casks of Whisky, and stabling for 20 horses. The buildings and ground adjoining cover fifteen acres.

The Green Distillery is almost of similar proportions, but of somewhat less contents. The John Street Distillery, which consists principally of Warehouses and Granaries is somewhat larger.

No. 13.

Midleton Distillery, Midleton, co. Cork.

PROPRIETORS, THE CORK DISTILLERIES' COMPANY, LIMITED.

MUCH to our regret, the journey to Midleton was a short one, being only thirteen miles from Cork. The railway runs some distance along the banks of the River Lee, under hanging woods and beautiful hill slopes. After leaving the river, the route traversed was through a well-cultivated country, both hilly and luxuriant. On reaching the terminus, we hailed a car and drove through the town to the Distillery.

Midleton is an interesting place. In olden days it was known by the name of Chore Abbey, so named from a famous Cistercian Monastery, founded in 1180 by Barry Fitzgerald: "chore" signifies a ford. The present name is derived from Midleton, being half-way between the towns of Youghal and Cork. It is situated on an inlet of Cork Harbour, and the tide flows up to the town. There is a river at each end of Midleton, one of which flows by the walls of the Distillery; these rivers abound in salmon, and are the favourite resort of anglers. The town is planted in the Vale of Imohally, a healthy and fertile country, screened on all sides by lofty hills and embellished with plantations. In the neighbourhood are numerous ruins of castles and abbeys, each with its legend and ghostly tale, of which our driver gave us a specimen; and as we evinced no signs of horror, nor did our hair stand on end, he did not repeat the experiment. But to return to the subject of our visit. The Midleton Distillery is one of several similar undertakings that have been absorbed in the Cork Distilleries' Company, Limited, Mr. Murphy, the former proprietor, remaining in the concern as a managing director.

The success of this enterprising Company was assured from the very first, when the former proprietors of the Distilleries, all practical men, decided to remain in the Company and undertake its personal management. The establishment at Midleton covers upwards of eight acres of ground, and was built by one Marcus Lynch, at a cost of £20,000, at the latter end of the last century, who at that time carried on an extensive woollen manufactory. The venture proved unsuccessful, and the buildings were subsequently sold to the Government, who made additions to them and turned them into military barracks. The premises eventually came into the hands of Lord Midleton, who, in the year 1825, sold them to Messrs. Murphy & Co. This firm converted them into a Distillery, and shortly brought the output up to 400,000 gallons annually, employing some 200 men in its manufacture.

We spent a most interesting time at the Distillery, and were more than ever convinced that woollen mills and barracks are not only suitable, but more convertible buildings for distilling purposes than any other, possessing, as they do, height, space, light, and large courtyards. The close proximity of the railway and water carriage, and the locality being a large corn-growing district, made the Midleton Distillery a desirable property for the Company to acquire. A carriage drive, which leads to the Distillery, runs alongside the river, which is shaded with lofty trees and forms a beautiful border to the grey-stone buildings of the establishment.

We drove up the centre of the big quadrangle, and through a crowd of carts and waggons laden with corn, to the Manager's Office, which adjoins the Corn buyer's department; and whilst waiting for the before-mentioned gentleman's appearance, we amused ourselves by watching the proceedings. The farmers were busy offering their samples, while among the crowd were several groups of laughing girls, who had accompanied their friends for the sake of an outing. As soon as the manager arrived, we commenced our inspection of this large work, at the Granaries. The first we entered was a handsome stone and brick structure, 99 feet long and 33 feet wide, and six stories high. On the opposite side there is a second building used for malting, whither we bent our steps. It has four floors, of large dimensions; the top being used for barley, which falls through sluices on to the three Malting floors beneath. The Steeps on these floors are composed of concrete, and are capable of working 350 barrels at one time. About twenty yards progress brought us to the Kilns, of which there are three, each measuring 40 feet by 31 feet. We passed through one of them, and found ourselves in the Malt-storing Department, which consists of four separate rooms, sheltered from the light and quite enclosed. Descending two or three steps, we passed through the Malt-meal Loft, which completed our tour of this range of building. We next retraced our steps to the Grain Lofts first visited, and, after passing through a pathway of corn, we came to the two handsome Corn Kilns, both of which communicate direct with the Dried Corn Floor. The dried barley is sent from this place by an endless belt into the Mill, which was the next object of our attention. Proceeding up a stone stair-case, we entered the Mill Room, which contained, beside the ponderous machinery and nine pairs of Stones, four large Malt Crushing Rollers, the malt being delivered here from the Maltings by elevators. Crossing the Mill Floor, we next come to the Grist Lofts, passing on our way four Heating Coppers, each with a capacity of 22,000 gallons, and all heated by steam. These Lofts are very spacious, and coveniently arranged for communication with the Brewing House.

The grist is conveyed through closed troughs to the Mash Tuns, where it undergoes the first process in Whisky making. Following our guide, we descended a flight of steps and found ourselves in the Mash House, a well-lighted apartment, and containing three Mash Tuns—two holding 21,000 gallons and the other 30,000 gallons, all possessing the patent revolving stirring gear. In close proximity to these vessels there is a large Underback, capable of containing 15,000 gallons of Wort. Passing along, we came to a place where two thoroughfares diverge, and turning to the left soon found ourselves in the Tun Room, an extensive gallery, ranged along the walls of which are 16 Washbacks—fine timber vessels; 14 of them hold 24,000 gallons each, and two 40,000 gallons each. From these vessels the Wash is pumped to the Wash Charger, which holds 20,000 gallons, and is placed at an elevation to command the Stills. We left this department for a time, and followed our guide across the court into the grounds attached to the house formerly occupied by Mr. Murphy, which are beautifully wooded and very picturesque, to see the coolers which are placed in the bed of a stream flowing from a rocky cavern, the waters of which are icy cold even in the hottest summer. Besides these there are also three sets of Morton's Refrigerators in the Distillery.

Returning to the scene of our labours, we passed the Worm Tub, 40 feet in diameter and 14 feet deep, and entered the Still House, the outward appearance of which is somewhat different from other places of the kind we have visited. It must have formerly been a drill hall or canteen in its old barrack time, and is well adapted to its present use. It contains, besides a Coffey's Patent Still, three old Pot Stills, of the following capacities:—a Wash Still, containing 31,648 gallons; and two Spirit Stills, each holding 10,000 gallons. Going forward a little to the right, we reached the Can-pit Room, wherein are placed, besides the usual Safe and Sampling Safe, five handsome Receivers, as follows:—one Spirit, two Feints, and two Low-wines Receivers, each with a capacity of 5,000 gallons. In close proximity is the Spirit Store, wherein are two vats, each of which holds 20,000 gallons. In this place the spirit is reduced, racked off into casks, weighed, and taken an account of by the Excise, and then sent to the different Warehouses, to which buildings we next directed our steps. They are seven in number, dry and well ventilated, and contained, at the time of our visit, 7,000 casks. After perambulating through these Warehouses, we paid a visit to the Cooperage, where casks are manufactured, cleaned, and sweetened; afterwards to the numerous industries of this large undertaking, consisting of smiths', carpenters', and harness makers' shops. On returning to the east quadrangle, we inspected the Engine Department, which consists of three handsome engines, of 30-horse power; four steam-boilers, measuring 30 feet long by 8 feet in diameter, and seven sets of powerful three-throw pumps. The three chimney stacks, which uplift themselves from the centre of the works, are upwards of 100 feet high, and add much to the appearance of the Distillery, all the buildings of which are of good structural and architectural proportions.

There is a capital fire engine on the premises, and the arrangements for extinguishing fire are as complete as those at North Mall. The whole of the establishment is lighted by gas, and there appeared to be sufficient coal stored in the yards to supply the inhabitants of Midleton during the winter.

Mr. A. Ross, who has an assistant under him, is the distiller, and there are upwards of 200 men employed on the premises. Mr. Davies is the supervisor, and there are seven other Excise officers. The Whisky manufactured at Midleton is called "The Cork Whisky Make," and the annual output is a little over 1,000 000 gallons.

No. 14.

The Glen Distillery, Kilnap, Cork.

PROPRIETORS, THE GLEN DISTILLERY COMPANY, LIMITED.

A DRIVE of about two miles from the "Beautiful City" brought us to Kilnap Bridge, at which point there is also a magnificent and graceful viaduct, containing seven arches of immense span, over which the trains pass between Cork and Dublin; both span the valley and river of the Glen. From the bridge we had an excellent view of the Distillery, which, although nearly a quarter-of-a-mile higher up and embosomed in the steep green depths of the wooded valley, seemed placed almost at our feet. This old-fashioned structure was used as a mill for nearly a century, but some few years since was converted into a Distillery, and we were surprised to find so quaint a building—its walls mostly covered with ivy and ferns—containing the very latest inventions of modern distilling.

This old-world structure is placed almost at the head of the valley, on the banks of the river Glen, and within fifty yards of the waterfall, where the river comes tumbling over the high rocks, some small portion of its volume having been previously imprisoned and conveyed through an aqueduct, which supplies a water-wheel of huge dimensions, capable of driving all the shafting, pumps, elevators, gearing, &c.

Half a century since this glen was a favourite holiday resort of the Cork citizens, and there are relics which testify to the fact that there was rollicking and merrymaking here in those days. The Distillery and buildings cover about six acres, and are approached by a short drive off the main road. The corn buildings of three floors are on a level with the road, and from this point we descended the hill to the Distillery proper. All the work is done by gravitation and water-power, of which there is always an abundant supply, indeed there is no steam engine on the premises.

The Corn Lofts above referred to contained about 7,000 barrels, and communicate direct with the Kiln, a building 36 feet square. The Mill, which commands the Dried Corn Loft, contains four pairs of stones, and adjoins the Grist Loft, which is over the Mash Tun.

The fine Boiler, 26 feet long and 8 feet in diameter, is protected by Dunne's patent lagging, which consists of woven hair, feathers, and other non-conducting material, enclosed within thin iron sheets, laid on in segments over the surface of the boiler, which has the advantage that every portion of it can be taken off at will; by this arrangement no heat is lost. The three Brewing Tanks, which supply the hot liquor for the Mash Tun, &c., are of the latest type, having steam distributors, or turbines, which consist of steam pipes, with wheel valves, and large copper globes, which inject the high pressure steam into the liquor at certain angles, thereby avoiding all vibration and noise.

The Mash Tun measures 17 feet in diameter and 8 feet in depth. It has double-action carriage rakes for stirring, and strainer plates. The two Underbacks are situated below the Mash Tun. There are two handsome sets of three-throw pumps, which send the liquor up to the Worts and Water Coolers and Refrigerators, situated on the top of the building, and also through cooling pipes laid in the bed of the river.

The six Washbacks hold 4,000 gallons each, and the Wash Charger 5,000 gallons. Near the Mash Tun there is a neat glazed office for the use of the distiller.

The Still House contains two "Old Pot" Stills, of the most modern make, containing 3,000 and 3,500 gallons respectively, with internal steam coils. These Stills work into two large worm tubs, which are placed some distance above them.

In the Can-pit Room there are two neat copper safes, of ingenious construction ; also five receivers, for the unfinished and finished spirit.

The Spirit Store contains two vats, each holding 600 gallons. There are at present three Bonded Warehouses, capable of storing 2,000 casks, and there is another large one in course of erection 200 feet long, which will hold about 8,000 puncheons of Whisky.

The Grains House and Spent Wash Tank are in the yard, and there are good Stables and Cart Houses. There are three houses on the premises which are used as dwellings and Excise office, and the company have just built a handsome villa, on the hill above the Distillery, for Mr. T. Creagh, the manager and distiller.

The water used for brewing and distilling purposes is of the best quality. Twenty workmen are employed. The Whisky made is pure Malt, and of a high-class quality, and the annual output about 60,000 gallons.

The City office of the Distillery is at No. 1, Carrol's Quay, Cork.

BANDON DISTILLERY.

No. 15.

Bandon Distillery, Bandon, County Cork.

PROPRIETORS, ALLMAN & CO.

THIS fine Distillery is situated at Monerone, a beautiful valley, half a mile from the thriving English-looking town of Bandon, and nearly three miles from the ancient and historic town of Innishannon, near which, on the lands of Barnas, there is an extensive circular fortress, surrounded by a double rampart and fosse, in which Barry Oge, who helped to make many a page of history, encamped when driven from Downdaniel Castle, which he had built.

It may be of some interest now, as the Bicentenary of the Revocation of the Edict of Nantes has lately been celebrated, to refer to an attempt made early in the last century to introduce the manufacture of silk into Innishannon. Mr. Addersley, the then owner of the village, invited some Huguenots, skilled in the rearing of silk-worms and weaving of silk, to settle there. He built houses for them, and planted out small plots of ground with mulberry trees. Owing to the unsuitability of the climate and other causes, however, the attempt proved an utter failure, but the survival of the names "Mulberry Field," where no fruit or trees of that description can be found, and that of "The Colony," whence the colonists have long since departed, attest the accuracy of this historical fact.

The lovely Vale of Innishannon, which extends almost to the Distillery, is covered with hanging woods, and the scenery is beautifully picturesque. Opposite the works, and on one of the hills on the other side of the river, Mr. Richard Lane Allman dwells in a stately stone-built mansion. The view therefrom of Bandon, the river, and surrounding country is all that an artist could desire. The River Bandon is navigable up to Innishannon, and flows past the Distillery, where it is joined by the Ordnagira, or Silver Stream, a lively dashing little rivulet, which runs right through, and in some places under the works; its water is used by Messrs. Allman for driving and distilling, and is noted for its brightness and purity.

A short distance from the Distillery is Kilbrogan Churchyard, where are buried three of Clancarty's soldiers, who were slain in the attempt to take the town of Bandon for James II.; but, beyond this, the district has been made classic by Spenser in his "Fairëe Queene." His daughter resided for a long time in Kilbeg Castle.

Having somewhat digressed, we now proceed with a description of the Bandon Distillery. It was in ancient times one of the old manorial mills, and dates back to the year 1700. We were able to trace the name of Allman in connection with the building to the year 1750, and at that time they were well known in the town and district for their patriotism and benefactions.

In the year 1826 the present proprietors turned the buildings into a Distillery, and when first fitted up, the works did not turn out more than 60,000 gallons yearly, but the Statistical Records of the county inform us that, after spending many thousands of pounds on improvements, in the year 1836, the Bandon Distillery was making nearly 200,000 gallons annually, and employing upwards of a hundred people. Even then, the Distillery buildings were of little note; now in this year of grace, 1886, they are the chief feature of the locality, and the proprietors are the largest employers of labour in any distillery outside of any city in Ireland.

The history of this fine establishment would occupy more than our available space; suffice it to say that from time to time every new patent and appliance known, and used in distilling, has been added, and the Messrs. Allman have spared neither time nor money in making this establishment as complete as possible.

The main block of buildings extends some 464 feet eastwards, whilst northwards they run back 340 feet, and nearly all of them are five and six storied. The works and grounds cover about eight acres, and their general appearance from the road and railway is commanding and picturesque; the premises are connected by a siding with the Cork and Bandon Company's line of Railway. The corn, which is principally grown in the district, is purchased at the Distillery and neighbouring markets. At the time of our visit the courtyards and roadway resembled a fair, so animated was the scene. The farmers' sons who had driven in the loads of corn, dressed in their Sunday best, were accompanied in a good many instances by their sisters (some of them real Colleen Bawns). We counted more than seventy carts laden with barley, each waiting their turn to deliver at the Granaries, and were informed that 1,200 barrels, on an average, are delivered daily, the payments for same from October 1st to Christmas amounting to about £800 per day.

Some of the Grain Lofts are of six floors, and at the time contained 50,000 barrels of grain, but this does not at all represent the requirements of the season. The mode of receiving the corn into these huge Granaries is unlike any we have seen in our travels. The loaded carts wait their turn in passing through a covered way to the Receiving Corn Hopper, which, in shape, is not unlike a pulpit, at an enclosed corner of which presides the corn sampling clerk, who duly tests the grain, which is tumbled from the sacks into this receptacle, where, through an opening at the lowest part, it falls into a metal scale below, which holds about a barrel of grain; here stands another clerk, who, without touching the scale, by the movement of a balance handle, registers the weight and tips the corn into a hopper below, across the bottom of which is stretched an iron riddle or grill to catch the straws or husks before the corn falls into the elevators. It may here be stated that the sampling clerk has the command of a semaphore on the top of the buildings, which indicates the destination of the barley, either for grinding or malting floors.

The corn is lifted to the various floors by patent elevators, which consist of ingeniously devised, malleable cast chains and wheels; the steel plate cans attached thereto are thin, light, and clean, and there is more than half a mile of these elevators in the establishment. The finest barley is selected from the stock for the two Malting floors, spacious and lofty apartments, which contain the usual Steeps. Connected with these floors there is a fine double Malt Kiln, with Hermann's patent wedge-section wire flooring, said to be the best and most durable yet invented. The chief Malt House is the second largest of its kind in Ireland, if not in the Kingdom; it consists of two growing floors, each 168 feet long, by 42 feet wide, and 8 feet high, and vies with those of Messrs. Guinness, of Dublin, which are only 4 feet longer and 2 feet wider.

MALTINGS, &c., BANDON DISTILLERY.

But to return to the Corn Department. After the grain has been thoroughly cleaned in the five machines, or separators, it is dried in the three Grain Kilns, and from thence lifted by elevators and belts, and conveyed by a series of shoots across the public road, at an altitude of 20 feet, from one section of the building to another, into the Mill, a three-flatted edifice, which adjoins the Mash House, and contains four pairs of stones, and a fine set of malt-rollers for crushing the malt. From here the pulverized grain is elevated to the Grist Lofts, which command the three Mash Tuns—two of them hold 33,000 gallons and the other 18,000, all of them having the usual patent stirring rake-shafts. The wort runs from these tuns into a huge Underback. We should here state that there are seven heating tanks for supplying the hot water to the Mash Tuns and other vessels.

There are four sets of three-throw pumps to send the liquor from the Underbacks through the coolers, which are laid in the bed of the millstream, and there is also a large Morton's Refrigerator commanding the fermenting Tuns. The 18 Washbacks, or fermenting Tuns, are fine timber vessels, each holding from 15,000 to 28,000 gallons, and the two Wash Chargers have a capacity of 15,000 gallons each.

The Still House, an angular stone building, with its outer walls covered with lichens, moss, and ferns, is the oldest part of the works, and contains five Old Pot Stills—two Wash and three Spirit—heated with open furnaces. Their contents are severally two of 16,000, one of 12,000, and two of 4,000 gallons.

The Worm Tub connected with the Stills is of timber, and placed in the open air; it contains 36,000 gallons of water, besides which there are other condensers at the rear of the Still House. The Running Room contains five Receivers, and the Safe commands them all, whilst they also command the Stills. There are in all, four Low-wines Receivers, capable of containing each 6,000 gallons, and one Spirit Receiver of the same capacity. The vat in the Spirit Store holds 15,000 gallons.

The fifteen Warehouses, dry and well ventilated, are conveniently arranged as basement and sub-basement to the Granaries, and contained 9,000 casks.

In the Boiler House we saw one of Galloway's Patent Steam Boilers, and there are two others besides, constantly working. Wilson, of Stafford, has just fixed one of his Patent Gas Producers, through which all the coal for steam-raising purposes is passed and converted; the gaseous products being finally consumed in the boiler flues in the usual manner.

All the work of the Distillery is done by gravitation and water power, the Millwheel over the stream is 36 feet by 8 feet. The aqueduct runs from a deep glen at the back of the Distillery, where the proprietors are making preparations to form an artificial lake (estimated to cover some 50 to 60 statute acres), for the ponding of water during floods, their requirements of power having of late years, so much increased. This lake will cost them a considerable sum. They are, however, assisted by the natural formation of the ground, the stream passing at the place chosen for the embankment and sluice being a narrow rocky gut of not more than 6 feet wide and 40 to 50 feet high.

CORN STORES, &c., BANDON DISTILLERY.

The firm also possess a fine spring of the purest water in the adjoining meadow, used only for reducing purposes. With the exception of Cadiz Sherry wood, which they have to buy, Messrs. Allman & Co. make all their own casks and have a fine cooperage. Their repairs are also done by their own workmen; hence there is to be seen quite a village of industries—carpenters, coppersmiths and fitters, engineers' and harness makers' shops, supplied with steam lathes and other machinery, and there is the veritable village blacksmith under the spreading tree.

Nearly 200 men are employed, and there is besides a large staff of clerks.

We noticed a fine bottling store, but were informed that Messrs. Allman and Co. bottle for export only, to oblige their customers in the colonies.

In a fine building there are capital offices for the general clerks, managers of departments and the partners, and good accommodation has been provided for the Excise gentlemen.

Messrs. Allman & Co. make both Old Pot Still Whisky, designated Irish, and Pure Malt Whisky, both of a superior quality, a large trade in which is done in Ireland; their principal business is, however, with England, Scotland, and the Colonies. The annual output is a little over 500,000 gallons.

The Partners are Mr. Richard Lane Allman and Mr. James C. Allman, J.P. The operative distiller and brewer is Mr. C. McPherson.

No. 16.

Birr Distillery, Birr, King's County.

PROPRIETORS, R. & J. WALLACE.

WE took Birr, or Parsonstown as it is also called, on our way back to Dublin, and unfortunately were obliged to stay in that town all night. We liked the town well enough, but the hotel we selected was not one of the best, and we have recollections of an uncomfortable night. The Distillery, which is near town, was established in the year 1805, and is built of solid limestone. The works are approached from the high road by a carriage drive or avenue, which runs for some distance along the river bank; a handsome stone archway, draped in ivy, gives access to the buildings.

The principal Grain Warehouses are situated on the opposite bank of the river, in an inclosure, entered by an old-fashioned pair of gates. Here are two Grainaries of five floors each, which contained 5,000 barrels of grain, and two Drying Kilns; the sub-ground floors are used as Bonded Warehouses. The corn is here delivered and weighed before being sent to the various Corn Lofts.

In the Distillery buildings there are altogether eight Grain Lofts, and the Mill contains two pairs of stones and a set of Malt Rollers. The Grist Loft, which adjoins the Mill, is above the Mash Tun; for supplying hot water there are four coppers. The Mash Tun is of the ordinary size and description, and near to it are four sets of three-throw Pumps. The six Washbacks have a capacity of 18,000 gallons each, and the Intermediate Charger is in the Still Room. In the Running Room there are five Receivers and the Safe. The Wash Charger is fixed on the roof of an annexe of the building.

The Still House contains two old Pot Stills, and adjoining there is a Spirit Store. In the yard there are thirteen Bonded Warehouses, which contained some 3,000 casks. We noticed a capital Cooperage, Stables, Engineers' and Carpenters' Shops. Forty men are employed upon the premises.

The following is a brief description of the arrangement of the Distillery. The centre court is called the Square Yard; the buildings on the north side are devoted to the Back House and Cooling Lofts, as also the Mill, worked by a powerful breast water-wheel, which discharges its waters over the Cooling Pipes, which are laid in the bed of the mill race, and over these pipes is the Worm Tub, fixed on an elevation of substantial stonework; those on the east, to Still House, Tun Room, Spirit Store, and Racking Room; on the west, Maltings and Kiln, Corn Floors for selected grain, Malting Steeps, and Bonded Warehouses; on the south side are Corn Stores and Bonded Warehouses.

The Whisky is produced from pure malt and grain; the annual output is 200,000 gallons, which obtains a ready sale in the principal cities and towns of Ireland and England, and shipments have been made to the Colonies.

No. 17.

Bishop's Water Distillery, Wexford.

PROPRIETORS, NICHOLAS DEVEREUX & CO.

ON our return we broke our journey at Dublin to visit the Bishop's Water Distillery, and to rest a few days before starting northward. By the advice of our Dublin friends we chose Brazil's Hotel, Kingstown, for this purpose, and were afterwards glad that we had done so. It certainly is one of the most comfortable and cosy little hotels in Ireland, and much frequented by Englishmen. The rooms are comfortable, the *cuisine* all that can be desired, and the attendance of the best. One of the waiters—who is a character in his way, and a very witty fellow, rejoices in the *soubriquet* of "Lord Pat" to his friends, but is plain "Pat" to the general public—studies every newspaper that comes into the place, and gives you the cream of it all whilst you are at breakfast; he is, of course, a Nationalist, and says he hopes to get into Parliament one day, "When he will settle Home Rule once and for aye." His great delight is to inveigle you into an argument, and ten to one he will get the best of it. From the windows of our room we had an expansive view of Dublin Bay, the Hill of Howth, and Kingstown Harbour, and we took great interest in watching the arrival and departure of the English Mails. The Hotel is a convenient place for tourists who wish to visit Bray, the Dargle, or Powerscourt Waterfall, as they are all within a driving distance.

It was a fine morning when we started on what proved to be a delightful journey to Wexford. The contrasts of scenery on the railway are very striking; now we travelled through a short valley, or passed at the base of lofty rocks, whose overhanging tops seemed to threaten our whole train; then by the verge of a precipice over the sea, or plunged into some deep tunnel: then perhaps a long stretch of beautiful country, well cultivated; anon across bridges, over streams and rivers, whose waters were sometimes flowing lazily along, or hastening impetuously in their progress to the sea. Some miles before reaching Enniscorthy, we had our first view of the celebrated River Slaney, whose banks in some places are beautifully wooded. We stayed a short time at Enniscorthy to see some friends, with whom we visited the new Catholic Cathedral and Castle ruins, also the fine Malting of Mr. Roche, who malts extensively for Messrs. A. Guinness and Son. The picturesque old Castle is one of the earliest military structures of the Anglo-Norman settlers, and its grey towers are still standing. It was at one time possessed by the Kavanaghs, and subsequently given by Queen Elizabeth to Spenser, the poet. After being taken by Cromwell, it was repaired by an ancestor of the Earl of Portsmouth, the present proprietor. Once more resuming our journey along the banks of the Slaney, we proceeded to Wexford, a half hour's ride. This glorious stream, which has often been compared to the Rhine, is crossed at Wexford by a new and handsome bridge, 1,500 feet in length, erected some years ago in lieu of the old bridge, and which with its approaches, is more than a mile long, forming a dry and pleasant promenade for the inhabitants, and on which a military band frequently plays during the summer months. Wexford, which is built on the south, bank of the Slaney, where that river discharges itself into Wexford Harbour, is an old Danish town, and at one time of great importance. It contains many ruins of abbeys and religious houses, and there are the remains of a fine old tower, which has been utilized as a windmill. Owing to its close proximity to the water, and being somewhat below sea-level, the railway station is built on piles, and at the time of our visit was being lifted up and renewed in several places. On our arrival, we drove through the centre of the ancient and picturesque town to the Distillery, the subject of our sketch. It is planted in the hollow of a hill, and running at the back is the celebrated stream called Bishop's Water, from whence the Distillery takes its name. This stream, which was blessed by a saintly bishop ages ago, issues from the heart of the Forth Mountain, and is said to possess rare qualities for brewing and distilling purposes. There is also a lovely little rivulet running through the works, which is made available for driving purposes.

The Distillery, which covers six acres, is built of fine Wexford stone, and was erected in the year 1827 by a small company of gentlemen in the locality. It afterwards passed into the hands of the Messrs. Devereux, who were original and the principal Shareholders and Directors of the Company. The works are enclosed by a stone wall, and at the entrance in Talbot Street, at the top of the hill, there is a handsome gateway; whilst at the bottom, in King Street, where the Wexford Corn Market is held, there is another entrance. The frontage in King Street is 582 feet, and the depth of the buildings therefrom nearly 200 feet, whilst the height is about 60 feet. The Distillery, being conveniently built on the slope of the hill, much of the work is done by gravitation, and home-grown corn only is used, which is delivered by the farmers at the large stores on the Quay, consisting of a three-storied building holding 2,500 barrels of grain, where it is dried in the Kilns adjoining, and afterwards carted to the Distillery. On reaching the latter place the dried corn is delivered by elevators to the dried corn lofts, which are at the top of a five-storied building; the lofts are 40 feet square, well lighted and ventilated, and in close proximity to the Distilling-house. From thence the grain falls through shoots into the Mill below, where there are three pairs of stones and a set of malt rollers. It then descends into the Grist Lofts, from which, through sluices, it falls into the Mash Tun underneath, a vessel 40 feet in diameter and 7 feet deep. On our way to the Mash House we passed the Malt Deposit Warehouse, a spacious building, which contained at the time of our visit 16,000 barrels of pure malt; also the Copper House, containing three coppers, which supply the hot water to the Mash Tun; all of which are very large and heated by furnaces.

From the Mash Tun the worts flow into the Underback, from whence they are pumped through the Coolers and three of Morton's Refrigerators into the Washbacks. We may here mention that the Worm Tub is a feature of this establishment, being erected on the slope of the hill, built up from the ground in solid stone and concrete work, 20 feet high and 90 feet long. It is quite the size of an ordinary town reservoir, and the only one of the kind in Ireland. This

Worm Tub is approached by a stone staircase, and the walls being some 6 feet thick, there is a fine promenade all round on the top, and we obtained a good view therefrom of the harbour and shipping.

Following our guide, we next visited the Back Loft, a large and well-lighted building. Along the wall there is one of the old-fashioned "continuous Spouts," which conveys the worts into these Washbacks, of which there are seven, each holding 30,000 gallons. From these Backs the liquor runs into the Wash Charger, a stone vessel, containing 25,000 gallons. It goes next into the Wash Still, which is capable of holding 18,000 gallons, thence through the pipes and Worm Tub to be cooled. Retracing our steps, we come to the Still House, a fine structure, which contains three old Pot Stills, with a capacity of 9,000, 11,000, and 18,000 gallons respectively, each having the old-fashioned revolving chains inside. From the Spirit Stills the perfected Spirit, which has already undergone three distillations, is pumped into a Vat, holding 16,800 gallons, in the Spirit Store, and there is also a smaller one holding 2,686 gallons. This Store forms an underground apartment, cut out of the limestone rock, and therefore as dry as a bone, and is similar to the Store in the Greenock Distillery before referred to. Here the Whisky is casked, weighed, and afterwards sent into the nine Warehouses distributed about the courtyard, which are capable of holding together 5,000 casks. As a matter of fact, there were at the time of our visit upwards of 3,000 in stock. Attached to the above, there is a duty-paid Racking Store to supply local wholesale customers. A few steps from this place is the Engine, of 30-horse power, and a Boiler, 30 feet by 7 feet. The engineer resides on the premises, and, with his assistant, does all the engineering work required. The Grains House is approached from the King Street entrance, and so arranged that there is no need for the farmers to enter the distilling part of the works to remove the grains and spent wash. There are capital Offices, a Cooperage, various workshops, and stabling for eighteen horses on the premises, and seventy men are employed.

The make is old Pot Still Whisky, and highly appreciated in Wexford and neighbouring districts, also in London, Liverpool, and Bristol. In the year 1882, Messrs. Devereux & Co. gained a Certificate of Merit in Class A for their Whisky at the Dublin Exhibition.

The annual output is 110,000 gallons.

No. 18.

Dundalk Distillery, Dundalk, co. Louth.

PROPRIETORS, MALCOLM, BROWN & CO.

CONTINUING our tour from Dublin, we arrived at the flourishing seaport town of Dundalk, wherein is situated the famous Distillery which heads this Chapter. From the railway we got our first view of this historic town, with its river, bridge, and harbour. The latter is formed by recesses in the bay, which is seven miles across at its mouth, and the same distance in depth. The English power was established in Dundalk about the twelfth century, and Dundalk, with other territories, was granted to Bertram de Verdon, who founded here a priory for Crouched Friars of the Augustine Order. In 1315, Edward Bruce took possession of the place, and caused himself to be proclaimed King of Ireland; but his assumed dignity did not last a year, his army being totally defeated, and himself slain by John de Birmingham. Up to the sixteenth century this town was constantly besieged, until it surrendered to Cromwell. At the east end of Dundalk are some fine ruins of a Friary, consisting of a lofty square tower, surmounted by a turret. Not far from the town is to be seen the Lady Well, resorted to by the pious on the patron day, September 29th. It is a fine spring of water, arched over, with ancient massive masonry.

The Dundalk Distillery and buildings, which cover ten acres of land, are within 300 yards of the entrance gates to the beautiful seat of the Earl of Roden, a richly-planted demesne of 274 acres, and close by the Assize Court, which is a handsome building of hewn stone, with a portico built after a model of the Temple of Theseus at Athens.

The works consist of several handsome blocks of buildings, mostly 65 feet high, and the statistical records of Dundalk state that the Distillery, in the year 1837, employed 100 men, and consumed 40,000 barrels of grain, producing 300,000 gallons of whisky of superior quality. Since that time great additions have been made to the buildings, and the trade considerably increased, until the output has more than doubled these figures. The water used in the works is of a fine quality, and comes from the Corthill Lough. All the machinery in the establishment is driven by steam power.

The present proprietors are John, Malcolm, and Henry Murray, three brothers, and it was a grand uncle of theirs who purchased the Distillery. Close to the entrance gates, and on the estate, is a picturesque house, the oldest in the district, at present occupied by the working partner. It was built by the Dutch settlers, and in the basement they carried on the business of a cambric manufactory. It is a charming old place, with a flat Dutch garden in front and a fruit orchard behind, round which are built the two Maltings, here, a separate department of the Distillery. One of them is a four-decker, built of stone, and pointed with brick, having two Kilns floored with iron tiles. These two houses are capable of malting 1,200 barrels a month. Each Malt House possesses a fine stone Steep, and the Kilns are heated by open furnaces. Opposite the entrance gates are the Corn Stores, a handsome block of buildings, with five floors, having a frontage of 200 feet, with a depth of 80 feet. In the old Corn Stores, which covered the same site, Cromwell quartered a troop of horse on his march.

At the time of our visit, which was in October, the firm were purchasing 1,200 sacks of corn per day, which would continue up to Christmas. The farmers deliver the corn to the weighing shed, where are to be seen in use a pair of old-fashioned Beam Scales, said to be 200 years old, in which the sacks of barley are weighed. Here the attendant tips the sacks into a hopper, from whence the corn is conveyed by elevators to the top of the buildings, and thence by endless screws to the different departments. The firm are also purchasers of Indian corn, and on one floor alone we saw 3,000 barrels piled up to the very ceiling. The dry Corn Kiln is, of course, contiguous to the Granaries, and is on the same principle as those of the Caledonian Distillery, Edinburgh, and heated by hot air. The grain is sent by elevators and screws direct to the Mill—a separate building of four floors, 50 feet by 28 feet, containing three pairs of stones and a set of Malt Rollers—which, although it was rebuilt in 1807, is still called the New Mill. It turns out 14 barrels per hour, or 336 barrels every 24 hours. The Grist Room is over the Mash Tun, and there are five immense Brewing Coppers, heated by steam, for boiling water. The Mashing House contains two Mash Tuns, 25 feet in diameter and 9¼ feet deep. One of these for patent Whisky is made of fine steel plates and enclosed, and mashes 160 barrels at one time. Several louvres in the roof of this building take away the hot air from these tuns.

The worts run from the Mash Tuns to the Worts Coolers, over the Back Loft, and are each capable of cooling 24,000 gallons of worts every three hours. The fifteen Washbacks are of large capacity, holding 24,000 gallons each, and we saw another of these handsome vessels in course of construction, of the same capacity. In this department also is placed the Underback and a Wash Charger holding 24,000 gallons. There are eight three-throw pumps, four Morton's Refrigerators, and two Worm Tubs. The huge Water Tank is on the roof of the Back Loft.

The Still House contains four old Pot Stills, as follows:—Two Wash Stills holding 10,700 gallons each, a Low-wines 8,000 gallons, and a Spirit 6,000 gallons, also a fine Coffey's Patent Still. The two Spirit Receivers are of the following capacity:—No. 1, 2,600 gallons, and No. 2, 20,700 gallons, and we noticed that the two Vats in the Spirit Store were registered to hold 13,000 gallons and 14,000 gallons respectively.

At the back of the Distillery, in a separate courtyard, there are nine Bonded Stores, and some idea of their size and capacity may be ascertained by the fact that they at the time of our visit contained over 7,000 casks, and that there is a whole street of workmen's houses in front of them inhabited by some thirty families. Close by there is a ponderous steam Crane for lifting the casks, and a Cooperage, which employs some twelve or thirteen men. The Grains Tank and Spent Wash Tank are so arranged that farmers can remove their contents without coming into the Distillery. The industries of the establishment consist of a large Engineers' Shop, fitted with two steam Lathes, a Saw Bench, and Boring Machine, all worked by steam, and other appliances; also a Carpenters', Painters', and Harness Makers' Shop, and large Smithy. The Stable contained seven horses for carting the Whisky to the boats and rail, and adjacent to the Stable are Cart Sheds and other buildings. The two lofty chimney stacks are a landmark for the mariners on the sea.

Returning to the Distillery proper, we were conducted to the Engine House, and were shown a wonderful Engine of 40-horse power, which has been working for half a century and shows no signs of decay, also a powerful Donkey Engine for feeding the five Boilers, each of which is 20 feet long and 6 feet in diameter. The fire arrangements are very perfect, sunken pipes through the yards, with a strong pressure of water on every floor of the buildings are available, and, besides this, there is a large Shand and Mason's fire engine on the premises. The Racking Store is conveniently situated near the Spirit Store, and there is also a duty-paid Warehouse for the convenince of local customers.

During the last few years the enterprising proprietors of this Distillery have added most of the new machines and patents used in distilling, and the annual output is close upon 700,000 gallons, a large quantity of which is consumed in the district, and the remainder goes to England and Scotland.

Before leaving, we were conducted to the top of one of the highest buildings to enable us to realise the extent and dimensions of the establishment, and to get a view of the delightful scenery of the neighbourhood. In front of us the Guillon Mountains, engirdled here and there with bands of white mist, outlined by a density of silver shadows, and lower down a long stretch of mountain landscape. Descending by another way, we found ourselves in the courtyard, crowded with carts laden with corn, and the whole place as busy as a bee-hive.

Before leaving, we inspected the Office Building, which consists of spacious clerks' offices, and private rooms for the partners. The Excise officers also have been comfortably provided for.

No. 19.

Royal Irish Distilleries, Belfast, co. Antrim.

PROPRIETORS, DUNVILLE & CO., LIMITED.

PURSUING our pilgrimage from Dundalk, we arrived in Belfast, the capital of Ulster. The town is certainly the most celebrated in Ireland, alike for its manufactories, commerce, and the public spirit of its inhabitants. It is situated on the western bank of the river Lagan, which here expands into a noble estuary called Carrickfergus or Belfast Lough. Belfast itself is flat, being but six feet above high water-mark; nevertheless, its general appearance is most prepossessing and cheerful, and its streets abound with stately buildings and handsome warehouses. The surrounding scenery is richly diversified and mostly picturesque. From a stage on the roof of the Distillery we obtained a fine view of distant mountains and the famous Cave Hill, the latter the most prominent feature in the landscape, the slopes covered with a dusky mottling of dark green, dotted here and there with a bit of plantation.

The Distillery is situated in the outskirts of the town; it was built in the year 1869, and covers about seven acres of ground. The Company own some seven acres besides, whereon to build should they require so to do.

The Establishment is supplied with fine water from Lough Mourne, twelve miles distant, and there are two splendid wells on the premises 160 feet deep. The whole of the works are enclosed, and entrance is gained by a handsome gateway, or through the lobby of the office contiguous.

We were conducted, first of all, to the Granary, a modern four-storied red brick building of good architectural proportions, having a frontage of 160 feet with a depth of 80 feet, capable of holding 250,000 bushels of grain; at the time of our visit it contained 200,000 bushels. The grain is delivered to the receiving floor of this building, and, after being examined, is hoisted by elevators to the different floors. Connected with same is the Barley Kiln, exceptionally spacious; it is able to dry 1,600 bushels every twelve hours, and is floored with the patent steel plates, so much in vogue in the North of Ireland. The dried grain is sent by Archimedian screws across the roadway to the Mill-building which is a four-decker, where there are five pairs of stones; from thence the grist is moved on by the screws to the large Grist Lofts capable of holding nearly 100,000 bushels of meal. On our way to the Mash House we were shown the two Heating Tanks, of large dimensions, heated by steam containing each 30,000 gallons. The capacity of the three Mash-tuns averages about 30,000 gallons each, one of them a fine vessel being entirely enclosed, and the hot air carried off therefrom by Louvres. The two metal Underbacks are of a similar capacity, and in the same building are to be found the Refrigerators, by both Morton and Miller. In the Back Room we were shown sixteen Wash-backs, each with an average capacity of 36,000 gallons, and an intermediate Charger of similar capacity.

The Still House is a fine, lofty building, fitted up in a most complete and modern style; it contains three old Pot Stills, containing 11,240, 6,551, and 5,255 gallons respectively, which are worked by fire, and there are besides two Steam Stills, bright and clean. On the gallery of this building there are eight Receivers and two large Safes and Sampling Safes. Our conductor pointed out to us the ingenious method adopted for extinguishing fire, consisting of, first of all, a water tank which covers the whole roof, tapped in the centre by a large pipe, from which smaller ones are struck off like the branches of a tree, all of them perforated and so arranged that they cover the building in case of fire. On turning a tap a continuous stream of water drops like a heavy rain shower on and over every part of the establishment.

The Malting department is in close proximity to the other buildings, and conveniently arranged, each floor being reached by a covered outside stair-case, whilst a glass door gives admittance therefrom to each flat. The top floor, at the time of our visit, contained 800 tons of barley. Whilst it is being delivered a steam fan is in operation, which blows the dust out of the barley, and effectually cleans it before the delicate operation of malting commences. The three malt floors are below, and it may here be remarked that they are all 180 feet long by 90 feet broad, and that the stone Steeps connected herewith will work 80 tons of barley. Adjoining are two Malt Kilns forty feet square. From here the malt is sent through endless screws to the malt deposit room, thence it is landed on the top floor of the mill, to be ground and made ready for the Mash-tun.

The roof of this Malting is entirely covered with a water-tank, the size of a small lake; it is five feet deep, and covers at least 10,000 square feet. On the premises are two engines, one of them a fine machine of 40-horse power, fixed in a handsome room, and kept in a very bright state. There are several sets of ponderous three-throw pumps, and three boilers, 30 feet long by 7½ feet in diameter, as well as a very large Economiser, said to be equal to two boilers. The Chimney Shaft, a handsome erection 160 feet high, is an ornament to the Works, and in the Spirit Store there are two vats each containing 8,651 gallons and 8,709 gallons respectively.

Most of the bonded Warehouses are in the town, but there are three in the Distillery containing some 10,000 casks. The Company have fine offices in Calendar Street, where 50 clerks are employed; also the Board Room and other apartments for the use of the Directors, fitted up and decorated in a most princely style.

The bonded Warehouses are on a large scale, covering 13 acres of ground, and containing at the time of our visit some 30,000 casks of whisky. Here also there is a cooperage and bottling department, and about 300 men are employed.

The Whisky made by Messrs. Dunville and Co. is well known and is shipped to all parts of the world. The annual output is 1,500,000 gallons, and this Company are said to be the largest holders of Whisky in Ireland.

Messrs. Dunville and Co. have obtained first gold medals at every Exhibition at which their whisky has been exhibited.

No. 20.

The Irish Distillery, Belfast, co. Down.

PROPRIETORS, THE IRISH DISTILLERY, LIMITED

MANAGING DIRECTOR, A. M. KIRKER.

BEFORE leaving Belfast, to continue our Northern tour, we drove to Connswater to see the "Model Distillery." It is certainly the newest and most modern, for at the time of our visit it was not completed. After our experiences of more than a year, we are bound to admit that this Company have spared no expense to make their Distillery as complete as any we have seen.

The architects are Messrs. Russell and Spence, of Glasgow, whose junior member makes a speciality of this business, and the contractors, Messrs. Dixon & Co., Belfast. The works are built on the banks of the Connswater, a tidal river, and near to the Belfast and County Down Railway; and conveniently placed either for unloading malt or reloading spirits. The buildings throughout, built of red brick of special quality, are of handsome and lofty elevation, and when viewed along with a fine octagonal chimney stack, 160 feet high, present a stately and imposing appearance from every point.

This Distillery is a roomy concern, the estate connected therewith covering twelve acres of ground. The Malt and Barley Stores, and Bonded Warehouses, are being erected on the riverside, along the embankment of the railway, and facing the three Kilns, 35 feet square.

We next visited the Mill, a fine building of three floors, each 50 feet by 25 feet, and containing four pairs of stones, with machinery sufficient for other four pairs. The Storing Bins, which are fitted up throughout, are capable of containing large quantities of grain preparatory to being ground, and are supplied with machinery necessitating no manual labour whatever. A large water cistern is erected over the Mill-room, storing an immense supply of water, and commanding the entire works.

Proceeding a few steps, we came to the Mash House, which is 60 feet by 50 feet, and contains two Mash Tuns; one of them being a construction of steel, calculated to stand a pressure of 20 lbs. per square inch, and is used for pulping the grain previous to the usual mashing process. The other is of cast iron, for mashing purposes, and has all the latest improvements. The first is 20 feet in diameter, and 8 feet deep; the second is 27 feet diameter, and 8 feet deep. On a gallery are three large wooden vessels for brewing liquor, each capable of containing 25,000 gallons, and two of Miller and Co.'s Refrigerators; a Wort Receiver, 34 feet by 10 feet by 4 feet, the Underback below being of the same dimensions. Near to the Mash House is the tank for draining grains, and having three flats underneath for storing them.

Following our guide, we reached the Tun Room at the back of the Boiler

House, which is 116 feet long by 46 broad, and is the best building for the purpose we have seen, both in ventilation and lighting. It contains twelve Washbacks, splendid vessels, each with a capacity of 25,000 gallons. The Still House is a large and lofty building, said to be the finest in the North of Ireland. One portion of it is allotted to the two Coffey's Patent Stills, each capable of distilling 4,000 gallons of Wash per hour. The other portions contain the old Pot Stills, all of large capacity. In connection with the Coffey's Stills are two Wash Chargers, each 25 feet in diameter, and a third, to command the Pot Stills, at a higher elevation. There is a large Feints and Spirit Receiver in this room, and three Spirit Safes, constructed of brass moulded in elegant designs.

Retracing our steps, we arrived at the Spirit Store, a large paved room, exceptionally well lighted, containing three Vats, each of 5,000 gallons capacity, and here we observed every appliance that can be thought of for the work. Adjoining the Kiln is the Engine House, 48 by 22 feet, built of brick with solid concrete floors, and handsomely laid off in coloured tiles. It contains a fine engine, compound tandem-surface condensing, of 250-horse power, made by Messrs. Combe, Barbour and Combe, Belfast, and is constructed on the most approved principles. The cylinders (one behind the other), are each supported in the centre, and connected to the bearings of the crank shaft by strong wrought-iron straps. Rods are placed in line with cylinders, so as to be in line of the strain, thus taking the direct thrust and pull of the steam. The valves are on the Corlies' principle, fitted with the makers' improved cut-off gear, and acted upon by a high-speed governor of handsome design.

The surface condenser, air pump, and circulating water pump are well placed and easily accessible. Another engine, made by Messrs. W. Malcolm and Co., Belfast, is placed in the Still House, and drives the Coffey's Still Pumps, which are of an extra substantial make, being of solid brass throughout. This engine, which is of 40-horse power, also drives the stirring gear of the Wash Chargers and Wash Still, and a centrifugal pump. The steam power to work this large concern is derived from three large boilers, made by Messrs. Victor Coates & Co., Limited, at their Prince's Dock establishment, in Belfast. Each boiler is 28 feet by 7 feet 6 inches diameter. They are high pressure, 80 lbs., constructed of mild steel on the most modern principle. The mountings are also of the very best description, the flues are welded in the longitudinal seams, and the cross-joints flanged after the Adamson principle.

Crossing the court, we come to the Bonded Warehouses, fine buildings and easily worked, having a neat hydraulic lift to each flat. In front of them are the Company's offices, which are solidly constructed and handsomely furnished throughout. The whole of the buildings are of brick with iron roofing, slated and plastered; every doorway in the establishment has double iron doors and every room is fully provided with fire appliances, should fire be subtle enough to find anything to live on.

We were informed that the output of this Distillery will exceed 2,000,000 gallons yearly, and its success is undoubtedly secured, all the owners being largely engaged in the wholesale trade, and easily able to dispose of the entire quantity this place could manufacture.

All the buildings and offices are lighted by electricity, erected by J. H. Greenhill, of Belfast. The only firms having an interest in the concern being Messrs. Kirker, Greer & Co., Limited; Messrs. Mitchell & Co., Limited; and James Wilson & Son Distillers, all of Belfast.

No. 21.

Avoniel Distillery, Belfast.

PROPRIETOR, WILLIAM HIGGIN.

THIS Distillery is about half a mile from that described in the previous Chapter. The proprietor stands conspicuous as being unwilling to allow an inspection of his works—for what reason we are unable to explain. The works are large, and we learned from his son that the Distillery was built in the year 1882 by the present proprietor, that it is a Patent Grain Distillery, and that the annual output is 850,000 gallons.

No. 22.

The Upper Distillery, Comber, co. Down.

PROPRIETORS, COMBER DISTILLERIES' COMPANY.

Resident Partner: MCCANCE BLIZARD, ESQ.

BELFAST has been called the "Athens of Ireland," the "Manchester of Ulster," the "Glasgow of Antrim." On every side are evidences of prosperity and indefatigable industry—there is no town in Ireland where the population has so rapidly increased. It is the emporium of art, trade, manufactures, and commerce, the seat of science, and the patron of letters. We spent several hours in visiting some of the principal public buildings before starting on our short railway journey to Comber, and regretted that we had not more time at our disposal.

We left the Royal Avenue Hotel in a very tipsy-looking jaunting car, with a driver to match the vehicle. His coat had evidently been handed down from a past generation, its skirts touching his heels, whilst his battered white hat and his knee-breeches were of like ancient date. He assured us on his honour that he would catch the Comber train; he kept his word, but it was at the peril of our lives. He bowled us along almost upsetting us at every corner, we collided with other vehicles, almost ran over one old woman and three street urchins, and we inwardly vowed we would never again let a jarvey know that we were in a hurry. Our short railway journey of eight miles to Comber, took us through thriving suburbs, past pretty country villas, and a fine agricultural district. The town, which derives its name from an Irish word signifying the meeting of water, consists of three streets and a large square, and is on the main road from Belfast to Downpatrick. The celebrated Royal Bog, from which great quantities of peats are sent to Belfast and other places is in this neighbourhood.

The Parish Church occupies the site of an old Abbey, founded in the year 1201, by Brien Catha Dun, to the honour of the "Blessed Virgin." It was inhabited by some Cistercian monks from Wales; the last Abbot was John O'Mulligan, who voluntarily resigned the Abbey in 1543, and, sad to relate, soon after, James I. gave this splendid pile of buildings to Sir James Hamilton, who committed the vandalism of pulling it down and using the materials in erecting a mansion called "Mount Alexander," which is now a heap of ruins. Comber derives its name from the river, on which it is situated, which flows into Strangford Lough.

The Distillery, which was originally a brewery, is about half a mile from the station. It was converted into a Distillery in the year 1825 by the late Mr. John Miller, J.P., who, in the year 1871, disposed of it to Mr. Samuel Bruce, the senior partner in the present firm, who retained the staff, and continued to make the Whisky on the old lines and of the same quality. The water used in this Distillery comes from Ballymaliddy Lough, about 2½ miles distant.

The arrangements of the establishment, so far as the Mash Tun, Fermenting Backs, &c., are very similar to those described in previous Chapters. There are two old Pot Stills, and the annual output is nearly 150,000 gallons. There are capital Granaries, capable of containing a thousand tons of barley, an extensive range of Malt Barns, and Bonded Warehouse, capable of containing 4,000 casks.

No. 23.

The Lower Distillery, Comber, co. Down.

PROPRIETORS, COMBER DISTILLERIES' COMPANY.

THIS Distillery is but a short walk from the work described in the previous Chapter. It has the same water supply for distilling purposes, and is under the same management.

Originally a paper mill, it was converted into a Distillery by Messrs. Burns and Griffithin about the year 1825, and subsequently became the property of the late Mr. John Miller, who disposed of it, along with the Upper Distillery, to Mr. Samuel Bruce in the year 1871.

It is situated on the River Inlet, which receives its supply of water from Ballymaliddy Lough and several rivulets rising in the neighbouring hills.

The establishment is built on the same lines as the Upper Distillery, and contains a similar number of vessels and two old Pot Stills. In the yard of the works are to be found a Cooperage, Blacksmiths' and Carpenters' Shops, Stables, &c. The annual output is nearly 150,000 gallons.

Five Excise officers are employed in the two Distilleries, the chief being Mr. Thomas Galway.

No. 24.

Bushmills Distillery, Bushmills, co. Antrim.

PROPRIETORS, THE BUSHMILLS OLD DISTILLERY COMPANY, LIMITED.

Registered Offices: 1, HILL STREET, BELFAST

Secretary: W. S. MITCHELL.

FROM Coleraine we proceeded to Portrush, the nearest stopping station to the Distillery which heads this Chapter.

We stayed over Sunday at Portrush, and on Monday morning started for Bushmills by the celebrated Electric Railway, which for nearly six miles climbs the hills and rocks overhanging the sea; after crossing the River Bush, we found ourselves at the old-fashioned town of Bushmills, and within a few minutes' walk of the Distillery. This very old work is about two miles from the Giant's Causeway, which attracts a large number of tourists during the season, from all parts of the world. The Bush, from which the town takes its name, is a fine salmon river, and one of its tributaries, a clear and beautiful stream, called "Saint Columb's Rill," passes through the Distillery, being used by the proprietors in the manufacture of their celebrated Whisky.

The first record we have of this, no doubt the oldest Distillery in Ireland, is in the year 1743, when it was in the hands of a band of smugglers; but in 1784 we find it recognised as a legitimate Distillery, making about 10,000 gallons of Whisky per annum, most of which, at that time, was exported to the West Indies and America. For nearly a century its progress was very limited under its different proprietors; but in recent years, since the present Company came into possession, there have been continual extensions to the plant, and, from the present rate of progress, we expect in a year or two to see it cover a much larger area of ground than it now does. The Company have recently increased the capacity of their old Pot Stills, and erected the electric light on their premises, which has a very pleasing effect, and shows that they are alive to all modern inventions.

The Manager first conducted us to the conveniently-arranged and capacious Barley Stores, which are, during the working season, always filled with home-grown barley. The proprietors use nothing but superior quality, and, therefore, encourage the farmers of the district to grow barley in large quantities by giving them a fair price for it; thereby doing away with the necessity of buying foreign grain.

Underneath the Barley Stores there is a range of Malt Floors, Kiln, &c., used for the manufacture of Malt. In connection with these buildings are the Store Rooms, from whence, through shoots, the malt is dropped into the two

Malt Deposit Rooms, where it is weighed into sacks ready for use, and wheeled across a gangway into the loft; thence through a hopper in the floor, it drops into the Mill-room below, where it passes through a fine set of patent Malt-rollers. The Malt-grist is sent from the Mill by elevators into the Grist-loft—a well-lighted floor, over the Mash Tun, where it is weighed into bags of 168 lbs. each, afterwards being emptied into a shoot which conveys it into the Mash Tun, a circular metal vessel, having the usual double-action stirring-gear. From the Mash Tun the Worts are drained into the Underback, holding 1,500 gallons; whence, by a double-action plunger pump, they are sent into the Worts Receiver in the Tun Room. This latter apartment is a lofty building—a model of brightness and cleanliness, containing four Washbacks, each holding 9,500 gallons; also a Wash Charger and four Low-wines and Feints Chargers. The large Patent Refrigerator is placed on a gallery in this building.

From this department, we were conducted to the Still House, a very large building, containing two old-fashioned Pot Stills, holding 2,500 and 1,500 gallons respectively; and space has been left for two more equal to those at present in use. The Running Room is an elegant place, containing the Safe and Sampling Safe, four Low-wines and Feints Receivers, holding 1,800 gallons each, and three double-action plunger pumps. In a separate room adjoining there is a fine new Spirit Receiver, of about 2,200 gallons content.

The Engine Room contains a 20-horse power engine for occasional or extra use, and a boiler for heating the coppers. On a brick pier in the yard we noticed a metal Worm Tub of large dimensions. Next we proceeded to the Spirit Store, opposite the Still House, containing a Vat capable of holding 5,000 gallons.

The four Bonded Warehouses are built on the side of the hill, and at the time of our visit were well stocked with Whisky of various ages. As in other Distilleries, large or small, there is a Grains House and Spent Wash Tank, the contents of which find a ready sale to the farmers in the locality. The Racking Store, Excise offices, and Store Warehouses adjoin the Distillery buildings. The Whisky is carted to the depôt of the Electric Railway, which conveys it to the Portrush Railway Station and Harbour for delivery to all parts. The annual output is 100,000 gallons. The Company have lately erected very fine offices in Belfast, consisting of Board room, sampling room, secretary's and general offices.

The Distillery is under the direct and personal management of Mr. James McColgan, one of the directors.

Mr. H. R. Mayer is the chief Excise officer.

No. 25.

Coleraine Distillery, Coleraine, co. Londonderry.

PROPRIETOR, R. A. TAYLOR.

FROM Belfast we again started on our "spiritual wanderings," and travelled by railway through towns and villages given up to the growth of flax and the manufacture of linens, until we came to the town of our quest, to pay a visit to the first "all malt" Distillery we have seen in Ireland. There are only two such, therefore we must particularize them a little more fully than others.

Coleraine is the second important town in the county, and is a sea-port. It is planted on the River Bann three miles from its influx to the sea. The river is navigable up to Coleraine for vessels of considerable tonnage, and a regular cross-channel steamboat trade to Glasgow, Liverpool, &c., is now established. Very extensive navigation works have lately been completed at the entrance to the river, where a sand-bar previously existed. These works, consisting chiefly of two extensive and almost parallel moles carried out into deep sea water, were designed by Sir John Coode, and have been worked out under his superintendence, the result being highly satisfactory—in fact, a complete success. The whole outlay will be £90,000, of which about £35,000 has been given by the hon. the Irish Society.

The history of this old town dates back to the year 540, and is very interesting. It was the royal seat of the Kings of Dalnaruidhe, and, at the date mentioned, it possessed a Priory of Canons Regular, of which St. Carbreus, a disciple of St. Finian and first Bishop of Coleraine, was the first Abbot. The establishment was continued until the year 930, when it was plundered and destroyed.

The Irish Society also settled some of their members here. Twenty years since were to be seen in the Diamond and Church Streets, some ancient houses of timber-cage work, said to have been framed in London and sent over for the settler's use. Alas! they have disappeared, and more modern dwellings have taken their places.

The neighbourhood abounds in charming scenery, and the air is extremely salubrious. The town is celebrated for manufacturing a fine linen called "Coleraine," and Malt Whisky. The greatest attraction, however, is its incomparable salmon river, called the "Bann," or "White River," a short distance from the Distillery. Upwards of eighty tons of this fish are annually taken at the Cutts, where the river makes a rapid fall of 12 feet over a ledge of rocks, which the salmon cannot ascend. There is a wooden bridge, on which one can stand and see them working their way up the foaming torrent. The River which runs swiftly through the town, is always a scene of beauty, with its verdant slopes and plantations stretching down to the water's edge. As we

FALLS ON THE BANN, COLERAINE.

stood on the bridge the rays of the setting sun were just falling on the distant hills and penetrating the thick branches of the trees.

At the time of our visit, the Distillery had just commenced active work, and the farmers were busy delivering barley which had previously been purchased at the public corn market, which adjoins the Distillery. The street was literally blocked with carts, and presented a very animated sight. The Distillery proper was an old manorial mill at the end of the seventeenth century, and was converted into a Distillery in the year 1820. It is entered from New Market Street by means of a handsome gateway, and is entirely enclosed. The Barley Stores consist of a fine lofty building, over 60 feet high, fronting the main street. The barley is raised by steam-hoists to the different floors. Besides these there is another, a fine building, having 150 feet of frontage, which contains five Barley Lofts, each 150 feet long. From here the Barley falls through a shoot into a large timber Steep, made of pitch pine, which takes up the entire end of the building, Here the first process commences—viz., that of steeping the barley for about forty hours. It is afterwards strewn on a carefully-swept concrete floor. There are two of these Malting Floors at this establishment, well ventilated and lighted. The barley is turned two or three times daily, so that each particle may come under the necessary atmospheric influence. After several days, when the acrospire has properly developed, it is taken from the floors and placed in the two large Kilns, both of which have an open roof, of the modern kind, each possessing two doors at different altitudes, connecting them direct with the Malting Floors. When the malt is dried it is sent to the Malt-mill, in which it is crushed between a fine pair of metal rollers driven by steam-power; thence it is conveyed to the Malt Deposit Floor, and weighed into sacks of 168 lbs. From here it is removed by a communicating gangway into the Grist Loft over the Mashing House. The two heating coppers in this establishment are heated by steam, and each contains 3,000 gallons; and now commences the first process of distillation. The grist is conveyed by means of a funnel to the Mashing Machine, which consists of a square wooden spout or shoot, connected with a copper pipe possessing a stopcock, through which flows the hot water from the coppers already referred to. As the grist falls down, it comes in contact with the water at the junction of the spout, and is well mixed by a little machine before it falls into the Mash Tun, which is a clean vessel, holding 7,000 gallons. Here it is subject to the process called mashing. This consists in the crushed malt being beaten about by a double-acting revolving stirring rake driven by steam. The object of this is to extract the saccharine matter from the malt, and great care is required during the process. When the mashing is finished the Worts are drained from the Tun into the Underback, a vessel containing 2,000 gallons. From here they are pumped up by a three-throw pump—there are three on the premises—into the coolers on the top story, which cover the whole of the roof of the Still House and Tun Room. The coolers are on the old-fashioned fan principle, and here the worts are reduced to the required temperature. They then descend into the Washbacks, of which there are six, each holding 5,000 gallons; and now commences the duties of the Excise officials. Fermentation having subsided, the liquid changes its name and becomes wash, and is ready for the various refining processes of distillation. The wash runs from the Washbacks into a vessel called a Wash Charger, holding 5,000 gallons, an intermediate receptacle, before the wash runs into the Wash Still. The first operation in the Still House now commences. A part of the wash goes by gravitation into the Wash Still, holding 2,700 gallons, where the process of distillation begins, and is carried on in different forms until the pure spirit is obtained. On leaving this Still it is called Low-wines, and after passing through the Worm Tub, a circular vessel containing 7,000 gallons of water, and placed out in the open, it descends into the Low-wines Receiver, a wooden vessel holding 1,500 gallons. From here again, by gravitation, it goes into the Low-wines Still, holding 1,500 gallons; from thence again through the Worm Tub into the two Feints Receivers, of same capacity as the former one. The Feints, as they are now called, run into the two Spirit Stills, each holding 550 gallons. Again it goes through the Worm Tubs, and descends into the Spirits Receiver, a circular wooden vessel holding 3,000 gallons. It is now perfected Spirit, having undergone three distillations.

Here we must pause to say that, in all our wanderings through Erin's Green Isle, for cleanliness, order, and regularity, we have seen no Distillery to beat this. The Stillmen seem to take a delight and pride in their work, and regard all these old Pot Stills with veneration. They are kept as shining as gold, and every bit of brass work, even the frames of the Safe and Sampling Safe, were polished and bright enough for a jeweller's show case.

From the Receiver the Spirit is pumped into a vat holding 3,000 gallons, which is placed in the Spirit Store, where it is reduced to 11 o.p. The Whisky is then racked into casks, weighed, and deposited in the Bonded Warehouses, of which there are nine at present, containing 5,000 casks, until required for consumption. The Engine-room contains a 30-horse power engine, also a fine machine which lifts about 300 tons of water from the well every twenty-four hours ; and there are also four huge double-acting pumps. The Iron Water-tank is fixed on the roof of the Export Bottling Warehouse. In the yard are to be found an extensive Cooperage and Carpenters' and Joiners' Shop. In both of these a number of hands are constantly employed in making cases and repairing and constructing casks. In a line with the office are extensive coal sheds, which, we were informed by our conductor, contained over 2,000 tons of coal.

The offices are at the side of the gateway and consist of two stories, the ground floor being occupied by the clerks, and the floor above by the principal and manager. Opposite the Coal Stores there is a bottling store for the export and home trade, also a similar building opposite the Distillery for duty-paid Whisky. We were informed that no Whisky is bottled under ten years of age. We noticed that all the bottles and cases bore the trade mark of "H.C," and on asking for an explanation we were informed that since the year 1845 this Whisky has been supplied to the House of Commons, and therefore the proprietor had adopted "H.C." as a trade mark. The water used in the Distillery comes from a noted well on the premises, 8 feet broad and 25 feet deep, containing several springs, and said to have been blessed by St. Finian. It supplies water for every purpose, and is of the finest quality. The Whisky made at this establishment is pure Malt.

Besides the Bonded Warehouse referred to in the Distillery account, there are others in Brook Street, a square pile of stone buildings, by the side of a small mill stream, which contained a large quantity of Whisky.

The annual output of this famous Malt Distillery is 100,000 gallons.

James Feehan, a local poet, thus wrote of the Coleraine Whisky :—

"The Spaniard may boast of his shadow,
The Frenchman his sparkling champagne,
But if a man wants to be merry
I'd advise him to thry Ould Coleraine.

"If you search in the annals of hist'ry
Till the time of the Roman and Dane,
You'll find it was reckon'd a mist'ry
How they made such good stuff in Coleraine.

"You've all heard of Barney McCleary,
And the buttermilk waterin' the plain,
And the pitcher, the pride of the dairy,
That Kitty got smash'd near Coleraine.

"But I'll tell you a saycret this minit,
I know you won't tell it again,
Of milk sorra taste there was in it,
She was smugglin' a drop of Coleraine.

Chorus—"Then hurrah for the trim little boro',
And the Bann as it runs thro' the plain ;
Its waters they banish all sorrow,
When mixed with a drop of Coleraine."

No. 26.

Limavady Distillery, Newtown, Limavady, co. Londonderry.

PROPRIETORS, YOUNG, KING & CO., LIMITED.

MANAGING PARTNER AT THE DISTILLERY, JAMES MCLOUGHLIN.

A SHORT run from Coleraine, on the Northern Counties Railway, mostly along the coast, with a fine sea view and a long stretch of landscape, brought us to Newtown, Limavady, wherein is situated the above interesting and old-fashioned Distillery, which stands on the hill, about ten minutes walk from the railway station.

Limavady is a market town, and a place of great historic interest, for here, on the brow of a romantic hill called Lima-vaddy, signifying "The Dog's Leap," from which the town takes its name, stood the Castle of the O'Cahan, who was the head of a powerful and warlike Sept. The estimation in which they were held appears from the fact that Desmond O'Cahan was summoned by Edward II. to attend him with his force on his disastrous expedition against Scotland. Desmond obeyed, but instead of joining the Army of the Invader, he was found in the ranks of the Scottish King at Bannockburn. A lineal descendant of these O'Cahans, a stone mason by trade, resides in the town, and built a chimney-stack of the Limavady Distillery.

The Castle was several times besieged, once for an entire winter, but in the end the Irish Army was successful, and burnt the whole town, church, and Castle. The town was rebuilt after the Revolution; hence the name of Newtown. From the lands adjoining the Distillery, the property of the Company, we had a fine view of the surrounding country. The environs of the town are exceedingly beautiful. To the north-west is the rich vale of Myroe, extending to the shores of Loch Foyle. To the east and north-east is the lofty range of Benyevenagh, and to the south the summits of Donald's Hill and Benbradagh, the latter standing out in bold relief against the sky, and covered with a roseate suffusion of colours reflected from the autumn sun which threw its crimson shadows on the heights and into the crevices; at our feet, below the hill, the Roe or Red River, so called from the colour of its waters, runs its course through the fertile flat, until it falls into Lough Foyle at Myroe. But to return to the Distillery. It is a most antiquated work, built early in the century, and covers about two acres of ground. The estate consists of upwards of 10 acres, which Messrs. Young, King & Co., ultimately propose to utilize.

The water used comes from the Well-glass, a spring in the hills, bubbling up for ages past, and mentioned in old records as the Fairies' looking-glass, from its transparent beauty. Here, it is said, these sprites came from the dells and glades to arrange their tresses and bind on their floral chaplets. This stream, clear and sparkling, is conveyed by a conduit, three miles to the Distillery, where it is used in the manufacture of the Limavady whisky, so well known, and which moistens the lips and cheers the heart of many an "Exile of Erin" in distant Colonies of the Empire.

The works include two large Grain Stores, 100 feet by 36 feet. To one of these is attached a large Kiln, floored with perforated Worcester tiles, and heated by open furnaces. The Malt House is spacious and well ventilated, and has one of the old-fashioned Stone Steeps, so easily cleansed and sweetened. Over the bonded Warehouses there is an extensive dry Grain Loft, holding some hundreds of tons of grain. In the Mill building we noticed all the usual appliances, such as Malt Rollers, pairs of Stones, &c. The Grist Loft is contiguous to the Mill, and underneath this Loft are several Mash-tuns capable of containing 10,000 gallons each, and having patent double-action stirring rakes. The heating tanks have an average capacity of 4,000 gallons each, and are advantageously placed for economising fuel. From this department we were conducted into the Tun Room, containing a number of Washbacks, holding from 6,000 to 10,000 gallons each, a Miller's Refrigerator, a large Underback, ponderous sets of three-throw pumps, a Wash pump, and a Wash Charger of large capacity. Passing along to the Still-house, we were shown some Pot Stills. They are heated by steam casings, and are the only kind used in this establishment. The Worm-tub, containing 20,000 gallons of water, is fixed on an outer building.

In the Running Room are to be found Receivers for Spirits, Low Wines, and Feints, besides the usual safes. We next passed the Spirit Store, containing an enormous vat, thence to the Engine House containing two boilers, 20 feet long by 5½ feet in diameter; also an excellent engine of 12-horse power.

The Buildings include, of course, a Cooperage, Carpenters' Shops, &c.

The three bonded Warehouses contained 3,000 casks of Limavady Whisky, of various ages.

The head-quarters of the Company are at Belfast, which we visited on our return journey. They are situated in Talbot and Robert Streets, and consist of a noble pile of buildings, with a frontage in both streets of 270 feet. The general offices are at the lower end of Talbot Street, and are entered through a fine vestibule paved with encaustic tiles, screened off by a handsome glazed partition. This lobby leads into the general counting-house, fitted with mahogany desks and brass ledger rails, also to private offices and sampling rooms, the walls and ceilings of which are lined with polished pitch-pine. All these apartments are elegantly decorated and furnished.

The Bonds, Cooperage, etc., are at the back of the offices, and are all in direct communication with the offices by telephone.

The Annual Sale in bond at this Establishment is said to amount to 900,000 gallons, which is mostly shipped to the wholesale houses of England, Scotland, and the Colonies.

The annual output of the Distillery, however, is about 250,000 gallons.

No. 27.

Abbey Street Distillery, Londonderry.

SOLE PROPRIETOR, ANDREW ALEXANDER WATT.

IT was almost with regret that we once more entered the train, as we realised that with the next stoppage our pleasant Irish Distillery Tour would come to an end. On leaving Limavady Junction, the rail runs close by the shores of Lough Foyle, and we were soon in sight of the Donegal Mountains. The tops were cloud-capped, here and there broken by a conical peak which appeared as though it had detached itself from the mass; the shadows of the setting sun were falling on the slopes, and the whole range had a mournful and oppressive look. On the right we caught glimpses of gentle hills, covered with plantations; here and there a village, and anon some ancient church, with its tower rising above the trees. All too quickly we found ourselves gliding into the station, and as we neared we had a view of Derry, the ancient city, and the prominent chimney-stacks of the Abbey Street Distillery. On emerging from the station we drove across the fine bridge, which is an ornament to the river and city, and sought our hotel for rest and refreshment.

The old-established Distillery which heads this Chapter, is the largest in Ireland; the buildings alone cover eight acres of ground. It is situated in the heart of the picturesque old city, the chief town of the county. The original name of the city was Derry, and it still retains its popular title. The name is from the Irish "Doire," which signifies a place of oaks. About the year 1613 the English prefix of London was imposed upon it by the Irish Society, incorporated by charter of James I.; the name of Londonderry was retained for many years by the colonists, but has now fallen into popular disuse. The town is of ancient date, and was many times besieged and plundered by the Danes. In 1689 occurred the famous siege of Derry, and the gallant struggle of the besieged, and how they were relieved, are matters of history.

The Distillery is close to the walls of the city, which are in a perfect state of preservation, and the ramparts thereon afford a fine promenade all round the town. "Roaring Meg" is still there, but let us hope she will never be called upon to frighten another enemy. But to return to the Distillery. It would be impossible to describe fully the shape and position of the buildings, as they cover such a large area of ground. They are erected on the slope of a hill, and have, from time to time, been added to by the grandfather and the father of the present proprietor. At the end of the last century, it is recorded in the statistics of that period, that it was then used as a Distillery. In 1826 it came into the hands of Mr. Andrew Alexander Watt, grandfather of the present proprietor, who was a leading merchant and alderman of the city, and head of most of the principal charitable institutions.

The water used in the Distillery comes from the Glashaugh Hills, and is collected in reservoirs on the Distillery property; besides this supply, there are wells in the yard for reducing and cooling.

The Wheat and Maize Stores are of immense proportions, as the following figures will testify:—No. 1 Building consists of three floors, 200 feet long by 150 feet, and contains 2,000 tons of wheat and barley; No. 2 Building is 200 feet long by 60 feet broad, and contains 1,000 tons of maize; No. 3 Building is also 200 feet long by 80 feet broad, and holds 2,000 tons of maize; No. 4 Building has four floors, each 150 feet long by 60 feet wide, and at the time of our visit contained 1,600 tons of grain. On the opposite side of the way there are two lofty Barley Floors, connected by a bridge. The floors are 200 feet long and 160 feet wide, and contained 2,000 tons of home-grown barley. Adjoining this is another four-storied building, 150 feet long by 60 feet wide, which contained 1,600 tons of barley, oats, and maize. The corn is elevated to the various floors and buildings by a steam-hoist. There is a Flour Mill in connection with the premises and business, the property of the proprietor, where a large trade has been carried on for some years past.

Adjoining No. 4 Building, there is a large dry Corn Kiln, called the "Malakoff," with the old-fashioned cone at the top; there is an archway through it leading to the Distillery buildings; the Kiln is capable of drying thirty tons every twenty-four hours. Attached to the Barley Floors there is another huge Kiln, which will dry thirty-four tons every twenty-four hours. The Malting House, No. 1, is one of the largest floors we have seen on the island; it is 300 feet long and nearly of the same width, and is capable of seating 2,500 persons; sixteen tons are malted here in one Steep four times a week. The Steep is of metal 50 feet long and nearly 9 feet wide, and is on the same level. Attached to this floor there are two Malt Kilns and two Deposit Rooms. All the Kilns are covered with wire-cloth flooring. No. 2 Malting House is of the same size and proportions, except that the Malt Deposit Room is somewhat larger; here is a timber Steep. The maize and malt are both sent by elevators into the Mill building, which has six pairs of stones. The Grist Loft is said to be the largest in the Kingdom, being 300 feet square. Screws and elevators take the grist into the Hoppers, which are placed over the Maize Tun, a fine timber vessel, entirely closed, 22 feet in diameter and 20 feet deep, having the patent double-action stirring gear. The malt runs through Shoots from a Grist Loft overhead into the three Mash Tuns. It must be borne in mind that the Maize Tun also discharges an equal quantity of its contents to these three Mash Tuns.

The Draining Tuns are of the following measurements:—Nos. 1 and 2 are 14 feet in diameter and 8 feet deep, No. 3 is 24 feet in diameter and 8 feet deep. From these vessels, the liquor goes, by gravitation, into two large Underbacks, each containing 4,000 gallons. From thence it is pumped by three-throw pumps into Worts Receivers, thence through three of Morton's Refrigerators on to the Washbacks, of which there are fifteen, averaging 27,000 gallons each. It then goes, still by gravitation, into two Wash Chargers, fine stone vessels, one of them capable of containing 50,000 gallons, the other (the intermediate) not so large. The worts are then pumped into the two Coffey's Patent Stills, situated in the Still House, a large and lofty structure, seven stories high.

Here there is also a fine double-action plunger pump to feed the Wash Still, which is on the ground floor of the building. The spirit then passes through a Morton's Patent Spirit Refrigerator into the two large Spirit Receivers. Here is a splendid Safe, also a Sampling Safe. The spirit then runs into the four Vats in the Spirit Store, each capable of holding 10,000 gallons. The fusel oil from the Stills is used for lighting purposes, and supplies all the lamps in the place; it has a spiritous smell and an all-pervading odour unmistakable.

In the sub-basement of the Still House there is a small engine, used for pumping water by a large set of three-throw pumps from a deep well, which gives a continuous supply of icy cold water winter and summer. The Engine House is arched in with brick, so that it would not be affected in case of fire. It contains one of the finest and largest engines in any Distillery in Ireland—of 230-horse power. There is also a smaller one of 50-horse power for use in the event of a break-down. We also noticed five of Galloway's patent boilers, 30 feet long by 7 feet, and four Heating Tanks, capable of holding 12,000 gallons each. As a prevention against fire, main pipes are placed all over the buildings, with stop-cocks and hose. There are on the premises five huge Warehouses, containing at the time of our visit, some 30,000 casks of Whisky.

The Cooperage is on a large scale, the Engineers' and Fitters' Shops are supplied with an engine and steam lathes. Adjoining them is a Carpenters' Shop, large Stables, and general stores. The two chimney stacks are 130 feet and 160 feet high respectively, and are landmarks for shipping in the river; 160 men are employed upon the premises

The make is Patent Grain Whisky. The annual output of this Distillery is about 1,260,000 gallons; the plant, however, is capable of making up to about 2,000,000 gallons if required.

No. 28.

Waterside Distillery, Londonderry.

SOLE PROPRIETOR, ANDREW ALEXANDER WATT.

ON leaving Abbey Street, we drove with our conductor, the polite and courteous distiller, to the Malt Distillery, which is situated about a mile distant, passing various objects of interest on the way. Near the Roman Catholic Chapel, outside the walls, are to be seen the St. Columb's Wells; the waters therein contained are considered by the pious country people to be a specific for diseases of the eye, but in Derry itself they are not held in much repute. Adjacent to these wells is St. Columb's Stone; on each side of it are two oval hollows, of which various legends are related. It is said that the water deposited in rain in these hollows possesses a miraculous power in curing certain diseases.

The Distillery is placed on the side of a steep hill, and is within a few minutes' walk of the river Foyle. Just above the works we had a fine view of the city with its picturesque surroundings. The establishment covers three acres of ground, and the water used is derived from a huge Reservoir covering nearly three acres of ground, some little distance away from the town, and the property of the Distillery. Besides this supply, there are two deep wells on the premises, from which water containing fine properties for mashing and distilling purposes is obtained.

The following is a brief description of these compact works, which are entirely walled in, and entered through an old-fashioned archway:—The No. 1 Granaries are two-decker buildings 300 feet by 200 feet, and contained 2,000 tons of barley. Nos. 2 and 3 are larger, but of one floor only, and adjoin this building; they each contained 1,000 tons. No. 4 is smaller and contained 600 tons. The No. 1 Maltings have three floors each 250 feet by 50 feet; No. 2 is not so wide, but is 100 feet long. Each of these five floors is concreted, and there are three metal Steeps, each of which can work 16 tons of barley at a time. In close proximity are the five Kilns, each about 50 feet square, floored with patent tiles and wire cloth, each having open furnaces. The dried malt is conveyed by Elevators and Screws to the Mill building, which contains four pairs of stones. From thence the grist is sent to the Meal Loft, where it is put into bags and shot through a sluice into the Mash-tun below, which vessel is 16 feet in diameter and 9 feet deep. There are two heating tanks holding 120,000 gallons. The Underback is a fine vessel and is placed under the Mash-tun. Most of the work in the Distillery is done by gravitation. On a gallery in the tun room are placed two of Morton's Refrigerators. In the Tun-room there are seven Washbacks, each holding 16,000 gallons, and a Wash Charger of a similar capacity, which commands the Wash Still. The latter vessel holds 8,000 gallons. Here we were shown the new patent condenser by Willison, of Alloa, said to be an improvement on the other kinds in use.

Passing to the Still House, we were shown the following vessels:—A Low Wines Receiver, holding 6,000 gallons. A No 2 Low Wines Still, holding 4,422 gallons. Two Feints Receivers of similar capacity. No. 1 Low Wines Still, holding 2,261 gallons, and a Spirit Still. These Stills are all of the Old Pot shape; there are no others in the Distillery.

The two Worm-tubs are placed immediately outside the Still House. From the Still House we were conducted to the Running Room, which, besides the usual safe and sampling safe, contains the Spirit Receiver, holding 2,000 gallons, also Feints and Low Wines Receivers. Thence we passed to the Spirit Store, which contains two Vats, each with a capacity of 3,000 gallons; and finally to the Bonded Stores, of which there are five, where, at the time of our visit, were stored some 20,000 casks.

The Cooperage, Carpenters' and Engineers' Shops, and other industries, are all to be found within the enclosure; there is a capital Engine of 100-horse power, also two boilers 25 feet by 7 feet diameter.

The annual output is 200,000 gallons, and the make is Old Pot Still Whisky only, no Patent Stills, as we have before said, being on the premises.

ENGLISH DISTILLERIES.

In England there are ten licensed Distilleries, most of them confined to the manufacture of Plain Spirit for rectifying and manufacturing purposes, but the following four have been selected as coming within the scope of the present work.

No.	NAME OF DISTILLERY.	WHERE SITUATED.	NAME OF PROPRIETORS.	No. of Page.
1	VAUXHALL ...	*Liverpool*	ARCHIBALD WALKER & CO.	445
2	BANK HALL ...	,, ...	R. W. PRESTON & CO., LIMITED ...	448
3	BRISTOL	*Bristol*	THE BRISTOL DISTILLING CO., LTD.	451
4	LEA VALLEY ...	*London, E.* ...	THE LEA VALLEY DISTILLERY CO., LD.	456

No. 1.

Vauxhall Distillery, Liverpool.

ARCHIBALD WALKER & Co.

IT is a far cry from Belfast to Liverpool, and a long tedious journey. The sea-passage from Larne to Stranraer, which occupied about three hours, was the pleasantest part of our homeward route; the railway journey by night, if you cannot sleep, is certainly very tiresome. We had to change carriages at Carlisle, and it was far into the small hours when we reached Liverpool. After resting a short time, we hired a trap and drove to see the Docks and other places by the waterside. What a wonderful place is this "Second City" in the Queen's Empire! From the year 1761, when there were only three docks, down to the present time, Liverpool has increased in magnitude, prosperity, and commercial importance, unexampled in the world. No town in England has received greater improvements, and none possess so much elegance and commercial accommodation. The natural convenience of its harbour, enhanced to an immense extent by the never-ending increase of the Docks, which are connected by canals, railways, and steamers with every part of the empire, are among the causes of its greatness, and have made it fit to be the capital of any country in the world.

Within the memory of living man, the city has started up like an enchanted palace, and enlarged its borders day by day. We drove for more than three miles alongside the Docks, and then had not exhausted them, returning to the Adelphi Hotel by way of the Distilleries we intended visiting. The next morning we secured one of the smart cabs, for which Liverpool is famous, and drove to the Vauxhall Distillery, situated about two miles from the centre of the city.

It was founded in the year 1781 by Messrs. Robert Preston & Co., and in 1857 came into the occupation of the enterprising firm of Messrs. A. Walker and Co., of the Adelphi Distillery, Glasgow, and the Limerick Distillery, Ireland. The buildings, which are all lofty and of an imposing appearance, cover three acres of ground, and are entered from the Vauxhall Road. Mr. Godwin, the Operative Manager, proffered his services as guide; and, after giving us the necessary information, conducted us first of all to the Granaries, which have a frontage to the public road. They are three-storied buildings, 115 feet long by 36 feet wide, and are used for the storage of maize, malt, and oats. On the ground floor is the Kiln, one of the largest we have seen, which is floored with metal plates, heated by open *chauffeurs*, and capable of drying 75 quarters at one time. Adjoining and forming a continuation of this building is the Mill, which contains, besides the machinery, nine pairs of stones—six of which are used for maize and the other three for malt. After inspecting the Mill, we ascended some steps into the next building, of similar dimensions to the Granaries, and found ourselves in the Grist Loft, under which is the Receiver Room. Here the grist is filled into sacks of 168 lbs. each, and wheeled across a gangway to the grist deposit, ready for being emptied into the wetting or soaking tank, for the purpose of "being treated" before it goes through the Steel's Mashing Machine. We next visited the Mash House, a lofty building lighted from the roof, wherein are two metal Mash Tuns, 25 feet in diameter and 7 feet deep, each with the double-action stirring gear. In the centre of each of these Tuns there is a sluice, through which the draff is dropped into a creeper, called in Scotland a "screw," which screws it away into elevators to the required height, when it is again started off by creepers to a distant part of the work. Adjacent to the Mash Tuns are two cast-iron Underbacks, each of 4,000 gallons content; also at an elevation, the Wash Charger holding 21,000 gallons.

Following the process, we proceeded to the Fermenting Department, which consists of two spacious enclosed Tun Rooms and one large open gallery, the latter opposite the entrance gates, from which point the lofty vessels, smartly painted, have a very imposing appearance. The buildings, which are respectively numbered 1, 2, and 3, are separated from the Brewing Department by a covered archway, wherein are three heating tanks for hot water, all heated by steam, each of 19,000 gallons content; also the Grist Steeper, or pulping vessel, before referred to, where the grist is steeped before it goes to the Mash Tun. Leaving these vessels we passed into the No. 1 Tun Room, where ranged along the centre are to be seen eleven Washbacks, each holding 20,000 gallons; and then to the No. 2 Tun Room, a lofty apartment, containing three Washbacks, each holding 41,000 gallons, and from thence, through a doorway at the western end, to No. 3 Building already referred to, containing four Washbacks, lofty timber vessels, each with a capacity of 42,000 gallons. Passing through a doorway, we came to the Pumping Room, wherein are two Wash Chargers of similar capacity to the one before mentioned, three Hot Feints Receivers, and four steam-pumps, three of which are horizontal and the other vertical; all are fixed in the north corner of the building, and form a portion of the Engine Department. Passing through an archway, we found ourselves in the No. 1 Still House, a lofty apartment, containing a Coffey's Patent Still, also a handsome beam-engine, of 14-horse power, used for pumping wash to the No. 2 Still and for working the mashing and tank machinery. A few steps progress brought us to the No. 2 Still House, a tower-like structure, wherein are two Coffey's Patent Stills and all the necessary appliances.

Crossing the alley we ascended a handsome staircase, to the right of the buildings, which leads to the Receiving Room, built on a level with the top of the Stills. It contains three sets of patent vertical copper Refrigerators, by Laurence, of London, a Safe and a Sampling Safe, and two circular Receivers; the latter, handsome timber vessels, as clean as a new pin, each holding 6,000 gallons, and possessing the patent index gaugers. Our guide here pointed out to us the singularity of the construction of this room, being entirely supported by heavy iron girders and columns, capable of bearing 100 tons. Contiguous is an apartment, appropriated for the reception of malt and oats; it is a large place, 80 feet square, well arranged for the exclusion of light and dust. Continuing our inspection, we climbed a zig-zag staircase to the No. 2 Receiver

House, which contains two Feints Receivers, of the same size and capacity as those already mentioned. In the centre of each of these vessels there is a floating-index-measuring rod, and, by an ingenious arrangement, a gas jet, with a circular reflector, throws the light directly on to the small figures of the measurer, to enable the Excise officers to check the contents with rapidity and ease. Overhead is the Worm Tub, which we inspected by mounting a steep staircase; it is a square metal vessel, supplied with water direct from the main of the Liverpool Waterworks. Stepping out on to a spacious parapet, we came to a small house, which encloses a circular Vat, with appliances for making condensed water for reducing the spirit to the required strength.

We next returned to the Mash House, to follow the course of the worts to the Coolers, which are in another building. Following our guide up several flights of stairs, we came to the top floor of a lofty structure, covered with metal Coolers. They consist of a shallow open tank, covering the entire floor, which is 60 feet square, and there are latticed ventilators all round the apartment. On leaving these Coolers, the worts flow through a copper Refrigerator, and afterwards fall into a tank on the floor below, 57 feet square, from whence they run by gravitation into the Washbacks before referred to.

Crossing the quadrangle, we next visited the Spirit Store, which contains three Vats, each with a capacity of 7,500 gallons, and the usual casking apparatus, and then inspected the Grains House and spent wash receptacles. Passing from thence we came to the ten Bonded Warehouses, which are very extensive, and hold upwards of 8,000 casks of Whisky. Leaving these Warehouses behind us, we bent our steps to a large building, on the left of the Tun Rooms, devoted to the manufacture of patent yeast. It is quite a work in itself, and many hands are employed. Here, by a patent process, the purified "barm" is made into a firm substance, put up into small bags and sent to the English and foreign markets. We saw a large quantity packed and piled up to the ceiling waiting for shipment. This yeast is said to be of a superior quality, and well known both at home and abroad. The Engine House next claimed our attention. It contains a powerful engine of 60-horse power and eleven boilers; two of them, of the ordinary kind, are 32 feet by 8 feet, the others are Galloway's patent steel boilers: one 28 feet by 7 feet, for 70 lbs. pressure; two 24 feet by 6½ feet, for 100 lbs. pressure; and one 28 feet by 7 feet for 80 lbs. pressure. Adjoining is the Engineers' and Fitters' Shop, a large Cooperage, and other industries. At the rear of the establishment, and commanding all the departments, is an old-fashioned mansion, which in former days was the residence of the proprietors. The upper part is now devoted to the partners' private offices, also the resident manager's, and the ground floor is used as general offices.

The offices for the eight Excise officers are splendid rooms, placed near the gateway and conveniently arranged. Mr. Bargery is the supervisor.

The firm store most of their grain at the public Warehouses, which are at a convenient distance from the Distillery and contiguous to the water-side. There are also large Bonded and Grain Stores belonging to the firm in Lightbody Street, Blenheim Street, and Maguire Street.

The spirit produced is pure Grain Whisky, which matures rapidly, and after five or six years' maturation is said to be almost equal to old brandy.

The annual output is 2,000,000 gallons; and there are 150 persons employed in the establishment.

No. 2.

Bank Hall Distillery, Sandhills, Liverpool.

PROPRIETORS, R. W. PRESTON & CO., LIMITED.

THE next day, as arranged the previous evening, our party of three walked from the hotel to St. George's Hall, one of the lions of Liverpool. It is a noble building, with a magnificent central hall, round which are ranged the law courts and municipal offices. After this we adjourned to the Walker Gallery, the munificent gift of a generous citizen, which contains priceless treasures of art, which we regretted that we had not time to study. We then adjourned to the Athenæum, as one of our friends wished to unearth some information respecting the derivation of the name of Liverpool. The Athenæum, which consists of a library and reading-rooms, was opened in 1799, and was the first of its kind in the country, and gave rise to those of London, Manchester, and Bristol. The origin of the name of Liverpool is very obscure; some say it is derived from a species of liver-wort found on the sea shore—others, with more probability, ascribe it to the Welsh words Lle'r-pwll, signifying "the place on the pool." The pool on the borders of which the original town stood occupied the site of the Custom House. Baxter supposes this to have been the port of the *Sestantii*, mentioned by Ptolemy, but this is doubtful, as it is generally supposed that the town did not even exist at the time of the Conquest. In the beginning of the sixteenth century, Leland gives this description of it: "Lyverpoole, a paved towne hath but a chapel, Walton at 4 miles off, not far from the se is paroche chirch"; and in 1571 the place is mentioned in a petition to Queen Elizabeth as "her majesty's poor decayed town of Liverpool." In this reign, however, a mole was formed to lay up the vessels in during the winter, and a quay for shipping. It was in the reign of William III. that Liverpool was made into a distinct parish from Walton-on-the-Hill, and since that time the town has grown into a great city, and the greatest port in the British Empire.

On leaving the Athenæum, we drove to the Bank Hall Establishment, distant from the hotel three miles. It is a modern work, built of stone, with a frontage to the main road of 450 feet, and covers five acres of ground. Owing to the close proximity of the public grain warehouses, it is not necessary to keep a large stock on the premises; nevertheless, the Company have devoted several floors of one of their large buildings to that purpose. The grain from the public warehouses is delivered by waggons to the Distillery, and raised to the various floors of the Corn Lofts and Mill buildings by a steam hoist.

On presenting our credentials, we were conducted, by one of the junior partners, over the establishment, and commenced our inspection at the Mill building, which is entered from the road, and consists of several floors. Part of the ground floor is appropriated to the ponderous grinding machinery, driven by an engine of 40-horse power; the remainder to the storage of maize in sacks. Before reaching the mill crushers, the grain is passed through a "Joggler," which effectually cleans and separates from it all dirt and foreign matter.

The floor above is supported by strong iron columns, and contains thereon four pairs of stones, a Roller Mill, a Disintegrator and other machinery. From this floor the grist is screwed away direct into the Mash or Brewing House. Returning to the road, we entered the Distillery through a pair of gates, and found ourselves in a quadrangular court, round which the various buildings are erected. On the left are the general offices, and on the same side the Mash and two Still Houses; facing us is the Engine and Boiler House, and on the right the Inland Revenue Office, and then comes the Methylated Spirit House and Spirit Store. Following the pulverized grain, we mounted a staircase to the Grist Lofts, where several workmen were busy filling the meal from the Screw Hopper into bags and placing them ready for use. Descending by another way, we found ourselves in the Mash House, a lofty apartment, 150 feet square, which contains five Mash Tuns. No. 1 is 26 feet in diameter and 9 feet deep, and will hold 30,000 gallons; No. 2, which is 22 feet in diameter and 8½ feet deep, holds 25,000 gallons, with stirring rakes driven by steam power; No. 3 holds 2,600 gallons, and Nos. 4 and 5 each 10,000 gallons. Passing through a doorway, we found ourselves in another Mash House of almost similar dimensions, wherein is placed the Corn Tun, which holds 22,000 gallons. There are two Underbacks connected with the Tuns, holding together 7,000 gallons, and close by three Worts Receivers, so placed as to form the roof of the Back Loft.

Following our guide, we came to the No. 1 Back Loft, 84 feet by 45 feet, floored with iron plates, which contains six Washbacks, each of 30,000 gallons content, and two others, each 17,000 gallons content. Descending a few steps, we reached the No. 2 Back Loft, a smaller apartment, containing two Washbacks, each of 30,000 gallons content, and afterwards crossed the passage to the No. 3 Back Loft, which contains other two Backs, each holding 35,000 gallons. On leaving this department, we were taken to the Refrigerator Room, where there are three patent Condensers, each machine consisting of copper plates, V shape, and of eight divisions, through which steam and water run in alternate frames; there are also three of Miller's Refrigerators. But to return to the process; the wash runs by gravitation into a Wash Charger, constructed of slate, placed under the No. 1 Back Loft, which contains 27,000 gallons. From this vessel the wash flows into an intermediate Charger of similar capacity under the Stills, from whence it is easily pumped into the latter vessels. We next visited the Still House, a lofty building of neat elevation, where are to be seen two of Coffey's Patent Stills; these handsome machines are each capable of condensing and working 4,000 gallons of wash per hour. Besides these, there are two handsome Pot Stills—a Wash Still, containing 4,000 gallons, and a Spirit Still, 2,600 gallons, for the manufacture of Malt Whisky. In close proximity are the usual vessels and Receivers connected with the Patent Stills, except the two Spirit Refrigerators, which are placed on iron columns outside. We next entered the Safe Room, which contains, beside the Safe, two Spirit Receivers, holding 5,500 gallons and 3,200 gallons respectively, also a Feints Receiver, of 1,200 gallons content. At the south corner of this room there is a tank for distilled water, lined with white enamelled brick, and conveniently placed for reducing purposes. On returning to the quadrangle, we inspected the Engine Department, which contains, besides the engine referred to (which drives the Mill), a 30-horse power engine, various sets of three-throw and other pumps, and four of Galloway's patent double steam boilers, each fitted with Henderson's patent stoker.

Progressing a few yards, we entered the Spirit Store, a handsome and spacious building, wherein are three Vats, each with a capacity of 3,745, 5,054 and 4,833 respectively. In close proximity, but in no way connected with the Store, is the Methylated Spirit House, where methyl is added to the pure spirit for manufacturing purposes. At an elevation in the open we observed the large water-tank, which is supplied from the Waterworks Company, which holds 35,000 gallons, and over our heads a continuous screw, 280 feet long, which conveys the grist to the Mash House. Having completed our tour of the establishment on the south side of the road, we crossed a bridge, which is suspended from one floor to the other over the public way, and found ourselves in the Maltings and Stores. These buildings stand on the site of what was once the favourite seaside residence of the ancestors of the present Lord Derby, and close by the spot where formerly stood the bathing house from which the noble lords were wont to take their "headers." They consist of a noble block, seven stories high, each floor measuring 120 feet by 80 feet. Three of them are used for Malting Floors, laid with tiles, contiguous to which are two splendid Kilns, each of which is capable of drying 120 quarters at one time. We passed through several of the other floors by a spiral staircase, and from the top obtained a grand view of the river, extending on the right to beyond the Fort at New Brighton, and the left Eastham.

We next bent our steps to the Vatting Store, which is the length of the whole building, and contains five Vats, each of 12,500 gallons content, and a small one, 1,400 gallons. The sub-basement and basement of this building form two large Bonded Warehouses, each 140 feet square. Through a doorway we passed into the Cooperage, quite a manufactory, where ten persons are contantly employed. and from thence to the Blacksmiths' Shop, where all the smith's work of the firm is done. Emerging from this place, we found ourselves in the courtyard, which runs along the back of the Maltings, the end of which overlooks a deep cutting of the London and North-Western Railway. At the bottom is situated "Preston's Siding," constructed for the firm at the expense of the company. At the top of a solid granite wall, there is fixed a powerful hydraulic crane, which raises 30 cwt. of coal at a time, or lowers down a dozen casks of spirits.

Ninety men are employed on the works, and the make of the Distillery is called "British Plain Spirit," Grain Whisky, and Malt Whisky, the largest proportion being Plain Spirit, and the annual output is 1,500,000 gallons.

The Managing Directors are Robert Wheeler Preston and Richard Percy Preston.

No. 3.

Bristol Distillery.

PROPRIETORS, THE BRISTOL DISTILLING COMPANY, LIMITED, BRISTOL.

MANAGING DIRECTOR, JOSEPH THOMAS BOARD.

FROM London to Bristol by the "Flying Dutchman" is one of the fastest railway journeys in England, and after our recent experience of the iron roads in "Erin's Isle," was certainly an agreeable change. We stayed the night at the Talbot Hotel, said to be one of the most comfortable in the West of England, and the next morning explored the ancient city. There is an old world appearance about the houses truly fascinating, whilst its fine old churches and narrow streets add much to its picturesque appearance. We have many times visited Bristol and explored the beauties of the Cathedral and the church of St. Mary, Redcliffe, but had never made ourselves acquainted with its Docks and Shipping, and thither we bent our steps.

The recent acquisition by the Corporation, and subsequent amalgamation of the Docks at Bristol, Avonmouth and Portishead, has revived the name and fame of this ancient maritime city, and brought into prominence its unrivalled position as a point for the landing and distribution of traffic, and for the export of coal, iron, salt and manufactured goods. The ease with which Bristol can be reached from London, and its being so much nearer Queenstown and New York than Liverpool, evidently points to its being the future American Mail Port of the Kingdom. The "Old City Docks"—now made accessible, in consequence of extensive river improvements, costing between £80,000 and £90,000, to sea-going vessels of considerable draught and size—comprise an area of 85 acres, while the docks at Avonmouth and Portishead, situated at the mouth of the Avon, afford safe accommodation for transatlantic and other steam liners of the largest class. The Foreign tonnage of the Port is considerably on the increase, and it is noteworthy that there are no export dues on either vessel or cargo.

Bristol occupies the position of being the leading grain port in the Bristol Channel, the rates for handling grain being much lower than those in force at the other leading ports. The line steamers running to the port from the United States and Canada, include vessels of the Dominion, Anchor and Great Western Steam-ship lines, and at each of the Docks there is a perfect system of warehouses and transit sheds; rails run alongside from the Great Western, Midland and London and South-Western Railways. Mr. F. B. Girdlestone, Queen Square, Bristol, is the General Manager of the Port and Docks Company.

Bristol, in days gone by, was the chief port in England for Wine, and the statistical reports of the Old City give some interesting information thereon.

King John was the best customer the Bristol Vintners had on their books. In 1205 he commanded his merchant to present his beloved Justiciary, the Earl of Essex, with 20 casks of his good wine at Bristol, and twenty days after, ordered payment to be made of forty-one shillings and sixpence for carriage of thirty tuns of wine from Bristol to Tewkesbury, etc. During the next month he commanded that forty tuns be in readiness for the King's messenger; and the records state that the constable of the castle is ordered to pay out of the fee farm of Bristol, 97½ marks to the merchants of whom the wine was purchased. Also a few weeks after, the Baron of the Exchequer is instructed to pay to John de la Warre and others £586 for wine purchased by the King's orders. On the 7th of June, in the same year, John ordered 70 casks, twenty of them for the castle and fifty for the King's use at Portsmouth and other places. We are indebted to Mr. John Taylor, the Curator of the City Libraries, for the foregoing particulars, also the following, which is somewhat quaint. In 1208 John ordered "that in Bristol a tun of Poitou wine should not be sold for more than twenty shillings, nor wine of Anjou for more than twenty-five shillings, unless it were so good that any person would give at the highest two marks for it; that Poitou wine should not be sold for more than fourpence per gallon, nor white wine for more than sixpence"; and the King appointed twelve officers who were to take care that these regulations were observed. It is said that Sack and Malmesbury Wine were first shipped to Bristol, and that for many centuries it was the principal emporium for those celebrated Wines. Rumour further has it, that the original of "Old Simon, the cellarer," lived in this city. But having somewhat digressed, for which we apologize to our readers, we now return to the object of our visit to this city. From the Talbot Hotel we drove through Bath Street across St. Phillip's Bridge, past the Churchyard, so prettily laid out and planted as a recreation ground, and down Cheese Lane, at the bottom of which we came to the famous Distillery, said to be the most ancient in England. We entered the enclosure through a spacious gateway, and turning to the left passed through the general and public offices to the Managing Director's room, where we received a cordial welcome from Mr. Board, who afterwards conducted us through the establishment.

The Bristol Distillery is said to be one of the oldest in England, having been founded in the 17th century. In the days when Bristol was one of the chief wine emporiums of the kingdom it flourished, and was an extensive work. In 1761, when the Duke of York visited Bristol to receive the freedom of the city, the old malt spirit made in Cheese Lane is said to have been freely distributed among the populace. In the year 1863, Mr. Board, the father of the present managing director, who was previously connected with the Distillery, formed it into a Limited Liability Company, but none of the shares were offered to the public. No alterations were made in the working of the place or the buildings by the Company, except turning some substantially-built houses on the property into Bonded Warehouses. The establishment is on an extensive scale, and replete with machinery and vessels of a most scientific type. The premises, which occupy both sides of the street, cover an area of 73,930 square feet; all the buildings, which are mostly of granite, are very lofty, and built round various quadrangles and paved courtyards, entered by spacious archways, and reminding us, as we passed through, of some Spanish convent, all being so quaint in style and construction. The narrow street divides the Distillery and Corn Stores from the Bonds and Spirit Store.

We first entered the Corn Stores, which comprise a block of buildings, four stories high and run over the archway leading to the southern quadrangle, where, in the two upper lofts, the various kinds of malt and grain are stored previous to their being treated before going to the Mill. They are capable of holding 4,000 quarters of grain, and are connected to a second block, which faces the entrance gates by a gangway, and the top floor therein is also used as a Corn Store. At the time of our visit all these great floors were so full that in many places we had to walk on the sacks of corn some five feet from the floor to reach the different divisions.

Arriving at the end of the top floor of the first-mentioned Corn Building, we followed our guide up a narrow stair to a platform, some 8 feet wide, which runs through the roof of the next building, abutting on the river. It leads to the trap door or landing stage, hanging over the water some 60 feet, and is used for unloading the grain direct from the steamers below. When the grain reaches the platform, it is shot into the various open bins underneath or wheeled to the Stores where required. Retracing our steps to the starting point, we turned to the right, and passed through an arch protected by a stout iron door in case of fire, which swung back lazily to our touch, and gave admittance to the Mill Building, which contains several floors, the first being the Grinding Room ; here there are six pairs of Stones, a Grist and Malt Mill, and other machinery. Ascending to the floor above, we found ourselves amid clouds of dust, for here many persons were busy weighing off the meal into sacks of four bushels each, and stacking them up to the roof. Mounting another ladder, we reached the Hopper Loft, where the grain drops from the spout of the elevator into the Hopper which feeds the Mill. Over this floor is a Meal Loft. Immediately adjoining there is another building of two stories devoted to the same purpose; also over the Draff House a spacious Meal Loft, which was filled to the ceiling with meal in sacks ready for tipping into the Mash Tun feeder. We passed into another apartment at the back of this house, which is also a Meal Loft, and adjoins two other floors, used for storing the grist. All these Meal Lofts are round and about the Brewing House, and conveniently communicate with the Tuns.

Leaving the West Meal Loft behind us, we entered the Mash House by the platform over the Mash Tuns to inspect the Heating Coppers. They are of the most ancient pattern, and yet most suitable, being made of three old Pot Stills, in which the Malt Whisky was made when George the III. was King. They are all heated by steam, the old furnaces being closed up, and hold respectively 10,000, 7,000, and 6,000 gallons. This Mash House is a large building, some 50 feet high, with open roof and skylights, and contains two metal Mash Tuns, with the usual stirring gear and draining plates. One of them is 30 feet in diameter and 8 feet deep, the other, which is cased with timber, is 16 feet in diameter and 10 feet deep. The Draff House is close to this building, and contains an automatic machine, a registering index and an elevator, all combined and worked with a switch lever. Below the Mash Tuns are two metal Underbacks, one oblong and the other circular, the former holding 3,000 and the latter 4,000 gallons. On the Western side of the Mash House are five sets of open Coolers on an extensive scale, which form the roofs of the Back House and other buildings, and contiguous there is a large Refrigerator. Just above the Coolers we were shown an apparatus for softening water before it runs into the boilers. It consists of four timber vessels, into which two kinds of water, hard and soft, run from one to the other. The water from one vessel is previously softened by passing through a preparation of lime, and on falling into the lower vessel the two waters meet, and are afterwards filtered; the whole affair is automatical and requires no attention. The worts run by gravitation from the Coolers referred to, into the Backs; thither we followed them. Descending a short flight of steps, we found ourselves in the No. 1 Back House, a lofty and spacious apartment, containing nine Washbacks, constructed of timber, capable of holding from 12,000 to 50,000 gallons each. Leaving this house we crossed a gangway bridge, nearly 100 feet long, over the roof of a low building and alongside the river, to the No. 2 Back House, which contains six Washbacks, holding from 19,000 to 20,000 gallons each. Passing downwards from this place, and crossing a paved passage, we suddenly found ourselves in a very gloomy apartment called the Pumping Room, erected over a celebrated well, which supplies the water used for brewing purposes. It is 120 feet deep, and the water is lifted by a powerful three-throw pump to a reservoir at the top of the building. In the adjoining lobby there is a set of wash pumps, also two sets of worts pumps, and two cooling pumps. We next descended a few steps, and passed under a low archway to the Refrigerator Vaults, under one of the Meal Lofts, to inspect a set of Refrigerators. They are upright machines, 30 feet long, and were manufactured on the premises by the Company's own workmen. Leaving this subterraneous, chilly place, we returned to the main lobby to visit the Distilling Department, passing on our way the No. 2 Charger Room, a light, clean and spacious apartment, the walls painted white, and the floor paved with stone. It contains the No. 2 Wash Charger, of 30,000 gallons content.

The Still House is the loftiest building in the works. The first object which attracted our attention was the No. 1 Wash Charger, placed on a suspended gallery, and holding 18,000 gallons. The Wash Regulating Receiver, which receives the Wash from this vessel, is placed in the adjoining building. At the western end of the house is the large Coffey's Patent Still, to which is attached a patent Rectifying Still, an invention of Mr. Board's, and patented in 1882. It consists of a large Old Pot Still, united to a Coffey's Patent Still, which rectifies the spirit produced by the Coffey Still, by means of the waste heat from the spent wash, thereby keeping a low and uniform temperature, resulting in a rectified spirit superior to that produced by fire or steam. Its advantage is, that there is no loss in the operation, and works so regularly that it requires no attention.

Fixed on the wall we noticed a handsome set of Wash Pumps, for pumping the liquor from the Wash Regulating Reservoir to the Stills, and a self-containing one of gun-metal, for pumping water into the Refrigerators, which is driven by an Otto Gas Engine. In a section of this building there are three Spirit Receivers, of 5,000, 4,000, and 2,000 gallons content, two Safes, a large Worm Tub, two upright Refrigerators, and a Lawrance Patent Refrigerator. We next passed through the large quadrangle to a smaller one, in the centre of which are four large spent Wash Tanks. Our guide next conducted us to the Engine Department, and led the way to the principal Engine-house, a lofty stone structure, of neat elevation; the roof is of an oval shape, and the dome lighted by ornamented glass; part of the paved floor is raised several feet, and reached by handsome stone steps. It contains a noted "Watt" steam-engine, kept beautifully bright, erected in 1821, of 70 indicated horse power, which works as well as any of the new engines.

Another house contains a condensing beam engine, of 20-horse power, of even more ancient date. There are three steam-boilers for the Still; one of them is a double furnace Lancashire boiler, 32 feet long and 9 feet in diameter; the others are 20 feet long and 5 feet in diameter. After inspecting these, we crossed the roadway to the Spirit Storage Department; the buildings connected therewith are all enclosed. We first entered the Spirit Store, containing five timber Spirit Vats, holding together 37,360 gallons; and then the four large Bonded Warehouses, the walls of which are all twenty inches thick; one of them is more lofty than the others, and is fitted with gauntree platforms five stories high. The Vatting Warehouse is the largest we have seen, and contains eight vats, reaching from floor to ceiling, which contained at the time of our visit 71,556 bulk gallons. On our way back to the Distillery proper, we noticed a massive pipe across the road overhead, stretching from the Receiver to the Spirit Store, allowed under an old Act of Parliament.

Beyond the offices, on the left of the quadrangle, is the Cooperage, containing all the steam appliances and machinery for sweetening and repairing casks; also a Cask Shed, and adjoining a carpenters', engineers', and blacksmiths' shop; stables for eight horses, cartsheds, &c., and eighteen mechanics are employed in these industries.

We next drove to the various Malting Works connected with the Distillery, and first inspected the David Street Maltings, which cover an area of 3,600 square feet, and are three stories high, one of which is used for storing barley, and the other two for malting, and each contains a cemented Steep, capable of wetting 120 bushels at one time. At the end of these floors there is a Kiln, 24 feet square, floored with Worcester tiles and possessing open furnaces. Continuing our explorations, we came to the Bread Street Maltings. They cover an area of 3,500 square feet, and consist of a Barley Loft and two Malting Floors, with Steeps and Kiln, the same as the others.

Unity Street Maltings, which cover 2,400 square feet, are similarly arranged, but are of smaller dimensions. The next place visited was Dundas Wharf, Redcliffe, where the Company have large bonded stores and corn lofts, a lofty block of buildings, covering an area of 12,360 square feet, with landing stage and appliances for unloading and loading direct into or from the steamers. The basement and ground floors contained at the time of our visit over 300 butts and hogsheads, and here also there is a blending and bottling room. Over the Warehouses are three Corn Lofts, and a donkey-engine of 6-horse power is used for hoisting the grain to the different floors.

A ten minutes' drive brought us back to the Distillery, where we collected a sample of the maize, white oats, barley, and malt used in the Distillery to take with us to London.

One hundred persons are employed in the Distillery, and six excise officers. The "make" is Grain Whisky and plain spirit, the latter being sold to Rectifiers for the manufacture of gin; the former is sent to Scotland and Ireland to make a blended Scotch and Irish Whisky, for which purpose it is specially adapted, and stands in high favour.

The total annual output is 637,068 gallons, which is sold principally in Leith, Belfast, London and Bristol.

No. 4.

Lea Valley Distillery, Stratford, London.

PROPRIETORS, THE LEA VALLEY DISTILLERY CO., LIMITED.

Managing Director: E. A. BROCK.

Secretary: W. A. CARDEN.

THERE are several ways of reaching this Distillery, which is five miles from the City. Tram-cars run from Aldgate, omnibuses from the Bank, and trains from Fenchurch Street and Liverpool Street Stations; we chose the tram-car, which landed us nearer our destination than any other route. When the Distillery was built, the whole district was a country suburb, and land was very cheap; now, with the exception of a few fields at the back of the works, every inch has been built over and almost absorbed in the great City. Lea Valley is the only Malt Distillery in England, and it was certainly a bold experiment to make a trial in the very heart of the Kingdom, so far away from the hills and mountain streams; the proprietors find, by experience, that they did wisely, and the demand for their Whisky has led to the erection of other buildings and the enlargement of those existing. The Company have also gone in for the manufacture of Grain Whisky, and possess all the appliances and vessels used by the Scotch Distilleries for that purpose. The managing director, who is a practical distiller, received us most courteously, and himself conducted us over the establishment.

The Distillery was founded by Mr. E. A. Brock in connection with Mr. Geo. Phillips, who sold it to the above Company, Mr. Brock remaining as managing director. The buildings, which cover one acre, are planted on the banks of a section of the Canal, and are erected entirely of brick, after the plans of Mr. Brock. The Maltings are all at Ware, in Hertfordshire, and the malt is brought direct therefrom by canal. We first inspected the Granary building, a lofty structure of four stories, which abuts on the canal, and is 120 feet long by 45 feet broad; the grain is lifted by hoists direct from the barges and spread out in the Lofts. One of the lower floors is appropriated to the Mill machinery, and contains five pairs of stones, the others are used for storing the grain.

Adjoining the Granary, is the Heating Tank Room, wherein are three wrought iron Tanks, made by Fraser, of Bromley, two hold 24,000 gallons the other one 20,000 gallons. They stand on iron columns and girders, and are heated by steam, the space underneath being utilized as a Smithy and Fitters' Shop. We passed from the second floor of the Granary on to the top floor of the next house, which constitutes the Grist Loft, and is over the Mash House

It is a light and spacious apartment, 85 feet long by 45 feet wide and placed in its centre is the Grist Hopper, which feeds a Steel's Mashing Machine. Descending a stair ladder, we reached the Mash House, of same dimensions as the Grist Loft, where we inspected the metal Mash Tun. This vessel, which is 26 feet in diameter and 8 feet deep, contains a set of double revolving rakes and the usual draining plates. There is another Mash Tun in the same house in course of construction, which will be of similar dimensions, and both are by Turnbull, Grant and Jack, of Glasgow. The Underback, holding 12,000 gallons, is placed under the paved floor, and the worts are pumped up therefrom to the Worts Receiver, placed on iron columns, 32 feet high, close to the Back House. This Receiver is a prominent object from the railway, and is a very handsome vessel. Underneath, by a neat contrivance, there is a hanging Grains Receiver, containing an automatic measure, which registers the quantity of draff as it falls into the farmers' carts. The Mash House is well and conveniently arranged, and the walls are painted white.

Passing through a doorway we next found ourselves in the Tun Room, a long gallery, 90 feet by 40 feet. On either side of the walls are four Washbacks, unlike any we have seen before, being composed of thick metal plates, 16 feet in diameter and 18 feet deep. On the half-landing above are placed two of Morton's Refrigerators, of 60 barrels capacity per hour. We next went through an opening in the wall, and descending a long flight of steps found ourselves on a platform level with the heads of the Stills in the Still House, a lofty apartment, 60 feet long by 25 feet wide, containing three handsome Pot Stills, made by Fleming, Bennet, and McLaren, and all heated by steam. They consist of a Wash Still, holding 4,000 gallons; a Feints Still, 3,000 gallons; and a Spirit Still, 1,500 gallons. Connected with these Stills is the Wash Charger, holding 15,000 gallons, and on a gallery there are four Low-wines and Feints Receivers, holding 2,500 gallons each, and one Spirit Receiver, containing 2,000 gallons.

Our guide then conducted us to the No. 2 Still House, 65 ft. long and 25 feet broad, which contains a Coffey's Patent Still, made by John Dore and Sons, of Bromley; two Spirit Receivers, holding 2,500 and 2,000 gallons respectively; two Wash Chargers, each 25,000 gallons capacity: two Feints Receivers, each 1,000 gallons content; and also a Morton's Patent Vertical Refrigerator, the first ever erected in a Distillery for cooling spirits. We next made an inspection of the Engine Department, containing a 30-horse power engine, by Deakin and Parke, of Manchester; there are also four others, of less horse-power. Adjacent are three steam-boilers, by Galloway and Fraser; two of them are of 60-horse power and the other 50-horse power, all 31 feet long, by 7½ feet in diameter. Here also are three sets of three-throw pumps, by Hunter and English, of London, and several patent pumps for water, worts, &c., by Picking and Hopkins, of Arnold Works, Bow. Crossing the yard we entered the Spirit Store, a detached building, containing two vats; one holding 10,000 gallons, the other 450 gallons. In close proximity there is a larger building used for storing spirits in vats. The Warehouses are three in number, and contain together a little over 1,800 casks. On the premises there is a Cooperage and Cask Shed, Distillery, and Revenue Offices, a private office for the Managing Director, Foreman's house, and capital stables. Forty persons are employed in the works. The water used is from the New River and the Whisky made is both Grain and Malt; the annual output of the former is 305,000 gallons, of the latter 155,000 gallons.

ADVERTISEMENTS.

IMPORTANT TO BREWERS, DISTILLERS, &c.

By Her Majesty's Royal Letters Patent.

ROBERT MORTON & CO.'S

IMPROVED PATENT

VERTICAL REFRIGERATOR,

For Cooling Brewers' and Distillers' Worts and other Fluids, the Condensing of Steam, the Cooling and Condensing of Spirits in Distilleries, &c.

GOLD & SILVER MEDALS, for Refrigeration, Awarded to ROBERT MORTON & Co., Burton-on-Trent.

These Refrigerators are made of a series of Hand-drawn Copper Tubes with rounded edges, fitted into gun-metal frame, with loose Caps, readily removable for cleaning inside the tubes; also with improved Wort inlet and outlet Troughs. The top Trough is constructed so as to equalise the distribution of Worts over the Refrigerator.

Very Economical with Water.

The advantages of these Refrigerators are as follows:

Being made of MORTON'S Patent Tubes, which, by a new process, are drawn nearly as hard as steel, they will stand a very great pressure (although made of a metal in substance little thicker than a sheet of writing paper), thus combining great strength with unequalled cooling power.

Every part is perfectly accessible, so that both inside and outside the tubes can be readily cleaned with the greatest ease.

These new Refrigerators are most easily repaired, and in case of a tube bursting by frost or accident, it can be replaced with a new one within an hour, extra tubes being supplied with these Refrigerators at a small cost.

Each Refrigerator is tested to 50 lbs. pressure before leaving the works, and another great advantage is they will stand pumping through.

These Refrigerators are made of Seamless Tubes and fitted with two water inlets and outlets when required.

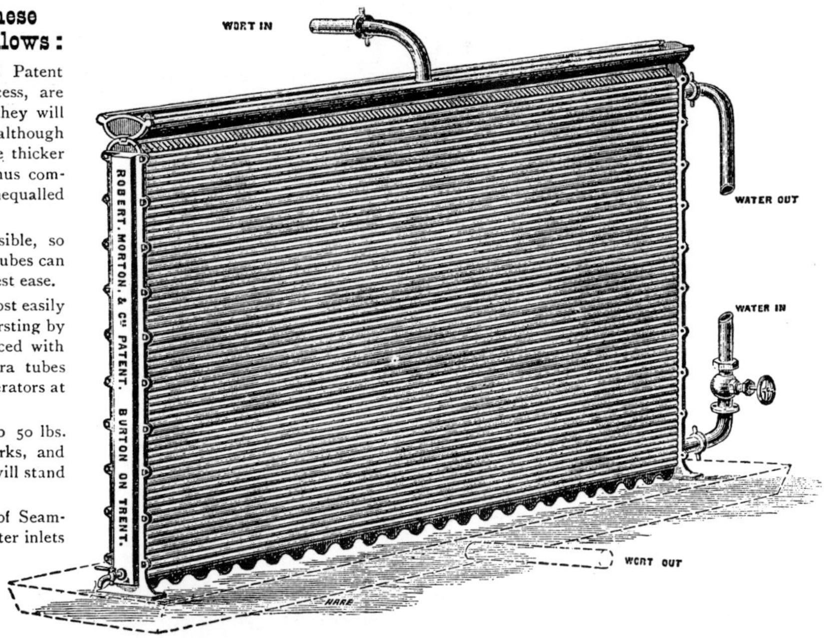

PATENTEES AND SOLE MAKERS—

ROBERT MORTON & CO.

(LATE SOUTH DURHAM WORKS, STOCKTON-ON-TEES),

Brewers' Engineers, Brass and Iron Founders, Coppersmiths, &c.,

TRENT WORKS,

BURTON-ON-TRENT.

DANL. MILLER & CO.,

ESTABLISHED 1809.

Coppersmiths and Brassfounders,

DUBLIN COPPER AND BRASS WORKS,

29, CHURCH STREET,

DUBLIN,

Manufacturers of every description of Distillery and Brewery Plant.

CENTRIFUGAL PUMPS & PUMPING ENGINES,

For Docks, Circulating Purposes, Salvage Work, Distilleries, &c.

The Cheapest and most Efficient Pump in the Market.
From Newest and most Improved Patterns.

Specialities:—Centrifugal Pumps, Baking Machinery, Leather Dressing Machinery, Hydraulic Presses and Pumps, Hydraulic Cranes, Accumulators, Hydraulic Rivetters, Lifts of all kinds.

DRYSDALE & CO.,

Bon Accord Engine Works, GLASGOW.

FLEMING, BENNET & McLAREN,

Distillers' & Brewers' Coppersmiths,

CRANSTONHILL, GLASGOW.

Makers of Fire Stills, Steam Stills, Coffey's Patent Stills, Steam Coils, Condensers, Refrigerators, Mashing Machines, &c. Brewers' Wort Coppers, Mash Tuns, Spargers, Attemperators & Skimmers. Gun Metal Cocks and Valves of all kinds, and General Copper and Brass Work for Brewers and Distillers.

TELEGRAPHIC ADDRESS:
"COPPERSMITH," GLASGOW.

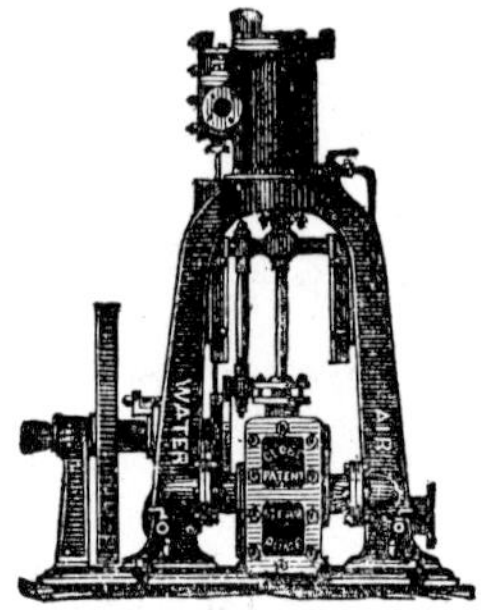

STEAM PUMPS.

KESSON
AND
CAMPBELL,

Carntyne Foundry & Engine Works,

PARKHEAD,

AND

GREENFIELD FOUNDRY & ENGINE WORKS,

NEAR HAMILTON.

SOLE MAKERS of the "Globe" Patent Double-Acting Steam Pump, the best Pump in the market for Distilleries, Brewers, Chemical Works, Contractors, &c.

Makers of Lockwood's Patent Oscillating Furnace Bars, and General Ironfounders, Engineers, Millwrights, Machine Makers, Smiths, &c,

Prices, with Testimonials and Particulars, on Application.

EMPTY CASKS.

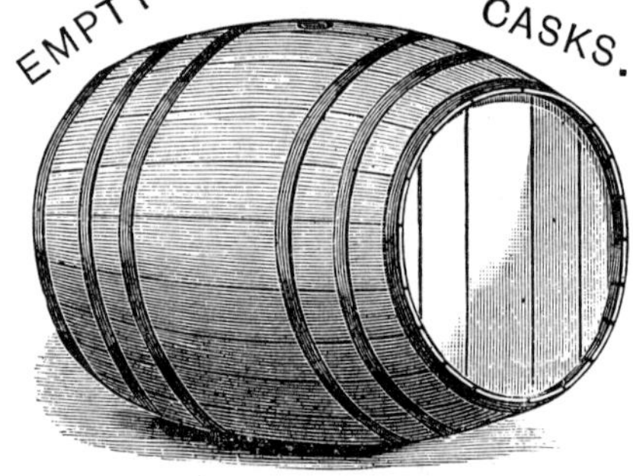

All descriptions of sound fresh-emptied

WINE & SPIRIT CASKS

Supplied for Home & Export Trade.

RE-COOPERED CASKS ALWAYS IN STOCK.

C. DREWE HARRIS,

60, MARK LANE, LONDON, E.C.

Cooperage & Stores:

Weston Street Arches, Tooley Street, S.E.

Wine Merchants having any Casks for disposal should apply for List of Prices.

VAN GELDER, APSIMON & Co.

(LIMITED),

Victoria Iron Works,

SOWERBY BRIDGE (YORKS), & 3, OLD ROPERY, LIVERPOOL,

MANUFACTURERS OF THE MOST PERFECTED MACHINES FOR

CLEANING AND SEPARATING GRAIN.

"LIVER" SEPARATOR (Patented).

THIS MACHINE WORKS WITH A DETACHED FAN.

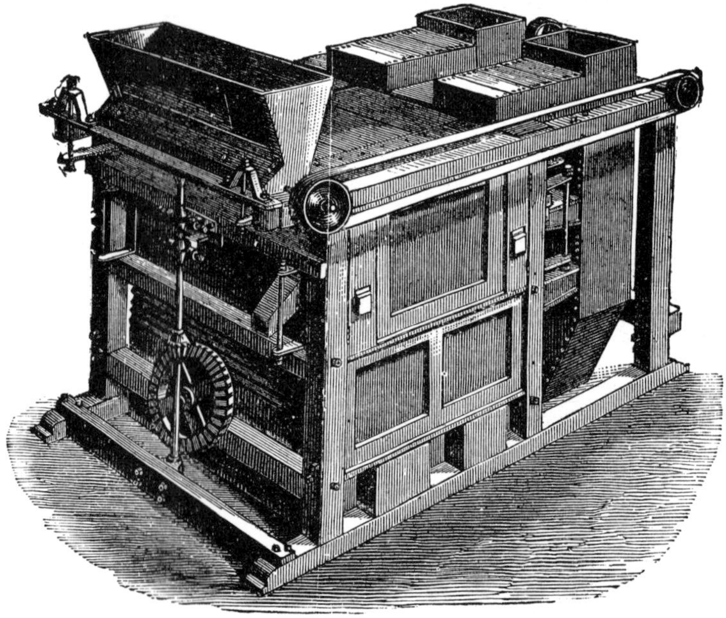

The "Liver" Separator is used in hundreds of Mills, and at St. John's Lane Distillery; St. James's Gate Brewery, Dublin; Lion Brewery, West Hartlepool; The Brewery, Newark-on-Trent, &c.

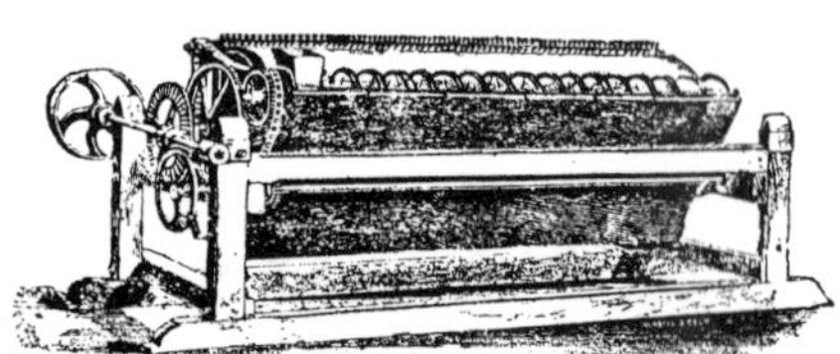

The VICTORIA SEPARATOR

(Patented),

For Extracting Seeds, Half Corns, Stones, &c., from all kinds of Grain.

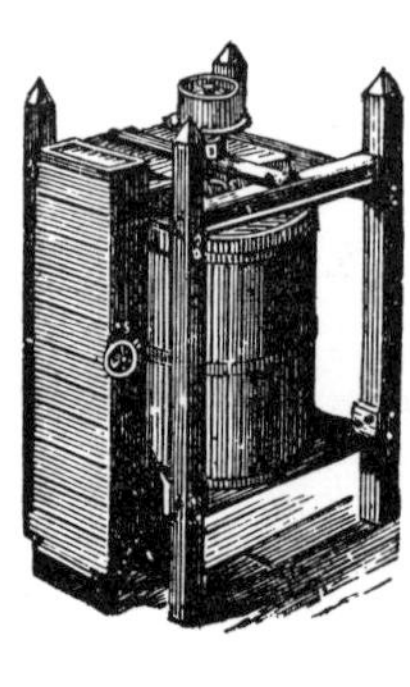

The

Improved "VAN GELDER"

MALT POLISHER

AND

GRAIN SCOURER,

In use at

Messrs. Barclay, Perkins & Co., London;

The Brewery, Newark-on-Trent, &c.

Harper's Weekly Gazette.

THE WEEKLY ORGAN OF THE WHOLESALE WINE AND SPIRIT TRADES.

THIS Publication has been successfully established to supply the Wholesale Houses with a Weekly Paper containing all news and information of interest to the Trades it represents.

It is published every Saturday, being posted in London Friday Evenings in time for delivery by the Saturday Morning Mails, in the Provinces, Scotland and Ireland.

It is supplied to Subscribers only, in the Wholesale Trade, at a Yearly Subscription of 25/- post free, dating from the first of any month in the year.

It contains a Weekly Report of the Foreign and Home Markets, having responsible and reliable correspondents in all the chief centres of Trade both at Home and Abroad. Reports of the principal market sales are regularly given, with descriptions and prices realized. Original articles on current Trade topics, and all information of general or particular interest to the Trade appear each week. Reports of the chief failures in the Trade in England, Scotland and Ireland, together with list of the creditors and full particulars, form a prominent feature of the paper, and every care is taken in the editorial department to study the interests of the trade in every way.

HARPER'S
Weekly Gazette.
DEVOTED TO THE INTERESTS OF THE WINE, SPIRIT AND BREWING TRADES.
No. 95.—VOL. IV. OCTOBER 23rd, 1886.
MESSRS. SOUTHARD & CO., Sworn Brokers
MR. WILLIAM THOMAS RESTELL
MESSRS. W. & T. RESTELL
MR. JOHN W. BASHFORD, Sworn Broker
MESSRS. NORRIS and GILBEY
MESSRS. SCOTT, WRIGHT & CO., Sworn Brokers
WINE & SPIRIT ASSOCIATION
FINEST EXTRA QUALITY CHAMPAGNE.
MOIGNEAUX'S
LONDON BRANCH HOUSE—26, Crutched Friars, E.C.
J. R. PARKINGTON & Co.
DEUTZ & GELDERMANN.
ROPER FRÈRES & CO.,
VINE GROWERS' COMPANY.
J. DUTRÉNIT & CIE.
CHAMPAGNE
E. MERCIER & Co.,
Epernay.
T. C. STEVENS, 8, NEW LONDON STREET, E.C.
FINEST HIGHLAND MALT WHISKIES
WILLIAM & KEITH JOPP,
Whisky Merchants,
ABERDEEN.
ESTABLISHED 1817.
D. J. FOX,
17 CORN EXCHANGE CHAMBERS,
SEETHING LANE, LONDON, E.C.
OUR OLD HIGHLAND WHISKY
TEACHER'S
HIGHLAND CREAM,
THE
Cream of Highland Whisky.
WM. TEACHER & SONS,
GLASGOW
AND 26, PHILPOT LANE, LONDON, E.C.

FAC-SIMILE OF FRONT COVER.

As an advertising medium HARPER'S WEEKLY GAZETTE presents unusual facilities, circulating as it does among the principal Houses in the Trade, in the United Kingdom, Abroad, and the Colonies. Application for advertisement spaces can be made to the Office of the Paper—

39, Crutched Friars, London, E.C.

LLEWELLINS & JAMES,

Castle Green, BRISTOL,

Manufacturers of all descriptions of Distillers', Brewers' & Refiners' Plant & Machinery,

ARCHITECTS, ENGINEERS, COPPERSMITHS, BELLFOUNDERS, &c.

IMPROVED MALT MILL.

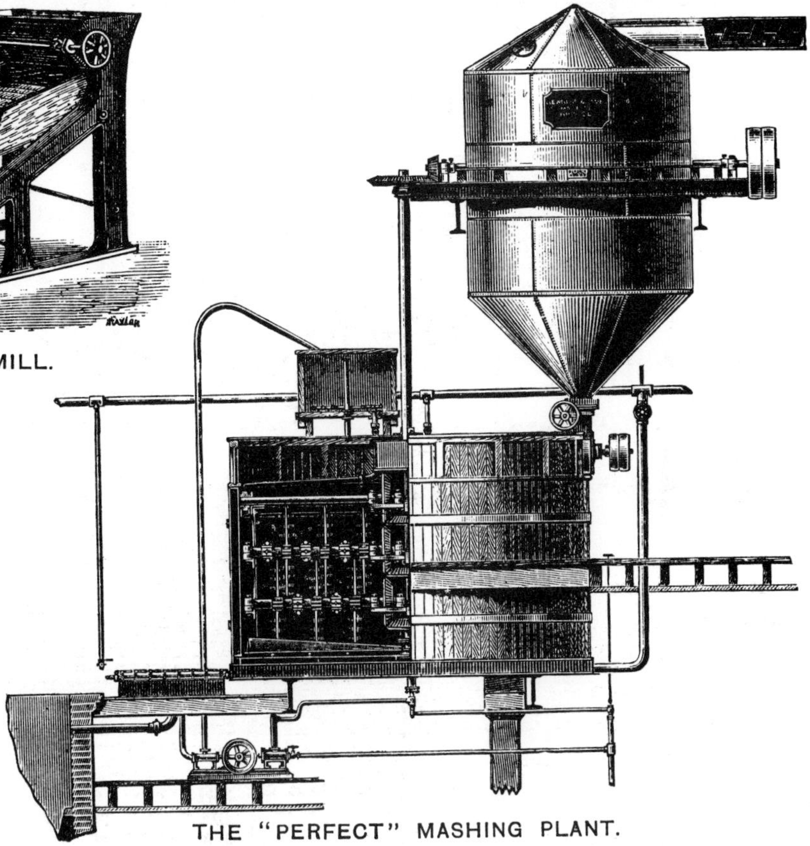

THE "PERFECT" MASHING PLANT.

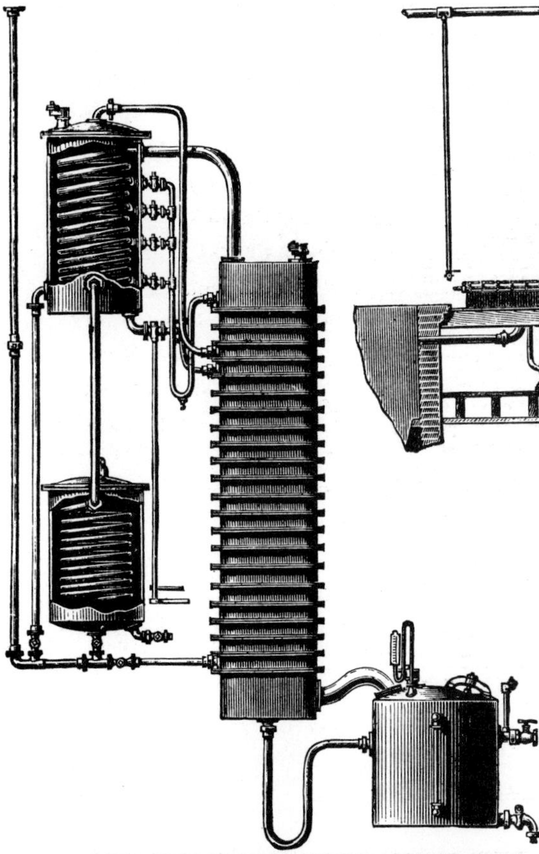

IMPROVED CONTINUOUS STILL.

PATENT RAW GRAIN MASHING MACHINE.

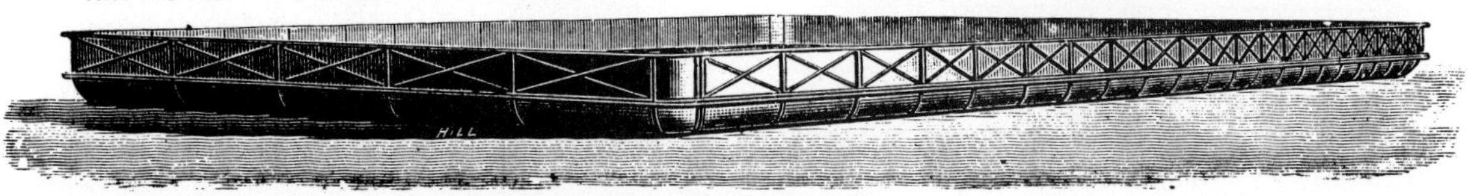

CAST IRON COOLER.

SUMMER TOURS IN SCOTLAND.

THE

ROYAL  ROUTE.

GLASGOW AND THE HIGHLANDS

Via Crinan and Caledonian Canals.

TOURISTS SPECIAL Cabin Tickets issued during the Season.

Giving the *privilege* of the run of *all the undernamed Steamers to any part of the Highlands* at which they may call during the time specified.

For One Week, £3; Two Weeks, £5; or Six Separate Days, £3 10s.

NEW ROYAL MAIL STEAM SHIP "GRENADIER."

Columba	Mountaineer	Claymore	Lochiel
Iona	Pioneer	Clansman	Fingal
Chevalier	Lochawe	Clydesdale	Lochness
Gondolier	Glencoe	Cavalier	Ethel
Glengarry	Linnet	Islay	Inveraray Castle

THE ROYAL MAIL SWIFT PASSENGER STEAMER "COLUMBA" OR "IONA"

Sails daily from May till October, from GLASGOW at 7 A.M., and from GREENOCK about 9 A.M., in connection with Express Trains from London and the South, Edinburgh, and Glasgow, &c., for KYLES OF BUTE, TARBERT, and ARDRISHAIG, conveying passengers for OBAN, GLENCOE, INVERNESS, LOCHAWE, STAFFA, and IONA, MULL, SKYE, GAIRLOCH, STORNOWAY, THURSO, &c., &c.

A WHOLE DAY'S SAIL BY THE "COLUMBA" OR "IONA."

From GLASGOW to ARDRISHAIG and back (180 miles),

CABIN FARE	6/-,	or including Breakfast, Dinner and Tea ...	12/-
FORE CABIN FARE...	3/6	do. do. do. do. ...	7/-

TOURS TO THE WEST HIGHLANDS

(Occupying about a week), BY STEAM SHIP

"CLAYMORE" or "CLANSMAN,"

Via Mull of Kintyre, going and returning through the Sounds of Jura, Mull and Skye, calling at Oban, Tobermory, Portree, STORNOWAY, and intermediate places.

CABIN RETURN FARE, 45s.

The Route is through scenery rich in historical interest and unequalled for grandeur and variety. These vessels leave **GLASGOW** every Monday and Thursday about 12 noon, and GREENOCK about 5 p.m., returning from STORNOWAY every Monday and Wednesday.

Breakfast, Dinner, and Tea, 7s. per Day.

Passengers continuing the voyage to **THURSO** and back pay 10s. extra fare.

The Steam-Ship "CAVALIER" will leave GLASGOW every Monday or Thursday at 11 a.m. and GREENOCK at 4 p.m., for INVERNESS and back (*via* Mull of Kintyre), leaving Inverness every Monday or Thursday morning. Cabin Fare for the Trip, with First-Class Sleeping Accommodation, 30/-; or including Meals, by Steamer leaving Glasgow on Mondays, 60/-

OFFICIAL GUIDE BOOK, 3d.; ILLUSTRATED, 6d; CLOTH GILT, 1s.

Time Bill, Map and List of Fares, sent free on application to the Owner,

DAVID MACBRAYNE, 119, Hope Street, GLASGOW.

FAMOUS SCOTCH WHISKIES.

ALEX. FERGUSON & CO.,

REGISTERED A F TRADE MARK

106 & 108, WEST REGENT STREET,

GLASGOW.

Proprietors, BRADALBANE HIGHLAND WHISKY,

AND OTHER FAMOUS BRANDS.

SOLE AGENTS, BENACHIE DISTILLERY, N.B.,

PURE HIGHLAND MALT.

Also Standard Blends of the oldest and choicest Whiskies always on hand, these are vatted and bottled under supervision of Excise Officials.

CUSTOMERS SUPPLIED WITH THEIR OWN BRANDS ON CASKS AND CASES FOR CONTRACTS.

BONDERS AND HOLDERS OF

GLENLIVET'S, ISLAY'S, HIGHLAND AND LOWLAND WHISKIES.

Quotations and Samples from all Wine Merchants, and from—

HEAD OFFICE AT GLASGOW,

LONDON: CROSBY BUILDINGS, E.C.

W. & J. RUSSELL,

Sole Proprietors of the following celebrated Blends of OLD HIGHLAND MALT WHISKEY.

FINEST OLD SCOTCH WHISKY

AILSA  BLEND

AILSA CRAIG

W. & J. RUSSELL,

EDINBURGH & LEITH

TRADE MARK REGD.

Auld Reekie

BLEND.

KENNEDY & CO.S

Old Scotch Whisky

In Bond in Leith and London, in Butts, Hhds., Quarter-Casks and Cases.
Prices and Samples to be had on application.

Offices: 1, NORTH SAINT DAVID STREET, EDINBURGH,

AND

FOWKE'S BUILDINGS, GT. TOWER STREET, LONDON, E.C.

ESTABLISHED 1820.

HENDERSON & TURNBULL,

SCOTCH WHISKY MERCHANTS,

Registered Proprietors of the Famous Blends of Choice Old Scotch & Highland Whiskies—

FAC-SIMILE OF LABEL AND BRAND ON CASKS AND CASES.

GREEN LABEL.

"Acorn Brand"

AND

"The Corrychoillie" Blend.

In Casks and Cases, for Home and Export Trade.

Samples and Quotations on Application.

LABELS.

FAC-SIMILE OF LABEL AND BRAND ON CASKS AND CASES.

50, BERNARD STREET, LEITH.

Telegraphic Address "CORRYCHOILLIE," LEITH.

KIRKER, GREER & CO., LTD.,

DISTILLERS,

BELFAST AND GLASGOW.

GOLD MEDALS AWARDED AT

Calcutta Exhibition, 1884,
South Australia Exhibition, 1881.
Western Australia Exhibition, 1882,
New Zealand Exhibition, 1882.
Highest Award, Melbourne Exhibition, 1880,

For their Old Irish and Scotch Whiskies.

Liverpool Office: **H. B. McBRIDE, Grecian Chambers, Dale Street.** *Glasgow Office:* **58, Dundas Street.**

London Office: **Mr. D. J. FOX, 17, Corn Exchange Chambers, Seething Lane, E.C.**

SAMPLES AND PRICES ON APPLICATION.

"WHISKEY AT ITS BEST."

HUDSON & CO.'S DUBLIN WHISKEY.

O'CONNELL MONUMENT BRAND (Registered)

(Seven years old) as shipped to Europe, Asia, Africa, America, and Australasia,

Home and Export Warehouses—NORTH WALL, DUBLIN; *Telegraphic Address,* **"HUDSON."**

London Office—OLD TRINITY HOUSE, WATER LANE, E.C.; *Telegraphic Address,* **"POTHEEN."**

Glasgow Office—58, WEST REGENT STREET; *Telegraphic Address,* **"NOTAP."**

Liverpool Office—57, DALE STREET; *Telegraphic Address,* **"MONUMENT."**

New York Office—112, PEARL STREET; *Sole Agents, U.S.A.,*

Messrs. JAMES LOUCHEIM & CO.

The *Irish Times*, August 8th, 1886—alluding to the visit of the Colonial and Indian Exhibition Deputation to the Custom-House Whiskey-Vaults, Dublin—says "that many were the ejaculations of surprise on seeing the vast amount of Whiskey stored therein. Mr. Hudson, of Hudson & Co., guided the distinguished party through the subterranean passages; the celebrated Blend of O'Connell Monument Whiskey was then sampled, their conductor explaining that good Whiskies by different makers, when blended, were superior to the Whiskey produced by an individual distiller. The Lord Mayor concurred with the general opinion that the blended Whiskey tasted well.

PARIS, 1878.

LONDON, 1884.

W. WILLIAMS & SONS,
ABERDEEN.

OLD HIGHLAND WHISKY.

Branches and Agencies.

LONDON.	CAPE TOWN.	KIMBERLEY.	PERTH, S.A.
ADELAIDE.	COLOMBO.	MELBOURNE.	ROCKHAMPTON.
BARBADOES.	HALIFAX, N.S.	MONTREAL.	SYDNEY.
BRISBANE.	KURRACHEE.	NEW YORK.	TOWNSVILLE.
CALCUTTA.	MAURITIUS.	NORMANTON.	WELLINGTON.

W. W. & SONS will be prepared to appoint Sole Buying Agents for the sale of their well-known Whisky anywhere not mentioned above.

W. WILLIAMS & SONS are the largest Blenders, Holders and Exporters of Highland Whisky in the North of Scotland, and have received Diplomas of Merit at Paris, 1878, and Prize Medal at London, 1884, for the excellent quality of their blended Whisky.

JOHN DEWAR & SONS

ESTABD. D A.D. 1846

Old Highland Whisky

PERTH, N.B. & LONDON

MEDAL—EDINBURGH EXHIBITION 1886. SAMPLES & QUOTATIONS ON APPLICATION.

THE TALISMAN WHISKY

CHARLES WATSON.
GLASGOW.

THE CANTIRE WHISKY.

THE CANTIRE BLEND is fully matured, and is perfectly free from fusel and other oils. It is blended from some of the finest distilleries in Scotland, being matured by age and not by a doctored process, and thus can be relied upon as a thoroughly safe and wholesome stimulant.

Sole Proprietors:

L. ROSE & CO.,

WINE AND SPIRIT MERCHANTS,

11, CURTAIN ROAD, LONDON, E.C.; Also LEITH, N.B.

Sole Agents for

JOSE COREIRA ... ... Oporto.
HERMANOS MARCEZ Xerez de la Frontera.
JEAN PIERART & CIE. ... ... Cognac.
PEDRO DEL CAMPO ... Tarragona.

GREENLEES BROTHERS,

BONDED VATTING
AND
BOTTLING WAREHOUSE PROPRIETORS.

Vattings & Bottlings made in Customer's own name.

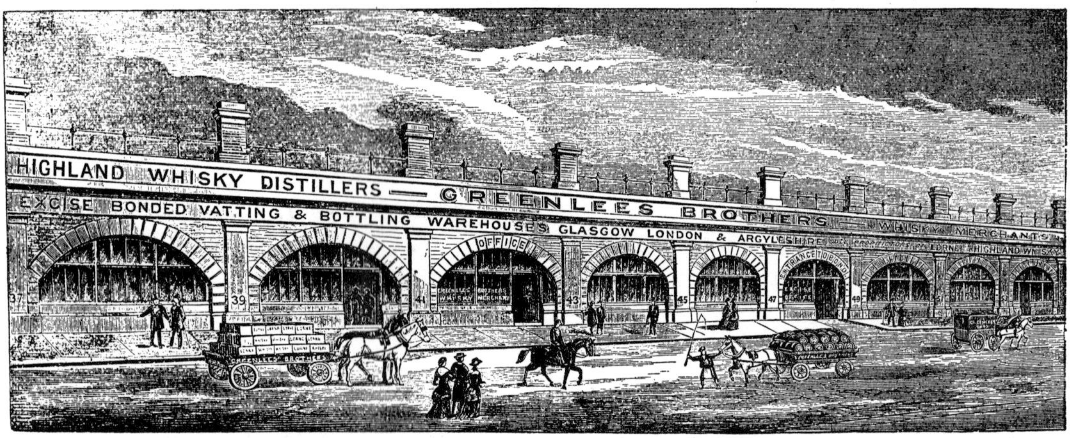

DIMENSIONS.

Frontage	-	384 Feet.
Superficial Area		56,502 Sq. Feet.
Cubic Area	-	739,158 Feet.

OPERATIONS 1886.

Received	1,302,060	Gallons.
Vatted	1,470,726	,,
Delivered	1,378,998	,,

Bonded and Bottling Warehouses:

37 TO 53, AND 59, OSBORNE STREET,

Offices:

38, STOCKWELL STREET, GLASGOW.

Alexander, A. & Co.,
55, COOPER STREET, LEITH.
Sole Proprietors of the
" Dandie Dinmont Scotch Whisky."

Baxter, Charles R., DUNDEE,
" Baxter's Barley Bree."
Established 1800.

Black & Ferguson,
Blenders of the Finest Old Scotch Whiskies,
23 and 30, ADELPHI, ABERDEEN, N.B.

Buchanan, James & Co.,
Proprietors of the celebrated " Buchanan" Blend,
20, BUCKLERSBURY, LONDON,
LEITH and GLASGOW.

Catto, James,
Fine Old Highland Whisky,
Prize Medals awarded PARIS 1868, LONDON 1884,
21, ADELPHI, ABERDEEN.

Dewar, John & Sons, PERTH.
Celebrated Highland Whisky.
Established 1846.
Silver Medal EDINBURGH Exhibition, 1886,
London Offices:
5 and 7, WARWICK STREET, CHARING CROSS.

Kidd, Eunson & Co.,
Whisky Brokers and Distillers' Agents,
Holders of Finest Old Scotch Whiskies.
QUALITY STREET, LEITH.

Mackie & Co.,
Whisky Brokers,
Parcels of old bondings from 1 to 6 years always in bond.
5, DIXON STREET, GLASGOW.

Mackie, N. M. Scott & Co.,
" Red Deer Brand."
Finest Blend of Old North County Malt Whiskies.
17, ASSEMBLY STREET, LEITH.

Mackinlay, Charles & Co.,
Whisky Brokers, Distillers' Agents and Blenders,
LEITH AND LONDON.

McEntire, J. V.,
Holder of the Oldest and most celebrated Highland Whiskies.
16, ROYAL EXCHANGE EDINBURGH.
Telegraphic Address: " MCENTIRE, EDINBURGH."

Mitchell & Co., of Belfast, Limited,
BELFAST AND GLASGOW.
Belfast Office: 84, Tomb Street.
Glasgow ,, 167, St. Vincent Street.
Newcastle-on-Tyne Office: 32, Grainger Street.
Liverpool Office: 62, Dale Street.
London ,, 2, Fowkes' Buildings, Gt. Tower Street, E.C.

Russell, W. & J., EDINBURGH,
Scotch Whisky Brokers and Blenders.
Established 1830.
London Office:
FOWKES' BUILDINGS,
GREAT TOWER STREET, E.C.

Stewart, J. & G., EDINBURGH.
Established 1779.
Old Vatted Scotch Whiskies,
Sole Address: 111 & 113, HIGH STREET.
Telegraphic Address: "STEWART, EDINBURGH."

Walker, William & Sons,
Established 1827.
Holders and Blenders of the Finest North County Malt Whiskies.
52, UNION STREET, ABERDEEN.

Watson, Charles,
205, WEST GEORGE STREET, GLASGOW,
" The Talisman Blend,"
Fine old Scotch Whiskies.